Books by T. HARRY WILLIAMS

Huey Long (1969)
Hayes of the Twenty-third: The Civil War Volunteer Office (1965)
The Union Sundered (1963) } (Vols. V and VI of
The Union Restored (1963) } *The* Life *History of the United States)*
McClellan, Sherman, and Grant (1962)
Romance and Realism in Southern Politics (1961)
American History: A Survey, with Richard N. Current and Frank Freidel (1961)
Americans at War (1960)
A History of the United States, with Richard N. Current and Frank Freidel (1959)
P. G. T. Beauregard (1955)
Lincoln and His Generals (1952)
Lincoln and the Radicals (1941)

Books Edited by T. HARRY WILLIAMS

Hayes: The Diary of a President (1964)
Every Man a King, by Huey Long (1964)
Military Memoirs of a Confederate, by E. P. Alexander (1962)
Abraham Lincoln: Selected Speeches, Messages and Letters (1957)
With Beauregard in Mexico (1956)
Selected Writings and Speeches of Abraham Lincoln (1943)

THE HISTORY
OF AMERICAN WARS

T

OF AME

From

HE HISTORY
RICAN WARS
1745 to 1918

By T. Harry Williams

Louisiana State University Press   Baton Rouge and London

Grateful acknowledgment is made to G. T. Sassoon and Viking
Penguin Inc. for permission to reprint four lines from "Attack" from
Collected Poems by Siegfried Sassoon. Copyright 1918 by E. P. Dutton.
Copyright renewed 1946 by Siegfried Sassoon. Reprinted by permission
of Viking Penguin Inc. and G. T. Sassoon.

Library of Congress Cataloging in Publication Data
Williams, Thomas Harry. (Date)
The history of American wars, from 1745 to 1918.
Bibliography: p.
Includes index.
1. United States—History, Military. I. Title.
E181.W64   1981   973   80–2717
ISBN 0-8071-1234-8 (paper)

Louisiana Paperback Edition, 1985
Published by arrangement with Alfred A. Knopf, Inc.

For

Robbie

Cissy

Minou

Madge

CONTENTS

Preface   ix

Introduction   xi

I · *The First Wars*   3

II · *The Revolution: The American Military Organization*   21

III · *The Revolution: The Armed Forces and the First Battles*   40

IV · *The Revolution: 1776 to the End*   55

INTERLUDE *1783–1812*   83

V · *The War of 1812: Origins and Organization*   93

VI · *The War of 1812: Battles on Land and Sea*   110

INTERLUDE *1815–1846*   135

VII · *The Mexican War: Origins and Objectives*   144

VIII · *The Mexican War: The Campaigns*   161

INTERLUDE *1848–1861*   186

IX · *The Civil War: Origins and Beginnings*   198

X · *The Civil War: Means and Measures*   219

XI · *The Civil War: Strategy and the First Shots*   245

XII · *The Civil War: The Battles*   267

INTERLUDE *1865–1898*   303

XIII · *The War with Spain*   317

INTERLUDE *1898–1917*   343

XIV · *The World War: Origins and the American Reaction*   358

XV · *The World War: The American Experience*   382

Bibliography   417

Index   427

PREFACE

THE AUTHOR PLANNED THIS BOOK to be "an account of all American wars from the colonial period to Vietnam, comprehensive enough to give a well-rounded picture . . . and yet succinct enough to fit into a single volume." A knowledge of our military history is important for Americans, he believed: "some of the most serious shortcomings in our military policy have come about because soldiers and civilians have had an inadequate or inaccurate appreciation of our history."

To enable the reader to follow the development of the armed forces, the author has discussed each major war in from one to four chapters, bridging the years between with "interludes." These interludes systematically trace the evolution of the militia (now the National Guard), the army and navy, and the beginning of the air force; military training and schooling of officers; weaponry and artillery strength; national strategy; and economic and political influences on the military establishment. Also included in the interludes are the so-called Indian wars. Taken together, the war chapters and the interludes give a comprehensive, yet compact, picture of American military history—although not up to the present: the book concludes with the end of World War I.

History is never finished, and no one was more aware of this than T. Harry Williams. His original manuscripts are heavily interlined, for he was continually reappraising and revising his own interpretations of historical events and reviewing the interpretations of other scholars. He saw the events of each successive day as an addition to the vast drama of history, to the study of which he devoted his life. His awareness of history as a living force, his fascination with it, and his contagious enthusiasm for it made him a memorable lecturer and writer.

It may therefore be appropriate, although tragic (as history often is), that the author's unexpected death in July, 1979, left this work unfinished. His story of World War II and of the Korean and Vietnam conflicts will be sorely missed. Most of all, perhaps, one might have hoped for a concluding section giving his appraisal of his country's military situation, present and future.

E.S.W.
for
T.H.W.

January, 1980

INTRODUCTION

THIS IS A MILITARY HISTORY of the American people and the American nation—an account of our wars from the colonial period to Vietnam, comprehensive enough to give a well-rounded picture, it is hoped, and yet succinct enough to fit into a single volume.

The writer of such a history is immediately confronted with a question: what is war? Or put another way, how is he going to define a war? The question may seem unnecessary or even absurd to some of his readers, but in actuality formulating a satisfactory definition of war is a difficult task, as anyone can see by looking at some of the attempts. A standard explication is that war is conflict carried on by force of arms as between nations or states (international war) or between parties within a state (civil war). This definition is helpful but incomplete; a number of encounters in history would fall outside its scope. For example, in the American experience the white expeditions against Indians would be excluded because the tribesmen were neither sovereign states nor parties within a state, and the incursions of marines and other forces into Latin American countries would not qualify as "wars" because the invaders were not fighting a foreign power but were merely "protecting" American property. Yet these episodes were clearly conflicts carried on by force of arms, and in some of them the size of a particular American force equaled or exceeded that of an "army" in a recognized war.

The military historian would probably object to any brief definition of war. He would say that war is too complex and varied a thing to be caught up in a few words. Nevertheless, he must have a concept of the nature of war, for without one he could not understand war. And if he is going to write about war, he will have to try to explain his concept to his readers.

As an obvious starter, it must be emphasized that war is an exercise in violence. The violence occurs between groups of men, small or large in number —from an indeterminable minimum up to millions—operating under some kind of direction, loose and vague in primitive societies, tight and specific in modern nations. The violence may be applied by various weapons—stones, clubs, bows, spears, swords, muskets, rifles, artillery, atom bombs, missiles— but regardless of the weapon, violence is the first ingredient of war.

The resort to this violence has traditionally been marked by ceremony. One or both of the contending groups indicates that it intends to use force: in primitive cultures one tribal chief might personally challenge another, and in modern states the intention has been formalized in a declaration of war by government. Ceremony has also marked the end of the violence. The defeated side signals in some way that it wishes to surrender, and the victor then imposes or negotiates a peace treaty. However, it should be noted that ceremony has not always been the rule. Many wars have been initiated without a formal declaration; or put more specifically, fighting has often preceded a declaration of war. These conflicts have occurred when one nation believed its chances of victory would be increased if it struck an enemy without warning, for example, the Japanese attack on Pearl Harbor in 1941. However, in most such wars the situation before the actual strike was so replete with tensions as to be a warning in itself, and after the attack both the aggressor and the victim proclaimed the existence of a state of war, thus recognizing the rule of ceremony.

The groups who engage in violence—tribes, nations, factions within nations—do so for various reasons. Often, and especially in wars between nations, the causes are incredibly complex and deviously tangled. Historians must deal with how wars are caused, but they have not been completely successful in their analyses. Their greatest problem has been to designate one cause as more important than another. It is understandable that they should have difficulties. The emotions and influences that bore on a people in a past age are not easy to recover. And even if these can be identified, it is a formidable task to separate their impact. One influence may have incited one portion of society, whereas another may have moved another part. Moreover, it sometimes happens that a people may not know all the reasons that have impelled them to war. The usual explanation of their ignorance is that they have not been fully and frankly informed of the issues by their leaders. This has occasionally occurred, in American history as in that of other nations, but the influence of official stealth has been slighter than supposed. A more likely explanation is that people in organized groups, like individuals, sometimes act for reasons of which they are unaware.

On the other hand, it is quite possible that the members of a group resorting to war will have a fairly accurate comprehension of their reasons. At least they always *think* they know why they are acting. In modern history the principal wagers of war have been national states, and their peoples and certainly their governments have had what seemed to them good reasons to fight. Nations fight wars to attain political objectives. This fact, so simple and obvious, has not always been grasped, especially in America and by soldiers, who have tended to view the violence that is war as an end in itself—to be fought and won just for the victory, like an athletic contest. Nobody has better defined the political purpose of war than the German generally ranked as its greatest student, Karl von Clausewitz: "War is not merely a political act, but also a real political instrument, a continuation of policy carried out by other means." By policy Clausewitz meant the aims which in peace a nation tries to achieve by diplomacy and other pressures. Failing to reach them, it resorts to war, the ultimate method.

The policy objectives of nations have varied throughout history. During the last half of the eighteenth century, when the American nation was born, wars in Europe were fought for limited objectives—to gain a strip of territory, to place a friendly prince on the throne of a rival nation, or merely to preserve "national honor." Just as the aims were limited, so were the ways of making war restricted. The armed forces consisted of professional armies and navies. In land warfare, which predominated, the relatively small armies maneuvered against each other but seldom fought (though the conflict was bloody when they did); meanwhile, the civilian masses at home remained almost unaffected. At the end the victor exacted a small concession, which was all he wanted or could demand and which the defeated could easily yield.

The close of the century saw the advent of a new and quite different kind of war. The wars of the French Revolution and of Napoleon introduced the concept of "the nation in arms." They were fought by mass armies and became conflicts of whole nations. If their objectives were not quite unlimited, they were still large—the subjugation of nations or peoples. Significantly, the new era in warfare developed coincident with the Industrial Revolution, which enabled governments for the first time to keep large equipped bodies of men in the field.

The appearance of mass warfare also coincided with the emergence of the United States as an independent nation and with the beginning of American military history. The war that achieved independence, the Revolution, was a combination of the eighteenth-century limited type and the new mass type. The Americans, at least, fought for an unlimited objective, independence from British rule. If they did not place large armies in the field, they could mobilize at short notice substantial bodies of militia or irregular troops; and being able consistently to call on this form of resistance, they were truly a "nation in arms." Although they usually relied on traditional battle tactics, they at other times violated accepted rules and frequently manifested a ruthless determination to win at any cost—a characteristic of the new kind of warfare.

The inception of mass wars did not mean the end of limited wars. The United States and European nations continued to wage limited conflicts: the War of 1812 and the Mexican War are American examples. Nevertheless, the trend was toward larger and more encompassing wars. The American Civil War marked the advent of what came to be called "total war," one that was fought for an absolute objective—the survival of a nation or the destruction of its evil enemy—and that demanded the entire energies and resources of society to win it. The new totality was even more apparent in the world wars of the twentieth century between coalitions of nations. Their effects were felt throughout the world and by nations not involved in the struggles, and they were accompanied by frightful destruction that weakened the victor as well as the defeated.

POLICY, the purpose for which a nation goes to war, is determined by the government of the nation, which in practice means by the men who comprise the government. The exercise of the determination has varied with the nature of governments. In the ancient, medieval, and early modern periods the decision usually rested in the hands of one man or a few men, the chief of state and his advisers—Alexander the Great, Frederick the Great, and Napoleon are examples. The chiefs also headed the military division of government and when war was joined, took command of the armed forces. Even in later times the determination was sometimes made by one man, like Adolf Hitler and Benito Mussolini, chiefs of state who did not actively command in the field but still exerted control over operations. However, in the modern era and since the rise of representative or democratic governments, the determination of policy has come to belong to a number of men who make up the civil branch of the government, which is sharply separated by law and custom from the military branch. Thus, in the United States the decision is vested in the president and the Congress, with the president being the dominant partner because of his power over the conduct of foreign affairs.

Once a government has decided on a policy, it turns to *strategy* to achieve its objective. The government, to cite the American experience, informs the military of the objective and indicates the human and material resources it can make available. The military then takes over the planning and execution of a strategy to accomplish the policy; in effect, it takes over the running of the war. This is the concept of strategy that appeared in early modern writings on military theory and that prevailed in America's first wars. There was always, however, a gap between the theory and the practice.

Strategy was originally defined as the art of command or the art of the general, the planning and directing of campaigns. As conceived of in American conflicts before the Civil War, it was a function of the military. Theoretically, strategy was framed and directed by a general in chief if operations were the charge of one man, or by several departmental commanders if, as was often the case, there was no single head. The actuality was somewhat different. Policy and strategy were so obviously related that it was recognized the latter could not be determined by generals alone. Therefore, even in the early wars, the civil branch exercised a degree of influence over strategy. In the Revolution this influence was exerted by the Continental Congress, and after the government of the Constitution was established, it could be brought to bear more directly by the president acting in his capacity as commander in chief of the armed forces. Presidential power was sometimes invoked, as by James K. Polk in the Mexican War, but its full possibilities remained to be realized. Strategy continued to be thought of as primarily the business of the military.

During the second half of the nineteenth century a new concept of strategy began to take form in the United States and Europe. Society was becoming more complex, and so were ideas on warfare. Consequently, strategy acquired a broader definition. It became less military. It came to include a combination of factors—political, economic, psychological, technological—and to involve in its formulation and direction a variety of individuals, civilians as well as military men. The change was first apparent in the Civil War, when Abraham Lincoln exerted a control over operations undreamed of by previous presidents and when civilians had to supervise the running of the military railroads. It was more apparent in the two world wars of our century. Britain's experience in the first prompted Winston Churchill to say: "Modern war is total, and it is necessary that technical and professional authorities should be sustained and if necessary directed by heads of government, who have the knowledge which enables them to comprehend not only the military but the political and economic forces at work and who have the power to focus them all upon the goal." Today strategy would be defined as the art of employing all the resources of a nation, or of a coalition of nations, to achieve the ends of policy. This total utilization is sometimes called *grand strategy.*

MAKERS OF STRATEGY, whether soldiers or civilians or both, have to consider a variety of factors in framing their plans—the human and material resources available to them, the physical features of the theater of operations, the intention and capacity of the enemy. But above all they must bear in mind the purpose for which they are planning—they have to produce a strategy that will attain the policy for which their government went to war. Clausewitz stressed this overriding objective in one of his neatest formulations. The aim of war and hence of strategy, he said, is "to compel our adversary to do our will."

Thus stated, the problem of the planners seems simple. Its implementation, however, may prove difficult. How do "we" compel the adversary to do "our" will? Clausewitz had an answer, and because it seemed so logical and because his reputation was so great, it was warmly embraced in Europe and the United States. Strategy should aim at the "complete disarming or overthrow of the enemy," he proclaimed. He appeared to advocate total destruction of the enemy, and his doctrine became known as the "strategy of annihilation." Actually, he was not as extreme as his language suggested. By *disarm* and *overthrow,* he meant only that the principal army or resisting force of a foe must be brought to battle and defeated so decisively that it could fight no longer; its government would then sue for peace.

The strategists who accepted and attempted to apply Clausewitz's doctrine neglected to ask one important question about it. If the purpose of war is to make the enemy do one's will, is it necessary to annihilate him, or his military machine, to accomplish the purpose? Or, put another way, is it possible to achieve one's will by means of another strategy? Clausewitz did not live to complete his work on the philosophy of war and was unable to consider these issues. Other, later theorists, however, did consider them and were led to produce an alternate doctrine, the "strategy of exhaustion." It could be employed in any kind of war, but was most likely to be used in a limited war, especially one of limited objectives. The strategy of exhaustion did not set up winning the "decisive battle" as the only, or the best, means of accomplishing policy. Instead, it stressed that the objective could be attained at less cost by depriving the enemy of the resources to wage battle, by invading and occupying vital areas of his territory and thus weakening his logistical base. Eventually he would be unable to fight effectively and would have to yield. He would do "our" will but would not be destroyed.

Elements of the strategy of exhaustion were, of course, employed in wars before the term was coined, just as the principle of the strategy of annihilation had been used before Clausewitz erected it into a faith. But stated as a formal doctrine, the strategy of exhaustion excited distrust and even resentment in the minds of many planners and directors of war. Especially in the United States, military thinking continued to stress the decisive battle as the aim of strategy. The first questioning of the strategy of annihilation came as a result of the wholesale destruction in World War I, and it was intensified after World War II. The new weapons that technology had devised held a grisly promise—that one side in a war could literally annihilate the other. After 1945 the development of nuclear weapons led to a virtual renunciation of Clausewitzian doctrines, at least by the nations possessing atomic bombs, and these are the only nations capable of waging big wars. Strategists of those nations would not dare to advocate an unlimited war—unless they were willing to risk national destruction.

BEFORE LEAVING the subject of the purpose of war and strategy, it is necessary to append some exceptions to the generalizations. It has been contended that the government and the people of a group resorting to war are likely to have a fairly accurate impression of what it is they want to attain. But whereas their objective seems apparent, it may not be intelligible or realistic, and hence not attainable.

An example of the fuzzy objective is afforded by British policy in the American Revolution. Britain sought to force the colonists to pay taxes to support the empire: the result was to cause rebellion. The British attempted to assert their authority, the main exercise of which would be to collect taxes from the Americans. But as historian William Willcox has pointed out, the British could gain nothing even if they suppressed the rebellion. "Britain would either have to conciliate the colonies by granting them a large measure of autonomy, or hold them down by military rule. Conciliation would mean surrendering all hope of a colonial revenue; the cost of military rule would absorb whatever revenue might be raised." As a result, Britain's will to win was sapped by doubts as to "what winning would achieve."

A more recent example of the blurred objective was provided by American policy in Vietnam. Although the full story of that conflict has yet to be told, it seems clear that it was a civil war, and if there is one thing we know about civil wars, it is that they have to be fought out to a decision. Thus, in Vietnam both sides were fighting for an unlimited objective. Into this war the United States intervened with a limited objective—free elections, shared power, other compromises. Neither adversary could accept these aims, and the United States, as if realizing the dilemma it put itself into, could not pursue a realistic strategy.

An even larger qualification must concern the very purpose of war. It can be argued that in the past war often had a social utility. Some wars accomplished great results that probably could not have been brought about by any other means. Most important, war, or the threat of war, was a way of preserving international order. And these results were achieved at a comparatively small cost—as long as wars were fought with weapons of limited destructive power and involved principally the contending military forces. But this was no longer true after the advent of total war. Warfare became so destructive that its costs were almost as high for the victor as for the defeated, so high, in fact, as to render victory hollow. Moreover, the great wars of the modern era had an increasing tendency to impose their own conditions on the humans who thought they could control them—to force the wagers of war to adopt policies to achieve victory they had not considered at the outset of war and often did not want to adopt. War as a means of accomplishing political ends was becoming an unreliable instrument.

CLOSELY RELATED to strategy are *tactics,* the arrangement and direction of forces in battle, or the art of fighting. Tactics will be discussed as they appear in various wars but not in detail, because they can become wearisome and obscure the main outline of the story. Nevertheless, they have to be treated, for sometimes they may be a more decisive element than strategy. As the British historian Cyril Falls has emphasized, the commander who has suffered a strategic reverse may remedy everything by a tactical success; for a serious tactical reverse, however, there may be no remedy whatever.

With tactics is associated a set of subterms. In land warfare, armies are arranged in a *tactical formation*. These formations have varied throughout history, depending on what weapon or weapons are dominant at a particular time. When shock weapons—for example, clubs or swords—have predominated, a mass formation has prevailed. When missile weapons—bows or rifles —have ruled, a line formation has been the rule. An army moving to attack advances from its *base of operations* in home or friendly territory along a *line of communications,* which may consist of roads, railroads, waterways, or air routes. When it finds the enemy, it may employ various movements to defeat him. The simplest one is a *frontal assault,* relying on sheer physical superiority. More subtle is an *envelopment,* which involves attacking on the enemy's flank and toward his rear while holding him in front. Most difficult of all to pull off, but most fruitful if it succeeds, is a *double envelopment*—attacking on both flanks of the enemy while occupying his center, which can result in destruction or surrender.

Ranking in importance with strategy and tactics is *logistics,* which was originally and simply defined as the art of moving and maintaining forces. The definition still holds, but as warfare has become more technological, the exercise of logistics has become incredibly complex. The most unglamorous and unrecognized of military activities, it is one of the most vital ingredients of victory. We will have occasion to review campaigns that were well conceived and executed but that faltered or failed because the problems of supply were neglected.

I HAVE SPOKEN of the difficulty of defining war or deciding when an exercise in violence is a war. Still, a choice has to be made. This book will deal mainly with international wars—conflicts between the United States and foreign foes. The Civil War may be considered an exception, but it actually was a war between two nations. However, note will be taken of those "other kinds of wars"—with Indians, and in imperialistic adventures. These conflicts will be described in sections summarizing military developments between international wars. The treatment of the formal wars will include as much as space allows of the clash of battle, the making of strategy, the mobilization of manpower and resources—all the varied factors that are a part of the violence we call war. It is vitally important that we understand this violence. As Walter Lippmann once said: "War will never be abolished by people who are ignorant of war."

T. HARRY WILLIAMS

THE HISTORY
OF AMERICAN WARS

CHAPTER I

The First Wars

IN THE SPRING OF 1745 the town of Boston in the colony of Massachusetts hummed with martial activity. Soldiers marched through the streets and ships crowded the harbor. The mother country of Great Britain was at war with France, and her New England colonies on their own initiative were preparing an expedition to seize the strongest fortress in French Canada, Louisbourg. Boston, the principal town of the region, was serving as the main point of assemblage. In Boston a doctor with a penchant for sarcastic expression watched the gathering of forces with amused scorn. What most impressed him was the amateur quality of the enterprise. It had, he wrote, "a lawyer for contriver, a merchant for general, and farmers, fishermen, and mechanics for soldiers."

As matters turned out, the doctor's sneer was undeserved. The amateurs captured Louisbourg, a fortress constructed according to the latest European standards and garrisoned by French regulars—greatly outnumbered, it is true, but still regulars. The attackers had a piece of initial luck—the French had left a strong position undefended—but luck alone did not explain their success. It was, rather, the determination and skill, even professional skill, with which the operation was conducted. The troops, militia volunteers, charged with an almost reckless enthusiasm. Equally important, perhaps more so, their leaders displayed an unsuspected knowledge of European methods of siege operations.

The expedition to Louisbourg was an epitome of colonial military undertakings. Impulsively planned, it was carried to completion with a kind of frantic efficiency. Naively conceived in optimistic anticipation of easy success, it met unexpected obstacles, but the dogged determination of the leaders and the men overcame them. Combining British-European and American practices of war, it expressed an emerging new way of warfare. In this it was like the colonies themselves, an emerging society that was evolving new institutions while retaining vestiges of the institutions of an older, parent society.

THE PEOPLE WHO SETTLED the thirteen English colonies on the Atlantic seaboard were predominantly of British origin. However, groups from other sources could be found in pockets throughout the colonies—French, German, Irish, Scots, and Scotch-Irish. Because the majority had an English heritage and because the first colonists had come from England, the social patterns of the colonies developed along British lines. This was most apparent in the evolution of political institutions, especially the popular assemblies modeled on the British Parliament that contested for power with royal or proprietary governors. It was also apparent, but not to the same degree, in the development of military institutions. In this area European influences were evident, transmitted in part from Britain, which during the colonial period shifted to continental methods of war. But in part they came directly from Europe. The Americans, a people of diverse origins and reasonably well informed, had at least a general knowledge of how wars were conducted in that larger world of which they considered themselves a part.

The kind of warfare the colonists knew was that practiced in the period of settlement, the seventeenth and eighteenth centuries. Although there were some changes in tactics and weapons during these two centuries, the basic methods of fighting remained constant, becoming so formalized finally that the system took on a name, eighteenth-century warfare.

The continental nations fought their wars with professional armies and navies. So also did Britain after the seventeenth century. She had formerly relied on a citizen, or militia, army, but when she became an imperial power and had to fight in foreign lands, she was forced to turn to professionals. In all countries the raising of an army was an onerous and expensive task. The officers came from the nobility and gentry and were easily enlisted. But the rank and file had to be recruited from the lowest classes, from men who had no other place to go and were amenable to offers of bounty or threats of force. Once raised, a professional army was a resource to be husbanded—it was difficult and perhaps impossible to replace. Therefore, commanders did not risk battle unless they were reasonably certain of victory, or had no choice but to fight.

Armies were composed predominantly of infantry, with cavalry and artillery as supporting units. During the seventeenth century an infantry formation normally included a number of pikemen, who protected the musketeers while they reloaded. By the end of the century, however, the pike sections were disappearing. As the relatively new gunpowder weapons were improved, commanders came to rely more on the volume of firepower that an army could deliver and less on the effect of shock weapons like the pike. Moreover, a way was found to give the musket the power of shock—by fitting a small pike, the bayonet, onto the end of the barrel without plugging it.

The standard handguns of infantry in the seventeenth century were first the matchlock and then the wheelock. The names suggest the problem of the designers of the first muskets, which was to provide a firing mechanism that would ignite the powder in the priming pan and propel a lead ball out of the muzzle in the direction of the massed enemy. When a musketeer pressed the trigger of a matchlock, a slow-burning fuse or match fell into the powder pan; when he triggered a wheelock, a small steel wheel struck sparks from iron pyrites which were transferred to the pan. Both guns were hard and slow to load, and in bad weather were uncertain in discharge. By the eighteenth century they had been supplanted by the flintlock, which was easier to load and fire, surer in discharge, and superior in range and accuracy. This musket remained in use, in American and other armies, until the 1840s. A remarkable weapon, it merits description.

Although the flintlock was lighter than earlier small arms, it was still a cumbersome piece. Six feet in length with the bayonet, it weighed ten pounds or more. It was loaded from the muzzle, the man doing the loading having to stand in an exposed position. He bit off the end of an envelope containing ball and powder, rammed home the charge, placed priming powder in the pan, and was ready to fire. On command, he pressed the trigger, whereupon, if everything went right, a piece of flint struck steel, producing sparks that ignited the powder. The process required seventeen motions, but a trained soldier could get off two to three rounds a minute if he did not become rattled in the din of battle.

The projectile discharged was a large lead ball that killed, or tore a gaping, ghastly wound, if it hit an enemy. It did not always hit, however. The barrel of the flintlock was a smoothbore—that is, it had no rifling; the ball bounced around within it and, when it left the barrel, was limited and uncertain in flight. The range of the musket was 200 yards, but at that distance it was inaccurate. Its most effective range was 50 to 100 yards. The Revolutionary officer who reportedly exhorted his men, "Don't fire until you see the whites of their eyes," was not making a statement for the history books but giving a necessary order.

Artillery, the second of the combat arms, had two functions. Siege artillery was used against fortresses or walled towns. The siege pieces were cumbersome and heavy, weighing up to 3,000 and 4,000 pounds, and fired mainly "solid shot," large iron balls. Field artillery was lighter, the pieces mounted on wheeled carriages pulled by men or horses, and was employed principally against enemy personnel. It fired grapeshot, a cluster of small iron balls attached to one another, or canister, a can of loose pellets. Like the handguns, the big guns were smoothbores and muzzle-loaders. They had a longer range than the handguns, up to 400 or 500 yards, but were not effective at that distance. Men who wanted to kill other men in the eighteenth century had to be able to see their intended victims.

Cavalry, the third arm, had with the advent of missile weapons sunk to a third place. In the Middle Ages, cavalry had relied for success on its shock tactics, a mass of mounted men armed with sword or lance riding over and through infantry armed with spears or short-range missile weapons. But now infantry bearing firearms might blow a cavalry force off the field before it came close. Consequently, the horsemen had to accept a subordinate role in battle. They were most likely to be used near the end of a battle, when a commander judged the enemy infantry was at the breaking point. Then the cavalry charged, firing carbines (short muskets) and pistols at close range and finally sweeping into the enemy ranks with sabers.

Tactics in the eighteenth century, as is always the case in warfare, were closely related to the prevailing weapons. They were also influenced by the terrain, which in Europe was usually open and level. Opposing armies had to approach near each other in order to deliver their fire, and on the fields of Europe they could do this easily. But they also had to approach in such a way that they could deliver their fire with the most effective impact, and this was where tactics came into play. Armies of the time employed formations known as linear tactics to distinguish them from earlier mass formations.

In an eighteenth-century battle, an army marched onto the field in columns and then deployed into line. A line of infantry, the core of the army, consisted of a number of regiments formed in three or more ranks, the men standing shoulder to shoulder. The artillery was deployed in line with the infantry, while the cavalry was posted on the flanks or in the rear. The opposing army was drawn up in the same formation.

The battle would be opened by artillery fire from both sides; then, the commander who thought he was strong enough to attack would order his men forward. Advancing in rigid lines which were constantly kept dressed—it was believed that only a uniform line could achieve an effective fire—the troops moved to within a hundred yards or less of the enemy. Here they were halted, and on command fired by volley at the enemy mass. All firing was by volley without aiming, because this was judged the best way to accomplish a quick fire, and besides, the muskets had no rear sighting device. After firing, the first rank passed to the rear to reload or knelt so that their comrades could fire over them. The enemy replied with his own volleys, and the exchange continued until one commander decided to try for a final decision with a bayonet or cavalry charge or both. If he won the field, he pursued the enemy as vigorously as he could. The defeated commander attempted to elude pursuit and regroup his army for the next battle. The tactics of such a battle—the measured volleys —could be executed only by highly disciplined troops who had been subjected to endless drill.

Not all engagements were fought on open fields. Sometimes an army on the offensive would find that the enemy had taken refuge in a fortress. Then, if the attacker wished to achieve a decision, he had to resort to siege operations. By the eighteenth century both the art of building forts and the art of taking them had been highly developed. Interestingly, both were based on the ideas of one man, a French military engineer, Sébastien Vauban. It was said that a fortress built by Vauban could not be captured and that a fortress besieged by him could not resist.

Vauban's fortresses were built in the shape of a star, the walls of stone or masonry covered with earth on which cannon were mounted. At intervals bastions projected from the walls to provide an enfilading fire along their length. In front of each main wall, or *scarp,* and around the whole ran a ditch, and in front of this was a smaller earthen wall, the *glacis,* intended to absorb the impact of hostile solid shot.

Vauban's system of siege was known as the approach by parallel lines. The attacking force first surrounded the fortress and then brought up heavy siege artillery to within range of the walls. Behind the guns a parallel trench was dug to protect the gunners and assault forces. While the siege guns thundered away, engineering troops ran smaller trenches several hundred yards forward to a point where a new parallel was opened. The guns were then moved forward, and the same process was repeated. By the time a third parallel had been constructed, the besiegers were so close to the walls that they could breach them and storm the fortress, whereupon the defenders usually surrendered. This complicated system was known to Americans, as were other European practices. It was a variation of the system that the New Englanders had used to take Louisbourg.

THE FIRST COLONISTS found themselves in a land that was very different from the built-up environment of Britain and Europe—vast in extent, heavily forested, without roads, sparsely populated. If the various tribes of native Indians were not initially disposed to be hostile to the newcomers, they soon became so, as more and more colonists arrived and the inevitable frictions between two diverse cultures developed. Thus, at an early date the colonists faced an enemy, and they had to devise a military organization to cope with him.

The organization they created deserves the attention of social scientists as a practical expression of a society's needs and resources. It reflected the military tradition of the English colonists but was also an outgrowth of the way in which all the colonies were established. It was a good instrument for the task of fighting Indians—was, indeed, the only available instrument.

The thirteen English colonies were founded one by one over a span of more than a century. Settlements in them came into being in the same piecemeal fashion. First, a single town or village would be established, and then other centers nearby; next, people moved out into the surrounding countryside to set up farms or plantations; and finally, as the population swelled, the line of settlement pushed farther inland. It was at these clusters of settlement or habitations near them that the Indians struck when they decided to resist further encroachment. Necessarily, the initial response to the Indian threat was at the local level, and the first military organization to appear was local in make-up, but almost immediately became a part of a larger organization—the colonial militia.

The tradition of the militia stretched far back into English history, to the Saxon fyrd of the time before the Norman conquest and to the Assize of Arms of Henry II in the twelfth century, which required all able-bodied freemen between the ages of sixteen and sixty to bear arms in defense of their country. From these beginnings emerged the institution of the militia, which was organized on a county basis but owed allegiance to the central government. The militia was based on the principle that a freeman had an obligation to fight for his country in war and to prepare to fight in time of peace. It was a part-time citizen army, to be called out in an emergency—to repel an invasion and then return to the citizen mass whence it had come. Established when Englishmen had feared a professional army as an instrument of tyranny in the hands of an ambitious king and before Britain had embarked on foreign ventures that demanded professional forces, it was declining in vigor while the colonies were being settled.

It was, however, the organization to which the colonists turned in their need, because it was the form they knew most about and because they retained the fear of a standing army. Even if they had been receptive to the idea of a professional army, they lacked the resources to support one. Moreover, for the kind of warfare they had to wage, a professional army was obviously not practical. Campaigns by and against Indians were generally of short duration, and a professional force would have been a needless expense.

A town militia outfit, usually the first unit to appear, consisted of a company or "trained band" of sixty-four men. The size of a company was increased as the population grew, until a maximum of two hundred was reached, whereupon a new company was formed. These early companies were infantry, two-thirds of the men being musketeers and the remainder pikemen. However, in the forests of the New World the pike was recognized to be an outdated weapon even before it was discarded in Europe. Thus, in 1675 a Massachusetts law declared the pike of "little use in the present war with the Indians" and ordered pikemen to provide themselves with firearms.

Laws regulating the militia were among the earliest enacted by the colonial assemblies. Typical of the importance attached to a proper organization was the statement of the Massachusetts General Court: "The well ordering of the militia is a matter of great concernment to the safety and welfare of this commonwealth." Although the laws varied in detail, they agreed on principle —all able-bodied males between certain ages owed military service to the colony and had to enroll in their local militia. Every colony enacted such a compulsory-training law except Quaker-influenced Pennsylvania, which permitted a volunteer militia.

The laws usually stipulated that males between sixteen and sixty were liable for service. Certain occupational deferments were allowed—to sheriffs, justices, ministers, teachers, and other public servants. Most colonies excluded one numerous group—Negroes. Some colonies excluded all blacks, others only slaves. The spectacle of blacks bearing arms was disquieting to many whites, and was especially alarming if the blacks were also slaves. Hence the exclusion laws were justified on the grounds that militia service was a prerogative of freemen. In times of crisis, however, such as an Indian raid, blacks were likely to be impressed into service in any colony.

Not only was every male within the age limits required to present himself for service, he had to provide his own equipment, musket, ammunition, clothing, and provisions, thus becoming in effect his own logistics service. At fixed times he reported to his town or township seat for drill. The training sessions were at first frequent, once a week, but as the Indian danger seemed to abate, ardor also declined, and the drill days were reduced to eight a year, and in some colonies to even fewer. At these meetings the men would engage in marching and other parade-ground formations and in musketry practice, and more often, as conditions became more settled, in social, festive, or political activities. On occasion the men of a local company trained with men from other units. Each colony provided, at least on paper, for a regimental organization, the companies of a county. In some colonies the regiments assembled once a year, but in others the rule was once in four years, and the practice was likely to present a rare spectacle, a colonial force of combined arms. Many colonies allowed cavalry companies, which operated as scouts with the infantry, and a few authorized artillery companies, which could perform the latest European evolutions with field and siege artillery.

The command system varied in detail from colony to colony but followed a general pattern. Supreme authority rested in law with the assembly of each colony, but the assembly in practice left the active management of military affairs to a less plural agency, sometimes to the upper house (in most colonies appointed by the governor), more usually to the governor himself. The governor, with the consent of the assembly, appointed the general officers and the "commanders," or colonels, who administered military districts. The company grade officers were elected by the men, a method inherited from the English. The practice has been condemned by later critics who think it introduced politics and hence inefficiency into the officer corps. It did this on occasion, but it was just as likely to result in the selection of men who were natural leaders.

In none of the colonies did the officer corps include a permanent staff—planning or "housekeeping" officers, commissary or quartermaster organizations to look after supplies. A permanent staff was not needed. Most campaigns against the Indians lasted but a few days, and the militia reported with their own weapons and provisions. If an expedition was to be of any duration, the colonial government took over the logistical problem, providing what supplies were needed and appointing temporary staff officers to distribute them. Procurement was a simple process compared with what it would become in later and more complex wars. Food could usually be secured locally. Although most arms had to be imported, there were some resources of production. Probably one-third of the muskets used by the colonists during the seventeenth century were made in small domestic plants, and gunpowder was manufactured in a number of mills. There were even a few foundries that cast cannon.

An expedition against the Indians was usually organized in a district or districts that had been attacked or were threatened by them. The assembly assigned quotas to the local militia commander, who first endeavored to fill them by calling for volunteers from the units under his direction. If the expedition was going to penetrate Indian country, he sought to enlist the younger, fitter men. Volunteers usually filled the quotas, but if they did not, the commander was authorized to draft additional men. The column finally marched forth, a true citizen force.

LITTLE IN THEIR military heritage had prepared the colonists for the kind of warfare carried on by the Indians. Accustomed to British-European rules and practices of war, the whites encountered an enemy who did not know the rules and did not care to learn them. The Indians' ignorance of convention gave them certain initial advantages, but the colonists were able to adapt to Indian tactics and themselves become unconventional. And, having a superior technology and social organization, the whites in the end prevailed.

When the whites came, the principal Indian weapon was the bow and flint-tipped arrow. Although its range was limited, it was an effective missile weapon, silent, accurate in the hands of a skilled warrior, and capable of use in all weather. For shock action at close quarters the Indians relied on the tomahawk and knife. Contact with the whites impressed them with the killing power of muskets, and they quickly converted to their use, securing the guns by trading furs for them with the colonists or as gifts from the rival French.

The weapons of the Indians might change, but their tactics remained the same. They lacked the social organization to plan and execute a complicated or sustained campaign. In preparing to attack whites, voluntary bands formed under war chiefs and took off, usually with only a vague objective in mind. The basic Indian tactic was surprise, a sudden strike at isolated cabins or villages; the Indians first surrounded the objective and then attacked, usually at dawn. In battle they moved in a scattered and loose formation, utilizing every possible cover, each warrior operating on his own and seeking an individual opponent. If resistance was unexpectedly stiff, they gave ground but might return when the pressure eased. If pursued, they lay in wait and tried to ambush the pursuers. They occasionally attacked the palisaded wooden forts that the whites erected on the frontier but hardly ever tried to storm them. The savage concept of war did not demand the sacrifice of life in a last desperate effort.

Faced by such an enemy, the whites had to modify the tactics of their European heritage. The Indians would not stand up and fight on an open field, and besides, in the American forests there were few open fields on which to fight. In part the whites met the problem by adopting Indian tactics, moving in a loose formation and taking advantage of cover. A force penetrating Indian country would seek to prevent ambush by sending ahead scouts, another Indian practice. The scouts were sometimes friendly tribesmen, but more usually were specially enlisted units of woodsmen known as "rangers." Similar to the rangers but an improvement on them were the light troops, a joint American-British creation, the name deriving from their lighter clothing and armament. They not only scouted but in battle took an advanced place on the line.

The rangers and some of the light troops were armed with a new handgun that was colonial America's most distinctive contribution to weaponry: the Pennsylvania or Kentucky rifle. Resembling the musket in size and firing device, it differed by having rifling in the barrel, which imparted spin to the ball. Consequently, its accurate range was much greater than the musket's—up to 300 yards. It was, however, a weapon of restricted use: it took three times as long to load as a musket, could not mount a bayonet, and hence was impractical on the battle line.

Eventually, the whites found that the most effective way to strike at the Indians was to attack them in their home territory and destroy their fields and villages, many of which were protected by log fortifications. Adopting the Indian tactic of surprise, the whites would surround a village at night and attack at dawn. They also learned to take advantage of the seasons, attacking in winter, when the Indian preferred not to fight. Their task was made easier by the curious Indian practice of never posting guards. Thus cornered, the Indians had to stand and fight, and against even militia only partly trained, they had little chance.

The Indians repeatedly tried to throw back the line of advancing white settlement. In 1622 and 1644 the tribes in the tidewater region of Virginia arose in bloody assault, but were finally crushed and forced to move. The Pequots in Connecticut struck back in 1637 and were almost annihilated. In 1675 a remarkable chief known to the settlers as King Philip incited several New England tribes to attack the whites; he was killed, and his followers were broken. The Tuscaroras of North Carolina, some 1,200 warriors, rose in 1711 and were defeated so badly that they had to leave their lands.

The most formidable uprising occurred in 1763–64 under the leadership of an able Ottawa chief, Pontiac, who had formed a confederation of the tribes in the area that later would be Ohio, Indiana, and Michigan. A combined British and colonial effort was required to suppress this outbreak. The last war took place in 1774 and was entirely colonial, undertaken by Virginia, which claimed present Kentucky and part of Ohio in its jurisdiction. In this western region the Shawnee and other tribes rose in sudden and bloody war. Virginia, under the leadership of its royal governor, Lord Dunmore, sent two expeditions of 1,500 men each to restore order. The columns moved by land and water to points opposite one another on the Ohio River—the movement was a considerable logistical feat—from which point they expected to unite. Before they could do so, one of the columns was attacked by a force of 1,000 Indians, who fought almost a pitched battle. It was a rare tactic for Indians, but the Virginians finally won, and their victory broke the resistance of the tribes.

The colonists learned more from the Indians than tactical innovations. The whole Indian way of warfare was a disregard of existing rules, and this disregard entered subtly into American thinking about war. In later conflicts foreign observers would note that the Americans were a people remarkably uncommitted to doctrine. Surely this flexibility resulted in part from the Indian experience. The colonists learned something else from the Indians—brutality. When the natives captured a settlement, they slaughtered every person in it except the few they elected to take prisoner. By the Indian concept all were enemies and had to be killed. The whites, however, were infuriated and retaliated by sometimes slaying every person in an Indian village. Their reaction was understandable, but they had not originally possessed such a concept of enemies. Thus they shed another layer of their European heritage.

THREE EUROPEAN POWERS had marked out colonial empires in North America. British colonies stretched along the Atlantic seaboard from Maine, then a part of Massachusetts, to Georgia. By 1700 the line of settlement was reaching toward the Appalachian Mountains, and beyond this range Britain claimed all the territory west to the Mississippi River and south of the Great Lakes and north of Spanish Florida. Some of the colonies contended that their charters gave them title to lands in this region.

France, the paramount continental power and chief rival to Britain in European politics, claimed a vast area of the North American mainland—all of Canada and the entire Mississippi River Valley, on both sides of the river and to the east as far as the Appalachians. Settlements within this expanse, however, were few and scattered. French colonial strength was dissipated in two widely separated centers—Canada, or New France, and Louisiana. In New France the principal settlements were on the St. Lawrence River, Quebec and Montreal; in Louisiana they lay on the Gulf Coast, New Orleans and Biloxi. Between the two centers the French erected what they hoped would be a linking line of posts in the Mississippi and Ohio river valleys. The population was not only dispersed but sparse. Frenchmen were reluctant to emigrate to the harsher American environment. By the middle of the eighteenth century the population of the French colonies had grown to only 75,000. By contrast the number living in the British colonies was over one million.

Spain's extensive colonial domain lay mostly outside North America and hence out of the area of clashing imperial ambitions—Central and South America, Mexico, and islands in the West Indies. Farther north she held only outposts, the California and New Mexico extension of Mexico proper, and Florida. Spain did not play a major role in the European and colonial wars of the seventeenth and eighteenth centuries. She was a declining power and was usually found in subordinate alliance with France.

Britain and France, the principal colonial powers in America, were the leading nations in the European system and on opposite sides in the four wars that divided that continent between 1689 and 1763. Britain supported whatever coalition of continental states opposed the ambitions of mighty France. France fought alone or with the feeble aid of Spain and occasionally of other powers. The first three wars originated in European dynastic rivalries but caused fighting in America between British and French and Spanish colonists. The colonists and the European principals gave these conflicts different names, possibly indicating that they were regarded as foreign wars. The War of the League of Augsburg (1689–97) was known in America as King William's War, the War of the Spanish Succession (1701–13) as Queen Anne's War, and the War of the Austrian Succession (1744–48) as King George's War. The fourth and last war was primarily American in origin, fought, at least by Britain, for the imperial control of North America. The Americans, as if recognizing the issue, dropped their European nomenclature. They called the Seven Years' War (1756–63) the French and Indian War.

Although the first three wars were European in origin and objective, the British colonies joined in the fighting. Or more accurately, some of them joined in—those that had a special motivation to fight. These were the northern colonies adjacent to Canada, that had suffered or might suffer French-inspired Indian attacks—the New England colonies and New York and, although with less zeal, Pennsylvania. In the south, South Carolina and Georgia similarly feared Spain. Most ardent of all were the New Englanders, stern Calvinists, who, in addition to harboring grievances about the Indians, viewed the French as heathen Roman Catholics who should be smitten hip and thigh. An expedition into Canada took on something of the character of an ideological crusade.

The sectional character of the colonial response pointed up a military weakness in the British colonial system. Although the population was much larger than that of the French colonies, containing a larger reservoir of manpower, it was impossible for the British government to mobilize this resource. No central agency of control over the colonies had been established and no centralized war effort could be mounted. By contrast, New France was governed much as a French province. Its royal governor had a smaller population behind him, but his word controlled it. The Canadian militia did not compare in size with the colonial forces, but it could be easily and quickly mobilized. Moreover, the governor did not have to wring money to support his force out of a reluctant colonial assembly; he could draw on the resources of his home government.

Both sides possessed advantages and disadvantages on the eve of the wars. In addition to their militia, the French relied on garrisons of regulars stationed at strategic forts on the St. Lawrence River or its approaches and on the Great Lakes. The garrisons were small, however, and even in conjunction with militia were not strong enough to undertake major or distant campaigns against the British colonies. For offensive operations the French recruited their Indian allies in the Great Lakes and Ohio Valley regions. These tribes resented the British, who penetrated their lands in numbers, as the French did not; they accepted firearms from the French and, acting with French troops, raided the colonial frontiers. These forays caused widespread death and destruction, but this irregular kind of warfare could not decisively affect the course of the wars.

Britain's greatest advantage was in her navy, the strongest in the world. Her control of the sea ensured her line of communication with America and enabled her to harass the French. It also raised the possibility of mounting naval expeditions against the French strongholds in Canada—if sufficient manpower could be joined with sea power. But Britain did not seem interested in supplying the manpower. She maintained regular forces in America but in even smaller numbers than those of the French and restricted them to seaport towns. Preoccupied with the conflicts in Europe, she did not exert herself until the last war to put sizable forces in America. If French power in Canada was to be struck, it would have to be done by the colonists, with Britain furnishing largely naval support.

The colonists were willing to attempt the task. At considerable expense and energy they organized several expeditions to invade Canada. Because such an expedition was intended to operate outside the boundaries of a colony, it was technically not a militia force. However, it was raised out of the militia, which served as a base of recruitment. The colonial government appointed as commanding officers popular leaders who could persuade militia units to join the endeavor. The men enlisted for short hitches, the expected duration of the campaign, and were paid by the assembly. These expeditions entered Canada on two routes, via the lake and river chain connecting the Hudson and St. Lawrence rivers or along the Atlantic coast to the mouth of the St. Lawrence.

The colonists carried on what fighting occurred in America in the first conflict, King William's War. Massachusetts raised 700 men for a land and naval attack on Port Royal in Acadia on the Nova Scotia peninsula. The operation revealed the strength and weakness of a colonial offensive. The attackers took the town but could not leave enough men to hold it, and the French eventually returned. Emboldened by this success, Massachusetts prepared a more ambitious project, an assault by a force of 2,000 troops and naval vessels on Quebec. This fortress was too formidable for a colonial army to crack, however, and the attack was abandoned. Simultaneously with the onslaught against Quebec, a column of New York and Connecticut volunteers started to move from Albany along the lakes-river route to Montreal. The column was small—some of the promised units did not arrive—and faced appalling logistical problems in this wilderness area, so its discouraged leader called off the invasion. In their various enterprises the colonists displayed a fair measure of competence and much ingenuity in planning. But they could not achieve a decision with their resources alone. No decision was reached in Europe either, and the war ended in 1697 with all conquests in America being restored. Both sides rested and prepared for the next round.

It came soon, in 1701, with the outbreak of Queen Anne's War. Again the colonists took the initiative in planning operations, and again they did most of the fighting, although Britain provided more aid than previously. In 1709 the governments of the northern colonies, displaying a sound instinct for the offensive, prepared a two-pronged attack on Canada, on Montreal by land from New York and on Quebec by sea from New England. Britain promised to support the latter movement with a naval convoy and five regular regiments. It was a project of considerable cooperation—seven colonies were involved—and was commenced with great enthusiasm. A force of 1,500 volunteers was assembled at Albany, and a contingent almost as large was gathered at Boston to await the coming of the British. Just as all was ready, the news arrived that the British were not coming—the troops were needed in Europe. The disgusted Americans were forced to abandon both expeditions. The following year, however, they raised 1,500 men to attack Port Royal and secured British naval support. They captured the town again, and this time they held it and the surrounding region of Acadia.

In 1711 the British government revived the plan to attack Montreal and Quebec, promising to provide warships and transports and supporting troops. Despite their recent bitter experience in cooperating with the British, the colonists were willing to try it again, and New England and New York pledged men and money. Fifteen hundred provincials assembled in Boston to join a British force of 7,000 and its naval escort for the descent on Quebec. Over 2,000 men collected at Albany for the strike at Montreal. The offensive should have succeeded—it was superior to anything the French could bring against it—but it failed because of the lack of resolution on the part of Sir William Phips, the admiral commanding the Quebec expedition. When he sailed into the St. Lawrence, several of his transports foundered on rocks and were wrecked, and he returned to Boston. This abandonment of one thrust of the invasion meant that the other would also have to be called off. When Sir Francis Nicholson, the commander of the Montreal column, received the news, he threw his wig on the ground, stamped upon it, and cried, "Roguery! Treachery!" He should have cried, "Incompetence! Cowardice!"

The war finally ended in 1713. Britain and her allies had the better of the fighting and were able to demand concessions from France and Spain in

America and Europe. France ceded the island of Newfoundland, Acadia, and the Hudson Bay region. The combination of colonial and British power was beginning to roll back the borders of the French domain.

The exhausting second conflict was followed by a long period of peace. But in 1744 the contestants renewed the struggle in Europe, and in America in King George's War. It was the shortest of the four wars, lasting only until 1748, and the least decisive. In America the British government made practically no effort. The New England colonies, however, exerted their strongest venture yet, the previously described expedition against Louisbourg. This fortress, sometimes called the Gibraltar of the New World, stood on Cape Breton Island, dominating the entrance to the St. Lawrence and menacing American fishing interests in northern waters. To capture it New England sent a force of over 4,000 troops and a small navy. Britain contributed three warships, but otherwise the operation was an all-American action, and its success was the greatest accomplishment of colonial arms. Small wonder that colonial feelings were inflamed when, in the treaty ending the war, Britain returned Louisbourg to France in exchange for one of its posts in India captured by the French.

The apparently senseless relinquishment of Louisbourg reflected the vagueness of Britain's objectives in the first three wars. She wanted to retain the colonial empire she had staked out in America and thought, but was not sure, that she ought to acquire Canada. To accomplish either aim she would sooner or later have to seek a decision with France, but she shrank from exerting the effort to achieve such a decision. The colonies, aggressively eager to strike at the French centers in Canada, displayed sounder military sense. But after 1748 Britain had to make a choice—one forced on her by France.

Between 1748 and 1754 the French extended and strengthened their line of forts guarding the approaches to Canada. The principal posts were Crown Point on Lake Champlain in northern New York, Fort Frontenac on the eastern tip of Lake Ontario, and Fort Niagara on the eastern bank of the Niagara River between Lake Erie and Lake Ontario. To the colonists it seemed that the forts were meant to serve more than a defensive purpose. They could be possible offensive bases; indeed, two of them, Crown Point and Niagara, stood on territory the colonies considered theirs. But this was not all. The French moved into the Ohio Valley and announced their claim to the entire region. To demonstrate that they meant to hold it, they erected Fort Duquesne at the juncture of the Allegheny and Monongahela rivers, "the forks of the Ohio"—dominating the passage to the west and blocking British and colonial hopes of expansion.

The London government was aware of these moves and was made more aware of them by colonial complaints. In response, it told the colonial governors that although they were not to take the offensive, they could repel "force by force," that is, they could resist French encroachment upon British territory. Virginia, which claimed part of the region seized by France, acted immediately. In 1754 it dispatched a militia force under a young officer named George Washington to expel the French from Duquesne. The French had no mind to be expelled and attacked Washington with a superior force, compelling him to surrender. War, shooting war, had begun in America, although in Europe Britain and France technically were at peace.

They were technically at peace but actually at war. In 1755 both countries sent land and naval reinforcements to their colonies. From Britain as commander in chief of British forces in America came General Edward Braddock, a veteran of continental warfare, with two regiments. Braddock, with as many colonials as he could induce to join him, had as his mission the capture of Fort Duquesne. He might have landed in Philadelphia and marched for much of his way through relatively settled country. Instead, he elected to arrive in Virginia, whence after leaving the coastal region his path would lead through wilderness terrain.

He set out with a force of 2,500 troops, most of them regulars but including a contingent of Virginia and North Carolina militia. Many Americans were discouraged from joining him by his sneers at their lack of competence. "Their slothful and languid disposition renders them very unfit for military service," he declared. Ahead of him went 300 axmen to clear the road and behind him toiled a heavy baggage train of wagons. The train so slowed his march—he averaged only two miles a day—that he finally left it to follow, while he pushed on ahead with 1,500 men. As he approached Duquesne, Braddock was suddenly attacked by a force of French and Indians concealed in the dark woods, an inferior force, actually, of some 300 regulars and militia and 600 Indians. Braddock had been warned of the Indian tactics of ambush and thought he had taken adequate precautions. But when the attack fell, he was too rattled to organize countermeasures. His men, as shaken as he, pressed together, trying to form a line and firing vainly at the unseen foe. Their casualties were appalling—sixty-three of eighty-six officers killed or wounded, including Braddock mortally wounded, and almost a thousand troops killed or wounded. At the end of three hours the remnant of the column fled the field and did not halt its retreat until the safety of the settlements was reached.

Out of Braddock's defeat an American myth was born—that European tactics were not suited to the American terrain or to Indian warfare. Like most myths, it was only partly true. Braddock's men could not have scattered and fought from cover, for they were not trained to fight so, and in such a formation they could not have delivered a mass fire. They needed to break out of their encirclement by attacking with part of their force the enemy's flank or rear, thus creating another front. They would do this on other fields, demonstrating that they had learned something from the battle in the American woods. They also had learned the value of better security and greater mobility. The trend to the use of rangers and light troops received new impetus after 1755.

Simultaneously with Braddock's move the British government planned attacks on Crown Point and Fort Niagara. These offensives were to be delivered by provincial troops, with Britain furnishing money and supplies. The New England colonies and New York responded enthusiastically. Approximately 3,000 troops were raised for the assault on Crown Point and 2,400 for the one on Niagara. The column moving on Crown Point got as far as Lake George, where it was attacked by a superior French force. The provincials repulsed the assault, but the leaders decided to call off the expedition. Also cancelled was the expedition against Fort Niagara, because of logistical difficulties. The colonies had not achieved a success in 1755, but neither had they suffered a disaster.

After fighting an undeclared war for two years, Britain and France went formally to war in 1756. Although both countries and their allies were committed in Europe, Britain decided to make her main effort in America. She was at last ready to fight for colonial mastery. During the course of the war she would send to America strong naval detachments and 25,000 troops and, after some initial bad choices, able generals. In many of the land engagements colonial troops served with the British, a small number enlisting in regular units, the majority preferring to fight as militia volunteers. They served under British direction, however, in what was now a British operation.

The weight of British strength did not make itself felt until 1758. In that year Louisbourg was taken by a British naval and land expedition. British officers led a predominantly colonial force of 3,000 to capture Fort Frontenac on Lake Ontario. Its fall severed French communications with the western posts and made their hold on Fort Duquesne untenable. When a combined British and colonial force moved through Pennsylvania on Duquesne, the French abandoned the place, which was renamed by the British Fort Pitt. Only one failure marred the record of victory. As the first step of a move into Canada by the lakes-river route, the British assembled in New York an army of 16,000 troops, over half of them provincials. Its first objective was to occupy Fort Ticonderoga, recently built by the French on Lake Champlain south of Crown Point. Advancing on the lake in an armada of transports, the army reached Fort Ti, but its assault was repelled with heavy losses.

In 1759 the British planned to deliver the knockout blow. An army of 9,000 men and a strong naval force were to enter the St. Lawrence and take Quebec. Commanding the army was perhaps the ablest general of the war, James Wolfe. At the same time another army of 11,000 troops, half of them provincials, under General Jeffrey Amherst was to capture Ticonderoga and Crown Point and advance down the water route to join Wolfe before Quebec. Amherst was commander in chief of all British forces in America and had discretion to pursue any other objective that he thought might weaken the enemy. He thereby detached a force that occupied Fort Niagara, an important stroke because it further severed French communications and left Fort Detroit and the far western posts isolated. Then he advanced on Lake Champlain. The French, inferior in numbers, abandoned their forts at his approach but took a strong position on the Richelieu River in Canada. Here they held up Amherst so long that he could not go to Wolfe's support.

Wolfe, however, had decided that he did not need aid. He had found a path up the rock on which Quebec sat, and his army suddenly appeared before the city in traditional battle line. The French commander, the Marquis de Montcalm, accepted the challenge and deployed his troops in the same manner. Thus the climactic battle of the war was fought in the classic style, and the better-disciplined British decisively defeated the French troops and militia. In the following year Amherst occupied Montreal, and the British conquest of Canada was complete.

The war actually ended at Quebec, but France would not admit defeat until 1763. When it came, her admission was humiliating. She had to cede to Britain her North American empire—Canada and the territory east of the Mississippi River except for the New Orleans area. Her ally Spain had to cede Florida to Britain, but was compensated by receiving New Orleans and the territory west of the Mississippi that had been claimed by France. Spain was weak, and Britain now stood as the only strong imperial power on the continent.

A GREAT HISTORICAL EVENT will often have an ironic result, and this was the case after Britain's triumph over France in the colonial wars. The departure of the French from America and the consequent lessening of the Indian danger had the effect of loosening the bonds between Britain and her colonies. The colonies, no longer so dependent on the home country for support and many of them persuaded that previously they had not really needed British support, became increasingly restive under imperial controls, increasingly disposed to claim an independent role in their own affairs. As another ironic turn, at the same time that they were asserting their self-sufficiency, they were relaxing their military strength. There was a marked drop in the quality of the militia after 1763. Drill was not taken seriously, and the training days tended to become a farce. Indeed, some colonies no longer attempted to enforce the laws requiring drill and relied instead on voluntary militia units, the forerunners of the later National Guard.

As the years went on, the colonists exaggerated their part in the war. But this has been compensated for by the disparagement of that effort by historians. Historical treatment of the colonial contribution is almost uniformly belittling. The colonies should have done more than they did, the historians claim. They should have formed a union, as a few of their leaders advocated, and raised men and money in a united effort for the struggle in which they had a large stake. Because they did not do this, the reasoning seems to run, their other efforts did not amount to very much.

These criticisms overlook the considerable contribution of the colonies. They bore the brunt of the fighting in America in the first three wars, and they raised substantial forces that helped to determine the final result, the erosion of French power. They did not establish a central government, but managed a fair amount of cooperation, involving on occasion five to seven colonies. It is hard to see how much more they could have accomplished. The colonies could not possibly have effected the kind of combination the critics demand. They were too widely separated by space and time. There was no system of rapid communication to arouse and inflame them to unite against the French danger, and no system of ready transportation to enable them to mobilize their resources in a common effort. Nor did they have as yet that sense of identity that draws a people together to fight for a cause. That would come later, when after years of controversy with Britain and after much agonizing the Americans decided they would try for independence.

CHAPTER II

The Revolution: The American Military Organization

THE REVOLUTION holds a special place in American history. It is the conflict in which the nation was born, and although theorists and predeterminists might argue that an independent America would eventually have emerged through the operation of natural causes and without war, the great fact remains that the nation came into existence as a result of war, and at a particular time. Had the birth of this nation been delayed, the future course of world history would have been altered, and perhaps not for the better.

The Revolution also has a special place in American military history and in general military history. It is the first American war—the first, that is, that was fought formally, conducted by a government and waged as a national endeavor. Until the Vietnam involvement it was the longest American war, lasting eight years, from 1775 to 1783. (The Vietnam conflict is regarded by many to be the longest war. But as American participation in it did not begin actively until 1965 and was ended by 1973, the two struggles were of equal duration.)

In the context of world military history the Revolution was a precursor of modern mass wars. It was the first revolutionary conflict of the modern era, anticipating the French Revolution in calling forth a popular effort to achieve victory, and it antedated the wars set off by the French movement in proclaiming a political ideal as its objective. The Americans were fighting for independence and for the values amounting almost to an ideology that they associated with independence, and they could not compromise their purpose. They had to fight to victory, or to defeat. This was no dynastic war waged for a strip of territory; it was a political struggle.

Because it was a new kind of war and because the Americans were a new people and not as bound as Europeans by old rules, the conduct of the war departed in significant ways from the eighteenth-century pattern. This was most apparent in the Americans' disregard of accepted rules of war, in part a legacy of their experience with the Indians. They occasionally embarked on winter campaigns, at the time a practice almost unheard of—partially because of the logistical difficulties involved but also because by the prevailing leisurely standards there was no need to fight in disagreeable weather.

The Americans performed in ways the British considered savage or treacherous. Their riflemen aimed at and shot officers, who as gentlemen were not to be fired at deliberately, at least not by common soldiers. A British officer stigmatized this American practice as showing a lack of "modern good breeding." Americans often resorted to unprecedented trickery. At the battle of Bennington a rebel militia force opposed British regulars who had been joined by Loyalist militia of the area. Neither militia group was in uniform, of course, but each wore distinguishing rosettes. A body of patriot militia fashioned Loyalist rosettes and infiltrated the British flanks and rear and from these vantage points poured in a devastating fire when the battle was joined. The result was a slaughter of the British and a shocking blow to feudal notions of honor in war.

Although the Americans disregarded some existing rules, they observed many others, and in general the war was conducted by both sides according to eighteenth-century practices. The Americans made frequent use of their militia in emergencies and for short service, but for the long pull and as their chief fighting instrument they created a professional army on the British model. It was also trained to fight like a British army, to advance in line on an open field and deliver a volley fire. In the area of tactics, however, the American spirit of innovation effected a change. A patriot army moved in line but was usually preceded by a large, loose body of skirmishers who felt out the enemy and drew his fire. The British responded by reducing their cumbersome line from three ranks to two and by developing skirmishers themselves. Tactics had taken a step toward greater flexibility.

EVERY AMERICAN WAR has aroused historical controversy as to its causation, some stirring wide and extended debate, others provoking relatively restrained comment. But each has had its argument, concerned mainly with the considerations of the American people in entering upon war. American motivation in the Revolution has not been resolved even after two centuries.

The colonists, as they embarked on war, provided numerous statements to explain and justify their action. The crux of their complaint against the mother country was caught up in the Declaration of Independence, in the charge that the British government had endeavored to create an "absolute tyranny" over them. As proof of their indictment, they offered various accusations: that Britain had refused assent to colonial laws, dissolved assemblies, imposed unjust taxes, and had done other hateful things, all charges coming down to one central accusation—that Britain had attempted to destroy American liberty. This was why the Americans were going to war, to preserve a set of liberties they had brought with them from England—the right to have their assemblies, to be taxed only by these assemblies, to be governed in essential matters only by these assemblies. They were fighting, in short, for home rule.

Historians who first wrote about the Revolution accepted the colonists' view of the war, and for a long time the traditional view prevailed: it had been fought to sustain home rule. But other historians came to challenge this idea. They argued that democracy—that is, popular participation in government—was only imperfectly realized in the colonies and that those Americans who wanted more of it had to contend not only against the aristocratic British government but also against native patricians. The Revolution was not, therefore, a movement for agreed-on principles or liberties. Its supporters advocated separation from Britain so that they could more easily overcome the colonial upper classes. In a phrase made famous by a leader of the new historical school, the issue was not only home rule, but who should rule at home.

These views prevailed until recent years. Then a still newer school emerged with an analysis that was remarkably close to the perception of the war held by the colonists themselves, that a large degree of democracy existed in the colonies. As Americans already enjoyed about as much democracy as they desired, they did not rebel to get more. Rather, they wanted to keep the democracy they possessed and cherished and that Britain had tried to subvert. This, of course, is another way of saying that they believed in a common set of liberties and fought to preserve home rule.

Whatever the correct interpretation, the Americans were clearly fighting for a political idea or ideas, and this objective invested their war with a particular character. The Revolution was a new kind of war.

THE THIRTEEN AMERICAN COLONIES challenged a formidable foe, the leading power of Europe. Britain possessed the greatest navy afloat and an army of 50,000 officers and troops. If her army was not as large as those of some continental nations, it compared with them in professional competence and was superior to anything the Americans had. Indeed, at the start of the war the Americans had no military organization and would have to create one, as well as other elements of a military machine in the stress of conflict.

As a going nation, Britain not only had a going military system but seemed to possess greater potential resources. The population of Britain was approximately 8 million, whereas that of the colonies was at most only 2.5 million. Measured in terms of available manpower, the disparity was even more striking. Of the American total, 500,000 were black slaves and hence disqualified from military service. In addition, a substantial minority of the whites were either loyal to the mother country, willing to actively aid her, or neutral, hoping to sit the war out. The number of Loyalists, or Tories, has been variously estimated but was probably around 500,000; it is known that 50,000 Loyalists served with the British armies. The number of neutralists has been estimated as 200,000. Thus the supporters of war constituted something more than one million of the white population, a militant but bare majority.

Britain enjoyed a similar preponderance in economic resources. The Industrial Revolution had begun, and although it was as yet in an initial stage, it was more advanced than in any other country and dwarfed developments in the colonies. Britain had tried to discourage competitive colonial manufacturing, and even when restrictions were not imposed, would-be American producers found it difficult to raise the capital necessary to launch large enterprises. The American economy was predominantly agricultural, and such manufacturing works as existed concentrated on making light or household goods. Few of them were capable of shifting to producing heavy goods, such as artillery and other implements of war.

A note of qualification has to be entered to the comparison of resources. Britain's advantages were not quite as potent as they seemed. Although her industry could produce in abundant amounts the goods of war, these goods were not immediately deliverable in America. They had to be transported over an ocean supply line of 3,000 miles, in crossings that might take as long as two to four months. The British navy was able to keep the line open, and British armies were generally better equipped than their American opponents. The navy could not, however, close the sea lanes to the colonies, and the Americans consistently managed to import from France and other sympathetic countries goods they could not themselves easily produce, such as gunpowder and artillery. This foreign aid was important, but even without it the Americans could have maintained armies in the field. In the eighteenth century, industrial capacity was not the decisive factor it would be in later wars. It was easier then to equip soldiers, and for a long time the Americans had been a populace in arms.

A similar caution is necessary in assessing Britain's apparent great advantage in population. Although her manpower pool was larger than the colonies, she could not mobilize for service in America a force commensurate with her numbers. The rebelling colonies were not her only military concern. She had to retain a part of her existing army in the home islands in the event of a European war and to station other units throughout the empire, in the West Indies, Canada, and India. For the American war she would have to rely on what forces remained, or try to increase the army.

It soon developed that she would have to raise additional troops. British generals in America estimated that at least 50,000 troops would be required to subdue the colonies, a number equal to the entire existing army. The government attempted to meet the call by the customary methods of recruiting volunteers and impressing vagrants. But this time the methods did not produce the usual response. Men who would have volunteered to fight a European foe were averse to taking up arms against a distant adversary who seemed to pose no threat to British soil. Others were reluctant to serve in a war that was not popular with a large section of the public (if American opinion was not united in support of independence, British opinion was not agreed on the necessity of coercing the colonies). In sore need, the government finally resorted to a practice occasionally used in the eighteenth century, that of hiring foreign troops. It secured them from the princelings of certain petty German states, Hesse-Cassel and others, employing in the course of the war some 30,000 of these mercenaries, who were hated by the Americans and known indiscriminately as Hessians. Drawing from this foreign resource and exploiting as best it could the domestic pool, Britain was able to maintain consistently in America some 35,000 men, more than the American national forces but not enough to accomplish policy objectives.

THE BRITISH OBJECTIVE was to suppress the rebellion and persuade the Americans to return to their allegiance to the empire. The expectation was plausible but not necessarily realistic. It did not follow that suppressing the Americans would make them submissive. They might continue to be recalcitrant, and Britain would then have to consider what she would do with her victory. As previously indicated, she would be required either to grant them a large measure of autonomy, thus abandoning hopes of colonial revenue, or rule them by military force, thus expending whatever revenue might be raised. The government had not thought through its war aim, had not considered that its objective might be unattainable.

The objective might be faulty, but it seemed logical and was, indeed, the only one Britain could have adopted—unless she chose to admit she could not control the colonies. Britain did enter the war with a purpose: she knew what she wanted to do. The Americans, on the other hand, began the war with a confusion of purpose and hence of will. They knew they were contending for a set of ideas, but were unsure as to how they could best achieve them. Should they try to force Britain to recognize their freedoms within the empire or strike for independence? They fought for fully a year before deciding for independence. That they should think they could fight and simultaneously profess loyalty to the power they were fighting seems absurd to the modern mind. But their action was understandable. Many colonists could not bring themselves to believe that Britain would refuse to confirm their rights, and the conviction that independence was the only recourse formed slowly. The most important factor influencing their delay was the absence of a central government to guide and announce their thinking. The Americans entered the war without an established government and lacked one until near its end. It is true that there was an agency that functioned as a government, but it was one by default—it had been created to fill another purpose and was used only because of convenience. In any listing of American handicaps the nature of this so-called government must occupy a high place.

The agency-turned-government was the Continental Congress, which came into being in 1774, elected by the colonial assemblies and charged by them to present to the mother country a united protest against the destruction of colonial rights. This First Continental Congress adopted a ringing Declaration of Rights and directed a boycott of British goods, in itself an act of rebellion, and then adjourned to await British reaction. Britain made no move to redress American grievances, and accordingly the Second Continental Congress convened in Philadelphia in May, 1775. In the previous month there had been a collision between the British force in Massachusetts and the militia, and the other New England colonies had called out their citizen soldiers to aid Massachusetts. These troops, although loosely organized and without a recognized commander, had nevertheless been able to lay siege to the British in Boston. The dispute between Britain and her colonies had come finally to the arbitration of arms, had come, although many Americans were reluctant to use the term, to war.

It was apparent that the colonies would have to put forth a military effort, and if it was going to be effective, it would have to be a coordinated effort—even the most dedicated parochialists recognized the impossibility of thirteen separate ventures. But in the rush of events there was not time to create a coordinating agency. There was a power vacuum, and the Continental Congress, displaying a true revolutionary spirit, stepped into it. On June 15, 1775, it took the militia around Boston into its service and named Virginia citizen-soldier George Washington as commander in chief "of all the continental forces, raised, or to be raised, for the defense of American liberty." At that hour the Congress ceased to be a vehicle of American protest and became an American government.

It had acted boldly but without appreciating the full implications of its action. In the remaining months of 1775 and the early months of 1776 the Congress regarded itself not as a government but as the superintending agency of the colonial effort to recover colonial rights—by fighting for them. Like the American people, it moved gropingly to recognize the reality of the situation: that if the colonists had to fight to secure their rights, they might as well fight to be independent. But it moved. In the spring of 1776 the Congress advised the colonies to act on the assumption that the authority of Britain had ended and to form new governments "such as shall best conduce to the happiness and safety of their constituents." The colonial governments needed little urging. Some of them had already made their own assessment of the situation and had asserted their independence of British control. Following the lead of Congress all of them announced formally their separation from the empire: by resolve of their assemblies they transformed themselves into "states." Congress, as the representative of these states, on July 2, 1776, adopted a resolution that "these United Colonies" ought to be "free and independent States," and two days later it proclaimed a Declaration of Independence—of the United States of America. A revolutionary action had been taken, not in revolutionary haste or fervor but with almost conservative deliberation and as a last and almost reluctant recourse.

The location of authority in America was at this stage dubious. In transforming themselves into states, the colonies stipulated that legislative and executive power within their borders rested with their assemblies. But they also declared they were acting at the injunction of Congress—"under the direction of the Great Continental Congress," ran one document. Did Congress then possess authority to direct the states or was it merely their agent doing their direction? In the confusion only one thing was certain—the American people wanted some form of permanent union, either as a device to prosecute the war or for its own sake. The resolves of the assemblies and numerous other expressions of opinion had called for union, and Congress accordingly appointed a committee to draw up a plan of government. The committee devised a framework of government to be called the Articles of Confederation, which Congress approved in November, 1777. Ratification by the states, however, was not accomplished until March, 1781. By that time active fighting had ceased, talk of peace was in the air, and the end of the war was only two years away.

In the meantime, in 1776 and after, the Continental Congress acted as the coordinator of the war effort, as it had since 1775 acted as the central government or civilian authority. Lacking a delegation of specific powers, it exercised such powers as the states would permit or public opinion support. In general, it adhered to the authority granted to the Congress of the as yet unratified Articles of Confederation. Thus it organized an army and navy, appointed commanders of these forces, sent diplomats to Europe, and financed its war effort by the revolutionary expedient of issuing paper money. Finally and most important, it asserted the right to determine policy and participate in the framing of strategy. These were proper powers for the civilian authority in a republic to exercise, but they were exceedingly bold ones for a government without statutory basis.

WHEN CONGRESS appointed George Washington as general in chief of the Continental forces, it attempted to spell out his command position. His commission read: "You are hereby vested with full power and authority to act as you shall think for the good and welfare of the service." This was a broad authorization, but it was followed by an exhortation of unmistakable meaning:

"And you are . . . punctually to observe and follow such orders and directions, from time to time, as you shall receive from this or a future Congress . . . or committee of Congress."

The language of the resolution seemed clear, but it left some things undefined. Washington was invested with broad powers to command, under Congress, the American land forces—those then in service, most of whom were under his direct control, and others yet to be raised. As a part of his responsibility, he was obviously expected to oversee the strategic operations of all American forces. But nothing in the document defined how strategy was to be formulated, and this vagueness left some hard questions to be settled. Who, for example, was supposed to initiate a strategic plan, the commander or Congress? If Washington, he must clearly secure the approval of Congress before acting. But if Congress, must it obtain his approval? Could a plural body like Congress formulate strategy? Or if it acted in consultation with Washington, how could it make its ideas known to him? An additional complication was the fact that Washington was also the commander of a field army, in the Middle Department, comprising lower New York, New Jersey, Pennsylvania, Delaware, and Maryland. The other two departments, the Northern and the Southern, had their own commanders. Was Washington expected to devise and direct strategy for their armies as well as his own?

At first the Congress attempted itself to exercise the function of making strategy. The delegates, meeting in secret session, laboriously framed several plans and transmitted them to Washington. Most of the schemes failed, although some of them were soundly conceived, and their failure brought wide criticism on the chamber. The more perceptive members came to realize that Congress as a whole could not actively direct the war. The process of formulating strategy by debate was too cumbersome, and besides, Congress had other affairs of state to occupy its time—foreign relations, finance, and the like. What was obviously needed was an agency that would represent Congress in the area of strategy and command, that would make its wishes known to Washington, and that could, if necessary, consult with the general in chief on strategic matters.

In deciding on the form of such an agency, there was little chance that Congress would settle on a single executive. The image of "royal tyranny" was still too sharp in colonial minds, and the fear of one-man power too present. Congress, as the guardian of American liberty, reflected the popular distrust of unitary authority. Moreover, because it was a plural body, when it thought of delegating authority, it thought instinctively of giving the delegation to a smaller plural body, or a committee. Thus when a shortage of salt developed in 1775 the Congress created a Committee for Salt; and when a shortage of meat developed, a Committee for Meat. Now, when there was need for more effective direction of the war, it would create a committee for war.

The committee was authorized in June, 1776, less than a month before the formal proclamation of independence, and was called the Board of War and Ordnance. Usually known simply as the Board of War, the agency consisted of five members of Congress and a paid secretary. The creating statute invested the board with responsibility for "the raising, fitting out, and dispatching of all such land forces" as might be "ordered out" in defense of the American cause. These were important powers, but if the board had been limited to them, it would have been largely a mobilizing and equipping agency. More important, it was to handle all congressional correspondence dealing with the conduct of the war, which meant that it was to transmit to the military branch the orders or suggestions of Congress.

The military situation did not immediately improve, and criticism of Congress resulted; accordingly, in 1777 the composition of the board was changed. Now it was to consist of three persons not members of Congress and was to include, at Washington's advice, military men. Still another alteration was made in 1778: the personnel of the board was fixed again at five, two members of Congress and three nonmembers. In 1781, when the government of the Articles of Confederation went into effect, Congress at last felt sufficiently secure to agree to a single military executive. It authorized an official called the secretary at war, the quaint title deriving from British usage. This minister had about the same powers and functions as the Board of War, and the creation of the office did not change in any way the relation between the civilian and the military branches of the government. Indeed, in this closing and relatively quiet period of the war the secretary was less active and influential than the board had been.

This then was the American command system during the greater part of the Revolution—a committee representing the civil authority, the Board of War, and a general in chief, Washington. It was far from ideal, but it was as good a system as the Americans could have devised. It worked surprisingly well, certainly better than is admitted in many of the histories of the Revolution. On the occasions when it did not work—and there were many—the failure was due primarily to the human elements in the system rather than to any flaw in the organization. The human element most at fault was Congress or, more specifically, certain members of Congress, and not Washington.

The general's private letters are filled with anguished complaints about the Congress, some of them justified and some not—he was suspicious and sometimes saw imaginary enemies or plots. But publicly Washington was the very model of the proper citizen soldier. He always acknowledged the supremacy of the civil branch over the military, refrained from open criticism of Congress, and kept that body or discreet members of it fully informed of his plans.

The Congress was not nearly as correct in its relations with him. Frequently it sent orders directly to commanders of departments. In 1780 the Congress removed the Southern Department from Washington's control, only to restore it when the delegates' hand-picked commander suffered a humiliating defeat. When the Board of War was reconstructed with military members, a step Washington recommended, known enemies of his were appointed to the new places.

These and similar congressional actions have usually been ascribed to that body's fears of a military dictatorship. The feeling existed, and with some members was an obsession. John Adams, the first chairman of the Board of War, exhorted his fellow legislators to keep always "a watchful eye on the army, to see that it does not ravish from them that liberty for which all have been contending." Men like Adams sought for opportunities to put the military in its place, sometimes elevating this objective above military efficiency. But the conclusion is inescapable that Congress's worst mistakes were caused by its neglect or disregard of good administration. The most serious indictment that can be made of Congress is not that it did too much but that it did too little. Too often it simply dawdled. Once Washington waited three months for the legislators to authorize him to increase his artillery forces and then acted on his own initiative. Congress even delayed to inform him of the French alliance, although the prospect of foreign aid was an important factor in strategic planning. Washington lamented that he would rather see prompt decisions against him than continued procrastination. But this American government had not been created to practice efficient administration. It had come into being to preserve American liberty, and this was its first interest, even in war.

The American command system was simple—Congress and its war committee, and Washington and his departmental commanders—and should have been easy to operate. The details of its operation are, however, not disclosed fully in the records. It is not always apparent who took the lead in formulating strategy, Congress or Washington; probably in most situations it was the general. But in most situations the issue was not important, because the Americans had little choice but to conform their movements to British strategy. Britain's policy was to reconquer the colonies, and this objective required an offensive strategy. The British owned the initiative—they determined where and when battles would be fought. The Americans were forced to meet these attacks and try to repel them, to hold places under threat or block British armies moving inland. In short, on the highest strategic level the Americans were forced into a defensive strategy; however, on a lower level they had the option of employing the offensive against individual British armies.

The British command system was somewhat more complicated. At its head was the king, George III, lately hated by the Americans as the instigator of the repressive measures that brought on the war and regarded now as the tyrant who was prosecuting it for their subjection. Both views were considerably exaggerated. Before the war the king had not solely determined British policy toward the colonies but had been influenced by his cabinet ministers.

and now that war had come, although he was insistent that the rebel Americans must be reconquered, he did not actively participate in the strategy. He left this function to his principal ministers, who met at stated intervals and took their projects to him for approval or disapproval. Two men in this group dominated the discussion, Lord George Germain, the secretary of state for the American Department, who planned the land campaigns, and the Earl of Sandwich, the First Lord of the Admiralty, who directed the sea operations. Sandwich owed his influence to his position: the navy was considered Britain's chief military arm. As an administrator, he was notoriously corrupt and inefficient. Germain, a man of great force and energy, seized his function. He did not have clear constitutional authority to act as land planner—there was a secretary at war in the cabinet—but he asserted the power and because of his closeness to the king was able to maintain it. He had ability, but not nearly as much as he thought. Overly sure of himself, he tended to make plans that were overly optimistic and too grand for the available resources.

Germain and his fellow planners did not appreciate the difficulty of their task. Looking at a map, they saw America as essentially a long coastal strip of 1,000 miles. It seemed easy to strike. The Royal Navy commanded the sea and, operating from bases in or off Canada and the West Indies, should be able to land troops at any point on the coast. Although the British would have to operate on exterior lines, the outside of a vast circle, they could move much faster than the Americans because water transportation was faster than that on land. For example, under favorable conditions a ship could run from Boston to Savannah in eight days. Troops marching that distance would require at least thirty days. The British could land on the coastal strip, but here their difficulty began. There was no vital center, political or economic, for them to maneuver against. The Americans had a capital, Philadelphia, but without symbolic importance. Its fall or the fall of New York or Charleston or even the defeat of an army defending one of these cities would not be sufficient to cause the rebels to quit the war. If the British were going to retake the colonies, they would have to advance inland and occupy every important center of American strength.

The British would attempt such an occupation, again and again, before admitting failure. The first problem here was transportation. Much of America was not coastal, as they pictured it: it was wilderness or semiwilderness, and an army moving inland on a land line of communication would have to be accompanied by a huge train of horses and wagons. Therefore, the British usually operated on a river line, preferably on a large stream that emptied onto the coast from far inland. The most tempting water line was the Hudson River. It offered the opportunity for a two-pronged offensive. A British army and naval force based on New York City could advance up the river to above Albany. At the same time another force could move south from Montreal along a lakes-river and land route (the one followed by the invading militia in the colonial wars), and eventually the two contingents would join. The juncture would cut the colonies in two, isolating New England from the others, and would be a serious blow to the American cause. Twice during the war the British attempted this move, and although coming close to success, twice failed. The reasons were several but boiled down to the fact that in an age of relatively slow transportation the British could not coordinate such a complicated movement with the precision required. As one disgusted general complained, carrying on a war in such terrain was "a damned affair." Another Briton said of the terrain that it "had absolutely prevented us this whole war from going fifteen miles beyond a navigable river."

The second problem of the British was they never had enough troops in America to occupy the whole country. They could concentrate in one area only by taking forces from another. Thus, when late in the war they decided to recapture the southern colonies, they had to wind down their operations in the North to a standstill. One other possibility remained to them, and this they would try, notably in the South. If they could conquer territory in the interior, they would arouse the Tories, who could be joined to the army or left as occupation troops (as later in Indo-China the French and Americans would attempt to use Vietnamese troops for occupation). They would fail in this hope as well, and again partly because of the American terrain and the transportation difficulty it imposed. Once a British army had moved away from the coast, as the British army in the South did, it had always to keep moving in search of supplies. Unable to stay long in any place, it could not hold territory and organize the Tories. An army that merely marched through the country could not force the Americans to battle—until they were ready to fight, which was when the invading army was desperate for supplies and cornered. In the meantime, the militia could be relied on to harass the invaders and hold the Tories in check. The British planners never understood that they had to subjugate an armed population. Their task was, as British historian Eric Robson has said, like "trying to hit a swarm of flies with a hammer."

FEW IF ANY governments at war have labored under such financial handicaps as burdened the Continental Congress. Called on suddenly to coordinate the American military effort, it had immediately to find money to create a military machine—to raise and equip an army and navy, to pay the salaries and wages of the personnel of these services, and then to keep supplies flowing to all parts of the machine. And it had to do these things without possessing the power to tax. It held, of course, no granted power of taxation, and this was a power it dared not grasp, because the charter of the Articles of Confederation, the general guide under which this Congress operated, denied to the Congress of that prospective government the authority to tax.

The lack of this most elementary power of government would have hampered the Congress in peacetime. In the stress of war it was crippling. Nor was this the only clog on Congress. It had to formulate a war-financing program in an economy of limited financial resources. This economy had experienced a significant expansion in recent years, but it was still relatively undeveloped. Despite promising industrial and mercantile beginnings, it was predominantly agricultural, and most of its few exports were agricultural. All American exporters, of whatever goods, relied heavily on British credit. There were no commercial banks in the country to extend domestic credit, and no supply of specie to underwrite a domestic issuance of money. Indeed, before the war most of the money circulating in trade consisted of foreign coins or bills.

The Congress was aware of its financial problem, but it had no time to consider a fundamental solution, such as asking the states for permission to tax, and even if there had been time, the request would undoubtedly have been refused. Money was necessary immediately, and Congress acted to get it by the only method available—issuing its own money. This was an exercise of power that Congress could justify by pointing to the right of issuance vested in the government by the Articles of Confederation, but it was still a bold and revolutionary action. Congress was in reality decreeing the creation of money, and in the nature of the American situation this was necessarily paper currency in the form of certificates and promissory notes. The first financial resolution of the Congress in 1775 authorized an issue of bills not to exceed $2 million. This issue was to be supported by tax quotas set for each state, to be paid in specie or Continental bills in four annual installments beginning in 1779.

The Congress had apparently found an ingenious method to finance the war. It had obtained money to expend without having had to seek the approval of the states. Moreover, the issue was thought to be sound because the states were certain to provide the funds to redeem the paper. At this juncture the members of Congress guiding its financial program had no intention of issuing large amounts of unredeemable currency. But events soon took the decision out of their hands. The states, because they lacked economic resources or feared to alienate public opinion, failed to collect the required taxes, the war went on and on and its expenses mounted, and Congress had to meet these expenses. It did so by authorizing more issues of bills, which were now supported by nothing but hope. The states also printed paper to pay their expenses, and by 1781 the total national and state money in circulation reached approximately $450 million, a staggering sum for that time.

As the money rolled off the printing presses, the inevitable economic law began to work—the value of the Continental paper dollar steadily sank and a runaway inflation set in. A hat came to cost $400, a pair of boots, $600, a suit of clothes, $1,600. A foreign officer serving in the American army exclaimed unbelievingly in a letter: "An ordinary horse is worth $20,000; I say twenty thousand dollars!" The skyrocketing prices dismayed many Americans, who either suffered from them or feared that they would depress popular morale. Several states attempted to place controls on prices and wages, a move which Congress endorsed, but the effort failed. It was too much at variance with prevailing ideas of the function of government and was not supported by popular opinion.

The situation did not improve until 1781. By that time the paper had become so worthless that it was no longer accepted, and some specie began to circulate again. At the same time Congress, moving toward unitary administration in finance as well as war, created the office of superintendent of finance and named to it Robert Morris of Philadelphia, one of the richest men in the country. Taking over at an opportune time, Morris was able to meet the costs of the remaining operations of the war. On occasion, he pledged his own considerable personal credit, and more important, he could utilize the resources of the Bank of North America, organized by him and associates and chartered in Pennsylvania. The first important commercial bank in America, it provided valuable services in extending credit, issuing notes, and handling import transactions. It could not have been organized, however, nor could Morris have carried on as he did except for timely foreign aid. France had recently shipped to America a supply of specie which buttressed the operations of both the government and the bank. Foreign loans and subsidies formed only a small part of the total American expenditures—some $9 million was received from France and Spain—but they generally came at crucial moments.

The funds expended by Congress went for various parts of the war effort, but the greater share was allotted to equip the land forces—to provide food, clothing, shoes, muskets, artillery, and gunpowder, the principal logistic requirements of eighteenth-century armies. Some of these items were available from the American economy. The farms produced sufficient amounts of food, and the home manufactories and small shops turned out enough clothing and shoes. Shortages of these developed in the armies, but they were generally the result of problems in procurement or distribution. Other items were in American possession at the outbreak of war, including a considerable supply of muskets held by men in the states where the militia tradition flourished. Additional weapons were secured from captured British supply ships, the victims of the privateers freely commissioned by Congress. More than 2,000 of these raiders were authorized during the war, and in the first two years of hostilities, before Britain resorted to countermeasures, they took a heavy toll of enemy commerce. However, the number of muskets was inadequate for a long war, and the supply of other war matériel was scanty. If the Americans were going to sustain their armies, they would have to develop domestic production and seek what aid they could from foreign sources.

The nucleus of an arms industry already existed. Numerous small gunsmith and blacksmith shops were accustomed to making muskets, and ironworks and foundries could convert to musket production and, it was hoped, to artillery manufacture. On the eve of the war several of the colonial governments had established public arms factories, and others followed suit. The Congress also created several foundries, the largest at Springfield, Massachusetts; but whereas the state works concentrated on small-arms production the federal arsenals were designed to make artillery. The states eventually decided that public manufacture of arms was too expensive and contracted with private producers for their weapons. The Congress also relied heavily on private arsenals, usually negotiating contracts with the owners through the Board of War.

Under the stimulus of the war the public and private arms industry expanded production. In the winter of 1775–76 the arms makers of Pennsylvania, a center of the industry, alone turned out more than 4,000 muskets. The production of artillery posed greater problems, but by 1775 the foundries in Philadelphia, Springfield, and other places were casting both bronze and iron guns that were almost as good as European pieces. Enough of these were made during the war to satisfy most of the requirements of the armies, and because of imports from France, American forces did not suffer serious shortages of guns. In another area of military procurement the Americans began and remained dependent upon foreign supplies. Relatively little gunpowder was manufactured in the colonies, largely due to a lack of saltpeter, and Congress and the states were unable to increase production. Over 90 percent of the gunpowder used in the war was imported, practically all of it from France.

The supply function of Congress did not cease when it created money to pay for the supplies or stimulated industries to produce them. They then had to be collected and distributed to the armies, and this would have to be done by a military staff. The Congress knew about the use of military staffs in European armies, and in 1775 it established its own. It authorized a number of offices, and appointed the holders of them, an adjutant general to handle records, a paymaster general to disburse money, and others. Two of these officials were concerned with supply and constituted what in later armies would be called the Services of Supply—a commissary general, who purchased and issued provisions, and a quartermaster general, who supervised the transportation of them to the armies. Later Congress appointed a clothier general, who received all clothing purchased by the Board of War. The various staff and supply officers were responsible to the Board of War, but the latter exercised only a loose coordination over them, and the administrative structure was thus highly decentralized.

This failure to provide unitary direction reflected Congress's disinterest in efficient administration. The attitude was particularly apparent in its regulation of the supply services, and particularly calamitous. Thus at one time it became disturbed that the commissary general's department was not procuring needed provisions. The solution was to split the office into two parts, a commissary general of purchases and a commissary general of issues. The apparent reasoning was that if the job was too big for one man it should be given to two;

the result, of course, was to divide authority still further. On another occasion the quartermaster general resigned, and Congress delayed for three months before appointing a successor, as though assuming that this important department could run itself.

The administrative indecision of Congress was one reason that shortages of certain supplies, particularly food, clothing, and shoes, appeared in the armies as early as 1776 and continued and grew worse every year thereafter until 1781. In the winter of 1777–78 Washington reported from winter quarters in Valley Forge that 4,000 of his men were "unfit for duty because they were bare foot and otherwise naked." A foreign observer wrote that "the unfortunate soldiers were in want of everything; they had neither coats, nor hats, nor shirts, nor shoes; their feet and legs froze till they grew black, and it was often necessary to amputate them." The troops were enduring a Pennsylvania winter, but those in the warmer South suffered similar privations. The commander of the southern army once complained: "For upward of two months more than one third of our men were entirely naked, with nothing but a breech cloth about them, and never came out of their tents. . . . Our beef was perfect carrion."

The supply shortages, coupled with the arrearage that often occurred in paying the troops, caused serious morale problems. On several occasions units up to the size of a division threatened to mutiny or did mutiny to secure a redress of their grievances. Usually officers were able to persuade the men to return to duty, but sometimes sterner measures were employed. Once Washington had three New Jersey regiments arrested and three men in each unit shot.

The suffering of the troops was not entirely due to administrative laxity. The goods in short supply were usually available in the country, but they could not be got to the armies. In part the problem was transportation. Just as the British had trouble in supplying their forces if they moved away from the rivers, so did the Americans. There were few good roads and almost none running north and south, and wagons were scarce. But the root cause of the problem was the Continental currency. As it depreciated steadily in value, producers tried to avoid taking it; many farmers preferred to sell to the British in return for specie. Congress was at last driven to recognizing the collapse of its currency system and the crisis of its supply system. Late in 1779 it authorized a requisition of "specific supplies" on the states. Quotas of various provisions, meat, flour, and other items, were assigned according to their resources. The states were expected to fill the quotas by assessing taxes in kind on their citizens. Barter was being substituted for currency.

The requisition system brought in some supplies but it was an unreliable method. When the states levied taxes in kind, they either got nothing—people avoided paying—or too much of one commodity and not enough of another. Requisitions were discontinued in 1781 when Robert Morris became superintendent of finance. Charged also with procuring supplies, Morris resorted to the contract method used in European countries whereby a government made agreements with businessmen to furnish stipulated supplies for stipulated sums. The Morris system worked reasonably well but largely because by that time the currency was on a firmer basis and the war was in its closing phase.

The usual judgment of the financial policy of the Congress is that it was a sorry failure—paper money, inflated prices, dire shortages of supplies. Actually, the accomplishment of the Congress was remarkable, and in the eighteenth century unexampled. Governments of that time did not engage in wars unless they had on hand a sufficient fund of coins to sustain their forces, a "war chest," in the contemporary phrase. If the chest was lost to the enemy, operations were likely to be suspended. The Congress had no chest or any hope of acquiring one, but it still continued the war. It created its own money and decreed that all must use it in the national interest. And it kept its forces in the field and eventually won the war. That Congress and the Americans were aided by other countries to achieve their objective should not detract from the accomplishment.

THE OUTBREAK OF WAR in America was observed with varying degrees of interest by the nations of Europe. The most calculating attention was shown by France, the leading continental power and England's imperial rival until humbled in the wars for empire. The French government and the ruling classes looked with sympathy on the American cause and hoped the colonies would win their independence. Their attitude was rooted in the realities of power politics: if Britain lost her richest colonial possessions, she would be weakened economically, and in the international arena she would suffer a diminution of prestige and influence; an independent but not strong America might well turn to France for support and guidance. This was the view of the ruling class, but pro-American sentiment took another form that the rulers should have taken account of. Among intellectuals and in certain court circles a fad of republicanism flourished, and these groups romanticized the self-governing Americans as representing the wave of the future. The French Revolution was not far off.

The leading members of the Continental Congress were well informed on the workings of European politics and were especially aware of the French ambition to strike back at Britain. The Congress sent envoys to various countries to seek recognition of American independence and material aid, but it was on France that the highest hopes were placed. Envoys to Paris were instructed not only to ask for arms and other supplies but to try to encourage French intervention as an American ally. The principal American representative was fortunately chosen. He was Benjamin Franklin, the Pennsylvania sage and savant. Sophisticated and cosmopolitan, he moved easily in the French court and performed with such subtle skill that he deserves to rank with the great American diplomats.

Franklin and the other envoys found that the French government was eager to provide the Americans with what in later times would be called aid short of war, to furnish enough military gear to enable the patriots to keep fighting. Because France was ostensibly neutral, the government supplied this aid covertly through a front, the exporting firm of Hortalez and Company, organized specifically to conduct this business by Caron de Beaumarchais, an adventurer and dramatist who felt drawn to the American cause. The company, supported by subsidies and loans from the government and also from allied Spain, shipped to America large supplies of artillery, muskets, gunpowder, tents, and blankets. Some of the artillery pieces came from official arsenals and were stamped with the royal insignia. In addition, the government encouraged its younger army officers to go to America and place their service and knowledge at American disposal (they would also gain valuable experience). One who went was the Marquis de Lafayette, who rose to the rank of major general and became an American legend. Another was Louis Duportail, who became the first chief engineer of the American army. He and other foreign military engineers were especially needed because there were few such technicians in America.

This material and technical aid was very helpful to the Americans and was appreciated by them. But they desired more—they wanted France to cast her full weight in the war as a participant. Franklin employed his greatest skills to this end but met always regretful rejections. The French government hoped the Americans would win independence and would aid them with weapons and supplies and would even enter the war if—if the Americans could achieve a victory that promised ultimate success. Or put another way, France was not going to get stuck with a loser.

The needed victory was won in 1777. At Saratoga in northern New York the Americans captured an entire British invading army. France was at last convinced. Early in the following year she and the United States concluded a military alliance whereby each party bound itself not to make peace with Britain without the consent of the other. Spain shortly declared war on Britain, and was followed by Holland, whose merchants hoped to exploit the trade of an independent America. By the standards of the time the American Revolution had become a world war.

The intervention of other powers altered the nature of the war. Britain now had to keep part of her naval strength in home waters to defend against possible French or Dutch attacks on her coast or commerce. France sent to America substantial contingents of troops and sizable naval forces. At one time France achieved superior sea power in American waters and although the advantage did not last, it enabled a combined American and French army to win one of the greatest victories of the war, leading to the end of the conflict.

It might have concluded with the same result had there been no foreign intervention; in the last years of the war the British retained possession of only a few coastal cities, and as they were obviously unable to conquer the continent, they would probably have abandoned the struggle. Nevertheless, foreign aid was an important factor in the war, and the participation of foreigners is a part of the story of the land and sea engagements of the Revolution.

CHAPTER III

The Revolution: The Armed Forces and the First Battles

AMERICAN LAND FORCES in the Revolution were made up of two components—the militia of the states and the Continental Army. The militia was a citizen army or, more accurately, thirteen citizen armies organized under state authority and placed under national command only temporarily, in emergencies. The Continental Army was a professional or regular force raised under national authority although not directly by the central government. The Continental Congress did not feel that it had the power to recruit men directly into a national army. Accordingly, it asked the states to furnish quotas of troops based on population. Thus a man came into the Continental Army through the medium of his state. A soldier from Pennsylvania was said to be in the Pennsylvania Line of the Continental Line.

The militia in its turn was organized in two segments, although the dividing line between them was shadowy—the regularly enlisted forces and the short-service forces. The only difference between them was in length of enlistment. Men in the first group were usually enrolled for terms of up to six months; men in the second were called out in emergencies for indeterminate but usually shorter terms. There was a great deal of passing back and forth between the groups, and the size of each fluctuated from year to year, with the short-service section generally being more numerous.

Evaluations of the performance of the militia have usually been negative. Washington set the tone, and most later historians followed him. Writing to Congress after a lost battle in which most of his militia troops defected, the general asserted: "If I were called upon to declare upon oath, whether the militia had been most serviceable or hurtful upon the whole, I should subscribe to the latter." He was writing in anger and out of a conviction born of his admiration for the British army model: that only regular troops could be depended on in battle. It was not a balanced assessment of the role of the militia.

Militia troops did often break on the battlefield. They fled because they lacked confidence in themselves: each man took for granted that the man next to him would flee and that he should get out first. The militia had not received the training that enabled troops to fight the stand-up battles of the time. Washington and other generals realized this deficiency but did not believe anything could be done to remedy it—the citizen soldiers could not be retrained because they were under state control and served short terms. They would have to be used in spite of their deficiencies, but only if regulars were not available.

In writing off the militia as a negligible factor, the generals overlooked some pertinent facts. On some fields the militia stood firm, particularly when they fought behind some kind of cover or had confidence in their immediate officers. They could also be used, as a few generals discovered, as a screening force in front of a line of regulars, to receive and blunt an attack before retiring. Their greatest utility, however, was in performing the function for which they were most often criticized—turning out for short service but on short notice to meet a British thrust. If the Americans had depended on their regulars to counter all the various enemy incursions, they could not have met them, because the regulars could not be transported rapidly enough from one part of the country to another. But at every invasion the militia swarmed out to contain the foe until regulars could arrive. In no crisis of the war did Congress or Washington contemplate calling for a levy in mass, a rising of the population, such as the French revolutionaries would summon in their wars. The American leaders were perhaps not as unorthodox as the French or, more probably, not in as desperate straits. In their citizen state armies they had almost the equivalent of a popular levy.

Both Congress and Washington preferred to place their main reliance upon a professional army modeled on the British example that they knew; they hoped, that is, to create a typical eighteenth-century army. Like other armies of the time, it would be small, large enough to drive the British forth but not so large as to become unduly expensive or to interfere with the normal lives of the people. It would be raised by voluntary enlistment, the men encouraged to come forward by offers of substantial pay and bounties. In one respect, it would be different from other armies. The terms of service were to be short—one year was the length first set by Congress—because this was expected to be a short war: when confronted with resistance, Britain would assuredly negotiate a peace; or if she fought, she would not sustain the struggle very long.

A professional national army could be authorized only by Congress. The delegates were willing enough to act and were in essential agreement on the pattern of the army, but in the hectic spring and summer months of 1775 when war was breaking, they did not have time to devise a considered military policy. They needed an army immediately and they got one, enlisting it not in accordance with a previously determined tidy formula but creating it out of materials at hand, which was the way other institutions of Congress were created in that crisis year.

In April British troops in Boston, then the only place containing a sizable "redcoat" garrison, had moved out to Concord to destroy a cache of military goods reportedly being collected by the local resistance leaders. At Lexington, on the way, they encountered hastily called out militia, and fire was exchanged. Going on to Concord, the British destroyed the supplies, but on their return they were attacked by ever-growing numbers of militia, who pursued them back to Boston. As the news of this British aggression flamed through the colonies, Massachusetts summoned its militia to arms and appealed to the other New England colonies for support. They responded with alacrity, and soon a New England "army" was besieging the British in Boston.

It was not really an army. Composed of troops from various colonies, it had no unified organization and no recognized commander, although by consent the officers of the other colonies deferred to the senior Massachusetts general, Artemas Ward. The only way it could become a true army was for it to become a national army, and various voices urged Congress to take it over, the loudest being that of Massachusetts, which had contributed most of the troops. Congress, recognizing that it could not resolve the dispute with the mother country unless it had force at its disposal, responded. On June 14 it voted to place the New England contingents under its control and appointed Washington to command them and other forces to be raised. The New England army had become the first Continental army.

Washington, however, was not sure that it *was* an army he had been given. After inspecting the troops, he defined them as "a mixed multitude of people." He was appalled at the lack of organization. Some of the units consisted of militia, others of volunteers raised out of the base of the militia. There was no uniformity in the arrangement of size of the units, no basic tactical formation, and no administrative agency above the various units to coordinate their operations. Washington set it as his first task to provide an organization. In the process he would invest the Continental Army with features it would retain throughout the war.

Using the British army as his example, he prescribed as the basic tactical unit the battalion or regiment. Above the regiment were the brigade and the division, but these were primarily units of administration, intended to facilitate operations off the field rather than on it. On the field the army would maneuver in regiments, under the control of the commanding general. This first national army was primarily an infantry force; a few artillery units were present, but there was no cavalry. An effective artillery adjunct was eventually developed, but there were never many horsemen in any Continental army. Washington, having had no experience with cavalry in his militia career, was unable to grasp its utility, and in any case, it could not be employed as it was in Europe in the wooded and rugged terrain of much of America.

Washington was determined to introduce discipline into the army. "Discipline is the soul of an army," he wrote. There had been little of it before he arrived. Officers exercised only a loose control over their units, the men drifted in and out of camp pretty much as they pleased, regular roll calls were not made, and no reliable strength returns were available. This laxity reflected the nature of the army—a mass of citizens summoned hastily from their homes under other citizens who happened to bear officer titles but were still a part of the mass, accorded some deference if they were liked or respected but otherwise regarded as ordinary fellows. One visitor to the camp was shocked to see a captain shaving his troops: he was a barber, and his skill was in demand.

Accentuating this casual attitude was the fact that the officers were physically indistinguishable from the men, for this was an army without uniforms. Everybody in it had come in whatever clothes he thought were proper or could acquire, which meant in most cases in civilian clothes. Washington was resolved that the army should have a distinctive dress, but he knew this would be impossible to achieve immediately (eventually a blue and buff uniform would become standard). He could, however, see that the officers were provided with insignia or symbols of authority in the form of colored ribands or cockades, and he could insist that their authority be recognized on pain of punishment. The effect on the troops was marked. One observer wrote that there had been "a great overturning in the camp as to order and regularity." He added, as though something strange and sinister had happened, "Everyone is made to know his place and keep in it."

The number of troops under Washington's command at this time has to be guessed at. The keeping of precise statistics was not then habitual, and contemporary appraisals of the size of any American army were but estimates and likely to vary. Washington probably had before Boston between 16,000 and 19,000 troops (perhaps 7,000 other troops were in national service elsewhere). It was a considerable force by eighteenth-century standards, one of the largest American aggregations in the war, but it would not remain in existence very long—the term of enlistment of the men would expire at the end of the year. Thus while Washington was reorganizing his present army, he had to raise another force, which in turn would have to be organized.

In planning the army of 1776 Washington conferred with a committee of Congress, and out of their discussion came a recommendation adopted by the legislature authorizing the enlistment of a Continental force of 20,000 troops to serve for one year. By the end of 1775, however, only 10,000 recruits had come forward. The initial enthusiasm inspired by Lexington and Concord had abated, and many who were willing to serve a short stint were reluctant to undergo a longer one. Washington, striving to reenlist his trained troops and finding the going hard, was near to despair. "Could I have foreseen what I have, and am likely to experience," he exclaimed, "no consideration upon earth should have induced me to accept this command." Eventually, the rate of enlistment picked up, and in 1776 the number of men in Continental service, in Washington's and other armies, approached 25,000 men.

As a result of his first experience in raising an army, Washington urged Congress to authorize longer enlistments, three years or the duration of the war, and to hold forth as inducements bounties of cash and land. The army should not again be forced to depend on a "limited Inlistment," he declared. The Congress was reluctant to take this step, but in the latter part of 1776 it did, and then with unexpected ardor. It not only provided for the longer enlistments and bounties recommended by Washington but authorized the raising of 76,000 troops. The projected total proved to be unrealistic—less than half that many recruits were secured for 1777, and not all of them came in under the provisions of the act. Many men preferred the shorter service in the militia, and others spurned the bounties, which were paid in depreciating Continental currency. In later calls Congress would set smaller quotas but would always have trouble in filling them. (States that did not meet their quotas sometimes drafted men out of the militia for twelve months, on the advice of Congress, and hence some one-year men still came into the armies.) Enlistments tended to come in bursts, depending on the fortune of American arms, and the size of the Continental forces fluctuated from year to year. They were probably at their greatest strength in 1777 and 1778, some 35,000 men; but by 1780 they had sunk to 20,000 men. The largest number of regulars ever under Washington's command was 17,000 men. By contrast, the largest British armies ranged from 28,000 to 34,000 troops.

The mobilization methods of Congress have been subjected to severe criticism by historians. They score it for not realizing immediately the need for long-term enlistments and charge that it did not adequately tap the available manpower resources. As for the enlistment issue, Congress in 1775 restricted recruitments to one year for good reasons; it expected the war to end shortly by a negotiated peace, and it feared that a call for longer service would dampen the popular hopes for reconciliation and thus weaken the will to resist. When it realized that the war would be of some duration, in 1776, it authorized long terms—only to witness a disappointing response. Certainly if Congress could not raise large forces for long hitches in that year and later, it could not have done so earlier. And even if it had been able at any time to enlist a large permanent force, there would have been trouble sustaining it. The relatively small and short-term armies that were raised were usually short of supplies.

The criticism that Congress failed to exploit adequately the available manpower rests on dubious comparisons with the American performance in modern wars. Thus, one historian estimates that the largest American force in any year, regulars and militia in all armies, was 47,000 men in 1776, or 3 percent of the population, and contrasts this total with the 10 percent of the population put under arms in World War II. Such analyses lack reality. In World War II the United States had a powerful central government, a relatively united people, and a conscription law and the machinery to enforce it. The government of the Revolution was weak, the people were not united in support of the war, and there was no draft—indeed, in an age of slow communication, there was no effective way to reach the masses with appeals for voluntary enlistment. And whereas in later wars it was considered patriotic to enlist, in the Revolution enlistment was for many men a wrenching act of rebellion.

A realistic analysis of the American mobilization performance would relate the number of men serving in the army to the number supporting the war, something over one million persons, who constituted the real manpower pool. Any conclusion reached, however, has to be tempered with a caution as to the unreliability of Revolutionary statistics. The total number of men serving throughout the war, regulars and militia, is estimated at 377,000 or 396,-000. The difference results from varying judgments as to the number of militia; there is general agreement that 232,000 Continentals were enlisted but dispute as to whether there were 145,000 or 164,000 militiamen.

The discrepancy is not important, for whatever the total was, it is misleading. It includes an indeterminable but large number of men who were repeaters, or duplicates, men who were called out again and again for short terms in the militia. In the Continental service it counts men who served for only one year and men who enlisted several times, usually individuals who jumped service to secure an additional bounty. To arrive at a meaningful appraisal of the size of the Continental forces, it is necessary to calculate the number of men serving for an appreciable period, three years or longer. One estimate reckons 150,000 such troops. This would be 15 percent of the population supporting the war and is probably too high a figure. A more likely one is 100,000 troops, or 10 percent of the population. Even if the number was somewhat less, it would seem that the Revolutionary government came close to approximating modern standards of manpower utilization.*

That Congress was alert to opportunities to tap all its human resources is shown by its reaching out to enlist men from a group hitherto excluded from military service—the blacks. The war had hardly started when free Negroes

---

*The accepted casualty figures for the Revolution have been 4,000 battle deaths and 10,000 deaths from all causes. However, a recent study, Howard H. Peckham, *The Toll of Independence* (Chicago, 1974), arrives at higher totals: 6,824 killed in battle, 10,000 died in camps, 8,500 died as prisoners of war, or an aggregate of 25,324 deaths. If the estimate is correct, it makes the Revolution one of the deadliest wars in our history.

in the northern colonies offered themselves for enlistment. Washington felt constrained to call a council of general officers to decide whether they should be accepted. Not surprisingly, the council voted unanimously "to reject Negroes altogether," free or slave. The decision was approved by Congress, but blacks, including some slaves, persisted in trying to enlist. Washington finally gave way and instructed recruiting officers to accept free blacks and recommended such a policy to Congress, which ratified it.

Thereafter free Negroes but also slaves, most of them in the northern colonies, entered the Continental Army through the medium of their state "lines." The slaves went in as substitutes for masters, or were promised freedom by their states to enlist. At least one all-black regiment from Rhode Island, with white higher officers, was formed, and at the battle of Monmouth fought with what its colonel called "desperate valor." Probably 5,000 Negro troops overall served in the Continental forces. Many of them were interspersed in units with white troops—in integrated units, which may indicate that less racial prejudice existed at the time of the Revolution than later.

The general officers of the Continental Army were appointed by Congress, whereas officers below that grade in the state lines were commissioned by their states. Altogether, Congress named seventy-three general officers. Of these, fifty-two held previous military experience, sixteen in the English army or in European armies and thirty-six in the colonial militia; only twenty-one were without experience. It cannot be said that there was any great difference in performance between those with experience and those without it. Charles Lee and Horatio Gates had served in the British army before settling in America and great hopes were placed on them, but they turned out to be disappointments; Richard Montgomery, who also had had British service, gave promise of becoming a fine fighting general before being killed early in the war. Some of the militia officers developed into good generals, but others did not. Two of the better generals were innocent of any experience but had learned their trade by reading manuals and military history—Nathanael Greene, who became a capable infantry leader, and Henry Knox, who organized Washington's artillery.

The supreme figure among the generals was, of course, George Washington. Congress could not have made a more fortunate choice to be supreme commander. He had his shortcomings. His militia experience had not acquainted him with all the problems involved in running a professional army. He was not well read in either strategy or tactics and would frequently err in handling troops on the field. But he had a good mind and learned from his mistakes and steadily improved his generalship. Above all, he had that indefinable quality called character, the ability to dominate a situation, that is vital to a general and enables him to surmount defects in experience or education. He and his Continental Army would have to do the sustained, year-after-year fighting of the Revolution.

EVEN AS IT WAS improvising an army, the Congress acted to establish a navy. It would find, however, that a sea arm was much more difficult to create than a land arm. An army, like the first Continental force, could literally be called into existence. Many of its members would arrive bearing their own weapons, and once assembled, its logistical requirements were relatively simple —artillery, ammunition, quarters, food. A navy, by contrast, was a material thing, a collection of vessels that were the largest and most complex machines of the time. The American government, having no navy, would first have to construct one and then arm it. It was an expensive and laborious undertaking.

An eighteenth-century navy consisted of three types of sailing ships, with variations in each type as to size and armament. Largest of its vessels was the ship of the line, the equivalent of the battleship in later navies, each one of which required 2,000 oak trees in the making. Its most distinguishing characteristic was the number of guns it carried, which varied from sixty to ninety-eight guns, with seventy-four guns being the usual complement. (Naval guns, like land pieces, had a limited range of accuracy; their most effective fire was at 300 yards.) Ships of the line had battle as their mission; as the name indicates, they fought in line against enemy ships also in line. Next in size was the frigate, the cruiser of later navies. The heavy frigate carried fifty guns and could if necessary be used in the line; the conventional frigate, with from thirty to forty-four guns, was used for reconnaissance, convoy duty, and commerce raiding. Last was the sloop, the later destroyer, lightly armed but useful in patrol or to prey on enemy commerce.

To build and administer the navy Congress turned to its favorite political device, a committee. In 1775 it formed the Naval Committee, later renamed the Marine Committee. At the same time, and demonstrating its talent to disperse strength, it authorized the states to create their own navies and to issue commissions to privateers. The Naval Committee was empowered to build and buy ships, appoint officers, and organize personnel (as a part of this last function it established a Marine Corps to provide combat troops aboard). The administration of naval affairs repeated the pattern of the army. In 1779 Congress became disturbed that so few ships were being built and abolished the Marine Committee. In its place a Board of Admiralty was created, the majority of whose members were "experts," seafaring men outside Congress. Finally, in the closing phase of the war, Congress entrusted direction to a single executive, an agent of marine.

Despite the changes in administrative arrangement, the Continental navy remained small. During the war only fifty to sixty vessels saw service and not all at the same time. The failure to achieve a higher production could not justly be attributed to poor administration. In fact, the navy attained its greatest single strength under the committee system, twenty-seven ships in commission in 1776. The basic reason for the deficiency was a lack of construction facilities. Congress authorized three ships of the line, but only one was completed, and so late in the war that it was turned over to France. Of the eighteen frigates voted, only six made it to sea; the other twelve either were never completed or were captured in port by the British. In startling contrast to the tiny American force, the Royal Navy numbered 270 ships at the opening of the war and 480 at the close.

What Congress hoped to accomplish with the navy is not entirely clear. Even if the construction program had been carried out in full, including the three ships of the line, the resulting fleet could not have challenged the might of the British navy. Members of Congress apparently did not possess a developed concept of the use of sea power or, if they had, did not detail their thinking. They seem to have intended their navy to have a limited function, to harass British commerce and thereby lighten or lift the enemy blockade of American ports. Such a restricted strategy was classic with weaker naval powers, and if Congress did not know the doctrine, it was still the only course open to the Americans.

The first mission ordered by the Naval Committee was a raid on British commerce. By late 1775 the committee had assembled at Philadelphia its first fleet of eight small vessels—sloops and brigs—that had been converted from merchantmen and hastily armed. They were officered and crewed with little difficulty. In recruiting personnel, the navy had the advantage over the army of being able to secure men who were already partly trained in their profession. Captains and sailors in the merchant trade knew all there was to know about sailing, and the crews had only to be drilled in gunnery.

Early in 1776 the Naval Committee appointed Esek Hopkins, a Rhode Island merchant captain, commander of the squadron and directed him to sail down the Atlantic coast as far as the Carolinas, to "take or destroy all enemy ships found," and on completing his "business" to return to American waters. Finding no enemy ships, Hopkins proceeded to Nassau in the Bahamas, captured some supplies from the surprised British garrison, and then made his way back to Rhode Island. It had been a successful if not a spectacular cruise, but Hopkins did not receive another assignment in the war, undoubtedly because he was resented by other captains. Jealousies ran deep in the small naval officer corps, more so than in the army.

These jealousies were one reason that Congress did not repeat the experiment of appointing an overall commander. In naming Hopkins, it had obviously intended him to act as a commander in chief, a naval counterpart of Washington. A larger reason was that such a title was ridiculous—the officer in command had little to command. Except for Hopkins's cruise, there was only one other important employment of a squadron by the Continental navy. American ships in general operated independently, raiding British commerce and occasionally offering battle to an enemy vessel of their own size.

The most daring and successful of the American raiders was John Paul Jones. Although only twenty-eight years of age at the beginning of the war, he had a greater knowledge of naval organization and tactics than any other American officer, having previously served as a midshipman in the Royal Navy and a captain in the British merchant marine. Given command of the sloop *Ranger* in 1778, he terrorized British commerce in the Irish Sea. In the following year he was out again in command of a frigate, really a converted East India merchantman given him by the French and named by him, in honor of Benjamin Franklin and the latter's famous "Almanac," the *Bonhomme Richard*. Accompanied by three supporting vessels, Jones appeared in the North Sea, where he sighted a British convoy guarded by the frigate *Serapis* and a sloop. Although he was outgunned by the *Serapis,* he engaged her, while his other ships went after the sloop. The two ships fought for three hours—at the last, muzzle to muzzle—before the British captain struck his colors. The sloop also surrendered, but in the melee the convoy escaped.

The exploits of Jones and other raiders aroused pride in America and boosted morale, and in the navy itself created a tradition for fighting. But such individual actions could not alter the fact of British sea power. The little rebel navy was unable to break the blockade of American ports or to prevent the Royal Navy from landing troops at will on the coast. Sea power shifted to the American side for only a brief interlude—after France and Spain entered the war and Britain in apprehension divided her fleet between the home isles and the colonies, thus permitting France to gain a temporary superiority in American waters. A significant American and French victory on land resulted, but it was the only success directly attributable to sea power. The war was for the Americans primarily a struggle on land.

No FORMAL DECLARATION of hostilities signaled the opening of the war. The first battle did not come about as a result of planning by either side but flared up spontaneously between British and colonial forces in Massachusetts. The beginning seemed accidental, but if it had not occurred there and then, it would have occurred later.

The British column of 1,800 troops that on the night of April 18, 1775, marched out from Boston to destroy the stores at Concord expected no trouble. However, the patriots had been alerted to their coming—it was easy to get word out from Boston—and when the column reached Lexington at dawn the next day, it found a militia company barring the way. While the British commanding officer was ordering the militia to disperse, a shot rang out, the first shot of the Revolution. It is not known to this day who fired it, a nervous militiaman or an infuriated Britisher. Thereupon the redcoated regulars, apparently without orders, fired a volley and then charged with the bayonet. The militia fled, leaving behind them eight men killed and ten wounded. The British continued on to Concord and destroyed what stores the patriots had not been able to remove.

Returning from Concord, the British were attacked by other militia who had heard the news of Lexington and swarmed out to take revenge. In the course of the day probably 3,000 militia assembled, although not all at the same time. Their tactics were simple: they positioned themselves on either side of the road the British had to take back to Boston and from behind cover shot at the redcoats. At intervals the British sent out flanking parties to clear the road, but increasingly they had to run a gauntlet of shot. One officer wrote that they had been "surrounded" by an "incessant fire," and another admitted that as they got closer to Boston "we began to run rather than retreat in order." They almost ran into Boston.

It is curious that British regulars should have been so demoralized by the American fire. Apparently, it was the weight of the fire rather than its accuracy that unnerved them. The British losses were only 273 men: 73 killed, 174 wounded, 26 missing, 15 percent of their total. If the average militiaman fired 20 of the 36 charges he was supposed to carry, the Americans that day must have discharged 75,000 shot—and scored only a few hundred hits. Or put another way, only one bullet out of 300 found its mark. The inaccuracy of the fire is not surprising. The attackers for the most part shot from a distance too great for their muskets to carry effectively, and these New England militia had received little training in shooting.

They had, nevertheless, driven the British into Boston; and when they were joined by the militia of the other New England colonies that arrived in response to Massachusetts's call, the combined force was able to lay the city under a modified siege. Stretched in a half-circle around it, they could prevent the British from breaking out, except at a costly loss of life. Conversely, they were not strong enough to break in, especially as they lacked heavy artillery. And so for a time the two armies watched each other, the Americans operating under the loose supervision of General Artemas Ward of Massachusetts while in Boston the British under General Thomas Gage waited for reinforcements and supplies to come by sea.

In June the reinforcements arrived, 1,100 troops that brought Gage's force up to a total of 6,500 men. With them to assist Gage came three generals who were thought to be among the best in the British army and who would play prominent parts later in the war: William Howe, John Burgoyne, and Henry Clinton. They convinced Gage to extend his lines so as to secure room to maneuver for an eventual breakout. Specifically, they proposed that he seize the Dorchester peninsula south of Boston and the Charlestown peninsula north of it. The plan was talked about in officer circles, and inevitably word of it seeped out to the American lines.

The news caused the convoking of a council of officers at the American headquarters. They decided to occupy the Charlestown peninsula immediately, thus forestalling the British in that area and possibly diverting their attention from Dorchester as well. The plan has been subsequently criticized as violating several principles of war, especially those of unity of command and of concentration. The occupying force would be isolated from the main army and largely dependent on its own resources. Moreover, it was being placed in a position of great peril, on a peninsula whose waters were commanded by enemy vessels. That it escaped annihilation is ascribed by the critics to British stupidity. Critics, however, tend to become unduly alarmed when viewing a position on a peninsula.

The American force of 1,200 men moved to the peninsula on the night of June 16. It had only a nominal commander, a reflection of the lack of organization in the besieging army. Originally, the intention had been to construct a fortification on an eminence called Bunker Hill. After arriving, however, the officers and an accompanying engineer decided to dig in on Breed's Hill, closer to Boston but actually less defensible. (The ensuing battle would take its name from Bunker rather than from Breed's Hill.) The men labored throughout the night and by dawn had thrown up a redoubt about forty yards square. Its outline greeted the British when they awoke the next morning.

The first reaction of Gage and his generals was military: the fortification posed a threat to Boston if the rebels could mount heavy guns, and an undoubted obstacle to British occupation of the peninsula. Mingled with this response was a feeling of outrage—British officers had great contempt for the fighting abilities of Americans, and now these miserable fellows had dared to approach the city. General Howe was given 2,200 troops and ordered to attack and disperse the rabble.

It was here, according to many historians, that the British blundered badly in strategy. In their contempt for the Americans they resolved on a frontal attack and disregarded the obvious move, which would have been to hold the rebels in front with a demonstration and land a force in their rear. Contempt was a factor, but it was not the only influence in the thinking of the British generals. They had to consider that other unseen rebel forces might be on the peninsula and that an amphibious landing in the uncertain state of the tide would be exposed to a counterthrust. Their perceived mission was to gain a beachhead and then expand it, to capture the position that was visible. In assailing Breed's Hill, Howe did not intend to rely solely on a frontal attack. While holding the rebels in front, he would flank their left, which from the redoubt to the Mystic River was protected only by a breastwork and a rail fence. He expected that his regulars would charge through an ineffective fire and overrun the defenders before they could reload and that they then would finish off the fight with the bayonet.

Howe could not know that the American officers had their men under unusual control—instructed to hold their fire until the redcoats were within a range of 100 feet. In conventional battle formation the British advanced, each soldier burdened with marching equipment weighing sixty pounds. The main body struck at the American left, while a secondary force tried to envelop the redoubt. The blast of fire from the American line was so devastating that the attackers wavered and fell back to re-form, a crucial delay that gave the defenders time to reload. Howe rallied his men and threw a second attack, this one at the redoubt. It met an even deadlier fire because as the British milled about, the rebels had time to load several times. Shaken but still determined, Howe ordered a third attack, and this one succeeded in turning the left and breaking into the redoubt, but mainly because the Americans were running short of ammunition. They retired in good order, and Howe had no stomach to pursue them. His total casualties were slightly more than 1,000, over 40 percent of his total, while the Americans had lost only 440 killed and wounded. "A dear bought victory," British General Clinton mused; "another such would have ruined us."

Bunker Hill was followed by no important strategic results. The two armies remained in the same positions they held before. The battle had, however, important psychological effects. The confidence of Americans in their ability to stand up to England was confirmed at the very outset—the British obviously were not invincible. Indeed, the showing of the relatively untrained American troops may have mistakenly convinced many Americans that militia alone could handle the British army. On the British the effect was sobering. They realized now that they faced a foe who would not yield easily and that hard fighting lay ahead. Howe and other generals thereafter would be extremely cautious in attacking Americans in fortified positions.

Shortly after the battle Washington arrived to take command of the army. While he was reorganizing it, no operations occurred. Washington was not going to move until his army was in hand and had accumulated heavy artillery to enable it to blast its way into Boston, a destructive process from which he shrank. Moreover, he thought, and correctly, that he would not have to fight for the city. Boston was a poor offensive base for the British. The only reason for the location of their army was that the town had been the center of American resistance to British measures. To reconquer the colonies, the British would require as a base a city at the mouth of a large river running back to the interior, such as New York. They would therefore leave Boston eventually, and in the meantime Washington would keep them under watch, try to nudge them out in due time, and then race to meet them at New York or wherever they returned.

While Washington was concerning himself with ways to meet British thrusts, Congress was occupied with studying possible offensives. Its attention had become fixed on the lake and river chain that connected the Hudson with the St. Lawrence River in Canada and that had been a colonial invasion route in the wars with France. Members were intrigued with the idea of using this route to seize Canada: they believed, as did many Americans, that the French *habitants* resented British rule and would rally to the patriot cause if a liberating army appeared among them. The opportunity for an offensive presented itself at an early date. In the spring of 1775 American militia had captured the British post at Fort Ticonderoga on the neck of land between Lake George and Lake Champlain, an obvious base, and Congress had assembled there a force of 2,000 men under the command of Philip Schuyler, a wealthy New York aristocrat. Now in June Congress directed Schuyler to move on Montreal and Quebec and take possession of the St. Lawrence Valley if "not disagreeable to the Canadians."

To this point the planning had been civilian and political, but eventually the project had to be presented to Washington. He saw immediately that it promised important military benefits. The lakes-river chain could also be used by the British; an army coming down it could join with an army coming up the Hudson, and the colonies would be cut in two. But if Canada could be occupied, the British would be deprived of it as a base. He therefore endorsed the plan and offered to detach 1,100 of his own army to participate in the expedition. This force was not, however, to join the column at Ticonderoga. Instead, Washington proposed to move it from near Boston by water to the mouth of the Kennebec River in Maine. It would proceed up the Kennebec in specially built flatboats or bateaux to a portage called by the Indians the Great Carrying Place, which led to the Chaudière River, which in turn led to the St. Lawrence at Quebec. Washington expected that the force moving from Fort Ti would capture Montreal and then move down to the river to join the one before Quebec, whereupon the combined columns would assault and take the latter fortress. He was here demonstrating one of his weaknesses as a strategist—to plan complicated movements without determining fully the difficulties in the way. He directed the move across unsettled Maine on scanty and, as it turned out, inaccurate information; he had been told of a map that showed the distance much shorter than it was and that did not indicate the terrible obstacles in the portage.

The Ticonderoga column moved out in September. Schuyler, possibly because he distrusted his ability to handle troops in the field, gave the command of it to a more experienced former British officer, Richard Montgomery. Advancing along the water chain, it was held up for a time by the enemy on the Richelieu River but pushed on to take Montreal from its small garrison on November 13. Meanwhile, the cooperating column, under the command of Colonel Benedict Arnold, was floundering through the Maine wilderness. Arnold would later reveal serious faults of character, but he was an officer of driving energy, and he displayed this quality now. The expedition proceeded on schedule till it left the Kennebec and attempted to cross the portage. But then it encountered ponds and rivers and rugged terrain not shown on its map. The men had to carry the bateaux, each one weighing 400 pounds, and their provisions from pond to pond, and many of them came near to breaking under the strain. Most of the boats eventually broke up in the rough waters, and the supplies that were not lost were shortly exhausted. Toward the end of the march the troops were on the verge of starvation, reduced to using cartridge cases, moccasins, and hide thongs as stock for soup. Over 300 of them turned back, but Arnold drove the rest on, and on November 8 they came to the south bank of the St. Lawrence opposite Quebec—675 of the approximate 1,000 that had begun the journey. It had taken 45 days instead of the expected 20, and from the mouth of the Kennebec they had traveled 350 miles instead of the 180 miles projected for them. It is one of the great logistical feats in American military history.

On the following day the ragged band crossed the river and encamped before the city. The British wisely retired into the fortress and refused battle. Not feeling strong enough to storm it, Arnold waited for Montgomery to join him and for the expected reinforcement from the Canadians. Montgomery soon arrived but, because he had left part of his force to garrison Montreal, with only 300 men. Nor did the *habitants* rally; they seemed completely indifferent to the outcome of the struggle between the two groups of Anglo-Saxons. Despite the smallness of their force, Montgomery and Arnold resolved to storm the city; the enlistments of half their troops would expire at the end of the year, and they could not wait. The attack was made on the night of December 30 in a snowstorm and was bloodily repulsed; Montgomery was killed and Arnold was wounded. Arnold, however, kept his stricken army before the city, hoping for reinforcements. They came eventually in bits, but Arnold did not dare to risk another attack. Nevertheless, throughout the winter the American army remained on Canadian soil and was still there when spring dawned.

Meanwhile, Washington had accomplished his purpose to edge the British out of Boston. He had found the means during the winter, a store of heavy artillery that fell in American hands at captured Ticonderoga. His chief of artillery, Henry Knox, had brought these guns to the army, transporting them on sledges pulled by oxen and horses over snow and ice and proudly presenting them to his commander as "a noble train of artillery." In March, 1776, Washington mounted the guns on Dorchester Heights, from where he could blast the British lines. The British commander, Howe (now Sir William), took the hint. He evacuated the city and went with his army to Halifax, in Nova Scotia. He was going to leave anyway to return to a more satisfactory base, but Washington had hastened his departure, so the outcome seemed to be an American victory. The British now had no foothold in any part of the colonies.

The first year of operations had gone well for the Americans. They had raised an army, started a navy, expelled the British from Boston and other posts, and launched an offensive into Canada. Their successes were, however, deceptive. Britain had yet to throw her full resources into the conflict. The war was just settling into the long, hard pull.

CHAPTER IV

The Revolution: 1776 to the End

IN 1776 BRITAIN PUT FORTH a mighty effort to crush the American rebellion —assembled, in fact, the largest expeditionary force England had ever sent forth. Additionally, the navy in American waters was increased to armada proportions. British strategy was to mount three coordinated offensives that would occupy key areas in America and ultimately break patriot morale and resistance. The plan was of such dimensions as to deserve the title of grand strategy. It would not, however, accomplish its objectives, partly because of American opposition, partly because of bad luck, but mainly because of its very grandness. Its success depended on the ability of the British to move forces by land and sea over long exterior lines and converge on a single point. Such delicate coordination was difficult to achieve in an age of slow communications, and the probability of success was made even more remote by the splitting of the British command in America.

Originally, all royal forces in North America had been under the command of one man, General Gage. London had expected the arrangement to continue when Howe succeeded Gage on the latter's return to England after Bunker Hill. However, the American invasion of Canada in 1775 forced a recasting of authority, intended to be temporary but retained throughout the war. Sir Guy Carleton, the governor of Canada, was given the supreme command there, and Howe was to command all forces south of Canada. There were several good reasons for the immediate partition. For one, Carleton needed independence to counter the sudden American thrust. And there were reasons even for its continuance—two such widely separated armies could not easily act in unison. Its ultimate effect, however, was bad, causing divided action in 1776 and divided planning later.

The two British commanders were at best soldiers of only average ability. Carleton is the more difficult to evaluate. He had long experience as a subordinate in the British army, but during the Revolution he led a field army only once. On that occasion he displayed competence but little aggressiveness or imagination. He was never really tested in battle. His greatest service was as governor of Canada: he won the respect if not the affection of the French people, and retained their passive allegiance during the American invasion.

Howe would hold field command for two years in some of the most important campaigns of the war, but he too is a puzzling figure. He knew his profession thoroughly and on the field was nearly always professionally efficient. He also had courage and was ready to risk attack to attain results. But he never achieved the expected results. Something was lacking in Howe—an absence of intellectual quality that limited his strategic grasp, an indolence of character that restrained him from urgent action. "He is as valiant as my sword," a Hessian officer snorted, "but no more of a general than my arse." The indolence may have been a reflection of his training—most eighteenth-century generals conducted war in a leisurely fashion—but it was more probably a personal trait. Handsome and sociable, he enjoyed good food and drink, gambling, and American mistresses. He liked Americans generally, and he came in 1776 to wage peace as well as war. His government commissioned him to offer concessions to the rebels if they would lay down their arms, and he and his brother, Admiral Richard Howe, who led the accompanying fleet, hoped to negotiate with Congress. The effort came to nothing because Congress would accept only independence, but William Howe's desire for peace may have been another factor accounting for his inertia. The instructions from his government revealed incompatible aims—it was pursuing peace while waging war, and doing neither effectively.

The British plan contemplated two major offensives and a third supporting movement. After being reinforced at Halifax, Howe was to sail for New York City, capture it, and then make his way up the Hudson and into New England. At the same time Carleton, after driving the Americans from Canada, was to proceed down the lakes-river route, recapture Fort Ticonderoga, and also turn into New England. The two armies, presumably to be combined, would regain Boston and conquer the entire region. The third offensive had actually been designed first and then fitted into the grand plan, an example of the laxity that often marred British planning. While the British were still at Boston, Howe's second in command, Henry Clinton, who did not admire his superior, had sought and secured permission to lead a land and sea expedition to the southern colonies. Clinton and the London government had been persuaded by the royal governors of these four colonies, who were then sojourning on warships off the coast of their former domains, that thousands of Tories would flock to the cause if only a British army appeared to support them. Clinton was to be joined by a fleet coming from England and was to provide this support. After reestablishing British authority, he was to go to meet Howe in New York, arriving, of course, just as Howe did.

None of the movements went off quite as planned or on schedule. Clinton left Boston late in January but stopped in New York harbor and at Hampton Roads to confer with the exiled governors of New York and Virginia. Not until March 12 did he reach the mouth of the Cape Fear River in North Carolina, where he was to rendezvous with the English fleet. There he found no fleet and learned that the promised Tory uprisings would not materialize; attempts had been put down by patriot militia, the latest one at Moore's Bridge in North Carolina. Clinton also learned that the fleet had been delayed but was coming. It did not arrive until late May under a bellicose admiral, Sir Peter Parker. Although the original purpose of the expedition, cooperation with the Tories, had evaporated, Parker insisted on attacking at some point. He decided on Charleston, the principal port and city in the South, and convinced a reluctant Clinton to accompany him.

The attack was not delivered until late in June, giving Charleston time to prepare for it. A small but determined force of Continentals and militia held the land approaches to the city, and artillery was mounted in palmetto-log forts commanding the entrance to the harbor. When the fleet rashly sailed up to one of these forts, Moultrie, it met a devastating fire and limped off without trying to land Clinton's troops. The expedition required three weeks to refit before sailing for New York to join Howe. It arrived on August 1—to find that Howe had been there a month, trying to build up strength to assault the city.

The British offensive from Canada could not begin until the Americans were driven from before Quebec and dislodged from Montreal, and Carleton did not feel equal to the task. He therefore waited for the coming of a promised new army from England. Actually, the American force on the St. Lawrence line was not much larger than Carleton's. Reinforcements had continued to limp in during the spring months, but other troops had gone home at the expiration of their service, and of those there at any time a large number were sick or enfeebled for want of food. Probably 8,000 troops were committed in the course of the campaign, but in 1776 the average American strength was only about 2,000, not all of them fit for duty. They were now under the command of General John Thomas, the wounded Arnold having retired to Montreal to recuperate.

In May the relieving expedition awaited by Carleton appeared in the St. Lawrence, a fleet of war vessels and an army of 10,000 regulars. Carleton disembarked only a few hundred of the troops before sallying forth with the Quebec garrison to attack the besiegers. He did not need any more, for the appearance of the fleet had thrown the Americans into a panic. They fled up the river with the British in pursuit and did not check their retreat even at Montreal. Back down the lakes-river route they went, pausing at Crown Point on Lake Champlain and coming to a stop only at Ticonderoga in July. They were at the moment more of a mob than an army; were, as one observer saw them, "disgraced, defeated, discontented, diseased."

The Americans were eventually brought under control by Arnold, who left Montreal in the retreat. Although they were a part of Schuyler's northern army, that general and other ranking officers were occupied elsewhere, and Arnold by assent exercised command. In the meantime, Carleton, now with a total of 13,000 men, had paused south of Montreal. His objective was Ticonderoga, but he knew that to take and hold it he would need a secure water line of communication back to Canada. He was therefore building a lake flotilla before venturing further. Arnold was equally alert to the importance of sea power on the lakes, and on the shore of Champlain he was constructing a navy of his own. The British would have to fight for control of the lake. Carleton has often been criticized for taking so long to construct his fleet that he could not move south until autumn. A more telling criticism is that he and other British planners should have realized the necessity of a lake fleet before embarking on the campaign.

The vessels in the two squadrons were row galleys and gondolas, small as compared with ocean-going ships, propelled by oar and sail and not very fast or maneuverable, and armed with light cannon. Carleton assembled his flotilla at St. Johns on the Richelieu River with the help of artisans from the naval force in the St. Lawrence; he was also able to transfer some of the small gunboats of the navy to the river. Arnold's task was more difficult. He had to requisition laborers and sail and other supplies from New England while axmen felled trees on the lakeshore to provide the wood for the vessels. Nevertheless, his boats were ready by early October, and with crews of soldiers he sailed up Champlain to challenge the British.

The squadrons met in the middle of October at the hotly fought battle of Valcour Island. Arnold lost most of his vessels, while Carleton suffered only slight damage. The British now possessed superiority on the lakes and an open passage to Ticonderoga. Carleton, however, abandoned his purpose to attack Ti and retired to winter quarters at St. Johns. He reasoned that the fort was too strong to be stormed and it was too late in the season to undertake a siege. The excuse is not quite convincing. Carleton, like other eighteenth-century generals, simply lacked a sense of exigency and saw no reason to do something now if it could be done more easily later. It is true that if he had captured Ticonderoga he could not, because of the lateness of the year, have gone on to cooperate with Howe. But if he had held it, the British would have had an advance base from which to operate in 1777. As it was, their only accomplishment was to expel the Americans from Canada.

Only the offensive directed by Howe achieved a distinct success, and although the result was limited because the movement was also plagued by delay, it almost destroyed the American cause. After leaving Boston, he had waited at Halifax for reinforcements and naval support to arrive. They did not arrive until June, and then not all the expected naval force, part of it having been diverted south to aid Clinton's expedition. Howe, nevertheless, embarked for New York and in early July landed his vanguard on Staten Island, across from the city on Manhattan Island. When his force was completely assembled, he would have an army of 32,000 professional and abundantly equipped soldiers. The naval squadron, when finally collected under Admiral Howe, would number ten ships of the line, twenty frigates, hundreds of transports, and 10,000 seamen. The expedition was slow in gathering, however, and did not reach full strength until late in August. Thereupon, General Howe decided that there was no time before winter to advance up the Hudson and into New England. Instead, he would capture New York and Newport, in Rhode Island, to open up another port, and from these bases launch an offensive in the following year.

Confronting the formidable British array in New York was Washington, with a smaller army and no navy. The American commander had moved to the city in April following the evacuation of Boston, and since that time had devoted his main energy to raising troops to fill his depleted ranks. By strenuous effort, he was able finally to assemble a force of nearly 20,000 Continentals and militia, most of them untrained and undisciplined. He had come to New York to hold it, realizing the city's strategic importance and also responding to the wishes of Congress. This decision has been a source of controversy among military historians. New York, it has been pointed out, was indefensible and potentially a giant trap. Situated at the southern tip of Manhattan Island, it was surrounded by the Hudson River on the west, the East River on the east, and the Harlem River to the north; and inasmuch as the enemy navy controlled the waters, it could land troops at almost any point on the island to interpose them between the Americans and their only escape route, across the Harlem River. To make matters worse, the city was dominated by Brooklyn Heights across the East River on Long Island. Washington could not maintain his position unless he occupied Brooklyn Heights, and to do this he would have to divide his army by water and expose either or both parts to capture.

The critics have theory on their side, but Washington and Congress had to take political factors into account. An attempted defense of New York was necessary: if the city had been tamely abandoned, the government's desire to prosecute the war in earnest would have been suspect. Granting this, it must also be said that the attempt would have been better made above the city on one of the rivers. New York would have been lost, as it would be in any case, but without the Americans' suffering a costly and humiliating defeat.

Washington had grasped the importance of Brooklyn Heights and posted there 10,000 troops, approximately half of his army. They were entrenched in field fortifications on the heights and in an advanced position on a tier of hills to the south. Unfortunately for the Americans, the roads in the area did not run laterally to their position but through the hills and toward their rear. It was on this detached and vulnerable American force that General Howe's eyes fastened when he was at last prepared to launch an attack in late August.

In a smoothly executed amphibious operation, Howe moved 20,000 troops from Staten Island to Long Island—transports guarded by warships transferred the men to landing craft, and they hit the beaches without opposition. With a force double that of the Americans, Howe was able to fight a classic battle. He struck at the American front on the hills and simultaneously attacked their left. The American general on this section had left one of the vital roads unguarded, and the British coming up from the rear smashed the entire flank. The Americans then broke along the whole line and fled to the fortifications on Brooklyn Heights. They suffered 2,000 casualties and were badly demoralized, and if Howe had attacked again, he might have bagged them all. Instead, possibly with memories of Bunker Hill, he halted and began to dig approach trenches, indicating that he intended to take the heights by a siege.

In the respite thus provided, Washington had time to consider his next move. Somewhat reluctantly, he concluded that he would have to evacuate his force from Long Island. The removal was carried out on the night of August 29, the troops being transported in small boats manned by soldiers of a Massachusetts regiment who were former fishermen. No enemy warships appeared in the East River to interfere with the movement, possibly because the weather was bad or because the Americans had placed obstacles in the river to prevent their entrance, perhaps because the British were not aware of the transfer until too late.

Washington now realized the advantage that sea power gave the British, and he tried to so dispose his troops as to counter it. Leaving part of the army in New York, he strung other sections of it all the way up the island to the Harlem River over a distance of 16 miles. He was still hoping to hold the city and at the same time guard his escape route, but his extended line was vulnerable to British attack. Howe realized his opportunity and struck again. On September 15 the British general moved up the East River and landed a force at Kip's Bay, intending to turn Washington's left and pin the American army against the Hudson. Washington had to evacuate New York hurriedly and concentrate his army at Harlem Heights. Here he occupied a position too strong for Howe to assault, and he had an escape passage over the Harlem River.

Howe, however, was not finished with maneuvering. In October he moved farther up the East River and disembarked at Pell's Point. Again he was in Washington's rear, and again the American commander had to move to escape entrapment. Washington now crossed the Harlem, leaving Manhattan Island at last, and moved up to White Plains. He had eluded Howe, and at White Plains he was in such a strong position that he easily fended off a British attack. But in the chase he had again let his forces become divided. The Americans had built two forts on the Hudson to obstruct British passage up the river, Fort Washington on the east bank and Fort Lee on the west bank. Although much of their importance diminished with the fall of New York, Washington was determined to hold them, and as he moved north, he left 6,000 troops behind their walls. He had separated his army in three places in the face of an enemy who possessed greater mobility.

Howe saw another opportunity. Moving quickly to Dobbs Ferry on the Hudson, he interposed himself between Washington's army and the forts. They were traps now and should have been evacuated, but Washington would not see the danger. He seemed uncertain as to what Howe would do next or what he should do himself. Leaving 8,000 troops at North Castle and Peekskill to guard the New York highlands, he crossed the Hudson at North Castle and moved into New Jersey, apparently intending to appear at Fort Lee. Before he reached it, Howe, with the aid of warships that came up the Hudson, stormed Fort Washington and captured it and 3,000 prisoners and immense quantities of weapons and supplies. Washington at last consented to evacuate Fort Lee, and with its garrison and the remnants of his army he retreated across New Jersey, pursued by a British column commanded by General Charles Cornwallis.

The pursuit ended only when Washington crossed the Delaware River into Pennsylvania, in early December. He took with him about 2,000 troops, all that remained of the original force of 20,000. His army had begun to evaporate during the retiral from New York City, and the dissolution continued as reverse followed reverse and reached a high point after the debacle at the forts. Both Continentals and militiamen deserted, or simply went home. Most of the 8,000 troops Washington had left at the Hudson passes also disappeared, although 2,000 eventually made their way to him, minus their commander, Charles Lee, who was captured by the British.

It was the darkest hour of the Revolution. Many were saying that it was hopeless to resist the British, that Congress should seek what terms of peace it could get. Even Washington was for the moment depressed. "I think the game is pretty near up," he confessed in a letter to a brother.

If Howe had continued the drive he undoubtedly could have taken Philadelphia, the largest city in America and, as the seat of Congress, the capital. He might also have taken the little American army or at least dispersed it, and the blow possibly would have destroyed the rebel will to continue the war. He was satisfied, however, with what he had accomplished: the expulsion of the Americans from New York and the occupation of New Jersey. To maintain his position, he established a line of posts from New York City to Trenton and Bordentown on the Delaware. He had secured his base, and in the spring he would move on Philadelphia, which from now on became a magnet to him. Howe's action was a prime example of the limitations of eighteenth-century generalship. He had halted a movement that could have provided a decisive victory because he did not see the need for a decision: winter was coming on, it was difficult to campaign then, and there would be plenty of time later to finish the job. And in fixing his gaze on Philadelphia he betrayed his belief that a place was a more important objective than an enemy army.

George Washington had revealed serious faults of generalship. They may be summed up as an unsureness of judgment and touch, a tendency to act without thinking of his available resources or of the difficulties in his way. But he had also displayed great courage and sound strategic sense. He now resolved to deliver a blow at the British even though it was winter, not primarily to win a military success, although he hoped for that, but to convince the American people that the cause was not hopeless, that the British could be defeated. In making his plan he showed a sensitive appreciation of the relationship between war and politics.

He was ready to strike by the end of December, when reinforcements of Continentals and militia had brought his army up to 6,000. The main attack was to be a surprise descent on the Hessian garrison at Trenton on Christmas night, to be carried out by 2,400 regulars under Washington's personal command. While this force was crossing the Delaware above Trenton, a body of militia was to cross opposite the town to block the Hessians' escape route. Another militia group was to cross at Bordentown and occupy the attention of the enemy there. The Pennsylvania side of the Delaware was scoured for boats, and a number of so-called Durham boats were collected, large canoes really, forty feet long, propelled by poles and sail. They were to be manned by men from the Massachusetts regiment that had evacuated the troops from Long Island.

The crossings were made on a cold and blustery night, through floating chunks of ice, and took ten hours. The two militia forces did not reach their destinations, but the main column under Washington appeared at Trenton on the morning of December 26. A surprised Hessian garrison of 1,000 men surrendered after a brief resistance. Collecting his prisoners, Washington retired to the safety of the Pennsylvania side of the river, satisfied with his work. But then he learned he had accomplished more than he thought. The British had been thrown into confusion by the raid, and their detachments on the river had pulled back 12 miles to Princeton. Emboldened to exploit his success, Washington recrossed the Delaware on the night of December 30 and took up a position near Trenton.

In New York General Howe, enjoying the social pleasures of the holiday season, was astounded and angered at Washington's temerity. He ordered Cornwallis, whom he had just given leave to visit England, to restore the situation. Cornwallis, collecting troops from the Jersey posts as he went, arrived at Trenton late on January 2. He could see the American camp nearby, but because of the hour and the fatigue of his troops he put off an attack until the following morning, assuming that the Americans would accommodate him by waiting to be trapped. That night, however, Washington, leaving his campfires burning deceptively, marched back to Princeton in the British rear.

Appearing there in the morning, he struck and scattered a British force moving to join Cornwallis. That general awakened to the sound of guns booming at Princeton and the sight of a deserted American camp, and in fuming haste he retraced his steps to Princeton. At his approach Washington retired into the rugged New Jersey highlands around Morristown. Here he could repel any attack the British were likely to mount in winter and, lying parallel to their line of communication, he could interrupt it at will.

Faced by this threat, Howe abandoned most of New Jersey, pulling in his outposts to near New York City. After all his efforts and victories, he held only New York, Newport, and a fringe of New Jersey. However, it was not the recovery of territory that was Washington's great accomplishment. He had demonstrated that the war was not hopeless, and had rejuvenated the American will to resist. Now he could hope that recruits would turn out to strengthen his army for the campaigns of 1777.

THE BRITISH strategic plan for 1777 was so bad as to be almost unbelievable. The product of several minds, it emphasized unrealistic objectives, divided command, and separated armies. The blame for it must rest collectively on its architects, Lord George Germain in England, General Howe in America, and a new figure in the British command structure in America, General Sir John Burgoyne. No one of them had great strategic ability, but they might partially have overcome this lack if they had kept one another informed of their thinking. The most astonishing feature of British planning in this year was the almost complete absence of communication among the planners.

First to advance a proposal was Howe. Late in 1776 he informed Germain that if he could be reinforced, he had a plan to assure victory. He claimed that losses in the recent campaign and the detachment of units to protect his bases had reduced his effective force to 20,000 and he requested his numbers be brought up to 35,000. Given such an army, he would leave substantial garrisons in New York, New Jersey, and Newport and launch two major offensives, one from Newport against Boston and another up the Hudson to meet at Albany a British army coming down from Canada. The conquest of New England completed, he would then reduce the southern colonies during the winter.

In suggesting a juncture on the Hudson, Howe was voicing an idea he knew would appeal to the planners in London. Possession of the Hudson-Champlain line was a fixed item in British strategic thinking. It had been attempted in 1776 when Carleton came down from Canada, and Howe was certain that it would be tried again. What he did not know for a time was that a specific plan for a movement down the lakes-river route to Albany had already been proposed by John Burgoyne, who sought command of the expedition. Burgoyne had served briefly in Boston in 1775, had gone to Canada in

1776 to fight under Carleton, and then had returned home to seek an independent command. Although technically subordinate to Carleton, he was to have a free hand in the field. "Gentleman Johnny," as he was known, was an attractive man of varied talents, a politician, playwright, and wit as well as a soldier. As a commander, however, he was to betray gross deficiencies. Overly ambitious, he was too optimistic and ignored possible difficulties until they were upon him and could not be met. An American observer judged him accurately: "sanguine and precipitate and puffed-up with vanity, which failings may lead him into traps that may undo him."

Although Howe had endorsed a Hudson meeting, he was probably only paying lip service to the project to please Germain. Certainly he never intended to commit to it any substantial part of his army. As he soon revealed, he had fixed on an entirely different objective. Early in 1777 he proposed to Germain that his main effort should be to take Philadelphia. What he expected to achieve by capturing that city he did not clearly explain. He apparently thought that thousands of Tories would rally to him and, if armed, could hold the city, enabling him to move to another, unnamed objective at an unspecified time. Knowing now that a force would be descending the lakes-river route, he stated that he would leave on the lower Hudson about 9,000 troops, who should be able to "facilitate in some degree the approach of the army from Canada."

Germain approved Howe's plan early in March, at the moment he was giving final consideration to Burgoyne's plan. His decision to approve the latter defies rational explanation. He agreed to a strategy that had one army moving down the Hudson to Albany to establish communication with the force in New York while that army was moving away from New York toward the Delaware. Germain may have thought Howe could capture Philadelphia in time to return and aid Burgoyne, plainly a fatuous hope. Eventually, he saw vaguely the dangers inherent in the division of the armies and sent messages to Howe urging him to take Philadelphia so that he could "facilitate" Burgoyne's movement. But he never explained clearly to Howe the mission of the northern army, which was to force its way to Albany, where it would come under Howe's command. Not understanding what was expected of him, and perhaps not wanting to understand, Howe felt free to pursue his move on Philadelphia.

For his part, the British commander was not completely frank in informing Burgoyne what aid he could render. He told his colleague variously that he could do little and that he would leave a corps on the lower Hudson that might be able to "act in favour." It is possible, however, that Burgoyne did not want or expect Howe to join him on the Hudson. Ambitious to make a name in the war, he preferred to make it largely on his own. His original statement of the plan indicated that he desired no more of the force on the lower Hudson than a diversionary attack to enable him to reach Albany. Once there, he would sustain his army and open communications with New York while Howe moved on Philadelphia. How he could sustain any army in the winter he apparently did not consider.

Howe and Burgoyne started their campaigns at approximately the same time, in June. Howe's beginning, however, did not take him from his position around New York: he merely maneuvered from it for almost two months, seeking to mask his objective from Washington. He still planned to move against Philadelphia, but now he had conceived a different line of approach from the one he had proposed to Germain. Instead of going by land across New Jersey, a distance of approximately 100 miles, he would travel by sea, entering Chesapeake Bay and landing his army south of the rebel capital, a distance of 300 miles. He considered an alternate and shorter water route, up the Delaware River, but came back to the Chesapeake route.

His reasons for choosing this long and roundabout way have been endlessly speculated on by historians and are still not clear. It has been said that he wanted to keep Washington's army in his front so that he could engage and possibly destroy it and that only the Chesapeake approach offered him this opportunity. If he had advanced on the land or the Delaware route, Washington could have escaped to the west or north. The argument is not persuasive. Washington was going to fight for Philadelphia on whatever route Howe advanced. Howe was merely making the bad British plan worse. He removed his force from between Washington and Burgoyne, making it easier for the Americans to reinforce their northern army, and he put himself even farther away from Burgoyne. The conclusion is inescapable that Sir William desired mainly to capture Philadelphia and was willing to take as long as he needed to place his army in the best base of attack.

Believing that he had ample time to accomplish his objective, Howe did not leave New York until late in July, having been assured that Burgoyne was well on his way down from Canada. Early in the month he learned that Gentleman Johnny had taken Fort Ticonderoga, so when his awaited supplies arrived from England, he set sail. He had not, however, been able to secure the reinforcements he had requested and departed with only 15,000 troops supported by a naval squadron of over 200 ships. Behind him on the lower Hudson he left 8,500 men under the command of Henry Clinton.

Washington was not drawn out of position by Howe's maneuvers. Although he had to consider that the British general might move up the Hudson to join Burgoyne, he decided that Howe would more probably advance on Philadelphia by land or water. Therefore he kept his army of 11,000 men so posted as to counter any thrust, and when the British left New York, he moved to meet them, first at the mouth of the Delaware and then at the head of Chesapeake Bay. His decision to defend Philadelphia has been criticized by some historians who say he should have marched north and united with the northern army to crush Burgoyne and then returned with a strengthened force to engage Howe. But Washington could no more have abandoned Philadelphia without a fight than he could have similarly given up New York the previous year.

It took Howe thirty-five days to make the passage from New York to his point of debarkation at Head of Elk in Maryland, about 50 miles south of Philadelphia. (If he had marched overland, he would have required at the most twelve days.) Landing early in September, he moved northward to find Washington barring his way at Chadds Ford on Brandywine Creek. Howe now displayed his skill in maneuvering. Demonstrating in Washington's front, he crossed a force upstream to come down on the American flank. The surprised defenders broke but escaped being entrapped. Still relying on maneuver, Howe continued to advance and entered Philadelphia on September 26. Because the Americans still held the lower Delaware, he had to distribute his army over a wide front. He posted 9,000 men at Germantown north of Philadelphia and the remainder in the city and across the river in New Jersey. The exposed force at Germantown invited Washington's attention, and the American commander resolved to strike it. His plan was characteristic, audacious but too complicated. Four columns were to move on separate roads and converge on the British at dawn on October 4. Such a pincers movement would have been difficult even for experienced troops to execute; for the largely untrained patriots, it was impossible. To make matters worse, the morning was foggy, and the columns, arriving at different times, could hardly tell friend from foe. After fighting for over two hours, the Americans retired with casualties of more than 1,000 men, compared to the British loss of 500. While Washington went into winter quarters at Valley Forge, Howe reduced the American forts at the mouth of the Delaware and opened up a shorter supply route.

Howe was now secure in the city he had set such store on capturing, but no great results ensued from his feat. The patriot army did not disperse in despair, the American government and public gave no indication of abandoning the struggle (Congress had removed to York, Pennsylvania), and few Tories came forward to offer their services. The most ominous outcome of the campaign did not seem to dawn on Howe as he prepared to savor the delights of another social season. He had taken Philadelphia so late in the autumn that he could not move very far from it. His dilemma was realized by shrewd old Benjamin Franklin in Paris. Told that Howe had captured Philadelphia, Franklin replied: "No, Philadelphia has captured Howe!"

While Howe was still preparing to move from New York to the Chesapeake, Burgoyne started down the water route toward his objective of Albany. He left his assembly point, St. Johns on the Richelieu River, with a force of close to 9,000 troops: some 8,000 regulars and Hessians, 250 French Canadians and Tories, and 400 Indians. He also had with him an indeterminable number of women—wives and camp followers—an immense baggage train (his personal supplies alone required thirty carts), and an unusually large collection of artillery. Mindful of Carleton's error in lacking a fleet, Burgoyne had a squadron of warships and transports awaiting him. However, he overlooked another precaution. Once past the lakes he would have to depend on land transportation, and he took with him, considering his baggage, only a small number of horses, oxen, and carts. He actually knew little about the region into which he was so blithely advancing—a largely unsettled area scarce in food and with hostile inhabitants. To furnish a diversion in his favor, he gathered at Oswego at the head of Lake Ontario a force of 875 regulars and 1,000 Indians under Colonel Barry St. Leger, which was to move down the Mohawk Valley and join the main force before Albany. Burgoyne thought that the appearance of this column would cause many Tories to rally; he did not realize that the large body of Indians would arouse fear and anger in the people of the valley.

Burgoyne and his flotilla moved down Lake Champlain undisturbed— there was no Arnold and a fleet to oppose them—and approached Fort Ticon- deroga on July 1. The American commander in the Northern Department, Philip Schuyler, had at the most 3,000 troops at his disposal, and he made but a token defense of the fort before retreating to Fort Edward on the Hudson. Schuyler was a devoted patriot but his command abilities were limited; his most serious deficiency was a lack of decisiveness. He was probably correct in thinking that he could not hold Ticonderoga, but its abandonment brought wide criticism, especially in New England, whose militia were reluctant to serve under him because he was a New Yorker and who wanted him replaced by his second-in-command, Horatio Gates.

At Ticonderoga, Burgoyne was only 70 miles from Albany. He could have entered Lake George and sailed to Fort George on its southern shore, which was a short land march to the Hudson. However, his advance column had pursued the Americans down to Skenesborough below the southern tip of Champlain, and Burgoyne decided to advance by this route on Fort Edward while shifting his artillery and heavy stores on water to Fort George. He was committing an incredible folly, which he tried to justify by explaining that a retrograde movement to Ticonderoga would have raised the morale of the rebels. It might have done so, but Burgoyne was incurring a grave risk to his own army. He had chosen a long and difficult route to the Hudson that took him farther away from his base of supply and would place him finally in an untenable position.

His line of approach ran through a wilderness cut up by ravines, creeks, and marshes, and the advancing army had literally to hack out a road. Schuy- ler, although he had received reinforcements from Washington, did not feel strong enough to offer battle, but he showed great resource in delaying tactics. His men felled thousands of trees across the route of the British, destroyed bridges, and even diverted streams across Burgoyne's way. The British general pushed on through the obstacles, but very slowly, and did not occupy Fort

Edward until July 29. His journey had consumed three precious weeks, and once at Edward he had to wait more weeks while his artillery and other gear were hauled through the woods from Fort George.

Burgoyne remained at Fort Edward more than a month. Even after his stores arrived from Fort George, he made no move except to push an outpost slightly to the south. He was pondering his situation, and something of its desperate nature at last began to dawn on him. His long supply line was not providing him with the supplies he needed. His field base was at Fort George, but his permanent base was at Montreal, 185 miles to the north. The region into which he had brought his army produced but little food, and his troops were beginning to feel the pinch of hunger. If Burgoyne was going to sustain his army, he would have to either retire to Canada, admitting failure, or go on toward Albany. But if he advanced, his line would become longer and he would be moving farther away from his water route and would have to depend on land transport. He sent a rush order to Montreal for hundreds of horses and carts—too late to have it filled.

While Burgoyne wrestled with his hard choices, he suffered two serious setbacks. He was informed that a large number of horses could be collected in the area around Bennington, Vermont, and seeing an opportunity to replenish his supply, he sent a column of 800 Hessians, regulars, and Tories to gather in the animals and whatever stores could be found. He knew that a force of rebel militia was in the neighborhood but had been told it was small and incapable of offering much resistance. It was actually much larger than his intelligence indicated, swollen by recent accessions. The New England frontier was inflamed at reports of atrocities committed by Burgoyne's Indians, and 1,500 vengeful militiamen had assembled at Bennington under General John Stark, a veteran officer. Stark detested Schuyler and had refused to obey an order to join the main army, but he was eager to engage the approaching British raiders. Attacking their front on August 16, he also enveloped one of their flanks—this was the battle in which some of the militia donned Tory cockades and passed to the enemy rear—and almost destroyed the entire detachment. A relief force sent by Burgoyne arrived only in time to be smashed back by a second American attack. Burgoyne lost more men than he could afford to lose, and with no gain.

During these same weeks of Burgoyne's delay, St. Leger and his force of regulars, Indians, and Tories had appeared before the only American bastion in the Mohawk Valley, Fort Stanwix, and on the refusal of its commander to surrender had laid it under siege. A relief force of New York militia attempted to fight its way to the fort but was ambushed by the Indians at Oriskany and driven away after a bloody battle. However, messengers from the fort reached Schuyler at his camp at Stillwater and begged for aid. The American commander, even though he lay only 25 miles from the British at Fort Edward, believed he could rely on Burgoyne's inaction, and dispatched a column of 900 regulars under Benedict Arnold, who had been assigned by Washington to help him. Arnold, as he approached Stanwix, employed a clever ruse. He sent into the Indian camp a friendly native and a half-witted Dutchman to spread rumors of the great size of his force. The half-wit was chosen because Indians looked on mental defectives with awe as possessed of spirits, and he was instructed to say, when asked the number of the Americans, as many as "the leaves on the trees." St. Leger's red allies were already bored with the routine of siege operations, and when they heard the Dutchman's disquieting news, they departed en masse. St. Leger had to retire to Oswego and then to Canada, and Burgoyne was deprived of a needed reinforcement.

Burgoyne did not decide on his next move until nearly the middle of September. It was the choice of a man who had to gamble—he would go on to Albany. He knew now he could expect little aid from Clinton in New York. In response to his appeals, Sir Henry promised no more than a minor diversion. The cautious Clinton was not inclined to risk his force in a possibly rash move, and besides, he had no orders from Howe to do anything specific or spacious in design. Still, Burgoyne determined to advance. He could not retire to Canada, giving up his dream of glory, and he could not winter his army where he was. If he advanced, he would cut his already long line of communications, but in Albany he might be able to sustain his army. He was on the east side of the Hudson and could have marched down it and crossed at Albany. Reasoning that a crossing there would be difficult, he moved to the west side and headed for Bemis Heights, where the Americans awaited him in an entrenched position.

The patriot army had a new commander. Responding at last to New England criticism of Schuyler, Congress had replaced him with Horatio Gates, who had served in the British army and had good administrative ability. As a field general, however, his talent was limited. Fortunately for the Americans, there were fighting generals in his command, men like Arnold and Daniel Morgan. His army was growing in size, reinforced by units from Washington and assembling militia. He would eventually have at his disposal 11,000 troops as compared to the 6,000 or 7,000 men remaining to Burgoyne.

Gates acted soundly in occupying a fortified position along Bemis Heights. He knew that Burgoyne would have to come to him, would have to attack him, and he placed himself advantageously. Burgoyne made his assault on September 19 at the battle of Freeman's Farm and was repelled with heavy casualties. For three weeks he did not venture another move. Hearing that Clinton had started up the Hudson, he hoped for relief. Then came the depressing news that Sir Henry had advanced only above Stony Point and could go no farther. Burgoyne's situation was now hopeless. His store of food was almost exhausted, and rebel parties were slipping around to his rear to cut his communications and drive in his foragers. As he lamented: "No foraging party could be made without great detachments to cover it; it was the plan of the enemy to harass the army with constant alarms and their superiority of numbers enabled them to attempt it without fatigue to themselves." Stubbornly he made a last effort to break through the American lines, attacking on October 7 in what is usually called the battle of Bemis Heights, and again failing after severe losses. He then retired to a fortified position at Saratoga to deliberate on when he would bow to the inevitable, which was to surrender.

It was a hard decision for the proud British general—to yield to a rebel, even though that man had once been an officer in the British army. But Burgoyne had no choice. "My army would not fight and could not subsist," he wrote later. On October 17 at Saratoga he surrendered approximately 6,000 officers and men and his still-great stores of artillery and ammunition. Because Gates was eager to secure the triumph, he allowed Burgoyne easy terms. The British were to be paroled and allowed to go to England on the promise not to serve in America again during the war. The Americans had little experience in handling large bodies of prisoners—previously those captured had been exchanged by individual generals—and Gates may have thought that Congress would not want to be burdened by his large bag. But as his arrangement would have freed 6,000 other troops then in England for service in America, Congress found reasons to repudiate the agreement. The British were eventually escorted to prison camps in Virginia and Maryland—although many dropped off on the march and merged into the local population—and were held in them until the end of the war.

Saratoga was the first great American victory of the war and is rightly ranked as one of its decisive battles. It lifted patriot morale to new heights and brought France to the American side. Years of fighting remained ahead, but after 1777 the tide turned in favor of the Americans.

AFTER THE FAILURE at Germantown, Washington took his army into winter quarters at Valley Forge 20 miles northwest of Philadelphia. His militia troops returned to their homes, but approximately 6,000 Continentals remained with him. They lived in tents until crude huts could be built, and they endured privations that have made the name of Valley Forge a synonym for sacrifice in American wars. Their suffering resulted from shortages of food, clothing, shoes, blankets, and other necessities and, in the consequent weakened condition of many of them, from exposure to cold, although the winter was relatively mild. The shortages were occasioned in part by a breakdown in the supply departments. The heads of the quartermaster and commissary agencies and various of their subordinates, disliking certain new regulations imposed by Congress, had resigned, and Congress took its usual time in naming replacements. Often supplies were available but were not moved to where they were needed. Just as often they were not available. Many farmers preferred to sell their products to the British for specie instead of the depreciated American currency, and many merchants chose to sell their goods to the British or civilians, in either case for exorbitant profits. Valley Forge is a prime illustration of the contrasts in human behavior released by war—heroism and denial at the danger line, greed and graft behind it.

The American army survived its ordeal and, indeed, emerged from it a more efficient force. Congress eventually reorganized the supply departments, and before the end of the winter, stores were again coming in, although the improvement was only temporary. More important and of more permanent effect, the army went through a training program that gave it a new professional competence. There appeared in camp a man who was to acquire the name of "drill master of the Revolution," Friedrich Wilhelm von Steuben, the most valuable of the foreign soldiers who enlisted in the patriot cause. In securing a commission Steuben had said he was a former lieutenant general in the Prussian army of Frederick the Great and a baron. Actually he had been but a captain and his title from a small German state was honorary. Despite his posturing, he was, as Washington soon realized, an officer of rare ability. His service had been in staff, and he had a thorough knowledge of European drill methods. Washington appointed Steuben inspector general and directed him to institute a training regime. The German introduced into the Continental Army such innovations as marching in columns of fours and in cadence, from which troops could deploy into line of battle quickly; reveille and inspection; and bayonet practice. He was much struck by the difference between American and European soldiers. He described it in a letter to a friend: "You say to your soldier, 'Do this,' and he doeth it; but I am obliged to say, 'This is the reason why you ought to do that': and then he does it." Thanks to him, the American army took the field in 1778 prepared to fight as European professional armies fought.

In February, 1778, the French and American governments concluded a treaty of alliance in Paris. Although it would not reach American shores to be ratified by Congress until early in May, it was known that negotiations were under way and that French aid was certain. Ironically, in that same month the British government extended a peace offer, more specific than the one it had previously put forward through the Howes: if the rebels would return to their allegiance, Britain would renounce power to tax them. The commissioners dispatched to America to discuss these terms, however, never had a chance to present them. Buoyed by the success of Saratoga and the promise of French help, the Americans would now accept nothing but their total objective. Before the commissioners arrived, Congress adopted a resolution declaring that the United States could not enter into any peace conference until Britain withdrew her land and naval forces "or else in positive and express terms" acknowledged the independence of "said states." American resolution was strengthened by the apparent inability of Britain to inflict retribution if her offer was not met. While the commissioners were trying to get through to Congress, the British army was evacuating Philadelphia and thus abandoning its only significant gain of the previous year.

General Howe had spent a gay winter in the American capital, but as 1778 approached, he realized that his usefulness in America had ended. Under criticism at home for failing to end the war and perhaps dissatisfied with himself, he requested and received relief from his command. In his place the government named Henry Clinton, who was somewhat more intelligent but who would suffer the same frustrations. His began with the reception of confused and confusing orders from London. Rumors of the French alliance had thrown Germain and his associates into a frantic reappraisal of strategy. Clinton was first told that he might have to evacuate Philadelphia and assume a defensive position at New York while detaching parts of his army to hold Canada and the West Indian islands; he was told, indeed, that he might have to retire all the way to Halifax. Next, when the alliance was announced by France in March, he was directed to evacuate Philadelphia by sea and proceed to New York, which he was to hold along with Newport; once there he was to detach a force to defend Florida and a larger one to attack French possessions in the West Indies; later he could consider mounting an offensive against the southern American colonies. Germain had shifted from a defensive strategy to one that was partly offensive, but in both he was promoting an unwise dispersal of the British forces. Historians once surmised that Philadelphia was abandoned because the government feared that a French fleet known to have sailed for America might bottle up the army there. The truth was that the objectives set by Germain could not allow for enough troops to hold the city.

Clinton decided to move to New York by marching overland across New Jersey, mainly because he had too many horses to crowd on his naval transports. His decision was defensible—he could reach New York more quickly by land—but it left his army vulnerable to attack, strung out in column of march with a heavy baggage train. As it lumbered through Jersey in a hot June, it was followed by Washington, who had occupied Philadelphia and then taken up the pursuit. He had perhaps 12,000 troops, most of them products of Steuben's training, while Clinton, after sending some of his force by sea, had 10,000 or more men.

The conditions were favorable for attack, but Washington hesitated as to whether to deliver a partial blow or risk a general action. Finally, on June 26, he decided to strike the British rear at Monmouth with almost half of his army. The employment of such a large force implied that he meant to bring on a general action, but if so he did not indicate his purpose to his officers. He perhaps was not sure of his intentions, and his indecision communicated itself to others. Charles Lee, recently exchanged from captivity, commanded the attack on June 27, and because of his innate caution or confusion as to Washington's orders or both, bungled it. Clinton managed to deploy his troops from march line to battle line and then to counterattack. The two armies fought for hours, with the Americans standing well on an open field, but in the end Clinton was able to continue his retirement and reach New York.

Chagrined that the British had escaped him, Washington still champed for action. A French fleet under the Comte d'Estaing and carrying 4,000 troops had arrived in Boston, and Washington urged the admiral to join in a land and sea attack on New York. D'Estaing agreed but on approaching the harbor concluded he could not get his larger ships in without foundering. The two commanders then decided to attack Newport, Rhode Island, but this plan too went awry. Just when the assault seemed at the point of success, a relieving British fleet appeared. D'Estaing sallied out to meet it, whereupon a sudden gale scattered both squadrons. The attack was abandoned, and d'Estaing limped off to Boston to refit. He then sailed to the West Indies to attack Britain's possessions there. The Americans had received a reminder, if they needed one, that although the French would help them, they would also pursue their own national interests.

With autumn coming on, Washington abandoned hope of a further offensive. He distributed his army in an arc around New York City, running westward from White Plains across the Hudson, where West Point was fortified to hold the river, to New Jersey. He had the British effectively shut up in the city, and although he did not feel strong enough to go after them, he was on the whole satisfied with the situation. "It is not a little pleasing, nor less wonderful to contemplate," he wrote a friend, "that after two years Maneuvering . . . both Armies are brought back to the very point they set out from, and that that, which was the offending party in the beginning is now reduced to the use of the spade and pick axe for defence."

For the remainder of the war no general action occurred in the northern theater. There were brisk outpost clashes on the Hudson between New York and West Point, but they did not develop into anything larger and resulted in no permanent advantage to either side. Washington managed to keep his army intact, although it continued to suffer from lack of supplies and the soldiers were angered by arrearage of pay. A crisis was experienced during the winter of 1779–80 when most of the army was encamped at Morristown, New Jersey. It was a season of biting cold, the weather more bitter than at Valley Forge, and the men were in a sullen and dangerous mood. Washington feared that unless the supply situation improved, the army would "infallibly disband in a fortnight." Some mutinies occurred and others were threatened, but the army survived the ordeal as it had previous ones. The cause it represented also survived, even in the face of the attempted treason of a highly placed and popular general. Ambitious Benedict Arnold, bitterly convinced that his talents had not been recognized by Congress, decided to go over to the British. He secured from Washington the command at West Point and then entered into secret negotiations with British agents to deliver the key fortress. The plot was discovered in time to foil it, although Arnold escaped to fight against his countrymen.

The only American successes in the North were minor ones over the Indian allies of the British who had been incited by agents at Niagara and Detroit to raid the frontiers of New York, Pennsylvania, and Kentucky, then a part of Virginia. The raids had been ordered by Germain to create diversions and draw off American troops from the main theater. A force detached by Washington dealt a damaging blow to the Iroquois who had been striking New York and Pennsylvania, and a small column of fewer than 200 men recruited by Virginia and under the command of Colonel George Rogers Clark captured the British posts in present Indiana and Illinois. As a result, the Indian danger was lessened although not removed. In the main theater Washington still hoped to attack New York. In 1780 a force of 5,000 French troops under the Comte de Rochambeau, accompanied by seven ships of the line, occupied Newport, which Clinton had evacuated to augment his forces elsewhere, and Washington urged the French general to join him in a combined attack on New York. However, a British fleet appeared to blockade the French, and Rochambeau admonished Washington to wait until France could achieve naval superiority in American waters. Meanwhile, with stalemate in the North, the theater of war had shifted to the South.

EARLY IN 1778 the British planners in London decided to make their main effort in the southern colonies, heretofore almost untouched by the war. The plan was developed gradually, its seed being contained in Germain's instructions to Clinton to evacuate Philadelphia: the British commander was told that after the West Indies and Florida were secured from French attack it might be possible to mount an offensive in the South. As the year progressed, the design was filled in. Clinton was to stand on the defensive in New York while troops drawn from his army and the Caribbean invaded the South. The striking force would be large enough to accomplish its objective and would be augmented by the numerous Tories waiting in Georgia and the Carolinas, the perennial illusion that had lured previous British generals to disaster. The southern colonies would be occupied one by one, and then a crippling blockade could be laid on the northern colonies, or perhaps an offensive launched against them by the combined southern and New York armies.

The men who produced the plan did not seem to know their precise objectives. Perhaps they had too many objectives to focus on one, or maybe they could not admit, even to themselves, that they had no realizable aim. Presumably the main effort was being transferred to the South because the British could transport forces there faster by sea, on what Washington called their "canvas wings," than the Americans could move troops by land, and this would enable them to occupy territory before the Americans could assemble to defend it. But it was not clearly established that occupation of the interior was the chief objective. The army was also to secure such ports as Savannah and Charleston to facilitate the shipment of supplies to the West Indies and to be in position to defend the islands if the French attacked. In addition to dispersing their objectives, the planners dangerously dispersed their armies, one in New York and one in the South, the two separated by 1,000 miles of water. If the French could attain naval superiority, even for a brief time, the army in the South would be isolated. Clinton realized the peril in the plan, although he concurred in it. Neither he nor the men in London could acknowledge the great failure of their strategy: the British could not bring Washington's army to decisive battle.

The Americans became aware of the new threat in the South in 1778, when British troops moving from Florida captured Savannah and overran the rest of Georgia. Forced to organize a quick defense, Congress sent General Benjamin Lincoln to Charleston to command the Department of the South. Lincoln had demonstrated administrative ability while serving under Gates, and it was hoped he would be able to create an army out of the few Continentals available in the South and the militia. He assembled 3,500 troops, mostly militia, and with this raw force managed to repel a British column that appeared at Charleston.

Lincoln's ultimate purpose was to recover Savannah, but even after his troops were better trained, he doubted he could accomplish the mission without naval support. Consequently, he sought the aid of d'Estaing's fleet still operating in the West Indies. The admiral obligingly arrived off the Georgia coast in the fall of 1779, and Lincoln with part of his army marched to meet him. The two commanders decided to make a combined attack on the town, which was protected by sea and land fortifications. If they had followed conventional tactics, on the land side they would have employed the siege method of approaching by parallel lines. But d'Estaing was in a hurry to get his ships out of waters exposed to seasonal gales and proposed to storm the works. The assault was made on October 9 and was thrown back with heavy losses; one man in every five of the attackers was killed or wounded. D'Estaing then returned to the West Indies and Lincoln to Charleston. Another attempt at Franco-American cooperation had ended in failure, and the British retained their base.

While this operation was concluding, Clinton in New York was planning another British offensive in the South. At the urging of the government, it was to be a major effort, aimed at capturing Charleston, which would become the base for future offensive operations. The movement strained Clinton's resources because he had to leave sufficient troops to hold New York. In order to augment his force he pulled in the garrison from Newport, now to be abandoned, and other outposts, and late in December sailed for Charleston with 8,000 men aboard transports. Encountering winter storms, he did not arrive off the South Carolina coast until February 1, 1780. After landing, he drew troops in from Savannah, bringing his army up to 14,000. In the face of this concentration Washington was able to send only small reinforcements south over the slow overland route. Lincoln in Charleston awaited the British attack with something over 5,000 Continentals and militia.

Charleston was protected on the sea side by Fort Moultrie and water batteries and on the land side by field fortifications, and Clinton, a careful general, was of no mind to dash his forces on these works. While his fleet invested the harbor, his army inched forward in conventional siege fashion, the heavy guns being moved behind parallel lines ever closer to the city. Eventually he was in position to bombard it by land and sea preparatory to an assault, and Lincoln, realizing his cause to be hopeless, surrendered early in May. The British here achieved their greatest victory of the war and secured possession of another important base.

Satisfied with this accomplishment, Clinton returned to New York with about a third of his force. The remainder he left under the command of Cornwallis, who had come south with him as second in command. Cornwallis had over 8,000 troops, including several regiments of Tories, who enlisted with fierce anticipation. The South Carolina Loyalists, like those in other states, suffered much before the coming of the British, having been subjected to personal indignities, legal discriminations, and confiscation of property, and now they saw an opportunity to repay old scores. Tory troops usually accompanied the columns of regulars that Cornwallis sent into the interior to establish a line of posts running from Ninety-Six to Rocky Mount and Camden. The invaders encountered little organized resistance—no American army remained in the field—but they had to endure constant harassment from local partisan bands led by Francis Marion, Thomas Sumter, and Andrew Pickens. The fighting that occurred was by eighteenth-century standards unusually savage, of the kind that later generations would call guerrilla warfare. The most ruthless practitioner of it on the British-Tory side was a regular cavalryman, Colonel Banastre Tarleton, who at the Waxhaws near the North Carolina border slaughtered a patriot band of 350 men even though they displayed a white flag.

The fall of Charleston shocked Congress to renewed effort. It scraped together at Hillsboro, North Carolina, a small Continental force, most of it from Washington's army, which was expected to form a rallying point for the local militia. Congress, without consulting Washington, appointed as commander the heralded victor of Saratoga, Horatio Gates. On arriving at Hillsboro, Gates found only about 1,500 regulars and but few militia. Nevertheless, he announced that he was going to march on Camden, one of the northernmost British posts in South Carolina, collecting additional militia as he advanced. It was a rash and risky move, prompted by Gates's exaggerated opinion of himself after Saratoga. He saw himself as a great field general who could win a victory even with a largely green army.

Gates approached Camden with about 4,000 troops, including the militia he had gathered. Cornwallis, warned of his coming, had hurried from Charleston with reinforcements, and the two armies met north of the town on August 16, 1780. Although he had only 2,000 men present, Cornwallis decided to attack. He struck first the militia, which Gates had posted on his left, and at the onslaught they broke in disorder. The Continentals on the right put up a fight but were also driven from the field. At small loss to himself, Cornwallis inflicted on the Americans one of their worst defeats of the war. Approximately 1,000 patriots were killed or wounded and another 1,000 captured; an untold number went home. Gates, who fled to Hillsboro 160 miles away, found there only 800 survivors of his force. Once again the Americans were without an army in the South. They were also without a commander, Gates having been relieved by Congress. As one of his friends had predicted, his "Northern laurels" had turned to "Southern willows."

The British possessed both a commander and an army, and that general wore the laurels of victory. Cornwallis had handled his army well in the recent campaign, but he had generally followed Clinton's direction. Now, however, he began to exhibit a restiveness under Clinton's restraint and to develop views on strategy sharply divergent from those of his superior. Neither he nor Clinton seemed to understand the strategic purpose of the other. Their lack of communication was not helped by Clinton's reluctance to issue flat orders to Cornwallis, known to be a favorite of Germain's, nor by the time required to transmit messages between New York and the South, which sometimes took up to six weeks.

Clinton wanted, while holding New York, to establish a post in the Chesapeake region of Virginia, preferably near Norfolk. From this base he would launch raids up the Virginia rivers to arouse the local Tories and discourage the local patriots. Once his base was secure, he would prepare a two-pronged offensive against Pennsylvania from the Chesapeake and New York. Only then did he propose to bring Cornwallis into the campaign—a substantial part of the southern army would join him, moving up along the coast so as to be always in touch with the Royal Navy and the supplies it would need. It was a cautious strategy, designed to husband the limited British land forces and avoid battle unless success seemed reasonably certain.

Clinton's plan would have restricted Cornwallis, for a time, to holding South Carolina and conducting short raids into the interior. Cornwallis rejected this passive strategy. Essentially a gambler, he preferred to risk for victory rather than wait to assure it. He told Clinton he could not pacify South Carolina unless he conquered North Carolina: "I see no safety for this province but in moving forwards as soon as possible." With Clinton's reluctant consent, he invaded North Carolina late in 1780. Instead of moving by the coast, as

Clinton suggested, he struck into the interior toward Charlotte, giving as his reason that he wanted to get the troops out of the unhealthful low country. He was moving away from his base at Charleston and away from the fleet that supplied the base and was his most secure link with other British forces. In the interior his army would have to keep marching in search of supplies, or starve. His movement was ominously reminiscent of Burgoyne's invasion of New York.

An episode suggestive of Burgoyne's fate occurred almost immediately. As Cornwallis advanced to Charlotte, he detached a force of 1,000 Tories under British Major Patrick Ferguson to the North Carolina backcountry to recruit additional Loyalists. The appearance of this force infuriated the patriots of the area, including those in southwestern Virginia and the "over-mountain men" in present-day east Tennessee. Approximately 1,700 militiamen assembled, animated by a single and simple purpose, to destroy the invaders. Ferguson, who could have retreated, chose to give them battle at King's Mountain on the border of the Carolinas. What followed was more like a gigantic game hunt than a battle. The militia encircled the elevation and methodically shot the Tories. Ferguson fell and almost 400 of his men were killed or wounded, whereupon the survivors surrendered; some of the Tories were slain after surrendering. It was Bennington over again. The militia delivered the prisoners to Continental authorities, and then most of them returned to their homes.

Although the militia disbanded, they had accomplished a solid success. King's Mountain discouraged the North Carolina Tories from rallying to Cornwallis and encouraged the patriot militia and partisan bands to increase their activities. More important, it set back Cornwallis's invasion schedule. Unable to determine the size of this enemy force that had suddenly appeared on his flank and fearful that it might threaten his communications, he retreated to Winnsboro, South Carolina. So alarmed was he that he sought and obtained from Clinton a reinforcement of 2,500.

In the meantime, a new American commander had arrived in the South. Congress, this time asking Washington's advice, appointed Nathanael Greene to succeed Gates. Greene had had no military experience before the war, but he had studied military science and served capably under Washington and as quartermaster general. Nothing in his record indicated distinction, but as commander in the South he would exhibit qualities of brilliance.

Greene assumed command at Charlotte early in December. His army consisted of only 1,500 troops, over half of them militia. He knew he must avoid battle until he could build up his force, but he knew too that if he hoped to rally the militia he would have to achieve some kind of success. He therefore resolved on a daring move. Dividing his inferior force, he moved with part of it to Cheraw just over the North Carolina border. He sent the other part under General Daniel Morgan far to the west around Cornwallis's left. The two American fractions were 140 miles apart, and according to the textbooks either could be destroyed by the British mass between them. Actually, Cornwallis at Winnsboro could not concentrate against one or the other without exposing his western posts or Charleston to attack. He too would have to divide his force, and this suited his purpose because he was still determined to occupy North Carolina. Moving most of his supplies up from Charleston, he sent Tarleton with 1,100 infantry to run Morgan down and with the bulk of his force moved into North Carolina to intercept Morgan, who was expected to retreat before Tarleton.

Tarleton came up with Morgan on January 17, 1781, at a place called the Cowpens, near King's Mountain. Morgan was willing to fight, and in the ensuing battle he achieved a minor tactical masterpiece. Avoiding the mistake of other American generals of putting the militia in the battle line, he posted his in front of the Continentals. They were instructed to fire until the British were upon them and then to pass to the rear, a movement they ordinarily executed without urging. The British advanced in battle order and although briefly checked by the militia fire, pressed on. But they wavered when they met the fire of the Continentals, and then a concealed American cavalry force struck them on the right, and the militia, having been re-formed in the rear, hit them on the left. Caught in a trap, the British were almost annihilated, suffering casualties of over 900 men. Only Tarleton and a few cavalry escaped. Cornwallis had lost another part of his army.

Morgan too had to make an escape, for Cornwallis was between him and Greene. Moving fast, he eluded the pursuers and joined Greene early in February. The American army was reunited but retreated before Cornwallis's advance, finally crossing the Virginia border. When Cornwallis stopped his pursuit, Greene returned to North Carolina but deliberately maneuvered to avoid battle. He was building up his force, however, and eventually commanded 1,500 Continentals and 3,000 militia. In March, 1781, he halted at Guilford Court House in northern North Carolina and offered battle. After hard fighting he abandoned the field, but the British victory was won at high cost—Cornwallis suffered casualties amounting to one-fourth of his dwindling army.

The British general was now in desperate straits. His troops were exhausted by the long marches he had required of them and were suffering for lack of food. He could not gather supplies from the country around him, for partisan bands harassed his foraging parties and prevented deliveries from his base at Charleston. His nearest water base was Wilmington, 200 miles away on the coast, and he took his bedraggled army there. To Clinton he wrote that his campaign had been completely successful, but Clinton and everybody except Germain knew better. An observer in London expressed the prevailing opinion: "Lord Cornwallis had conquered his troops out of shoes and provisions, and himself out of troops."

Cornwallis was hardly without troops. He brought with him to Wilmington about 1,500 men, and perhaps as many as 8,000 others were scattered in posts throughout South Carolina and Georgia. However, he could not pull in his detachments without abandoning the posts, and even if he had been willing to do this, he could not have subsisted them on the way. The troops at Wilmington were his only available field force, and after refitting them he had to decide what to do with them. He did not arrive at a decision until late in April. Then he heard that Greene was marching on South Carolina.

Cornwallis's instructions required him to defend Charleston, and he could have returned by water to meet Greene. He rejected this move as a disgraceful retreat; like Burgoyne, he could not turn back. He resolved to move to Virginia and join the forces sent there by Clinton. Successful operations in Virginia "would tend to the security of South Carolina and ultimately to the submission of North Carolina." He was trying to hide from the government and perhaps from himself that he had failed. Admitting he had not conquered the Carolinas, he proposed to reduce them by conquering Virginia, his ultimate absurdity. On April 25 he set out for Petersburg. He did not ask Clinton's permission for the move but merely informed his superior that he was coming.

While Cornwallis was marching north, Greene was moving south. The American commander had followed the British part of the way to Wilmington but had called off the chase. Persuaded that Cornwallis was at least temporarily harmless, Greene decided to carry the war into South Carolina. Explaining his move to Washington, he wrote that Cornwallis would either have to return to meet him, thus abandoning North Carolina, or chance the loss of the South Carolina posts. As Cornwallis chose the latter alternative, Greene faced only the opposition of the dispersed British garrisons. The commander, Lord Francis Rawdon, attempted to pull his forces together, and in battles at Hobkirk's Hill and Eutaw Springs held the field but suffered heavy losses. Greene, his army swollen by militia and partisans, continued to maneuver and attack and by the end of 1781 had captured all the interior posts. Of the territory the British had sacrificed so much to conquer, they retained only the coastal strongholds of Charleston, Savannah, and Wilmington.

Cornwallis, on arriving at Petersburg, took command of all the British troops in Virginia, with the addition of his own force, some 7,000 men. Confronting him were 2,000 Continentals sent down by Washington under the command of the Marquis de Lafayette. Before Cornwallis came, the British, at Clinton's orders, had restricted their activities to raids up the rivers. Cornwallis, however, believed that Virginia was now the main theater of the war, apparently because he was there, and proposed to occupy as much of the interior as he could. He advanced beyond Richmond and sent a detachment as far as Charlottesville, meeting only harassing opposition from Lafayette. Then, as though realizing he had gone too far, he retired nearer the coast.

Clinton had been appalled at the Earl's movement to Virginia. "My wonder at this move of Lord Cornwallis will never cease," he wrote, and he became even more disturbed when he learned of Cornwallis's advance toward the interior. He was sensitively aware of the presence of French sea power in American water—the large French fleet in the West Indies and a smaller one at Newport. If these squadrons could unite, they might achieve supremacy over the British fleet and bottle up Cornwallis's army. Clinton therefore ordered the Earl to retire to Yorktown or another point on the coast and establish a base whence he could be taken by water to New York or back to Charleston and where he could be supplied by sea. Cornwallis, having no choice, went to Yorktown and began to erect field fortifications. Lafayette followed him at a circumspect distance.

The danger to Cornwallis that Clinton saw was not immediately apparent to Washington. The American commander was still discussing with Rochambeau the desirability of a Franco-American land and naval attack on New York, which would depend on the presence of the French fleet in the West Indies. But on August 15, 1781, Washington learned that this squadron was not coming to New York but would arrive in the Chesapeake. He immediately grasped that he could trap Cornwallis—if he could achieve land superiority opposite Yorktown and if the French could maintain naval superiority in the bay. He and Rochambeau made their plan quickly. The French army moved from Newport to above New York while the French squadron at Newport slipped out to join the fleet sailing to the Chesapeake. On August 19, only five days after receiving the French intelligence, the allied armies were on the march.

The movement was masked to deceive Clinton. Two thousand troops were left above New York to demonstrate against the city, while the main force marched around it and into New Jersey as if it were preparing to attack Staten Island. From there it moved to Philadelphia and then southward down the Chesapeake in transports. Meanwhile, the French West Indies fleet reached the Chesapeake and landed 3,000 men to join Lafayette. Clinton and the British naval commander in New York, Admiral Thomas Graves, now realized the intent of the allied movement, and Graves set sail for the bay to relieve Cornwallis. The British and French fleets fought an indecisive battle off the Virginia capes, but while they were maneuvering for further action, the French squadron from Newport arrived in the bay. The French now had superiority, and Graves retired to New York to refit and reinforce. Temporarily, at least, the trap on the water side was closed on Cornwallis.

The allied armies arrived before Yorktown on September 26. They had completed a long journey—the French covered 756 miles from Newport—and by eighteenth-century standards accomplished a rare feat in concentration and logistics, the more remarkable because it involved forces of two nations. They showed the same cooperation in constructing operations against Yorktown. Washington and Rochambeau agreed that siege methods would be required to take the town, and French engineers supervised the approach by parallels. The allies had superiority in artillery as well as in numbers, and as the lines were driven closer, Cornwallis, although he knew that Clinton was preparing a relief expedition, decided he could hold out no longer. On October 19, 1781, he surrendered his army of 7,000 men, the prisoners being sent off to camps in Virginia and Maryland. The relief expedition arrived to find that the army they had come to save was gone.

Yorktown ended the major fighting in the war, although peace was not formally declared until two years later. In the North the British held on to New York, closely observed by Washington. In the South they abandoned Wilmington and Savannah and retained only Charleston, watched by Greene. They possessed the bases from which to conduct further operations, but after Yorktown they realized that any offensive would fail, that they could not reconquer the colonies. The London government fell, and a cabinet promising to enter into peace negotiations came into power. The new government readily accepted a mediation offer from Austria and Russia, and representatives from Britain, France, and the United States convened in Paris to conclude a treaty. In the long and tortured discussions, the American delegates displayed a tough realism and an undeviating concern for the national interest, even entering into separate and secret dealings with the British to secure what they wanted. The treaty that was agreed on in September, 1783, granted the Americans all that they could reasonably demand—British recognition of the independence of the United States and of American possession of an imperial domain stretching to the Mississippi River. The new nation had been born in war, and its martial origin would endure in the consciousness of its people.

INTERLUDE

1783-1812

THE ARTICLES OF CONFEDERATION, the form of government under which the Americans finished the Revolutionary War, embodied the political ideals for which they had resorted to war. Having decided to throw off the repressive authority of Britain, they took care in forming their own government to ensure that it in turn could not become repressive. The "sovereign" states comprising the confederacy delegated certain powers to the central government, which was to consist of a unicameral Congress in which each state had one vote. The powers of Congress were restricted to matters judged to be of common concern. It could conduct foreign relations, make war and peace, manage Indian affairs, provide postal service, and prescribe uniform standards of weights and measures. Denied to it were the powers to tax, regulate commerce, or enforce its laws directly on citizens of the states. The assent of nine states was required to enact laws of a substantive nature. A separate executive was not authorized, but Congress could appoint committees or "civil officials" to administer its measures. It was a system of government that was difficult to operate and that experienced many difficulties, and toward the end of the 1780s the states were constrained to create a new form of union: the government established in the Constitution.

Although the charter of the Articles vested in Congress the power to wage war, it was vague in stipulating how this power was to be exercised. Congress was authorized to "build and equip a navy," but the word *army* appeared only once in the document, where the legislature was forbidden to "appoint a commander in chief of the army and navy" without the consent of nine states. There were, however, several references to the right of Congress to raise "land forces." In times of crisis it could make requisitions of troops from each state "in proportion to the number of white inhabitants" thereof, and the troops so summoned had to "march to the place appointed" by Congress. Each state could commission its own regimental officers, but Congress reserved the right to name general officers. The document did not define how the states were to fill their quotas, but as each one was required to maintain a "well regulated" militia, it was undoubtedly intended that the troops should be volunteers from the base of the militia. The apparent avoidance of the word *army* has led some historians to conclude that the framers were registering an antimilitarist sentiment. It is more likely that they were simply uncertain as to what kind of wars the United States might wage in the future and hence uncertain as to what kind of military organization they should authorize. The young nation did not have a clearly defined strategic purpose to fulfill. It wanted to be able to preserve itself against foreign attacks, if any came from European powers, and to police the Indians on the western frontiers. But the leaders did not go beyond this simple formulation in their thinking. They had at least implied that Congress could raise a standing army, and this seemed enough.

The standing force that had come into being during the Revolution, the Continental Army, was demobilized by the end of 1783, only a regiment of infantry and a battalion of artillery, some 600 men, being retained to guard military stores. While the disbandment was being carried out, a committee of Congress was assigned to study the problem of what kind of peacetime military establishment the new nation should have. Understandably, the committee turned to General Washington for advice. He consulted with various of his generals and in due time submitted a plan entitled "Sentiments on a Peace Establishment." Interestingly, Washington, who during the recent war had voiced harsh criticism of poorly trained militia troops, now came out for a well-disciplined citizen force as the country's main military reliance.

Arguing that a large professional army was dangerous to liberty, expensive, and unnecessary, he asserted that 2,600 regulars should be sufficient to regulate the Indians and prevent surprise attacks by foreign foes. But to fight a war, the country should depend on its militia, which, however, needed to be made efficient. Washington proposed that all able-bodied males between the ages of eighteen and fifty be required to enroll in the militia of their states and that the militia be placed under national supervision and trained by officers educated at a national military academy. In a sweeping affirmation of the claims of mass warfare, he declared that every citizen owed "not only a proportion of his property" but also "his personal services" to the defense of the government, so that the "Total strength of the Country" could be called forth in emergencies. And, in a significant break with past practice, he recommended that the citizen soldiery should be provided with weapons by the state.

Congress took no action on Washington's report. Some members objected that it would entail too much expense and others that it would unduly increase the power of the central government; still others responded to the pressure of their militia organizations, who did not wish to be made efficient, at least not by centralized supervision. In 1784 Congress disbanded the 600 troops still in service, retaining only 80 to care for stores. Then, because it needed a force to guard the frontier, it called upon the states to supply 700 volunteers from the militia. Obtaining only a fraction of these, in the following year it requisitioned 700 men from the states for three years—it presumed, that is, that it was empowered to create a regular army. In 1786 Congress called for more three-year troops when a rebellion of debtor farmers in Massachusetts seemed to threaten state authority. On neither occasion were quotas filled. In 1788, the last year of the Confederation's life, there were only 595 men in national service. This "army" was under the command of the senior officer, Josiah Harmar, with the rank only of lieutenant colonel. The civil military administration consisted of Secretary at War Henry Knox, three clerks, and a messenger. The contingent expenses of Knox's office amounted to $176 for the year.

In 1789 the new government formed under the Constitution took over. It was a stronger government than the Articles had provided for, both in its structure and in its allocation of powers. Instead of just one branch, there were now three: legislative, executive, and judicial. The legislative branch, Congress, enjoyed powers denied to the old government; it could tax, regulate commerce, and enforce its laws directly on the citizens of states. Visible weaknesses in the government of the Articles had persuaded most Americans that a stronger authority was necessary—it had been in almost constant financial straits, and unable to conclude satisfactory trade treaties with other countries. Equally serious, it had failed to establish an effective military organization that could guard the western frontier, supervise the Indians, or repress domestic insurrection. Recognition of the military deficiencies of the old government was apparent in the provisions of the Constitution dealing with war.

The Constitution gave Congress the exclusive power to declare war and to provide an army and navy. In a significant difference with the Articles, it was stated unequivocally that Congress could raise and maintain an army directly, without calling on the states. Congress was also empowered to raise the militia for specific purposes, to execute the laws of the Union, suppress insurrection, or repel invasion. It could provide for organizing, arming, and disciplining the militia and for "governing" such parts of them as were called into national service, but the states retained the right to appoint militia officers and to train the militia "according to the discipline prescribed by Congress." Although Congress could raise armies and navies, it could not direct them. The power to command was vested in the head of the executive branch, the president, who was designated as "Commander in Chief" of the armed forces. The framers of the Constitution were determined that the military should always be under civilian authority.

The first president was understandably interested in military policy. Washington usually left the task of managing the administration's legislative program in Congress to subordinates, but he intervened actively to secure a law establishing what he thought was an effective military organization. The plan he recommended to the legislators was essentially the same one he suggested to the Congress of the Articles—a small regular army as the first line of defense and a large militia force trained under national supervision. A measure embodying his ideas was introduced, but it encountered the same kind of opposition that had stalled the earlier proposal. Finally passed as the Militia Law of 1792, it bore only formal resemblance to Washington's plan. It required that all able-bodied white males between eighteen and forty-five be enrolled in their respective militias and arm themselves. With Washington's idea of federal inspection amended out, the system of training was left to the states. Most of them prescribed a system but did not enforce it, and consequently the militia generally continued to be an undisciplined force. As ineffectual as the act of 1792 was, it did register an American tradition of long lineage, that citizens owed military service to their government in time of peace.

While Congress was delaying action on Washington's plan, it was taking steps to create a military establishment of more modest proportions. One of the first executive offices it authorized was a War Department, headed by a secretary who was to be the president's deputy in military matters. Henry Knox shifted easily from being secretary "at" war to being secretary "of" war; he was to direct somewhat more employees than before, ten instead of four, and was also to supervise naval affairs, although there was as yet no navy. Congress also authorized the creation of several staff offices to assist the secretary; the occupants were charged with supervising supplies and stores, but their duties were light because there was not much of an army to provision. Congress fixed the size of the army at 1,200 men who were to be enlisted for three years. These troops were scattered in the frontier posts and were loosely under the command of Josiah Harmar, now a brigadier general. The office of commanding general was not recognized in law, and Harmar exercised control only because he was the senior officer.

Almost immediately the inability of this establishment to meet a serious threat was cruelly revealed. Since the Revolution, settlers had been pushing west of the mountains into the lands known as the Southwest (south of the Ohio River) and the Northwest (north of the Ohio River). Although the Indians in both areas resented white encroachment, they resisted it more fiercely in the Northwest, and in 1790 the people in that region were pleading with the national government for protection. Washington was determined to put down the Indian danger, and with congressional authorization he called out 1,500 militiamen from Pennsylvania and Kentucky. They assembled at Fort Washington near the little frontier town of Cincinnati and joined 320 regulars under Harmar's command. Harmar was under orders to conduct a "rapid and decisive" move against the Indians, which was impossible with his green troops. With a column of 1,400 men he struggled northward through the wilderness, his militia becoming increasingly restive under discipline and threatening to mutiny. At the end of two weeks, near present-day Fort Wayne, he was attacked by Indians. In the confused fighting in the woods Harmar suffered 200 casualties and retreated with his bedraggled force back to Fort Washington. The Indians, emboldened by their success, stepped up their attacks along the whole frontier.

Washington was convinced that only a show of white might would awe the Indians, so he prepared to organize another expedition. But the most he could wring from Congress was authority to enlist an additional regiment of regulars and 2,000 special "levies" for six months. The quotas were slow in filling, and when the expedition was assembled at Fort Washington in the summer of 1791 it numbered only 2,000 troops, of whom 600 were regulars and the rest militia and levies. It was placed under the command of Arthur St. Clair, a Revolutionary veteran who had been governor of the Northwest Territory but was now commissioned a major general. He thus succeeded Harmar as commander of the United States "army."

Not until mid-September was St. Clair prepared to move out. Following Harmar's route, he marched even more deliberately, slowed by his stopping to build forts and perhaps by the noncombatant impedimenta he carried with him; according to one count some 300 women, many of them prostitutes, accompanied the column. By early November he had covered only 100 miles, his supplies were running short, and militia desertions and sickness had reduced his force to 1,400 effectives. While encamped near the headwaters of the Wabash River, he was surprised just before dawn by 1,000 Indians, because he had not taken proper scouting precautions. The militia and the levies broke, and a slaughter ensued. More than 600 Americans were killed and almost 300 wounded. St. Clair escaped with less than half his original force and retired from the army in disgrace.

The debacle did not influence Congress to think more favorably of Washington's militia bill, but it did shock the legislators into authorizing an increase in the regular army to 5,000 troops. At the suggestion of Secretary Knox, who had a taste for the classics, this force was called the Legion; its units of 1,200 men were called sub-legions, this form of organization temporarily replacing the regiment. A balanced force of infantry, cavalry, and artillery, it was expected to be able to cope with the Indians—if it was led well. Washington realized the part that hesitant or inept leadership played in the previous failures, and he selected a commander with great care. He appointed Anthony Wayne, who with the grade of major general became the ranking officer in the army. Wayne had been an aggressive infantry general in the Revolution, but he had acquired a reputation for rashness, reflected in his nickname, "Mad Anthony." Wayne proved to be anything but precipitate. He subjected his troops to rigorous training before moving to Fort Washington in 1793 and continued to train them there. Not until the following year did he move into the Indian country with 3,000 picked men. His care paid off when he was attacked by the tribesmen at Fallen Timbers, near present Toledo. His men withstood the assault and then in an attack of their own scattered the Indians, inflicting heavy casualties. In 1795 the cowed tribes agreed to make peace and to cede their lands in Ohio to the United States. The Indian menace was for a time ended.

While tranquility was being restored on the domestic scene, events in Europe threatened to involve the young nation in a foreign confrontation. In 1793 the wars of the French Revolution broke out and continued for the rest of the decade. The principal antagonists were France and a coalition of nations supported by Britain, and it was the clash of the two giants, Britain and France, that touched American interests. Britain instituted a naval blockade of France and seized neutral vessels suspected of carrying contraband goods to her enemy. The United States was the country most affected by this procedure, and American protests were loud and bitter. A possible crisis was averted by the negotiation of an agreement, Jay's Treaty, in which the United States recognized the British position on contraband in return for the evacuation of the northwestern military posts which the British had held on to illegally since 1783. (It was a mark of the military weakness of the United States and its low national standing that it had been unable to expel the British from these places.)

France interpreted Jay's Treaty as an American move to the side of Britain and retaliated by seizing American ships making for English ports. Now American anger flared at France, and as the depredations continued, there was talk that the United States should prepare to defend its rights by force, even against its ally of the Revolution with whom it still had an alliance. Responding to these pressures, Congress in 1794 authorized the construction of six frigates. The act stated that the ships were necessary to protect American commerce from attacks by "Algerine corsairs" in the Mediterranean Sea; but as accompanying acts provided for the construction of harbor defenses, it was obvious that the frigates were intended for protection against France. Whatever the reasons, a navy had come into being and was recognized, along with the army, as a principal line of defense. Its importance was underscored in 1798, when a separate Navy Department was created.

The possibility of a foreign war did not cause Congress to increase materially the size of the land forces. During the last year of Washington's second administration the strength of the regular army was 3,300 men, the largest force, except for the Legion, since the advent of the Constitution, but not large enough to repel an invasion by a major enemy. Such an attack was apparently not expected, as most of the army units were stationed at posts in the Northwest and the Southwest and only small garrisons were placed in the coastal towns. Wayne died in 1796 and was succeeded as commander by James Wilkinson, a mediocre career officer. Although the position normally carried the grade of major general, Congress, in an economizing mood, abolished that rank, and gave Wilkinson the status of brigadier. This was the military establishment that John Adams found when he became the second president in 1797.

Under Adams, French interference with American commerce became more frequent and flagrant, and the president, a doughty patriot, called on

Congress to strengthen the nation's defenses. The legislators, also aroused by France's high-handed attitude, authorized the enlistment of 10,000 volunteers for three years and the construction of 12 vessels of various types for the navy. More than 4,000 volunteers were mobilized during 1799, and Washington was called out of retirement to command them, with the rank of lieutenant general. Counting the troops already in service, the United States had perhaps 7,000 men under arms, and the strengthened American navy was cruising the coastal waters seeking out French raiders. This show of force impressed the French, who had other reasons for reaching an accommodation with the United States. France had more need of American trade than Britain had, and as she was about to pressure Spain to return Louisiana to her, she required a friendly neighbor to the north. In 1800 she agreed to a treaty in which she recognized the American position on neutral rights, thus averting the danger of an American war. The United States had also escaped the threat of war, and the provisional army was disbanded. The strength of the regular army was fixed at 5,400 men, although only 4,000 enlisted. Brigadier General Wilkinson again became the commander.

The military system of the new nation had been established under the auspices of the Federalist party, whose leaders had been prominent in the movement for the Constitution. The Federalists held certain beliefs that may be termed, with some exaggeration, their "ideology." They supported a strong national government, as strength in government was then understood, holding especially that it had a function to stimulate the economy. As a corollary to this conviction, they evolved a kind of mystique about the nation. America should be proud and respected, and one way for it to attain this position, in addition to a sound economy, was for it to be militarily strong. The Federalists were uncertain as to how great this strength should be—they had the common American fear of a large standing army—but they remained convinced that some power was justified. Thus they began by creating a small army and kept increasing it, and eventually they instituted a navy. Their military philosophy overcame their fear of the military—they became persuaded that an army was an instrument of society and could be a part of society.

Although their political and military accomplishments were significant, they lost control of the government in the election of 1800. They were defeated by the Republicans, a party with a different ideology.

Whereas the Federalists represented primarily the mercantile and financial interests, the Republicans were predominantly an agricultural party. Their political ideas were a reflection of the thinking of their constituents and of their leader, Thomas Jefferson, who became president in 1801 and retained the office for two terms. As a first principle, the Jeffersonians advocated a national government of limited functions. The central authority should exercise only the powers specifically allocated to it by the Constitution, leaving other powers to the states. It should not, by using implied powers, engage in such activities as stimulating the economy. As the Republicans envisioned it, government would be an inexpensive enterprise, and one of their main objectives as they entered office was to effect this economy.

A second objective was to keep the country at peace. The Republicans were not pacifists, but they had a horror of war and consequently an animus against those who were involved in making war—that is, the military. They recognized that the country had to have an army, but they thought it should be small, sufficient only to perform frontier constabulary duties. Unlike the Federalists, they did not conceive of the army as an instrument of society and a part of society. It was an evil to be tolerated. Secretary of the Treasury Albert Gallatin spoke the feeling of Jeffersonians when he said: "The distribution of our little army to distant garrisons where hardly any inhabitant is to be found is the most eligible arrangement of that perhaps necessary evil that can be contrived. But I never want to see the face of one in our cities and intermixed with our people."

Entranced with economy and confident of peace, the Republicans began immediately to reduce the military establishment. First to feel the knife was the navy. Most of the ships commissioned during the Federalist period were sold to other countries or laid up, only the larger frigates and a few other vessels being retained in service. Next, the authorized size of the army was cut from 5,400 to 3,200, a number deemed sufficient for frontier defense. Wilkinson remained in command of the army—as its only officer of general grade. The War Department consisted of the secretary and a dozen clerks, the Navy Department of a secretary and fewer clerks. Except for the secretaries, no person or agency in either department was responsible for control, procurement, or even record-keeping. The Jeffersonians had lofty ideals about the purpose of government but little interest in the efficient administration of it.

Hardly had the military machine been dismantled when the realities of European power politics intruded on the Republican dream of peace. The war that had racked the Continent during the 1790s had ended at the time Jefferson took office, but in 1803 another conflict began. The lineup of nations was much the same as before. France, now ruled by a military genius, Napoleon Bonaparte, was opposed to Britain and a coalition of countries that feared France. Again the principal antagonists were Britain and France, and again each sought to prevent the flow of war goods to the other by seizing American and other neutral ships on the high seas. American anger was directed at both nations, but most bitterly at Britain. Because Britain had a larger navy than France, she was able to enforce her blockade more tightly and to take more American ships. More antagonizing than the restrictions on commerce was Britain's presumption that she could impress men from American-owned vessels for service in her navy on the claim that these men were British citizens or deserters. In 1807 a British ship of the line attacked a United States frigate, the *Chesapeake,* in U.S. coastal waters and took sailors off her. Impressment was an insult to national pride and another indication that Britain did not respect American sovereignty. She was also suspected of inciting the Indians in the Northwest to attack the frontier and of plotting an invasion of New Orleans and the Gulf Coast, a part of the Louisiana Territory recently acquired from France.

Jefferson and his successor, James Madison, were resolved to uphold American neutral rights. But they shrank from resorting to war against either Britain or France, because they disliked war as an instrument of national policy and because war with a major enemy would place dangerous strains on the developing young nation. Instead, they decided to employ economic pressure to force the offending nations to recognize American rights, not admitting that this was itself a way of making war. Under Jefferson, trade with all countries was prohibited; American shipping was withdrawn from the seas. When this policy did not secure results, only trade with Britain and France was embargoed, with a promise to renew it with the country that repealed its restrictions. Under Madison, trade with both countries was reopened, but with a threat: if one of them acceded to the American position and the other did not, trade with the latter would be closed.

This experiment in economic war failed to secure its objective. Britain and France were hurt by the American restrictions, but not enough to make them yield; probably damaged more seriously was the American economy. Reluctantly, Jefferson and then Madison had to consider that a recourse to real war might be necessary, and undoubtedly against the main offender, Britain. Jefferson asked Congress for authorization to recruit 24,000 volunteers. The legislators refused permission, but did vote an increase of 6,000 men in the regular army. Madison also asked for a larger volunteer force, and this too was refused. Not until 1812, when relations with Britain were at the breaking point, did Congress bring itself to act. In January it authorized the president to raise the army up to 35,000 troops and to call out 50,000 militia. In June it declared war against Britain.

Ironically, it was the anti-war "liberal" party that took the nation into war. The same irony would appear again in American history. Most American conflicts have occurred under liberal administrations that disliked war but would not renounce its use.

The actual strength of the army at the outbreak of the conflict was probably only 6,700 troops plus several thousand very recent recruits. An accurate estimate is impossible because of the administrative shortcomings of the Madison government. Two weeks before war was declared, the Senate asked the secretary of war to state the number of troops under arms and their readiness for combat. The secretary passed the request on to the inspector general, who replied that he did not know the strength of the army because almost no recent reports had been received and he could not evaluate its condition because he had not inspected it. The incident epitomized the lack of order and control in the military system as the United States entered its second war.

CHAPTER V

The War of 1812: Origins and Organization

THE WAR OF 1812 has an unhappy reputation in the national historical record. As its story is usually presented, the United States rushed into conflict with Britain for reasons that were inadequate and ill advised, or that, if not confused, were base and covetous. Desiring war but unprepared for it, the Americans conducted their operations with a singular lack of skill, suffering numerous humiliating defeats and winning few successes. Consequently, the policy objectives of the government, whatever they may have been, were not achieved. It was a war without result, and, offering no military lessons, it is better forgotten. So goes the popular view of the second American resort to arms.

Actually, the American performance was not as bad as has been depicted. Although in the first two years of the war the land forces endured defeat and even disaster, in the final year, demonstrating steady improvement, they more than held their own with British armies. The navy, although not large enough to be a major factor in ocean warfare, proved consistently in ship-to-ship action that it was superior to the navy that ruled the seas, and on the inland lakes it generally exercised control and swung the military balance there in favor of the Americans. The war did offer some lessons, many of them negative. Some lessons were absorbed, and attempts were made to improve the military system, too late to affect the course of the war but influencing the future.

The war may be in low repute because it did not seem to have been "won," and Americans like to think, whether or not the facts fit the case, that they have never lost a war. The War of 1812 was not won, but neither was it lost. If the United States did not achieve its announced purposes in going to war, it was nevertheless in a stronger position at the end of the conflict than at the beginning, and such a result is certainly a test of a successful war. Britain finally realized she could not afford to antagonize the young American nation, that an unfriendly United States posed a constant threat to Canada, and the two countries entered on a long period of peaceful relations marked by mutual respect. But the most important and certainly the most enduring result of the war was its effect on the American spirit, on national pride. Although they had to ignore some facts to reach the conclusion, Americans felt they had stood up to the mightiest nation in the world—the nation that had crushed Napoleon —and had taught Britain that her recent colonial subjects could not be scorned. Secretary of the Treasury Albert Gallatin, who had experienced frustrations in trying to finance the war, understood this effect. "The war renewed and reinstated the National Feeling and character which the Revolution had given, and which were daily lessened," he wrote. "The people now have more general objects of attachment with which their pride and political opinions are connected. They are more American; they feel and act more as a nation. . . ."

THE OSTENSIBLE PURPOSE of the United States in resorting to war, proclaimed in statements of President Madison and speeches of members of Congress, was to force Great Britain to recognize American neutral rights—to make her desist from seizing American merchant ships and searching them for contraband goods, from blockading American harbors to intercept such vessels, and from impressing American merchant sailors alleged to be British deserters or citizens, of whom an estimated 6,000 had been coerced into British service. The war was, in a phrase that became popular then and later, a fight for freedom of the seas.

The contemporary account of the war's causes was for a long time accepted by historians as founded in fact. But, inevitably, the usual revisionary process set in. In the twentieth century various scholars looked at the vote in Congress on the declaration of war and were struck by its closeness—79 votes to 49 in the House, 19 to 13 in the Senate. Examining the vote further, they discovered a surprising result. The members voting for war were in preponderant numbers from the South, the West (Kentucky, Tennessee, Ohio), and Pennsylvania, and were Republicans. The members voting against war were almost entirely from the New England states and New York, and were Federalists. The distribution of votes seemed illogical. Why were legislators from the agricultural states and the agricultural party so ardent for a war to uphold maritime rights? And why were members from the maritime section and of the mercantile party, representing the interests directly affected by British policy, so opposed to the war? The historians who asked these questions were active in the period of disillusionment following the First World War, when intellectuals suspected that the official reasons given for wars were intended to deceive and that the real reasons were concealed. They readily concluded that the cry of neutral rights in 1812 was a mask for another objective.

That objective seemed apparent to some of the revisionists—the United States wanted to acquire Canada from Britain. As these historians analyzed the situation, the Republicans represented a dynamic agricultural imperialism that harbored ambitions to absorb the continent. During Jefferson's administration the Republicans had secured the huge Louisiana Territory by purchase, but they sought to obtain yet more lands for agricultural expansion, Canada by war with Britain and perhaps Florida by war with Spain. The advocates of the imperialism thesis found abundant evidence that apparently supported this view. Demands for the conquest of Canada filled the speeches of the young Republicans in Congress who had forced the declaration of war, who were dubbed by Eastern critics the War Hawks. Revealing of their confidence in America's might and destiny was an outburst by Henry Clay of Kentucky: "I am not for stopping at Quebec, but I would take the whole continent."

The expansionist explanation won wide acceptance among historians, and for a time was not challenged. Some scholars voiced doubts that the American desire to drive the British from Canada arose out of land hunger. Rather, they suggested, the American purpose was to eliminate the Indian menace on the northwestern frontier by depriving the natives of their British base of support —an objective that President Madison held forth, along with the necessity of maintaining neutral rights, in his message to Congress asking for a declaration of war.

The questioning eventually came, however, most of it in the decades after World War II, a period that saw many existing theses rejected as historians in a troubled world sought assurance by finding consensus in the past; and by the 1960s a new explanation of the causes of the War of 1812 had been developed and seemed on the way to winning acceptance. This latest interpretation, while not ruling out completely the influence of the expansionist surge, emphasized that the Americans resorted to war for primarily maritime objectives—they were determined to force Britain to cease her depredations on American commerce and particularly to renounce her practice of impressing American seamen. This was, up to a point, a restatement of the first concept of causation. However, the architects of the present thesis offered an addition that made their analysis more sophisticated, and more plausible. They suggested that the United States was contending for something even more important than maintaining its neutral rights. The Americans were a young people, proud and touchy, who felt that Britain had affronted their independence and even their existence. In challenging Britain on the issue of neutral rights they were in actuality asserting their right to be a nation.

In the view of present historians of the war, this fierce assertiveness explains the vote of the agricultural sections for war. The people of the West and the South were the most nationalistic of Americans, and in their definition of national honor they included American rights on the seas. It was not necessary to live in a coastal town to feel a sense of outrage at British violations of American maritime rights; a farmer in Ohio or Tennessee who had never smelled saltwater could burn with anger when he heard that the British had insolently impressed another group of American seamen. Rural Americans had an additional reason to resent Britain's maritime policy. For their well-being both farmers and planters depended on their ability to export surplus products abroad. But Britain's restrictive measures, and the American countermeasures, had shut off this trade, and the West and the South were experiencing a depression for which they blamed Britain—and for which they wanted to make her pay.

These historians also have an explanation for the vote of the Northeast against the war. Most of the members of Congress from this region were controlled by the ruling merchant class, who saw no reason to support war and many reasons to oppose it. Although the area was affected by the depression, the merchants blamed conditions on the maritime policy of the Republican administration, dominated by agriculturists, rather than on Britain. Moreover, the merchants were doing very well under the existing state of affairs. Although they might lose an occasional ship to the British, they reaped huge profits on vessels that got through the blockade. Consequently, they pressed their representatives to vote against war, against a war that if it added Canada to the United States would enlarge the influence of the agricultural majority in the government and thus further imperil the interest of the mercantile minority.

It is the question of Canada that weakens the case of the latest revisionists. Members of the war party pushed for the acquisition of Canada, and those of the peace party feared that it would be seized. Moreover, American strategy in the first two years of the war was directed to occupying large areas of the colony. The revisionists, while admitting the existence of an expansionist spirit, argued that the strategy was dictated by geography. The Americans could strike at Britain only by invading Canada—holding it, they could offer to return the colony in exchange for recognition of their maritime rights. This may possibly have been their purpose, but it seems unlikely that they would have gone to such an exertion merely to secure a bargaining counter, or that if they had secured Canada they would have relinquished it, even in return for acknowledgment of their rights on the seas. That other than maritime considerations influenced the Americans was revealed in an episode occurring soon after war was declared. The British government, unaware of the American action, announced that it was abandoning its claim to search neutral vessels, but not the policy of impressment. Word of the repeal reached the United States fifty days after the declaration of war, and to some officials on both sides Britain's concession seemed to offer a basis to negotiate peace. President Madison brusquely dashed these expectations. He instructed a general on the New York frontier who had concluded an armistice with the British to get on with the business of fighting the war.

The revisionists make their strongest point in suggesting that the United States was fighting to uphold its national honor. This phrase connoted to Americans a number of objectives which might or might not be related or realistic. As a Tennessean who would attain fame in the war, Andrew Jackson, put it: "We are going to fight for the reestablishment of our national character, . . . for the protection of our maritime citizens, . . . to vindicate our right to a free trade, . . . to seek some indemnity for past injuries, some security against future aggression, by the conquest of all the British dominions upon the continent of North America." The logic of Jackson's position might seem questionable—for one thing, the conquest and retention of Canada would assuredly not persuade Britain to recognize American neutral rights. But to Americans the purpose of the war was completely logical: they were going to show mighty Britain and the world that the United States was a nation that must be respected. If they were not quite certain how they would accomplish their objective, they were still going to make the effort. It was a war of a young nation determined to prove itself, and appropriately, and unlike some other wars, it was forced by young men—many of the War Hawks were in their late twenties or early thirties—who overcame the caution of the older men holding the nominal seats of power in the government.

THE CONFIDENT young nation was challenging one of the major powers of the world, and on paper the advantage lay heavily with the older, established nation. In the category of manpower, Britain could draw from a total population of 15 million people; the United States counted only 7.7 million, of whom 1.7 million were black slaves and not available for military service. The British regular army numbered approximately 300,000 men, practically all of whom could be dispatched overseas because of the large force of militia guarding the home islands. The American regular army, the bulk of it hastily assembled in 1812, totaled only some 11,000 troops, of whom 5,000 were very recent recruits. In naval strength there was no comparison. Britain's navy, which she was constantly augmenting, numbered over 700 ships of all types and some 150,000 men. Between 124 and 150 of the vessels—the estimates differ—were ships of the line and well over 100 were frigates. The American navy totaled between 16 and 20 ships—the estimates of it differ, too—and a personnel of but 4,000. Its largest vessels were frigates.

Britain enjoyed other advantages. She was still the leading industrial nation in the world and possessed the capacity to produce enough goods to satisfy the needs of her military machine, whereas the United States, although it had made significant industrial beginnings, was primarily an agricultural country. But as had been the case in the Revolution, Britain was not able to bring her full resources to bear on the American war. The bulk of them were committed to the campaign against Napoleon, and until the French menace was removed, the government would divert to the American struggle only those forces it could spare from the main effort.

Thus, of the great British navy, only 80-odd vessels were in American waters in 1812. These included 11 ships of the line, 34 frigates, and other assorted vessels, a larger force than anything the Americans could muster but small for the tasks it had to perform. Some of the vessels were based at Halifax and some in the West Indies, and from these scattered stations they had to escort British shipping to Canada and the islands, keep the St. Lawrence River open, and blockade American ports. Of the large British army, the greater part was fighting in Europe or guarding the colonies. Only 6,000 regulars were posted to Canada, and in 1812 this force and 2,000 local militia and perhaps 3,000 Indians constituted the defense of the province, holding a line that stretched from Quebec to Fort Malden opposite Detroit. The possibility of augmenting the defense with local levies was remote. The total population of Upper and Lower Canada was only 500,000, most of them of French origin who had accepted English rule but were not animated by any martial desire to fight in a war between Anglo-Saxons.

The War Hawks predicted that the conquest of Canada would be an easy matter. "Sir," cried one of them, John C. Calhoun of South Carolina, "I believe that in four weeks from the time a declaration of war is heard on our frontier, the whole of Upper Canada and a part of Lower Canada will be in our power." These anticipations have usually been dismissed as the bombast of politicians who did not realize the difficulties in the way of American arms. But the boasts were not without foundation. In view of the weakness of the British in Canada, it was possible that the Americans might have succeeded in conquering the province and thus in accomplishing their primary objective—if they had been able to bring their own resources to bear on the war. The failure of the central government to organize the national strength was one of the curious features of the conflict.

The first and greatest failure was that of mobilizing effectively the available manpower. On the face of the official records a vast force was called up, more than 500,000 men. However, this aggregate is highly deceptive. It breaks down into 56,000 regulars, 10,000 volunteers in national service from the militia, 3,000 rangers, and 450,000 militiamen. Only the regulars and volunteers enlisted for appreciable terms, some for a year, some for eighteen months, and some for five years. The militia total included many duplicates, and the great majority of the citizen soldiers served only for periods ranging from one to six months. This mobilization performance was inferior to that of the Continental Congress in the Revolution. That Congress, although a weaker government, succeeded in enlisting 231,000 regulars and employed only 164,000 militiamen.

The military legislation enacted in 1812, supported by the president and the administration leaders in Congress, provided for enlistments of one year.

Madison later explained the reasons for the shortness of term. Because it was considered difficult to raise an army for long service, "it was thought best to limit our first attempts to such a force as might be obtained in a short time, and be sufficient to reduce Canada from Montreal upward . . . ; trusting to the impression to be made by success, and to the time that would be afforded, for such an augmentation of the durable force as would be able to extend as well as secure our conquests." As the war progressed, Congress acquiesced to longer enlistments, offering generous bounties to prospective recruits, but the regular army never attained its authorized strength, standing generally at half or less of the total. Probably only 15,000 troops were in service at the end of 1812 and but 20,000 a year later; 35,000 or more men were enrolled in 1814 but many of these turned out in response to British invasions. As a result of the government's policy, the number of troops available for offensive operations against Canada during any one year was small.*

Only regular troops could conduct the projected offensive operations against Canada. The use of the militia for this purpose was impeded by the constitutional provision that they could be called out in war only to repel invasion; the citizen soldiers were quite aware of their rights, as they demonstrated on several occasions in 1812 by refusing to obey orders to cross into Canada. But even if the militia had not been so legalistic, they would have been an unsatisfactory instrument for offensive campaigns. For one thing, their term of service was too short to permit them to engage in a sustained operation. For another, they had not received the training that would enable them to stand up to British troops on the open field. The weapons employed in the war were those of the Revolution, the muzzle-loading, smoothbore flintlock musket and the muzzle-loading, smoothbore artillery piece, both having limited range and accuracy. Consequently, the tactics were virtually the same as those used in the Revolution. Infantry, in order to deliver a massed fire, had to move close to the enemy and attempt to maintain a line as it moved. Continental armies advanced in three ranks whereas the British marched in two, a formation they had employed since the Revolution and which enabled them to create a longer line. Regardless of the number of ranks, this kind of fighting required iron discipline—the result of rigorous drill.

Because of the policy of short enlistments, many regulars did not receive this training. Often the one-year men and eighteen-month men had to be rushed into battle soon after being inducted and with only the most elementary instruction. They might be given additional training subsequently or might learn by hard experience, but by the time they had become proficient, unless

---

*In relation to the number of troops mobilized, the number of service deaths in the war was slight. The conventional estimate is 2,200, but this apparently includes only men who died in battle. If a larger number died from other causes, as was true in other wars of this period, the total must be 6,000 or more.

they reenlisted, they passed out of the army. Many officers during the first two years of the war did little drilling of their men. Some of them failed to appreciate the importance of drill and others did not even know how to accomplish it. Officers who desired to train their troops—and these increased in number as the war continued—had to learn the evolutions by studying manuals, which in America were scarce and of inferior quality. Those that were available were adapted from European practices and prescribed a three-rank line, and this formation was the one favored by American officers. Usually it was unattended by skirmishers or light infantry, the Americans in this respect being less innovative than their forebears had been in the Revolution or than the British were in this war.

The neglect of training reflected the most salient characteristic of the officer corps during the first years of the war—a want of professionalism or expertness. This deficiency existed even though for the first time a cadre of professionally educated officers was present in the army. In 1802 Congress had authorized the establishment of a school for military engineers at West Point, New York, the origin of the institution that became the United States Military Academy. By 1812 the academy graduated eighty-nine cadets, most of whom remained in the army. They brought to its operations a needed technical capacity, but as technicians they held very junior commissions and did not direct troops in the field.

The American generals were incompetent, unlearned in the military art, and old. Those holding the highest grade had served in the Revolution, but in middle-level positions where they had no opportunity to command troops in numbers. Henry Dearborn, the senior major general, was sixty-one years of age; he was a lieutenant colonel in the Revolution but then left the army for a career in politics. The other major general, Thomas Pinckney, was two years older; in the Revolution he was a partisan leader in the Carolinas and since had served in diplomatic and political capacities. Of the nine brigadier generals, the senior, James Wilkinson, was fifty-five; he had been a minor officer in the Revolution and had remained in the army, where he acquired a reputation for intrigue but not for ability. The other brigadiers had been junior officers in the Revolution or militia officers or owned prominent political connections that were responsible for their commissions. The average age of the generals was fifty-eight years. Some of the older ones would reveal that age had sapped their physical and mental vigor.*

Why were such men chosen to lead armies? The usual, obvious answer is that there were none that seemed better. The source of officer supply was

---

*It is not contended here that there is a necessary relationship between the age of a general and his competence. Throughout military history older generals have performed well and even brilliantly. But there have been a larger number who in one war or another were affected adversely by their years.

limited, and these men were apparently the best that had been produced, the seniors with the greatest experience. Another possible explanation is that poor generals were selected because President Madison and his Republican advisers did not know how to identify good ones. Ignorant of war and innocent of administrative skill, they made bad appointments. Better generals would eventually be named, but these would be men who fought their way up to prominence and commanded attention by their deeds.

AMERICAN BOASTING on the eve of the war frequently included references to the economic strength of the nation, and consciousness of the expanding economy was one reason for the confidence to challenge the might of Britain. Although Americans exaggerated the extent of this growth, as they did all other manifestations of national development, they could justly take pride in the material progress that had occurred since the Revolution. The simple agricultural economy of the colonial era had evolved into a much more sophisticated system. Farming and planting were still the primary occupations, but industrial beginnings were abundant and promising. Factories, mills, and foundries dotted the northeastern states, where rivers provided water power for the machines of industry, and were starting to appear in the South and the West. The industrial boom was in part a natural development, the exploitation of the resources of a potentially rich country. Ironically, it was also stimulated by the prewar policies of the agricultural Republican party in control of the government—by shutting off trade with Britain and France the government had forced Americans to become more dependent on their own industrial productivity.

The leading American industry was textile manufacturing. But close behind it was the iron industry, with weapons production as one of its principal outputs. The development of iron manufactories was due in no small part to government patronage. Beginning in the Federalist period, the government deliberately nurtured the rise of an arms industry. It established two arsenals of its own, at Springfield, Massachusetts, and Harper's Ferry, Virginia, which produced small arms, ammunition, and gun carriages. Supplementary materials, such as gunpowder, were acquired by contract from private companies. The government also relied on private plants for artillery, contracting with producers to supply stipulated numbers of pieces. As a result, a respectable arms industry had developed by 1812. In that year the two government arsenals turned out 20,000 muskets, and officials predicted that domestic production would be sufficient to supply the armies during the war. The prognosis proved to be accurate, although a similar one that the civilian foundries could provide enough artillery ordnance was overly optimistic. Nevertheless, in this war American armies would not be handicapped by a lack of arms.

Weapons, however important, were only one of the items required by the armies. Others were uniforms, shoes, food, and medical supplies, and even if all these had been available, they were useless to the military effort unless they could be procured and distributed to the armies, a result that depended on the efficiency of the supply services. But in the years preceding the war no supply services had been provided in the army. The staff that had come into existence during the Revolution was disbanded at the war's end, and during the Confederation and Federalist period the functions of supply were assigned by Congress to civilian agencies, the office of the quartermaster general, the superintendent of military stores, and others. The heads of these offices fulfilled the modest needs of the small military establishment by contracting with private suppliers. One of the most important of the offices, that of the quartermaster general, charged with transporting men and supplies, had been abolished by the Jeffersonians as part of their economy program, its duties being assigned to contract agents.

As the probability of war with England loomed closer, Congress acted frantically to reinstitute the supply services. Within the space of three months in the spring of 1812 it established the offices of quartermaster general, commissary general of purchases, and commissary general of ordnance. The enacting laws did not clearly define the functions of the new departments; for example, the duties of the quartermaster and the purchase offices overlapped, the former responsible for some procuring in addition to distributing and the latter involved in issuing in addition to procuring. Created in haste and forced almost immediately to operate in wartime conditions, the supply services functioned poorly in 1812. Shortages of ammunition, clothing, and, especially, food afflicted all the armies. The failures were not entirely the result of the inexperience of the services. With American forces operating on the offensive, stores had to be moved over long supply lines, from the producing centers in the Northeast to the New York frontier with Canada, and most distant of all, to Fort Detroit in the western territory. Except where river transportation was available, supplies had to be moved through wilderness areas where roads had to be cut and with horse and wagon transport. The task would have been difficult even for an efficiently organized staff.

In 1813 Congress attempted to improve the organization. It enacted a law "for the better organization of the general staff of the army," marking the first time that the term *general staff* appeared in American legislation. As employed then, it had a different meaning from its present usage of a collective agency concerned with planning strategy and coordinating the military establishment. This general staff was not a collective body and it was not concerned with strategy. Rather, it was a group of administrative officers housed in Washington and responsible to the secretary of war, who discharged the housekeeping functions of the army—a quartermaster, a commissary of purchases, an inspector general, a commissary of ordnance, an adjutant general, and others, each one performing his duties with no consultation with the others. Although this staff did not possess the advantages of a collective group, it was an advance over the previous system. For the first time the secretary of war had professional advisers to rely on, and during the last year of the war the supply problems were better handled. The greatest shortage continued to be in subsistence, principally because Congress had not assigned the procurement of food to one of the supply services, preferring to entrust it to private contract agents.

The economy of the country being essentially sound, the government should have been able to finance the war without much difficulty. Instead, it failed miserably to exploit the means available to it. The costs of the War of 1812 came to $105 million, but this sum represented a small part of the nation's resources: by one estimate, only one-tenth of the aggregate, in proportion to population and wealth, that would be required later in the Civil War.

An adequate program was proposed to Congress in 1812 by Secretary of the Treasury Gallatin. An able and experienced financier, Gallatin recommended that Congress authorize a loan of $10 million, double the existing customs duties, once the chief source of revenue to the government but in recent years reduced by the disruption of overseas trade, and enact a wide-ranging set of internal taxes. The last suggestion horrified the Republican majority. Internal taxes were a contrivance of Federalists to victimize the people, and good Republicans would not hear of them. The party leaders agreed to a loan of $11 million, an issuance of $5 million in treasury notes, and an increase in the tariff duties—and then adjourned Congress. They seemed to assume that the government could meet the added expenses of the war with its normal, peacetime tax revenue.

But by early 1813 the government was experiencing serious difficulty in meeting its expenses. Even so, Congress was reluctant to enact a tax measure. President Madison finally had to call a special session, and only by appealing to party loyalty was the administration able to secure the approval of a number of internal taxes. Included in the bill was the rare expedient of a direct tax levied upon the states in proportion to their population and wealth. As the government had no power to enforce collection of this tax, little was realized from it. Nor was much revenue obtained from the internal taxes. By the time the Treasury Department had set up the machinery to collect them, the war was nearly over. Less than one-third of the total cost of the conflict was financed by taxation.

The financial plight of the government was not entirely due to its inexperience or inefficiency. There was a bitter opposition to this war, concentrated among the wealthy class, the controllers of credit, and in New England. When the government offered its first loan, the editor of a New York newspaper wrote: "We have only room this evening to say that we trust no true friend of his country will be found among the subscribers to the Gallatin loan."

To EVERY AMERICAN WAR there has been an opposition, varying in its strength and intensity and its capacity to hamper the military effort. Especially in the Revolution and the Civil War was there active resistance. But the most overt and persistent opposition, except for the Vietnam conflict, prevailed in 1812. And but for Vietnam, the War of 1812 was the most unpopular American war.

The opponents of the war were invariably Federalists. Members of this party felt they had ample reasons to protest the appeal to arms. Their resentment was the expression of a minority that believed its interests were being sacrificed in the political association of which it was a part. In their view, the Federalists and the mercantile class they represented had been ruled since 1800 by an agricultural majority that did not understand or care about the needs of the business minority. And now this majority, acting through the medium of the Republican party, had resorted to war to conquer Canada and augment still more the strength of the agricultural interests. Many Federalists thought that if the objective was attained, the time had perhaps come to calculate the value of remaining in the Union. In addition to nursing economic and political grievances, Federalists believed that the war was being fought against the wrong country—conservative, Protestant England instead of radical, godless France. Expressive of this feeling was a proclamation issued by Governor Caleb Strong of Massachusetts calling for a public fast to atone for declaring war "against the nation from which we are descended, and which for many generations has been the bulwark of the religion we profess."

Federalists lived in most states, and whatever their location, they felt the same way about the war. The party was strongest, however, in New England, where it controlled consistently the governments of four of the states, Massachusetts, Connecticut, Rhode Island, and New Hampshire, and shared control in a fifth, Vermont. Commanding these mechanisms of power, the New England Federalists were able to turn them against the national government and behind the shelter of their authority to conduct an opposition unlike that in any other American war.

In addition to issuing a constant torrent of denunciation of the war, the Yankee Federalist states manifested their opposition in three practical ways. First, the banks and creditors of the area, with rare exceptions, refused to lend the government money. This rejection would be a serious blow to the Treasury's bond program because during the war New England became the financial center of the country. The British naval blockade of the American coast had deliberately excluded friendly New England, and consequently the only imports coming into the United States had to enter at Boston and other nearby ports. Buyers of imports flocked to New England to snap up the scarce goods with the result that by 1814 over half of all the specie in the country was held in the region's banks. Yet this richest section subscribed only $3 million of the total of $80 million raised by the government through the sale of bonds. The withholding of credit was deliberate and was intended to have a political result—to force the administration to abandon its plan of conquering Canada.

The second expression of opposition took the form of trading with the enemy in Canada. Throughout the war New England merchants and to a lesser extent those in New York carried on a profitable although illegal commerce with the British and Canadian authorities. The goods sent north were principally items of food, usually livestock that could be driven across the border. An American general thus described this traffic: "The road to St. Regis is covered with droves of cattle, and the river with rafts, destined for the enemy. . . . On the eastern side of Lake Champlain the high roads are found insufficient for the supplies of cattle that are pouring into Canada. Like herds of buffaloes they press through the forest. . . ." Whether the American traders were trying to aid the enemy or were merely hoping to turn a profit, the fact remained that they were aiding the enemy. The British army in Canada could hardly have existed without this subsistence. The governor general of Canada admitted in 1814: "Two thirds of the army in Canada are at this moment eating beef provided by American contractors. . . ."

The third manifestation of opposition was the most damaging to the war effort. Invoking the doctrine of states' rights, the governors of the New England states either refused to place their militia at the disposal of the national government or put such restrictions on the employment of the militia that they were useless to the government. As constitutional justification for their action, the governors argued that the militia could be called out in war only to repel invasion and that no invasion had occurred; or that their state laws prohibited placing militia under national officers. Massachusetts contributed not a man; Vermont provided a fair number while it was under Republican control; the other states permitted some men to be summoned but forbade their being sent out of the state. Although the national government was thus deprived of an important source of manpower, it was more than compensated by the readiness of the loyal minority in New England to volunteer for the regular army. The five states provided thirteen regiments to the army as compared to fifteen from the Middle States and only ten from the South. More alarming to the government than the loss of possible manpower was the threat posed by the New England militia—well armed and drilled and responsive only to state authority. It was as a threat that the Massachusetts Federalists maintained their militia, 70,000 strong, a formidable state army. They believed that eventually the national government would be unable to raise men and money and would have to come to the states for support, and the states could then demand peace.

In 1814 it seemed that the government was almost at this last desperate strait. The war was going badly, the Treasury was almost bankrupt, and despondency gripped the administration. Some Federalists advocated that the New England states should seize this opportunity to secede from the Union, whereas others counseled that the states could now use the influence of their wealth and militia to force the government to end the war and accept amendments to the Constitution that would guarantee the rights of the mercantile minority. In the hope of reaching accord on a course of action, Massachusetts, the most predominantly Federalist state, issued an invitation to the other states to meet in convention at Hartford, Connecticut. Rhode Island and Connecticut promptly agreed to the call, but Vermont and New Hampshire, made more cautious by the presence of reinforced British armies in Canada, declined to send delegates. However, unofficially chosen representatives from these last two states attended the meeting.

The Hartford Convention met in secret in December. Although the more extreme delegates demanded secession, the moderates were in control and dictated resolutions setting forth conditions on which the New England states would remain in the Union. The right of a state to "interpose its authority" to protect its citizens from unconstitutional actions by the general government was asserted, and seven amendments to the Constitution were proposed. These were designed to limit the power of the agricultural majority and to provide the minority with a veto on the actions of the majority. One amendment restricted a president to a single term and forbade his being chosen from the same state as his predecessor, a blow at the Virginia "dynasty" that had dominated the chief office. Another required a two-thirds vote of Congress to admit new states—the intention being to exclude additional agricultural states—and another prohibited Congress from imposing an embargo on foreign commerce for more than sixty days. The most far-reaching amendment required a two-thirds vote of Congress to declare war unless the country was actually invaded.

The convention dispatched three of its delegates to Washington to bear its demands, and adjourned subject to being recalled by its president to convene in Boston. The delegates reached the capital early in 1815, simultaneously with the arrival of news of a great American victory at New Orleans. Shortly afterward word came that representatives of the United States and Britain meeting in Europe had signed a peace treaty. With the war ended on a successful note, the Federalist emissaries realized they had lost their leverage. Not revealing the purpose of their mission, they returned home. Only later did the proceedings of the Hartford Convention become known, and then the odium heaped upon it as a treasonable assemblage helped to bring about the downfall of the Federalist party.

The New England Federalists were not guilty of treason, but in their repugnance to the war they went beyond the bounds of a loyal opposition. They were an unusually determined and potent minority, and if the war had continued, it is possible that they could have imposed their will on the majority. As it was, they had seriously impeded the prosecution of the war. The fumbling performance of the government was not entirely the fault of poor administrators. President Madison and his colleagues were always painfully aware that they led a divided people.

THE MAKERS of American strategy had an onerous task—to devise plans to accomplish a policy that was not clearly defined. It could not be defined because it was composed of too many disparate elements, all the confused forces that had brought the government and the people to this war. Insofar as the government announced a policy, it was attempting to secure recognition of American maritime rights. But it also alluded to other objectives, vindication of national honor, tarnished by British violations of these rights, and removing the Indian menace on the frontier, instigated by British agents.

These were the official or admitted aims. But also announced, and at least semiofficially, were the demands of the War Hawks in Congress for the occupation of Canada, which was necessary, as some members put it, to force recognition of American rights and eliminate the Indian danger, or was, as others put it, a desirable end in itself. What then was the policy objective and why had it been decided on? A satisfactory answer to these questions was never provided. But one thing was plain: whatever end the Americans hoped to achieve, they could reach it only by invading Canada, the single part of the British empire they could strike at. They were fighting for a limited objective, maritime rights, but to accomplish it they had to employ a total strategy, the conquest of British North America.

The immediate problem of the strategy planners was to decide what area or areas of Canada should be invaded. The most obvious move was to mount one big offensive against a key point while possibly organizing secondary and diversionary thrusts in other theaters. Such a point was the city of Quebec, the center of British power in Lower Canada. The planners were aware of the importance of Quebec, but they rightly ruled it out as an objective—it was impregnable as long as the British navy controlled the St. Lawrence River, a condition that seemed likely to continue. The next most important target was Montreal, which could be reached by the old lakes-river route of the Revolution, and this city became the objective of the planners. But at the same time their attention was drawn to other places, Kingston and York on the northern shore of Lake Ontario, the British forts on the Canadian side of the Niagara River between Lake Ontario and Lake Erie, and Fort Malden opposite Detroit, and soon they were developing offensives against these points.

At first the planners intended the additional movements to be secondary and supportive to the attack on Montreal. But as their projects matured, the minor movements became equal to the main offensive. The planners thought they had good reasons for increasing the weight of the other offensives—for example, it was believed that an advance from Detroit would blunt the Indian threat—but they were dissipating American strength. The strategy of several more or less simultaneous attacks, which in military parlance is called a cordon offensive, could have been executed only if the Americans possessed the forces to sustain the attacks, which they did not. American strategy, like the policy, had too many objectives.

The command structure that devised the strategy was simple and informal in the extreme. The land campaigns were determined by Madison, the secretary of war, and whatever field generals the president chose to consult. Madison usually established priority objectives and then solicited plans that might achieve them from the secretary or from the senior generals through the secretary. Thus in 1812 he consulted with Secretary William Eustis, Henry Dearborn, the senior major general, who had overall direction of operations in the entire New York theater, and William Hull, who commanded in the Western Department. As a result of the discussions the president developed the plan for the invasion of Canada. The process was varied somewhat in other years, in that a larger number of generals was consulted, but the pattern remained essentially the same, lacking in coordination or system, the roles of the various individuals drawn into the process never fully defined or understood. No serious consideration was given to the possibility of designating one officer as general in chief to plan and execute overall strategy, the function Washington exercised during the Revolution. However, in 1813 a man appeared in the command apparatus who aspired to direct strategy, although in appointing him Madison had not intended he should have such authority.

After the 1812 invasions ended in fiasco, Secretary Eustis, a mediocre administrator, resigned, and to his place Madison named John Armstrong, a New York Republican, one of the few forceful men to hold office in the administration. Armstrong had not been Madison's first choice, and during his tenure he lacked the confidence of the president and his cabinet associates, who feared that he had presidential ambitions and resented his harsh criticism of Virginia's influence in the government. It was believed that he intended to use his office to build a national reputation—he would claim credit for campaigns devised by him and then get himself appointed lieutenant general, or general in chief. The evidence on this issue is inconclusive. Armstrong did for a time become the dominating figure in the command system; further, he made his office an instrument of power unequaled in American military history. It does not follow, however, that he had a conspiratorial purpose. He may have fallen into his role because of the kind of man he was and because of the nature of the administration he was serving.

A man of great energy and military pretensions—he had been a minor officer in the Revolution—Armstrong tended increasingly to impose his opinion and will on his pliant colleagues, including the president. Madison continued to set down strategic guidelines or priorities, but these directions were so general or imprecise that Armstrong, while seeming to follow them, was often able to exercise his own authority. He framed strategy and directed its execution, sometimes going in person to the theaters of war to oversee the carrying out of his plans. Indeed, he once proposed to establish his headquarters in northern New York, where he could personally command an invasion of Canada. Madison forbade this move, but in 1813 Armstrong took the War Department to Sackett's Harbor on Lake Ontario for two months to supervise an offensive against Montreal.

Armstrong might have pleaded that the slowness of communication made it necessary for him to be on the scene—it usually required two weeks for a letter to travel from Washington to the northern frontier and the secretary had no way to keep abreast of changing events. But it was not the proper function of the civilian deputy of the president to frame and direct strategy. Armstrong had made of his office something it was not intended to be and in an efficient military organization should not be. He was trying to function as a planner, in later terminology as a chief of staff, and as a general in chief. The combined role would have been too burdensome for even an abler man.

In 1814 Armstrong's power gradually waned. Madison, urged on by other cabinet members, began to tighten the reins on the secretary. Armstrong was instructed not to issue orders to departmental commanders without securing Madison's approval and was required to submit his strategic plans to the president and the cabinet for consideration. When one of his plans was held up, Armstrong exploded angrily that it was being delayed by "a discrepancy in the opinions of the Cabinet." Late in the year he was allowed to resign.

In informing Armstrong of the new state of affairs, Madison wrote: "On viewing the course which the proceedings of the War Department have not unfrequently taken, I find that I owe it to my responsibility as well as to other considerations, to make some remarks on the relations in which the Head of the Department stands to the President, and to lay down some rules for conducting the business of the Department which are dictated by the nature of those relations." The involved language was not that of a man who understood administration or who had a resolute spirit. Madison, the first president to act as commander in chief in actual war, did not really command. Rather, he cast himself in the role of an observer and a critic of the war effort, setting up goals and chiding those like Armstrong who failed to achieve them, but lacking the ruthlessness to remove his subordinates. He was perhaps too much the philosopher to be an effective director of war.

CHAPTER VI

The War of 1812:
Battles on Land and Sea

I F PRESIDENT MADISON GAVE but a general and gentle supervision to the making of land strategy, he was even less active in the planning of naval operations on the high seas. In 1812 he conferred occasionally with Secretary of the Navy Paul Hamilton and with senior officers who happened to be in Washington, but at these meetings only routine matters seem to have been discussed, the appointment of captains to particular ships and the assignment of missions to individual vessels. There is no record that a broad strategy was considered, although at the beginning of the war an important strategic move was feasible. This was to mass the available navy in north Atlantic waters and seek a showdown with the as yet limited British squadron. A victory would have lifted the damaging blockade of the coastal ports for at least a year and raised American morale, suffering at the time because of defeats on land.

In 1812 the only proposal for any kind of combined action came from Secretary Hamilton, a South Carolina rice planter. He suggested to the senior captains that they cruise in three squadrons, each consisting of a heavy frigate, a light frigate, and a sloop. But since he did not order this procedure, the idea was largely ignored. Hamilton, who had a weakness for liquor, resigned early in 1813, and was succeeded by William Jones, a Pennsylvania businessman and politician, who had served in both the merchant marine and the navy. Termed by Madison the "fittest minister" who had ever headed the Navy Department, Jones ran his agency with vigorous efficiency. But he seems to have offered no strategic proposals, and Madison apparently did not press him for any plans. As the president probably came to realize, it was impossible to develop a unified strategy. The small size of the navy restricted its strategic options, and although it was enlarged during the war, it remained inferior to the British fleet and an instrument of limited strength.

The nucleus of the American navy at the beginning of the war was its seven frigates, three of which were rated as heavy frigates—the *Constitution,* the *United States,* and the *President.* They were the most powerful vessels of their type in the world; indeed, the three largest in armament and dimensions compared to small ships of the line. Their formidable quality was the product of the genius of their designer, Joshua Humphreys, the chief of construction. Restricted by Congress to building frigates, Humphreys determined to create a ship of that class more mighty than any afloat, and he succeeded. Because his vessels were larger than conventional frigates, they could mount more guns; thus, the heavies were rated at forty-four guns but actually carried fifty-four. Built of fir instead of the customary oak, they were strongly resistant to shot and acquired a reputation for invulnerability. The *Constitution* became known as "Old Ironsides" when a British shot bounced off her hull and a seaman shouted: "Huzza, her sides are made of iron." The frigates had limitations, but they were potent fighting machines and the mainstay of the small navy.

Both the administration and Congress were amenable to increasing the size of the navy, and construction bills offered in 1812 and 1813 were enacted with little difficulty. By the end of the war the navy had attained a total of approximately 75 armed vessels plus over 200 gunboats, barges, and other smaller craft, and its personnel, including marines, comprised some 10,000 men. However, the result was not as impressive as it seemed. Some of the vessels that were authorized never saw service. Congress, in addition to providing for conventional frigates and sloops, authorized three ships of the line and three heavy frigates. These vessels were completed but too late to get to sea. Even if they had been finished earlier, they would have been doubtful economic and martial investments. They were expensive to construct and maintain and required large crews that could be obtained only with difficulty. Conspicuous objects, they could not easily evade a blockading squadron and probably would have remained penned in port.

The object of the government in authorizing the construction of such vessels is not clear. As was the case in the Revolution, the leaders did not enunciate a precise naval doctrine. A probable purpose was to prey on British commerce and thus force the enemy to weaken the blockade. But this result could have been accomplished more effectively by concentrating on the building of another type of vessel introduced during the war, the heavy sloop, designed to be as superior to the British sloop as the American frigate was superior to the British frigate. Three such ships were completed—the *Wasp,* the *Frolic,* * and the *Peacock*—and slipping through the blockade, they compiled a record of destruction that more than justified their construction.

The promoters of the large ships may also have hoped that they could challenge the British navy in American waters and force the lifting of the

*During the war there was a British *Frolic* and an American *Frolic.*

blockade. But this eventuality was remote after 1812. The British, adding to their own navy every year, were able to shift more vessels to the American theater in 1813, and they could always move as many as were necessary to maintain the blockade. Only one explanation of American naval policy seems plausible: its framers were not certain what they hoped to accomplish and did not have a firm grasp of the function of the navy. This lack of purpose was revealed in instructions issued by the Navy Department in 1812 to captains about to take to sea: "You are to do your utmost to annoy the enemy, to afford protection to our commerce, pursuing that course which to your best judgment may under all circumstances appear the best calculated to enable you to accomplish these objects as far as may be in your power, returning into port as speedily as circumstances will permit consistently with the great object in view." This directive must rank as one of the most opaque documents in naval history.

No uncertainty of purpose afflicted the officers of the navy. For years they had realized that at some time they might have to engage a European power, most probably England or France, either of which had a greatly superior navy, and they had considered how they would meet either foe. Naturally they had concentrated on devising means to counterbalance their physical inferiority. Their solution was to make what they had the best in the world, to produce a navy that ship for ship was superior to the probable enemy. One powerful instrument was at hand, the frigates designed by Humphreys that outgunned all other frigates. The next step was to ensure that the crews of these vessels and of the sloops were trained to a superb level. The seamen, recruited from the merchant trade, already knew the art of sailing; they had only to be taught the ways of war—the handling of the heavy guns and small-arms exercises to fit the men to board enemy vessels. Gunnery particularly was practiced, to such a degree that American crews were probably the most accurate shots of any navy. In making these preparations the officers were showing that they at least had a doctrine—they believed that a navy existed to fight. They were ready to apply their doctrine when war was declared against England.

But what in the British navy were they to fight, and for what ends would they fight? Secretary Hamilton had this question in mind when in 1812 he asked various senior officers to suggest a strategy. One officer, John Rodgers, proposed that American vessels should operate in small squadrons, preying on British commerce and giving battle to any opposing force they could engage profitably. Placed in command of a squadron of three frigates, a sloop, and a brig, Commodore Rodgers (as in the Revolution, a captain in charge of several vessels bore the nominal title of commodore) set out to prove his theory by capturing a British convoy known to be sailing from the West Indies to England. He chased the convoy almost to the English Channel, but missed it and returned home with only seven small prizes to show for his cruise. Although this scanty result did not invalidate Rodgers's strategy, no other such concentration was attempted during the war. The other captains simply rejected the strategy.

These officers commanded frigates, and they were enamored of their beautiful and powerful ships. They told Hamilton that the frigates had to operate singly, that they must not be encumbered by accompanying smaller or slower vessels. So insistent were the captains on this matter that they disregarded the secretary's suggestion to cruise in squadrons, and so eager were some of them to get to sea that they sailed without orders. Although they proclaimed an intention to harry British commerce, their larger aim was to seek out and engage enemy frigates, to demonstrate the worth of their craft in ship-to-ship battle.

The single-ship strategy seemed to promise lustrous results in 1812. In every encounter between frigates the American vessels were victorious over their rivals. The *Constitution,* under Isaac Hull, sank the *Guerrière.* The *United States,* under Stephen Decatur, disabled and captured the *Macedonian.* On a second cruise the *Constitution,* now under William Bainbridge, demolished the *Java.* At the smaller-ship level the American sloop *Wasp* defeated the British *Frolic.* Although in each battle the American ship was larger and heavier-gunned, the victories were not due entirely to physical weight but to superior seamanship and gunnery. The British vessels were riddled, whereas the American ships were hardly touched. These successes over the navy that had ruled the seas lifted American pride and morale to exuberant heights. The British government and public could hardly believe the news of the reverses.

Britain was only humiliated, however, not disheartened. In 1813 the London government increased substantially the number of ships of all types in American waters, and the blockade became even tighter than before. The strengthened squadrons maintained constant vigil off the ports where American frigates were resting, and in the face of this threat few of the American vessels ventured forth. The *Chesapeake,* captained by James Lawrence and manned by a green crew, put out of Boston harbor only to meet the waiting *Shannon,* and in a short bloody battle the American ship was shot to pieces. Although Lawrence suffered the first serious American defeat of the war and was himself mortally wounded, he gave the navy an enduring slogan, murmuring as he lay dying: "Don't give up the ship." At the end of 1813 only two American frigates were at sea, and one of these had been out since 1812.

The British maintained their restrictions for the rest of the war. In 1814 but three American frigates saw action. The *President* attempted to run out of New York harbor but was caught by three enemy frigates and disabled. The *Constitution* eluded the blockaders at Boston and in the last months of the war captured two small British ships. The *Essex,* under David Porter, had been at sea since late in 1812. In an epic cruise Porter sailed around South America and into the Pacific Ocean, becoming the first American commander to operate in that area in wartime. He swept the area of British commerce, but in 1814 he was trapped by two British frigates off Valparaiso and his ship was destroyed. While the frigates remained locked in port, the smaller ships, the sloops and the brigs, were able to slip through the blockade, and breaking into open water, ravaged British trade to the English Channel. Together with the approximately 600 privateers commissioned by the government, they provided the principal American naval punch during the last two years of the war.

The American frigates and sloops wrote some valiant chapters in the history of the navy. Their victories fortified the popular will to sustain the war. But apart from its exploits of glory, the navy accomplished little. It captured only 16 British naval vessels while losing twice that many to the enemy, and snared but a few of the 1,300 merchant ships taken during the war, the majority of which fell to privateers. The navy failed to lift or even to lighten the blockade, and it was not able to prevent British ships from conducting raids in the Chesapeake Bay area and on other parts of the coast. The navy's small size did hinder it from performing a larger function, but the officers did not seem to realize that a larger function was possible, nor did they seek a broader role. In rejecting a strategy of concentration, in insisting on single-ship actions, they betrayed a romantic concept of war—a longing to pit one strength against another merely to demonstrate that their own was superior, a satisfaction in victory as an end in itself. In contrast, the navy on the Great Lakes, operating usually in conjunction with land forces, fought in squadrons and proved to be one of the most effective instruments in the American arsenal.

AS FINALLY DEVELOPED, American strategy in 1812 called for three offensives into British North America: one proceeded from Plattsburg against Montreal, a second from Detroit against Malden, and a third from the Niagara River against the British forts on the other side. A fourth thrust from Sackett's Harbor against Kingston was discussed but not implemented. The purpose of the foray on Montreal was to occupy a key point in Lower Canada from which it might be possible to move on Quebec. The army from Detroit was expected to repress the Indians and then advance eastward into Upper Canada. The army on the Niagara could either move westward along the shore of Lake Erie or strike for York on Lake Ontario. Possession of these objectives, or of one of them, would interrupt British communication between Lower and Upper Canada and open the way to conquest of the latter province. In making these grandiose plans, the American strategists ignored the fact of enemy naval supremacy on the lakes: eleven armed British vessels against only two inferior American craft. The planners also overlooked the advantage to be gained from having the offensives jump off simultaneously. Contrary to the conventional historical view, no common time was set for the movements to begin. The planners were not that efficient.

The British command had no choice of strategy. Forced to fight a war that it viewed as an irritating diversion from the larger conflict in Europe, the government's only policy during the first two years of the war was to retain possession of Canada. Necessarily, the strategy was defensive, a holding action with whatever forces could be spared from the European struggle. At first the strategic decisions for the American war were determined in London—in theory by the king, George III, but in practice by ministers of the cabinet and often by one minister, Lord Bathurst, secretary of state for war and the colonies. Almost immediately, however, this procedure had to be abandoned. Events on the Canadian border broke so fast and communication between Britain and her colony was so slow that the government could not intelligently direct operations. Consequently it abrogated the making of strategy to generals on the scene in Canada—until 1814, when it was able to throw greater force into the American war and to adopt a new policy.

One officer commanded all British forces in Canada, Governor and Lieutenant General Sir George Prevost, who had been appointed late in 1811 when hostilities with the United States seemed probable. Of the four mainland provinces he was expected to defend, Prevost had little worry about Nova Scotia and New Brunswick, which were on the periphery of operations and were protected by the navy. His principal concern was for Lower and Upper Canada, both invitingly open to American thrusts, and he rightly decided that the former was more important. Consequently he made his headquarters at Quebec and actively directed operations in Lower Canada. Because of his distance from Upper Canada, he could give affairs there but a loose supervision and had to entrust its actual defense to the lieutenant governor, General Isaac Brock.

Despite Prevost's years of experience in the British army, he proved to be an indifferent commander. He did not possess the largeness of mind and spirit required in a general in chief. Too inclined to worry about details—he was a competent peacetime administrator—he lacked the resolution to dare for great results. Brock was an abler field commander, energetic and ambitious, although an impetuous streak sometimes led him to take unnecessary risks. The subordinates on whom Prevost and Brock had to rely were by and large of ordinary ability, men who had served in the European war and been found wanting. A provincial observer complained that any officer deemed unfit for service in Europe "was considered as quite good enough for the Canadian market."

Of the three American offensives planned in 1812, the first to get under way was one from Detroit under the command of General William Hull, who was also the governor of Michigan Territory. Its early start was the result of previous planning. Hull had gone to Washington during the spring, before war was declared, and had received his instructions from President Madison and Secretary Eustis. Shortly thereafter he left for the West, expecting that the government would inform him promptly when war was declared. His army of

1,500 Ohio militiamen and 400 regulars was being assembled at Dayton, Ohio. Hull took command on May 25 and within a few days started to march to Detroit, 200 miles away.

While the army was struggling northward through the Ohio wilderness, cutting a road as it went, Hull received on June 26 a dispatch from Eustis dated June 18, the day war was declared. "Circumstances have recently occurred," wrote the secretary, "which render it necessary you should pursue your march to Detroit with all possible expedition." Eustis had composed the message shortly before the vote on the declaration was taken and in anticipation of the result, but apparently because the outcome was not yet known, he chose to make his language somewhat vague. However, the implication of the order should have been clear to Hull: a state of war existed or was about to, and he should base his actions on that assumption. He apparently assumed that he was to operate as though peace existed until he was informed specifically that war had been declared. He did, however, obey the secretary's injunction for haste. Leaving his camp equipage behind, he pushed on to the mouth of the Maumee River on Lake Erie, arriving there on June 30. The British defenders in the area knew already that war had been declared, for communication between Lower and Upper Canada on the lakes was faster than that between Washington and the West on land.

When he reached the mouth of the Maumee, Hull was delighted to find an American schooner riding at anchor. Still assuming that a state of peace existed and thinking to rid himself of the heavy equipment that was delaying his march, he loaded on the schooner the officers' baggage and other gear and dispatched it across the lake to Detroit. Unknown to Hull, or so he claimed later, his son put on board a trunk containing Hull's muster rolls and his orders or plan of campaign. The army, relieved of some of its impedimenta, took up its march around the shore of the lake. It was barely on its way when a message from the War Department caught up with Hull, on July 1, informing him that war had been declared. On the same day he learned that British war vessels on the lake had captured the schooner, and the realization dawned on him that the enemy was aware of his plans and the force at his disposal.

Although shaken by the second piece of news, Hull continued on to Detroit, reaching the fort on July 5. His orders required him to cross the Detroit River and capture Fort Malden, about 20 miles south of Detroit on the Canadian side, and if he had moved quickly he might have accomplished his objective. At this time only a few hundred British regulars, Canadian militiamen, and Indians were in or around Malden, although Brock was known to be on the way there with reinforcements. Hull, however, showed little disposition to attack. He was becoming increasingly conscious of the danger posed by British naval control of the lake, which would enable the enemy to land raiding parties to cut his communications with Ohio, and he magnified in his mind the number of Indian allies available to Brock. "The

British command the water and the savages," he wrote Secretary Eustis. "You therefore must not be too sanguine."

Not until July 12 did Hull cross the river, and then he merely occupied the landing opposite Detroit. His principal activity was to compose a proclamation to the inhabitants which read: "Had I any doubt of eventual success I might ask your assistance, but I do not. . . . I have a force which will look down all opposition and that force is but the vanguard of a much greater." The bombastic language was but a façade behind which Hull's will was breaking. He knew that Brock had reached Malden and believed that the British commander brought with him large reinforcements. Actually Brock's force consisted of only 730 regulars and militiamen and perhaps 600 Indians, but he cleverly gave the impression that it was larger, boldly sending detachments across the river to raid Hull's communications. Hull was further dismayed by the news that Fort Michilimackinac on the straits between Lake Huron and Lake Michigan had fallen to the British. In his imagination he pictured hordes of Indians from the north descending on him.

On August 7, his nerve completely crumbled, Hull retired across the river into Fort Detroit. Brock immediately followed him and arranged his troops and artillery as if preparing to attack the works. Whether Brock would have dared an assault or whether he could have carried one is doubtful. He must have known that he could get the fort without a fight—Hull's communications with Ohio were so tenuous that soon he would run short of supplies and would have to retire southward. Brock, however, wanted a more signal and substantial triumph, the surrender of the American army. He secured it by playing a superb game of bluff. Summoning Hull to surrender, he hinted that if he had to storm the fort, he might not be able to control his Indian allies. To the amazement and anger of most of the American officers, who thought they could cut their way out, Hull acceded to the demand. The American militia were allowed to go home on parole, but the regular officers and troops were sent as prisoners to Montreal. Later Hull was paroled, but on returning to the United States he was subjected to a court-martial, found guilty of dereliction of duty, and sentenced to be shot. Madison, in consideration of the general's age and past service, remitted the sentence. Hull was not entirely to blame for the failure of the campaign: the British naval force on Lake Erie made it impossible for him to succeed. But he was responsible for the disgraceful outcome of the campaign. As a result of his irresolution, the first American offensive had collapsed, and with it American power in the West. The British stood at Detroit and dominated the entire region.

Hull expected to be aided in his operation by a diversionary offensive on the Niagara River front. However, the forces destined for this movement were slow in gathering, only a few hundred New York militiamen being on the Niagara when Hull crossed into Canada. One reason for the delay was that no one seemed to know who was in command in the theater. Supposedly, it was in the department of General Dearborn, whose headquarters were in Albany, but Dearborn tried to disclaim responsibility and refused to give any active direction. Finally the government appointed to the command with the rank of major general Stephen van Rensselaer, a New York militia officer and member of a powerful political family. Also tardily, the government pressed forward reinforcements, and by the end of September 6,500 troops, half of them militia, stood on the Niagara. Across the river were approximately 2,000 British regulars and Canadian militiamen.

The American army was dispersed along the 40-mile-long river. The largest concentration was under van Rensselaer's direct command, 3,500 troops, most of them New York militiamen, and was stationed at Lewiston, below Niagara Falls and opposite the Canadian village of Queenston. Farther to the north 1,350 regulars held Fort Niagara at the mouth of the river. At the southern end of the river, near Buffalo, was a recently arrived force of 1,650 regulars and nearly 400 militia under Brigadier General Alexander Smyth. Smyth's commission was in the regular army, which he entered in 1808 from the legal profession. Although a relative fledgling, he assumed that his status made him a superior soldier to militiaman van Rensselaer. Smyth did not openly deny the authority of his commander, but he avoided obeying orders from him.

Van Rensselaer had deficiencies as a soldier, knowing little of either strategy or tactics. He understood, however, that he had been placed on the Niagara to fight, and fight he would. His first thought was to deliver a two-pronged attack, making his main effort against Queenston and a secondary assault on Fort George opposite Fort Niagara. The river between Lewiston and Queenston ran between steep banks but was only 250 yards wide and could be crossed in a few minutes. Once over, van Rensselaer intended to seize the heights above Queenston and from this commanding position move to occupy the whole Niagara peninsula. It was a fairly good plan, designed to take advantage of the dispersed British forces on the river; but Smyth refused to cooperate, arguing that the attack should be made above the falls, where the river was wider but ran between lower banks. Apparently believing he could not control Smyth, van Rensselaer acquiesced to the loss of a third of the army. He decided to limit his offensive to an attack on Queenston.

The assault was made on October 13, almost two months to the day after Hull's surrender. Six hundred troops were ferried across the river in flatboats, and, landing on the beach, they fought their way to the heights overlooking the town. The attack surprised the British, who expected one at Fort George. Nevertheless, they rallied quickly. General Brock, who had come from Detroit to direct the defense, was at Fort George, and he personally led reinforcements to attack the American force on the heights. In a hot fight the Americans repelled the assault—Brock was killed in the melee—but their position was becoming precarious. More and more British troops were pouring toward the heights, and few American soldiers were coming over the river in support. On the other side van Rensselaer and his officers were trying to induce men to embark, with only slight success. Most of the New York militia troops refused to cross, standing on their constitutional right to remain on American soil. Those who crossed found the passage difficult because of British artillery fire. Only about 1,300 men were brought over, and no more than half of these were able to reach the beleaguered defenders. Late in the afternoon the Americans retreated to the beach and there had to surrender. Over 900 prisoners fell to the British, and in the fighting 350 Americans had been killed or wounded.

It was another American disaster, and in its wake, and amidst bitter criticism, van Rensselaer resigned his commission. Some of the strongest objections came from the man who was named to succeed him, Alexander Smyth, who by his refusal to cooperate in the campaign had helped to ensure its failure. On assuming the command Smyth revealed an ability to compose purple military language. In a proclamation to the army he announced: "In a few days the troops under my command will plant the American standard in Canada. . . . They are men accustomed to obedience, silence, and steadiness. . . . They will conquer or they will die. Will you stand with your arms folded and look on this interesting struggle? . . . Have you not a wish for fame? Yes!"

The troops to whom this nonsense was addressed resented it intensely, believing that Smyth had imputed cowardice to them. He might have recovered from its effect if he had displayed even ordinary competence in conducting operations. He proved, however, to be more inept than van Rensselaer, who had at least fought. Smyth, who was reinforced after Queenston, talked about fighting but never did. Twice in November he marched troops to the river preparatory to crossing and then drew them back, giving as his reason that not enough men could be assembled. The truth was that Smyth was losing control of his army. Disgusted at his indecision, the militia units one by one went home, and the regulars who remained lost their discipline. At the end of November the regulars were ordered into winter quarters. Smyth requested leave, which was quickly granted, and three months later his name was dropped from the army rolls.

While van Rensselaer had been trying to organize his offensive, his technical superior, General Dearborn, had remained inactive at Albany. His instructions from the War Department allowed him to set his "own time" in moving on Montreal, and he showed no disposition to make haste. Not until mid-November did he begin his movement, so late that winter would set in before he could reach Montreal. With 5,000 troops, part of them militia, he advanced to within a mile and a half of the Canadian border. There he encountered a force of 3,000 British, and his militia announced they would not cross into Canada. Dearborn seemed relieved. He marched his army back to Plattsburg and went into winter quarters. So ended the third and last of the American offensives, and so ended a year of humiliating failure.

THE FIRST OBJECTIVE of American strategy in 1813 was to recover Detroit and reinstate an offensive into Upper Canada. Preparations to this end had begun late in 1812 after Hull's disaster. Learning a lesson from that failure, the government planned to make this move with an army unusually large by the standards of this war, 10,000 troops, mostly militia from the western states. To command this host Madison selected, after some hesitation, William Henry Harrison, who was given a commission as brigadier general. The president's first choice had been James Winchester, a Tennessee planter who had served in the Revolution and in the militia, but political pressure from the West forced him to appoint Harrison. The forty-year-old Harrison was immensely popular in the states from which most of the militia would have to be drawn. Originally from Virginia, he had served in the regular army and then had become governor of Indiana Territory. In that position he had won an exaggerated reputation for military ability by defeating a band of hostile Indians in the battle of Tippecanoe. Winchester agreed to serve under Harrison, commanding the left wing. By late autumn 6,500 of the projected army had been collected, and in the West and the country at large demands for an offensive became ever louder. Although Harrison was dubious about the feasibility of a winter campaign, he was sufficiently impressed by the popular clamor, or was sufficiently ambitious for his own advancement, to undertake one. In January, 1813, he began to move his army toward the mouth of the Maumee River. A recent cold snap had hardened the swampy ground south of Detroit and frozen Lake Erie, and Harrison apparently thought he might be able to capture both Detroit and Malden.

First to move was the left wing under Winchester, about 1,300 Kentucky militiamen and regulars. While waiting on the Maumee for the main army to arrive, Winchester was informed that an enemy force, including Indians, was harassing the village of Frenchtown on the River Raisin, about 40 miles to the north. With no objective in view except to rescue the inhabitants, Winchester, with most of his force, pushed on to Frenchtown. Once there he took no security precautions to guard against the foe he knew to be in the neighborhood, a slightly larger force under Colonel Henry Procter. His negligence had a tragic result. In a dawn attack the British completely surprised the Americans, killing 300 troops and taking 500 prisoners. Fewer than 100 men straggled back to meet the main army on the Maumee. Some of the defenders were slain after they had surrendered, and the affair became known as "the massacre at the River Raisin." "Remember the Raisin" became an avenging cry that American troops would raise in later battles. Harrison was shaken by the reverse and retired, but shortly he returned and built Fort Meigs on the Maumee and Fort Stephenson farther to the east, strongholds in which he and his forces went into winter quarters. He was instructed by the government to defer further operations until American naval supremacy on Lake Ontario and Lake Erie could be accomplished.

The importance of controlling the lakes had been apparent to both sides from the beginning of the war. If the Americans maintained control, they could sustain their forces invading Canada. If the British had control, they could deny support to the invaders and compel them to retire. As vital as lake power was, neither belligerent acted vigorously to increase its own. In 1812 the British had only six vessels on Ontario and five on Erie, brigs and schooners mounting twenty guns or less. To oppose this force there was a lone armed brig on Ontario and an unarmed schooner on Erie. Not until late in 1812 did the United States government move to redress the balance. It appointed to command on the lakes Captain Isaac Chauncey, who had been commandant of the New York naval yard and who had a reputation as a skilled executive and builder. Sending supplies and workmen ahead, the forty-two-year-old Chauncey repaired to Sackett's Harbor on the eastern end of Ontario, which became his base of operations.

During the winter Chauncey demonstrated that his reputation as an executive was deserved. By the spring of 1813 he had acquired through construction and purchase a squadron of eight vessels. The British, also building, had a squadron of the same size on Ontario, although it was inferior in armament to the American ships. Both sides would add to their strength during the remainder of the war, first one and then the other attaining a slight advantage. But neither was able to achieve a clear mastery on the lake. Commodore (his courtesy title) Chauncey never challenged the British in a showdown battle. A master builder, he did not understand that the function of a fleet in wartime is to risk a showdown battle, given a reasonable chance of victory. He was perhaps too proud of his creation to endanger it.

In addition to the construction yard at Sackett's Harbor, there was a facility at Presque Isle on Lake Erie, and Chauncey was anxious to find a competent officer to command it. There had recently reported to him a twenty-eight-year-old lieutenant, Oliver Hazard Perry, who, unable to secure a suitable ocean assignment, had asked for service on the lakes. Chauncey, hard up for good officers, gave the Erie command to the new arrival. It was a more fortunate selection than Chauncey could have known. Perry turned out to be as good a builder as his superior. Driving the workers and sailors and soldiers assigned to him, by the end of the summer he had constructed a squadron of nine ships. Unlike Chauncey, Perry believed that a fleet existed to fight, and he cruised the lake looking for the rival British squadron. When the enemy refused to come out of Malden to meet him, Perry blocked the passage of supply ships heading to the fort and thus forced the British to fight. In September at Put in Bay on the northern shore of Lake Erie Perry destroyed the British squadron, disabling two of the vessels and compelling the rest to surrender. It was a complete victory, its luster not dimmed by Perry's advantage in numbers and armament. He handled his squadron with skill and resolution, and he was justified in sending his famous message to Harrison: "We have met the enemy and they are ours."

Erie was now an American lake, and Harrison could at last undertake his delayed offensive. He moved in September with a force of 3,500. Most of the troops were transported by water to Fort Malden while a regiment of mounted Kentucky militia made its way around the head of the lake to Detroit. Against this combination the British could offer little. Procter, now a general, had at his disposal fewer than 1,000 regulars and something over 1,000 Indians. He evacuated both Malden and Detroit and fell back along the line of the Thames River. Harrison caught up to him at a point 85 miles from Malden, where Procter's Indian allies demanded that he stand and fight. As Harrison was preparing to make a traditional infantry advance, the commander of the mounted Kentucky militia asked for permission to deliver a cavalry charge. Harrison assented, although he said later he knew of no rule of war that sanctioned opening a battle in this manner. Perhaps because it was unexpected, the charge succeeded magnificently. Riding through the enemy line, the troopers dismounted and opened a firing line in the rear, and the enemy broke in rout. Over 500 redcoats and Indians were taken prisoner, and among those killed was the famous Tecumseh, the genius of Indian resistance in the West.

The battle of the Thames was the first American victory of the war and was followed by substantial results. The lost territory in the Northwest was recovered, and the Indian menace in that region was eliminated. With this defensive accomplishment the Americans were satisfied. They abandoned efforts to launch an invasion of Canada from the Detroit base. It was too difficult and costly to supply an army operating in that far area, and the militia troops that would compose such an army could not be enlisted for terms sufficiently long to maintain an offensive. Curiously the two men who figured most prominently in the campaign would not appear again in the war. Harrison, who had demonstrated resolution if no great military skill, had incurred the distrust of Secretary Armstrong and, after enduring repeated slights from the latter, resigned his commission. Perry, promoted to captain, chafed under Chauncey's restrictions and returned east to seek ocean duty, which was not forthcoming because no frigate was available to him.

While Harrison's army idled on the shore of Lake Erie during the winter months, another American offensive was being organized on Lake Ontario. This movement was the conception of Secretary Armstrong, recently appointed to his office and determined to impress his ideas of strategy on the conduct of the war. His plan was shrewdly devised. Four thousand troops were to be collected at Sackett's Harbor under General Dearborn and another 3,000 at Buffalo. As soon as the lake opened, Dearborn, transported by Chauncey's budding squadron, was to move across Ontario and capture Kingston, the most important British naval station on the lake. This accomplished, the expedition was to proceed up the lake to York and destroy enemy vessels and stores known to be there. Thence it would move to the western end of the lake and, joined by the force at Buffalo, reduce the British forts on the Niagara River. The key objective was Kingston. If the Americans could occupy it or, failing that, destroy its facilities, they would disrupt British water communication to the west. York and the Niagara forts would fall for want of support, and virtually all of Upper Canada would come under American control.

The ensuing campaign was an instructive illustration of the danger of entrusting a strong plan to weak subordinates. Dearborn and Chauncey consulted together and, having heard exaggerated rumors of enemy reinforcements to Kingston, decided that it was too strong to attack. Coolly inverting Armstrong's plan, they informed the secretary that they were bypassing Kingston to attack York, after which they would move to the Niagara and then return to Kingston. Having no choice, Armstrong acquiesced to the alteration. The attack on York was launched in April, and after overcoming sharp resistance, the Americans seized the town. They held it for ten days, burning stores and public buildings, and then withdrew to their transports to sail to the Niagara. Dearborn remained on ship during the attack, claiming an illness that may have been induced by his growing irresolution.

The expedition reached the mouth of the Niagara late in May and debarked near Fort Niagara. Just across the river was its immediate objective, Fort George. The fleet opened a bombardment of George, which was followed by an amphibious assault that forced the British to retire. Dearborn, still ill, observed the operation from one of the vessels. Although several generals were ashore, the attack was really directed by Colonel Winfield Scott, one of several rising junior officers. Scott had entered the army in 1808 and by studying strategy and tactics had made himself one of its better technical officers. He was one of the few officers familiar with European drill procedures, and he drilled his troops rigorously at every opportunity.

Surprised by the sudden American thrust, the British abandoned Fort Erie at the southern end of the river and their other posts and fell back westward. A vigorous pursuit by Dearborn might have broken up the disorganized enemy and secured the entire Niagara peninsula. However, the general waited several days before moving, and then he sent out a force of only 2,000. This column moved to a place called Stony Creek and encamped for the night without taking proper security precautions. Meanwhile, the British had collected themselves, and a party returned to attack the sleeping Americans. After a confused battle in the darkness—two American brigadiers were captured—both sides retired. This minor setback shook Dearborn badly. Reporting it to Armstrong, he asked for instructions. The secretary, who could not understand that the enemy had been allowed to escape after being forced out of his forts, brusquely ordered Dearborn to concentrate his army. The commander responded by abandoning all the captured British posts except Fort George, where he assumed a defensive position. For their exertions in this campaign the Americans could show but one fort barely on Canadian soil.

One result of the campaign was not immediately apparent—the emergence below the top command level of a number of promising younger generals. One of these was Scott, who was promoted to brigadier. Another was Brigadier General Jacob Brown, who before the war gained experience in the New York militia. While the Niagara campaign was in progress, Brown had been left in command at Sackett's Harbor with only 400 regulars and 700 militiamen. General Prevost noted the weakened condition of the base and decided to deliver a land and naval attack on it in May. Brown, handling his troops with cool determination, repelled the assault with heavy losses. He was not a skilled technical soldier like Scott, but he had great resolution, understood the limitations of citizen soldiers, and knew how to lead them. He and Scott would later make an effective team.

Secretary Armstrong was becoming aware of the limitations of the senior generals and was determined to sweep them out. However, his judgment as to whom to put in their place was not always sound, and sometimes the replacement was as bad as the original. Thus in July the secretary persuaded Dearborn to resign, but to succeed him in the important New York theater, he selected another incompetent, his old Revolutionary crony, James Wilkinson. In the words of one historian: "Age and infirmity gave way to age and fatuity."

Armstrong had decided on Wilkinson for the assignment in March. Sending the general, then in New Orleans commanding the Southern Department, an order to repair to Dearborn's headquarters and a major general's commission, the secretary in a covering letter asked an intriguing question: "Why should you remain in your land of cypress when patriotism and ambition equally invite you to where grows the laurel?" Despite this injunction to haste and glory, Wilkinson journeyed northward at a leisurely pace. He did not arrive in Washington until July 31, and after conferring there with Armstrong he and the secretary went on together to Sackett's Harbor, which they did not reach until August 20. It was getting late in the season to gather laurel.

In Washington the general learned the reason for Armstrong's summons. The secretary wished to return to his original strategy of the spring, a move on Kingston, and he apparently believed that Wilkinson would be a cooperative instrument to execute his purpose. As Armstrong outlined his plan, an army of 7,000 troops, most of whom would have to be drawn from the Niagara front, would be assembled at Sackett's Harbor. With this force and naval support, Wilkinson was to attack Kingston or move down the St. Lawrence River to cut off the post's communication with Montreal. Or, the secretary added, Wilkinson could contain Kingston and move down the river on Montreal itself. If he should decide on Montreal, he would be supported by an army of 4,000 men at Plattsburg under Major General Wade Hampton, which would move up to join him at some point on the river. In wavering between two objectives, Armstrong was betraying an increasing uncertainty of purpose, and in entrusting a choice of objectives to Wilkinson, he was risking failure of the campaign. He was risking it further by staking so much on cooperation between Wilkinson and Hampton, who hated each other.

At Sackett's Harbor the secretary and Wilkinson spent all of September preparing the expedition—and arguing about which objective should be struck. Wilkinson was ill and feeble and seemed to want to place the responsibility for the decision on Armstrong; the latter appeared to sense that the movement would fail and tried to lay the responsibility on the general. Sometime late in October Wilkinson made his choice—he would bypass Kingston and go for Montreal. The troops were loaded on bateaux, and, guarded by gunboats, the expedition proceeded down the river. Hampered by bad weather, it moved slowly and by the first of November had traversed only 20 miles. At about this time Armstrong returned to Washington. It has been surmised that he saw disaster ahead and was leaving Wilkinson and Hampton to their fates.

Hampton seems never to have understood clearly the strategic objective he was to accomplish. Sixty-two years of age, he had been a partisan leader in South Carolina during the Revolution. Returning to civilian life, he had become a wealthy planter. In 1808, angered at Britain's disregard of American nautical rights, he reentered the army as a colonel, rising to general grade. Devoted as he was to the American cause, Hampton lacked the capacity to direct a large force, and although personally brave he was irresolute in the face of battlefield danger. In September he led his army north from Plattsburg to the Canadian border, but finding that drinking water in the area was scarce because of a recent drought, he turned southward to the Chateaugay River, which he followed westward. Armstrong instructed him to continue on the river to the St. Lawrence, and in October Hampton entered Canada for the second time. Encountering unexpectedly strong resistance—largely simulated by local defense forces—he decided that it was hopeless to continue and withdrew across the border, going into winter quarters. Armstrong unaccountably agreed with his decision, although by this time Wilkinson's expedition had left Sackett's Harbor.

Wilkinson was hardly on the St. Lawrence when he proposed to his generals that the army return to American soil. He was rapidly losing confidence in the offensive and in himself. Still ill, perhaps psychosomatically so, he gave but little direction to operations. The officers persuaded him to continue, and the expedition proceeded down the river. A British force followed it on the north bank, firing into the massed troops on the flatboats, and at intervals parties were landed to drive the harassers off. In November, as one of these columns was returning to the boats at a place called Chrysler's Farm, the British cut it up badly. The rest of the army fled down the river to St. Regis, where Wilkinson learned that Hampton had retired to winter quarters. He too was allowed to retire, both his and Hampton's army eventually being sent to Plattsburg. The two generals were later dropped from the army rolls.

Most of the troops for Wilkinson's army had been removed from the Niagara front, leaving that line thinly defended. In December the British took advantage of the situation to recapture Fort George and then crossed the river and seized Fort Niagara. Alleging that the Americans had burned towns on the Canadian side, the British in retaliation loosed their Indian allies on the New York frontier, which was ravaged for 30 miles. Earlier raiding parties from the British ocean fleet had looted the area of the Chesapeake and Delaware bays. A mood of savagery unusual in wars of this time ·was taking possession of both sides.

The year 1813 was another frustrating one for the Americans. Their offensives, except for the one at Detroit, had again collapsed in fiasco, and the success in the West was not followed by any important strategic result. However, there was a promising portent for the future. As a result of the year's failures, more of the older generals had been relieved and younger and abler commanders were coming to the fore.

THE CREDIT for bringing the new generals forward belongs to Secretary Armstrong. He saw the worth of Jacob Brown after the latter's defense of Sackett's Harbor and promoted him to major general and commander of the Niagara-Ontario theater. With Brown as second in command went Winfield Scott. To direct operations in the northern New York theater, with headquarters at Plattsburg, Armstrong named George Izard, recently raised to major general grade over several senior brigadiers. Izard, thirty-seven years old, was the only American general with a formal military education, having been sent to European schools by his wealthy South Carolina father. Although he was considered one of the more promising officers, he never achieved an important success. He seemed to lack confidence in himself and in his capacity to handle citizen soldiers.

Armstrong still dreamed of launching an offensive into Canada, and during the early months of 1814 he discussed possible objectives with Madison and the cabinet. A decision was not reached until June, when it was settled that the thrust would be made on the Niagara front. General Brown was ordered to cross the river at the southern end and capture Fort Erie and then advance northward to Lake Ontario. It was expected that Commodore Chauncey would leave Sackett's Harbor and come to the western end of the lake to afford Brown naval support. With the attack so coordinated, the invaders should be able to occupy the entire Niagara peninsula and, in the process, draw the British out of Fort Niagara. Indeed, Brown thought that the army might go all the way to Kingston. The British had 4,500 troops in the area, but they were scattered in posts from Fort Erie all the way up to York and might be destroyed in fractions. The American plan was well conceived, but now strategy seemed directed to a limited objective, the seizure of Upper Canada alone.

Brown, with 3,500 troops, crossed the river on July 3, easily overwhelmed the small enemy garrison at Fort Erie, and then advanced northward toward the Chippewa River. His sudden descent had thrown the British into momentary confusion. The supreme commander, the governor general of Upper Canada, Sir Gordon Drummond, was at Kingston, and the commander in the immediate theater, General Phineas Riall, was at York and uncertain of Brown's whereabouts. Assuming that Brown was besieging Fort Erie, Riall collected reinforcements and hurried to the fort. Just south of the Chippewa, on July 5, he came upon Brown's camp. The American general had halted to rest his men and give them a belated Independence Day celebration. Although Riall's force was smaller than Brown's, he resolved to attack; most of his troops were regulars, and he supposed that most of the Americans were militiamen who would flee at the first encounter. Whether his assault caught Brown by surprise is a matter of controversy. What is certain is that Brown was somewhat tardy in concluding that the enemy was in his front in force. Late in the afternoon he ordered Scott to bring his brigade forward to attack the British. Scott advanced his superbly trained troops in battle line (according to a doubtful story they were in formation for a parade when Brown's order arrived) against the approaching British line. Observing the steadiness of the Americans, Riall ejaculated in astonishment: "Those are regulars, by God." When within 70 yards of the enemy, Scott ordered a bayonet charge, and the British broke in disorder over the river. For the first time in the war an American army had fought a battle in the classic style, and had won it.

Following the victory, Brown advanced to Queenston, and from there he besought Chauncey to join him. "For God's sake let me see you," he wrote. Chauncey, however, found reasons to decline the invitation. The British had recently built up their naval strength on Lake Ontario, and although the rival squadrons were approximately equal in size, Chauncey feared to risk a battle. His refusal to come to the western end of the lake enabled the British to land raiding parties on the American side of the Niagara and cut Brown's communications, thus depriving him of needed supplies. (The lack of coordination in the American command system is revealed by the fact that apparently nobody thought to ask the president to order Chauncey to join Brown.)

In order to prevent the interruption to his supply line, Brown decided to move away from the Niagara, drawing the British after him. Retiring to the Chippewa to regroup, he proposed to move around the head of Lake Ontario to get in the British rear and on favorable ground to offer battle. On his march he collided with the British army under Drummond and Riall at a crossroad called Lundy's Lane. The ensuing battle began at dusk and raged until midnight, the opposing forces, about equal in size, engaging in what essentially was a slugging match. The casualties were frightful, each army losing over 800 men; Drummond and Riall were wounded and so were Brown and Scott, the latter so severely that he did not serve again in the war. Although both sides claimed a victory, it was really a drawn battle. The Americans, however, abandoned their offensive and retired to Fort Erie.

Drummond, receiving reinforcements, followed the Americans to the fort and laid siege to it. Brown eventually broke the siege, and shortly thereafter American reinforcements arrived. In August the War Department ordered General Izard at Plattsburg to march with 4,000 troops to Sackett's Harbor to effect a diversion to aid Brown or, if Izard chose, to move to the Niagara theater. Although Izard protested that his departure would endanger the American position on Lake Champlain, he obeyed the order. Moving out on August 29, he went to Sackett's Harbor, and in response to an appeal from Brown, from there to the Niagara, which he reached on October 5. He and Brown decided that the British were now too strong to be attacked, and early in November the Americans abandoned Fort Erie and withdrew to positions in the United States. During its long march Izard's force had been effectively taken out of the war and for no result—and at a moment when the British were about to launch a formidable offensive of their own.

On September 1, three days after Izard left Plattsburg, a British army crossed the New York border and, accompanied by a naval squadron, headed down Lake Champlain. The army, commanded by Prevost, numbered 12,000 men, most of them veterans from the European war recently shipped to Canada, and was the largest land force mobilized by Britain during the war. The naval contingent, in addition to transports, comprised four armed brigs and twelve gunboats. The size of the expedition indicated a new British strength in Canada, and a new policy and strategy in London. Napoleon had abdicated in April, and with the winding down of the war against him, Britain could throw her great resources into the American conflict. During the first six months of the war at least 15,000 troops were dispatched to Canada. Additional soldiers were sent to the West Indies, and the naval blockade was strengthened to include the entire Atlantic coast. No longer did Britain have to stand on the defensive.

The London government outlined its new aims in a directive to Prevost on June 3. He was instructed to provide first for the immediate security of Canada by destroying Sackett's Harbor and smashing the American naval establishments on the Great Lakes. Then he was to undertake operations to ensure the "ultimate security" of British North America. Fort Niagara and adjacent territory were to be retained, and Detroit and the Michigan country were to be occupied, with a view to making this area a buffer Indian state between Canada and the United States. If Prevost should decide that the frontier of Lower Canada could be made more secure by occupying territory "which extends towards Lake Champlain," that is, northern New York, he was authorized to conduct an offensive in that region. An additional objective of British strategy was naturally not communicated to Prevost: the occupation of New Orleans.

Surveying the options presented to him, Prevost decided that the American positions on Ontario and Erie were too strong to be attacked. Of the objectives remaining, he settled on Plattsburg, which could be reached with comparative ease on the traditional lakes-river invasion route. It was a valuable objective, and at the moment a vulnerable one. After Izard's departure the post was weakly held by only 1,500 regulars and an equal number of militiamen under Brigadier General Alexander Macomb. If the British seized it, they could control the entire frontier area, which they might retain or offer to return as a bargaining counter in peace negotiations.

Prevost arrived before Plattsburg on September 6, while the navy was still coming down the lake. Finding the base protected by fieldworks and also by a squadron of naval vessels, he decided to wait for his own naval support before attacking. The British ships appeared on September 11, and Prevost directed their commander to destroy the American vessels, whereupon he would launch his assault on land. Prevost was placing an unusual reliance on the outcome of the naval fight.

The American squadron consisted of four ships and a number of gunboats, about equal in size to its rival but outgunned by the longer-range British pieces. Its commander was a brilliant young sailor, Thomas Macdonough, only twenty-eight years of age. Macdonough realized that if he tried to conduct a classical battle of maneuver he might be blown out of the water before he could close with the enemy. Therefore he anchored his ships in an enclosed bay, forcing the British to come to him at short range; moreover, he used kedge anchors, a device that enabled him to swing his vessels round and present another deck of guns. In a battle of two hours Macdonough forced the two largest British ships to surrender and severely damaged the others, which withdrew from the fight. When the naval commander informed Prevost of the disaster, the general halted his assault and on the next day began to retire to Canada. Prevost has been criticized for giving up the attack, but he probably acted wisely. Even if he had taken Plattsburg, he could not have held it without a water supply line. The American naval victory was a decisive battle—it turned back one of the most dangerous British offensives of the war.

During the summer months, while Prevost was preparing his expedition, the British government organized a land and naval attack on the American coast to effect a diversion in Prevost's favor. Three thousand troops under General Robert Ross, a veteran of the Napoleonic war, were sent to Bermuda, where another thousand men and a powerful naval force were waiting. Ross's orders were to strike at Washington or Baltimore and adjacent areas and destroy stores and facilities that might be useful to the enemy, but not to hold permanent possession of any captured district. Included in the land force were several units of black West Indian troops, and while the British were in the

Chesapeake region, they collected a number of slaves who attached themselves to the army and were used as laborers or guides. The episode underlines a revealing fact about the war, that the British probably made more use of black manpower than did the Americans. Negro sailors served in the Great Lakes squadrons and Negro soldiers were present in a few regular army units, but the total number enlisted was small, smaller than the total employed in the Revolution. Apparently racial prejudices had increased since the war for independence.

The expedition left Bermuda early in August and two weeks later entered Chesapeake Bay. Landing a short distance from Washington, the army marched on an almost helpless capital. Although the Madison government had known that an attack was impending, it took few measures to meet it; indeed, there was little that could be done without draining men from the northern armies. Now, in a flurry of activity, it placed General William Winder, who had been captured at Stony Creek and exchanged, in charge of defenses and issued a call for militia from the surrounding area. Eventually Winder collected some 5,000 troops, militiamen, a few regulars, and 400 sailors and marines from the Washington naval yard. On August 24 this nondescript force attempted to block Ross's advance at Bladensburg, a village seven miles from Washington, but was easily brushed aside. The British marched into the city, and that night and the next day they burned the Capitol, the White House, and other public buildings. Although they claimed that they were exacting retribution for depredations committed by the Americans in Canada, some of the British officers professed personal satisfaction in their work. It was another indication of the hatreds unleashed by the war.

Leaving the flaming capital, the British returned to their ships, where Ross proposed that they go on to Baltimore. Winning over the naval commanders, he led the expedition up the bay. The foray on Washington had given Baltimore time to prepare, however, and its citizens used the time well. The defense that was organized was almost entirely a local enterprise. Samuel Smith, who had been a major general of the state militia, was appointed to direct operations. Over 10,000 militiamen turned out to serve under him, and a line of earthworks was constructed on the land approaches to the city. On the water side stood Fort McHenry, garrisoned by 1,000 regulars and sailors, the only sizable national contingent present. On September 13 Ross landed troops to probe at the land defenses while the navy bombarded Fort McHenry. The American resistance was strong on both fronts—Ross was killed in the action—and the British army and naval officers agreed that the attack should be called off (just two days before, Prevost had been turned back at Plattsburg). Leaving the Chesapeake, the expedition returned to the West Indies to join an operation previously planned, which was to have been commanded by Ross. At Jamaica a powerful land and naval force was being assembled to attack

New Orleans. The focus of the war was about to shift to the southern United States.

Before 1814 the war had touched the South but lightly. The Madison administration and Congress harbored designs to seize Florida from Spain, which was friendly to England, but plans developed to achieve the purpose were not implemented, the government doubting it could take on another war. However, the administration did approve an operation to occupy West Florida, claimed by the United States as a part of the Louisiana Purchase, and in 1813 a force of regulars under General Wilkinson captured Mobile. Later in the year the Creek Indians in Alabama rose in rebellion, and to deal with this threat the government authorized an expedition of the Tennessee militia commanded by Andrew Jackson, who was an aggressive fighter but lacked technical training. With 2,000 militiamen and 600 regulars, Jackson crushed the Indians in a ruthless campaign that did not end until the spring of 1814. For his service he was commissioned a major general in the regular army and designated to command the Southern theater. In the fall he was ordered to go to Mobile to meet a sudden British threat. The British had taken over Pensacola from the acquiescent Spanish and were converting it into a base for raiding operations. Collecting a force of 4,000 militia and regulars, Jackson captured Pensacola in October. He remained in the town throughout most of November, although he had been informed that the British expedition assembling at Jamaica was probably intended for New Orleans.*

The idea for an offensive against New Orleans, originated by Admiral Alexander Cochrane and other naval officers, found quick favor when broached to army officers and the government. The plan seemed to promise important results. Occupation of the city and of other points on the Gulf Coast would close the Mississippi River to American commerce and provide Britain with another bargaining piece (the movement was planned when it was thought that Plattsburg would fall) in the peace negotiations. In preparing instructions for the expedition, the government was explicit on one point: the commanders must "discountenance" any desire on the part of Louisiana inhabitants to place themselves under British rule. However, if the people manifested a wish to reattach themselves to Spain, they were to be encouraged to do so. It is possible that the government had in mind, if the peace negotiations should stall, returning Louisiana to Spain.

The force gathering at Jamaica consisted of 8,000 veteran troops and 50 ships of war and transports carrying 2,000 sailors. The new land commander was Sir Edward Pakenham, who had served in the recent war in Europe and was the brother-in-law of the Duke of Wellington. However, Wellington had

---

*At the end of the war the United States would retain the part of West Florida it had occupied, to a line slightly east of Mobile; however, Pensacola was returned to Spain.

never entrusted Pakenham with an independent operation and in summing up his relative had written: "Pakenham may not be the brightest genius," which in the Duke's lexicon was a condemnation. Regardless of his qualifications, Pakenham did not have much opportunity to display them. He did not reach Louisiana until Christmas Day, and by that time the nature of the campaign had been determined by others, principally by Admiral Cochrane.

The expedition left Jamaica on November 26 and after a leisurely voyage cleared the Louisiana coast on December 8. A hasty parallel journey was made by Andrew Jackson. Convinced at last that the British offensive was aimed at New Orleans and not at Mobile or Pensacola, he left the latter port on November 21 and reached New Orleans on December 2. The forces he had to defend it were widely dispersed. In the city he found 800 regulars and 1,000 militiamen. Other troops were on the way from Mobile and Baton Rouge, but it was a question whether they would arrive before the British attack. Fortunately for Jackson, the British delayed their approach, giving him time to concentrate and organize his army.

On reaching the coast, Cochrane and his council of officers were uncertain as to which route they should take to get up to New Orleans—one of the several mouths of the Mississippi or one of the numerous inlets of the Gulf, Lake Barataria, Lake Pontchartrain, or Lake Borgne. As one of the officers said, it seemed impossible to reach the city unless "assisted by the aerial flight of the bird of prey or astride the alligator's scaly back." Finally the council decided that Lake Borgne was the most feasible route, as it was easy to navigate and offered a landing place below the city on the east side of the river. The expedition entered Borgne on December 13 and with great exertion established a base in the marshes. A canal was dug from the lake to the Mississippi through which the British could pass small boats should they decide to operate on both sides of the river. On December 23 Jackson struck the advancing British in a successful effort to delay them and then retired to make his defense nearer the city. This was where Pakenham found him on December 25.

Jackson had finally collected a force of 5,000. It was literally a mixed aggregation—regulars, militiamen, civilian volunteers, coastal freebooters (the notorious "Barataria" pirates), and several hundred black troops. The nucleus of the last group was the Battalion of the Free Men of Color, a militia unit reluctantly authorized by the Louisiana government; Jackson saw it on arriving in the city and asked that additional black troops be called out. (The original battalion is probably the only all-black unit ever to appear in the militia of a state and survived until the 1830s, when it was disbanded during the rising agitation over slavery.)

The Americans were strongly posted, their front of only three-fifths of a mile anchored on its left to a swamp and on its right to the river. Across the river was a battery placed to command the water approach and on the river was a small armed ship. It was a tough position to take by frontal assault, as

Pakenham appreciated when he surveyed it. Nevertheless, he ordered an attack, the main effort to be made on the east side and a supporting effort on the west side by a force that would be crossed over the canal. The British general was overly confident of the steadiness of his regulars and overly contemptuous of the courage of Americans.

The attack was delivered on January 8. As the main force on the east side moved forward in traditional battle line, it was an impressive sight. But the British were heading for certain destruction. The Americans on their narrow front simply had too much massed musket and artillery fire. The assault line was shot to pieces, and a second advance led by Pakenham himself was also thrown back. Pakenham was killed in the charge, another general fell, and a third was badly wounded. The total British casualties were almost 2,000 men while the Americans lost only 45; put in percentages, the British losses were 34 percent of the total engaged to only 1.6 percent of the Americans. Meanwhile, on the other side of the river the attack on the battery was making progress. But the carnage on the east side so horrified the surviving major general and the naval officers that they decided to call the column back and abandon the offensive. Withdrawing slowly to the coast, the expedition paused to attack Mobile but on hearing that peace had been signed returned to the West Indies.

British and American negotiators had been meeting in Europe and had signed a peace treaty on Christmas Eve, the agreement to become final when ratified by both governments. Word of the treaty had not reached the United States when the battle of New Orleans was fought. Therefore it is sometimes said that the encounter occurred after the war ended. This is not quite accurate, because neither government had yet ratified the pact. Some historians have speculated that if the British army had been victorious and seized New Orleans, its government would have repudiated the treaty and continued the war. Their assumption seems dubious. The British public was weary of the American war and the long struggle against France and desperately desired peace. The government would have found it difficult to rally support for a war that promised no successful end. It had asked its great soldier Wellington if he would go to America to take command. He bluntly replied that Britain had no chance to win unless it could achieve naval supremacy on the Great Lakes, a condition that was obviously impossible.

The Madison administration had put out feelers to other governments to mediate a peace soon after the war started. The czar of Russia, Britain's ally, offered to bring the parties together, but the London government rejected the offer. Then in 1814 Britain indicated she was willing to undertake direct negotiations. Madison dispatched to Europe an able delegation which met with British representatives at Ghent, Belgium. The British negotiators were mediocre and minor officials, the principal leaders being at Vienna, remaking the map of Europe.

Beginning in August, the rival delegations wrangled for months over demands that neither side was able to enforce. The British wanted the creation of an Indian state in the Northwest, control of the sources of the Mississippi, the exclusion of American armed ships and fortifications from the Great Lakes, and recognition of the British position on maritime rights. The Americans demanded recognition of their neutral rights, indemnity for past damages to their commerce, and the cession of part or all of Canada. At one point the British offered to settle for territory presently held, when Prevost was approaching Plattsburg and the expedition against New Orleans was being prepared. When news arrived of Prevost's failure and there was silence from Louisiana, the British had to drop this request. Finally, the negotiators recognized that it was impossible to agree on a document settling the issues for which both nations had fought. They signed a treaty that simply ended the war, that exchanged no territory and confirmed no rights. As one of the American representatives said, it was "a truce rather than a peace."

However, as events turned out, the truce was a peace, and one that represented, even if indirectly, an American victory. Although the United States had not secured formal recognition of its perceived rights, it had demonstrated its capability of defending those rights. Hereafter it would be respected even by the British as a true nation.

INTERLUDE

1815-1846

AFTER 1815 the United States turned away from Europe and European politics and disputes and directed its attention and energies to national development. Concurrently, Europe turned away from America, its leading powers pursuing policies that were of remote concern to Americans. Only once did Europe seem to threaten interference in American affairs, and this intervention was not aimed at the United States itself but at neighboring areas in the western hemisphere. During the early 1820s Spain asked the other powers of Europe for aid in recovering her recently revolted Latin American colonies, now independent nations, and for a time it appeared that an international expedition might descend upon Central and South America. The project fell through, however, primarily because Britain, the world's strongest naval power, refused to participate. U.S. opposition was only of secondary importance in this instance, although it was expressed in a document that would subsequently become historically significant and influential. The Monroe Doctrine declared that the United States would view as an unfriendly act an attempt by a European nation to acquire colonies in the hemisphere (or reacquire old ones), or to establish its system of government in the hemisphere.*

Although the Monroe Doctrine was not a weighty factor in the international bargaining that forestalled the intervention, its promulgation was significant in the developing history of the young republic. It was an expression of the mood of nationalism that possessed the country after the War of 1812. In that conflict the American people had asserted their right to be a nation, and having, as they thought, proved this right, they were eager to demonstrate their nationhood, to themselves and to the world. They boasted constantly and loudly of the size and wealth of their country, of its expanding frontiers, now pushing into the Mississippi Valley, and of its burgeoning economy, no longer

---

*Britain's reluctance to assist Spain stemmed from several motives, the most important being that she saw trade advantages in a Latin America free of Spanish control. President Monroe's statement, contained in a message to Congress, did not become known as the Monroe Doctrine until thirty years later.

a simple system based on agriculture but one increasingly balanced by a growing industrialism. They boasted too about their political structure, the federal system capped by a national government strong enough to foster the welfare of a rising nation but not so strong as to threaten liberty; in their vaunting pride after 1815 they were willing to grant new and dramatic powers to this central government, a step that some of them, notably Southerners, would shortly regret. But in the years immediately after 1815 few opposed extensions of nationalism. Americans felt secure, optimistic, and isolated from and superior to Europe, and they were voicing this feeling in the Monroe Doctrine, telling Europe that the United States had primacy in the western hemisphere and would resent outside interference in this area of its destiny.

Without Britain's tacit backing the United States could not have upheld the Monroe Doctrine, either in the 1820s or in the next few decades. The various expressions of American nationalism had not included the creation of a large military establishment, and the government did not maintain forces adequate to repel a strong European invasion. At the time of the threatened intervention the regular army numbered only 6,000 troops, and the navy consisted of but 70 ships of all types, its nucleus being two small ships of the line and five frigates. This was the country's largest peacetime force, but it could not cope with a coalition of European powers or even a single major European nation. Nor did the size of the military establishment increase in the years after the era of nationalism and before the country's next foreign conflict, the war with Mexico in 1846. During this time the navy remained at approximately the same strength, and the size of the army was raised to 12,000 in 1838 but reduced to 8,000 in 1842.

The land forces could have been significantly strengthened if the militia had been integrated into the defense system, but the professional officers opposed this. The soldiers preached, and sold civilian leaders, the idea that militia could not be relied on in battle. The victories in the War of 1812 were credited to regulars and the debacles blamed on militiamen. Although these claims were not completely true, the idea of the superiority of regulars prevailed in the minds of those making military policy, and the concept of a serviceable citizen army began to fade from American military thought.

In comparison with the military establishments of European powers of similar resources, American forces were small, consuming but a minor part of the government's expenditures. The expanding young nation could have comfortably supported a larger establishment, but to all except certain professional officers the existing force seemed adequate to execute national policy.

The near-unanimity on adequacy was possible because nobody in the government or the military understood precisely what policy the army and the navy were supposed to execute. The United States still lacked a clearly defined national strategy. To the extent that the military had a mission, it was to defend the nation against foreign enemies. But who were the enemies, and over what issues would they engage the United States? The answers were vague and varying. For a time after 1815 some leaders believed there would be another war with Britain. John C. Calhoun, secretary of war between 1817 and 1825, thought such a conflict might develop from the efforts of both countries to control the fur trade in the far Northwest. Others opined that a war with Spain might erupt over Florida, a haven for hostile Indians and runaway slaves from the southern states. Neither eventuality materialized. Britain practiced careful restraint in her dealings with the potentially aggressive nation on the Canadian border, and Spain, unable to govern Florida effectively, ceded the colony to the United States in 1819.

Not called on to fight a foreign enemy, the armed forces performed domestic functions. The navy patrolled American waters and occasionally showed the flag in distant ports to remind possible depredators that it was available to protect America's growing overseas commerce. The army, its troops scattered in a hundred posts throughout the country, built forts and seacoast fortifications, ran surveys and conducted explorations in the West, and policed and fought Indians on the western and southern frontiers. Although such routine assignments were tedious to the officers charged with them, they were important to the welfare of the nation. The army in particular was playing a vital role in fostering national expansion. As long as the nation's policy remained essentially defensive, the two services were adequate to execute it, and during these years they generally did so at least with competence and occasionally with expertness.

Their performance can be credited to improved administrative arrangements at the top level of command and increased knowledge of the military art in the officer corps. In a word, the services were becoming more "professional." The most important changes occurred in the army, which for eight years was under the strong and imaginative direction of John C. Calhoun, who must be ranked as one of the great secretaries of war. His first accomplishment was to complete the establishment of the General Staff organization under the War Department. The various staff bureaus had been created in 1813 and originally consisted of their directors and a few assistants headquartered in Washington. But as time went on, and with Calhoun's encouragement, the directors not only added to their personnel, bringing to the capital officers who were specialists like themselves, but also expanded their functions. Although the bureaus were concerned with purely "housekeeping" functions, supply and administration, and although each director performed his work individually, not meeting with the others to discuss broad policy, their mere presence was an immense asset to the secretary, who could turn to them for technical advice or the delegation of authority. Calhoun was careful to select competent staff officers and also to maintain his authority over the bureau heads, who according to army regulations were responsible to him. Being a strong person, he was able to exercise control, but succeeding secretaries found the job difficult. The bureau chiefs, having the security of seniority, tended to resist civilian mastery, and their expert knowledge in narrow areas enabled them to fend off the interference of any but a determined secretary.

In another administrative development of the Calhoun era, the office of commanding general was established as a permanent institution. No officer had led the army as a whole since Washington had emerged from retirement during the quasi-war with France, and in an administrative sense no officer had acted as general in chief since Washington's tenure in the Revolution. While a succession of officers had been recognized as commanding generals—St. Clair, Wayne, and others—they had been field commanders, chosen for their supposed ability to lead troops in battle rather than for their administrative skills, and none had held the position for more than a few years. Calhoun himself did not propose the creation of the office, apparently preferring to retain overall control of the army in his own hands. In a reorganization plan submitted to Congress he recommended that the top command consist of two major generals and four brigadier generals. However, the legislators rejected his plan and in 1821 provided for a top command of one major general and two brigadiers. Although the act did not stipulate that the major general should be the commanding general, this was its implication, and Calhoun accepted the interpretation. He ordered the senior major general, Jacob Brown, to make his headquarters in Washington, thus formalizing the creation of the office. Hereafter the commanding general would be at the disposal of the secretary, and under his direct supervision.

Brown held the office until his death in 1828, and was succeeded by Alexander Macomb, who also died in office in 1841. Winfield Scott then was appointed to the position and retained it until 1861, when he retired at the age of seventy-five. All three men served long enough to put their stamp upon the army, Scott especially. Brown and Macomb were extremely competent soldiers. In addition, Scott, as he would demonstrate in the Mexican War, was a great battle captain. The fact that men of such quality chose to remain in service showed that the rewards and prestige of a military career were becoming sufficient to attract able officers, that the profession of arms was attaining respectability in the American scale of values.

Not all officers in the higher command levels were of the caliber of Brown, Macomb, and Scott. Among the brigadiers and the colonels there were some competent men, but also some who were only average and some who were mediocre and even worse. These senior officers were career soldiers who had spent most of their adult lives in the army and militarily were self-educated: they had learned whatever they knew about their trade from experience or reading and not from having had a formal military education. For officers such as these who desired to increase their knowledge, a number of tactical manuals were available, one of them prepared by General Scott. Ambitious officers could also improve their proficiency by instructing at the first of the army's specialist schools, the artillery school of instruction, established with Calhoun's encouragement at Fortress Monroe, Virginia, in 1824, or at the infantry school of practice organized at Jefferson Barracks near St. Louis in 1827. (Unlike modern specialist schools, these institutions instructed whole units rather than individuals.)

In contrast to the self-educated, or uneducated, senior officers, most of the junior officers possessed a formal education. By 1846 the Military Academy at West Point had graduated approximately a thousand cadets, of whom about one-half stayed in the army. The others, after performing their required tour of duty, resigned their commissions, either because they despaired of promotion or because they were seduced by the promise of more lucrative positions in civil life. Those who chose to remain in service were products of a school that was a greatly improved model of the original institution. With the encouragement of Calhoun and under the leadership of Sylvanus Thayer, who became superintendent in 1817, West Point developed into a first-rate officer-training school, broadening its curriculum and reforming its methods of instruction. Although it retained its original emphasis on engineering and stressed tactics to the neglect of strategy, the academy turned out graduates who were well trained in the technical aspects of the various branches of the services, who could command in the engineers, infantry, artillery, or cavalry. Many of the graduates who had gone into civilian occupations would return at the outbreak of the Mexican War, and for the first time in a war American armies would contain large numbers of officers with a formal military education.

ALTHOUGH THE UNITED STATES remained at peace with other nations between 1815 and 1846, it conducted three wars against Indians during this period. Two were short in duration, and the troops engaged in them, regulars and militiamen, were victorious over relatively weak opposition. However, the third encounter was a grim and difficult struggle, perhaps the longest, bloodiest, and costliest Indian war in American history. The regular army would be called upon to fight a kind of war it was not prepared for, a kind it did not like to fight and did not fight very well.

The first of these conflicts began on the border between Georgia and Spanish Florida. Late in 1817 war parties of Seminoles and Lower Creeks fell on outlying settlements. The Creeks were a faction of the tribe that had fled to Florida after that once numerous "nation" had been crushed by Andrew Jackson in 1814. The Seminoles were an amalgam of peoples from several southeastern tribes who for various reasons had left their tribes and collected in Florida: the name Siminole or Seminole meant "separatist" or "runaway." Accentuating the uniqueness of the Seminoles was the presence among them of a number of runaway slaves, some of them held in nominal bondage, others being free and in some cases the actual leaders of particular clusters of Indians.

The attacks on the Georgia frontier illustrated the problem posed for the United States by the presence of the Spanish in Florida. Spanish authority was so weak as to be almost nonexistent, the few royal officials rarely venturing out of the principal towns and exercising no restraint over the various tribes roaming the swamps and forests. Those Indians who crossed the Georgia border were incited by British adventurers who told them, falsely, that their former lands in south Georgia had been returned to them by the Treaty of Ghent. As long as Spanish authority remained in Florida, such incursions were obviously going to continue. To eliminate them, the United States itself would have to act against the Indians, or drive out the Spaniards.

The government was prepared to move vigorously. It instructed Major General Andrew Jackson, commanding the Southern Department, to employ "necessary measures" to terminate the raids, even to the extent of crossing the border into Florida in pursuit of the Indians. Jackson was eager to exercise his authorization to the hilt. He believed that the government wanted him to find a pretext to occupy Florida for permanent retention—the government would later deny such a motive—and he conducted his campaign on this assumption.

To accomplish his purpose, Jackson had a force of 800 regulars and 1,000 Georgia militia, later augmented by 1,000 militia volunteers from Tennessee. Although he had to dispose some of his troops in forts and supply bases, his army was ample to deal with any opposition he might meet. He encountered little as he moved over the border in February, 1818, brushing aside remonstrating Spanish officials and executing two British citizens accused of inciting the Indians. The Indians melted into the swamps at his approach, and by May Jackson was in possession of central and western Florida. His actions aroused the anger of Spain and Britain, however, and the U.S. government had to express regrets to both nations. But at the same time it impressed on Spain that the United States could not permit Florida to become a base for hostile Indians, that Spain must either provide order in the province or cede it. Unable to establish order, Spain chose the alternative of cession in return for financial compensation. Thus, the principal result of the conflict was to complete the expansion of the United States on its southeastern border. It had been a war with very little fighting, especially by the Seminoles, whose subjection had been the original objective of the Jackson expedition. Nevertheless, the episode became known as the Seminole War, and when still another conflict was required to pacify these Indians, it was designated more precisely as the First Seminole War.

The next Indian conflict erupted in the upper Mississippi Valley, and the natives who engaged in it fought bravely and skillfully. But because they were few in numbers and chose to operate in a white-settled area, their cause was hopeless, and in the end they were crushed bloodily. These Indians were of the Sac and Fox tribes and had originally lived in the Rock River region of western Illinois. Induced by the government to cede their lands to accommodate migrating whites, they moved over the Mississippi River into present-day Iowa. But they still cherished memories of their home region, and Black Hawk, a leader of the Sacs, preached that the cessions had been illegally obtained and that the Indians should reclaim their lands. In 1832 he recrossed the river with 500 warriors (additions from allied tribes swelled this total to perhaps 800) and over 1,000 women and children. He had obviously come to stay, and the struggle known as the Black Hawk War had begun.

The incursion stirred the U.S. government to frantic activity, in conjunction with the Illinois authorities. The War Department ordered Colonel Henry Atkinson, commanding at Jefferson Barracks, to move against Black Hawk with all the regulars he could muster, and also instructed General Scott to collect 1,000 troops from the East Coast and proceed to Illinois via the Great Lakes.* The governor of Illinois called the militia to assemble, and 2,000 volunteers, the majority of them mounted, joined Atkinson's field force of 500. An army comparable in size with some of those in the Revolution or the War of 1812 was raised to deal with fewer than 1,000 Indians.

Against such a force Black Hawk had no choice except to retire. Closely pursued but carrying his women and children with him, he moved into Wisconsin Territory, hoping to escape across the Mississippi. The mounted volunteers caught up to him at Wisconsin Heights on the Wisconsin River and killed sixty-eight of his warriors before he could withdraw. He was brought to bay finally at the confluence of the Bad Axe River with the Mississippi, and here he had to fight. In a battle lasting three hours Black Hawk's followers were almost destroyed. Approximately 150 Indians were killed, and an equal number were drowned trying to swim across the Mississippi. Of the original band of over 1,500 persons, fewer than 300 succeeded in recrossing the river. Black Hawk was captured, and his war was ended. He never had any chance of success. His small tribe could not oppose the power the whites brought against him, and he made the mistake of moving through relatively built-up country in a compact or mass formation, of maneuvering as a white force might have done.

The third of the Indian conflicts occurred in a very different kind of terrain, the swamps of Florida, and the Indians who fought it, the Seminoles, employed tactics very different from Black Hawk's visible formations. The Second Seminole War began in 1835, when the tribe repudiated a treaty in

---

*The force under Scott did not arrive on the scene until after the war ended, and then with only a part of its original complement: cholera broke out on the transports and killed or disabled one-third of the troops.

which they had agreed to move to lands west of the Mississippi. Led by an able half-breed named Osceola, they ambushed and massacred a detachment of regulars, and the war was on. It would last until 1842, requiring an expenditure of $30 million and engaging forces totaling 10,000 regulars and 30,000 militiamen, of whom approximately 1,500 would lose their lives in battle or from disease. One general commanded almost 9,000 men, a larger force than Washington led in many of his campaigns. Some of the best generals tried their hands at subduing the Seminoles—Scott was one of these—and most of them left in frustration. The war came to be considered a graveyard for military reputations.

The war lasted so long because the army insisted on employing traditional or conventional methods of warfare against the Indians, marching columns of soldiers to attack the natives in strongholds where it was rumored they were collected. Thus, on one occasion Scott divided his force into three columns in an attempt to encircle Osceola. But when he attacked, the Seminoles were not there: they had melted away into the swamps and forests. This experience would be repeated many times. The Indians generally avoided a direct confrontation with the army. Instead, they struck at small parties or unguarded points, and when pursued, they disappeared. It was guerrilla warfare, and the army was puzzled as to how to deal with it, how to cope with a foe who would not fight a conventional battle. "Could the enemy be brought to battle even in his own strongholds, the war would soon be closed," one officer lamented.

Various devices were attempted to flush the Indians. One officer, Zachary Taylor, hit on the plan of dividing the peninsula into districts, each of which contained a fort and a garrison. The commander of each post combed his district every other day seeking hostiles to attack, a tactic that in a later war would be called "search-and-destroy." This method brought some results, but it demonstrated that the army, made desperate by the continuing struggle, was becoming more ruthless and abandoning some of the principles of so-called civilized warfare. The army demonstrated this regression in other ways, resorting to such treachery as inviting Osceola and other chiefs to conferences under a flag of truce and then taking them prisoner. In the end the army adopted even more extreme practices. One of the frustrated generals had defined the problem of dealing with guerrillas. "To rid the country of them you must exterminate them," he declared. The army finally did almost exterminate the Seminoles, attacking them during the summer season, when they did not expect it, and destroying their crops and dwellings and forcing those who were not killed to accept submission.*

The Second Seminole War was the first conflict in which the army en-

---

*The Seminoles numbered perhaps 4,000 persons, of whom about 1,000 were warriors. One remnant of the tribe was moved west of the Mississippi, but another refused to go and was eventually assigned to a restricted reservation.

gaged a guerrilla enemy. The army won in the end, but it had great advantages—the Indians were confined to a peninsula and had to depend entirely on their own resources. Even so, the army suffered maddening frustrations, and it had obviously been unprepared to fight an elusive enemy who seemed determined to fight interminably. In future conflicts the army would have to fight guerrillas who enjoyed support from outside powers, and then it would experience even greater frustrations than in Florida.*

*Many writers of today make a distinction between partisan and guerrilla warfare, although the methods in each are similar—sudden attacks by small and mobile forces. Partisans fight to establish or restore a native authority, to expel an outside power. Thus, Marion's and Sumter's bands in the Revolution were partisans. Guerrillas fight to overthrow an existing native authority, to incite a revolution—the Chinese Communists or, by their own definition, the Viet Cong are examples. It has been said that a government dealing with guerrillas has three choices: to exterminate them, to yield to them, or to fight endlessly. Western nations, including the United States, have usually had trouble in fighting guerrilla wars. Powerful and industrial, they have attempted to bring their might to bear on an evasive enemy, and when the desired result was not achieved, they have lacked the patience to wage a protracted war. At the time of the Second Seminole War the United States was becoming a built-up country, and it tended to employ conventional methods of warfare against the Indians. It is possible that the Americans of the colonial or Revolutionary eras were better prepared to deal with Indian guerrillas.

CHAPTER VII

The Mexican War: Origins and Objectives

T HE MEXICAN WAR has always occupied an ambiguous position in the national historical consciousness. Depending on the prevailing mood of intellectuals and historians, it has been denounced as a wicked war of aggression against a weaker neighbor or justified as an inevitable phase in the expansion of a virile and superior people. In recent decades the latter view has prevailed, but the former interpretation has retained adherents and was given a new lease on popularity by the spasm of war guilt that seized on the American people after the Vietnam conflict.

Perhaps because Americans have had lingering doubts about the purpose of the war, they have shown little interest in its events. Except for the specialists, there are few who can name its leading generals or recount its principal battles. This obscurity is undeserved, because the Mexican War was an important episode in our military and general history. As a case study in nineteenth-century warfare, the conflict offers a number of significant lessons, several of which pointed to the future. In the context of general history, the war is important because of its results; indeed, the results of few wars were so important or enduring. During the administration of James K. Polk, the chief executive during the war, over one million square miles of territory was added to the domain of the United States, the greater part of it wrested from Mexico, and the nation's boundaries were advanced from the Louisiana Purchase line to the Pacific Ocean. The acquisition of the new lands eventually strengthened the nation and the bonds of nationality, but the immediate effect was to cause internal sectional division and thus weaken the ties of union. The area secured became a prize to be contended for between the South and the North, between the forces of slavery and antislavery, a struggle that culminated in the secession of Southern states from the Union. Thus, the Mexican War led almost inevitably to a greater conflict, the Civil War.

In American military history the Mexican War is significant because of the number of "firsts" associated with it. It was the first overseas war. Although some American forces were moved into Mexico from adjacent areas in the United States, others were transported on water to bases on the Mexican coast, from which they penetrated inland. In moving these troops, land and naval officers learned a great deal about the problems of water transportation and the conduct of joint amphibious operations, lessons that would be later put to use in the Civil War. The forces dispatched to Mexico were carried largely in sailing ships, still the main reliance of the navy. However, the majority of the men brought to points of embarkation in the United States were carried in river steamboats, and the Mexican War thus became the first steamboat war.

It was also America's first successful offensive war, the first in which the strategic objectives were laid out with some clarity before hostilities were joined, and the first to be conducted with a large measure of technical proficiency and with relative efficiency. Finally, it was the first war in which the president really acted as commander in chief. In the War of 1812 Madison had not actually used his powers to control operations, but Polk influenced every aspect of the conflict. In the apt words of one historian, Polk "proved that a President could run a war."

THE WAR HAD its origins in events that occurred years before its inception, events that involved not only the United States and Mexico but also certain European nations. The story of these relationships is a complicated record of conflicting ambitions and complex diplomatic maneuverings that here can only be summarized. On the American side the account reveals that ideological and economic forces can influence the making of foreign policy and determine military objectives.

The America of the 1830s and 1840s was an expansive and an expanding nation. Its western boundary stretched from the Sabine River, between Louisiana and the Mexican province of Texas, in a northwesterly direction until it finally touched the Rocky Mountains. Large portions of this imperial domain remained unsettled—the upper eastern Mississippi Valley and the region beyond the Mississippi River. But during these decades the restless American population, constantly being augmented by natural growth and by an influx of European immigrants, began one of those great westward pushes that have characterized the occupation of the continent. Settlers laid the basis for the new state of Michigan and the soon-to-be state of Wisconsin, and moved across the Mississippi into adjacent areas that became the states of Arkansas and Iowa. By the time of the Mexican War the line of settlement reached from Louisiana to Minnesota Territory.

While some Americans were casting calculating eyes on Oregon, others were showing a similar interest in the Mexican provinces adjoining the United

States on the southwest—New Mexico, Upper California, and Texas. These areas had once been part of Spain's colonial empire in North America, but in 1821 they had passed under the authority of the newly born republic of Mexico. The transition meant little in the lives of the Mexican inhabitants, descendants of Spanish colonists and few in number. Under Spanish rule they had been subjected to only the lightest supervision from the government of the distant viceroyalty in Mexico City, and this condition continued under the republic. The Mexican government lacked the power or the administrative machinery to enforce its will on these remote areas, and Mexico did not have a large enough population to increase its influence with migrants.

American interest in New Mexico came about because of the province's economic isolation. During the Spanish period the inhabitants exported their few products to Mexico City or Vera Cruz and from these centers imported their meager finished goods. It was a difficult and costly way of effecting exchange, and when Mexico became independent, she let it be known that traders from the United States would be welcome in New Mexico. The result was to create the colorful enterprise known as "the Santa Fe trade." Every year the American merchants engaged in it would collect at some point west of the Mississippi, usually Independence, Missouri, and, traveling in a caravan of wagons loaded with simple manufactured goods, would set out on the 800-mile-long trip to the metropolis of New Mexico, Santa Fe. Their business transacted, the traders would return bearing gold, silver, furs, and other exotic items. Although this "commerce of the prairies" aroused wide public interest, its economic importance was modest; the total volume of the trade was small, and the number of Americans concerned with it was few. Nor did the traffic lead many Americans to settle in New Mexico, although some traders and other entrepreneurs did decide to remain there. The real significance of the Santa Fe trade was in its influence on future expansion. It fixed American attention on New Mexico and revealed another area that invited penetration.

Even more distant from the homeland than New Mexico and equally dependent on outside trade was California, and it was the hope of profits to be derived from trade that brought the first Americans to that province. They were maritime traders or captains of whaling ships who put into California harbors to barter goods or acquire supplies. Following them came merchants who established trading posts, imported merchandise, and carried on a profitable exchange with the 7,000 Mexicans in California and the Indians. These first settlers came by sea, but soon others began to arrive by land, farmers and their families who had been attracted by the spreading stories of the province's rich soil and salubrious climate. By 1845 some 700 Americans had settled in California, the majority of them hopeful that one day their adopted home would be joined to the United States.

The national government had shown an interest in California even before many Americans had moved there, primarily because its harbors offered convenient bases from which to support the whaling trade in the Pacific or to expand American trade with Asia. President Andrew Jackson during the 1830s and President John Tyler during the 1840s considered trying to buy all or part of California from Mexico, each of them inspired by rumors that England wished to acquire or dominate the area. No formal offer of purchase was made, but a possessive interest in California was clearly developing in the United States, and this was emphasized in 1842 by a curious incident. The commander of the American naval squadron in the Pacific heard a report—a false one, of course—that war had broken out between his country and Mexico and that a British naval force was heading for California, probably with aggressive designs. Executing what he thought was the policy of his government, he sailed into Monterey harbor and took possession of the town. An embarrassing situation followed when the falseness of the report became known, with both the officer and his government presenting quick apologies to Mexico. Mexico was placated, but now she, and Britain, knew that the United States had marked California off for possible acquisition. Regardless of what the United States might do, California was for practical purposes soon lost to Mexico. In 1845 the native inhabitants, out of patience finally with the fumbling rule of the home government, set up a semiautonomous administration, and Mexico was forced to recognize their regime.

More accessible to Americans than California or New Mexico was Texas, which received the largest influx of settlers from the north. Ironically, in view of later events, the first of them came on invitation from the Mexican government, which during the 1820s offered land grants to enterprising Americans who would promise to settle a stipulated number of families on their concessions. The government's motive in inviting immigration was largely economic in origin: by increasing the population of Texas it hoped to expand the economy of the province and eventually the tax revenues derived from it. However, the action revealed the weakness of Mexico's hold on Texas, and on the other northern provinces. Unable to populate them herself, she was forced to import foreigners. The process might promise immediate economic benefits, but it held the seeds of future danger: if the Americans entered in sufficient numbers, they might eventually be able to throw off Mexican control. The Americans came, more and more of them, until by 1835 there were 35,000 in Texas.

Almost from the beginning friction developed between the settlers and the Mexican officials in Texas and Mexico City. The specific issues involved such matters as land titles and taxes, but behind these was a more fundamental cause of difference—two cultures had come into contact and into inevitable conflict. The points of contention became more numerous and bitter as time went on, until finally the Mexican government decided that its authority over Texas was being challenged. In a move to exert control it abolished the self-governing powers of the various states of the republic, a measure that the Texans took to be aimed specifically at them. Determined to maintain their rights, they rebelled in 1836 and proclaimed the Republic of Texas.

The Mexican government was equally determined to retain Texas, and sent a large army to subdue the rebels. Its commander, Antonio López de Santa Anna, who was the real power in the government, won some initial successes but eventually was defeated at the battle of San Jacinto and he himself taken prisoner. He won his freedom by offering vague promises to withdraw Mexican authority from Texas, promises which his government promptly disavowed. Mexico made no immediate attempt to reconquer the province, however; Texas had won a precarious independence.

It was precarious because Texas lacked the resources to sustain an independent existence. The population, now grown to perhaps 50,000, was small in comparison with that of Mexico, always a potential menace on its southern border, and insufficient to support the expenses of a national government. Most Texans realized the dangers in their situation and wanted to be annexed to the United States, not only to gain protection but also because the great majority of them were Americans and desired to be a part of their own country. Consequently, in 1837 Texas asked the United States for annexation. President Andrew Jackson was sympathetic but forbore to place the proposal before Congress. Although sentiment for annexation seemed strong in all sections of the country, there was also opposition to it, particularly from antislavery forces in the Northeast, who denounced the incorporation of a new slave area. Fearing to provoke a sectional controversy, Jackson merely recognized the independence of Texas just before he left office. In 1844 President John Tyler persuaded Texas to apply again for annexation, and a treaty of acquisition was submitted to the Senate. It received a majority of the votes but, because of the opposition of antislavery members, not the required two-thirds majority.

Tyler, a Southerner eager to expand slave territory, had been inspired to act by reports that Britain was plotting to extend her influence in Texas. These reports were partially true. Texas, rebuffed by the United States, had sought recognition and financial support in Europe. Some Texas leaders played with the thought of maintaining a separate existence but with close dependence on Britain and France. These governments were receptive to the prospect of an independent Texas, which could be a barrier to further expansion by the United States, and considered guaranteeing the independence of the republic and also the present boundaries of Mexico. However, Britain and France moved too tardily to accomplish their designs and were unable to persuade Mexico to recognize Texas's independence. Rumors of British activities, exaggerated to include the actual occupation of Texas and perhaps of Oregon as well, excited anger and apprehension in the United States.

On the eve of the presidential election of 1844 the question of the nation's interest in all the areas to which Americans had moved—Oregon, California, New Mexico, and Texas—loomed large in the thinking of many voters. Although some politicians did not realize it, a majority of Americans had gradually been possessed by a swelling sentiment for the expansion of American rule. An editor who approvingly observed this urge to dominion gave it a name that has endured, "Manifest Destiny." As he explained the term, speaking for many persons less articulate, the American nation was destined to occupy most or perhaps all of the continent of North America, not through the "agency of our government" but "in the natural flow of events, the spontaneous working of principle." Manifest Destiny, it appeared, was a superhuman force.

OF THE TWO MAJOR PARTIES in the 1844 election, the Whigs and the Democrats, the latter were more representative of the masses and hence more attuned to prevailing trends in popular opinion. The Whig managers, somewhat aloof and insulated, did not seem to realize the strength of expansionist sentiment in the country; indeed, they feared they would lose votes if they endorsed expansion. The managers especially wanted to avoid taking a stand on the most immediate issue of expansion, the annexation of Texas, which they believed would generate a damaging sectional division. Consequently, at the Whig convention they forced the nomination of a candidate who favored ignoring annexation, Henry Clay, and their platform omitted any reference to Texas or to expansionism generally.

Some of the Democratic leaders also preferred to avoid the problem of Texas, and this strategy was supported by the chief candidate, former President Martin Van Buren. However, other Democrats were determined to embrace annexation—men from the West and the South who sensed the appeal of Manifest Destiny in their sections and in the country at large. The latter were in control at the national convention, and discarding Van Buren, they engineered the nomination of James K. Polk, an expansionist, and the adoption of a platform demanding assertion of American title to all of Oregon and annexation of Texas. In a bold affirmation of the expansionist spirit, the platform proclaimed that the "re-occupation of Oregon and the re-annexation of Texas" were "great American measures" that must be consummated at the "earliest practicable period."

The "re's" in the platform must have seemed a curious use of language to some foreign observers. However, the Democrats had a definite purpose in employing them. They wanted to make the proposed acquisitions appear legal and just to other nations: Oregon had always belonged to the United States, and Texas had originally been a part of the Louisiana Purchase.* In the realm of domestic politics the Democrats were using shrewd tactics by combining

---

*Actually, the United States had in 1819 renounced its claim to Texas in the treaty with Spain providing for the cession of Florida.

Oregon and Texas: they had separated the expansion issue from the slavery controversy. Obviously, one territory would eventually add to the strength of the free states, the other to that of the slave states. No one could accuse the Democrats of sectionalism; rather, they stood forward as the champions of *national* expansion.* They had caught the mood of the country, and in November they swept to victory. Polk rolled up a decisive electoral majority, although his popular margin was narrow.

The result could fairly be viewed as a mandate for expansion, and this was the interpretation placed upon it by outgoing President Tyler. However, Tyler chose to read the returns as a command to secure only Texas. An ardent advocate of the interests of slavery, he saw no reason to wait for Polk to acquire the province. Professing it to be still threatened by British designs, he proposed to Congress that Texas be annexed by joint resolution of both houses, a device that would circumvent the requirement of obtaining a two-thirds vote in the Senate for ratification by treaty. The resolution was carried in February, 1845, although by close majorities, and Texas at last became an American possession. One of the two proclaimed territorial objectives of the Democrats had been accomplished before Polk assumed office.

The incoming president was not displeased that Tyler had anticipated him on Texas. On the contrary, he was delighted that the province was finally secure in the American fold, and he publicly and officially defended Tyler's action. Thus, in his inaugural address, speaking particularly to foreign powers, Polk asserted that the annexation was not "the conquest of a nation seeking to extend her dominion by arms," but only "the peaceful acquisition of a territory once her own, by adding another member to our confederation with the consent of that member." Although Polk agreed with Tyler that taking Texas promptly had been necessary, he viewed the result from a different perspective. Tyler had been concerned merely with acquiring additional territory for slavery. But to Polk, Texas was only the first step in a program of continental expansion.

Continuing his inaugural address, Polk asserted American title to Oregon, the second proclaimed territorial objective in the Democratic platform. The right of the United States to the region was "clear and unquestioned," he declared, and would be not only asserted but "maintained." "Already are our people preparing to perfect that title by occupying Oregon with their wives and children," he concluded. He seemed to be promising that Oregon would be acquired by peaceful means, that it would fall to the United States because of the sheer numbers of American settlers.

*The political journalist Walter Lippmann once pointed out that through the years the Democratic party (or its political ancestor) has been the "party of bold designs," and in support of this statement, he cited the annexation of Texas. Other examples that Lippmann listed were the Louisiana Purchase, the Monroe Doctrine, and the occupation of the Southwest, including California.

In his public pronouncements on Oregon, Polk espoused the official Democratic position, implying that the United States would demand all of the area up to the fifty-fourth parallel. In private discussions with his advisers, however, he indicated a willingness to negotiate for a division at the forty-ninth parallel, the boundary that previous administrations had offered to Britain, and a proposal to this effect was placed before the British minister in Washington. Polk's motives in agreeing to compromise American interests are not evident and have been variously interpreted by historians. Probably he realized that to insist on a more northerly boundary would provoke England to war, and he was satisfied with as much of Oregon as he could get without war. Whatever the case, he saw his proposal to negotiate ignored; the British minister in Washington rejected the American offer without ever referring it to his government.

Polk thereupon assumed a more belligerent stance. Declaring that the United States should look arrogant John Bull "straight in the eye," he specifically claimed American title to all of Oregon and hinted that the nation might have to protect its rights by war. In December, 1845, he asked Congress to authorize giving notice to England that joint occupation of Oregon would end in a year, and the legislators complied. By thus invoking the abrogation clause of the 1827 treaty Polk was throwing the initiative for a settlement back upon Britain, who would now have to negotiate or, if she took Polk's threats at face value, fight. With little hesitation the realistic men in the British government chose negotiation; they believed it would be rank folly to fight for a region most of which was settled by Americans. Accordingly, the government submitted to the United States a proposed treaty dividing Oregon at the forty-ninth parallel, the line in Polk's original offer. The president now said he was opposed to any compromise of American claims, but he was obviously talking only for the record. He was easily persuaded by his cabinet to send the agreement to the Senate for its advice, and that body ratified the treaty in June, 1846. The United States had secured the greater and the better part of the Oregon country and all that it could have realistically expected to get.

Polk's actions throughout the Oregon confrontation were puzzlingly inconsistent. He first offered compromise and negotiation, but when this course was rejected, he abruptly threatened to use force. He apparently believed that in certain diplomatic situations a nation had to assume an aggressive posture in order to induce favorable negotiations later. The strategy worked in the case of Oregon, but it was one that reduced his choice of policies. If Britain had not backed away, the United States would have had to fight or back away itself. Polk would employ the same kind of pressures in dealing with Mexico, but in these maneuvers he ran out of choices.

The republic to the south engaged Polk's immediate attention. When he entered office, the two countries did not enjoy diplomatic relations. The break had resulted from American action in regard to Texas. Mexico, which had never recognized its loss of Texas, had angrily protested the act of annexation, and when Texas was admitted as a state late in 1845, the government broke off formal contacts with the United States. Polk was determined to restore diplomatic relations, but on terms that he would define. The nature of those terms is not fully revealed in the documents that have survived, and the president's objectives are still disputed among historians. Here it is possible only to state what his probable purposes were.

About one of Polk's objectives there is no doubt. He was determined to force Mexico to recognize Texas as a part of the United States, actually and legally. Although this was a legitimate American ambition, Polk realized that the Mexican government would experience political difficulties if it yielded on Texas, and in order to enable it to save face he was willing to offer an indemnity. Previously, Mexico had admitted owing several million dollars to American citizens residing or doing business in the country for damages to property, unsatisfied debts, and other losses, but she had not honored the obligations. Polk let it be known that the United States would assume these claims if Mexico admitted the loss of Texas.

Recognition of American title to Texas was not the only concession Polk intended to wring from Mexico. He also hoped to effect the transfer to the United States of the provinces of California and New Mexico. These territories had not been demanded in the Democratic platform, and in moving to secure them the president tried to conceal his actions from public view. Because of the semi-secrecy attending his maneuvers, his course was not always apparent and different interpretations of his purposes are possible. Some critics, political enemies of his time and later historians, have ascribed sinister motives to Polk. They charge that he never intended a peaceful settlement with Mexico, that in his various machinations he was trying to provoke war, with the objectives of acquiring California and New Mexico and possibly other territory in northern Mexico and of settling the Texas question finally. The most extreme advocates of this "plot" theory do not concede that Polk was animated by goals of national glory but contend rather that he was seeking in war partisan advantage for the Democratic party.

Polk's actions that have aroused the suspicion of critics occurred during the summer of 1845. At that time he sent secret instructions to American representatives in California, and he dispatched other agents to the province to cooperate with the representatives already there. What he wanted these various persons to do is not completely clear; or to put the problem differently but perhaps more accurately, what they may have *thought* he wanted them to do is not clear. The language in the written instructions was sometimes ambiguous and could have been interpreted in several ways by the recipients. Probably Polk was attempting to invest his agents with a large degree of discretion so that they would be free to respond to any of several situations that he thought might arise in California. As it turned out, he selected men who could not be trusted with discretion.

Polk had directed the commander of the Pacific naval squadron to stand in close to the coast and to seize the principal ports if he heard that Mexico had declared war (this indicated that the president realized that his policy might lead to war) or that the British squadron in the area seemed about to occupy the ports (Polk ever feared the ambitions of England). Another directive went to the American consul in California, Thomas Larkin, a resident merchant and an ardent annexationist. Larkin was given a characteristically Polkian list of choices. He was told to avoid provoking the nominal Mexican authorities, to conciliate the inhabitants, to assist them if they attempted to throw off Mexican rule, and in the last event to impress on them that they must not accept the protection of any foreign power except the United States. Similar instructions were carried by Captain John C. Frémont of the army's corps of topographical engineers, who led an exploring expedition into California, appearing there with a large and well-armed party that aroused suspicion in the Mexican officials. Frémont, like Larkin, was an annexationist, and also a very impulsive man, and he and the consul decided they should incite the American and whatever native inhabitants they could influence to revolt. They may have thought they were executing Polk's wishes, but they were exceeding the letter of his instructions.

While the president's zealous agents in California were risking provocation of Mexico, he himself committed an act that was certain to antagonize her. He ordered a force of regulars under Colonel Zachary Taylor to move from Louisiana into Texas to a point "on or near" the Rio Grande that could be readily "adapted to repel invasion."

In making this sudden display of strength, Polk was serving notice on Mexico that he supported Texas in claiming as her southern and western boundary the Rio Grande from source to mouth, an assertion that would have placed a good part of New Mexico in Texas. The claim was based on doubtful legal grounds, inasmuch as under Spanish rule the boundary had never been defined. Texas naturally wanted to extend her limits, and Polk felt that he had to stand behind her. Later the Mexican government would assert that the rightful boundary was the Nueces River, farther to the north, and American critics of Polk took up the allegation, charging that to provoke Mexico into war he had sent troops into Mexico or at the least into "disputed" territory.

At the time Polk acted, however, Mexico claimed *all* of Texas, and she would have resented the presence of American forces anywhere in the area. Her later proposal of the Nueces line was probably a last-minute recognition of the reality of American occupation and an attempt to negotiate as favorable a boundary as she could. At this stage Polk was possibly amenable to settling for the Nueces line. With his permission Taylor stopped at the river, encamping at Corpus Christi at its mouth. His column was eventually reinforced to 4,000 men, half of the entire regular army.*

In pushing a military force into Texas and toward the Rio Grande, Polk was employing his favored tactic in diplomacy, mingling aggression and bluff in order to pressure an opponent to negotiate. He still hoped to get what he wanted from Mexico without resorting to war. Working through special agents, he had secured assurances from the Mexican government that it would receive from the United States a "special commissioner" to negotiate the "unsettled questions" between the two nations, by which Mexico meant only that she would consider recognizing the loss of Texas if the United States expressed regret for having annexed her and canceled the damage claims as a form of indemnity.

Although Polk understood the limited nature of the Mexican offer, he affected to regard it as an invitation to negotiate all the issues that had strained relations between the two countries. He appointed as his representative to Mexico not a special commissioner but a "minister plenipotentiary," John Slidell, a prominent Louisiana Democrat, whose first assignment was to reopen diplomatic relations. In addition, Slidell was instructed to secure Mexico's assent to the Rio Grande boundary of Texas, in return for which the United States would assume the damage claims, and to negotiate the cession of New Mexico for a payment of $5 million and of California for a sum of $25 million. Slidell arrived in Mexico City late in 1845, when the faction in control of the government was under threat of overthrow by a more militant group. Conscious of its weakness, the government refused to receive him officially, citing as its reason the presumption of his title, which implied that Mexico had consented to resume diplomatic relations. Even so, the rival party shortly took over control, and having risen to power partly by denouncing the American offer, it was even more adamant in refusing to negotiate. After weeks of waiting, Slidell finally informed Polk that his mission was hopeless. Immediately on receipt of the report, in January, 1846, the president ordered Taylor to advance to the Rio Grande. It was a provocative action, whether or not he so intended it. He had asserted that the river was the boundary of Texas and had said to Mexico, in effect: this is the line between peace and war. He had nearly exhausted his options.

Taylor, now a general, prepared his movement somewhat dilatorily and did not reach the Rio Grande until late in March. Once there, however, he acted with energy, disposing his troops along the north bank of the river opposite the Mexican town of Matamoros and constructing near its mouth a fort, Fort Texas, from which he could block navigation. His appearance infuriated the Mexican government. President Mariano Paredes, charging that

---

*Most of Taylor's force had been transported by sea from New Orleans to Corpus Christi; a mounted unit had moved by land.

the Americans were occupying Mexican territory, reinforced his army on the south bank to 8,000 troops, twice the size of Taylor's force, and in a proclamation dated April 23 declared a "defensive war" to expel the Anglo invaders. Two days later a Mexican column crossed the river and attacked an American reconnaissance party, killing eleven and capturing the survivors. Taylor announced the clash to Washington in a terse dispatch the following day: "Hostilities may now be considered as commenced."

While the general's news was traveling slowly northward, in Washington Polk was discussing with his cabinet the probability that the United States would have to resolve its problems with Mexico by war. There was no longer any hope of negotiating American grievances, the president declared. Although he thought the Mexicans might attack Taylor, he was not willing to wait for their action to inaugurate hostilities. He decided to ask Congress to declare war on the grounds that Mexico had not honored her obligation to pay the damage claims and had insulted the United States by rejecting the Slidell mission. While Polk was considering the draft of a war message, Taylor's dispatch arrived on May 9, announcing the attack on his force. Quickly and with elation the president recast his message to emphasize this development. Sending it to Congress on May 11, he charged that Mexico had "passed the boundary of the United States and shed American blood upon the American soil." Since war existed "by the act of Mexico herself," the United States had no recourse except to recognize the situation. "We are called upon by every consideration of duty and patriotism to vindicate with decision the honor, the rights, and the interest of our country," the president concluded. Nowhere in the message did he specifically state the objectives for which the nation should fight. He merely asked Congress to authorize him to prosecute the war to a "speedy and successful conclusion," which could mean expelling the Mexican "invaders," assuring the Rio Grande boundary, settling the damage claims— or conquering California and New Mexico.

Two days after receiving the president's message, on May 13, Congress declared that a state of war existed with Mexico. The vote was overwhelming in both houses: 40 to 2 in the Senate and 174 to 14 in the House. But many members voted for the declaration with great reluctance, and only because they felt that the troops on the Rio Grande had to be supported. Some legislators realized that a "first" had occurred in American history: the president had informed Congress of the existence of a war before war had been declared, and in demanding recognition of this condition had divested Congress of its war-making power. John C. Calhoun predicted the consequences of the precedent: "It sets the example, which will enable all future Presidents to bring about a state of things, in which Congress shall be forced, without deliberation or reflection, to declare war, however opposed to its convictions of justice or expediency."

Calhoun and other critics of Polk were right in ascribing to him a large share of responsibility for the events leading up to the war. However, they gave too much weight to these immediate events as causing the war and consequently magnified the president's role in them, which is what some later historians have also done. Polk alone did not "make" the war, nor did he conspire or stampede the nation into conflict. He was, rather, an agent of powerful and impersonal forces rooted in the past and in the national consciousness that irresistibly moved him and his country into war—the principal agent, it is true, and a willing one, but still only an instrument.

The origins of the war lay far back in history, in the beginning sweep of the American people across the continent and in their determination to press onward, no matter what physical or human barrier stood in their way. It was not merely a hunger for land that drove them, although this was a factor, nor a desire to achieve greater national glory, although this was present in their minds. They were also impelled by a mystique, or an idea—that it was their Manifest Destiny to bring, even to force, the benefits of American liberty upon "lesser" lands and peoples. It was the misfortune of Mexico to stand in the path of American expansion and to attempt to oppose it. "Miserable, inefficient Mexico," the poet Walt Whitman exclaimed, "what has she to do with the great mission of peopling the New World with a noble race? Be it ours, to achieve that mission!"

In his diplomatic maneuvering before the war Polk was seeking to attain legitimate national ends. Only the United States had the population and resources to settle California and New Mexico. They would fall to the United States sooner or later by a natural process. In resorting to war to realize them, Polk was only hastening an inevitable result.

AMERICAN WAR POLICY was never defined precisely or publicly. In debating the bill to declare war, members of Congress—either ignorant of Polk's purposes or desiring to conceal his ends—limited their remarks to threats of punishment to be visited upon the Mexican invaders. "Let us enter the Mexican territory and conquer a peace at the point of the bayonet," one senator cried. "Let us move on till we meet reasonable proposals from the Mexican Government."

The president himself was not completely decided on his objectives. Just as in conducting diplomacy he was inclined to improvise step by step, so in conducting war he was capable of moving from aim to aim, or retreating. He pronounced one objective, to compel Mexico to recognize the Rio Grande boundary. Another, and to him a more important one, was not proclaimed, or at least was not emphasized: to compel Mexico to agree to a peace in which she ceded the territory the United States had previously attempted to purchase, California and New Mexico. Polk considered still a third objective, to require Mexico to yield additional territory on her northern border, but finally rejected this as being too difficult to realize. He revealed these aggressive designs to his colleagues in the command system as he began to formulate strategy for the war.

Polk was determined to be a true commander in chief, to control every aspect of the war effort from the strategic level on down. He also scrutinized the civil functions of his office, trying to oversee the routine and details of all the executive departments. This spare, worn, and outwardly ordinary man was actually one of the strongest presidents of the century, possessed of an abnormal capacity for work and a fervid conviction that the chief executive should dominate the government. He brought his energy and resolve to the running of the war, maintaining constant contact with the War and Navy departments and demanding frequent reports from their heads, supervising the General Staff offices and prodding those in the area of supply to greater endeavors, selecting the commanders of all military expeditions, and checking on such relatively minor matters as the promotions of junior officers and the sailing dates of ships. Naturally he assumed he should take the lead in framing strategy.

On May 13, the day he signed the war bill, he summoned Secretary of War William L. Marcy and commanding general of the army Winfield Scott to a strategy conference. Little was decided at the meeting, but the following day the president outlined a plan of operations so detailed as to suggest considerable previous thinking on his part. The plan seemed logical and related to the requirements of policy. To attain the objective of acquiring New Mexico and California, American strategy had to be offensive in nature, and Polk proposed to occupy the two provinces as soon as adequate forces were available. He realized, however, that this limited action alone would not bring Mexico to terms. Therefore, as an added form of pressure he advocated reinforcing the army on the Rio Grande and placing it under Scott's command to invade the northern provinces of Mexico and, as he expressed it in his diary, to "seize and hold them until peace was made." Marcy and Scott agreed to the plan, and the latter consented to take the proffered command. While Polk was thus arranging the land strategy, he was also getting the war at sea under way. The commander of the Gulf squadron was ordered to blockade Mexican ports and if possible to occupy Tampico as a base of supply for the army that would be operating in Mexico. The commander of the Pacific squadron was instructed to execute his contingency orders to seize the port of San Francisco and blockade other California ports.

Polk had offered the command of the army in Texas to Scott only because he thought this was due to the senior general. However, he distrusted the huge and hulking soldier, viewing him accurately as a Whig aspirant for the presidency and fearing he would exploit his war record as a personal platform. He also doubted Scott's military capacities, thinking him "rather scientific and visionary in his views," and he saw his reservations confirmed when he re-

THE HISTORY OF AMERICAN WARS / 158

ceived the general's proposed plan of operations. Scott indicated he would spend the summer months in Washington organizing his expedition and would not advance into Mexico until September. His plea for time to prepare an adequate force infuriated Polk, who was convinced that a relatively small army could subdue the Mexicans. The president instructed Secretary Marcy to tell Scott to "proceed very soon to his post, or that I would supersede him in the command."

Marcy informed the general of the president's displeasure at the delay but did not communicate the threat of removal. Scott received the reprimand at the same time he learned that the administration had recommended to Congress a bill authorizing the appointment of two new major generals and four new brigadiers. Being abnormally protective of his prerogatives and inordinately suspicious of the motives of those he viewed as enemies, he jumped to the conclusion that the administration was plotting to staff the army with Democratic officers. "I smelt the rat," he said later. Being also a noted epistolary brawler, he immediately expressed his sense of outrage in a long letter to Marcy. It was a remarkable document, of a kind seldom received by a civilian superior in American history. Addressing the secretary but by implication the president, Scott declared that he was too old a soldier not to realize the importance of protecting himself against political intrigue. He ended it with an unmistakable meaning: "I do not desire to place myself in the most perilous of all positions:—*a fire upon my rear, from Washington, and the fire, in front, from the Mexicans.*"

What Scott hoped to accomplish with his blast can only be conjectured. He was probably attempting to gain a free hand in conducting his operations, to remove himself from any supervision by the civilian authorities. He was an early example of a type of soldier who has occasionally appeared in American history and is best described in a figure from another discipline: he was a military artist who was convinced that only he knew how to play the piece and who would play it his way with no interference. Officers like him have always posed problems of control to their civilian superiors, but Scott was dealing with a superior who would not permit such a problem to develop. Polk coldly remarked that Scott's bitter "partisan feelings" unfitted him for command, and Marcy was directed to order the general to remain in Washington and make "arrangements and preparations" for prosecuting the war, or in less polite terms, to confine himself to routine office duties. The command of the army in Texas would stay with Zachary Taylor.*

With the commanding general relegated to the sidelines, Polk had no

---

*Scott's letter was improper by military standards. Its tone justified a rebuke or even removal. However, Polk considered that the general had committed a political offense in criticizing the administration. Both Polk and Scott acted more like political rivals than like principals in a command system.

professional expert on whom he could call for advice. However, he did not seem to feel a need for such assistance. As had been his practice from the outset, he continued to take the lead in forming strategy. Now he discussed his plans with the cabinet, using it largely as a sounding board to test his views and usually reserving the ultimate decision to himself. Through this simple command system he achieved a remarkable coordination of the war effort. All his plans succeeded. The northern provinces of Mexico and California and New Mexico fell to American arms, but the Mexican government refused to admit defeat and come to the peace table. Polk then had to resort to another strategy and a more unlimited kind of war, and at this stage General Scott would again appear in the command structure and in a command function.

SOME AMERICANS opposed the war with Mexico, as, earlier, others had opposed the Revolution and the War of 1812. However, the opponents in this struggle were not as large a proportion of the population as in the previous conflicts, nor were they as well organized or as dangerous to the war effort. Theirs was a vocal and often a bitter opposition, but it was ineffective in influencing the conduct of the war.

The dissent was centered in the Whig party in the New England states, but it counted some Whigs in all sections. In addition to politicians, it included editors, clergymen, social reformers, antislavery leaders, and some of the leading literary figures of the day. New England contributed a disproportionately small fraction of the military forces. Most of the volunteers came from the Mississippi Valley, where the war drew its greatest support.

The Whig opposition was ineffective because most of the party's members of Congress felt they could not vote against appropriation bills to carry on the war. They might disapprove of what they considered Polk's partisan motives in desiring war or his surreptitious methods in precipitating hostilities, but they believed they had to support the war once it was begun. They demanded that the conflict be negotiated to an honorable conclusion, but they offered no alternative if Mexico continued to fight. In short, their opposition was politically inspired and their objective was to gain political capital. By denouncing "Mr. Polk's war" as unnecessary and unconstitutional they hoped to return their party to power.

Quite different motives influenced other critics of the war—the small band of "radical" Whigs in Congress, so called because they were antagonistic to slavery; and idealistic individuals who had no partisan axes to grind. These groups denounced the conflict as a war of conquest against a smaller country, a naked grab for land, and they demanded that it be stopped immediately with or without an "honorable" settlement. Typical of their expressions of disgust were resolutions adopted by the Massachusetts legislature in 1847, which declared that "such a war of conquest, so hateful in its objects, so wanton, unjust and unconstitutional . . . must be regarded as a war against freedom, against humanity, against justice. . . ." Some opponents went so far as to admit they desired an American defeat. "We only hope that, if blood has to flow, that it has been that of the Americans," an antislavery editor wrote, "and that the next news we hear will be that General Scott and his army are in the hands of the Mexicans."

The war's opponents were powerless to influence its course, but in the perspective of history their protest deserves notice. For the first time a sizable number of Americans opposed a war not for political or economic reasons but because they considered it unjust and immoral.

CHAPTER VIII

The Mexican War: The Campaigns

IN ENGAGING MEXICO the United States was for the first time fighting a weaker power. The American population was approximately 17 million, that of Mexico only 7 million. Although the Mexican regular army of 32,000 men outnumbered the American army of 8,000, the United States had a greater manpower reservoir and could put larger forces into the field. Moreover, the Mexican army was not as formidable as its numbers indicated. Its elaborate organization contained too many generals in relation to the total of enlisted men, and some of the senior officers were of poor quality, having risen to their place by bribery or intrigue. In sea power there was no comparison: the American navy of over seventy fighting vessels of all types dwarfed the minuscule Mexican fleet, which during the war dared not venture out of port.

The United States had other material advantages. Its burgeoning industrial economy was capable of producing most of the supplies required by the armed forces—small arms, artillery, uniforms, and the like—and supplies that could not be manufactured domestically were imported from Europe. The Mexican economy, in comparison, was primitive. Although a few factories existed, they were inadequate to support the needs of the army, and the government was accustomed to purchasing most of its weaponry from European countries. The American naval blockade of the Gulf Coast shut off this source of supply and forced Mexico to rely on the stock of weapons she had on hand.

Maintaining the blockade was only one of the important services performed by the navy during the war. Control of the seas enabled the United States to overcome its greatest disadvantage, the need to conduct an offensive war at a great distance from the home bases of men and supplies. The navy escorted the transports that carried American armies to Mexico, assisted the land forces in securing lodgments on the coast, and then guarded the captured ports to maintain a continuing flow of reinforcements and supplies. It is no exaggeration to say that without the navy the United States could not have carried on the war.*

In view of the American material strength, one may wonder why Mexico resorted to war, why she did not accept Polk's offer of compensation for territory that was of little value to her. Nations, however, do not compute their chances in war as realistically as do later historians, especially if they are a prideful people like the Mexicans. Mexican leaders were inordinately proud of the martial quality of their soldiers, who were undeniably brave and good fighters, and contemptuous of the Yankees. General Santa Anna reportedly threatened that if necessary he would plant his flag upon the Capitol at Washington, and a Mexican officer told an American diplomat that his country's cavalry could break infantry squares with their lassos alone. Mexico was quite as ready as the United States to resolve the difficulties between the two countries by war.

PRESIDENT POLK insisted to political intimates that the war would be a short one, lasting at the longest only a year. There was an element of political wishfulness in his analysis in addition to a miscalculation of Mexican powers of resistance. He feared that a long war might cause voters to turn against the Democratic party or enable Whig generals to win military reputations.† Although his prediction seemed foolish and rash to some observers, it turned out to be not far from the mark: hostilities lasted sixteen months from the time of the declaration of war to the capture of Mexico City.

Polk's recommendations were embodied in a bill enacted by Congress coincidentally with its declaration of war. This measure authorized the president to call for 50,000 volunteers, of whom 20,000 were to be enlisted immediately, "to serve for twelve months . . . or to the end of the War." General Scott had advised that the regular army be increased in size and constitute the chief fighting force, but Polk thought, with some justification, that the process of filling up the regular ranks would consume too much time. Congress did

---

*The Gulf squadron of twenty-nine vessels was believed to be the largest aggregation of ships ever assembled under the American flag. It contained one of the relatively new steam frigates, of which there were several in the navy. The authorized personnel strength of the sea arm during the war was 10,000 men, although only 8,000 were actually enlisted.

†Polk knew that Scott was a Whig, and to his disgust Taylor turned out to be one also. Hoping to reap some partisan benefit from the war, the president at one time considered asking Congress to create the rank of lieutenant general, intending to appoint to the post a prominent Democratic senator, Thomas Hart Benton of Missouri. He abandoned the scheme when he realized that Congress would not go along with it.

authorize an increase in strength of the regulars to 15,000 troops and eventually to 32,000. However, men electing the regular branch had to sign up for five years or the duration, and understandably most of those who wanted to fight Mexicans chose the volunteers.*

A total of 104,000 troops was raised during the war, the aggregate breaking down into 60,000 volunteers, 32,000 regulars, and 12,000 militiamen, who were used but briefly. Over half of the soldiers served for periods of twelve months or less, 65 percent of them if the militia are removed from the total. Volunteer units usually went home at the end of their term, and others had to be enlisted to take their place, a practice that delayed generals in conducting their campaigns. General Scott, when he finally got to Mexico, had to halt his campaign deep in enemy country for months while he discharged some units and waited for reinforcements. Because of the fluctuating rate of volunteer enlistments, the total number of troops under arms at a given time, volunteers and regulars, was probably never more than 50,000. As this amount had to be distributed among several armies operating in widely separated theaters, the size of each one was small. The largest single aggregation numbered only 14,000 men: Taylor commanded this many early in the war, and Scott, after borrowing part of Taylor's force, led about the same number in the final campaign. However, neither general could put his full strength into battle; units had to be detached to guard communications or garrison key points, leaving but 10,000 or even fewer men available for fighting. In most of the engagements the Americans were outnumbered.†

The president selected the army commanders and also had a large hand in choosing their subordinates, the divisional and brigade leaders, appointing some of them directly and passing on the assignment of others. In picking army commanders Polk turned to career officers in the regular army, either because he thought they were the most competent or, more probably, because he feared political repercussions if he went outside the service. Three generals directed armies: Taylor and Scott, who served in Mexico, and Stephen Kearny, who led a small column to New Mexico and then went on to California. A fourth officer, John Wool, exercised independent command briefly, taking a small force into northern Mexico. On meeting no resistance, he joined Taylor and became a divisional commander under him.

In selecting officers to command divisions and brigades, Polk had the greater freedom of being able to go outside the army to find qualified men. There were simply not enough regular officers to man the new units created

*Although the records are inadequate, it seems that few blacks served in the land forces. They were barred from joining the regular army and in practically all states would not have been welcomed into the volunteer units.

†The estimated number of service deaths from all causes during the war is something over 13,000, 14 percent of the 92,000 under arms and thus a fairly high proportion.

during the war, and some of those available were not competent to command units as large as a division, which in this war appeared for the first time as a combat group.* Polk did name some professionals for division command— William J. Worth and David E. Twiggs, officers of seniority and experience, were examples—but in filling other posts and in finding brigade commanders he took men out of civilian life. His standards were not clear. Some of them had been officers in their state militia, but others had as a qualification only service to the Democratic party or friendship with the president. Interestingly, despite their backgrounds, the level of ability among the subordinate officers did not vary significantly. The professional Worth was probably the best handler of troops in the army, but he was also erratic and quarrelsome and was embroiled in almost constant controversy with his superiors. Twiggs was an aggressive fighter, but his only idea of tactics was a frontal assault, and he was likely to blunder into traps. Some of the civilian officers proved incompetent, the worst of them being Gideon Pillow, Polk's former law partner. But others developed into highly capable leaders, comparable to any of the professionals. John A. Quitman, a Mississippi Democratic politician, became one of Scott's most trusted division commanders. Considered as a group, the unit officers were competent and probably the ablest collection of subordinates yet to appear in an American war.

The army commanders were competent, and one, Scott, merited an even higher mark. Two of the others had limited command experience. Kearny led his small force to California capably and handled it adeptly after arriving there, and perhaps he would have performed equally well if he had commanded a larger levy; but he was not tested by heavy administrative burdens or in the ordeal of battle. Wool conducted his small column ably in its long march into Mexico, but he commanded too briefly and uneventfully to reveal how he could react to pressure.

The commanders of the two largest armies, Taylor and Scott, were fairly tested, and their conduct in the council and on the field provides an adequate basis for evaluating them and also affords an insight into the quality of American generalship before the Civil War. Taylor was the first hero of the war, and his reputation survived beyond its end. He was of the stuff of which legends are made. Thickset and corpulent in body, and with short legs, he seemed the very model of what a general should not look like, and he accentuated his image by the costumes he affected. He scorned the wearing of a uniform and appeared in a dusty gingham or linen coat, his head topped by a straw hat or an oilcloth cap. In speech he was rough and ungrammatical, and he delighted to aim pungent barbs at "spick and span" professional officers and self-important West Pointers. His soldiers loved him—he was "Old Zack" or "Old

---

*Divisions had existed in previous wars, but they were largely administrative units.

Rough and Ready," who looked like a cherished father or uncle back home. The public loved him too. He was a soldier, but he acted like a civilian. He was a professional, but he seemed to be contemptuous of specialized knowledge, a characteristic that most Americans admired.

Taylor's reputation was in part deserved. He was a brave and inspiring leader on the field, and no other general in the war was so capable of arousing the devotion of troops. In battle he was aggressive, and although only a fair tactician, he knew how and when to put his men in. He also had defects. He was a mediocre strategist and a worse administrator. His greatest shortcoming was that he would not admit the handicap of his lack of technical knowledge. Largely unread in military science, he was reluctant to take advice from officers who were so read, particularly West Pointers. He preferred to throw troops against a strong enemy line rather than ask the academy engineers serving with him to reconnoiter it. He was victorious in every battle, but his successes may have been as much the result of luck and the valor of the troops as of his own design.

Scott too won victories, a sequence of triumphs that ended the war and were clearly the result of his design. Yet he failed to attain the fame and popular devotion that fell to Taylor. The reason lay in his personality, which was such as to repel rather than attract a largely volunteer army and an unsophisticated public. In contrast to Taylor, Scott did not seem "folksy" or like anybody back home. Towering four inches above six feet in height and weighing at least 250 pounds, he was always resplendent in full uniform when he appeared before troops, and he insisted on the observance of every detail of military punctilio, from which he derived an obvious delight. The soldiers derisively called him "Old Fuss and Feathers," and although they might respect him for winning objectives with small losses of life, they were not likely to set up a cheer when he rode by. His ability to achieve success without losing many men did not impress the populace, who thought that a fighting general should incur heavy casualties, as Taylor did. To the average citizen Scott appeared to be what Polk had thought him, too "scientific."

Scott was a scientific soldier. Appreciating his disadvantage in not having had a formal military education, he had read widely in the available literature, particularly in the writings of the eighteenth century, which stressed maneuver and the occupation of territory as the primary elements of strategy and cautioned against battle confrontation unless imperatively necessary. This was the strategy he would employ in Mexico, and for him in his situation, leading a small army in an enemy country and pursuing a limited objective—bringing the enemy to accept peace—it was the most appropriate. In executing it, he would show that he was a complete soldier—a consummate strategist, tactician, and logistician. His march of 260 miles from Vera Cruz on the Gulf Coast to Mexico City was a minor masterpiece and entitles him to be ranked with the great American captains.*

Not one of the generals, not even the professionals, had received a formal military education. However, a large number of educated officers were present in the lower command levels, the several hundred West Point graduates who now experienced their first taste of actual war. They appeared in all branches, in the engineering corps, the infantry, the artillery, and the cavalry, and they provided a store of expert knowledge that had not been available in previous wars. Although some senior officers failed to make adequate use of their skills, others turned to them gratefully. Scott in particular recognized their value, especially that of his engineers, whom he assigned to conduct reconnaissances and make maps and whom he also drew into strategy conferences. His engineers and other academy graduates serving with him constituted, in fact, a field and planning staff, the first such group to approach adequacy in an American war. Scott called them his "little cabinet," and after the war he said that without the contributions of "our graduated cadets" the conflict would have lasted "four or five years" longer than it had.

THE WAR COST the United States $118.5 million, of which $100 million was consumed in direct expenses; the remaining sum consisted of $15 million paid to Mexico under the peace treaty as compensation for the loss of California and New Mexico and $3.5 million of damage claims against Mexico that the United States assumed. The expenditure was small in relation to the wealth of the nation, and the government should have been able to defray the war costs with relative ease, meeting a substantial share of them from current revenues and thus avoiding the necessity of having to borrow large amounts. However, this method would have required the Polk administration to seek an increase in current revenues by asking Congress to enact additional taxes, and this the president refused to do. His reluctance to face up to this need was one of the few instances in which he acted timidly, and represented one of the few failures of his presidency.

Polk explained that he did not want to increase taxes because the war would be short and could be prosecuted to a decision without placing additional burdens on the people. He may have believed, or have convinced himself, that he was influenced only by economic considerations, but a suspicion persists that his motives were primarily political, that he thought enactment of a tax bill would damage the prospects of his party. The taxing power of the federal government was a rarely used instrument, and the mass of people of

---

*Scott completed his movement without a reverse in six months, with a field force that numbered only 10,000 men. In 1861–63 it would take a French army of 30,000 regulars eighteen months to travel the same distance, and en route the French suffered a bad defeat.

the time had never felt its effect: not since 1817 had the government levied duties that reached a considerable number of persons—excise, stamp, inheritance, or other like taxes. To reimpose a national system of taxes would be to break with past practice, and Polk appeared to fear that voters would react negatively. Apparently it did not occur to him to appeal to the patriotism of the people and ask them to make a financial sacrifice.

The only income the government derived through current sources during the war came from customs and public land sales. These monies were small in amount and barely sufficient to support the normal peacetime operations of the government; they could sustain only a fraction of the new expenses required by the war. The government had to have money immediately to begin the war and then more to support the operation. To secure the necessary sums it resorted to issuing treasury notes and floating large loans. The Treasury Department had little trouble in placing its bonds—the banking community considered them profitable investments—but the process was a costly one in that it left the country with an unnecessary debt. Such an undue reliance on borrowing was possible only because the war ended quickly. If the conflict had lasted much longer, the Polk administration would have faced serious financial problems. Continued borrowing might have strained the resources of the banks and certainly would have become more costly. To ask Congress for enactment of a tax bill would have been to admit an earlier failure of judgment and hence to invite defeat. It was fortunate for President Polk that his prediction of a short war turned out to be accurate.

The monies obtained by the government were expended to provide the usual matériel of war—weapons, ammunition, uniforms, rations, and the like. Most of these items were secured in the United States, a few, like small-arms weapons, by requisition from government arsenals, the majority by purchase from private manufactories. In placing orders for many articles, the government speeded up delivery by using a revolutionary new device in communication, the telegraph, sending its requests over the more than 1,000 miles of telegraph lines that linked the cities of the industrial Northeast.

The supplies that were thus procured had to be moved long distances to field depots on the Gulf Coast and in Texas for transshipment to the battle zones. In accomplishing this endeavor the government took advantage of recent technological developments that had quickened transportation. The growing railroad system was of limited use in the war: although lines webbed the northeastern states, they were just beginning to reach the Mississippi Valley and had not yet crossed the river itself. Of more importance were the steamboats that plied the Ohio and Mississippi rivers and the coastal waters, carrying substantial supplies to New Orleans and ports in Texas and even in Mexico. So necessary to the war effort was water transport that the quartermaster's department maintained its own fleet of seventy steam and sailing vessels.

The development of steam power enabled abundant supplies to reach the rear of the battle zones quickly, but no similar rapid facilities were available in the zones themselves. American armies operating in Mexico relied on the horse-and-wagon transportation used in previous wars. Even a small force required a large number of wagons to carry its assorted gear: one wagon for each ten soldiers was the ratio favored by most generals. An insufficient stock was on hand at the outset of the conflict, about one hundred wagons that had been commissioned by the quartermaster general in 1845. This official hurriedly ordered the construction of over a thousand additional vehicles, seeking out every firm in the country that made wagons and announcing that price was no object if delivery was quick. He saw his orders completed within a few months and with some justification was able to boast that his department now had more wagons "than the service required."*

The problem of the wagons illustrates the way that the heads of the War Department bureaus, the officers of the General Staff, functioned during the war. They had not engaged in any preplanning as to how they would operate —nobody in the command structure had instructed them to be prepared—and they had to improvise procedures, or scramble for supplies, after hostilities started. But once they were given an assignment, most of them had the technical proficiency to execute it. Those officers charged with producing and distributing supplies were particularly effective. Shortages occurred occasionally, but generally the armies were adequately supported.

American forces were especially well equipped with weapons, the available supply being larger than in any previous conflict. There was, however, a difference in quality in the small arms carried by regulars and volunteers, with the latter, surprisingly, having the superior gun. In the years immediately preceding the war, an important transition in small-arms manufacture had been occurring in European countries and in the United States: the mercury cap was being substituted for the flintlock as a firing mechanism, and the percussion musket was taking the place of the flintlock musket. The new device was more reliable than the flintlock—a percussion arm could be fired with reasonable confidence in rain or snow—and government arsenals in the United States had stopped making flintlock muskets in favor of percussion weapons, in addition to converting accumulated stores of flintlocks to take mercury caps. On the eve of the war an ample supply of the percussions was available to the regular army, but few were issued. General Scott objected to them because they had not been sufficiently tested to prove their worth in field use.

No such doubts restrained the volunteer officers who raised units in their states and led them into national service. These men, coming out of civilian

*The temporary shortage of wagons threatened to delay General Taylor's advance into Mexico, forcing him to resort to hiring 1,900 pack mules.

life, were more aware than regular officers of the technological changes occurring in American industry and more receptive to innovations in weaponry. They grasped quickly the superiority of percussion muskets and insisted to their state governments that the volunteer troops be provided with the new weapons. Few states cared to resist the demand, coming as it often did from influential politicians turned soldiers, and the volunteers went to Mexico better armed than the regulars, who still bore flintlocks. Percussion muskets were eventually issued to the regulars, as the advantage of the guns became apparent, and in some battles they were in the hands of a majority of the soldiers. The percussions, like the flintlocks, had a smooth bore and hence a range no longer than the older weapons; however, their greater reliability produced a more constant rate of firepower.

Artillery differed but little from that employed in the Revolution or the War of 1812. Field artillery still consisted of muzzle-loading, smoothbore pieces of limited range. However, there were significant changes in tactics, adapted from European systems. The field arm was now highly mobile. Batteries were hauled into battle by horses, and during combat they were maneuvered with almost the flexibility of cavalry. Sometimes called the "flying" artillery, the American batteries were superior to the Mexican service not only in mobility but also in the number and weight of their guns, and in several battles the artillery was responsible for the American victory.*

ZACHARY TAYLOR'S ARMY on the Rio Grande fought two battles before war was declared by Congress. Immediately after informing Washington of the Mexican attack on his reconnaissance party, Taylor learned that other enemy forces were operating north of the river and threatening to cut communications with his field base at Point Isobel, 26 miles up the coast. If they should succeed, Taylor's 4,000-man force at Fort Texas would soon be bereft of supplies and unable to maintain its position. The general therefore decided to march to Point Isobel with the bulk of his army, make that place secure against attack, and return with added supplies to Fort Texas. Leaving at the fort about a third of his troops, he set out for Point Isobel on May 1, and after spending a week there, began his trip back accompanied by 200 supply wagons. On May 8, when he was barely started, he found a Mexican force barring his way at Palo Alto, about 4,000 troops commanded by General Mariano Arista, who had come up from Matamoros. The Mexicans, outnumbering the Americans almost two to one, and eager to prove their superiority over the Anglos, attacked with impetuous bravery, the infantry advancing in lines and the cavalry, many of

*The Mexican army possessed only a few heavy pieces, along with a number of lighter guns of varying age and quality; its artillerists, by and large, were indifferently trained. Mexican foot soldiers were armed predominantly with flintlocks, although some carried percussion weapons.

the riders armed in the romantic tradition with lances, trying to take the defenders in flank. They never got close to the American line. Taylor's artillery blasted every attempt with fearful losses and, as the general admitted, was responsible for the victory. After suffering over 600 casualties, the Mexicans retreated. American losses were only some 50 men.

On the following day Taylor resumed his march and early in the afternoon encountered Arista again at Resaca de la Palma, a dry riverbed surrounded by ravines and thick chaparral. Here the Mexicans had dug in, and this time they intended to force the Americans to come to them. Taylor was anxious to get through to Fort Texas, which he had learned was under enemy siege, and he sent his troops forward in attack. Because of the nature of the terrain, he could not make full use of his artillery or give much centralized direction to the assault, which developed into an infantry battle of small parties. The Americans rooted the Mexicans out of position after position, and the defenders, demoralized under the pounding, finally fled. Arista suffered close to 1,000 casualties (American losses were about 120 killed and wounded), and large numbers of his men deserted on the retreat, which stopped only when it reached Matamoros. Taylor returned in triumph to Fort Texas, now renamed Fort Brown in honor of the slain officer who had directed its successful defense. He probably could have captured Arista's army if he had continued on to Matamoros.

Taylor was urged by several of his officers to occupy Matamoros, but he demurred and remained at Fort Brown over a week. On May 18 he crossed the river and took possession of the town, which the Mexicans abandoned at his approach. He gave as his reason for delaying the lack of any pontoon bridge equipment—rubber-covered small boats lashed together to form a span, a device that had been developed during the Second Seminole War. This was probably an excuse, as he eventually crossed without pontoons, using boats rounded up in the area. A more probable explanation is that he was in doubt as to what the government wanted him to do. He had previously told Washington that if war came it should be carried into the enemy's country, and as a likely objective he had fixed on Monterrey, one of the principal towns in northeastern Mexico and a center of roads radiating to all parts of the region. However, he had received no order to advance, and while awaiting instructions, he did not move very far beyond Matamoros.

The instructions were delayed partly because of the time required to transmit a communication from Washington to the Rio Grande, usually two to three weeks. Moreover, although President Polk decided immediately to order the Rio Grande army to invade Mexico, he intended that Scott rather than Taylor lead it. But then Polk and Scott had fallen into the rancorous dispute that led the president to conclude that Old Fuss and Feathers was unfit for field command and to confine him to desk duty. Although Polk also had doubts about Taylor's ability, there was no recourse but to leave him in command, and it was only after reaching this decision that he could assign a definite mission to the general.

The directives Taylor eventually received must have caused him to wonder whether the planners in Washington had a clearly thought out strategy. Secretary Marcy, writing for the president, suggested that Taylor move southwestward and occupy Monterrey. This was definite enough and accorded with the general's own thinking, but Marcy went on to speculate that the capture of Monterrey might not be enough to bring Mexico to ask for peace. In that event, could Taylor advance farther south and possibly to Mexico City itself? And if such a move was not feasible, should American efforts be directed to seizing a port on the coast, Tampico or Vera Cruz, and striking from it at Mexico City? In posing these questions to Taylor, Marcy revealed that the administration was beginning to doubt that its limited strategy of holding a line in northern Mexico would achieve its policy objective.

Old Zack refused to give an opinion on the matter of seizing a base on the coast: the making of grand strategy was not to his taste. But he did avow his readiness to capture Monterrey. His army had been reinforced to over 14,000, and he proposed to move the bulk of it westward to Camargo on the Rio Grande, marching the men and sending his heavier stores on river steamboats. He would establish a supply base at Camargo and from there would advance on Monterrey. However, it would be impossible for him to continue on to Mexico City, he warned Washington. The distance between Camargo and the enemy capital was approximately 1,000 miles, and a line of communication that long could not be maintained. Therefore he would confine his operations to "cutting off the northern provinces." Taylor was correct in emphasizing the logistical difficulties involved in conducting an offensive from northern Mexico, but he may have had an additional reason for refusing to be drawn into one. He was obsessively convinced that the Polk administration was not giving him proper support, because back in the states he was being groomed as a presidential candidate by prominent Whig politicians. His victories had made him a national hero, and although his political preferences were unknown, the Whigs claimed him as one of their own. Outwardly coy at their approaches, the general was actually highly receptive—and was persuaded that his partisan commander in chief resented his fame and wanted him to fail. His attitude was another expression of the poisonous jealousies engendered among the generals by the political atmosphere in which the war was conducted.

Although Taylor started part of his army up the Rio Grande early in June, he was not able to assemble his full force at Camargo until August, and he did not begin an advance toward Monterrey, about 125 miles distant, until late in the month. He moved with a column of over 6,000 troops, half of them regulars and half volunteers, and four batteries of field artillery but only three heavy or siege guns. His failure to take more of the big pieces reflected one of his shortcomings as a general: he would not trouble to secure adequate information about an objective he was to attack, and he relied too strongly on the ability of his troops to storm a strong point with the bayonet. He was approaching a place of extraordinary strength. Monterrey was a city of stone, set in a mountain pass and protected by field fortifications. In it waited General Pedro de Ampudia, with a Mexican army of 7,000 well equipped with artillery. The Americans would need siege guns.

Taylor arrived at Monterrey on September 19, and after receiving reports from his engineers on the defenses, he decided to attack on the following day. His battle plan indicated that he was somewhat impressed by reports of the strength of the place. Dividing his force, he sent a column under General Worth to his right and westward to deliver a flank assault while he drove at the city from the front. Although he hoped that the flanking movement would divide the enemy's attention, he intended to rely mainly on a bayonet charge by his own men. He was contemptuous of the Mexican fieldworks in his front, as he revealed in an order that is surely one of the most casual battle directives in the history of war: "Colonel lead the head of your column off the left, keeping well out of reach of the enemy's shot, and if you think (or you find) that you can take any of them little Forts down there with the bay'net you do it—but consult with Major Mansfield [an engineer officer], you'll find him down there."

Both attacks succeeded, but only after three days of hard fighting and at a heavy cost in casualties. The Americans broke through the ring of outer fortifications and the city walls and then in house-to-house fighting pressed the Mexicans into the center of the town. At this point, on September 24, Ampudia, who had also sustained large losses, offered to yield the city on condition that his troops be permitted to march out in safety and that an eight-week armistice would prevail. Curiously, Taylor agreed to this proposal. In reporting his concurrence to Washington, he explained that he had incurred damaging casualties, a total of over 800, and that he probably could not have taken the city by continued assault. His action infuriated Polk, who declared that Taylor must have been mad to let the Mexican army escape and ordered the armistice terminated and hostilities resumed. The general, more than ever convinced that he was serving an ungrateful administration, responded by moving 1,000 men westward to occupy Saltillo, another road center. He was still determined to observe a limited strategy of holding territory.

While Taylor was establishing his defensive line, two other offensives, both planned by the president, were getting under way. In November the Gulf squadron under Commodore David Conner seized Tampico, which Polk and Marcy hoped to convert into a base for an advance inland. The Mexicans yielded the town without a defense, knowing it could not be used for the American purpose—the roads from Tampico led to no vital area. The captors also soon realized that the port offered no strategic advantage; nevertheless, an army garrison was placed in the town, and several months later it would serve as a staging point in Scott's campaign.

The other offensive moved on land and was directed at the state of Chihuahua. Polk had been informed that the people of the region were disaffected under Mexican rule and would welcome the Americans as deliverers, and he thought that possession of the province would increase the pressure on the Mexico City government to make peace. Accordingly, an army of 3,000 was assembled at San Antonio, Texas, under the command of General John Wool, whose force was ready to move by October. As Wool marched southward, encumbered by a large wagon train, he encountered no opposition. The Mexican forces in Chihuahua retired, and civilians along the way, according to one of Wool's officers, treated the invaders with "nothing but kindness and hospitality." Deciding that Chihuahua could be taken by a small force at any time, Wool won permission to join Taylor. He arrived at Parras, west of Saltillo, in December, having accomplished a remarkable march of 900 miles. American forces now held a long line in northeastern Mexico, extending from Matamoros to Parras, and one of Polk's objectives had been achieved.

THE ACQUISITION of New Mexico and California was the primary policy objective of the Polk administration, and it was to attain this end that all the military movements planned by the president were directed. Thus, Taylor was dispatched into northern Mexico not to secure territory for permanent retention but, by occupying part of the country, to force Mexico to cede the provinces. However, Polk was not satisfied to exert merely an indirect pressure upon Mexico. To ensure that the United States would retain New Mexico and California, he proposed to occupy them with American forces.*

Movements to conquer the provinces were set in operation in May, 1846, immediately after war was declared. Orders went to the commander of the Pacific squadron, Commodore J. D. Sloat, to execute his previous instructions to seize San Francisco and other ports. Another directive went to Colonel (soon to be brevet brigadier) Stephen Kearny, the commandant at the far western post of Fort Leavenworth (in present Kansas near the Missouri border). Kearny, with only a regiment of regulars under him, was ordered to call on the governor of Missouri for volunteers, and when he had a force he judged sufficient, to march to New Mexico and occupy Santa Fe and other towns. Shortly he received an additional order, to continue to California after completing his work in New Mexico and there to cooperate with the navy in reducing the province.

Kearny assembled his force quickly, having available by the middle of

---

*Again, attention is called to the extensive area of New Mexico. It included the present states of New Mexico, Arizona, Utah, and Nevada, and parts of Colorado and Wyoming.

June some 1,800 troops, including his regulars and Missouri volunteers, some of whom were mounted. Giving this aggregation the somewhat grand title of "Army of the West," he began his long march late in the month, and making good time (averaging 100 miles a week), he entered New Mexico in August. Although the governor of the province had threatened to fight the invaders to the death, he retired hastily at their approach, and Kearny occupied Sante Fe on August 16 without firing a shot. The inhabitants seemed resigned to American rule, as did the residents of other communities, and the apparent calm persuaded Kearny that only a small force was required to hold the province. He therefore decided to detach a column of 1,000 mounted Missouri volunteers under the command of Colonel Alfred W. Doniphan to occupy Chihuahua; and knowing that a relief officer was on the way, he determined on the latter's arrival to move to California with 300 troops.*

As it turned out, Kearny did not wait either to greet his relief officer or to see the Chihuahua expedition get under way. Becoming impatient to reach California, he left Santa Fe late in September with his small column. On October 6, while still in New Mexico, he met a courier from California on his way to Washington with a dispatch from the commander of the Pacific squadron. The messenger carried surprising but reassuring news: California had already been occupied by American forces. Kearny naturally assumed that he would need only a small force to garrison the conquered province, and sending the bulk of his contingent back to Santa Fe, he resumed his march with an escort of only 100.†

The courier's appraisal of the situation in California had applied when he left the province in late August—American forces were indeed in control of the principal towns, and the native population seemed to acquiesce to American rule. But a formidable revolt then broke out, and Kearny would arrive to find an area torn by conflict.

The war in California began amidst confusion and doubts—the American representatives there, because of their isolation from Washington, were not certain that war had been declared—and it was conducted by an odd and divided command structure and force that is unique in the annals of military history. The first events were set in motion by Captain John C. Frémont, the leader of the exploring expedition that appeared in the province early in 1846.

---

*The situation in New Mexico was not quite as secure as Kearny had thought. In January, after his departure, a revolt broke out; it was, however, quickly suppressed.

†The Chihuahua expedition, which did not get under way until December, was one of the most dramatic episodes of the war. "Doniphan's Thousand," after defeating a Mexican force, occupied Chihuahua in early March. Then, because the terms of the men were almost up, they were ordered to join Taylor at Parras, from where they were taken to the coast and shipped home. In their movement from Missouri to New Mexico and Mexico, they must have covered 3,500 miles. It was a striking physical and logistical feat, although it had no important effect on the course of the war.

Ordered by nervous local officials to depart, he had moved northward toward the Oregon boundary, but in June he returned and attempted to incite the American settlers and whatever Californians would join with him to revolt (he claimed later that he had been acting on orders brought to him recently by a messenger from Polk, but he apparently went beyond the instructions). Although few natives supported him, he and his party and the settlers proclaimed on July 4 the independence of California and hoisted its emblem, the Bear Flag. Immediately afterward news came that war had been declared, and the rebels hastily pulled down their flag and ran up the Stars and Stripes and proclaimed that they were now in the service of the United States.

In the meantime, Commodore Sloat, who was in ailing health and expecting a relief officer, was anxiously awaiting word of the war so that he could execute his contingency orders. Early in July he learned of the battles of Palo Alto and Resaca de la Palma, and assuming that a state of war must exist, he occupied San Francisco and Monterey. At this point his replacement arrived, Commodore Robert Stockton, who bore certain information that war existed and who had been instructed to grasp as much of the interior as he could. But before Stockton could move, Frémont marched into Monterey with his followers, now styled the California Battalion, and announced that he was prepared to cooperate with the navy in reducing the province. However, he would cooperate as supreme commander, a demand which Stockton resisted. The controversy, a persistent one in American wars when the two services have had to act in concert, was resolved by an agreement that Stockton would act as overall commander but Frémont would retain tactical control of his own men.

Once the command issue was settled, the Americans turned to the more important matter of conquering California. They had to operate with a small force: Stockton's approximately 400 sailors, Frémont's column of about the same number, and two companies of regulars that had been dispatched by sea. Nevertheless, the occupation was accomplished easily and quickly. The Californians offered no resistance, and the Mexican government could spare no troops to defend a place so distant. By the middle of August the Americans were in possession not only of the principal seaports but also of Los Angeles and other inland towns, and the conquest seemed complete. This was the situation that had been reported to Kearny.

The elation of the victors was suddenly shattered in September. A secretly organized revolt erupted in the towns of the south, and by early December, when Kearny arrived, the rebels had pressed the Americans back into the seaport cities. Kearny, with his tiny force, could do little to aid Stockton, who, indeed, declined to take direction from the general, but the commodore and Frémont were eventually able to reorganize their forces and recover Los Angeles and the other lost towns. In January, 1847, the rebel leaders agreed to cease their resistance, and California again and finally came under American control.

By the end of 1846 the United States had achieved the strategic objectives that Polk set forth in the spring. American forces occupied the principal cities of northeastern Mexico and held a secure defensive line in that area. Other forces were in possession, or apparently in possession, of New Mexico and California. The president had thought that when his goals had been realized, Mexico would recognize defeat; but its government had not asked for peace and gave no indication of intending to negotiate. The problem posed by Mexico's attitude was expressed aptly by a Whig senator. "Mexico is an ugly enemy," he said. "She will not fight—and will not treat."

The stubbornness of Mexico in the face of great adversity was a reflection of the pride of her leaders and people, the same pride that led them to think they could engage a nation as powerful as the United States, and that still ruled them and made them think they could win. This arrogance was exemplified in the person of the man who late in 1846 emerged as the dominating figure in the government, General Santa Anna, a veteran and powerful politician and the country's ablest military leader. Ironically, Santa Anna was able to gain his place because of an action by President Polk. He had been living in exile in Havana, Cuba, at the beginning of the war, after one of the frequent revolutions that characterized Mexican politics had brought a government hostile to him to power. Through intermediaries he made it known to Washington that if permitted to return to Mexico, he could recover control and would be amenable to concluding a satisfactory peace treaty. Polk, eager to end the war quickly, swallowed this bait, and gave orders to the naval officers in the Gulf that if Santa Anna attempted to elude the blockade he was to be allowed "to pass freely." Santa Anna landed at Vera Cruz in August and announced that he had come to fight for his country. Within a month he was named commander of the Mexican army, and by the end of the year he had taken over the government as president.

The refusal of Mexico to discuss peace terms forced Polk and his advisers to consider whether a different strategy would be necessary to end the war. Some members of the cabinet, as well as General Taylor, advocated a variation of the present limited strategy: strengthen the defensive line in northern Mexico, organize territorial governments in New Mexico and California, and throw the initiative for continuing the war back onto Mexico. The proposal carried a certain logic. The United States could undoubtedly maintain its positions, and eventually Mexico would become tired of fighting and agree to peace. Its drawback was that it required a popular patience to support a war of indeterminable duration—an indulgence, Polk suspected, that would not be forthcoming. The president was convinced that a bolder strategy would have to be employed to bring Mexico to terms, and in October he discussed with the cabinet a plan to land an expedition at Vera Cruz, with a view that this force might be able to penetrate inland. Coincidentally, General Scott, who had been a model of decorum since his subordination, presented a plan to occupy Vera Cruz and move from there to Mexico City. In November Polk decided to adopt this plan, and although he still distrusted Scott's abilities, he felt he had no choice but to name the general commander of the offensive.

Scott asked for a minimum of 10,000 troops to conduct his operation, and Polk agreed to the number. But nowhere near this total was available in the United States. Some units could be assembled from posts in the Northeast and the South, but the bulk of the projected force would have to be drawn from an existing army. The obvious source was Taylor's army, and accordingly, with the president's concurrence, Scott went to the Rio Grande in December to tell Old Zack that he would have to take some of his troops. When Scott arrived at Camargo, Taylor was absent, ostensibly attending to defensive arrangements farther south but probably seeking to avoid a meeting with his superior. Scott detached 8,000 of Taylor's troops, ordering them to rendezvous at Tampico and at the Brazos Islands near the mouth of the Rio Grande. With this accession Scott had over 14,000 under his command. Taylor was left with slightly under 7,000 and orders from Scott to stand on the defensive at Monterrey. When Taylor returned and read these orders, he was enraged. Now, he thought, Scott was trying to efface him, as Polk had tried. In a state of suspicion bordering upon morbidity, he decided to interpret the orders as "advice" that he could observe or not as he pleased. Leaving garrisons at Monterrey and Saltillo, he moved with 5,000 troops to a hacienda called Agua Nueva, 18 miles south of Saltillo. What he hoped to accomplish is not clear, but if he was trying to tempt an attack, he succeeded. His troops would shortly have to fight the hardest battle of the war.

Santa Anna was aware from reports in American newspapers of the impending movement on Vera Cruz, and from captured documents he learned of the division of the invading forces and of the small number of troops left to Taylor. Assuming that Vera Cruz could hold out against Scott, he decided to gather a large army and march northward to smash Taylor, after which he would return to face Scott. Some 200 miles south of Agua Nueva, he collected 20,000 troops, and early in February, 1847, he moved forward. His way led through a barren desert waste, and many of his men dropped off on the trek. Even so, he approached Taylor's position with 15,000 men, three times the number of the American army.

Warned that a large enemy force was advancing on him, Taylor fell back to Buena Vista, a few miles south of Saltillo. There the road north ran through a network of ridges, ravines, and gullies that constituted a natural defense, partially nullifying the Mexican superiority in numbers. Despite the strength of the position, Santa Anna believed he could carry it, and for two days, on February 22–23, he sent his men forward in attack after attack. Several times the American line seemed about to break, but in each case it held because of the timely arrival of reserves or of the mobile artillery that moved rapidly from spot to spot. "Without our artillery we could not have maintained our position a single hour," an infantry general admitted after the battle. Both sides suffered heavy casualties, the Mexicans losing probably 2,000 men killed and wounded to about 750 for the Americans. Although the proportion of losses was about the same, Santa Anna had had more than enough. On the night of the second day he withdrew from the field and began the long march back to his base, proclaiming as he went southward that he had destroyed the Americans at Buena Vista.

If Santa Anna had actually won, he might have been able to break up the entire American line in northeastern Mexico and threaten Texas; such a success would have forced the cancellation of the Vera Cruz expedition and prolonged the war indefinitely. As it was, any threat to the lower Rio Grande was ended, and the Vera Cruz offensive was not interrupted. Taylor had conducted the battle with great tactical skill, moving his units with a sure hand from one weakened place on the line to another and inspiring his men by his calm presence. But his strategic conception had been highly deficient. If he had remained at Monterrey, his position to receive an attack would have been much stronger. Indeed, he might not even have had to fight a battle.

IN PLANNING HIS CAMPAIGN, Scott was conscious that his objectives, although large, were limited. His purpose was to capture the enemy capital, not to retain it but to persuade the enemy government to halt the war. He believed that Mexico City so completely dominated the political life of the country that its fall would cause all resistance to collapse. Just as his objective was limited, so were his ways of making war. He did not punish or destroy the cities he occupied. Instead, he proclaimed to their inhabitants that he came in a spirit of conciliation and would protect their rights and property. Nor did he attempt to smash Mexican armies in bloody battles. Although he fought when he had to, he avoided battle if he could, achieving victory by turning the enemy out of position by flanking movements. He thus conserved the lives of his own men and brought them before Mexico City with remarkably small losses.

Scott rendezvoused his troops first at Tampico and then at the Lobos Islands, about 50 miles south of the port city and a few miles off the coast, where he conferred with Commodore Conner on landing procedures at Vera Cruz. On March 2 the men were loaded on Conner's vessels, and the flotilla set sail. Three days later the Americans saw the domes and cupolas of Vera Cruz rising above its hexagonal walls, and on approaching closer, the castle fortress of San Juan de Ulúa in the harbor. Many of Scott's young soldiers had never seen a foreign city, and they thought this one exotically beautiful. They would continue to marvel at the alien charm of Mexico as they pressed inland, the more literate reflecting that they were following in the path trodden by Cortez's Spanish conquerors three centuries earlier. It was an age when men could still think of war as a romantic adventure.

Viewed as a military problem, Vera Cruz seemed to present formidable obstacles to an attacker. Behind its walls and in the Ulúa fortress was a garrison of about 5,000 and an array of over 200 guns. However, its appearance was deceptive. Some of the walls were in a state of disrepair, many of the guns were unserviceable, and the supply of powder was scanty. Moreover, the strongest defenses were on the sea side; those on the land side were more vulnerable, and it was against them that Scott planned to operate, landing his army on a beach three miles to the south and coming at the city from its strategic rear. Always conscious of the smallness of his force, he ruled out trying to take Vera Cruz by storm. Instead, he intended to rely on the slower but surer method of siege, mounting artillery to batter the walls and moving the guns behind infantry protection closer and closer to the target.

Scott and Commodore Conner made careful preparations for the landing, the first joint amphibious operation in American military history. To transport the soldiers through the shallow water off the beach, Scott had ordered 140 surfboats, the first boats in an American war specifically designed as landing craft, of which 65 had been delivered at the time of the operation; each boat carried about 40 soldiers and 8 sailors to work the oars. According to the landing plan designed by Scott and Conner, the surfboats would be towed to a line of departure by steamers and at a signal would head for the beach. They would be followed for a distance by light-draft gunboats and steamships that would cover them with fire if the Mexicans attempted to oppose the landing. As each surfboat deposited its contingent, it was to return to the fleet in a prescribed order to pick up another load.

The landing was carried out on March 9, a beautiful sunny day. As it began, warships of the English, French, and Spanish fleets drew near so their officers could observe the performance of the Americans. The operation went off without a hitch. To the surprise of Scott and his officers, the Mexicans offered no opposition, preferring to await attack in the city. Ten thousand troops were landed in about four hours, and Scott had his beachhead. The operation had been planned so well that even if the Mexicans had attempted opposition, it probably would have succeeded.

Immediately after the landing, Scott started his troops toward Vera Cruz. However, the siege could not begin until the artillery batteries and their horses and other heavy stores had been placed ashore, and the landing of these supplies was delayed by a storm that lasted for four days. After the guns were delivered, they had to be dragged inland over hastily cut roads and put in position; to prepare one battery required the labor of 100 men and 20 horses for a day and a night. Not until March 22 did Scott have everything in readiness. His troops were stretched in an arc of seven miles in the rear of the city, cutting it off from succor, and his batteries were mounted. After serving a demand for surrender on the Mexican commander and being refused, he opened his bombardment.

As the shells arched toward the city, one officer described the bombardment as "a sublime spectacle." But although impressive in sound, it was not effective in impact. Scott's only siege guns were mortars and howitzers, and their projectiles were not heavy enough to breach the walls. Consequently, the general felt compelled to ask for naval guns from the newly arrived commander of the fleet, Commodore Matthew Perry. Anxious to preserve the prestige of his service, Perry answered: "Certainly, General, but I must fight them." Scott protested that he had enough artillerymen of his own to man the guns, but Perry stood firm, and naval crews accompanied the naval guns. Six heavy pieces were landed and dragged before the city to join in the bombardment. Their shot not only shattered the walls but fell in the city itself, demolishing buildings and homes; some Americans heard people screaming as the shells struck. The Mexican commander, appalled by the destruction, surrendered the city on March 27. Having no facilities to care for a large body of prisoners, Scott paroled the Mexican army. He was satisfied to have secured a port base for his advance inland, and to have grasped it at a small cost in life, only 14 men killed and 59 wounded.

Although Vera Cruz was serviceable as a base, it was not a place where a large body of Americans could be quartered very long: situated in the low coastal area, it was subject to epidemics of yellow fever, the season for which was approaching. Scott therefore prepared to move inland as quickly as he could, heading for Jalapa, about 75 miles distant in the highlands. However, he had to collect enough wagons and pack mules to carry his supplies, and not until April 8 was he ready to proceed. On that day his advance division under David Twiggs moved out on the National Highway leading to Mexico City, the other divisions of the army following later. The size of the army, after units had been detached to guard Vera Cruz and other locations in the rear, was probably about 10,000 troops.

Twiggs, advancing confidently, learned from his scouts on April 11 that a large Mexican force under Santa Anna stood across the road at a pass called Cerro Gordo. Approaching the place the following day, he discovered the Mexicans in a very strong position. Although he had a deserved reputation for rashness, Twiggs on this occasion displayed prudence; he halted and waited for the rest of the army to come up. Scott arrived on April 14 and set his engineering officers to reconnoitering the position. They confirmed that Santa Anna did, indeed, occupy a formidable position.

The Mexican general had returned from Buena Vista to find in his capital a growing despondency as to the outcome of the war and a simmering opposition to his continued rule. Energetic and courageous, he faced down the opposition, and declaring that the war would go on, he collected an army and marched to stop the Americans before they broke out of the lowlands. He chose the position at Cerro Gordo wisely. His right rested on a river and ran northward on ridges to the National Highway; immediately south of the road he mounted batteries to command it. North of the road he placed other batteries and troops on a high hill called Cerro Gordo or El Telégrafo; his left ended at a lower hill called La Atalaya, held by a small number of troops because Santa Anna thought that the area on this flank was impassable. In neglecting to fortify Atalaya, he was making a frequent mistake of generals in war: assuming that the enemy would attack the defenders' strongest point.

Scott's engineers, reconnoitering before Atalaya, found a path that could be traversed and that would bring a flanking column in on the Mexican rear. He thus decided to employ his favored strategy of turning the enemy out of position: he would work a force around to Atalaya, and while it was cutting in behind the Mexican line, he would divert Santa Anna's attention by seeming to attack in his front. Preparations were completed by the night of April 17, and the following morning the operation began. The attack in front failed to deceive Santa Anna because it had been entrusted to the incompetent hands of Gideon Pillow, who did not press it vigorously. But the flanking movement succeeded brilliantly. Too late, Santa Anna realized the threat on his left and rushed troops there. The Americans, sweeping over Atalaya, struck the Mexican rear, instigating a panic that caused the entire opposing line to collapse. Santa Anna himself led the flight to the safety of the mountains. Scott had forced the Mexicans out of his way at a small cost in casualties, losing fewer than 500 men, of whom only 64 were killed. Santa Anna lost 1,200 men, many of them killed. An American surgeon walking over the field of Cerro Gordo after the battle was sickened by the "putrid stench" that arose from hundreds of decaying bodies.

On the day after the battle, April 19, Scott marched on to Jalapa. Here he had to pause to discharge about 4,000 volunteers whose terms were up, thus losing almost half of his army. While waiting for replacements to arrive, he pushed his advance on to Perote and then to Pueblo, the second-largest city in Mexico, which was occupied on May 15. Scott, with the rest of the army, moved to Pueblo before the end of the month. As the soldiers tramped along the road, they exulted over the news that the general had abandoned his communication line with Vera Cruz and would draw supplies from the country. " 'Forward' is the word," one young officer exclaimed in a letter home, "the 'Halls of the Montesumas' our destination."

Entrance into the fabled halls was to be delayed, however. Scott remained in Pueblo for ten weeks before resuming his march. He had to wait for his reinforcements, and the last of these did not arrive until late in July, bringing his army up to a size of 10,000 again. But he was also engaging in a peace negotiation, not offering peace himself as the head of a victorious army but acting as a co-agent with a representative of the civilian branch of the government. This representative had been sent to Mexico by Polk, and his presence with the army constituted a unique experiment in civil-military relations.

In April the president, continually seeking to bring the war to a quick conclusion, decided to dispatch a special emissary to travel with Scott's army; this agent was authorized to judge if the Mexicans were ready to treat and, with Scott's concurrence, to enter into negotiations. The man selected was Nicholas P. Trist, chief clerk of the State Department, who spoke Spanish fluently. After arriving at Vera Cruz in May, he later joined Scott at Pueblo. Trist bore the draft of a proposed treaty and a letter from the secretary of state to his Mexican counterpart, explaining Trist's mission. At first Scott resented Trist's presence, deeming it an infringement on his own powers, but after an acrimonious correspondence the two men resolved their differences. Subsequently, Trist, with Scott's approval, contacted Santa Anna through the medium of the British embassy in Mexico City. Santa Anna's reaction to the approach seemed promising. He indicated that he would discuss peace terms in return for a down payment of $10,000, with $1 million to be paid on conclusion of a treaty. Scott provided the down payment out of his "secret service" fund, but the Mexican dictator, apparently fearing domestic repercussions if he negotiated with the Americans, did not follow up the agreement (although he kept the $10,000). It was evident that the Americans would have to conquer their peace.

On August 7 Scott gave orders for the army to march to its last goal, Mexico City, some 80 miles distant. The men trudged along the National Highway, which wound up through the mountains. Reaching the final crest on August 12, they gazed on the magnificent panorama of the Valley of Mexico and saw dimly in the distance the city they sought. The advance under Twiggs descended to the hamlet of Ayotla, about 15 miles from the capital, while the remaining divisions followed close behind. So far the Americans had encountered no resistance.

At Ayotla, however, opposition appeared—Santa Anna was going to fight to hold the capital. Under criticism again after Cerro Gordo, he had repressed his enemies and organized a new army of 25,000 men. Determining to make his stand near the city, he took skillful advantage of the natural defenses of the area. Here the National Highway wound through a maze of lakes and marshes, becoming in effect a causeway. On an eminence just south of the road called El Penon, the Mexican general stationed batteries to command the approach and supporting troops and confidently awaited the Americans. They would have to come up the road, he believed, and he would then blast them to destruction.

On arriving at Ayotla, Scott was impressed with the strength of the Mexican position. Immediately his thoughts ran to a flanking operation—if he could move on another route to the capital he could turn Santa Anna out of his stronghold on El Penon. His engineers reported the existence of two other roads, one to the north and one to the south, but both seemed impracticable. The northern road stretched far around the lakes and marshes and would take a long time to traverse, and the southern one was narrow and rough and apparently incapable of supporting artillery. As Scott was considering that he might have to try to storm past El Penon, his engineers, making another scout, reported that the southern road, although indeed difficult, could be used. Scott decided to move on this route, to emerge at San Augustine, a few miles south of Mexico City.

As Scott's troops toiled along the road, Santa Anna, apprised of the movement, evacuated the position he had thought impregnable, and moved back to confront the Americans at San Antonia. Thus, when Scott reached San Augustine, he found the Mexicans barring his road to the north. Again he resorted to a flanking maneuver. To the left of the road was a 15-mile-wide lava bed called the Pedregal and beyond it a road that led to the capital. Although the Pedregal was considered impassable, the engineers found a path through it, and Scott crossed a part of his army under General Pillow to the hamlet of Contreras. Near Contreras was a Mexican force that attempted to interrupt the Americans in building a road over the lava bed, and Pillow attacked it on August 19. His assault was repulsed, but that night reinforcements came from Scott, and on the following day the Americans routed the defenders. As the Mexicans fled, Scott sensed that a decisive moment had arrived. He ordered both wings of his army to sweep forward and united them north of the Pedregal. The fighting of that day was not ended, however. Santa Anna evacuated San Antonia but took up a position at Churubusco, and Scott, seeking to sustain the momentum of his movement, attacked him here, resorting for the first time to a frontal assault. The Mexicans resisted fiercely but finally broke in disorder, retreating to the defenses of Mexico City. In the battles of August 20 Santa Anna lost over 4,000 killed and wounded and an undisclosed number of deserters and prisoners. Scott also suffered heavy losses in his small army, 900 killed and wounded.

After Churubusco, Santa Anna again professed a desire to discuss peace terms. Scott, hoping to avoid the severe casualties that an assault on the city would entail, agreed to an armistice and asked Trist to conduct the negotiations. Polk's agent bargained with representatives of the Mexican government for two weeks but could not induce them to accept a treaty. It finally became apparent to him and to Scott that Santa Anna had no intention of concluding an agreement and was, in fact, using the armistice as an opportunity to bring in reinforcements and strengthen the fortifications of the city. On September 6 Scott ordered the discussions ended; he would have to take Mexico City to end the war.

In assaulting the capital, Scott had two routes open to him. One was from the south, over three narrow causeways that ran through marshes. The troops would be restricted to the roads and vulnerable to damaging artillery fire, but they would encounter only weak forts at the end of the roads. The other route was from the southwest, over a broader road and on comparatively high ground, but the road was commanded by the fortress of Chapultepec that would have to be captured en route. While Scott was deliberating which route to choose, his attention was called to a complex of low stone buildings known as El Molino del Rey, situated just west of Chapultepec, where the Mexicans were reportedly casting cannons, and on September 8 he attacked and took the place, although at heavy cost. His reason for making the assault is puzzling. It could not have been merely to secure the cannons, of which few were found. He was probably leaning toward the western route, and decided to reduce the Molino as a preliminary move.

Still undecided on a route, however, he called a conference of his generals; significantly, he invited also the engineer officers, who were of junior rank. Most of the generals and a majority of the engineers voted for the southern approach. However, one engineer, Lieutenant P. G. T. Beauregard, made a lengthy argument for the western route, emphasizing that after Chapultepec was taken, the attackers could move quickly on the city. Scott, probably already half convinced, announced his decision—the army would capture Chapultepec and go in from the west.

The operation against Chapultepec began with a day-long bombardment on September 12. Although the fire damaged the walls, it did not force a surrender, and the following day Scott ordered an infantry assault. The first attack was repulsed, but scaling ladders were brought up, and the Americans swarmed over the walls, hoisting their flag in triumph. As the remnant of the garrison fled toward Mexico City, General Quitman, in charge of the assault column, started his men in immediate pursuit. At the same time Scott sent other troops forward on a road to the north. By nightfall the victors had gained two of the western gates. Santa Anna with his few remaining troops moved to a village to the north, and at dawn the next morning a delegation came out to offer surrender of the city. At seven o'clock the American flag was raised in the Grand Plaza, and a little later Scott and his staff rode in to a tremendous roar of exultation from the weary troops. The great city of over 200,000 had yielded to an army that by this time numbered at the most 8,000 men.

It remained to negotiate a peace treaty, but before this could be done, a responsible Mexican government had to be organized. Santa Anna resigned as president, and for two months there was no clearly recognized authority. Eventually a government was formed and it indicated to Trist its readiness to discuss terms. In the meantime, Polk had become irritated at the stalemate. Blaming Trist and Scott for the lack of progress, he sent orders recalling Trist and directing Scott to resume the war. His dispatches arrived as Trist was entering into serious negotiation, and the envoy, believing he could get a favorable treaty, decided, with Scott's approval, to ignore the order and continue the conversations. He finally extracted a treaty that conformed to Polk's original instructions: Mexico agreed to cede California and New Mexico to the United States in return for a money payment and to recognize the Rio Grande boundary of Texas. At the last minute the Mexican negotiators insisted on signing the treaty outside the capital, probably to avoid the appearance of acting under constraint of the American army. At the hamlet of Guadalupe Hidalgo north of the city they affixed their signatures on February 2, 1848.

Although angry with Trist for disregarding his instructions, Polk had little choice but to submit the treaty to the Senate. It secured the objectives for which the United States had gone to war and could not be repudiated by the president without arousing political opposition. The agreement was ratified by the Senate on March 10 and, after some delaying resistance, by the Mexican government on May 30. Only then did the American army evacuate Mexico City and start on its long journey home.

The war that had originated in the restless, reckoning desire of the American people to achieve their Manifest Destiny was over. If it had not pushed the national boundaries as far as some advocates of the destiny hoped, it had still extended them to new and spacious limits. The United States had won an empire.

1848-1861

T HE SUCCESSES of the Mexican War evoked an outburst of national pride
that persisted for several years after its end. The generals and the
battles were celebrated in numerous books written for popular consumption,
a representative title being *The Mexican War and Its Heroes.* Some of the
paragons rode into political office on their war reputations, and the general
who most caught the national fancy, Zachary Taylor, was elected president in
1848. However, the public's interest was restricted to the martial deeds of
individuals. Little attention was given to the more serious aspects of the war,
and its events had no discernible effect on thinking about military policy.
Although the United States had acquired vast new territories, and hence new
responsibilities, neither the voters nor their political representatives seemed to
feel that the nation needed to greatly expand its military establishment. And
few persons in government or out thought the country might now need something it had never had: a national strategy.

The size of the military establishment in the years after the Mexican War
was not much greater than it had been before. At the end of 1848 the authorized
strength of the regular army was reduced to 10,000 troops, a pitifully small
force to man the coastal defenses and patrol the western territories. In succeeding years the War Department persuaded Congress to provide increases, but
they were modest: at the outbreak of the Civil War in 1861 the authorized
strength was only 18,000 and the actual strength but 16,000. Probably 3 million
men were carried on the rolls of the state militia, but this number represented
a phantom force; the bulk of the militia received little or no training, although
in some states there were efficient volunteer units, the forerunners of the later
National Guard. The small size of the regular army did not seem to concern
the framers of military policy. It was assumed that in the event of a foreign
war the nation would have time to augment its forces by calling out volunteers.

The navy was also held to a moderate rate of expansion. Numbering about
70 craft in 1848, it was built up to over 90 ships by 1860. However, this listed
total was deceptive: it included a number of vessels that were obsolete or in
a state of disrepair. Only 42 of the ships were in seagoing condition. Although

smaller in numbers than the navy before the Mexican War, this force was stronger. It carried heavier guns and was more mobile, over half of the vessels being steam propelled. Steam power was becoming dominant in European navies, and in adopting it, the navy was following a world trend. Another European development, an increasing reliance on ironclad ships, had not yet influenced the navy. American designers were aware of this trend but were unable to secure from Congress the funds required to construct their own ironclads. The navy remained a wooden flotilla.*

Although naval spokesmen liked to boast that their vessels constituted the nation's first line of defense, they must have known that this was an exaggeration; the small force would have been helpless to repel an attack by a first-rate European navy. In more realistic moments naval strategists might have admitted that defense against a major power was not one of their missions. The navy had more limited assignments, and these it was adequate to perform—to patrol coastal waters, to police the illegal slave trade, and to show the protection of the flag to the country's expanding foreign trade.

The regular army also had its supporters, who considered it a vital line of defense: it was expected to hold off an enemy until larger forces could be raised out of the population. In peacetime its assignments, like the navy's, were limited. Before the war with Mexico its functions included the conducting of explorations in unmapped western territories, constructing roads and forts in these regions and on the coast, and policing the Indians on the frontier. These tasks, as a result of the war, were even more onerous—the army had to explore the huge area acquired, erect a string of posts throughout the far West, and, most important, ensure that the restless Indian tribes along the frontier submitted to the oncoming settlement by whites.

The technical aspects of the army's work, the exploring and mapping of unknown areas, were accomplished with efficiency and relative ease by the corps of topographical engineers. The knowledge gained of the western country and its trails would facilitate settlement. However, this information was more important for the future than for the present. The army's immediate problem was to provide for the safety of the horde of settlers who were about to erupt into the Indian lands beyond the westernmost line of expansion, and over the tribes in their way. Then and later, as the westward surge continued, things were done to the natives that have since lain heavily on the American conscience. However, the situation was very complex. A modern observer, Richard Goodwin, has emphasized that there was another side to it. Thousands of migrants, many of them poor and seeking a better life, went to the margin of rich lands that were virtually empty, and inevitably they appro-

---

*Congress appropriated money to aid one designer, Robert Stevens, who proposed to build an armored steamer intended to protect harbors. Although the funds were voted in 1842, construction lagged, and the vessel was still uncompleted in 1861.

priated them. "Great wrongs were done," Goodwin writes, "but the clash was unavoidable and the moral questions were ambiguous."

The line of settlement in 1848 extended from Texas to Minnesota Territory. West of this line, beginning at the borders of Arkansas and Missouri and stretching to the western edge of the Louisiana Purchase, was the expanse of territory called popularly the Indian Country—officially, the Permanent Indian Frontier. The titles derived from an arrangement put into effect by the national government during the 1830s. Responding to a widely held belief that the unorganized portion of the Louisiana Purchase was unfit for "civilized" —that is, for white—habitation, the government set aside this area as a reservation for the tribes resident in it and for other tribes originally living east of the Mississippi that were forcibly removed there. Originally the eastern boundary of the Indian Country ran from the northern border of Missouri through eastern Iowa and across northern Wisconsin. But within a few years after the boundary was drawn, settlers began to push across the Mississippi into Iowa and Minnesota, and the government had to relocate the tribes in these territories in smaller tracts. Even at this early date, it was apparent that the Permanent Indian Frontier was not going to be permanent.

Approximately 160,000 Indians lived in the areas west of the boundary line. Slightly over half of this total, about 85,000, were concentrated in one area, present-day Oklahoma. They comprised a sedentary group that the whites called the Five Civilized Tribes; they had originally resided east of the Mississippi, but when they were forced to move west of the river, they continued to practice their simple agriculture and were generally peaceful. In the remaining and larger portion of the Louisiana Purchase lived another 75,000 Indians, nomadic tribes that moved throughout the lands they claimed as their own, warred occasionally with other tribes, and resented the few whites who dared to intrude on their domain. Those whites who attempted to enter the reserved region had little trouble in slipping by the thin line of eight army forts that picketed its eastern boundary.

The territorial acquisitions of the 1840s placed an additional 200,000 Indians within the limits of the United States, the tribes residing in the southwestern area acquired from Mexico and in California and Oregon. These natives lived beyond the edges of the Indian Country and did not enjoy the protection of its guaranteed boundaries; their lands were open to white settlers unless the government, in an unlikely event, should choose to restrain settlement—or unless they were able to repel the invaders. The probability of white settlement in the new acquisitions posed a threat also to the tribes living in the Indian Country itself. Migrants moving westward would have to pass through the reserved lands, and the Indians had no assurance that the whites would move on. Some migrants might decide to remain on lands that had caught their eye, and in that eventuality the natives would have to fight to hold their country. The situation inevitably produced tensions and clashes between whites and Indians, and the burden of dealing with it fell on the small regular army.

The bulk of the army was assigned to the frontier during the 1850s, as many men being sent there as the War Department thought it could spare from other areas. Thus, in the middle of the decade, when the authorized size of the army was about 13,000 and the actual size was 10,000, over 8,000 officers and soldiers were stationed in the West. This force was adequate, although barely so, to perform the routine duties expected of it. But policing the Indians in the vast area of the Indian Country and beyond would place a severe strain on the army's resources and capacity, for there were many warlike tribes who were certain to resent white intrusions on their lands.

The army had to deal with two problems in the West. On the central Great Plains it had to protect migrants moving through the Indian Country to California or Oregon, and to persuade or compel the tribes residing along the routes, the martial Sioux, Cheyennes, Arapahoes, and Comanches, not to interfere with the travelers. In the Southwest the army had to defend the lives and homes of persons already settled in the area, on the Texas frontier and in New Mexico Territory, to repel raids by the aggressive Kiowas, Comanches, Utes, and Apaches, and, if possible, to punish the raiders. In both regions the army found that it had to conduct offensive expeditions against the offending tribes. These operations involved only small forces of several hundred troops, but they were known in the army and to the public as "wars," each one designated by the name of the tribe against which it was waged. According to one estimate, the army fought twenty-two Indian wars during the 1850s, an astonishing number in view of its other duties. Also remarkable was the army's success. Although not every expedition achieved its objective, the army was able to preserve a degree of order among the tribes, because of techniques and tactics developed by the officers and men of the frontier force.

The army began its mission of preserving order by constructing a network of forts throughout the Indian Country and the Southwest. Eventually, there were fifty-two of these stations, stretching from the eastern rim of the Great Plains to the Pacific coast. If the approximately 8,000 troops on the frontier had been distributed equally among the forts, the garrison of each post would have numbered slightly more than 150 men. The distribution was unequal, however, since forts in some areas required larger aggregations, either because of their exposed location or because of unusual Indian activity in their vicinity. Hence, many forts were held by fewer than 100 men, only a company and its supernumeraries.

The company became the basic tactical unit in the frontier army, patrolling the area around its fort and, if depredations by the Indians occurred, making sweeps against them. On occasion, if a tribe or a large portion of it went on the warpath, a number of companies from several forts would be combined into a column to seek out the raiders; at various times during the

1850s, forces numbering between 500 and 600 infantry and cavalry were assembled for offensive action. But many a company served throughout the decade without ever taking the field with another unit. Only a few of the major offensives resulted in important or lasting successes; the Indians usually found it easy to elude a large force marching through their country. Actually, some kind of small-unit organization, a company or several companies operating together, was more likely to run the quarry down. This lesson was partially learned by 1860 and would be put into fuller effect after the Civil War.

The men of the frontier army learned many other lessons, most of them by hard experience. Most of the officers were professionals, over 70 percent being graduates of West Point. These men went to the West with a good grounding in military fundamentals. They knew how to drill a company or a regiment and how to put troops into battle against a conventional enemy, but nothing they had learned at the academy prepared them to deal with such an elusive and tricky foe as the Indians. The only men in a unit likely to know much about Indian ways were veteran noncommissioned officers; even one good "noncom" could be invaluable to a company commander just out of West Point.

In adapting to small-unit tactics, the frontier army demonstrated that it was not bound to orthodox methods of making war. It revealed a readiness to learn new ways in other actions: it hit Indian encampments by surprise and, in skirmishes, experimented with formations more flexible than the usual linear advance. The sharpest break with past thinking was in the outlook that the army acquired toward Indians. Both officers and men lost quickly any notions that they were dealing with a traditional adversary and should employ "civilized" methods against him. Confronted by an enemy who did not know the rules of conventional warfare, an enemy who had his own rules, the army adopted many of his ways. It became increasingly harsh in its treatment of the Indians. Commanders took the view that a tribe was responsible for the acts of all its members and punished the whole group for the transgressions of a few braves, although this concept was in conflict with known principles of Indian government. Much the same transition had been made by colonial military forces and by the army in the Seminole Wars.

In 1860 the frontier army could look back on a decade of accomplishment. Despite some failures, it had preserved an uneasy peace in a vast area that but for its presence would not have known peace. Its dominion rested on the network of half a hundred forts that stretched across half a continent. Referring to this network as it existed in 1855, historian Robert M. Utley has written: "It was a thin covering, to be sure, but the flag that floated over each post brought the appearance and in places the substance of U.S. authority to an empire that a short decade earlier had owed allegiance to four separate flags."

THE MILITARY ESTABLISHMENT could regard the 1850s as a time of progress. Officers of the army and the navy kept abreast of technical developments in European forces and labored, within the restrictions imposed by the limited appropriations allowed to them, to install the latest advances in their services. The army officers were more fortunate than their naval counterparts in enjoying the support of a strong and able civilian superior, Jefferson Davis, who was secretary of war from 1853 to 1857 and who as a graduate of West Point and former soldier had unusual professional competence.

Although Davis attended to all matters relating to his department, he was particularly interested in weaponry, and this interest led him to study a new kind of small arms being developed in Europe, which he then pushed for adoption by the army. The piece that excited him was a musket with a rifled barrel that fired a lead projectile named, after its inventor, the Minié ball. Known as a rifle musket, the weapon had longer range and greater accuracy than previous shoulder guns. American arsenals began making rifle muskets in 1855, ceasing to produce smoothbores, and Davis directed that new units be provided with these new guns. Eventually, rifle muskets were distributed to other units, but because the capacity of the arsenals to turn out the guns was as yet limited, many soldiers in 1860 still carried the old smoothbores.

Several models of the rifle musket were developed in government and private arsenals. All of them were of basically similar design. The model adopted by the army, the Springfield, was a .58 caliber percussion muzzleloader. Although its rate of fire was similar to that of a smoothbore musket, employment of the Minié-type projectile in the new Springfield's rifled bore greatly increased accuracy. Aimed fire at individuals became practicable at distances up to 300 to 350 yards, as compared to the 50 to 75 yards that smoothbores allowed.*

Technology brought less traumatic change to the artillery. A new light fieldpiece designed by the French and named the Napoleon after their emperor, Napoleon III, won acceptance in the United States. The weapon, though lighter, cheaper, and more easily handled, still fired the standard 12-pound projectile. A smoothbore, it fired shot and shell (an iron projectile detonated by a crude time fuse) to ranges of a mile, while at closer ranges canister and similar projectiles (small iron balls or metal scrap) turned the weapon into a giant shotgun. The Napoleon superseded the 6-pounder in the field artillery. Larger and more effective smoothbores, invented by Major Rodman and Cap-

---

*Experiments with breech-loading rifles were conducted during the 1850s, and several models, of which the Sharps was the best known, were placed on the market; a model of a repeating rifle, the Spencer, was developed in 1860. However, neither gun was produced on a mass basis because neither received government patronage. The breech-loaders exhibited certain technical deficiencies, the most serious being a leakage of gas at the breech, and the repeaters remained untested. Moreover, to produce them would have required an expensive and extensive retooling process. The problem of conversion remained troublesome during the Civil War.

tain Dahlgren, and firing heavier shot, quickly replaced older smoothbores in shipboard and fortress use.

Captain Robert Parrott, among others, perfected a rifled fieldpiece. Though these pieces outranged smoothbores by a two-to-one factor, and were more accurate, they were not overly popular or effective. Fumes for the elongated projectiles and sights capable of exploiting the greater accuracy were thirty years in the future. Further, the elongated solid shot burrowed into the earth (the muzzle-loaders' iron balls tended to ricochet among massed infantry formations). In effect, the smaller bores and rifling of the newer weapons decreased effectiveness at short range with canister as compared to similar-sized smoothbore pieces. The Napoleon and the rifle musket were enough; massed infantry could be killed from farther away and in greater numbers than ever before.

MILITARY EDUCATION during this period underwent few changes. The academy at West Point continued to provide its students with the same kind of instruction that it had furnished in Sylvanus Thayer's time, turning out graduates with an adequate knowledge of fundamentals but little of the higher art of war. The curriculum still placed its emphasis on producing engineers. About 70 percent of total classroom hours was devoted to engineering, mathematics, and natural philosophy (science), while only 30 percent was given to all other subjects, including strategy and tactics. The apparent assumption behind this division was that an engineer officer would be a good fighting soldier, or could become one by extra study.*

Officers who wanted to learn more about their profession could find various ways to do so, and many took advantage of the opportunities. Those interested in infantry or artillery underwent instruction at the specialist centers, the schools of practice at Jefferson Barracks, St. Louis, and Fortress Monroe, Virginia. The cavalry went to Carlisle Barracks, Pennsylvania, which offered training in traditional tactics and also experimented with a new method of employing horse troops that took advantage of their mobility: to have the men ride to a point of contact in battle and dismount to fight. Officers could also improve their proficiency by studying the various texts that were published during the period. Several helpful infantry manuals appeared, the most widely used being *Hardee's Tactics* (by William J. Hardee) and an artillery

*West Point was no longer the only officer-training school in the country, although still the principal one. During this period other institutions were founded, some by state or local governments, others by private promoters; these schools adopted a system of training similar to that of West Point. Formal training for naval officers was not available until 1845, when the United States Naval Academy at Annapolis, Maryland, was established. This school received inadequate support from the government and had graduated only a small number of junior officers by 1860.

manual by Alfred Mordecai, the first full description of the army's system of artillery.

Although the manuals systematized existing tactical doctrine, they proposed no important changes in battlefield formations. The omission seems curious in view of the effect that the new weapons were certain to have on infantry attacking in the conventional line. With artillery and shoulder arms being able to kill at longer distances than in previous wars and to deliver a greater firepower at any range, a force advancing in rigid lines offered an inviting target; it would be subjected to a galling fire almost from the time it started to move and might be shattered before it could get close enough to the enemy to break through his position. The authors of the manuals were aware of the problem, but they offered no precise solution to it. The effect of the sweeping fire could be reduced if the attackers advanced in a looser or more spread out formation, in what is called "extended order," and some of the experts contemplated such an arrangement. Thus, Secretary of War Davis sponsored an official manual that prescribed "light infantry tactics." Although the term suggested a more flexible formation, the work proposed only a slight alteration, to reduce the line of the infantry from three ranks to two and to send a larger number of skirmishers ahead to draw the fire of the defenders. No greater alteration was recommended in the other manuals, which generally adopted the two-rank formation. The army was still being trained to fight in a relatively compact formation, in "close order."

This failure to adapt formations to fit the development of weapons is usually ascribed to military conservatism. In part, the criticism is justified. Like those in other professions, military leaders are usually committed to practices that have worked in the past and are perhaps less inclined to embrace new, unproven ways. The officers of the pre-Civil War era were no exception to the rule. They were familiar with an assault formation they had seen work or had been told would work. In it, the infantry was drawn up in two ranks with an interval of about twenty-four inches between each man and of thirty-two inches between the first and second ranks. A brigade so aligned would occupy a front of 1,300 yards and a division attacking in a "column of brigades," a frequent formation, a front of similar length. The line was to be held parallel as it advanced so that if it was halted to fire, it could deliver a massed or uniform volley. More important, it was believed that a parallel line would have a greater shock effect when it struck the defenders than an irregular line. Military men realized that such a rigid arrangement was vulnerable to enemy fire and would endure many casualties, but they believed that an attack coming in successive lines would eventually overwhelm the defenders and carry the field.

Although this devotion to traditional tactics seemed to represent a conservative aversion to change, military men had a real reason for adhering to close order. Many officers would have been willing to experiment with a more dispersed formation if they thought they could keep command over their men, but the difficulty of maintaining communication baffled them.

The problem of tactical control is an old one in warfare, and one of the hardest to solve. How can the commander of an army, or of a unit within an army, direct men who are operating beyond his range of vision or voice? The problem was not satisfactorily solved until the advent of field radio in World War II, and even with this device, control was not guaranteed. In earlier wars commanders attempted to maintain direction through simpler methods. A general might issue battle orders to his principal officers in council or send orders down by staff aides. When battle was joined, he might transmit additional orders by messengers, or ride around the field and give directions in person. The European manuals, on which the American texts were based, assumed that battles would be fought in built-up country, on a flat and open space, and that visual and voice contact would usually be possible.

Like the Europeans, the American manual writers relied heavily on command by voice, on orders issued personally or through staff messengers. However, the authors, and their readers, realized that this method was more difficult in America than in Europe. Much of the United States was still not built up, and in the rugged countryside, where battles were likely to be fought, a line of advancing infantry would be out of sight and sound of its higher officers soon after it moved off. Even the commander of the smallest tactical unit, the colonel of a regiment, would probably lose sight and hence verbal direction of his men once battle was joined.

The only way that an officer could establish contact, either to issue his own orders or to transmit those sent down from above, was through the "field music," composed of the regimental buglers and drummers whose instruments constituted a primitive form of radio. By bugle call or drumbeat a colonel might make a variety of orders known to men scattered over a wide field. One manual prescribed twenty-six bugle calls for all troops and twenty-three for skirmishers, and fifteen drumbeats for all troops and twenty for skirmishers. Not surprisingly, the calls did not always have the desired effect. Sometimes they could not be heard above the din of conflict, and sometimes a call for one unit might be heard and obeyed by another group. The method would work reasonably well if troops were kept in a relatively compact formation, or in close order, but if the formations had been extended, control was impossible. There had been a revolution in weapons but not a corresponding one in tactical communication.

In contrast to their concern with tactics, the military writers of the time showed relatively little interest in strategy. Few books on the higher art of war appeared to complement the growing body of tactical literature. In neglecting the subject, American thinkers were only following a traditional path. Grand strategy for a whole war, as contrasted to narrower battlefield strategy, had never been an object of serious study in the United States. The geographical position of the nation and its relations with other countries seemed to make the development of a national strategy unnecessary.

Isolated from the great powers of Europe by an ocean and confronted by weaker neighbors on their continental borders, Americans had little fear of a sudden formidable attack by any enemy. The nation most able to deliver such a thrust was Great Britain, with her naval might, but she and the United States had maintained generally peaceful relations since 1815. As for other European nations, the United States had renounced interest in their affairs in the Monroe Doctrine and felt that they had a similar lack of interest in its own affairs. Nor had the nation seen a need to develop a strategy to deal with such possible enemies as the Indians or Mexico, against whom the mere strength of the United States would be adequate. Thus, those soldiers who thought it important to study strategy and to formulate a national strategy were in a very real sense writing on a blank slate; they had no set objectives to guide their thinking. Naturally, they turned for inspiration to European writers, who presumably were steeped in the experience of centuries.

The European military experts most admired by Americans were the French. Virtually unknown in the United States was the German strategist whose ideas would possess American thinkers in a later era, Karl von Clausewitz. His great work *On War,* although published during the 1830s, was not translated into English until after the Civil War. Even if it had been available, his concept of war as maximum application of violence probably would not have appealed to Americans of the 1850s.

The works of many of the French writers were available in translations, some of them provided by the few army officers who could read French. They were considered by Americans to be the last word on strategy, the thinking of men representing the best army in Europe. One of these authorities was esteemed above all others, Henri Antoine Jomini, a Swiss-born officer who had served under Napoleon and who wrote a number of books on war. His most highly regarded work was *Summary of the Art of War,* which for a time was used as a text at West Point and which influenced the thinking of a whole generation of officers. Although the book was later dropped as a text, its tenets continued to be presented to cadets in the form of abridgments or in the lectures of faculty members. The extent of Jomini's influence has been exaggerated by some observers—it has been said that many a Civil War general went into battle with a sword in one hand and a copy of *Summary* in the other —and questioned by others, who have argued that the time devoted to the study of strategy at the academy was so short that students could have learned little of its principles. The truth of the matter is largely on the side of the exaggeration. Most army officers were exposed in some way to Jomini's ideas, studying his writings or abridgments of them as cadets or reading him or his disciples as commissioned officers. More than any other European, he was responsible for American strategic thinking.

Those Americans who studied all of Jomini's works could draw various and even divergent conclusions from them. Like any seminal thinker who writes voluminously, he threw out ideas right and left, so many that some were certain to run counter to others. The reader looking for guidance could pick and choose in this wealth, selecting dictums that supported his own predilection as to what was correct doctrine.

Jomini's announced purpose was to introduce rationality and system into the study of war. He believed that rules prevailed in war as in other areas of human activity and that commanders should know and follow these rules. His most emphasized principle was that of concentration or mass. A commander should so maneuver as to bring the major part of his force to bear upon the decisive area of the theater or field war, which was where the enemy was weakest, or as Jomini put it, bring his mass to bear on a fraction of the enemy. To explain how his principles should be applied, he devised twelve model battle plans based on geometrical formations. In each plan there was a theater of operations, a zone of operations, and a line of operations. The intelligent commander chose a line of operations that would enable him to dominate three sides of a rectangular zone of operations. This accomplished, the enemy faced certain defeat—unless he retreated.

Jomini professed to be interpreting and advocating the ways of war introduced by Napoleon: the quick and massive concentration of an army before battle, then the smashing offensive blow followed by an energetic pursuit. And when he discussed the advantage of the offensive in war, he did seem to be glorifying Napoleon's methods, as well as coming to substantial agreement with Clausewitz's misnamed "strategy of annihilation." But at other times he appeared to advocate a return to the limited warfare of the eighteenth century, to a more humane and less destructive way of war. Actually, as Jomini confessed, his "prejudices" were in favor of the eighteenth century, with its "chivalric" mode of conflict as opposed to the "organized assassination" of his own time. He revealed his devotion to the older kind of war in many passages. Thus, he stressed repeatedly that a commander might win a war without fighting a decisive battle, that he might, for example, maneuver so adeptly as to seize the capital and other important cities of the enemy and thus force a satisfactory peace. And even in his celebration of the offensive Jomini did not envision that the movement would necessarily result in a showdown battle— all his plans to enclose three sides of a zone allowed the enemy the option of retiring.

The influence of Jomini weighed heavily on the only two Americans who attempted systematic treatments of strategy, Dennis Hart Mahan and Henry W. Halleck. Their books, published in the late 1840s, reproduced the French master's ideas and principles and sometimes even his phraseology.

Mahan, a graduate of the military academy, joined its faculty in 1832 and became professor of civil and military engineering and the "art of war." His lectures were popular, and he eventually turned them into a book with an awkward seventeen-word title: *An Elementary Treatise on Advanced-Guard, Out-Post, and Detachment Service of Troops* . . ., it began. Usually it was known simply as *Out-Post.* Halleck studied under Mahan and served in the army before resigning his commission to become a lawyer and businessman. Of a scholarly cast, he was sufficiently conversant with French to translate the writings of Napoleon and Jomini into English editions for the American market. His own book, *Elements of Military Art and Science,* was largely a rehashing of the French works, but he provided a more systematic examination of strategy than Mahan had.

Both Mahan and Halleck praised the advantage of the offensive in war. It is evident, however, that their admiration was more rhetorical than real, an obeisance they felt they had to make to Napoleon. As they developed their treatment, they brought in qualifications, cautionary admonitions, and counterpraise to the advantage of the defensive, until finally, as historian Russell Weigley has written, "the original encouragement to offensive war" was "almost diluted out of existence." In taking this course, Mahan and Halleck were, of course, following the lead of Jomini. Like him, they really preferred an eighteenth-century kind of strategy, a war of maneuver to seize enemy places instead of an all-out attack to destroy an enemy army. The offensives they envisioned were limited in force and fury and were to be employed in a war for limited objectives such as to pacify Indians or to acquire a strip of territory from a neighbor like Mexico.

In adopting Jomini's concept of limited warfare, American thinkers believed they were framing a strategy calculated to serve the United States in any war in which it was likely to be involved. They could not foresee a conflict that demanded a Napoleonic or a Clausewitzian strategy of annihilation. The only possibility of a major war was that a European power might invade the United States to achieve a limited objective. Even in that event, an all-out effort would not be required. A well-prepared system of defenses could hold the aggressor away from vital areas and a limited offensive would easily persuade him to withdraw. It would all be over quickly with a minimum expenditure of means and men—a traditional, Jominian, war.

This was not at all the kind of conflict into which the United States was plunged in 1861.

CHAPTER IX

The Civil War:
Origins and Beginnings

NO OTHER AMERICAN CONFLICT—indeed, no other episode in our history—has so gripped the popular imagination as has the Civil War, the struggle between the United States and the Confederate States, the North and the South. It is the most written about, read about, and known about of all our wars.

The reasons for the war's enduring hold have been speculated on by many observers, including some who have admitted its fascination even while lamenting the national preoccupation with it. Critics have suggested that this war prompts attention merely because its story possesses unusual human interest and rare drama, and without conceding to their opinion, it must be said that the conflict had these qualities. It offers the reader an unparalleled cast of military characters—heroes and greats, might-have-been greats, and failures. It also offers speculative suspense—fateful battles that either side might have won, when, in contrast to later wars, men rather than machines clearly controlled the fighting.

More perceptive commentators have conjectured that the war has the attraction of a great tragedy. For the first and only time in their history Americans were unable to resolve differences between themselves through the normal political process and resorted to four years of bloody war. In this view the Civil War represents a national failure. It is a crimson gash across the success story that is American history, an episode that should not have happened, that "strange sad war" in the memorable phrase of the poet Walt Whitman.

The Civil War *was* a great dramatic experience and a searing national tragedy. But drama and pathos in themselves would never have ensured the place it has obtained in the public consciousness. There is something more. The American people, with a sound instinct, have sensed that this war was the pivotal event in their history. It determined to a large extent the direction the nation would take in the future. One of the war's results, the abolition of slavery, settled an issue that had brought on the conflict but left a new problem, the place of the black race in American society, to be dealt with by later generations. But the political result was never questioned after 1865: it was decided forever that the Union was indivisible. Even the defeated side accepted the verdict, an outcome that has not always occurred after civil struggles. Indeed, the ties of union were strengthened by the war, a development that intrigued a former Confederate general. Contemplating in the early 1900s the nation that had emerged from the war, Edward Porter Alexander was led to write: "Its bonds were not formed by peaceable agreements in conventions, but were forged in the white heat of battles, in a war fought out to the bitter end, and are for eternity."

PREVIOUS CONFLICTS had only minor effects on the structure of American society. Afterward, the position of the United States might be more secure vis-à-vis other nations or its pride or boundaries might be enlarged, but the basic social institutions remained essentially the same as before the war. The Civil War, however, compelled change in important areas of national life and left in its wake altered or new institutions.

The war forced change through its dimensions. The first big American war, it was also the first big American undertaking of any kind. The people of the United States, at least those of the majority North and to a lesser extent those of the minority South, were called on to do something that had never been required of them before—to put forth a supreme effort to achieve an objective so precious that every resource had to be employed and every obstacle had to be overcome. In the North the object was to maintain intact the Union, the great American experiment in popular government, which when threatened with destruction suddenly assumed hitherto unexpressed values, both mystical and material, in the minds of men. To preserve the Union, the Northern people would submit to controls from the central government that prior to the war they would have considered abhorrent—if they had even conceived that such restraints could exist.

Before the war the average citizen was, of course, conscious that a government existed in Washington, but he was unlikely ever to feel its hand as he went about his everyday activities. He paid no taxes to the government, because it did not have to levy general duties to sustain its modest functions; it could derive what revenue it needed by selling public lands or collecting import tariffs, exactions that affected only a small portion of the population. He handled little national currency, except coins, because the government issued hardly any paper notes of its own; most money consisted of notes put out by state banks. He could pass a lifetime without encountering directly the force of a federal law or even seeing a federal enforcement official, because only a few national laws applied to the ordinary citizen and only a small number of federal employees were retained to administer these laws. The absence of centralism in the political system was reflected in the social system. American society, viewed as a whole, was loosely and locally organized; its institutions were characterized by an absence of mass and a lack of shape.

The amorphous structure was ill fitted to conduct a great war or, indeed, any large undertaking, and under the strains of the Civil War its institutions and organization underwent important changes. In each section, or nation, the principal agent of change was the central government, but the men in that government were themselves often only the agents of forces beyond their control, of the implacable demands of the war. Thus the two presidents, Abraham Lincoln in the North and Jefferson Davis in the South, at times proposed measures they did not wish to advance but that seemed necessary to victory. The Civil War revealed a significant and an ominous truth about great wars—like the even more encompassing world conflicts of the twentieth century, it enforced its own conditions on the human beings who thought they could direct it.

The most important change caused by the war was a greater concentration of power in government. In both sections it was realized that this struggle would require a more centralized direction than had been necessary in previous conflicts, nothing less than a mobilization of mass endeavor to attain a mass result, and the central governments almost immediately gathered large new powers unto themselves. The Northern government was more successful in this centralization than was the Southern, and some of the accretions of authority were retained even after the nation was reunited in 1865.

One example of centralization occurred in the area of finance. In order to meet the huge costs of the war, both governments had to impose taxes and issue large amounts of paper money. Both devices were intended to be temporary wartime arrangements, but after 1865 the federal government found it expedient to retain paper notes and some of the special levies. Thus, as an unforeseen result of the war, the country acquired a national revenue system and a national monetary system.

By far the most striking exercise of central power, and to many people in both sections a frightening exercise, evolved out of the need of the rival governments to raise mass armies. Each government initially assumed it could enlist adequate forces by calling for volunteers, the traditional American method of mobilization, and in the first year of the war, when martial enthusiasm ran high and the war promised to be a short and glorious one, volunteering did serve to fill the ranks. But soon enlistments dwindled, and it became evident that the volunteer system would not provide the mass armies the war was going to require. Forced by the manpower crisis to act drastically, both governments resorted to conscription, the Confederate States in 1862 and the

United States a year later—the first time in an American war that national conscription was employed. Although the draft was accepted in both sections, its enforcement was a wrenching experience to people who had hardly known the authority of government; it seemed wrong for the hand of government to reach into a community, pick up a young man, and dress him in uniform. Almost as alarming was the action of both administrations in suspending civil law and placing opponents of the war under military arrest. The American people were learning a hard fact about war, that if its stakes are great enough, customary liberties have to be sacrificed to maintain national existence.

The demands of the war also altered the economy of each section but most affected the industrial system in the North. There the central government was forced by developing pressures to enter into new and direct relationships with industrial producers. Having created mass armies, the government thus had to supply them, and it became for the first time in an American war a massive buyer and devouring consumer of matériel, of arms, uniforms, shoes, and other items. Placing its orders for the required products with its own arsenals and with private manufacturers, the government demanded from either source quick delivery, holding out as an incentive high prices and promises of future orders. The result was to stimulate production and growth in some industries and to force the first extensive use of speeded-up manufacturing methods, of techniques resembling the modern assembly line. Mass production was emerging in American industry as an inevitable answer to the needs of mass armies.*

The demands of the war also stimulated the Northern railroad system, which was called upon to perform herculean tasks of transportation.† The raw materials required to manufacture military goods often were hauled long distances to factories, and the finished products carried similarly long distances for distribution to the military forces, functions that only the railroads could perform. Moreover, the large bodies of troops that were raised in all parts of the country had to be moved from mobilization camps to the fighting fronts and into the South and at times from one theater of operations to another, again services that only the railroads could render. Thus, the conflict hastened a turn to mass movement as well as to mass production. Surveying the changes in production and transportation and all the other transforming effects of the war, Howard Mumford Jones has written that it "dramatized ingenuity, it accustomed people to mass and size and uniformity and national action, it got

---

*A similar development occurred in the South, as will be discussed later, but the effort was not as successful as in the North. Some historians question that the war caused economic growth in the North. Utilizing elaborate data, they argue that the requirements of war industries deprived other industries of raw materials and labor and thus that the war retarded general growth. There were industries affected adversely, but it seems clear that others experienced significant growth and that the war hastened the development of mass production methods.

†The Southern rail system, consisting of fewer and shorter lines, almost collapsed under heavy usage and the enemy's depredations.

them used to ruthlessness," which is to say that it gave shape and size to their institutions.

HISTORIANS OF THE CIVIL WAR are often criticized, sometimes with justice, for exaggerating the importance of the conflict. Perhaps most controversial is their claim that the struggle was the first of the modern wars. However, these historians are trying seriously to view the Civil War from other than a domestic perspective, to place it against the backdrop of general military history. Specifically, they regard it as a harbinger of the greater conflicts of the twentieth century, the two world wars.

The Civil War seems modern because many of the features that distinguish modern wars initially appeared in it. It was the first conflict in which the massive productive capacities of the Industrial Revolution were placed at the disposal of the military machine. It witnessed the first prominent use of mass production of goods to sustain mass armies, mass transportation on railroads, and telegraphic communication between different theaters and on the battlefield. It saw also the first use of such devices of the future as armored warships, breech-loading and repeating rifles, rifled artillery, land and sea mines, submarines, balloons, precursors of the machine gun, and trench warfare. It is true that some of the innovations had appeared in previous wars. The government of Revolutionary France, for one example, had raised mass armies, and some of the "new" weapons had been employed in earlier conflicts.* Nevertheless, the fact remains that in no previous war had so many of the methods and weapons made possible by modern industry been so apparent. In its material manifestations alone, in its application of the resources of technology to the business of killing, the Civil War presaged the later world wars.

The Civil War also antedated the twentieth century in a more important way, in the spirit in which it was fought. This was not a struggle to induce another nation to recognize a maritime right or cede a border territory, as were the War of 1812 and the Mexican War. The Civil War was a war of ideas, the North standing for nationalism and, later, for emancipation, and the South for localism and slavery. Because it involved great and emotional ideals, it was a war of unlimited objectives. The North was aiming to restore the Union by force; the South was trying to establish its own independence by force. Between these purposes there could be no compromise, no partial triumph for either side. One or the other had to achieve a complete victory.

The totality of these objectives led some historians to call the Civil War a total war. The label is somewhat exaggerated, as neither side put forward the

*Some of the weapons of the Civil War, such as submarines and balloons, were employed on few occasions or in small numbers and had little effect on operations. But this scant usage was also true of former wars.

absolute effort required of many nations in World War I or World War II. Citizens were conscripted and industry was encouraged to shift to war production, but this was not the complete mobilization of resources that characterizes total war. Still, the Civil War missed totality by but a narrow margin. It became a rough and ruthless war, involving in its lethal path the civilian populations, especially those in the South. Because new and deadlier weapons were available, it was more destructive of lives and property than any previous American war. If it was not the first modern war, it was ominously prophetic.*

THE LITERATURE on the causes of the Civil War is vast, diverse, and often angry. Historians have been debating the coming of the war for generations, the first serious treatments appearing in the 1890s. In arguing their opinions they have sometimes displayed a fierceness of spirit reminiscent of the fervor with which the conflict was fought. Even yet, there is no general agreement on the nature of the causes, and the war of words goes on.

The various views that have been set forth may be summarized in the approximate order in which they appeared:

1. The war arose out of differing concepts of the nature of the Union held by the North and South, nationalism versus states' rights, with slavery being a secondary cause of dissension.

2. The war was a conflict between two rival economic systems, the industrial North and the agricultural South.

3. The war represented a clash of two cultures or societies, the urban, modern-looking North and the rural, unchanging South.

4. The war came because politicians on both sides, but particularly in the North, aroused emotions on slavery, which was not an important issue, and then refused to allow reasonable compromise.

5. The war was a struggle between conflicting ideologies. Each section held to a set of beliefs or values that it was unwilling to give up—differing concepts of the nature of the Union, of the way the economy should develop, and of the organization of society. Central in each ideology was a clashing view on the place of slavery in the American system. The issue of slavery, which was also an issue of race, was a moral question and hence not easily susceptible to compromise.

The proponents of these schools of thought were, of course, influenced by the intellectual currents of their own time and culture. That is, in advancing particular causes of the Civil War, they reflected contemporary ideas about the causes of war itself. Thus, historians who argued that the war resulted from

---

*For Americans the Revolution was a war of ideas and eventually a war for an unlimited objective. However, the Revolution did not, like the Civil War, inspire a new military cycle; the two wars that followed it were limited conflicts. Conversely, the cycle begun by the Civil War may have ended with World War II; the wars since 1945 have been limited in objectives and methods.

avoidable blundering of politicians were writing in the 1930s, when disillusionment with World War I ran high; repelled by that conflict, they concluded that wars never have basic causes, have no effects that would not have come otherwise, and should always be prevented by compromise. However, this tendency to apply present standards to past wars should not in itself make the interpretation of a particular school suspect.

What ought to be questioned is whether the ideas prevailing at a particular time helped or hindered scholars in attempting to explain the causes of the Civil War or wars in general. The answer must be that in most periods the ruling concepts were not very helpful. Thus, the view that the cause of the war was economic, an explanation that flourished in the 1920s, when intellectuals were disturbed by the excesses of industrial capitalism, appears naive to today's scholars, who doubt that men would begin shooting each other because of differences over a tariff or banking system. The view of the 1930s, that the war was precipitated by blundering and evil men, also seems too simple to later scholars. Contemporary historians doubt that a few fanatics could stir up a war, and the great majority of them reject the idea that slavery was a false or an unimportant issue.

Most of the present analysts of the causes of the Civil War regard it as a conflict between rival ideologies. Like the scholars of previous eras, they have been influenced by the ideas and events of their own time. Living in a world divided into hostile blocs, they have been persuaded that this division stems from differing perceptions of moral values concerning the correct ordering of a society. Reading their opinion back into history, they have become convinced that most wars of the recent past have been caused by similar clashing ideologies. Many of them were profoundly moved by the civil rights revolution, and in trying to determine the causes of the Civil War, they were struck with the parallels that seemed to exist between the civil rights and antislavery movements. Slavery was the central issue between the North and the South, they decided, and was the focal point around which all the other conflicting sectional values clustered.

Slavery was an old issue in American life. There was criticism of the institution in the colonial period which continued in the early years of the republic, voiced by concerned individuals and members of small religious sects. But for a long time the movement against slavery was ineffectual and little noticed, lacking strength and, above all, organization. Then in the 1830s the abolitionists burst on the national scene, dedicated men and women who denounced slavery as a moral evil and demanded its extirpation and who possessed the advantages afforded by organization: newspapers, lecturers, and other means to publicize their views. The abolitionists were a small minority of the population of the free states, comprising only about 200,000 persons, but their impact on opinion transcended their numbers, thoroughly frightening Southerners and finding in Northerners an audience disposed to accept their views on the wrongness of slavery.

The majority of the Northern people were never persuaded to the abolitionist position that slavery should be ended immediately or in the near future. But most of them came eventually to believe that slavery was an immoral institution and an offense against the American dream of freedom and equality and that it should ultimately be eliminated. Northerners were responding as much to influences in the outside world as they were to the demands of the abolitionists. Opposition to slavery was one of the strongest forces sweeping Western civilization during the nineteenth century. It had been abolished in the British empire and in most countries of Latin America, surviving only in Cuba, Brazil, and the southern United States. American opponents of slavery were reflecting one of the compelling urges of their time.

Americans intent on getting rid of slavery faced difficulties not encountered by abolition leaders in countries without written constitutions or federal systems. In the United States there seemed no way to remove the institution. Congress could not legislate slavery out of existence because it was protected in the Constitution. An amendment to the fundamental document could accomplish abolition, but ratification would be impossible because of the certain adverse vote in the Southern states. Northern antislavery advocates were aware of the barriers in their way, and being conservative by nature, they were willing to accept a conservative solution. Slavery must be prohibited from expanding into the national territories, and penned up in the states where it already existed. Thus restricted, it would wither on the vine, so to speak, and when it became unprofitable, eventually slaveowners themselves would be amenable to its disappearance. When that time came, a plan could be devised to bring about gradual emancipation with compensation to masters. It would solve the fundamental problem, although it took no account of the position of the former slaves in society. Moreover, it would be a long time in the working and would require remarkable patience from the Northern people. Nevertheless, the idea found wide acceptance among Northern voters and became the official position of one of the major political parties, the Republicans, whose strength was centered in the North.*

The white South reacted to the attack on slavery with injured surprise and then with a closing of ranks to defend the institution. Slavery had always been two things in the South: a system of labor supply and a device for white supremacy. Even if slave labor had not been profitable, Southerners would have maintained the institution because they could conceive of no other way

*Antislavery partisans said little about the social and legal status of the former slaves. They apparently envisioned few rights for blacks beyond their becoming free laborers; many antislavery leaders specifically ruled out equality for blacks. Only the abolitionists advocated equal rights for blacks, and even they seemed embarrassed about the question. Racial prejudice ran high in the North, and the opponents of slavery had to take it into account. It was enough, they felt, that they should advocate partial freedom for people of another race.

to ensure the subordination of a race they considered inferior and barbarian. But in the decade preceding the outbreak of the Civil War, slave labor seemed increasingly profitable. The price of cotton rose steadily during the 1850s, and with prosperity the slave system took a firmer hold than ever. No voices were raised in the South to suggest negotiation with the majority section for a settlement of the slavery controversy, to offer emancipation at a distant date in return for financial compensation. Even had they been so disposed, Southern leaders would have never dared to recommend a compromise on slavery to their people. Even gradual emancipation involved an adjustment of race relations that white Southerners were not willing to make.

ONE OF THE RUNNING DEBATES in Civil War literature has been over the question of the inevitability of the conflict. Some scholars have disagreed that it was an "irrepressible" conflict and have affirmed that it could have been avoided if men had shown reason and restraint and compromised their differences. Their view is appealing to those who want to believe that every war can be averted, but it is not convincing. Resting on an exaggerated concept of human rationality, it assumes that we possess the capacity to solve any problem. The truth is that Americans of the 1850s had worked themselves into a controversy that could not be solved by normal and rational methods. The majority was determined that slavery must be ended and demanded that a plan be devised for its riddance. The minority was determined to retain slavery and refused even to consider a plan for abolition. In this impasse something had to give. Either the North had to cease agitating the slavery question or the South had to accept a procedure for eliminating the institution it regarded as basic to its way of life. Since neither side would yield, the only remaining solution was a resort sooner or later to violence. The solution was tragic, but a tragic resolution was the only one possible.

Historians who have viewed the war as a struggle of ideologies are close to the truth. And they are clearly correct in thinking that slavery was the most divisive issue between the sections. The political and economic differences could have been tolerated or adjusted, but the question of the continued existence of slavery could not be compromised. Slavery alone did not cause the war, but without its presence war would not have come. This truth was recognized by the man who was the keenest observer of the currents of opinion of the time. In 1865, near the close of the war, Abraham Lincoln discussed its beginning and spoke of what he called the "slavery interest." He added: "All knew that this interest was somehow the cause of the war."

THE PRESIDENTIAL ELECTION OF 1860 was the most momentous contest of its kind in American history. No other election has been fraught with so many serious and shattering consequences for the body politic. For the first and the only time in the history of the republic the losing side decided it could not live with the result and withdrew from political association with the victors.

Four parties nominated candidates in 1860. The Republicans, flushed with hopes of victory after a strong showing in their first presidential campaign in 1856 (the party had come into being only in 1854), nominated Abraham Lincoln and adopted a platform pledging opposition to the expansion of slavery into the national territories and support of legislation to foster the growth of Northern industrial and agricultural interests.

The Democrats, sorely troubled by internal division on the question of slavery in the territories, split into a Northern and a Southern wing. The Northern segment nominated Stephen A. Douglas and, seeking to subordinate the slavery issue, recommended that the status of slavery in the territories be determined by "popular sovereignty"—that is, by the vote of the settlers in a territory as to whether slavery should be permitted; devised to placate the South by avoiding exclusion of the institution, popular sovereignty was actually an antislavery formula, since most settlers would be from the free states. The Southern Democrats, scorning this or any other subterfuge, nominated John C. Breckinridge and demanded a "slave code" for the territories, the right of slavery not only to enter the national domain but to be protected there by the power of the national government.*

As if three parties were not enough, a fourth joined the contest, the newly formed Constitutional Union party, which nominated John Bell. Led by elder statesmen, most of whom had been members of the conservative Whig party, now defunct, this organization advocated no platform except the Constitution and the Union. These vague sentiments masked both a partisan and a patriotic purpose. The promoters of the party feared that the election of any of the other candidates would create a dangerous sectional crisis, and by avoiding a stand on the slavery issue, they hoped to win enough states to throw the election into the House of Representatives, where their own moderate candidate might be chosen president.

The election in November was a victory for Lincoln, who received 40 percent of the popular vote and 180 electoral votes, a clear majority. Breckinridge had 72 electoral votes, Bell 39, and Douglas, who was second in the popular tally, only 12. Lincoln carried every free state except New Jersey, which he divided with Douglas. Breckinridge captured the lower South and three upper South states. Bell won in three border slave states. Douglas carried only Missouri and split New Jersey's vote with Lincoln. Although Lincoln was a minority president, with a popular vote about a million votes less than the total of his opponents, he was a legitimate electoral victor; he would have won

---

*Although the strength of each wing was centered in its own section, each had supporters in the other section.

even if the opposition had been united, because he would still have swept most of the populous Northern states with large electoral votes.

The meaning of the election has perplexed analysts ever since. Seeking to determine whether the results indicated a popular mood or mandate, they have been able to offer only tentative answers. Some observers have thought it significant that Breckinridge's popular vote in the slave states was less than that of Bell and Douglas, possibly revealing the South's reluctance to take extreme action. Others, reckoning Breckinridge and Lincoln as the extreme candidates, point out that each carried his section, the lower South and the North respectively, and attracted more popular votes than his opponents; they suggest that this demonstrated a tendency to extremism in the country as a whole. These and other explications read too much back into the voting patterns of the election. The voters, beset by the conflicting claims of four candidates and platforms, did not express a clear opinion and certainly did not register a mandate, extreme or otherwise. But a large majority indicated approval of an ultimate action. Almost 70 percent of them voted for Lincoln or Douglas, each of whom was committed to excluding slavery from the territories, and in so voting they recorded a condemnation of slavery itself and a resolve to eventually bring about its demise. This was the result of the election that counted, and was the one that impressed the South.

Extremist leaders in the lower South, the part of the region that contained most of the slaves and was most devoted to maintaining the slave system, had foreseen the possibility of Lincoln's election and had been preparing their people to act when the crisis came. Almost a year before the election Robert Toombs of Georgia proclaimed that if the Republicans should win, "I see no safety for us, our property and our firesides, except in breaking up the concern. I do not think it wise for the South to suffer a party to get possession of the government whose principles and whose leaders are so openly hostile not only to her equality but to her safety in the Union. . . ." And after the election Toombs advised the Georgia legislature to break up the "concern" immediately. "Nothing but ruin will follow delay," he cried. "Then strike, strike while it is yet time."

Toombs and other leaders wanted the South to adopt secession, a procedure in which as many states as felt threatened by the Republican victory would individually leave the Union. The doctrine was of long standing in the South, developed to protect the minority status of the section and intended to be used as a last resort to avert majority tyranny. It rested on a constitutional postulate, that the Union was an association of sovereign states; these states had formed the Union and could, whenever they wished, withdraw from it and assume their inherent status as independent principalities. Although secession was a legal process, it was a very serious one, and could not be undertaken lightly. A special ritual was necessary to accomplish it, and Southerners had devised one. The governor and the legislature of a state would call an election for delegates to a convention which would represent the sovereign power of the people, and this assemblage could, if a majority of the delegates favored secession, enact an ordinance that would take the state out of the Union. Because the convention came directly from the people, its action would not have to be submitted to popular ratification.

Advocates of secession in the lower South were determined to take advantage of the four months that would elapse between Lincoln's election and his assumption of the presidency in early March. Consequently, they counseled their states to take immediate action, to secede before the government was taken over by the Republicans, or, as some of them put it, by the "enemy." In pressing their demand, they encountered few opponents who denied the right of a state to secede; on this question there was virtual unanimity in the lower South. But the seceders did meet resistance from many who held that Lincoln's election was not sufficient cause to secede. These men, moderate by instinct, argued that the South should wait until the Republicans made a hostile move before acting. In the meantime, a Southern convention could be convened to formulate a set of conditions on which the section would remain in the Union. Advocating delay and collective action, this group was sometimes called the "cooperators."

The seceders won the battle for the mind of the lower South. Between late December, 1860, and February 1, 1861, seven states left the Union. They were, in the order of their going, South Carolina, Mississippi, Florida, Alabama, Georgia, Louisiana, and Texas. But the margin of victory varied from state to state. In South Carolina, Mississippi, and Florida the advocates of immediate action had huge majorities in the conventions and enacted secession against virtually no opposition—in South Carolina, in fact, by a unanimous vote. But in the Alabama and Georgia conventions the cooperators were strongly represented and almost succeeded in passing resolutions to delay action.* There was also considerable cooperator sentiment in Louisiana, but it was not manifested in the state's convention. By the time that body convened in late January five states had already seceded and a bandwagon psychology was beginning to take hold; most of the Louisiana cooperators simply jumped on the wagon. Also affected by the momentum of the movement in other states was Texas, the last of the seven to secede, although support for immediate action was stronger there than in Louisiana.†

It is evident that the citizens of the seven seceding states viewed the breaking of their membership in the Union with mixed feelings. Some left in exultation, some in sadness, and some in no clearly defined spirit but simply

---

*It is interesting to speculate on the outcome if these two populous and strategically located states had refused to secede. The process would probably have come to an embarrassed halt.

†Many cooperators in the conventions, notably in Alabama and Georgia, after having lost their fight, voted for secession in order to demonstrate unity to the North.

swept along in the excitement of the moment. Modern historians, surveying these responses, have wondered whether the decision for secession represented the considered opinion of the people in these states, or was even a majority opinion. Some have speculated that many were stampeded into acting by the leaders of the movement, who created a false crisis and frightened or intimidated voters to support secession.

There is some evidence to support a theory of conspiracy. The secessionists were obviously prepared to act quickly—many of them had long hoped for a propitious time to secede—and were much better organized than the cooperators, who seemed surprised at the result of the election and were slow in mounting their opposition. Several secessionist governors helped to create a crisis psychology by ordering federal installations in their states seized before separation was accomplished, thus spreading the impression that secession was inevitable. However, none of this was sufficient to demonstrate that masses of people in the lower South were rushed into making a choice they were not prepared to make. They were influenced by their leaders, it is true, but they were receptive to being influenced. For years they had been told that secession might be necessary to preserve slavery and the racial system associated with it, and they believed those leaders who assured them that the time of peril had now come, that, as one secessionist put it, the Republicans were determined to "use all the power of the Federal Government, as well as every other power in their hands," to break slavery down. To avert this danger, the cooperators proposed only delay, a continuation of the crisis. The seceders offered a simple and direct remedy that promised to snap tensions that were becoming unbearable.

And so the secession of the lower South was accomplished, as its adherents hoped it would be, before Lincoln assumed the presidency. Not only had seven states left the Union, but representatives of these states met in Montgomery, Alabama, in February, 1861, and formed a political association of their own, a different kind of union, the Confederate States of America. A new nation stood proudly though somewhat self-consciously before the world.

While the process of secession was being rushed to its conclusion, Northerners watched with mingled amazement and anger. Accustomed to hear Southerners threaten to leave the Union, they could not quite believe the threats were becoming reality. Although resentful of what they considered hasty and unjustified action by the South, they were uncertain as to how to deal with the crisis. Their disposition was to maintain the Union, but few voices were raised to counsel the use of force. At this stage most Northerners clung to the hope that some kind of compromise could be devised to induce the departed states to return.

One man with a large hand in framing a policy was the incumbent lame-duck president, James Buchanan, a Democrat. Buchanan, however, hesitated to take a firm stand, restrained both by the indecision of the Northern people and by his own personal indecision. Thus, he denied a state's right to secede but also said that the national government lacked the power to coerce a state back into the Union. His hope was to persuade Congress to adopt a satisfactory compromise plan, something that body was unable to do, and if this failed, to hand over the problem to his successor in office. On one issue, however, he stood steadfast. As the various states seceded, they seized all federal properties within their borders. But lacking naval strength, they were unable to take possession of certain offshore forts: Fort Sumter, in the harbor of Charleston, South Carolina; Fort Pickens, adjacent to the coast at Pensacola, Florida; and Fort Taylor, near Key West, Florida. First the governments of the states claiming jurisdiction over these places, and later the government of the Confederacy, demanded of Buchanan that he give them up. He rejected every request, and the forts were still under national authority when Lincoln was inaugurated on March 4, 1861.

Before coming to Washington, Lincoln had decided on a policy to deal with the secession crisis. He had outlined this program in private communications to associates, and he gave it fuller expression in his inaugural address. Naturally, he did not spell out every detail of his plan, leaving himself options to act differently if he had to. Although the new president did not rule out the possibility that the seceded states might return to the Union voluntarily if they were assured he would not interfere with slavery, he thought it probable that they would not come back unless they were coerced. He was prepared to use force, if necessary, to maintain inviolate the American experiment in self-government, that Union he later called "the last, best hope of earth."

Thus, in his inaugural address Lincoln spoke in conciliatory terms to the people in the seceded states and to Southerners generally, assuring them he would not interfere with slavery and begging them to refrain from any extreme action that would make a peaceable restoration of the Union impossible. "We are not enemies, but friends," he intoned. "We must not be enemies." He was saying, in short, that the departed states were welcome to return to the fold but that they would not be granted any favorable conditions to induce them to return. Elsewhere in the address he indicated what his policy would be if they did not come back and showed the iron fist that underlay the soft glove of conciliation. He asserted that no state of its own volition could leave the Union and that the ordinances of secession were unconstitutional. This was tantamount to saying he would not recognize the governments in the seceded states as legal entities, and he followed by declaring that he intended to enforce federal laws in all the states. Most important, and most disturbing to the Confederate government, he announced that he would maintain possession of federal property in the seceded states, which meant the offshore forts, those hated symbols of the old authority in the new Southern nation.

Lincoln felt little fear for the security of two of the forts, Pickens and Taylor, which were situated so far from the coast that they could be readily supplied by sea. But the third one, Sumter, sat in the middle of Charleston harbor and was ringed by hostile batteries and troops under the command of General P. G. T. Beauregard. Before the Confederate government took over the forces in Charleston, the South Carolina authorities permitted the small garrison of seventy or so men to draw food and other supplies from the city, but Beauregard, acting on instructions from Montgomery, ordered this traffic halted. Soon the troops in Sumter began to suffer for food, and the commandant, Major Robert Anderson, informed Washington that unless he received fresh provisions shortly, he would have to evacuate the fort. His message presented Lincoln with a difficult choice. The president had said the forts would be held as a means of maintaining the Union, and if he now abandoned one of them, he would seem to be abandoning his policy of patient firmness. On the other hand, if he moved to succor the fort, he would run the danger of starting war. Lincoln deliberated long over the problem and finally decided, against the counsel of his civil and military advisers, to send a naval relief expedition to Sumter. In a carefully worded dispatch he notified the South Carolina authorities of his decision (he could not recognize the Confederate government), explaining that although the ships carried troops and weapons, no attempt would be made to land them if reprovisioning of the fort was permitted.

In resolving his own dilemma, Lincoln had placed the Confederate government in a greater one. If Montgomery allowed the expedition to land supplies, it would extend the tenure of the Federal stay in Sumter; worse, it would seem to be bowing to Federal authority, to be admitting that it did not mean to sustain an independent existence. The only alternative seemed to be to attack, reducing Sumter before the relief expedition arrived—but this would not only invoke war but place the Confederacy in the role of aggressor. After hours of anguished discussion the men in Montgomery decided they had to risk the latter, that a continuation of the present stalemate was unbearable. Accordingly, Beauregard was ordered to demand the surrender of Sumter, and if this was refused, to take the fort. The general served his summons and, on receiving Anderson's rejection, opened a bombardment of the fort on April 12. The firing was renewed on the following day with severe damage to the works, and Anderson, recognizing his situation as hopeless, surrendered on the fourteenth. War had come at last.*

The attack on Sumter aroused the Northern people to fury. From all quarters demands pressed upon the government to avenge the humiliation to the flag, to punish the aggressors, to use whatever force was necessary to preserve national authority and the Union. "There are only two sides to the

---

*The relief expedition approached the harbor entrance during the bombardment but made no attempt to run the ring of fire. The Sumter garrison was permitted to board the ships and return to the North.

question," declared a Democratic leader who had heretofore favored a moderate course. "Every man must be for the United States government or against it. There can be no neutrals in this war; only patriots or traitors." The disposition to maintain the Union had existed from the beginning of the secession crisis, and it needed only the spark of an incident like that at Sumter to stir it to fighting pitch. The accusation is sometimes made that Lincoln maneuvered the situation at Sumter to create an incident, to provoke war. The charge is unjust. He did not want war, but realized he might have to resort to war to preserve the Union, an end that was worth even war. He so maneuvered at Sumter that if war came, it would be started by the other side, that his government and his cause would stand in the best light before his people and the world.

After the fall of Sumter, Lincoln on his own authority increased the regular army and called on the states to provide militia to deal with what he called "combinations too powerful" for the ordinary agencies of government to suppress. At this indication that the government meant to employ force to restore the Union, four more slave states, unable to accept this exercise of national authority, seceded and joined the Confederacy: Virginia, Arkansas, Tennessee, and North Carolina.* However, four other slave states, although torn by conflicting loyalties and emotions, remained in the Union: Maryland, Delaware, Kentucky, and Missouri. The last choices had been made, and both sides began to mobilize forces for the ultimate test of strength.

SOME MODERN CIVIL WAR SCHOLARS have marveled that Southerners ever thought they could prevail against an adversary so superior in material resources. Looking at the indicators of physical strength in the two sections, these historians have concluded that the Southern venture in independence was conceived in reckless disregard of reality and was foreordained to fail.

The supporters of this interpretation overlook an important fact, that the Confederacy, for all the odds against it, was able to carry on the struggle for four years. But there is a measure of logic in their argument. All the great material advantages were on the side of the United States, or the North, and these advantages did influence the outcome of the war. This material superiority was apparent as the war began and became more obvious and more important the longer it continued.

---

*After Virginia seceded, the capital of the Confederacy was transferred from Montgomery to Richmond. In making this move the government was in part paying deference to Virginia's honored position among the Southern states. But it also needed more commodious quarters than those afforded in Montgomery, and Richmond, a city of 40,000, seemed able to provide adequate facilities. The problem of finding a place large enough to house the government was a real one. New Orleans and Charleston could have served but were vulnerable to attack by sea. However, Richmond lay only about a hundred miles from Washington.

First of all, the North had a substantial advantage in population and hence a larger manpower reservoir from which to draw its armed forces. The twenty-three "loyal" states had a population of over 21 million, whereas the population of the eleven Confederate states was but 9 million. However, these totals give a somewhat misleading impression of the relative strength of the two sections. The Northern aggregate included over half a million people in the Pacific coast states, an area too distant from the conflict to provide a direct contribution to the military effort, and the inhabitants of the four loyal slave states, which sent thousands of recruits to the Confederate armies. On the other side, the total Confederate population included over 800,000 in Tennessee, whose eastern mountains contained a pro-Union population, and an indeterminable number of Union partisans in the mountain areas of other states where slavery was almost unknown. Complicating the problem of evaluating Confederate strength was the presence in the Southern population of over 3 million slaves, so that the white, or military, population was less than 6 million. If the slaves are counted in the Southern total, the Confederacy faced human odds of more than two to one. If the slaves are subtracted, the odds were almost four to one.

However the disparity is calculated, it is evident that the North enjoyed a substantial advantage in manpower. But the South was able to offset its inferiority in total numbers by making real, if indirect, use of its slave population. Not only did slaves serve as military laborers and in other capacities in the armed forces, but by their assured presence as agricultural laborers they freed a large number of white men for military service. Moreover, the South mobilized its forces somewhat more quickly than the North, and until 1863 maintained armies that were not appreciably smaller than those of the North. It is true that after 1863 Northern armies increased in size while Southern forces decreased, but until that time the Confederates possessed such strength that they might conceivably have won a decision on the field. Finally, at all stages of the conflict the North had to divert large portions of its armies to the maintenance of long lines of communication in the invaded South and to the garrisoning of occupied areas. Preponderance of numbers in itself has never guaranteed victory in war, especially if the superior side must invade and hold a large hostile area—as witness the failure of Britain to conquer the American colonies.

More marked than the North's edge in manpower was the superior potential of its economy to provide the matériel of war. In the North were 81 percent of the nation's factories and 67 percent of the farms. Even this overwhelming preponderance does not convey an adequate appreciation of the South's backwardness in production. The great majority of the region's factories were small establishments, actually not factories but shops, the average plant representing a modest capital investment and employing but a few workers; more serious, the typical factory was not mechanized but relied on hand labor, which had a limited productive capacity. In contrast, the more numerous Northern factories were, usually, larger in capital investment, in number of workers employed, and in annual value of products. But the most important difference between the rival industrial systems was that the larger Northern plants had installed labor-saving equipment that increased vastly their productive potential. Machines, such as the reaper, drill, and thresher, were also in use on Northern farms; such devices were unknown in Southern agriculture.*

The importance of the North's greater economic potential was soon apparent. During the first year of the war both sides had to purchase arms and other supplies in Europe, but by 1862 the Northern industrial system had converted to producing war goods, and after that year Northern reliance on Europe practically ceased. The South, in contrast, never achieved self-sufficiency. Although the Confederacy's industrial capacity was expanded, it was not able to provide its armies with anything like the amount and variety of goods they required, and was even less able to satisfy the wants of the civilian population for consumer goods. For every step forward the South took in production, the North took several that were much longer.

Few persons in either section in 1861 foresaw the role that Northern industry would play in the war. One who did was former army officer William T. Sherman, later to become a Northern general. Sherman warned a Southern friend: "You are rushing into war with one of the most powerful, ingeniously mechanical and determined peoples on earth—right at your door. You are bound to fail." There was some exaggeration in his prediction but much truth. Economic inferiority alone did not doom the South to defeat, any more than did inferiority in size of population. But inadequacy did contribute mightily to the eventual result and was a major reason for the Confederate downfall. After 1863 Southern morale sagged badly from the realization that the South faced a foe with apparently limitless resources.

Still another advantage possessed by the North was its transportation facilities, superior in every way to those of the South. The North had more and better inland-water transport, in the form of steamboats and barges, and more surfaced roads and wagons and animals. But the North's greatest advantage lay in its railroads, which had become the dominant form of transportation in the country before the war. The North had over 20,000 miles of railroads, whereas the South, comprising at least as large a land area, had but slightly more than 9,000 miles. However, the superiority of the Northern system was even more marked than the trackage totals indicate. Many of the Northern lines had been built by big companies and were "through" roads, providing

*A statistical comparison of Northern and Southern industry is revealing. In 1860 there were in the North 110,000 plants, representing a capital investment of $850 million, employing 1,130,000 workers, and making annually products valued at $1 billion. For the same categories in the South the figures are: plants, 20,000; capital, $95 million; workers, 110,000; value of products, $155 million.

continuous connections between distant points. In contrast, the Southern roads had largely been constructed by small concerns and were short lines; a railroad map of the region reveals long gaps between key places. The few through lines that existed, like the connection between Richmond and Memphis and that between Richmond and the Carolinas, ran close to the land border or the sea and were highly vulnerable to Northern raiders.

Both rail systems performed prodigious feats during the war, especially in moving troops vast distances from one theater to another. The Northern network was able to bear easily the burden placed upon it; rolling stock that became unusable was quickly replaced, and the total trackage was even extended somewhat. But the Southern system gradually broke down under the unusual strains and by 1864 was almost in a state of collapse. Locomotives, freight cars, and rails simply deteriorated and became unusable; other stock was destroyed or damaged by Northern raiders. None of the equipment could be replaced. Before the war Southern roads purchased their rolling stock from Northern factories or from the few large Southern ironworks that cast rail supplies. The war cut off the Northern source and diverted the Southern source; Southern iron plants turned to producing armaments and did not make a single car during the war.

The prostration of the rail system affected the Confederacy's war-making ability in several adverse ways. During the last half of the war it became increasingly difficult to move large bodies of troops any distance by rail, even to shift men within one theater. Equally serious, it became harder to transport food and other bulk supplies from producing centers to the armies or to the cities and towns that depended on outside sources for sustenance. The problem of feeding soldiers and civilians became especially acute the longer the war continued. Agricultural production declined as Federal forces occupied or devastated large areas and as thousands of slaves deserted the plantations and farms to flock into the camps of the invaders. But despite the drop, the South up to near the end was probably producing enough food to meet its minimum wants. Often, however, the provender could not be carried by the railroads to where it was needed, so hunger afflicted the armies and large sections of the civilian population. Although the privation was severe, its effect was more psychological than physical, intensifying the mood of hopelessness that grew on the populace after 1863. The collapse of the railroad system was not a decisive factor in causing Confederate defeat, but it was an important force in weakening the Confederate will to fight.

A final advantage enjoyed by the North was its preponderant sea power. At the beginning of the war the United States Navy numbered some 90 ships of all types, not all of them serviceable, and a personnel of 9,000, a small force compared to the squadrons of the larger European powers and inadequate to perform the task first demanded of it, to blockade the long Southern coast. However, rapid expansion converted the navy into one of the major sea forces of the world and enabled it to play a major part in the conflict—by 1864 it numbered approximately 670 ships of all types and boasted a service of over 50,000 men. The Confederacy had no navy, but it set out immediately to build one. It was never able to match the North's superior construction facilities, however, being able to put together but about 130 vessels that enlisted a personnel of only 4,000 men or so, and Northern sea power remained dominant throughout the war.

The Northern navy performed two important strategic functions. First, it attempted to seal off the Confederacy from intercourse with the outside world. The effect of this effort has been questioned by some historians, who have pointed out that a large number of vessels slipped in and out of the blockade. There can be no doubt that the blockade was "leaky"; it was impossible to close off completely the extensive coastline. However, most of the ships entering Southern ports were small craft that rarely carried heavy equipment like armaments and that often brought in luxury items to dispose of at a high profit. And fewer and fewer of these vessels got through as the navy became ever stronger and was able to tighten its stranglehold. The consequence of its labor has been stated aptly by historian D. P. Crook: "The blockade forced the Confederacy to breathe through a constricted windpipe, and the effort became more debilitating with time."

Northern naval power also supported Federal land forces operating in the Western theater, the region between the Appalachian Mountains and the Mississippi River. In this area the invading Federals advanced along the larger rivers, which were navigable to small ships of war and transport vessels, and the navy moved with the army, carrying supplies and joining in attacks on Confederate strongpoints. The combined assaults were the first large amphibious operations in American military history and represented a new degree of cooperation between the land and sea services.

THE SHEER WEIGHT of Northern material superiority has persuaded observers that the result of the war was inevitable. The odds against the South were indeed great, but not so preponderant as to render the cause of the Confederacy hopeless. As previously indicated, Confederate armies might have achieved such decisive victories before 1863 as to force recognition of Southern independence—if fortune had shifted her favor on one field or another. Even without a smashing military success, the Confederacy might have secured its policy goal simply by tiring the North out, by convincing the enemy that it could not be conquered. The South was fighting for something concrete, something easy for its people to support. It wanted only to be independent; it had no aggressive designs on the North. For its part, the North was fighting for an abstract principle, to maintain the Union, and this was a goal the North could abandon without incurring direct harm. The United States could have peace and still be independent by simply quitting the war. That the Northern citizenry did not succumb to this temptation can be ascribed to several factors—to the fact that the military situation never seemed to be completely hopeless, to the leadership of President Lincoln, but primarily to its own determination to see the war out.

CHAPTER X

The Civil War:
Means and Measures

A T THE START OF HOSTILITIES the majority of ordinary folk in both sections, and most of the leaders, thought the war would not last long. One big successful battle would convince the other side that it was beaten, the predictions ran, and the war would be over within a year or even less. These cocksure opinions sprang in part from American memories of the short Mexican War but fundamentally from the feeling of superiority that each section had developed about itself, or from the converse of this, the conviction each one held that the other was inferior and hence would be an easy victim. Thus, in the North many observers forecast that the "rebels" would be whipped "before the next cotton crop," and in New York City men were knocked down in the streets for merely suggesting that Southerners might fight well. In the South, where the conditions of plantation culture encouraged men to think of themselves as knights without peer, confidence in the result was even higher, and more unreal. Southerners dismissed as unimportant the North's greater resources, particularly its ability to raise more troops; those "popinjays" and "scurvy fellows" of the cities could not possibly be a match for the "hot blooded, thoroughbred, impetuous men" of the Confederacy. "Let them come South and we will put our negroes to the dirty work of killing them," one newspaper trumpeted.

More thoughtful men in both sections did not indulge in these fantasies. The two presidents especially, Lincoln and Davis, realized that the war was likely to be a long and hard-fought struggle, and their concern was reflected in the manpower policies they recommended to their respective congresses. Lincoln after Fort Sumter called on the states to provide 75,000 militia for three months' service, the maximum period allowed under existing law. His action was intended as only a symbolic assertion of the purpose of the government to uphold the Union. He knew the militia could not be utilized in a long

war, but with Congress not in session he decided to summon every force available to him. In his determination he employed even a power denied to him by the Constitution, the stipulation that only Congress can augment the size of the armed forces. By proclamation he authorized an increase of 23,000 men in the regular army and the enlistment of 42,000 volunteers for three years.*
He asked Congress to legalize his acts when it convened in regular session in July and further induced it to provide him authority to raise a total of 500,000 volunteers for three years' service. Because of Lincoln's insistence the North was off to a good start. It had called into being a large force that could be held under arms for a significant period of time, and avoided the error of creating a short-term army for a short war. Undoubtedly the great majority of congressmen who accepted the president's recommendation believed that the conflict would take much less than three years.

President Davis was not so fortunate in dealing with his Congress. Although he earnestly and frequently warned that the war would be a long one, not many heard him. The first military legislation enacted by the Confederate Congress provided for enlistment of only 100,000 men, for a service of twelve months. Later laws authorized Davis to accept up to 500,000 volunteers for terms of not less than one year or more than three years, and as many as would volunteer for the duration. But the damage was already done. Over 300,000 came forward in 1861, as contrasted with 600,000 in the North, but at least one-third and possibly two-thirds of them enrolled under the twelve-month law and were slated for discharge in the spring of 1862.†

Both governments thus appreciated that this war was going to be more encompassing than any previous American conflict; nothing like these hosts had been contemplated in earlier struggles. But in choosing a method to mobilize troops they were not so realistic. Both administrations assumed that they could raise and then maintain armies of sufficient size by calling for volunteers, the traditional way of creating a fighting force, but one that had been developed for smaller wars. The volunteer system turned out enough men in 1861, when martial enthusiasm and expectations of a brief war ran high in both sections, but as 1862 dawned, much of the earlier ardor was fading. Now the signs were obvious that the war was going to be a long, hard struggle. Volunteering fell off badly in both sections, but the decline affected more adversely the Confederacy, the side with the smaller manpower resources.

As the spring of 1862 approached, the Confederacy seemed threatened by a dissolution of its armies, and this in the face of expected large Northern offensives. Despite urgent appeals from Richmond, few volunteers were com-

*The size of the regular army after Southern defections was about 13,000 officers and men. Even with wartime increases, it remained a small force and played a minor part in the conflict. The Civil War was fought by both sides with citizen soldiers.

†Evidence indicates that more than 100,000 men were accepted under the twelve-month law; some estimates place the number so enrolled at 200,000.

ing forward to augment the ranks or to replace men who were leaving. And many were threatening to depart. The twelve-month men, trained and battle-hardened veterans, showed little disposition to reenlist. Their attitude was that they had done their bit—and now they would go home and rest for a time while others took up the burden. Where to find the "others" was the problem that worried the government.

The Confederacy met the crisis with bold action. At Davis's recommendation, Congress enacted in April a measure imposing conscription on the white male population, the First Conscription Act, the numbered title being applied later to distinguish it from subsequent draft laws. The act declared that all able-bodied white males between the ages of eighteen and thirty-five were liable to military service for three years and would be called up at the will of the central authority. In an equal assertion of power, designed to retain veterans in service, the measure decreed that men already in the army were to continue for three years from the date of their enlistment, getting credit for one year but having to serve two more. As the war continued, Congress enacted two additional draft bills, each a response to a worsening manpower situation. The Second Conscription Act (September, 1862) extended the upper age of men liable to service to forty-five years. The Third Conscription Act (February, 1864) fixed the lower and upper age limits at seventeen and fifty. In its desperation the Confederacy was said to be reaching toward "the cradle and the grave."*

With its larger manpower resources, the North was able to maintain its armies by relying on volunteers longer than its adversary. But by the latter part of 1862 Washington was also having difficulty in inducing sufficient men to come forward, and the president and legislative leaders began to consider that conscription might be necessary. However, action was slow in coming; not until March, 1863, did Congress finally enact a draft measure. Entitled the Enrollment Act, it declared that all able-bodied males between the ages of twenty and forty-five if unmarried, and between twenty and thirty-five if married, were liable to be called up for service for three years.† Ironically, in view of the differing constitutional traditions of the two sections, the Northern law did not provide for as great an exertion of national authority as did its Southern counterpart of the previous year. It did not actually impose a direct draft but held forth the threat of conscription in order to stimulate enlistments. Each state was divided into enrollment districts and at a call for troops was assigned a quota of men to be raised based on its population. If a state or a

---

*The upper age limits in the second and third acts brought in men who in a modern army would be considered too old to serve actively; in extenuation of Confederate policy it should be said that the government hoped to use the oldsters in home defense. The lower age limit of seventeen is not out of line with modern practice.

†The act applied to black as well as white males. Congress had authorized the use of Negro soldiers in the previous year.

district could fill its quota, by offering cash bounties or through other appeals, it escaped the draft completely. If the quota was not met, the government stepped in to draft enough men to make up the difference. The state naturally exercised great efforts to avoid the necessity for national interposition, and some states and many districts went through the war without ever seeing conscription agents.*

The men in the two governments who drew the draft laws were attempting to provide a method of mobilization without benefit of precedents from the American past. Conscription had been employed in colonial times to maintain the militia, it is true, but then it had been invoked by local governments and in wars that forced men into service for only very limited periods of time. For the kind of conflict the Civil War was becoming, the modest practices of the colonial era offered little direction, and needing a model, legislators turned to the laws of European nations with long experience with conscription. They took from these measures the principal provisions of their own acts and also the European usage of exempting some men from service, a procedure that was partly favoritism to the richer classes but also recognition of the fact that some citizens had to be held out of uniform to perform vital functions on the home front.

The Northern conscription act, because it was intended to work indirectly, allowed few exemptions, occupational or any other kind. Ranking national and state officials and clergymen could claim deferment, and so also could a son of a dependent widow or of dependent parents. However, it was possible to escape service by purchasing exemption. A man who was called up could hire a substitute to go in his place, or, if he did not feel such an urgent rush of patriotism, could remain at home simply by paying the government a "commutation" fee of $300.

In contrast, the several Confederate draft laws provided numerous exemptions. A conscripted Southerner could escape service by employing a substitute. But, unlike a similarly situated Northerner, he could not get off by paying a cash commutation. The fee in the North set a maximum top price on substitutes, but the Southern law had no such brake, so the price demanded by proxies mounted ever higher as the war continued, reflecting both a decreasing pool of manpower and an increasing supply of depreciated paper currency. It eventually reached as high as $10,000, and became a form of escape that only the wealthiest could afford.

Most Confederate exemptions were allowed to men assumed to be in an occupation important to the war effort. Although the purpose of the government was laudable, and its practice strikingly modern in anticipating the later principle of "selective service," it erred badly in choosing those to be deferred. The laws permitted too many occupational exemptions and included numer-

*It is estimated that only 46,000 men were drafted directly into service.

ous groups that by no realistic standards could be said to be performing necessary war work. Moreover, although the intention was more unconscious than deliberate, some of the exemptions had the effect of relieving from service men in the upper classes. Thus, exemption was extended to railroad employees, workers in mines, foundries, and furnaces, telegraph operators, and doctors and druggists, individuals who were obviously important on the home front. But it was granted also to Confederate and state officials and clerks, factory owners, college presidents and professors, lower school teachers with twenty or more pupils, militia officers certified by their governors as needed locally, and newspaper editors. The most overt example of class favoritism was a provision exempting one white man on each plantation containing twenty or more slaves, referred to scornfully by non-slaveholders as the "twenty-nigger law." The various indulgences allowed to the upper groups aroused wide and bitter class discontent and caused many ordinary men to say, as some in the North said too: "It's a rich man's war but a poor man's fight."*

To many people in both sections conscription came as a new and ominous exercise of national power, a startling interference with traditional freedom of choice. The majority accepted it as something disagreeable that had to be endured to achieve victory, but minorities denounced the draft as unnecessary or unjust or unconstitutional, and often as all of these. In the North resistance was strongest in the poorer sections of cities, among laborers who considered that the draft law discriminated against men of their class, and among immigrants who had come to America partly to escape conscription in their own lands.

There was opposition on different grounds in the Democratic party. Most Democrats supported the war, but some governors and other leaders contended that the national government had no power under the Constitution to draft men. One faction centered in the rural northwestern states, the Peace Democrats, opposed the war on principle, calling it an evil attempt of the Northeast to acquire dominance over the agricultural sections, and condemned conscription.

Although the opponents of conscription were moved by different influences, they shared one belief: all of them objected to fighting to free slaves or to elevate in the slightest way the condition of blacks. Usually critics of conscription limited themselves to denouncing it in speeches or the press. But occasionally feelings among the poorer classes boiled up to such a point that violence erupted. The most spectacular instance occurred in New York City

*Eventually the cash-commutation clause was repealed in the North and the substitution practice was ended in the South. The available evidence does not indicate that men of means in either section evaded service in large numbers. Most planters in the South seem to have sought service. Moreover, recent research in enrollment lists in several Northern districts reveals a surprising fact, that many men of average economic circumstances were able to pay the commutation fee and stay out of uniform.

in 1863. Excited by news that a new draft call had been issued, mobs of protesters rioted for four days, killing a number of whites and blacks and holding parts of the city in their grip until dispersed by troops sent in by the national government.

In the South, opposition to drafting did not take a violent turn. But a form of passive resistance developed, beginning in the summer of 1863, when military reverses convinced many people that the war could not be won, and becoming stronger as subsequent reverses pointed to the inevitable end. Thousands of men who were called up did not report, remaining hidden at home by friends or families or taking to the hills or woods to escape detection by government agents. Thousands already in the army deserted, going home to see to their families, or joining other evaders congregated in foothill areas in such numbers as to be able to defy attempts by the government to bring them back. A woman who saw such men trudging by her door in 1865 wrote in anguish in her diary: "I am sure our army is silently dispersing. Men are moving the wrong way, all the time. . . . They have given the thing up."

Another form of resistance was a kind of legal sabotage of the draft laws, a method of opposition that reflected the Southern tendency to define the rightness or wrongness of every issue, including even military policy in a desperate war, in constitutional terms. Southerners who in the old Union had fought the centralizing tendencies of the government did not lose this habit now they had a government of their own. Many of them opposed Confederate authority when it sought to exercise certain powers in connection with the war effort, being most aroused by the adoption of conscription, which in their view was an unconstitutional use of power. These states' righters, as they were called, controlled the governments of Georgia, South Carolina, and North Carolina, and the governors in these states used a variety of methods to impede enforcement of conscription. The law allowed deferment to militia officers, and the governors decided they needed more officers, many more. In fact, it seemed that at times the militia in these states had more officers than men. In 1864 the governor of North Carolina certified 16,000 members of his force as exempt, and in Georgia in the same year it was estimated that more men between the ages of eighteen and forty-five were in the militia than had gone into the army. A governor could also claim that his troops were needed at home for local defense, and if he could make a case or felt strong enough to withstand national authority, he could keep them there. In 1864 and 1865, with the Confederacy tottering to destruction, the governors of the three dissenting states virtually defied the Richmond administration to enforce conscription within their boundaries.

The draft policies of the two governments seem defective if compared to later practices. They contained too many loopholes that facilitated too many evasions. But their architects were pioneering in a new form of mobilization, whereas the framers of modern laws had the benefit of the Civil War experience. The Union and Confederate acts should not be judged by their shortcomings but by their results, and those were impressive. Both sides raised by drafting and by volunteering large numbers of men.* The statistical methods used by the two governments do not permit an accurate statement of the total numbers enlisted, including, as the records do, men who enrolled for short terms or joined up several times under different names to claim bounties. But it is possible to estimate with reasonable accuracy the number of men who served for a meaningful period, three years. The appraisals indicate that 1,500,000 long-term soldiers served in the Union armies and that 900,000 such men served in the Confederate forces. The latter total was an exceptionally high percentage of troops to be raised out of a white population of 6 million.

The Confederacy got its maximum strength onto the field at an early date in the war and then saw it drain away, whereas the strength of the Union began gradually but increased steadily. The South, resorting to conscription first, had 500,000 men under arms at the end of 1862 and during the first half of the following year. At the end of 1863, 465,000 men were carried on the army rolls, but not more than 230,000 were actually present for duty. The situation grew even worse during the desperate year of 1864. At its close, only 200,000 were on the rolls and probably not more than half were present for duty; an estimated 100,000 men had deserted and gone home. The Union armies, in contrast, expanded constantly. Conscription had the anticipated effect of spurring enlistments, and in 1864 the North had 500,000 men in service and hundreds of thousands more waiting in enrolled reserves. The arithmetic of manpower at last caught up with the Confederacy.

WHEN MILITARY HISTORIANS refer to manpower in conflicts before the Civil War, they are referring to white manpower. Black men had served in the earlier wars but never in numbers large enough to influence the outcome, or to cause whites to appreciate their contribution. The Civil War was the first struggle in which blacks participated in substantial numbers and the first in which their presence helped to determine the result. Admitted reluctantly into Northern armies, they won commendation of their efforts from civil and military leaders, including President Lincoln.

The Northern Congress authorized the executive branch to employ "persons of African descent" in the armed forces in the summer of 1862. Although black and abolitionist leaders had urged that Negroes be given a chance to prove their worth in combat, the appeals were not the primary influence in moving the government to act. Rather, it was responding to increasing de-

*Both governments continued to accept volunteers after imposing conscription.

mands from whites that blacks be compelled to share the perils of battle. Why should white blood be shed when black blood was available, was a question being asked by more and more whites.

Even after the doors were opened, the government moved slowly to enlist blacks. Not until 1863, when emancipation was proclaimed as an objective of the war, was there an active recruitment policy, concentrated in occupied areas of the South and on the former slave population. The War Department sent an officer of general rank to the lower Mississippi Valley to raise troops from among the freedmen of the area, and this man eventually organized fifty regiments. Also active in enlisting former slaves were some state governments, which sought by this method to fill the quotas assigned to them in troop calls and thus to escape the draft; agents of the northeastern states offering generous bounties were especially successful in this endeavor. So effective were the combined programs of the federal and state governments that of the approximately 180,000 blacks enlisted about 65 percent were raised in Southern states.*

Black soldiers, whether freedmen or free men from Northern states, suffered various discriminations. They served in segregated units and were initially paid less than white soldiers, although the monetary discrepancy would be eliminated. They also had to serve under white line officers, the government refusing to entrust them to leaders of their own race; only one hundred blacks were commissioned as officers, and none attained a rank higher than major. Used at first as laborers or rear-zone troops, black regiments were eventually placed in battle by officers who came to have confidence in them or who were forced by a lack of white troops to use them. They acquitted themselves well in various engagements, winning a grudging but increasing respect from whites. Whatever their performance, blacks added important manpower to the Union armies when more strength was needed. Lincoln declared several times that without this accession the war could not be maintained.†

From the beginning of the conflict, the Confederacy made important use of its slave manpower. As previously indicated, the mere presence of the slaves as agricultural laborers freed a larger percentage of white men to fight than would otherwise have been available. Slaves also were impressed to serve as military laborers, and they comprised half or more of the work force in the larger armament plants and of military hospital staffs. But this indirect participation did not seem enough to some. As the war wore on and white manpower

---

*Blacks also served in the navy. One estimate places their number at 29,000, but this total is probably too high.

†The performance of the black troops has to be placed in the context of soldier behavior in battle. Men under fire, regardless of race, will conduct themselves in various ways; they may fight well or passably or badly. The black troops at different times exhibited all of these qualities.

ran down, various military and civilian leaders suggested that the Confederacy should exploit this unused source of strength, should employ blacks as soldiers. The proposal horrified most whites. A general in the western army reflected a common reaction in denouncing "this monstrous proposition . . . revolting to Southern sentiment, Southern pride, and Southern honor."

The resistance to using black soldiers crumbled only in the face of impending defeat, when the white leadership realized it had no alternative but to call slaves into service. In February, 1865, Congress authorized President Davis to requisition 300,000 black troops, a quota being assigned to each state based on its slave population. The act did not promise that slaves who fought would be freed after the war; Davis, however, wrote in his instructions to the War Department that no man was to be asked to fight as a slave but, with the consent of his master, was to go into service free. But the decision to accept black soldiers came too late to help the Confederacy. Before the government could take action to implement the law, the war was over.

In both sections the decision to employ black manpower had been forced by the demands of the war—the totality of the conflict compelled use of all human resources. These demands also caused the use of another group hitherto excluded from participation in war making, women. Although women were not permitted to serve directly in the military forces, they rendered important support, doing work that otherwise would have had to be performed by men. Dorothea Dix, who had been pioneering for two decades in better treatment for the insane, spent the Civil War years as superintendent of women hospital nurses. Thousands of women served as nurses and aides in hospitals, as workers in textile and other factories, and as clerks in government offices. They also were active in the various private organizations that sprang into being to minister to the wants of soldiers, such as the United States Sanitary Commission in the North. The appearance of these groups was yet another indication of total involvement demanded by the war.

IN HIS MESSAGE to Congress in December, 1864, President Lincoln pointed out an interesting fact to his countrymen, intending also, one suspects, to reach the enemy with his message. The war, with all its demands, had not depleted Northern resources, he said. Instead, they had increased and were continuing to grow. The nation had more men than when the war began, and its supplies were "more complete and abundant than ever." He concluded: "The national resources, then, are unexhausted, and, as we believe, inexhaustible."

The picture was not quite as bright as Lincoln painted it—in 1865 the government had to make strenuous efforts to maintain the flow of men into the armies. But he was not exaggerating when he emphasized the health and the growth of the economy. Despite what later statistics may seem to reveal, that economy, or significant parts of it, expanded during the war; the impression one gets from studying economic developments, particularly in industry, is of furious activity and feverish acceleration. Old factories were enlarged and new ones were built. An important factor in increasing production was a greater use of labor-saving machines, especially the Howe sewing machine that put uniforms together quickly and the McKay shoe-stitcher that affixed uppers to soles.

The industries that experienced the greatest growth were those receiving orders from the government for war supplies—textile and shoe manufacturers and, above all, makers of arms and munitions. At the end of the war seventy companies were producing ordnance, and the capitalization of the arms industry had increased by 60 percent. It is significant that this expansion occurred without being directly abetted by the government. Although the administration stimulated growth by means of orders, it did not attempt to mobilize the economy as it did men. There was no setting of priorities or allocating of raw materials or direct fixing of prices. That the North was able to achieve new and previously undreamed-of levels of production through a largely voluntary association of private enterprise and government attests to its solid economic base from which to conduct a great war.*

The South did not possess such a base; it was not equipped to wage a war demanding vast amounts of matériel, and the frantic but futile attempts to overcome its deficiencies illustrate the truth that an agricultural society cannot wage modern war—unless aided and supplied by an outside power.

The South lacked factories, raw materials, machines, managers who knew how to organize production, and skilled laborers. The largest ironwork in the section, and the only big installation of any kind, the Tredegar plant in Richmond, Virginia, had to operate at half or less of its capacity throughout the war because it could not procure sufficient supplies of pig iron. The Tredegar and other mills also suffered from a shortage of trained workers. A majority of the workers were originally from the North; many went back at the start of hostilities and some who remained were drafted. The government attempted to encourage men in nonindustrial occupations to accept jobs in factories, but its efforts were of little avail. "Laws cannot suddenly convert farmers into gunsmiths," an official admitted sadly. "Our people are not artisans, except to a very limited degree."

The government acted on several fronts to stimulate industrial expansion. Indeed, it exerted a more direct influence on the economy than did the Union

---

*Congress enacted a number of measures that benefited important economic groups and had the ultimate effect of fostering economic growth: subsidies to a transcontinental railroad, increased tariff rates, free homesteads to western settlers, aid to agricultural education, and a new banking system. The very fact that such momentous legislation could be considered in the midst of war indicates that the North had energy to spare for purposes other than war and that it faced the future with confidence. No such looking forward was possible in the embattled South.

administration, its efforts anticipating, although crudely, the central mobilization of production that would occur in later wars. Some of its measures were astonishing exercises of power in view of the Southern tradition of limiting the functions of government—ventures, actually, in a form of "state socialism." In one striking experiment it entered into a kind of partnership with private enterprise that presaged the subsidization programs of modern governments. The executive branch, backed by legislative authorization and appropriations, extended generous loans to new or existing companies which agreed to make specified war materials and sell two-thirds of their product to the government. Nor was this arrangement the boldest of the innovations; not satisfied to rely only on private producers, the government engaged itself in the manufacturing process. Under the direction of the able chief of ordnance, General Josiah Gorgas, a number of armament and munition plants were established in Alabama, Georgia, and South Carolina—placed in the lower South to remove them from possible enemy attacks and, in another interesting anticipation of modern thinking, dispersed widely to prevent their being destroyed at one stroke.

The various efforts of government and business accomplished wonders in production—if measured against what the South started with. But the region began with very little, and it could not go fast enough or far enough to compete with the established facilities of the North. No government action could create suddenly efficient habits of production or supply in needed numbers labor-saving machines or skilled laborers. Examples of the South's backwardness are many. Its largest textile factory and principal producer of uniforms, in Atlanta, Georgia, relied entirely on hand labor, employing 3,000 women as seamstresses. In the biggest shoe plant, at Columbus, Georgia, workers had to sew uppers to lowers by hand; its maximum capacity was 5,000 pairs of shoes a week, or, if this output was sustained, 260,000 pairs a year. In the North, on the other hand, machine production enabled the shoe industry to produce 2,500,000 pairs by the end of 1863. Another example of the superior Northern potential was in the vital area of arms production. By 1862 the 38 largest Union arsenals were capable of turning out 5,000 muskets a day. Southern plants were never able to complete more than 300 muskets a day, and often, because of shortages of materials or laborers, could not achieve even this modest total.

Not only was the South unable to match the North in turning out military materials, it could not sustain its prewar capacity to produce nonmilitary supplies, the decline in food output being particularly serious. In fact, in concentrating on the war the South consumed many of its existing resources. The story of the Confederacy is in large part a record of a people having to make do with substitutes—clothes made from carpets, newspapers printed on the back of wallpaper, dyes produced from bark, pins contrived of dry thorns, and the like. Countless instances like these reveal a nation subsisting on its accumulated wealth. Abraham Lincoln could say truthfully to his people that they were gaining in resources as the war continued. Jefferson Davis, if he had dared to be realistic with his citizens, would have had to tell them that their resources were rapidly running down.

PRESIDING OVER an expansive and expanding economy, the Union government should have been able to finance its military effort with little difficulty. The costs of the conflict were great, the direct charges amounting to over $3.5 billion, but they represented only a fraction of the North's wealth. They could have been sustained easily out of the abundant available resources if the men in charge of framing financial policy had been willing to exploit these resources.

The policy makers were Secretary of the Treasury Salmon P. Chase, a politician with ability and experience but without much knowledge of financial matters, congressional leaders who had made fiscal issues their area of special concern, and officials of the larger Eastern banks who stood ready to advise the government and also to reap profits by aiding it. Almost without exception these individuals assumed that the war would be short and could be financed without placing new exactions on the people. Chase, in particular, opposed raising taxes, professing to believe that higher duties would depress popular morale. Supported by his advisers, the secretary in 1861 embarked on a program to support the war by raising loans from banks.

The sale of the first bond issues went rather slowly, and it soon became evident that this method alone would not produce enough income to meet the mounting costs of the war and that taxation would have to be resorted to. With Chase's reluctant concurrence, Congress enacted an "internal revenue" act in 1862, a sweeping measure that included duties on sales of most goods, income taxes, stamp levies, and occupational license taxes. Although the law caught in its net a large number of economic activities, the rates were low and the revenue modest. Taxes, including tariff receipts, paid about 20 percent of the war costs, a respectable proportion but small in relation to the resources available. The government continued to rely mainly on borrowing, the income from the sale of bonds providing approximately 63 percent of the wartime revenues. Although the banks advanced the sums required by the government, they exacted certain concessions in return, buying some bonds below par and reselling them at a profit and taking other bonds at high interest rates and long-term maturation periods, a practice that added to the indirect cost of the war.*

In addition to borrowing and taxing, the government issued a new and

---

*Not all the bonds were offered to banks. The Treasury launched a campaign to persuade the average citizen to buy a bond and disposed of securities totaling $400 million by this method, the first example of mass financing of a war in our history.

special paper currency called popularly, because of its color, "greenbacks." It resorted to this expedient in 1862 to meet suddenly soaring costs, and it continued the process, eventually printing $450 million in notes. Intended to be temporary wartime money, the greenbacks were not redeemable in gold and hence their value declined in relation to gold dollars, thereby causing an inflation in prices. The issuance of paper has been criticized by conventional economists as placing an unnecessary hardship on consumers, but the government had no other real recourse. As historian Fritz Redlich has pointed out, this "early modern mass war" could be financed only by creating "purchasing power," that is, by either the government's or the banks' creating money. The administration chose to issue irredeemable paper money, which was inflationary, but the alternative was irredeemable bank notes, which would have been more inflationary. The amount of paper currency was not sufficient to cause a runaway rise in prices—it represented only one-sixth of the total war costs—and was modest in comparison to the deluge of paper in the Confederacy.*

Few governments in modern times have embarked on war with such scanty financial resources as the Confederacy; the Southern nation, in its lack of fiscal assets and fiscal institutions and experts, was similar in many respects to contemporary undeveloped countries. The region depended for its principal income on selling cotton and other crops to Europe and the North, but this source of wealth came to an abrupt end with the war and the blockade. The wealth within the South was tied up in land and slaves, and not readily convertible into liquid forms; this fact was reflected in the relatively small amounts of money on deposit in Southern banks, as compared to sums in Northern banks. There were few large banks in the section, and hence few men who were skilled in handling large financial transactions; the only really large institutions were in New Orleans, and this city remained in Confederate possession for only about a year. Finally, in the South there were no mines to supply gold, the element employed by governments of that time to support other forms of money. The Confederate government held only $21 million in gold, most of it secured from occupied federal mints: in all the banks there was but $27 million in gold reserves. Any one of these conditions, and certainly all of them together, should have warned the government of dangers ahead, but none of them seemed apparent to the men who were charged with making financial policy.

The Southern secretary of the treasury, Christopher G. Memminger, was a South Carolina lawyer and politician who was appointed to his position because he was the most available person to represent his state in the cabinet. Although he was conscientious and hard-working, he had little experience in

---

*According to reliable estimates, the price index in 1865 was about 80 percent higher than it had been in 1861. Average wages rose probably 60 percent.

fiscal affairs and turned to other men for technical advice. In this he was like Chase, but whereas the latter had various experts he could call on, including veteran employees in his own department, there were few persons near Memminger who were proficient in finance, and no established civil service. Before he could think of what taxes he might recommend to Congress, he had to create an administrative system to collect them.

Memminger professed to believe that high taxes were necessary to finance the war. But he refused to urge adequate levies on Congress, either because he lacked the courage of his convictions or because he thought such a program would be unpopular with the citizenry. Equally disinclined to resort to taxation were the legislators, most of whom held the common delusion that the war would end quickly. The only revenue measure enacted by Congress in 1861 provided for a direct tax on property to be levied through and collected by the states, a procedure which underscored the administrative weakness of the central government. The act allowed a state to meet its quota by paying the sum itself, and this was what most of the states elected to do, issuing their own bonds or notes and thus adding to the inflationary pressures that were rapidly building up. The revenue realized was disappointingly small, and in 1863 Congress passed an internal revenue bill that imposed duties similar to those in the Northern act and in addition a tax "in kind": every person engaged in agriculture had to contribute one-tenth of his annual produce to the government. Not even this bolder measure brought in much return. Resentment and evasion of the produce tax were widespread, and the Treasury Department was never able to create an administrative service capable of collecting efficiently any of its liens. Of the total amount of money raised by the government, only about one percent, by the estimate usually accepted, came from taxes; the highest estimate is a mere five percent.

The first borrowing venture of the government was as cautious as its first taxing attempt. In 1861 Congress permitted the Treasury to sell $15 million in bonds, a pathetic sum in view of the mounting costs pressing on the government. The issue was subscribed fully, most of it being taken by banks which advanced specie; however, two-fifths of the total had been contributed in one city, New Orleans, the South's only financial center. Encouraged by this success, Congress later in the year authorized a loan of $100 million to be paid in specie, paper notes, or produce. The last item was included in the expectation that food and other commodities would be acquired for the army or that cotton could be secured and stored to guarantee additional loans. The loan "in kind" was an imaginative device, but it failed to produce the anticipated revenue. Many of the goods were pledged but not delivered, being held by the owners in hope of a rise in prices, or spoiling in storage, or falling into enemy hands. Nevertheless, the government continued to follow the practice in offering later loans, and after 1861 it offered issues every year. In fact, so many bonds were presented that people came to doubt they could ever be redeemed, and stopped buying them. All the issues together realized only one-third of the total costs of the war.*

The combined revenue in 1861 from taxes and bonds provided only about one-third of the military cost in that year. Forced to find money quickly, Memminger and his advisers turned to an easy solution—they secured congressional authorization to issue paper money. The action had justification. As proved to be true in the North, additional purchasing power had to be created to finance the war, and paper currency was the obvious answer. The first issue was moderate in amount and enabled the government to meet current expenses. But having used the device once, the government was tempted to resort to it again and again, the urge becoming ever stronger as income from taxes and bonds dwindled. Issue followed issue until it seemed that the printing presses might break down and the South be buried under paper. The total amount issued reached eventually the staggering total of $1.5 billion, and paper notes accounted for two-thirds of all the revenue raised during the war. In 1864 the Treasury, appalled by its own work, attempted to fund a portion of the notes: to persuade holders to exchange them for bonds. The effort met with little success. Southerners had no more faith in the government's bonds than they had in its money.

Because the notes were issued in such volume and because the redemption depended on Confederate victory, a prospect that became ever dimmer, their value depreciated steadily. Prices rose astronomically, the rate of inflation exceeded in modern times only by the ruinous climb in the German Republic in the aftermath of World War I. Some prices of 1863–64 reveal the full grimness of what happened: flour, $300 a barrel; cornmeal, $30 a bushel; chickens, $35 a pair; broadcloth, $125 a yard; men's shoes, $125 a pair; dressing combs, $200 a dozen; and so on. People submitted to paying the sums demanded in a mood of numbed resignation. "We fell into the habit of paying whatever was asked," one man recalled, "knowing that tomorrow we should have to pay more." But many could not pay, people who lived on fixed incomes

---

*A recurring controversy in Confederate historiography concerns the failure of the government to ship cotton to Europe in 1861. Critics have written that if it had exported the available supply, it would have gained a secure basis from which to negotiate foreign loans. Actually, the bulk of the 1860–61 crop was sold in Europe and the North before the war began, and even if the whole crop still had remained in the South, 4,000 vessels would have been required to ship it to Europe. The government might have stored cotton and negotiated loans on the promise of future delivery, but success would have depended on foreign investors' believing that the supply would eventually, in case of Confederate victory, get out. The Confederacy secured one loan, in France, based on cotton. But rather than trying to use cotton as a financial lever, the South employed it as a diplomatic weapon. With national sanction, state and local agencies discouraged producers from planting cotton, the hope being that shutting off the supply would force Britain and France to intervene in the war on the side of the Confederacy.

or resided in towns and had to purchase food and other necessities. The diary of a man in both circumstances, J. B. Jones, a clerk in the War Department in Richmond, is replete with instances of sufferings endured by his family. "I cannot afford to have more than an ounce of meat daily for each member of my family of six," he wrote in a typical entry. "The old cat goes staggering about from debility. . . . We see neither rats nor mice about the premises now. This is famine." The evil of inflation gnawed incessantly at popular morale and as much as any factor was responsible for eroding it. One of the several secretaries of war did not exaggerate when he said that the constantly rising prices were more demoralizing to the people than even the "dire calamities of war."

The financial policy of the Confederate government has been strongly criticized by historians, and on several counts it is open to censure. The Richmond administration practiced a halting and inadequate taxation program, it floated too many bond issues, and, worst of all in the view of the critics, it issued paper money with abandon and caused an undue inflation of prices. Yet, given the lack of material and financial resources it is hard to suggest any alternative. More and higher taxes could have been levied and the paper money could have been held within smaller limits or funded, but inflation would still have occurred and the government would still have faced difficulty in meeting expenses. The shortcomings of the policy should not obscure what was accomplished. The Confederacy created armies and navies and for four years maintained war against a superior foe—all this with only slightly more than $20 million in gold in its possession. Not many governments in modern times have done as well.

THE MEN WHO LED the cotton South out of the Union harbored no illusions that their states could exist as separate sovereignties. Although they insisted that each state secede individually, they advocated this action only because it seemed the most proper legal procedure. They intended, when the process of leaving was completed, to bring representatives of the states together to create a new confederation to which they hoped the other slave states would eventually adhere. This association would be based on the principle that the South had espoused in the old Union but had seen "perverted"—a central government of limited powers, the kind of framework envisioned by the authors of the United States Constitution in 1787. The architects of the Southern nation-to-be did not regard themselves as leaders of a revolution looking to a brave new future but as restorers of an idyllic system that had existed in the past. Theirs was a conservative revolution.

Acting according to schedule, delegates of the first seven states to secede met at Montgomery, Alabama, in February, 1861, and proclaimed the Confederate States of America. As a first step in nation-making, they prepared a "provisional" constitution,* and in this document they also established a provisional government. The delegates constituted themselves into a one-house Congress and authorized themselves to elect a president and a vice-president, choosing Jefferson Davis of Mississippi and Alexander H. Stephens of Georgia, respectively. The provisional constitution, after undergoing minor revisions, was approved by the Congress as the permanent constitution in March, and sent to the states for ratification. Elections held under the permanent constitution in November returned Davis and Stephens as permanent president and vice-president and also chose members of a permanent two-house Congress. The Southern nation had been created quickly and in an obvious mood of urgency.

The authors of the Confederate Constitution followed closely the model of the United States Constitution; indeed, they claimed later that their document differed from the older instrument only in clarifying ambiguous language or in providing technical improvements in the operation of government. The claim was in part true. In establishing the structure of their national government, the Confederate framers reproduced almost exactly the three-part system they had lived under in the old Union: an executive branch headed by a president and a vice-president; a legislative branch represented by a Congress consisting of a Senate and a House of Representatives; and a judicial branch presided over by a Supreme Court. To complete the duplication, members of the three branches were to be selected in the same way as prescribed in the United States Constitution. The president and vice-president were chosen by electors appointed by the states. Senators were elected by state legislatures, and representatives by popular vote. And court justices were appointed by the president with the approval of the Senate.†

The Confederate framers endowed the central government with some of the powers possessed by the old government: it could levy taxes, issue money, and raise armies and navies. But they also introduced significant differences in the Southern constitution.

The men at Montgomery set out to create a particular kind of union, very different from the one they had abandoned: not a federation in which sovereignty was divided between the central government and the member states, but a *con*federation in which the states were sovereign. Consequently they wrote into their constitution a statement declaring specifically that each state in the league was sovereign, and numerous clauses in the document provided

---

*Actually, representatives of only six states participated in framing the provisional constitution. The delegates from Texas arrived too late to share in the proceedings but signed their names to the document.

†The president was chosen for a term of six years, instead of the four years stipulated in the original Constitution, and was not eligible for reelection. The court system authorized at Montgomery was never instituted. Objections in the Confederate Congress to national courts were so strong that an attempt to provide a judicial branch was abandoned.

practical assertion of this principle. In general, the powers delegated to the central government were fewer than in the original Constitution and the powers reserved to the states were greater. Some powers enjoyed by the Washington government, such as imposing protective tariffs or constructing internal improvements, were forbidden to the Confederate administration. Other powers could be exercised only if they received approval of an exceptional legislative majority. Thus, a two-thirds vote of both houses of Congress was required to admit a new state or to enact an important money bill. These and similar provisions enabled a minority to veto the will of a majority and reflected the minority psychology that the South had acquired from its experience in the Federal Union. Southerners had a union of their own now, but they were reluctant to invest its government with too many powers.*

The young Confederacy embarked on war with a near-unanimity of popular support that an older, established government might have envied. Some of its citizens might regret that the section had separated from the Union, but once the decision was made, they were ready to join with the secessionists in sustaining a separate and independent South. Only the inhabitants of the mountain regions dissented from the consensus, and they constituted less than 10 percent of the white population. As has been indicated, many people who embraced the cause in 1861 later lost heart as the war turned sour and became resigned to defeat, but their despair was passive. They did not attempt to translate their feelings into active resistance to the government or to the military effort.

The only organized opposition to the war appeared in the mountain areas. That the people of the highlands would be cool to the bid for independence was no surprise. Isolated physically and socially from the residents of the more flat and fertile lands, the mountaineers lived almost in a different world and cherished different values and beliefs. Slavery was unimportant in their economy of small farms and small manufactories, and the concept of the Union had for them a mystic attraction unknown to other Southerners.†

In addition to their general sense of alienation, they nourished specific grievances against their state governments, believing that they were underrepresented in the legislatures and slighted in the allocation of roads and railroads. Their resentments were known to Confederate leaders, some of

*A striking difference between the two constitutions was in their treatment of slavery. The framers of the old Constitution acknowledged the existence of slavery only indirectly; they carefully avoided using the words *slave* and *slavery*. The Confederate framers specifically recognized the institution, used the taboo words a number of times, and included a provision forbidding passage of legislation interfering with slavery.

†The mountain people were not unanimous in their support of the Union. For one reason or another, some adhered to the Confederacy, and some wanted to have nothing to do with either side. Those who lived in north Georgia were the most ardent in defending the Confederacy, because the state had built a railroad into their region and had thus removed their grievance of being isolated from outside markets.

whom expected that the mountain people would attempt to avoid participating in the military effort. But only the most discerning Confederates anticipated the active resistance that flared up in some areas. In western Virginia some forty counties repudiated secession and set up their own "loyal" state government. Federal troops quickly occupied the section and with the aid of the inhabitants held it against Confederate counterattacks; in 1863 the mountain counties became the new state of West Virginia. Another center of resistance developed in eastern Tennessee, which comprised about one-third of the state's territory and had cast a strong vote against secession. The Unionists had no opportunity to move for statehood, because Confederate forces occupied the area immediately and held it until late in 1863. But they manifested their sympathies by conducting a persistent irregular warfare against the occupiers, destroying railroad bridges and ambushing small Confederate detachments. The opposition in the mountain areas posed no serious military danger to the Confederacy, being largely vocal except in Tennessee, but it was a propaganda victory for the North, revealing that Southerners were far from solid in supporting Southern independence.

A potential source of opposition that could have given great trouble to the Confederacy never developed—there was no uprising of slaves, no black "fire in the rear." Some whites worried that the slaves might take advantage of the absence of so many men of the dominant race in the army to engage in organized revolts or in random killings. Their fears, which were not publicly expressed, proved groundless. The slaves remained quiet throughout the war, offering, as far as the records disclose, their usual outward demeanor of respect to whites. Their inner feelings were quite different. Through the oral grapevine that was their only form of communication, they realized that the war was being fought because of them and over them, and they sensed that the North would eventually proclaim emancipation. In whatever ways they could, they tried to aid their potential liberators, providing military intelligence to Union officers, guiding Northern prisoners to escape, and performing other indirect services. Their greatest contribution to Northern success resulted from their desire to be free. Whenever a Union army appeared in a particular locality, slaves in large numbers would desert the plantations and farms and flock to the camp of the invaders, a process that gradually deprived the South of the bulk of its agricultural laboring force.*

The most serious division in the Confederacy did not occur over normal democratic differences, nor were the men who provoked it completely normal politicians. The instigators were known as the "states' rights party," although they did not have a tight enough organization to qualify formally as a party,

---

*The relative passivity of the slaves both before and during the war has been explained in different ways by historians. The simplest explanation is that the isolation of the slaves in a rural region prevented them from planning and executing large-scale uprisings.

and they included members of Congress, several governors, and state legislators; their most prominent figure and leader was Vice-President Stephens. The group has been previously referred to as leading the opposition to the central government's conscripting of men into the armies. They denied the government's authority under their constitution to draft citizens and charged that Davis's real purpose in asking for conscription was to arm himself, as Governor Joseph E. Brown of Georgia put it, with "imperial power." They were equally vehement in opposing another grant of power requested by the president of Congress: the right to suspend the writ of habeas corpus and detain persons suspected of disloyal practices under military control. Stephens stigmatized the suspension as "a menace to public liberty," accusing Davis of plotting to become a dictator. Although critics of the government used states' rights arguments as a convenient tactic to attack it, most of the group were committed to the doctrine as to a theology. Having become accustomed to opposing centralism in the old Union, they could not change their ways. They did not wish to achieve independence at the price of diminishing state sovereignty. Stephens told the Georgia legislature he would rather see "all go down in a common ruin" than sacrifice the rights of the states. "Without liberty," he cried, "I would not turn upon my heel for independence."

The opposition of the states' righters seriously impeded an efficient conduct of the war effort. Not only did they sabotage enforcement of conscription in several states, but their attacks on the Davis administration, combined with the sniping of other critics, gradually undermined the original mood of unity felt by the people, prevented the development of a true sense of nationalism, and blunted the popular will to sacrifice in order to create a nation. If Jefferson Davis had been the kind of leader the states' righters charged him with being, a ruthless grasper and user of power, he might have been able to counteract the forces of individualism and localism and make a nation. But like practically every other Southern leader, he was a conservative constitutionalist who believed he should observe every constitutional punctilio. Although the section in the Confederate constitution dealing with habeas corpus, which was derived from the old Constitution, was ambiguous as to whether the right to suspend the writ lay with the president or with Congress, Davis assumed that the power rested with Congress. He requested the legislators to grant him the authority —and received a limited permission. Watching Davis's meticulous attention to "proper" procedures, an official in the Confederate War Department observed shrewdly: "All the revolutionary vigor is with the enemy. . . . With us timidity—hair splitting."

That Richmond official discerned one of the great ironies of the war. The Confederacy, despite all the constitutional gloss that was applied to secession, was in reality a revolution, a newly born enterprise struggling to make itself permanent. Yet Davis and other leaders acted as though they headed an established government. They were not exactly timid, but neither were they consistently bold; they observed their constitution and laws and would not have thought of violating either one. The United States was a going nation and government, but Lincoln and some of the men around him acted on occasion as though they were leading a revolution. Lincoln used the war powers of his office with artistic abandon, skirting some provisions of the Constitution and violating others. The established nation was more ruthless and radical than the nation that was striving to establish itself.

The Northerners entered the war with a united purpose—in preponderant numbers they were willing to support the use of force to preserve the Union. Differences developed among them as the conflict continued, but most of these, like similar divisions in the South, were the kind of normal issues that appear in any democracy at war, divergences on such questions as taxation, conscription, and military policy. The men on either side did not wish to impede the war effort but to make it more efficient as they understood efficiency, or to gain a concession for themselves or their class or group. The most bitter issue of dispute arose, oddly, within the dominant Republican party, convulsing the party and eventually the public. Although all Republicans were antislavery, some were more so than others. One faction, the Radicals, demanded that the government seize the opportunity of the war to destroy slavery, that it make emancipation as well as preservation of the Union a war aim. Conservative Republicans, fearing the effect of an abrupt change in the racial status quo, opposed wartime action against slavery and supported gradual emancipation to be achieved after the war. President Lincoln was caught in the middle of the struggle. He preferred the conservative approach to emancipation, but above all he was determined that whatever was done about slavery must contribute to his larger goal of saving the Union.

The Radicals were men of righteous resolve, unusually moralistic and high-principled for politicians, and they denounced Lincoln and all who stood in their way with fierce invective; the president once referred sadly to what he called their "petulant and vicious fretfulness." But it must be emphasized that they did not oppose the war. On the contrary, they were among the strongest supporters of the military effort and were as determined as Lincoln to restore the Union. They differed from him in insisting that a new Union must be constituted without the great evil of slavery.

In the contest for the control of party policy, and for the popular mind, the Radicals were victorious. They had the great advantage of time on their side. The Northern people were simply not going to fight very long to preserve the principal social institution of the enemy. They were certain to demand that slavery be struck down. In the summer of 1862 Congress passed an act confiscating the property of persons aiding the rebellion and declaring the slaves of such persons free. Although the measure was a "paper" edict with no immediate practical effect, it was an important indication of the way opinion was turning: the representatives of the people had proclaimed that emancipation must be made an objective of the war. The indication was not lost on Lincoln. If his party and the people as a whole demanded the wartime destruction of slavery, he would have to accept the verdict; otherwise he would divide the supporters of the war and imperil his goal of saving the Union. Forced to act, he issued on January 1, 1863, the Emancipation Proclamation, which declared free the slaves in the Confederacy, basing his authority to issue this sweeping measure on the war powers of his office. He had said earlier that he hoped the conflict would not "degenerate into a violent and remorseless revolutionary struggle." But now he himself moved in the direction he feared. His action was yet another sign that the war was imposing its own conditions.

The only outright opponents of the war were Southern sympathizers in the slave states which had not seceded and Peace Democrats in the Northern states, most of them centered in the northwestern section. The Peace Democrats, who have been referred to previously as denying the right of the government to conscript men into the armies, professed to favor a restoration of the Union. But they insisted that this reconstruction could not be accomplished by force. "Union is consent and good will and fraternal affection," one of their leaders stated. "War is force, hate, revenge." Therefore, they advocated that a truce to the fighting be called and that the seceded states be invited to attend a national convention to amend the Constitution to the end of preserving states' rights—of guaranteeing the existence of slavery. It was an impractical formula—the Confederate states would have interpreted a truce as a recognition by the North that it could not win the war—but it was nonetheless a Unionist formula. However, not all Peace Democrats were Unionists. Some of them were so devoted to sectionalism as to advocate the formation of a Northwestern Confederacy, and some were so antagonized by the centralizing tendencies of the government as to organize secret societies that plotted treason. Or, at least, the charge of treason was leveled by Republicans during the war. Later historians have doubted that the societies had treasonable intentions, and have argued that they were merely political apparatus that became the victims of war hysteria.

The exact nature and aims of the secret societies will probably never be known. Whatever their purpose, they and the Peace Democrats generally seemed to many Northerners to be disloyal opponents of the war, potentially or actually as dangerous as Southern sympathizers in the border slave states. Both groups would feel the repressive hand of the national government. They may or may not have been victims of hysteria, but they were certainly sacrifices to the enforced unity that modern war demands.*

*Some contemporary historians are convinced that the Peace Democrats, including those in the societies, were a "loyal opposition." However, it seems curious that loyal men would organize semimilitary groups within a political party. Possibly some members of the societies felt they had to organize to protect themselves against intimidation by Republicans. Others may have considered treason, but never found the courage or opportunity to bring anything off.

Against the Democratic and border-state opponents of the war Lincoln used the weapon of military arrests. Disregarding the ambiguous language in the Constitution as to which government agency had the authority to suspend habeas corpus, he assumed that the power rested with the president, who could act more quickly than Congress in a crisis. At first he suspended the writ only in specified areas, but in 1862 he proclaimed that all persons who discouraged enlistments, resisted the draft, or engaged in "disloyal practices" were subject to military arrest. Under the operation of this sweeping edict, over 13,000 persons were arrested, some of whom were held for varying periods and released without being brought to trial; others were tried before military tribunals.

Lincoln offered several justifications for his suspension of the civil writ. Although he was careful to contend that he was acting in accordance with the Constitution, he once said that a president might in a crisis such as a war have not only a right but an obligation to violate the fundamental charter. Referring to his revocation of habeas corpus, he asked: "Are all the laws but *one* to go unexecuted, and the government itself go to pieces, lest that one be violated?" He himself was prepared to disregard a part of the Constitution to save the other parts. On another occasion he declared: "I shall do *all* I can to save the government." He had a revolutionary spirit, and because he would do what he had to do, he preserved a nation.

Even with this daring flexibility, Lincoln had no control over the election of 1864, the first to be held in the midst of a great war. For a time there was even doubt whether the president would be nominated by his party, because the Radical Republican wing remembered Lincoln's slow acceptance of emancipation and were afraid he would "favor a mild and forgiving policy" for the South in the postwar period. There was, however, no Republican strong enough to oppose him, so when the party met in June, Lincoln received the nomination, although with only chilly assent from the Radicals. Andrew Johnson of Tennessee, who had refused to follow his state into secession, was named to the second place on the ticket to replace Hannibal Hamlin.

As the summer months wore on, weariness settled on the Northern people, many of whom believed the war was hopeless, that the South could not be conquered. All signs indicated an election defeat for Lincoln, and he himself thought he would lose. The Radicals decided to ask him to withdraw rather than drag the party down to defeat; if he refused, they were ready to force him off the ticket and replace him with an uncompromising Radical.

Before they could act, however, political and military events forced a recasting of strategy. In August the Democratic convention met and nominated George B. McClellan, former Union general and an object of hatred to all good Radicals. The Peace faction got their plank into the platform. McClellan repudiated it, but the Democrats stood before the country as the peace party.

The Democratic convention gave the Radicals pause. Lincoln was bad enough, but McClellan and a peace platform were worse. Just at this time several military victories, particularly the capture of Atlanta early in September, rejuvenated Northern morale and gave promise of Republican success in November. The Republicans thereupon closed ranks behind Lincoln as the lesser of two evils.

The outcome of the election was a smashing electoral triumph for Lincoln, who received 212 votes to McClellan's 21. The president's popular majority, however, was uncomfortably small, 2,213,000 to 1,805,000, an advantage of only 400,000 votes. A slight shift of popular votes in some of the more populous states would have changed the result.

THE CIVIL WAR is one of the few major domestic conflicts in history that did not turn into an international war. No outside power or powers intervened on one side or the other; the Americans were left to themselves to fight their quarrel to a conclusion. The South actively sought intrusion and assistance from the great powers of Europe, while the stronger North labored to forestall interference. Foreign intervention in favor of the Confederacy was possible several times during the struggle, but the threat never materialized. That it did not develop was due to the working of several factors: the skill, or lack of skill, displayed by key members of the respective diplomatic corps, an area in which Northern personnel showed to advantage; the complications of European politics, which deterred action by the only nations capable of intervening; and, above all, the military situation in America, in which the tide of victory never seemed to turn toward the South.

In the diplomatic struggle between the North and the South the key nations were Britain and France. They were the greatest powers in the western world, they had global economic and political interests, and they possessed sufficient naval and land strength to intervene in the American struggle if they decided that their interests would be affected by its outcome. Their intervention could be decisive because it would have been a joint action: they were bound in an entente that pledged them to act collectively in foreign policy, with Britain taking the lead in the American sphere. The third power of Europe, Russia, had no direct interest in the outcome of the war and lacked the strength to interfere in an area so remote from itself.

Although both Britain and France had national legislatures as part of their political systems, in neither country was the popular voice very influential in determining government policies. The right of suffrage was restricted by property qualifications, and power rested with the ruling or upper classes, the landed gentry, and the commercial and manufacturing brotherhood, minorities that had always viewed the practice of majority control in the United States with distaste and fear.

The attitudes of the British and French upper classes toward the war in America were compounded of several motives and can only be summarized here. Most members of the elite groups felt varying degrees of satisfaction that the American Union was broken up by secession and hoped that the Confederacy would be able to establish its independence. Those of the landed aristocracy cherished sentiments of class kinship with Southern planters. Manufacturers and merchants believed that an independent South would become a market for English products. Elitists generally saw the American division as an irrefutable demonstration of a proposition they had long defended, that democracy would not work in a large and populous country. And some of them hoped for Confederate success for simple reasons of power politics. The existence of two American nations would ensure that neither one could dominate the western hemisphere, and the way would be opened to Britain and France to exercise added influence in hemispheric affairs.

The pro-Confederate bias of the upper classes was especially apparent in Britain, the nation that would lead in determining American policy.* But this opinion was not positive enough or active enough to move the government to intervene in the war on the Confederate side. It was a passive kind of opinion, a hope that the "right" people would win in the American conflict, and that if Britain could give them a hand without becoming too actively involved she would do so, but that was as far as she should go. Only a minority of elitists favored intervention from the start of the war, and their numbers never swelled appreciably. The government itself was content to follow a watch-and-wait policy. It extended recognition to the Confederacy as a belligerent, as did the other powers of Europe, but it refused to grant the South diplomatic recognition as a nation, its example again being followed by other powers. The government permitted Confederate agents to contract for the building of commerce-raiding ships by British companies, but this was the only material assistance extended to the South. Several times during the war Britain and France considered offering mediation, and if the North refused the bid, as it surely would, to intervene militarily and force a peace based on Confederate independence. But on each occasion something occurred to prevent action. Either the war in America failed to take an expected turn in favor of the Confederacy or a situation developed in Europe that required the entente powers to keep their attention and might at home. Their refusal to transform avowed sympathies into practical action in the end turned a large part of

*Not all members of the upper classes in either Britain or France favored the Confederacy. Some individuals in both countries supported the Union because they disliked slavery and foresaw that the war would destroy the institution, or because they admired the democratic ideals that they believed were exemplified in the United States. The attitudes of members of the lower middle and laboring classes to the war are difficult to determine. The traditional view that the laborers stood for the North has been denied by some recent historians; an authoritative conclusion will have to await fuller investigation.

Southern opinion against them. Speaking of Britain but probably with France also in mind, a Richmond paper raged that "it is hard to say which are our bitterest enemies, she or the Yankees."

Russia and the United States occupied similar places in the international hierarchy—both were rising powers on the periphery of the ancient seat of power, Europe, and both felt that their legitimate ambitions were being blocked by the pretensions of Britain and France to dominate areas of the world that they themselves should dominate. The two nations had, in the words of the Russian minister of foreign affairs, "a natural community of interests and sympathies."

The Russian government made no secret of its sympathy for the North or its hope that the Union would be preserved. Russia was not in a position to render any material assistance to the United States, but repeated expressions of goodwill by Russian leaders made a deep impression on many Americans; in a world that seemed filled with people who wanted to see the Union fall, the Russians were rare friends.

Some American observers of the European scene sensed that Russia might dominate the continent in the future—and that she and the United States might have a continuing "community of interest and sympathies." A New York paper offered an interesting prediction:

In the Eastern hemisphere the destiny of Russia is to absorb all minor states around her, and she is every day making rapid progress in that policy. She will soon be, if she is not already, the Great Power of Europe and Asia. In the Western World the United States is destined to play the same part. One of these governments is an absolute despotism; the other is a representative democracy. But both are suited for the regions and the races where they prevail. Both . . . will fulfill their destiny without coming into collision or competition with the other. Not so the milk and water governments that stand between them.

CHAPTER XI

The Civil War: Strategy and the First Shots

T HE RIVAL AMERICAN GOVERNMENTS, in characteristic American fashion, entered on war without previously prepared plans of general strategy, indeed, without much serious thinking about strategy.

The Confederate government, having just sprung into existence, had lacked time for military preparation except to create a skeleton organization. The United States Army had an established structure, which could have formulated a strategic design, but producing strategy was not a function assigned to the military system; no person or agency within it was charged with the task of studying and preparing plans for wars the nation might face. The need for a planning group had never been apparent to men in government or to military thinkers—the only wars confronting the country were likely to be against weak neighbors or Indian inhabitants.

Before the war only a few army officers gave attention to grand planning, and these men merely discussed methods of repelling an attack by a European power, which they thought could be handled easily and quickly. None of the officers considered that a great domestic conflict might occur. They could not, perhaps, bring themselves to address such a dire eventuality. Thus, in 1860–61 General in Chief Winfield Scott, instead of contemplating strategy, was devising schemes to avert secession. Hence, the war strategy had to be worked out after the commencement of hostilities, designed to fit conditions of a terrain over which soldiers on neither side had ever thought they would fight, and directed to attain a policy which statesmen on neither side had ever imagined they would seek to achieve.

United States policy was to restore the Union, to force the states that had seceded to return; the original purpose was to effect this restoration without striking at slavery, but later emancipation became a secondary objective. The North needed an offensive strategy, but one more extensive than might have sufficed against a foreign foe. In this civil struggle, the North had to do more than capture the enemy capital or defeat hostile armies. It had to convince the opposing people that their cause was hopeless, in effect, to subdue a whole population. It could accomplish this end only by invading and occupying large portions of the South.

As Northern strategy was finally created, there were three principal objectives: to capture Richmond, but more important, to smash the army defending the capital; to grasp the line of the Mississippi River, thus splitting the Confederacy into two parts; and after the second objective had been achieved, to seize Chattanooga on the Tennessee River line, thereby securing a base from which to launch an offensive to divide the Confederacy again. The areas in which Northern armies operated were designated as theaters: the Eastern theater, between the Atlantic coast and the Appalachian Mountains; the Western theater, between the mountains and the Mississippi; and the Trans-Mississippi theater, the area west of the great river.

The Confederate policy was to establish its independence and to compel the North to desist from attempting to subdue the South and recognize the existence of the Southern nation. To attain these objectives, the Southern planners, dominated by President Davis, relied on an almost completely defensive strategy. In part, they had no choice in the matter—with the North undertaking offensives, the South had to meet the thrusts directed against it. But the adoption of a defensive stance was also a deliberate determination, decided on because it seemed so logical, so expressive of the purpose of the South in seceding. As its leaders never tired of emphasizing, the Confederacy had no aggressive designs on the North, no desire to secure Northern territory; it simply wanted to be let alone. It could best demonstrate peaceable intentions by remaining on the defensive and repelling Northern attacks until the aggressors tired of the effort.*

In depending on a defensive strategy, the Confederate planners yielded the initiative to the North—the South had to wait until the enemy moved before it could move. Not only that, the leaders thought they had to counter every Northern advance, to attempt to hold every threatened point, a position that led them to disperse their inferior forces over a wide area. Their decision has been censured by various historians as revealing a fixation with places; the critics contend that the government should have shortened its line of defense, attempting to hold only the most defensible areas or those containing important re-

---

*The decision to stand on the defensive did not envision that Confederate forces should on every occasion wait to be attacked. A Confederate army, if the conditions were favorable, might attack a Federal army *within* the South.

sources or possessing symbolic values. But the government had a political problem. Although Davis and his advisers sometimes seemed to want to hold territory for its own sake, simply because it was within their boundaries, they had
valid reasons for such action—if the new Southern government abandoned any
regions, it would be confessing its inability to hold them and would have risked
losing some of its popular support. A sounder criticism is that, considering the
advantage that improved firepower gave the defense, the government detached
more men to secondary areas than were necessary to hold them. Thus, in 1863 in
North Carolina 27,000 Confederates confronted 16,000 Federals, and in southwestern Virginia 6,000 Confederates faced 7,000 Federals.

Many of the troops scattered around the circumference of the Confederacy could have been used to better purposes in other operations. They could
have been employed with particularly good effect in offensive operations directed *into* the North. That the Confederacy eschewed aggressive designs upon
the North was no reason for it not to attack its adversary. The South needed
to demonstrate it could not be conquered and chose to prove its strength by
undertaking a successful defense. But its point could have been made more
effectively by invading the North in the early years of the war, when its
manpower resources were at their greatest, and winning victories on enemy
soil, not to seize permanently any territory, but to establish its own invulnerability. On three occasions the Confederacy did go over to the offensive, but
these attempts failed, and in part because the government refused to commit
enough men to them, holding back troops to defend other areas. Jefferson
Davis once complained that "the means" to conduct offensives were "wanting." It was not the means that were lacking, but the will and the daring to
employ those means that were available.

The strategy of each side was conceived and directed by individuals in the
political and military structure who did not have a formal existence or title, but
who constituted what in modern terminology is called a command system. The
two systems were essentially similar in arrangement, the Confederates repro-
ducing, as they did in other areas, the organization they had known in the old
government. There were, however, differences in the way the systems were
operated, differences that reflected the character of the men in the various
offices, which in turn was influenced by the cultures from which they had come.

The Northern structure consisted of the president, the commander in
chief of the armed forces, his two civilian deputies, the secretaries of war and
the navy, and the bureau chiefs under the secretaries, those in the War Department being known as the General Staff.* In command of the land forces was
the general in chief, the senior officer, whose position was recognized by

---

*It must be emphasized again, particularly in view of the modern name of the army chiefs,
that in neither the North nor the South was the group a collective or a planning agency. The head
of each bureau did his own business and advised his secretary only about his own affairs.

congressional enactment, although his duties were not defined. No corresponding position existed in the navy. The highest rank in the sea service was captain; if several captains operated together in a squadron, the senior member bore the courtesy title of flag officer or commodore.

In both systems the dominating personage was the president. Each executive, of course, was invested with constitutional power to command and held in his hands the right to make "the ultimate decision." But investiture of power does not in itself ensure that a president will run a war. Madison did not truly act as commander in chief in the War of 1812. A president must want to command, and both Lincoln and Davis did, the former because he exulted in using power of any kind and would employ every bit he possessed to save the Union, and the latter because he fancied himself a military expert and thought he was qualified to impose his will on civilian advisers and generals. The two executives stretched their authority to the constitutional limits, exercising control over the war-making process that anticipated the practice of twentieth-century presidents.

If modern computer-calculators had been available in 1861, they would surely have forecast that Jefferson Davis would be a great war director and Abraham Lincoln an indifferent one. Davis came to his high office with apparently superior qualifications. He was a graduate of West Point, he had served in the regular army and as a volunteer officer in the Mexican War, and he had been secretary of war. Lincoln, in contrast, lacked technical qualifications. He had no military education and, indeed, little formal education of any kind, and he had no military experience except his brief and, as he admitted, inglorious service as a militia soldier in the pursuit of Black Hawk. And yet it was Lincoln who turned out to be the great war president whereas Davis achieved at best only competence. The command careers of the two men confirm the truth of Clausewitz's dictum that experience in military affairs is not the principal requirement in a director of war but that "a remarkable, superior mind and strength of character" are more important.

By the power of his mind and character Lincoln dominated the Northern command system and finally determined the nature of Northern strategy. His ideas of strategy were sounder than those of the generals with whom he had to deal during the early years of the war. Thus, Lincoln realized that numbers were on his side and, as has been recounted, called in 1861 to enlist 500,000 men, a larger force than most of the trained experts thought would be necessary. He understood almost immediately that the proper objective of his armies should be to engage and defeat Confederate armies and urged this end on his generals, most of whom, being Jominians, preferred to occupy places. Always he prodded his commanders to move, to attack. "Tell him to put it through," he wrote in preparing instructions to one general, and to another he said tersely: "You must act."

The most original element in his thinking was to propose a cordon offensive, constant and simultaneous attacks along the whole strategic circumference of the Confederacy. "We have the *greater* numbers," he explained to one general, and if we menace the enemy with "superior forces at *different* points at the *same* time" we will eventually find a place he cannot defend, and we will make a breakthrough. It was an idea that ran counter to what military men had been taught. As Jominians, they clung to the principle of concentration, which they interpreted to mean only one big effort at a time. Lincoln would have to search for three years to find a commanding general who was willing to adopt a cordon strategy.

Lincoln's first commander was Winfield Scott. In his day Scott had been a fine soldier, but that day was past. He was seventy-five years old in 1861 and although his mind was still reasonably sharp, dropsy and vertigo had rendered him incapable of sustained physical activity. Even a younger and healthier Scott probably would not have been able to adjust his thinking to the requirements of the forthcoming struggle. He had gained his experience in limited wars and his knowledge of military organization was restricted to small armies. But his reputation was towering, and Lincoln naturally turned to him for advice. Specifically, the president asked the general to propose a plan of overall strategy.

Scott's continued engrossment with political policy was evident in the plan he presented to Lincoln. Obviously prepared in haste,* it proposed a naval blockade of the Confederacy's coastline and the occupation of the Mississippi River down to the Gulf of Mexico by a combined land and naval force. This objective accomplished, the South would be enclosed within a ring from which it could not break out—this feature of the design caused it to be dubbed the "Anaconda Plan." As Southerners became subjected to an increasing economic and psychological squeeze, those among them with Union sentiments would make their voices heard and demand a return to the old government. Scott was confident his plan would end the war. "I will guarantee that in one year from this time all difficulties will be settled," he proclaimed.

The general's plan possessed elements of obvious soundness, and these were adopted by Lincoln. A naval blockade was begun, and seizure of the Mississippi line became a major objective. But taken as a whole, the Anaconda was an inadequate strategy. Indeed, in important respects it was not a military strategy but a political or diplomatic offensive. Scott assumed that a substantial Union sentiment existed in the South and that the Unionists would be able to make their views prevail, both highly dubious suppositions. The plan revealed

*There was a curious similarity here with Scott's procedure at the start of the Mexican War. He had no ready plan, and when asked by President Polk to produce one, he was forced to act hurriedly.

much about the military mind of the time. Generals like Scott believed that wars should be limited in objective and could be won without engaging in serious fighting.*

Scott retired on November 1, 1861, partly because he felt his years and health handicapped him in performing his duties and partly because he realized that Lincoln and others in the government and in the military structure were becoming convinced he was to blame for the inaction of the armies. One of those dissatisfied was the man Lincoln appointed to replace him in the supreme command, George B. McClellan, who was also the commander of the Army of the Potomac in the Eastern theater. McClellan had complained to the president and to other high officials that Scott was holding him back from mounting an offensive, and Lincoln, eager to get some kind of action going, was willing to believe him.

The president had probably intended for some time to appoint McClellan to Scott's place. He had called the young general, not quite thirty-five years of age, to Washington in July to assume command of the Federal forces that had recently been defeated at the battle of Bull Run, or Manassas,† and he had formed a favorable opinion of him. McClellan's reputation was high in the first days of the war. A graduate of West Point, he made a good record in the old army before retiring to enter business. After Sumter he volunteered his services and commanded a small force that routed a Confederate force in western Virginia. As soon as he arrived in Washington after Bull Run, he quickly organized the defeated troops and the masses of recruits that the government placed at his disposal; no general in the war was a better trainer of men. Always he radiated confidence. When Lincoln tried to impress on him the burden he would have in commanding a field army and directing other armies, he replied calmly: "I can do it all."‡

McClellan would shortly reveal that he lacked the qualities required in a field commander. At this time he gave distressing indications that he did not possess the breadth of vision required in a general in chief, the ability to think realistically about the war as a whole. In August, Lincoln, in a move that indicated he was considering McClellan for the chief command, asked the general to prepare a plan of overall strategy. McClellan responded with a detailed scheme. The main Union effort should begin in Virginia, with only supporting operations being conducted in the West. The force in Virginia

---

*Scott also proposed the raising of an army of 300,000. It is not clear from his writings whether he intended eventually to employ this force in battle or to hold it in reserve to show the South the seriousness of Northern purpose. He thought the Mississippi line could be occupied by 60,000 troops.

†The Federals named battles after the nearest natural feature in the area, usually a river or a stream, and Confederates after the nearest community.

‡Actually, the responsibility of dual command was too great for any general to bear. General Grant realized the problem in 1864 and avoided direct field command.

would be under his command and should number 273,000 men. He proposed to move this host by water to the seacoast and march inland and capture Richmond. Then he would reembark the troops and proceed down the coast, taking various port cities as he went and ending up at New Orleans. The successful execution of his plan would end the rebellion at "one blow," he assured Lincoln.

McClellan's proposal was defective on almost every count and revealed his considerable talent for fantasy. The government could not at that time raise the number of men he demanded or feed and house them in the Eastern theater, and it did not possess the water transport to carry them to distant points on the Southern coast. Even if these conditions had been met, the strategy would not have brought the Confederacy to its knees. McClellan, a confirmed Jominian, would make but one big effort at a time, and places instead of enemy armies would be his objective. Like so many other of Lincoln's generals he assumed that a war could be won without doing much fighting.*

What Lincoln thought of McClellan's plan is not known. He filed it without comment and never asked the general to implement the strategy. Nor did McClellan press for adoption of his ideas or offer any other serious strategic suggestions. During the next several months he prepared his army for operations in the spring, and he appeared content to let matters of strategy drop. When he finally took the field in March, 1862, Lincoln removed him as general in chief, presumably to enable McClellan to devote full attention to running his own army, but probably also because the president was doubtful about his strategic ability.

Lincoln possibly was beginning to nourish doubts about the capacity of military men generally—and to feel that he himself was competent to direct strategy. He did not name a successor to McClellan but for five months acted, in effect, as his own general in chief. During this period he coordinated whatever movements he could persuade his generals in the Western theater to undertake and supervised McClellan's slowly developing offensive in Virginia. Although he made the big decisions, the president did not act entirely on his own. He conferred regularly with Secretary of War Edwin M. Stanton and other officials in the War Department, and because of Stanton's initiative he had the benefit of some institutional military advice. The secretary created an agency called the Army Board, which consisted of the several bureau chiefs and was presided over by a senior officer brought out of retirement. This was, of course, only the General Staff under another name, but it was now converted into a formal group, and its members, although certainly not strategists, could

---

*With the exception of Richmond and Montgomery, the cities that McClellan proposed to occupy were on the coast. Even if he could have secured all of them, which is doubtful, the Confederacy could have remained strong and defiant in its heartland.

provide the president with professional counsel. A forward step had been taken.*

Although Lincoln seemed confident in directing strategy, he was not sure that he had handled every problem correctly or that he would be able to deal with even more troublesome problems that were threatening to develop. He needed a military man near him, one who could counsel him and frame and direct strategy. In July, 1862, he called to Washington General Henry W. Halleck, then departmental commander in the West, and named Halleck "to command the whole land forces of the United States, as general-in-chief."

Halleck appeared an ideal choice for the position. A graduate of West Point, he had served creditably in the army and prosperously in the business world. He was known most widely before 1860 as a student of and writer on the higher art of war, having translated various of Jomini's works and published a book of his own on strategy, winning for his efforts the sobriquet of "Old Brains." In addition to possessing theoretical knowledge, Halleck had a reputation as a practical and successful field general. In his department in the West important victories had been won, and although these were largely the accomplishment of one of his subordinates, Ulysses S. Grant, the credit for them in official estimation went to Halleck.

Lincoln intended that Halleck should actively plan and direct strategy. To generals who asked him what moves to make, as they had become accustomed to doing, he would say: "You must call on General Halleck." And for a brief time Halleck did act the role expected of him. But this phase lasted for only slightly more than a month. Complaining that he was being unfairly blamed for a battle lost by a field general, Halleck announced that although he would advise the president on a particular situation, he would make no decisions and issue no orders as to what should be done. As Lincoln ruefully described what had happened, Halleck simply "broke down." His collapse was a symptom of his unfitness for high command. He was essentially a "desk man"; he could advise doers but he could not do himself. Nevertheless, Lincoln retained him in his position precisely because he could advise, could at least provide professional knowledge to the president, who again had to make the big strategic decisions himself.

Lincoln exercised the function of general in chief until March, 1864, when a new command system was brought into being. The structure had several architects, Lincoln and Stanton certainly, Halleck perhaps, and General Grant, its principal military figure. But essentially the system was the product of many minds, or of a mass mind, an outgrowth of the evolving mili-

---

*The War Department was now a more efficient administrative agency, Congress having authorized the employment of three assistant secretaries. There was only one assistant secretary in the Navy Department.

tary experience of soldiers and civilians and an expression of the national genius to improvise an arrangement to fit the needs of the moment.

Congress provided a basis for the system when with Lincoln's approval it created the rank of lieutenant general, then the highest grade in the army, and declared that the officer the president designated to the rank might also be appointed general in chief. Everybody agreed who should receive the promotion and the position: Ulysses S. Grant had emerged as the Northern military hero, and Lincoln immediately named him to both. Charged with framing and directing strategy on several broad fronts, Grant realized he would have to leave the West and establish his command post at or near the seat of government, where he could be in quick communication with the president. He ultimately decided to set up his headquarters with the Army of the Potomac in Virginia, from where he could travel by train to Washington or be in telegraph contact with Lincoln. Grant gave as his reason for resorting to this unusual and somewhat awkward arrangement that he disliked the political atmosphere in the capital. More probably, he wanted to give direct attention to the Federal army that confronted the most dangerous Confederate force, Robert E. Lee's Army of Northern Virginia.

As the structure of the system evolved, Halleck received a new office, being designated chief of staff. It is not known who suggested the position or the title, which in modern usage connotes a planning and command function. Halleck had none of the powers of a modern chief of staff. His duties corresponded roughly with those performed in the present system by a service secretary. He was essentially a liaison man, a channel of communication between Lincoln and Grant and between Grant and his seventeen departmental commanders. He transmitted to Grant many of Lincoln's directives, and he read and summarized for Grant a vast correspondence from subordinates. The right man in the right job, he relieved Grant of a heavy burden of paperwork and was a major reason the new system worked.*

Shortly after arriving in Washington, Grant submitted to the president a plan of grand strategy. It called for simultaneous advances by all Federal armies and for the attackers to make enemy armies, rather than places, their objective. Recognizing that this was the cordon offensive he had so long championed, Lincoln gave his hearty approval. He also gave Grant a relatively free hand in carrying out the strategy, although not as free as the general later claimed in his memoirs. As compared with his relations with McClellan, Lincoln interfered little with Grant. He did not have to, because Grant was executing Lincoln's own strategy.†

---

*Through civilian and military telegraphs Grant and Halleck were in ready communication with generals in all theaters.

†When interservice coordination became necessary, it appears that Lincoln, Secretary of War Stanton, and Secretary of the Navy Gideon Welles would confer with each other and with officers with command roles in the proposed operation. In the amphibious operations on the

Southern command arrangements did not achieve the complexity or the ultimate efficiency of those in the North. The relative simplicity of the Confederate system resulted in part from the dominant command role exercised by President Davis. Completely convinced of his military ability, he wanted to be general in chief as well as commander in chief. He did not like to delegate authority to persons below him, he did not take advice easily, and he could not brook criticism or contradiction. But even if Davis had been a different kind of man, he, or any other individual who might have occupied the presidential chair, would have found the creation of an efficient command system difficult. The imperatives of Southern culture militated against experimenting in new ways in any area, including in war. Southerners were conservative, inclined to prefer institutions that had long existed, and parochially averse to accepting direction from a central authority except under necessity. They probably would have opposed a system that was not traditional and simple and that left the process of decision making in any but the familiar hands of the president. In this regard the thinking of Davis and his people for once coincided.

At the beginning of the war the military structure of the Confederacy was identical with that of the United States, except that the office of general in chief was not provided for. Early in 1862 Davis asked the Confederate Congress to authorize the position, not because he thought it was desirable or necessary to have a commanding general, but because he hoped by such an appointment to still critics of the War Department in Congress. The latter responded with legislation, but the president, thinking that it infringed on his prerogatives as commander in chief, vetoed the measure. Still seeking to achieve his object of placing a buffer between the War Department and Congress, Davis on his own authority created the office of general in chief in March. To hold it he named General Robert E. Lee, esteemed in military circles but at the time virtually unknown to the general public. Davis's directive charged Lee "under the direction of the President with the conduct of military operations in the armies of the Confederacy."

The phrase "under the direction of the President" was the key to Davis's concept of the office. Essentially he restricted Lee to acting as a provider of counsel and information. He usually asked Lee's opinion on strategic issues and sometimes accepted the general's suggestions, but he did not permit Lee to initiate or direct any large strategic operations. He also laid off on the general many minor matters. Lee's lack of authority was widely recognized. A Richmond newspaper spoke accurately when it said that his position was merely "complimentary" and that he was "simply an adviser."

Lee vacated the office in June to assume field duty, having been appointed by Davis to command the Army of Northern Virginia. Davis left the position

---

western rivers, officers of the two services on the scene usually arranged their own form of cooperation.

vacant for approximately twenty months, an indication of his opinion of its importance. During this time the president formulated strategy without professional advice except that which he chose to elicit from departmental commanders.

Davis did not resurrect the command office until February, 1864, after several recent defeats had brought strong criticism upon the government. He named to the post Braxton Bragg, who as a field commander in the West had been responsible for a disastrous defeat and whose removal had been forced on Davis by public clamor. In making the appointment, the president may have intended only to defy his critics. More probably, he was seeking to fill the position with a pliable instrument. Bragg, a personal friend, understood his place and restricted his function to providing advice when requested, and to praising Davis's military wisdom without being asked.

Disasters continued to strike Confederate armies. Demands that a military man be entrusted with the supreme command became ever louder, with some influential individuals demanding a dictator. Responding to the agitation, Congress in February, 1865, created the office of general in chief, and members made it clear they expected Davis to appoint Lee. Having no choice but to follow the mandate given him, the president did name Lee to the position. However, in his directive to Lee, he was careful to state that he was still commander in chief. The general, who had great respect for civilian authority, was careful to state in his letter of acceptance that he would serve as the president's subordinate.

The war ended two months later, before the new arrangement could be fairly tested. It certainly would not have worked. Even if Lee had been disposed to initiate an overall strategy, which on the evidence he was little interested in, he could hardly have done so while burdened with a field command. The problem of high command in a modern war was beyond solution by the unmodern Confederacy.*

BOTH SIDES USED a variety of weapons during the war, but generally they were the same ones. These arms, which came into use and were tested during the 1850s, were employed without important alteration throughout the conflict. Several new weapons were introduced, but produced in such small quantity as to have no significant effect on the course or the outcome of the war.

The basic small-arms weapon of the infantry soldier was the rifle musket, a single-shot, muzzle-loading piece with a range of about half a mile, but most

---

*Whether or not Lee had an overall view of the war has been argued by historians. Some have contended that he did see the war as a whole, but was never given a fair opportunity to frame general plans. The view here is that he was obsessed with the conflict in his native Virginia and had but a perfunctory interest in strategy on other fronts.

effective at 300 yards or less. Although several models of this weapon had been developed and were used during the war, the parts in them were essentially standard, and the guns could be produced in mass by the tooling machines available to manufacturers. Models of breech-loading and repeating rifles had been developed before the war, and the advantages offered by these weapons, a longer range and a faster rate of firepower, were apparent to ordnance officers. But despite their superiority, only a modest number of breech-loaders and repeaters were contracted for during the conflict. The failure to produce larger quantities was usually ascribed to the conservatism of ordnance bureaucrats, but these men had sound reasons for concentrating on turning out rifle muskets. An extensive retooling process was required to fabricate breech-loaders and repeaters in quantity, and neither government could afford to take the time to make the transition. Each one wisely decided to rely on the weapon it could already produce in mass amounts.*

Because of the distinction between field and heavy artillery, there was no basic artillery weapon. The most widely used fieldpiece of the war was the "Napoleon," a single-shot, muzzle-loading gun with a range of a mile, but most effective at half that distance or less. Pulled to a field by horses, a battery or batteries of Napoleons spewed forth shell, case shot, and canister and were effective dealers of death in the cramped spaces in which most of the battles of the war occurred. Rifled guns were also employed in the field service but in relatively small numbers. Although they had approximately twice the range of the Napoleons, they were no more effective than the latter at close distances, if as much so, and because of elementary sighting devices they were inefficient in searching out a remote or concealed foe. They were most frequently used to "soften up" an enemy position by bombarding it before the infantry attacked.

The heavier artillery was employed against fortifications, permanent or field, and in naval engagements. Most of the heavy pieces were muzzle-loading, single-shot smoothbores, the Rodmans or Dahlgrens developed before the war or models similar to them. Rifled cannon were also introduced, the most effective being the Parrott gun, which also was developed before the war. Although the rifled pieces had no faster rate of firepower than the smoothbores, being also single-shot muzzle-loaders, they possessed longer ranges, some of them being able to hurl a projectile as far as four to five miles. But at anywhere near their maximum range they were erratically inaccurate and were, like the rifled field cannon, unable to "locate" a distant or concealed target.

---

*The Northern Ordnance Department supplied the armies with nearly 4 million small arms in four years, a remarkable production achievement. The department may be criticized for not giving more attention to constructing the improved weapons after Northern arsenals went into full production of rifle muskets.

The weapons that came into use during the 1850s produced much greater firepower than anything possessed by armies in earlier conflicts—a force on the defensive could now strike attackers with artillery and musket shot almost from the time the latter started to move out. Students of tactics realized the threat that the new weapons posed for advancing infantry and considered the possibility of adopting a more dispersed or extended formation to make the attackers a less inviting target. But baffled by the problem of controlling large bodies of men beyond voice or vision, commanders continued to rely on a relatively rigid and close line formation. The number of lines was reduced from three to two but the men still moved forward in a dense conformation. The favored attack formation was in a "column of brigades," three brigades of a division aligned from front to back, and it was believed that the brigades, striking in successive waves, would be able to carry an enemy position.

Attackers in a Civil War battle usually opened by bombarding an enemy position to cripple opposing artillery and prepare the way for advancing infantry. Hardly ever was a bombardment effective. The defending infantry, employing rifle muskets, could keep artillery at a distance of a mile or more, and at this range the fire of cannon was ineffective. Consequently, when the attacking infantry finally moved out it encountered an unshaken enemy and received devastating fire from artillery and muskets the moment it started to advance.

As the attacking lines went forward, officers attempted to keep them parallel, perfectly dressed. One reason for this effort was that if a line halted to fire it could deliver a more massed volley if held parallel; more important, a regular line would have a maximum shock impact when it struck the defenders. Sometimes the insistence on maintaining uniformity had eerie results—men hit by bullets fell in parallel positions. A Confederate officer at Gettysburg saw a sight he described as "sickening and heart-rending." He counted seventy-nine rebels "laying dead in a straight line. I stood on their right and looked down their line. It was perfectly dressed. Three had fallen to the front, the rest had fallen backward, yet the feet of all these dead men were in a perfectly straight line." The principal result of adhering to a rigid line was tremendous casualty rates; men advancing in this formation were a vulnerable target and in hard-fought battles went down in windrows. Many units in both armies sustained total losses, killed and wounded, of 40 to 80 percent in a single engagement; at Gettysburg two out of every ten Union soldiers and three out of every ten Confederates were hit by bullets. The aggregate of service deaths on both sides was 618,000, a number almost equal to the deaths in all other American wars combined.*

---

*On the Union side approximately 360,000 deaths occurred and on the Confederate side about 258,000 deaths; the Southern total is less well documented but probably accurate. In both armies more men died of sickness or disease than in the field. Disease was a greater killer than bullets in American conflicts until World War I.

Frontal assaults in lines did not often succeed in Civil War battles. If the defenders were roughly equal in number and in a strong position, they could issue a fire that would shatter the attackers short of the defensive line or, if the latter continued, that would prevent them from making a real break-through; even a smaller defensive force, if sheltered by field fortifications, could usually hold off an attack.* The attackers, raked by artillery fire from the first and then by artillery and musket fire, tended to lose their formation; the successive lines ran together and approached the defenders bunched into a crowd and thus lost much of their shock effect. Even if a penetration was made, the surviving attackers were too few to exploit it into a breakthrough, and their reserves were too distant to aid them. Subject to a counterattack, the penetrating force had to retire or risk capture. The problem of the attackers was expressed aptly by a Confederate private at Gettysburg. Referring to the inability of the rebels to gain a foothold on Cemetery Ridge, he said: "It ain't hard to get on that ridge, the hell of it is trying to stay there."

Despite the failure of most frontal assaults and the frightful losses incurred in the dressed-line advances, generals continued to rely on the traditional formation throughout the war. They could always hope an attack would succeed, as some assaults did, and they remained convinced that only a close-order formation would assure them control of their troops. Some commanders adopted a modified version of the frontal attack. Feigning an advance on their front, they attempted to pass a force around the flank of the defenders, thus forcing the latter to abandon their prepared position and fight on less favorable ground. Other generals experimented with new and more extended formations. One innovation came to be called the advance by "rushes"; it probably originated by chance and was then employed by officers who saw its efficacy. An example of its use occurred in the Federal assault on Fort Donelson. Two lines of infantry coming under heavy fire lay down, the second forming on the left of the first. When the enemy fire abated, the line rose and rushed forward until pinned down again by fire. Rising and rushing in this manner, the attackers eventually carried the position with slight loss.

Another development was to strengthen the line of skirmishers, who ordinarily had no other mission than to feel out the enemy position. A general might advance half the strength of regiments in the front line of advance while holding the rest in support. This arrangement gave skirmishers for the first time a combat mission but enabled officers to retain a measure of control over the whole body of troops.

The various tactical innovations modified but did not seriously disturb the

---

*The advantage that firepower gave the defense is shown in the smaller number of troops required to hold a mile of position. In the Napoleonic wars 20,000 men to the mile were thought necessary. But in the Civil War 12,000 to the mile were regarded as ample, and in some sieges as few as 5,000 to the mile were found sufficient.

dominant role of firepower in the war. To the end, the plunging shot of artillery and muskets ruled most fields. Indeed, in the closing campaigns armies disappeared into the earth, both attackers and defenders digging into entrenchments before engaging in operations. Long forgotten were the parade-ground formations and the cheering crowds and the hopes of easy victory of 1861.

THE YEAR 1861 was for both sides a time of testing and trial. Each government was just beginning to mobilize land and sea forces, and neither was prepared to undertake a major effort. Nevertheless, both ventured campaigns. Some of the resulting battles occurred because one government or the other felt it had to make a move in a particular area to assert its authority or to retain, or to grasp, the human and material resources of the area. And behind these first thrusts was a feeling that a decisive success might end the war then and there —one smashing victory and the other side would quit. These hopes of a quick triumph ended in frustration. The North took several small encounters and the South won one big battle, but neither nation showed any indication of giving up, and at the close of the year the sides began to buckle down for a long war.

The small engagements won by the North had large results. As a culmination of one campaign, the crucial border slave state of Missouri was held for the Union. In Missouri supporters of secession and the Union confronted each other in armed organizations, and as the course of the state obviously would be determined by the side that could muster the greater force, both governments sent in troops to bolster their adherents. In August a Federal force of 5,000 under General Nathaniel Lyon attacked a Confederate army twice its size at Wilson's Creek. Although the Federals were defeated and Lyon was killed, the Confederates were not able to follow up their victory. Eventually the Federals attained numerical superiority and controlled most of the state. For the rest of the war the fighting in Missouri consisted of savage encounters between irregular bands of secessionists and Unionists that often seemed to have no relation to the main conflict. In saving Missouri the Federal government won an important strategic success. If the Confederates had secured Missouri, they could have used it as a base from which to attack the northwestern states.

In another campaign of small armies and battles, the North grasped a portion of Virginia, the forty-odd mountainous western counties that refused to recognize the legality of the state's act in seceding and had set up their own "loyal" state government. The mountain region attracted the early and covetous attention of both the Confederate and the Union governments, partly because it contained valuable resources, including deposits of salt, but mainly because it seemed to offer military advantages to the side that held it. The Confederacy wanted to reassert authority over this area within its claimed domain, and Southern military leaders saw the region as a possible base from which to cross the Ohio River and invade the North. For its part, the United States desired to "liberate" these Union-sympathizing people of a Confederate state, to score a propaganda victory by demonstrating that not all Southerners supported the rebel cause. Northern leaders also foresaw military possibilities in occupying the disaffected counties—from this mountain bastion Union armies might be able to move eastward against Confederate Virginia and Richmond itself.

Despite the importance that each government attached to western Virginia, neither was prepared in 1861 to send large forces into the area. The Federal government, using nearby Ohio as a staging area, eventually assembled about 20,000 troops under General George B. McClellan. The Confederacy never put in more than 15,000 men. These were the total forces, but the field columns that contested in several battles were even smaller, numbering from 5,000 to 9,000. The Federals were victorious in most of the encounters and at the end of the year held possession of the greater part of the region. However, the predicted strategic benefits did not materialize. Federal armies had such difficulty in moving in the rugged mountain terrain that the idea of a thrust to the east was abandoned. The battle for Virginia would have to be fought in another theater.

The year's only engagement involving sizable armies was fought between the two capitals of Washington and Richmond, a scene of frequent and furious conflict during the war. Everything that occurred in connection with this encounter, as was true later on, was influenced by the peculiar geography of Virginia—the land affected the prebattle planning, the determination of objectives, and the movement of troops to the scene of action.

In Virginia the Federals were usually on the offensive, and for them the most obvious objective was Richmond, lying about 100 air miles south of Washington. Richmond had symbolic value to the Confederacy and was also an industrial center of importance, and a Federal thrust at the city would force the Confederates to give battle in its defense. The most feasible way to move on Richmond seemed to be to march an army southward from Washington, and this approach was the one usually favored by Federal planners. Advancing on this route, the Northern armies were on the shortest road to Richmond, but it was one that presented troublesome problems in terrain. Northern Virginia was laced with rivers flowing from west to east, some of them broad and deep, and each of these streams was a potential Confederate defensive line.

Another route between the two capitals lay farther to the west. It was, however, only an alternative or a secondary way, and although it figured in the fighting that occurred in Virginia, it never became a principal theater of conflict. Just beyond the Blue Ridge mountains stretched the rich, rolling region known in Virginia as "the Valley," consisting actually of several concavities but dominated by one, the Shenandoah Valley. It was this last area that Virginians called the Valley which held forth particularly enticing possibilities

to the Confederates. It was a fertile source of grains and other supplies necessary to sustain Southern forces in the state. But more important, Southern
planners saw military rewards to be won by operating in the Valley. The
configuration of the great declivity favored the Confederates. Beginning in the
southwestern part of the state, it ran northeasterly until it reached the Potomac
River. Thus, a Southern force moving northward in the Valley would be
coming ever closer to Washington; and even if the Confederates could not
commit an army large enough to take the Northern capital, they could seem
to be menacing it and might frighten the Northern government into detaching
troops from its forces operating against Richmond.* Conversely, a Northern
army advancing southward in the Valley would be moving away from Richmond, and for this reason the Federals did not use it as an invasion road. They
had to try to occupy it, however, if only to deny its use to the Confederates.†

DURING THE SPRING of 1861 the Union and the Confederate governments
concentrated most of their hastily raised forces around or in front of their
capitals, each obviously expecting, when ready, to make a major effort in the
Virginia theater. Just south of Washington the Federal government assembled
an army that by early summer numbered over 30,000 and placed it under the
command of General Irvin McDowell, a regular army officer of apparent
competence. Guarding the northern end of the Shenandoah Valley was a
second Federal force of 15,000 under General Robert Patterson, who as a
volunteer and militia officer had served in both the War of 1812 and the
Mexican War.‡

The Confederate forces in Virginia were substantially north of Richmond,
placed so as to be able to make a defensive stand at a distance from the capital
or to menace Washington. The largest body of troops was stationed in and
around the hamlet of Manassas Junction, 30 miles southwest of Washington.
These 22,000 men were under the command of General P. G. T. Beauregard,
the Southern hero of Fort Sumter. A smaller force was watching Patterson in
the Valley, about 11,000 under General Joseph E. Johnston, who, although
holding a lesser command, ranked Beauregard. The two Confederate generals

---

*Here it is necessary to clarify terms used in describing movements in the Valley. The
Shenandoah River emptied into the Potomac. Hence, a Confederate force marching north is said
to be going *down* the Valley and a Federal force marching south is said to be going *up* the Valley.

†A third possible approach to Richmond existed, to come at the capital from the east and
on water. The Federals would attempt this in 1862.

‡McDowell and Patterson were representative of the officers on both sides who in the first
year of the war were entrusted with high command. McDowell, a graduate of West Point, had
attained the rank of major but had no experience in directing troops in numbers. Patterson, who
was sixty-nine years old, had led a division in Scott's small army in Mexico, but his service had
been undistinguished. The only Northern officers who had commanded men in numbers were
Scott and John Wool, who were both in their seventies and unfit for active service.

were officers in the old regular army with combat experience in the Mexican War; Johnston had also been quartermaster general in 1861.*

No general on either side contemplated undertaking a major movement in the early summer of 1861, or, indeed, even later in the year. They wanted more time before attempting to do anything, time to train and equip their green recruits, time to organize staffs, time to learn the art of commanding masses of troops. This last requirement weighed especially heavily on the generals. McDowell once complained that there was no officer in the army or, in fact, in the whole country, who had ever had to "handle" 30,000 men. He might have added that no officer in previous American history commanded as large a force as was under him around the capital. The largest single aggregation of troops in an earlier war was the 19,000 men Washington led for a short time in 1776.

McDowell's army was large only in comparison with forces in previous wars. But to the Northern public it seemed a mighty host, and as summer dawned, there were demands that the army move. "Forward to Richmond" was the cry emblazoned in a leading newspaper, and the phrase ran like wildfire throughout the North.

The clamor for an advance reached a peak late in June, and coincidentally President Lincoln instructed General Scott to ask McDowell to prepare a plan of operations against the Confederates at Manassas. It has been often said that in taking this action Lincoln was yielding to popular pressure. But more probably he was governed by military considerations. He indicated the direction of his thinking at a conference with Scott, McDowell, and members of the cabinet. McDowell was superior in numbers to Beauregard, Lincoln said, and should be able to smash the Southern army, disperse the remaining enemy forces in the state, and march unopposed to Richmond, perhaps ending the war at one stroke. When McDowell objected that he needed more time to train his troops, Lincoln replied: "You are green, it is true; but they are green; you are all green alike."†

McDowell realized he had to obey the president's wishes, and he presented a plan to turn the Confederates out of their position at Manassas and force them to fight on less favorable ground. Worried that he would lose his advantage in numbers if Johnston came to Beauregard's aid, McDowell asked for assurance that the Confederate force in the Valley would be contained. Scott replied that if Johnston moved, Patterson would follow "on his heels."

*The highest rank in Confederate service was general. Johnston was a general in 1861 while Beauregard was a brigadier. The highest rank in Federal service was major general until 1864; in that year the grade of lieutenant general was created, but was held only by Ulysses S. Grant.

†The remark quoted is from McDowell's account of the conference. McDowell did not attribute the statement specifically to Lincoln, but it certainly came from the president. In thinking that McDowell possessed the capacity to win a victory, Lincoln was reasoning soundly. He was wrong in believing that one Union success might convince the Confederacy to give up the war.

Relying on this promise, McDowell went ahead with his preparations, and on July 16 he moved out toward Manassas. His advance was advertised to Beauregard in the press and by spies.

Beauregard had thrown part of his army forward of Manassas, but on learning of McDowell's movement he withdrew his entire force behind the line of Bull Run, a small stream that ran just north of the village. A Louisiana Creole of French ancestry, Beauregard became excited easily, and the news of McDowell's approach stirred him to alarm. Asserting that he faced attack by a greatly superior foe, he called on his government to order Johnston to join him immediately. President Davis, however, refused to be stampeded. He and his military adviser, Robert E. Lee, reasoned that if Johnston joined Beauregard too soon, Patterson would go to McDowell and the numerical odds would tip even more heavily to the side of the Federals. Not until late on July 17, when the Federals were nearing Bull Run, did Davis order Johnston to proceed to Manassas, slightly over 50 miles by rail. Easily concealing his departure from Patterson, Johnston and his army reached Manassas on July 20.* The armies on either side of Bull Run were approximately equal in size, about 30,000 or so men in each force. McDowell would have to fight his battle without enjoying the numerical advantage he had counted on.

McDowell's battle plan was to occupy the Confederates by threatening to move on his front while sending a column up Bull Run to cross and come down on their left and turn them out of position. On the other side of the stream Johnston and Beauregard were also preparing an offensive, believing they should attack before Patterson could join McDowell. Although Johnston was the ranking general, he entrusted the planning of the battle to Beauregard, who knew the ground. Working all night, the Creole planned to throw a strong force across Bull Run on his right and turn the Federals out of their position, the same movement McDowell proposed to make. The opposing generals put their troops in motion early on the morning of July 21 in the battle called Manassas and Bull Run.

Beauregard was never able to get his offensive into operation. His hastily drawn and too complex plan was not fully understood by brigade commanders or his inexperienced staff, and perhaps not even by himself. After hours of effort he was able to move only a part of his attack force over Bull Run. In the meantime, McDowell's movement was going well. His attack, or right, column crossed the run, and coming down on the weak Confederate left, threatened to carry the field. Hurriedly Beauregard canceled his offensive and moved with all the troops he could collect to the point of danger. On the left he found the Confederate line facing almost due west and, although severely battered, still holding. Bringing up more units, Beauregard built his strength

*Johnston used his cavalry as a screen to mask his withdrawal from Patterson, who remained in the Valley.

on the left up to about 15,000 troops, as opposed to 13,000 Federals, and after his forces repelled a renewed assault, he ordered a counterattack. Previously Beauregard had displayed faults as a commander, the most serious being a tendency to make plans too grand for his resources, but now he showed a sure instinct for the kill—he seized the moment that often comes in a battle when victory will go to the general who dares to be bold. The sudden Confederate attack struck panic into the Federals, forcing them over Bull Run in what soon became a rout. McDowell, unable to get his troops in hand, ordered a retreat to Washington.

The Confederates, almost as demoralized by victory as the Federals were by defeat, were unable to organize an effective pursuit. And lacking adequate wagon transportation and bridging equipment, they lacked the capacity to cross the Potomac River barrier guarding Washington. During the remainder of the year the two armies occupied approximately the same positions they held before the battle. Both governments endeavored to increase the size of their forces, with the United States having the greater success. Lincoln, surveying his gathering host, decided that a bigger man than McDowell was needed to lead it, and called in the victor of the recent campaign in western Virginia, George B. McClellan.

BY THE LATTER PART OF 1861 the Federal navy was beginning to make its weight felt in the war. Although small in size—some forty vessels, of which about half were steam-driven—it had set up a blockade of the Southern coast and seized islands off the Carolinas and Georgia to serve as at-sea bases. The Navy Department, headed by Secretary Gideon Welles, started a feverish program of construction, concentrating on vessels equipped with steam power and rifled guns, that promised to make the blockade increasingly more effective and the United States a first-rate naval power.

The threat to the Confederacy posed by the rising naval strength of the North was realized early by the Southern secretary of the navy, Stephen R. Mallory. In the Senate of the old Union Mallory had specialized in naval matters, and he brought to his office a keen knowledge of the latest technical developments and a determination to build a sea force that could achieve realistic strategic aims.

Mallory proposed that the Confederacy adopt a dual naval strategy. First, it should commission in Europe fast and lightly armed vessels that would prey on Northern merchant ships in international waters and force the North to detach ships from the blockade to chase after them. Second, the government should have built in Europe and in Southern shipyards a flotilla of ironclad rams armed with rifled guns that could disrupt the blockade and perhaps even challenge the Federal fleet for superiority.

Mallory decided to rush the building of an ironclad vessel, and he had the skeleton of one available. When Virginia seceded, the Federal officers in the Norfolk navy yard tried to destroy everything that might be useful to the Confederates; unable to burn the frigate *Merrimack,* they scuttled her to the bottom of the harbor. Mallory had the hulk raised and ordered that it be plated with iron. Fifteen hundred workers toiled day and night on the job, and by the early spring of 1862 the ship, renamed the *Virginia,* was ready for action. She was slow and unwieldy and her engines were undependable, but she was an ironclad and, as far as the Confederates knew, the only one in either navy.

On March 8, 1862, the *Virginia,* or, as she is usually known in naval history, the *Merrimack,* steamed out of Norfolk to attack the squadron of wooden blockading ships in Hampton Roads. The blockaders had no chance against the iron monster. She easily destroyed two of the Federal vessels and forced the others to scatter. Then, with her engines beginning to sputter, she returned to anchorage, obviously intending to complete her work of death on the morrow. Jubilation reigned in Richmond at this seeming indication that the Confederacy possessed a weapon to break the blockade.

The Federal Navy Department had placed orders for the construction of several ironclads, and Secretary Welles, on learning that the Confederates were armoring a ship, directed work on one of these vessels, the *Monitor,* to be rushed. Construction was completed in a mere three months, an impressive feat, and although the ship had not yet been tested in rough waters, she was ordered to proceed with all haste to Hampton Roads. She arrived on the night of March 8, to a thankful welcome from the stricken Federal squadron.

When the *Merrimack* returned the next day, she was met by the *Monitor,* and there followed the first battle in history between ironclads.* The antagonists presented striking physical contrasts. The *Merrimack* stood high in the water and fired from portholes; the *Monitor* was low, almost flat, and armed with a rifle cannon in a revolving turret amidships. The two vessels fought for three hours, but neither possessed guns strong enough to penetrate the other's armor. The *Merrimack* finally broke off action and returned to Norfolk. The battle was a draw, but the Confederacy had lost the advantage of possessing a new and unique weapon.

All of Mallory's high strategic hopes ended in similar frustration. The commerce raiders almost swept Northern trade from the seas, but the Northern government accepted the loss rather than weaken the blockade. Mallory was never able to get together a flotilla of rams strong enough to challenge Union naval might or even to disrupt the blockade. Four ironclads were

---

*Such ships had operated in European navies but only against land fortifications, never against other ironclads.

contracted for in Europe, but in the face of Northern protests were not delivered. Twenty-two armored vessels were constructed in the South, but because of delays in building and for other reasons they were never available at the same time, and they offered no serious challenge to the ironclads being turned out by the superior Northern industrial plant.*

*After the summer of 1862 most of the Confederate ironclads were designed to serve as river and harbor defense vessels rather than to venture into open waters. A number of vessels were destroyed before or after completion to prevent their capture by Federal sea and land forces. Thus, the *Merrimack* was burned when the Federals advanced up the James River in the spring of 1862.

CHAPTER XII

The Civil War: The Battles

FEDERAL OFFENSIVE OPERATIONS in 1862 began in the Western theater, and in this large area laced with waterways the navy and the army worked in close cooperation. The primary objective was to seize control of the Mississippi River line, and to achieve this end the Federals moved with land and sea forces on the river itself or on streams parallel to it, flanking the Confederates out of position. Naval vessels, some of them traditional wooden craft and some small ironclad gunboats, not only carried supplies for the armies but also provided telling fire support in many of the engagements. This interservice cooperation was the first example of large-scale amphibious warfare in American military history.

As the year opened, Federal land forces in the West were distributed in two departmental commands. One comprised all of Kentucky except the extreme western tip and was under the direction of General Don Carlos Buell, who at his base at Louisville was busily training a force he estimated to number 50,000 effective troops. The second department included western Kentucky and the territory west of the Mississippi and was commanded by General Henry W. Halleck, whose headquarters were in St. Louis. Two separate armies operated under Halleck, 20,000 in Kentucky under Ulysses S. Grant and 30,000 in Missouri under Samuel Curtis. Buell and Halleck had been appointed to their commands in November, 1861, but in the ensuing months they had refused Lincoln's pleas to undertake offensive action, claiming they needed more time to organize their forces. Both generals were good administrators, but neither possessed an instinct to engage the enemy. Buell went so far as to contend that a commander could win a campaign by maneuvering, without ever fighting an important battle; he liked to proclaim: "War has a higher object than that of mere bloodshed."

All Confederate forces in the West, on both sides of the Mississippi, were in a single administrative department under the command of one general, Albert Sidney Johnston, an arrangement that proved cumbersome and was later abandoned. In Kentucky 50,000 troops were spread over a line 150 miles long, from Bowling Green to Columbus on the Mississippi. In Arkansas stood a detached left wing of 20,000 under Earl Van Dorn. Johnston was a handsome and impressive man who was regarded by President Davis and others as destined to be the South's greatest general. At this time, however, and in the campaign about to begin, he acted more like a troop leader than a departmental commander. He kept his headquarters at Bowling Green, from where he could give only the loosest supervision to his far-flung line.

The Confederate line not only was thinly held but was marked by a serious weakness in the center. Here the Confederates relied on the strength of two forts, Henry on the Tennessee River and Donelson on the Cumberland River, streams flowing northward to the Ohio River. But they had built the forts when Kentucky was asserting neutrality, and out of deference to the state had located them just over the border in Tennessee. The unfortunate result was that the center was thrown back from either flank and, resting on navigable streams, was vulnerable to an amphibious attack. A Federal commander imaginative enough to combine land and sea forces could come up one or both rivers and, capturing the forts, could isolate the flanks.

One Northern general realized early the possibilities offered in the Confederate center. Ulysses S. Grant was as yet relatively unknown, but he was about to demonstrate fine strategic ability and the instinct of the great battle captain to strike hard at a weak spot of the enemy. Late in January he won permission from Halleck to attack Fort Henry and enlisted naval support from Captain Andrew Foote, who commanded a flotilla of ironclad gunboats. Grant and Foote made their plans carefully and were ready to move early in February.

Fort Henry fell to the assault with almost no resistance, its defenders overly awed by the firepower of the gunboats. Grant had intended to go no farther, but realizing he had the momentum of victory, he secured approval from Halleck to attack Fort Donelson. His troops marched across the 12 miles separating the forts while his naval support moved to the Cumberland. At Donelson the Confederates put up a fight, their artillery fire damaging severely the ironclads that ventured too close to its walls. Grant finally had to invest the place with his troops. When the Confederate commander proposed an armistice, Grant replied with almost brutal directness that he would offer no terms except "unconditional surrender." The fort capitulated on February 16, and with it came a bag of 15,000 prisoners.*

Grant's move on the forts threw Albert Sidney Johnston into what can

---

*Grant was reinforced by Halleck during the attack to 27,000 troops. Probably 20,000 Confederates were in Donelson, but a number of them escaped before the surrender.

only be described as a state of "command shock"; some of the Confederate general's actions following the fall of Henry seemed hardly rational. Alarmed that Grant was between his flanks, and believing that Buell was also advancing, Johnston concluded he had to pull back his forces at Bowling Green and Columbus. His decision was soundly based, but at the same time he sent additional troops into Donelson just as it was about to be attacked. Apparently he thought the garrison could delay Grant while the flanks retreated and then escape itself, but he succeeded only in delivering more prisoners to Grant.

During the withdrawal Johnston continued to act more like a troop leader than an army commander. He insisted on shepherding the small force at Bowling Green toward Nashville, where, he said, he would make a stand. The withdrawal of the left flank he entrusted to General Beauregard, who was serving as his second in command, having recently been exiled to the West after quarreling with President Davis. Partly because the movement lacked central direction, it became more and more precipitate. But it would have been hurried in any case because the Federals in the center could march faster— Buell advanced on Nashville, forcing Johnston to retire again, and Grant returned to Fort Henry to start up the Tennessee, threatening to isolate the left wing and Confederate positions on the Mississippi. The Southern retreat did not stop until the two wings met at the railroad center of Corinth in northeast Mississippi late in March. The reunited army had saved itself, but its cause had suffered a stunning setback. The fall of Henry and Donelson were like the opening of a door—through the gap the Federals poured to grasp all of Kentucky, the western half of Tennessee, and adjoining Confederate strongholds on the Mississippi. They were also advancing west of the river. Early in March Curtis defeated Van Dorn at Pea Ridge in Arkansas and began to occupy the northern part of that state.

Halleck, Grant's superior, had done little to achieve the recent successes except to support his aggressive subordinate. But now he claimed credit for the victories and demanded as a reward command of all forces in the West, including Buell's army. Hoping that unity of command would bring additional victories, Lincoln approved the request. Halleck, acting as though he had been infused with some of Grant's vigor, directed the latter to advance up the Tennessee River toward Corinth and ordered Buell to move from Nashville to join him. But Halleck's cautious Jominian thinking was evident in his instruction to Grant not to bring on a general engagement. "We must strike no blow until we are strong enough to admit no doubt of the result," he warned.

Mindful of Halleck's restraint, Grant debarked his army of 40,000 on the west bank of the Tennessee at a place named Pittsburg Landing, about 30 miles from Corinth. His camps lay on rolling forested land near a little log church called Shiloh, between two creeks flowing into the river. Here Grant waited for Buell to join him and for permission from Halleck to resume his advance.

He took almost no security precautions, assuming that the Confederates would obligingly remain at Corinth until he was ready to attack. His error was one likely to afflict successful generals—he believed that the enemy would do what he wanted him to do.

The enemy had no intention of cooperating with Grant. At Corinth, Johnston and Beauregard were aware of the Federal build-up on the Tennessee, and they came to an obvious decision—to deliver a surprise attack on Grant and destroy him before Buell arrived. With their army reinforced to 40,000 men, they moved forward on April 4 to attack on the next day. Beauregard drew up the march and battle order and made it characteristically complicated. The plan called for the Confederate right to roll up the Federal left and sweep the whole Federal army away from the river and from the approaching Buell, pinning it against a creek to the north, where it could be destroyed.

A series of frustrating events seemed to threaten the success of the movement. The march did not start on time or proceed on schedule, and units of the three corps became mixed with each other and had to be disentangled before they could be deployed. It was late on April 5 before the confusion was cleared up, and Beauregard, convinced that the possibility of a surprise had been lost, wanted to call off the attack. But Johnston, in this crisis showing moral courage, insisted that it be made. "I would fight them if they were a million," he said.

In what must be one of the most sensational misreadings of intelligence in American military history, Grant and his corps generals refused to believe that the Confederate army was lying within a few miles of their lines. They knew through patrols that enemy soldiers were out there in the woods, but they brushed off this information as indicating only a reconnaissance in force. Hence, when the Confederate attack jumped off early the next morning, it caught the Federals by tactical surprise. The rebels drove easily through the forward Northern lines, but soon Federal corps and other unit commanders organized new lines of resistance and slowed the advance. Grant arrived on the scene from downriver and ordered the field to be held at all cost.

The fiercest Federal resistance was on the left, the flank the Confederates had hoped to turn. Protected by a sunken country road, the defenders here bloodily turned back eleven attacks. Meanwhile, the advance on the Confederate left was pushing slowly ahead. But the assault plan was off schedule—instead of moving the Federals away from the river, the attack was shoving them toward it. Concerned by the turn of events, Johnston rode to the right to spur his men on. As he observed a charge, he was struck by a stray bullet that severed the artery in one leg, and he bled to death in a few minutes. Beauregard, who was directing movements in the rear, came up to take command and press the attack. At five-thirty in the afternoon the Confederates finally broke through at the sunken road, but only after committing their last reserves. As darkness drew near, Beauregard called off his offensive. His men were exhausted after fighting for thirteen hours, and his units were disorganized and scattered. He hoped on the morrow to drive the Federals into the river.

Unknown to the Confederates, most of Buell's troops had arrived on the other side of the river, had been there, in fact, since the previous day. During the night of April 6, after the battle, 17,000 of them were ferried over the river, bringing Grant's strength up to 40,000 again. Thus reinforced, Grant went over to the offensive on the following morning. Because of his losses and of straggling by his troops, Beauregard could put only something over 20,000 men in line, and after hours of hard fighting he withdrew to Corinth. The battle of Shiloh, as the engagement became known, was costly to both armies: over 10,000 men in each killed and wounded, or one-fourth of their totals. The Confederates lost the field, but, more important, they failed in their strategic purpose, to destroy Grant singly. The two Federal armies were united and in position to move on Corinth.

On the railroad line from Charleston to Memphis, Corinth was an important objective in Mississippi, and to effect its capture General Halleck himself arrived at Pittsburg Landing with reinforcements that brought the Federal army up to 90,000. Moving slowly and cautiously, Halleck took most of May to get into position before the town, and then, becoming even more cautious, he elected to take it by siege. In Corinth Beauregard had 50,000 men, having been joined by Van Dorn from Arkansas, but he realized that he could not stand a siege and that if he remained, he would lose not only the town but his army. Consequently, he evacuated Corinth on the night of May 30 and retired 50 miles southward to Tupelo. A master of deception, an art not often practiced by American generals, Beauregard ran an empty train back and forth through the town to make Halleck think that Southern reinforcements were arriving. The army marched away to safety while the Northern general waited nervously to be attacked.

Halleck had been made to look foolish, but still he had secured Corinth, and other forces under his command were grasping at points on the Mississippi River. By June naval and land forces had occupied Memphis. Slowly but inexorably the Federals were possessing the line of the great river.

They were also coming up the Mississippi from the South, aiming first a naval blow at the port city of New Orleans. In April there appeared in the Gulf of Mexico the mightiest concentration of vessels yet assembled in an American war, 46 craft packing a total of 286 guns, under the command of Captain David G. Farragut, who would later become the first American admiral. Heading the squadron were four big wooden sloops, on which Farragut placed his main reliance. There were some ironclad gunboats with him but Farragut had a veteran's distrust of their capabilities, calling them "those damn teakettles."

Farragut made his move late in April, smashing past two weakly defended forts on either side of the river, defeating a smaller Confederate flotilla that tried to intercept him, and running up to New Orleans. The city was defenseless, the Confederate government having expected any attack to come from above, and was surrendered by its civic authorities. Farragut then sailed farther up the river and accepted similar surrenders at Baton Rouge and Natchez. His easy success convinced him and his superiors in Washington that the navy alone could seize every enemy stronghold on the lower river. But when Farragut probed at the defenses of Vicksburg, he met such a fire he had to retire; he reported that the cooperation of land forces would be required to reduce Vicksburg and its sister fortress at Port Hudson, farther south.

The Federals had been stopped on the lower river, but they had achieved an important success. They had seized the South's largest city, depriving the Confederacy of its financial and industrial resources, and they had closed off the mouth of the Mississippi to enemy trade. Land forces followed the navy in and occupied approximately the southern third of Louisiana, ensuring a base for possible future operations.

After the fall of Corinth, Halleck was called to Washington to become general in chief. Before departing, he again split the command in the West into two departments, under Grant and Buell. His assignment of missions to the commanders was curious, revealing the prejudices of the traditional military mind. Grant, the hardest-fighting Northern general yet to appear, was left with over 60,000 men but given the relatively unimportant task of guarding railroad communications along the Mississippi. Careless in dress and informal in manner, Grant did not fit Halleck's image of a soldier. He was "able" on the field, Halleck admitted, but he did not know how to "regulate" or "organize" an army. Buell, who had done almost no fighting, was awarded an important combat mission, to move eastward with 55,000 troops along the Memphis and Charleston Railroad to capture Chattanooga. He was a "proper" soldier, correct in manner and conduct and able to cite Jominian precepts.

Meanwhile, the Confederate army at Tupelo received a new commander. Beauregard came under wide criticism for allegedly throwing away Johnston's victory at Shiloh, and he had aroused Davis's displeasure by abandoning Corinth. Learning that the Creole had left his post on sick leave, Davis used this as a pretext to remove him, appointing in his place one of the corps commanders, Braxton Bragg. Stern in demeanor and sour in manner, Bragg became the most controversial general in the Confederacy and was probably the most disliked. But whatever his personal defects, he was capable of acting vigorously, and he now made a move that changed the face of the war in the West. Leaving holding forces at Tupelo and Vicksburg, he moved with the bulk of his army, about 32,000 troops, to Chattanooga. Because he could not move straight eastward on the railroad Buell was advancing on, he shipped his men by rail to Mobile and then northward, a journey of 776 miles over six different lines. Nevertheless, he reached Chattanooga in late July while Buell was still miles to the east.

Bragg's reasons for shifting his base to Chattanooga were not entirely clear. He went there in response to a plea from the Confederate commander in eastern Tennessee, Kirby Smith, who wired he could not hold the city against Buell. But Bragg must have known the obvious advantage Chattanooga offered as an offensive base from which to strike northward through Tennessee and Kentucky and recover the territory the Confederacy had recently lost. Also unclear is what occurred between Bragg and Smith when they discussed the strategy they should employ. Apparently they considered invading middle Tennessee to "cut Buell off" from his advanced base at Nashville. But Smith became increasingly enamored with the idea of moving directly into Kentucky, and early in August he struck out for Lexington with 20,000 troops. Bragg moved separately into western Kentucky with about 30,000, either drawn along by Smith's impetuosity or persuaded of the soundness of the plan. The plan *was* good, even if neither of the principals understood it clearly. The Confederate presence in Kentucky would force Buell to follow with the bulk of his army, and if the Confederates could get between him and his supply base at Louisville, they could force him to fight on ground of their choosing. If victorious, they could restore their line in Kentucky.

All the bright Confederate hopes crashed in failure. While Smith lingered around Lexington, Bragg interposed himself between Buell, who was approaching with 45,000 men, and Louisville. But he did not offer battle. Grown suddenly cautious and conscious of his numerical inferiority, Bragg permitted the Federals to pass by to their base. In Louisville Buell brought in reinforcements that raised his force to over 60,000 and then came out looking for Bragg, who had also been reinforced and had perhaps 40,000 men. The two armies stumbled onto each other at Perryville on October 8 and fought an indecisive battle in which neither commander committed his full force. Bragg, however, had had enough of offensive action. He yielded the field and retired to Chattanooga. Making no effort to pursue, Buell returned slowly to Nashville. His failure to follow up his success disgusted Lincoln, who shortly relieved him from command of the army.*

In Buell's place Lincoln appointed William S. Rosecrans, who under Grant had demonstrated an aggressive spirit and an apparent strategic aptitude. But on being given the responsibility of high command, "Old Rosy" seemed to change—like other generals similarly elevated, he lost his appetite for action. At Nashville he called for reinforcements and then more reinforcements and resisted urgings from Lincoln to advance. "I will not budge until I am ready," he said defiantly. Threatened with removal, he finally went forward in December. At the same time, Bragg, also urged on by his government, advanced, and the two armies met on the last day of the year at the battle

---

*While Bragg invaded Kentucky, the forces under his command in Mississippi struck at Corinth and Iuka but were repelled by troops under Grant.

of Murfreesboro, or Stone's River. Although slightly inferior in numbers, Bragg attacked the Union right and bent it back but could not break it; he waited a day and then struck the Union left and was bloodily repulsed. In both offensives he suffered heavy losses and was forced to retire, leaving the Federals closer to Chattanooga.

The year 1862 was a bad one for the Confederates in the West. They lost important territory and large numbers of men and, ominously for the future, they were slowly but surely being moved from the Mississippi River line.

WHILE FEDERAL FORCES in the West were grinding forward with success after success, the army in the Eastern theater was meeting with defeat and frustrating failure. Every one of its efforts to beat the Confederate army in Virginia and capture Richmond was turned back, and at the end of 1862 it seemed no closer to its goal than it had been at the beginning of the year.

All through the fall and winter months of 1861–62 George McClellan organized the masses of recruits the government placed at his disposal, the number eventually reaching 150,000. He called his host the Army of the Potomac and boasted of its discipline and condition. Nothing he said was exaggerated. McClellan was perhaps the best trainer of troops of the war, and he created a superbly trained army and a potentially formidable fighting force.

Whether McClellan would ever fight his fine army was a question that increasingly worried many observers, including President Lincoln. During the winter months Lincoln repeatedly urged the general to act, or at least to propose a plan of action, but always McClellan demurred, protesting he was not yet ready. He was the supreme Jominian, reluctant to move unless he could do so with overwhelming superiority and hopeful that victory could be achieved without costly fighting. The odds were never what he wanted them. He lived in a world of fantasy that he filled with many and diverse enemies. Some of the enemies were men in his own government who wanted him to fail —"those hounds in Washington" was an epithet he once applied to his civilian superiors—but the most dangerous foe was the Confederate army, which he always calculated as at least twice its actual size. Thus, he insisted to Lincoln that Joseph E. Johnston's Confederate force at Manassas numbered 100,000, although it had at the most only 50,000.

McClellan's tendency to lose his grip on reality appeared in his strategic planning for operations in the spring. He settled on a plan during the winter, but did not immediately inform Lincoln of it, apparently feeling no obligation to discuss strategy with his civilian superior. His scheme departed boldly from conventional thinking as to how to approach Richmond—he proposed to come at the capital from the east and by water. Specifically, he would move his army in naval transports to the mouth of the Rappahannock River and then upstream a short distance to a landing at Urbana. Arriving there before Johnston could shift south to meet him, McClellan would stand between the Confederates and Richmond and could either force them to fight on unfavorable ground or march into the city ahead of them. His strategy would end the war at one stroke, he told intimates.

The plan had undoubted merits. Operating from Urbana, the army would have a shorter land route to cover than moving from Washington, and it would be on a secure water line of communication. But the plan ignored the political situation, as McClellan discovered when he finally revealed it to Lincoln. The president was naturally and rightly concerned to keep Washington safe, and he objected that taking the army to the Rappahannock would open the capital to a strike by Johnston, who was only 30 miles away at Manassas. Tolerantly McClellan explained that Johnston would have to move south to meet the Federal thrust and that Washington would be in no danger. Lincoln, however, demanded that sufficient troops be left "in and around" the city to make it "entirely secure," and a minimum force of 40,000 was eventually agreed on. Even then the president's assent to the proposal was given reluctantly. The episode was a classic example of how not to conduct a civil-military relationship. The general had insisted on a plan that the civilian authority distrusted and therefore would not fully support. The president agreed to the plan but imposed conditions as to the defense of Washington that hampered the free movement of the general. McClellan should have shifted to a strategy that Lincoln would accept—or Lincoln should have found himself another general.

Early in March, as McClellan was preparing to get his operation under way, he received embarrassing news. Johnston, anticipating some kind of advance by the Federals and thinking Manassas too exposed a position, pulled his army back behind the Rappahannock line, back to where McClellan had intended to place his own army.* McClellan could gain nothing now by going to Urbana, but it was characteristic of him that he could not change a plan he had fixed in his mind. He was still intent on coming at Richmond from the east, and if he could not move on the Rappahannock, he would take another water route. He proposed to move his army by ship to Fortress Monroe, on the bulge of land between the York and the James rivers known as the Peninsula, about 75 miles from Richmond; landing here, he could use one of the rivers as his line of communication.† Lincoln disliked the change—it would take the army even farther from Washington—but he felt he had no choice but to allow McClellan to go ahead.

McClellan embarked for the Peninsula late in March. On boarding ship the general dispatched a note to the War Department listing the number of

---

*McClellan occupied the deserted works at Manassas, which became a Federal outpost. As it could be said that he had now taken the field, Lincoln chose this time to remove McClellan as general in chief.

†The Federals, utilizing their naval power, had held Monroe since the beginning of hostilities.

troops left to defend Washington. His action was a striking demonstration that he did not know how to deal with his civilian superior. Knowing that Lincoln was sensitive about the safety of the capital, he should have explained his arrangements in person. What was worse, he had not complied with the president's directive—his figures were juggled so as to give an impression that he had detached more men than he had. On being told of the deception, Lincoln concluded that his general had not been sufficiently concerned about Washington. Concerned himself, the president ordered McDowell's corps of 30,000, which had not yet gone aboard ships, to remain near the capital; eventually it was stationed opposite Fredericksburg, on the Rappahannock, about halfway between the capitals and in position to cover Washington. McClellan had been deprived of approximately one-fourth of his army, a loss he might have averted had he been frank with Lincoln.*

Even after losing McDowell, McClellan clearly retained a numerical superiority over the forces immediately confronting him. He began operations on the Peninsula with about 100,000 men, and reinforcements kept his army at around that size throughout the campaign. The only Confederate force in front of him as he moved up the York River, the stream he chose as his line of communication,† consisted of 11,000 troops at Yorktown. They were behind field fortifications, however, and their commander so disposed them as to give an impression of greater numbers. McClellan paused before the works long enough to allow Johnston time to reach the Peninsula, and then decided to reduce them by the certain but slow method of siege. His operation consumed a month, the defenders abandoning Yorktown at his approach on May 5. His leisurely procedure had allowed the Confederates to collect almost 70,000 troops to oppose him.

Johnston, however, did not choose to offer a strong opposition. He told Jefferson Davis that he wanted to draw McClellan farther away from his base before fighting, to defeat the Federals near Richmond and destroy them while retreating. Davis and his adviser, General Lee, disliked the strategy as involving an unnecessary loss of territory, but felt they had to let the commander in the field have his way. Davis's compliance, like Lincoln's earlier acquiescence to McClellan's operation, demonstrates an interesting truth about war: that a civilian authority frequently cannot control a general on the scene.

Moving forward against only delaying opposition, McClellan was within 20 miles of Richmond by mid-May, and by the latter part of the month his advance units were but 5 miles from the city. He was closing in, but his army

*McClellan had intended to operate with something over 130,000 troops. Actually, he had allotted enough men to secure Washington. However, a large part of the force was in the Valley, and he had not explained its defensive function to the president.

†McClellan's correspondence indicates that he elected the York River because of the supposed strength of Confederate defenses on the James. The presence of the *Merrimack* in the James may have influenced his decision.

was divided by the Chickahominy River, a stream that took its rise above Richmond and flowed east and then south into the James. Approximately a third of the army lay south of the stream and the remainder north of it. McClellan felt the division was necessary. Richmond was on the south side, and to get at it, he would eventually have to cross the bulk of his force. But he needed to retain a portion on the north bank to safeguard his communications on the York, and he thought he must keep the larger portion there. He expected a significant reinforcement to join him shortly, and he was keeping his right strong to make contact with this force.

As he advanced up the Peninsula, McClellan besought Lincoln to allow McDowell to join him. Ever inflexible, he insisted that McDowell come by water, although the latter, opposite Fredericksburg, was only two days' march, but a week's voyage away. Lincoln finally agreed, on May 17, that McDowell could go to McClellan—but by land, so as to remain in position to cover Washington. Marching directly south, McDowell expected to unite with McClellan's extended right somewhere above the Chickahominy.

The Confederate high command knew that McDowell was coming—like most movements of the war this was almost public knowledge—and realized the peril his reinforcement would pose for Richmond. There was need of a plan to keep him near Washington, and Davis and General Lee quickly devised one. They found a ready tool to execute their design in General Thomas J. Jackson, who commanded a little army of 5,000 in the Valley. Jackson had earlier gained fame in the battle of Bull Run by standing his ground so firmly as to win the sobriquet "Stonewall." Assigned to command in the Valley, he had a reputation for dash and mobility; previously, in May, he and his fast-marching soldiers, becoming known as Jackson's "foot cavalry," had drubbed and driven back a Federal column under General John C. Frémont trying to push into the Valley from the west. Now he was reinforced to 17,000 and directed to move north and create an impression that he was advancing on Washington.

Jackson performed his mission brilliantly. Moving fast and employing deception to mask his marches, he easily outmaneuvered the Federal commander in the Valley, Nathaniel P. Banks. Banks's forces were stationed in two separate positions before Winchester, and Jackson struck them before they could unite, driving the defenders in precipitate retreat toward the Potomac. Boldly exploiting the momentum of his victory, he followed the Federals all the way to the river crossings.

Jackson's approach alarmed many civil officials in Washington; it was widely believed that the capital was in danger. Lincoln, however, was not deceived. Appreciating that Jackson was trying to magnify his threat, he saw in the raider's movement to the northern end of the Valley an opportunity to lay a trap. If the several Federal forces in the area could converge on Jackson, they might destroy him and end the enemy menace in the Valley. Acting like a general in chief, Lincoln disposed his pieces. He ordered Frémont to return to the Valley, Banks to move southward, and McDowell, who was preparing to march to McClellan, to come in from the east. To McClellan he explained that the decision to use McDowell had been a "painful" necessity.

On each of the three generals engaged in the movement Lincoln impressed one order—to catch Jackson they must march fast. It was "a question of legs," he told McDowell. None of the generals was quite up to the task. Apprised of the trap closing on him, Jackson pulled back to safety, even delivering sharp blows at the advance forces of Frémont and McDowell as he escaped. His campaign was a spectacular success. He had inflicted serious losses on the enemy, but even more important, he had accomplished his strategic mission. McDowell's corps was so exhausted by its marching that it was unable to go to McClellan. The latter would have to fight with what he had.

While the Valley campaign was coming to an end, Johnston at last struck his promised blow at McClellan. On May 31 and June 1 he attacked the part of the Federal army that was south of the Chickahominy, at Fair Oaks and Seven Pines. His assaults pushed the Federals back slightly but did not break their line. McClellan, warned of danger to his left, altered his dispositions. Now he placed two-thirds of his army south of the Chickahominy while retaining one-third north, to guard his communications and to make contact with the reinforcements he continued to hope would come.

Johnston was badly wounded in the fighting and had to give up the command. To his place Davis named Robert E. Lee, who had previously served in minor commands and as the president's adviser. On taking over, Lee gave his forces a new name, the Army of Northern Virginia. The title indicated how he intended to use the army. He wanted to return the war to the frontier of the state and the Confederacy and even to take it, if possible, into the North. He would become the South's greatest general, and its hero. As a strategist, his most striking quality was audacity, a willingness to risk greatly for victory. "There is always hazard in military movements," he once wrote, "but we must decide between the positive loss of inaction and the risk of action."

Lee showed his audacity immediately. Determined to destroy McClellan if the opportunity presented itself, he saw that chance in the altered division of the Federal army—the weakened right wing north of the Chickahominy invited attack. Quickly Lee made his plan. In order to provide himself with greater striking strength, he brought Jackson from the Valley, raising his own army to 85,000. He proposed to mass the bulk of his force, about 56,000 troops, against the Federal right and crush that fraction. McClellan, with a third of his army smashed, would have to retreat, probably along the line of the York, and Lee intended to follow and finally destroy him. The plan involved a risk —if McClellan discovered the small size of the Confederate force south of the Chickahominy, he could almost walk into Richmond. But Lee reasoned that the violence of the Confederate attack would unnerve his opponent and cause him to think only of safety. The Virginian had read his enemy better than he knew. McClellan was apprehensively aware that Lee had received reinforcements, and he informed Washington that he was about to be attacked by an army twice the size of his own, by 200,000 men! His interpretation of Federal intelligence reveals a significant fact about war—that often a general may operate not on the basis of an actual situation but of the perception in his mind.

Lee struck his blow on June 26, and this engagement and others that followed became known as the battle of the Seven Days.* The fighting did not go at all as Lee had planned. He mauled the Federal right but could not destroy it. Inexperienced in commanding large bodies of troops and served by an inadequate staff, he was unable to make his army conform to his orders. Thus, on the first day he got only 14,000 of his 50,000 troops into action, and in later meetings he did only somewhat better. McClellan retreated but not, as Lee had expected, along the York River. Abandoning his base on that stream, the Federal commander pulled his wing above the Chickahominy back to the south side and retired toward the James River, where the navy was setting up a new base for him at Harrison's Landing. (This shift in bases was a striking demonstration of the flexibility that sea power afforded Northern armies.) Lee followed, trying again and again to deliver the finishing blow but always failing. After a last bloody repulse at Malvern Hill on July 1, Lee gave up the pursuit. He had not accomplished his objective of destroying the Federal army and he had suffered frightful casualties, 11,000 killed or died of wounds.†

At Harrison's Landing, McClellan was still only 25 miles from Richmond and on a secure water line of communications. The Federal high command—Lincoln, Secretary of War Stanton, and General in Chief Halleck—would have been well advised to leave the army where it was and let it resume the advance on Richmond. Lincoln and his counselors considered this possibility, but rejected it, and in the end directed the forces in the Peninsula to be evacuated by sea to northern Virginia, there to join an army of 45,000 that had been collected under General John Pope. The combined forces would be commanded by McClellan and would move against Richmond on the overland route. McClellan bitterly protested the decision, but he was to blame for it. He demanded impossible reinforcements as a condition of renewing operations and continued to insist that Lee's army numbered 200,000. If an enemy army of that size stood between the two Federal armies in Virginia, it behooved the Federal government to unite its troops.‡

The Federal army in northern Virginia consisted of the three forces that

---

*The principal battles actually took place over a space of six days, from June 26 to July 1. A preliminary clash on June 25 was counted as a battle when the campaign received its name.

†Lee's total casualties were 20,000 men. McClellan lost heavily in equipment and had over 15,000 casualties; of the latter, however, 10,000 were prisoners later exchanged.

‡Halleck influenced Lincoln to order the withdrawal by citing textbook maxims stating that two armies separated by an enemy were in danger. In this case, the separation was more technical than real because the navy controlled the waters between the armies.

had operated so ingloriously against Jackson, and Pope had been brought in from the West to command it. Originally Lincoln hoped to send Pope against Richmond from the west while McClellan was coming in from the east, but the sudden collapse of the Peninsula campaign compelled a recasting of plans. Now Pope was directed to maneuver below the Rappahannock and wait for McClellan and his army to arrive. He could not have looked forward to coming under the latter's command. An aggressive and arrogant man, Pope had expressed contempt for McClellan's lack of resolution. He also infuriated his soldiers by boasting of his own prowess. "I have come to you from the West, where we have always seen the backs of our enemies," he began one announcement. In the East he had heard too much talk of lines of retreat, and he wanted no more of this: "Let us study the probable lines of retreat of our opponents, and leave our own to take care of themselves."

McClellan's withdrawal was observed with keen interest by Lee. Satisfying himself that the Federals were really leaving and that Richmond was in no further danger, the Confederate commander resolved on a typically audacious move—he would shift the bulk of his army northward and defeat Pope before he was joined by McClellan. There now ensued the spectacle of two great armies moving in the same direction, one on water and the other on land, and to the same destination. On the outcome of the race hung the fate of John Pope.

Lee moved the two corps in which his army was organized to the Rappahannock in shifts, sending Jackson's corps on ahead and himself following with James Longstreet's corps.* At Jackson's approach Pope, who was still maneuvering below the river, retired to the north side. The Federal general was unsure of the strength of the force that had suddenly appeared opposite him, but he suspected it was formidable and called on the government to speed reinforcements. The high command also sensed danger and seized on the only reinforcements available, those units of McClellan's army that had arrived near Washington or were in the process of arriving. Orders went to McClellan to press his troops forward to Pope, but he was not to go with them. The combined forces would in the developing crisis operate under Pope, the general on the scene. McClellan complied with the government's wishes, but neither he nor his corps leaders showed much concern to reach Pope quickly; McClellan spoke callously of leaving the latter "to get out of his scrape." Only two corps of the Army of the Potomac were with Pope when he had to fight.

In the meantime Lee crossed the Rappahannock to attack Pope. As a deception he sent Jackson on a long, flanking march to the left that brought Stonewall to the Federal rear. When Pope discovered an enemy force behind him, he swung back to meet it and came on Jackson near the site of the earlier battle of Manassas. Pope had McClellan's talent for fantasy in reverse—he

*For administrative reasons Lee preferred to operate with two large corps.

refused to recognize dangers that existed. Although he must have realized that a Confederate corps would not be where it was without nearby support, he convinced himself he could destroy Jackson before help arrived. On August 29 he attacked Jackson in what became known as the battle of Second Bull Run, or Second Manassas. Relying on his superiority in numbers, about 75,-000, he sent his men forward in piecemeal assaults that got nowhere. Unknown to him, Longstreet had joined Jackson, bringing the Confederate strength up to 60,000 and giving Lee an offensive capacity. On the following day Pope resumed his pecking attacks, and after several failed, Lee suddenly threw Longstreet's fresh troops forward in a savage counterattack that swept the surprised Federals from the field. The withdrawal soon became a rout, and Pope's troops reeled into the Washington defenses looking more like a mob than like an army. In an ironic ending to his earlier boast, Pope had left his lines of retreat to take care of themselves.

As the shattered troops approached the capital, Lincoln directed that McClellan take command of all the forces in the defenses, and he later relieved Pope of command. The president did not blame Pope entirely for the defeat, knowing that the McClellan coterie had not given him full support, but he realized that the men would not serve under the beaten general. Moreover, with Lee's army not far away, Lincoln needed a commander who would quickly whip the disorganized mass of troops back into shape, and he knew McClellan was that man. "If he can't fight himself," Lincoln observed of McClellan, "he excels in making others ready to fight." The president intended McClellan's position to be temporary. Before the army took the field, he hoped to find for it a commander who would fight.

Lincoln lacked the time to look for a general. Early in September Lee suddenly moved his army over the Potomac into Maryland. His motives in undertaking an offensive were several. Most immediately, he wanted to get the contending armies out of Virginia while the crops on which his own force depended for supplies were harvested, and he also thought that the presence of his army might induce Maryland to secede. Beyond these objectives, Lee hoped to fight and win a victory on enemy soil, the only kind of victory, he believed, that would convince the North to quit the war. The Confederate threat needed to be met, and Lincoln had to allow McClellan to meet it.

As McClellan moved across Maryland, he had a remarkable piece of luck. A captured Confederate order revealed that the Southern army was divided —Longstreet's corps and the cavalry were in Maryland, but Jackson's corps was engaged in reducing a Federal garrison at Harper's Ferry, at the head of the Valley. McClellan's cue was to advance rapidly and hit the Confederate fraction in Maryland before the troops then at Harper's Ferry could arrive. He advanced with what was for him unusual speed, but still with unnecessary caution, giving Lee time to pull his forces together behind Antietam Creek, near the town of Sharpsburg. All of Jackson's corps but one division had joined up by the time McClellan approached. Lee had perhaps 50,000 troops, McClellan almost 90,000.*

After spending a day scouting the Confederate position, McClellan attacked on September 17. He flung three assaults in order at the Confederate line, from left to center to right. The fighting in each was fierce and sustained, and the Confederates, with no reserve available, were hard pressed to hold— but they did. The last onslaught on the right, made late in the afternoon, seemed on the point of breaking through, but at that moment Jackson's missing division arrived from Harper's Ferry and plugged the sagging line. Even then, McClellan probably would have won the field if he had put in his reserve. But he could not bring himself to take the last risk, and called off the battle. The next day the two armies watched each other, and when McClellan gave no indication of moving, Lee retired across the Potomac to the safety of Virginia. Ten thousand Confederates had been killed and wounded in fighting, and 12,000 Federals, making Antietam the bloodiest single day of the war.

McClellan made no effort to pursue Lee, or even to follow the Confederates to Virginia. He told the government his army was exhausted by the recent campaigns, and he would require more men and more supplies before he could advance. Not until the first week in November did he cross the Potomac and move to Warrenton, west of Manassas. Lincoln had watched him crawl on with mounting impatience and sent an order to Warrenton relieving him of command. To a friend who remonstrated against removing McClellan, Lincoln said that the general had the "slows." At the same time Lincoln got rid of Buell. He was looking again for generals who would fight.

To replace McClellan, Lincoln named Ambrose E. Burnside, who had commanded a small army on the North Carolina coast and been a corps general under McClellan. Burnside was a good subordinate, but he lacked the intellectual capacity to direct a large army. He realized his deficiency and tried to decline the command.

The responsibility thrust upon him, Burnside decided to move the army eastward and cross the Rappahannock River at Fredericksburg, from there driving south on a railroad line to Richmond. The initial stage of his plan might have worked if he had got opposite Fredericksburg before Lee could shift to meet him. The Federal advance reached the crossing first, but Burnside halted to await the arrival of the pontoon bridges he had ordered. The delay enabled Lee to reach Fredericksburg. Burnside would have to fight to get across the river.

Burnside had more than 100,000 men to Lee's 70,000. But the Confederates were in an exceptionally strong position, holding a seven-mile line on hills

---

*Many Confederate soldiers refused to fight outside the South; they dropped off on the march to return when the army returned. Their action is an interesting indication of the individualism of the Southern soldier and of the loose discipline in Confederate armies.

behind and below Fredericksburg. Their front was most formidable in the town, and here for some reason Burnside chose to make his main attack on December 13. His men had to fight their way through a narrow space swept by artillery and musket fire before they could even approach the main line, and they never had a chance. Brigade after brigade made the attempt only to be shot to pieces; a Federal officer likened the disintegration of each unit to "snow coming down on warm ground." At the end of the day Burnside had lost 15,000 killed and wounded and withdrew his forces over the river. He was tormented by his failure and the criticisms of some of his subordinates, and in January, 1863, he asked to be relieved. Believing that a successor should come from the army, Lincoln named one of the corps commanders, Joseph Hooker.

The war in the East had been frustrating to the Federals. Every attempt they made to reach Richmond failed, and at the end of 1862 they were no closer to their goal. Not so apparently, the Confederates had also been frustrated. They had driven back the Federal invaders but had not been able to do what leaders like Lee knew they must do to win the war: destroy a Federal army. Their own offensives, into Kentucky and Maryland, had been turned back. And all the while the numerically smaller Southern manpower was being bled grievously.

AS THE EARLY MONTHS OF 1863 unfolded into spring, Federal armies were stirring and preparing to move on all fronts, on the Mississippi and the Tennessee lines in the West and in Virginia in the East. First to engage in battle was the Army of the Potomac, which resumed its advance on Richmond under its new commander, Hooker.

He had seemed an obvious choice to succeed Burnside. A senior corps general, he enjoyed a reputation for hard-hitting and aggressive leadership— "Fighting Joe" the newspapers had christened him—and in addition was known to be a good administrator. But he also was a loud-mouthed braggart and an inveterate intriguer. His criticisms of Burnside had played a part in bringing about that officer's removal. Lincoln was aware of the general's faults. "Hooker talks badly," the president observed regretfully. However, Lincoln hoped that "Fighting Joe" possessed sufficient military ability to outweigh his personal shortcomings. If Hooker lived up to his name, he would at least fight, and this was important to Lincoln.

Lincoln was right in thinking that Hooker had ability. The general proved to be a good organizer and trainer, and he rapidly brought his army, reinforced to over 100,000, up to a new peak of efficiency. He also possessed a talent for strategic planning, as he would demonstrate shortly. But all his virtues could not compensate for his one fatal flaw—Hooker lacked that quality of character or resolution required in a great commander. He could devise an excellent plan and up to a point could execute the plan. But then something happened inside

Hooker; he hesitated, drew back, or in plain words, lost his nerve. His constant boasting masked an inner uncertainty. "If the enemy does not run, God help them," he cried in one outburst. It was as though he hoped the Confederates would retreat without fighting.

Hooker revealed his strategic ability in making a plan to attack Lee. His army lay on the north side of the Rappahannock above and below Fredericksburg, while the Confederates remained in the strong position they had occupied during the battle in December. Hooker needed to get his army over the river without being led into the fire trap that had destroyed Burnside, and he hit on an operation that bore the marks of brilliance. First, he proposed to send his large cavalry force on a sweeping raid in the Confederate rear to divert Lee's attention. Then, while leaving two corps conspicuously opposite Fredericksburg and concealing two additional corps in reserve, he would move three corps 30 miles up the river to cross and come down on Lee's left. At the same time the corps opposite Fredericksburg would cross, and if the turning column could advance far enough to uncover a ford above the town, the reserve corps could also come over. Hooker would have Lee in a vise. The only weakness in the plan was that it sent the cavalry units so far away they could not return in time to scout for Hooker; he would have to fight the battle without his "eyes."*

Hooker began his operation late in April. At first, all seemed to go well. The turning column, under Hooker's personal command, crossed the river and advanced eastward through a desolate area of underbrush and scrub trees known locally as the Wilderness, and the force opposite Fredericksburg crossed and demonstrated against the town. Lee, preoccupied with the latter movement, seemed unaware of the danger approaching his left.

Pushing through the Wilderness, Hooker made his first contact with Confederate troops on May 1. The clash awakened Lee to the threat on his left, and he reacted vigorously, reinforcing that sector and striking hard at the Federal vanguard. The unexpected opposition seemed to demoralize Hooker. Halting his advance, he retired to a hamlet called Chancellorsville and announced he would wait for the Confederates to attack him. He had abandoned his plan—to break out of the Wilderness and uncover the ford that would enable him to cross troops at will—and he had yielded the initiative. He had, in fact, already lost the battle.

Lee quickly took Hooker's measure: this was an opponent with whom he could take great chances. Although Lee had about only 60,000 troops with him —part of his army was absent on a supply-gathering expedition—he resolved to attack the Federals at Chancellorsville. Leaving a small containing force at

---

*Most Civil War generals made a similar improper use of cavalry. They did not understand that the most useful function of cavalry was to reconnoiter enemy movements. Hooker's cavalry did not divert Lee, and the raid, like most forays, caused little material damage.

Fredericksburg, he moved to the left with 42,000 men and Jackson. There he learned from his cavalry commander that the Federal right flank was unanchored and vulnerable. Immediately he and Jackson came to an audacious decision—Jackson would take 28,000 men and make a wide march westward and come in with a surprise attack on the enemy right while Lee engaged Hooker's attention with the remaining 14,000 troops. Jackson was expected to roll up the flank of the Federals and cut them off from the river, and at the same time Lee would drive in from his front to complete their destruction. The audacity of the plan was that Lee was dividing his forces to attack a superior foe. Hooker had crossed the river with 45,000 men but later had shifted over other units to bring his force up to over 70,000.

Jackson began his march on May 2. His column moving west was observed by the Federals, but because Hooker had sent his cavalry away, they could not determine the destination of the Confederates. At headquarters it was speculated that the enemy might be retreating, and Hooker and his generals took no precautions against an attack. But near dusk soldiers on the right noticed large numbers of animals running toward them through the woods— and then Jackson's men burst forward in a charge.

The first impetus of the attack broke the Federal right. But gradually the defenders rallied and set up holding positions that slowed the onslaught. Jackson, frantic at the possibility that the Federals would not be cut off from the river, raged forward to press the attack. In the confusion in the darkening woods he was mistaken by Southern troops as a Federal and was shot and wounded so badly he had to be carried to the rear. As night fell, the battered Federals were still hanging on.

The next day Hooker shortened his lines, which enabled the Confederate forces to unite. Although his troops were in a cramped position and pounded by a galling artillery fire, he still might have pulled out a victory. With his superior numbers he could have gone over to the offensive and broken out of the encirclement. But all the fight had gone out of "Fighting Joe." He could think now only of escape, and on the night of May 5 he withdrew his army over the Rappahannock.*

Lee had won another victory. His conduct of the battle had been almost faultless. But he had failed again to accomplish his objective of destroying a Federal army. And his own losses were severe, over 10,000 casualties. His most grievous loss was Jackson. The brilliant subordinate, weakened by his wound, died from the complicating effects of pneumonia.†

---

*Lee, while holding Hooker at Chancellorsville, had detached sufficient troops to drive the Federals at Fredericksburg back over the river.

†After the battle Lee, realizing that with Jackson gone he would have to exercise more direct command over his units, reorganized his army into three corps. The First Corps continued under James Longstreet, and the two new corps commanders were Richard Ewell and A. P. Hill.

WHILE HOOKER WAS MOVING to frustration and failure in the Wilderness, on the Mississippi River line Grant was pressing an operation that resulted ultimately in bringing the great stream under Federal control. Having incurred the displeasure of Halleck after Shiloh, Grant had been held inactive during the later half of 1862. But in December he won Halleck's permission to undertake an offensive against Vicksburg, which with Port Hudson (in Louisiana) guarded the corridor between the Confederate states east and west of the river.

Grant first tried to come at Vicksburg by marching south from Memphis toward Jackson, from where he intended to wheel east. At the same time he sent a corps down the river under his most trusted subordinate, William T. Sherman, to demonstrate against the city and divert the attention of Confederate commander John C. Pemberton. Grant began his movement with about 45,000 troops. The Confederates had in Mississippi a total of 60,000 men, but their forces were separated—30,000 in the garrison at Vicksburg and another 30,000 divided among various points in the state. All of them operated under a loose supervision by Joseph E. Johnston, who was coordinating the operations in Mississippi and Tennessee.

Grant's initial effort ended in failure. The Confederates ripped at his supply line so effectively that he had to halt his advance, and Sherman was repulsed when he assaulted the strong Confederate works north of Vicksburg. But Grant would not give up. He returned to Memphis and brought his army, supported by a naval flotilla, down the Mississippi and debarked above Vicksburg on the Louisiana side late in January, 1863. Having secured reinforcements, he now commanded 75,000 troops.*

Grant placed his army in Louisiana in order to get it on relatively high and healthful ground. But he was on the wrong side of the river, and to operate against Vicksburg he would have to cross to the east bank. His problem was difficult. Vicksburg sat on high bluffs and was defended by batteries on the river and fortifications extending north and south. The terrain above the city was low and marshy and crisscrossed by rivers and bayous, and the ground immediately below was only slightly more passable. The river batteries seemed to forbid passage by the Federal naval squadron, and consequently Grant decided to strike at the city from above.

His efforts consumed the winter months, and all of them ended in failure. The army, assisted by the navy, attempted to penetrate the network of waterways and reach high ground to the north and east of Vicksburg, but each expedition either bogged down in the miry terrain or was turned back by Confederate defenders. As the frustrations mounted, discussions at Grant's

---

*Grant's decision to move downriver may have been influenced by a command problem that developed in his forces before Vicksburg. Lincoln had authorized the political general John A. McClernand to raise a force to operate on the river, and McClernand, ranking Sherman, claimed command of all the troops around the city. Only by coming to the scene personally could Grant control McClernand.

headquarters turned to the possibility of operating below the city. Someone suggested digging a canal where the river made a great bend; the navy could then pass the batteries and meet the army and transport it to the east side. Thousands of men worked on the project, but when it was completed not enough water flowed in from the river to float the vessels. Grant said later he had little confidence that any of his various moves would succeed. At some time during the winter he settled on a plan to take Vicksburg and waited only for the arrival of spring. But in the meantime he had to keep his army busy, if for no other reason than to conceal his real intentions from the Confederates.

The final plan was an outgrowth of discussions between Grant, various of his officers, and the commander of the naval squadron, Commodore David Porter. Porter thought he could run his vessels past the river batteries at night. In the meantime, the army would march down the west bank to a point about 50 miles below the city and meet the navy and be ferried over to the east side. Striking east and north, Grant would be at last on high ground where he could maneuver. In order to turn Pemberton's eyes away from the river while the movement was in progress, Grant sent a cavalry force under Colonel Benjamin Grierson ripping southward from near Memphis. Grierson rode the length of the state and into the Federal lines at Baton Rouge, 600 miles in 16 days, disrupting Confederate communications and engaging all of Pemberton's attention. It was one of the few really effective cavalry raids of the war.

Porter ran past the river batteries with slight damage on April 16. Meanwhile, the army had moved to the rendezvous point and was crossed to the east side two weeks later. Once over, Grant moved with a speed that thoroughly confused Pemberton. First, he struck east toward Jackson, where Joe Johnston was collecting troops, drove the Confederates from the city, and occupied it. Then he turned east against Vicksburg. Pemberton, at last locating Grant, attempted to bar the way but was defeated in two battles and had to retire into his defenses. Eager to keep the momentum of his offensive going, Grant assaulted the works on May 23 and was repulsed. Realizing the strength of the fortifications, he settled down to take them by siege.

In the campaign just concluded, Grant, who was outnumbered at the start, had marched 200 miles in 18 days, had won four battles while inflicting 8,000 casualties on the enemy, and in the end had shut up an army in a fortress. His audacity gives the lie to the contention that he was only a slugger who relied on superior numbers.* The campaign is also instructive on the Confederate side, illustrating the confusion that results from divided command. Johnston besought Pemberton to join him so as to maintain a mobile army, but the latter thought President Davis wanted him to hold Vicksburg at all costs, and allowed himself to be entrapped.

*Grant crossed the river with about 45,000 men, although he was later reinforced. His 60,000 opponents were, of course, divided.

The siege lasted over six weeks. The Federals drove their lines ever closer to the city, subjecting the defenders and the civilian inhabitants to artillery bombardment day and night.* Many civilians abandoned their homes and went to live in caves, emerging only in lulls in the firing. "As the first shell again flew they dived," a girl diarist recorded, "and not a human being was visible." The scene was prophetic of the air bombings of the twentieth century.

Eventually Pemberton realized his cause was hopeless. The troops were running short of food, the civilians were running short of everything, and no relief was going to come in from the outside. He entered into negotiations with Grant and surrendered the city on July 4. Unwilling to burden his government with a large influx of prisoners, Grant allowed the Confederates to be paroled.†

At the same time Grant laid Vicksburg under siege, General Nathaniel Banks, commanding the Department of the Gulf, came up from New Orleans with 15,000 men and invested Port Hudson. When the defenders of Port Hudson heard that Vicksburg had fallen, they also surrendered. The Federals now controlled the entire length of the Mississippi and had accomplished one of their main strategic objectives—they had divided the Confederacy and effectively isolated the three states west of the river. A great turning point in the war had been reached.

GRANT'S INVESTMENT OF VICKSBURG caused grave concern in Richmond. Knowing that if the fortress fell, the whole Mississippi line would be lost, Davis and his advisers considered ways to force Grant to draw off. One favored proposal was advanced by James Longstreet, corps commander under Lee, who recommended standing on the defensive in Virginia and sending a part of Lee's forces to Bragg in Tennessee; Bragg could then undertake an offensive to relieve the pressure on Vicksburg. Lee, however, objected to the plan. Confident of himself and his army after Chancellorsville, he wanted to embark on an offensive of his own. He proposed to invade Pennsylvania. Although he argued that his movement would ease the threat on the Mississippi, he actually desired it for its own sake. He had always believed that only by winning a decisive victory on Northern soil could the Confederacy bring the war to a victorious conclusion.

Davis agreed to the plan, but balked at giving Lee as many troops as the general desired, refusing to strip defensive areas farther south. Lee began his movement early in June with 75,000 men. Shifting forces westward in spaced units, he entered the Valley and headed north toward the Potomac. Although

---

*A besieging force still employed the methods established by Vauban for reducing a fortified place.

†Pemberton, a Pennsylvanian who chose to fight with the Confederacy, reasoned that Grant would like to capture Vicksburg on the national holiday and would parole the garrison in exchange. He thus gave the Federals something extra to celebrate.

he attempted to screen the march with cavalry, he let most of his horsemen get away from him. He had directed the commander of his cavalry corps, J. E. B. Stuart, to move north on the right flank of the army but had given Stuart a discretionary order as to the route to be followed. Stuart was an excellent cavalryman, superb at gathering intelligence. He also had a juvenile penchant for engaging in spectacular exploits, and he took advantage of the discretion given him to ride around Hooker's army, which cut him off from Lee until July 2. The Confederate commander would have to operate in Pennsylvania without his eyes.

No movement as large or as extended as Lee's could be concealed very long, and Hooker soon discovered that the Confederates had left his front and were heading north. Reporting to Lincoln that the enemy was moving toward Maryland or Pennsylvania, Hooker made a strange proposal: he requested permission to attack the Confederate rear, which was still near Fredericksburg. When this was refused, he put forward an even more unreal suggestion. While the Confederates were marching northward, could he not go down and attack Richmond? Lincoln read the general a lesson in military science. "I think Lee's army, and not Richmond, is your true objective," the president wrote. Hooker should follow Lee on "the inside track," Lincoln instructed, and seek the opportunity to fight a battle.

Hooker finally started northward with 90,000 men. But, as he revealed in correspondence with Lincoln, he had no heart to fight again the man who had defeated him at Chancellorsville; he had let Lee gain a psychological ascendancy over him. He complained constantly that he was not being properly supported, and when troops he requested were refused, he asked to be relieved. Lincoln appointed in his place one of the corps commanders, George G. Meade, a competent and courageous officer but not one gifted with great talents.

Meade took over on June 28. His army, moving in a broad formation, was approaching the rear of the Confederates, as yet undetected. As Lee moved into Pennsylvania, he spread out his three corps, under Longstreet, Ewell, and Hill, to seek supplies. Without Stuart he did not realize that the Federals, moving on the "inside track," were so close to him. Learning at last of their presence, he began to draw his columns together. At the same time, Meade was pulling his corps together and moving northward to find a good defensive position; the Federal general reasoned that Lee, in enemy country at the end of a long supply line, would have to fight or retire, and believing his rival would attack, Meade sought the most favorable ground on which to receive the blow. Feeling for each other, the two armies converged, by a kind of natural process, on the town of Gettysburg, which was the hub of twelve roads in the area.

Confederate and Federal outposts clashed near Gettysburg on the last day of June, and on July 1 advance units of the two armies began to move into the area. The Confederates held numerical superiority, and they pushed the Federals out of the town and onto two heights to the south, Culp's Hill and Cemetery Hill. As additional Federal troops poured in—they kept coming even after darkness fell—they were posted on an eminence below the hills called Cemetery Ridge. The Federal line, which resembled an inverted fishhook, extended about four miles. The Confederate army lay in Gettysburg and opposite the Federal front on Seminary Ridge. The Confederate line from the town to the right flank was over five miles long. Ewell's corps was on the left, Hill's in the center, and Longstreet's, all of its units not yet up, on the right.

That night Lee discussed with his corps generals plans for the morrow. Longstreet spoke against an attack, arguing that the Federal position was too strong; he advised maneuvering the enemy out of his line and forcing him to fight elsewhere. But Lee decided to attack. He was too committed to disengage, he explained, and besides, he was confident his men could break the Federal line. At first, he considered making his main effort on the left with Ewell's corps but then decided to send in Longstreet's corps on the right. Longstreet was to attack the next day as soon as he could get his troops up and deployed. At the same time Ewell would demonstrate against Culp's Hill, and if the main assault succeeded, A. P. Hill was to come in to complete the victory.

Longstreet did not get his force deployed until mid-afternoon on July 2.* His attack crumpled up an advanced Federal corps and drove the defenders back on Cemetery Ridge. But as darkness fell, the Federals held their main line. Still, Lee was cheered at the result. Longstreet had won a partial success, and Ewell had secured a lodgement on the lower slope of Culp's Hill. The Confederate commander believed one more attack would finish the Federals, and announced that on the next day he would smash through the enemy center. To this task he assigned 15,000 troops, most of them from Longstreet's corps but some from Hill's, under the immediate command of General George Pickett.

On the afternoon of July 3 the Confederates opened a bombardment of Cemetery Ridge that lasted for almost two hours. The tremendous barrage was a certain indication to the Federals that an attack was coming and, ceasing their own fire, they pulled their guns behind the crest of the ridge to conserve ammunition. At about three o'clock the cannonade stopped, and the assault force lined up and moved out. The Confederates had to cross a mile of open space to reach the Federal position, and as they swung forward in the conventional brigade formation, they constituted a splendid sight. Here was "the grand pageantry and color of war in the old style," historian Bruce Catton has written. Another author, Fairfax Downey, has called the advance "the last great charge in the old tradition." It was also a charge that had no chance of success against modern firepower. First the artillery shells tore at the ordered

*After the war, critics of Longstreet charged that he stalled in making the attack. Actually, he moved with all possible speed.

ranks, and then musket fire struck them. The lines wavered and broke off to one side or the other or halted. Only 5,000 men reached the crest of the ridge, and they were either captured or forced to flee back to their own lines.

The two armies watched each other on July 4, while Vicksburg was surrendering, and when Meade gave no indication that he would attack, Lee withdrew and retired across the Potomac to Virginia. Meade followed but seemed content merely to harry the Confederates ahead of him. Lincoln, who was anguished at the dilatory pursuit, later told the general that he had acted like "an old woman trying to shoo her geese across the creek." Meade fought competently at Gettysburg, but he lacked the instinct to destroy an enemy.

In the invasion of Pennsylvania, Lee lost more than an opportunity to smash up a Federal army—he suffered approximately 25,000 casualties. Federal losses were almost as large, 20,000, but the North had replacements and the South did not. Never again would the Army of Northern Virginia be able to risk an offensive. Now Lee would have to fight defensively, a way he knew would result eventually in defeat. On the slopes of Cemetery Ridge the war had taken another decisive turn.*

VICKSBURG AND GETTYSBURG were sore setbacks to the South. But the Confederates still had a chance to halt the deadly shift against them. They retained Chattanooga on the Tennessee line, and as long as they held that city, they had a base from which to mount an offensive in the West. And if this did not prove possible, they could at least deny to the Federals entrance into the lower South. They were not, however, allowed to rest in their position undisturbed. In that fateful summer of 1863, General W. S. Rosecrans resumed his advance on Chattanooga.

During the first part of the summer, when Vicksburg was under siege, Rosecrans occupied himself with writing letters to Washington complaining that he was not being properly supported. Urged by Halleck to undertake an action to prevent Bragg from reinforcing Johnston in Mississippi, he replied with the curious argument that if he drove back the enemy, he would put them closer to Johnston. The correspondence revealed that Rosecrans was cracking under the strain of command. Finally, the government issued him orders to advance. He moved forward late in June and brought his army to Tullahoma by July 3. Here, with Chattanooga about 80 miles away, he paused to regroup.

Rosecrans remained at Tullahoma almost two months. Although he required time to prepare the next step of his advance, he took more than necessary. He expended much of his energy in writing carping letters to Lincoln and Halleck, revealing the continued rise in his inner tensions. Again

*Meade followed Lee back to Virginia, and for the rest of the year the opposing armies maneuvered against each other without coming to battle.

the government had to order him to move, and he advanced late in August. Maneuvering with his customary skill, he arrived at Chattanooga without fighting by September 9. Bragg evacuated the city and retired over the state line into Georgia. At the same time a smaller Federal force under Ambrose Burnside, who had been given a minor independent command, occupied Knoxville, farther north. The Federals were at last liberating the Union-sympathizing section of Tennessee.

Excited at having grasped Chattanooga, Rosecrans plunged after the Confederates, moving his army in three separate columns over the mountain roads. He forgot he was not pursuing a defeated and disorganized enemy— Bragg had yielded Chattanooga in order to secure room to fight. He had hoped to hit the Federals while their units were separated, but he postponed attacking to wait for the arrival of reinforcements from Lee's army. With the Virginia front stalemated, Lee let Longstreet and most of his corps go to aid Bragg. Three advance brigades from Longstreet arrived on September 18, and Bragg, unwilling to lose any more time, decided to attack the next day. In the meantime, Rosecrans, alerted to the danger on his front, had pulled his forces together behind Chickamauga Creek.

The Confederate assault on September 19 made little headway: although some units crossed the creek, they were unable to penetrate the Federal line. However, that night Longstreet and the remainder of his corps reached the scene, giving the Confederates a numerical superiority, about 70,000 to 60,000. The next day Bragg resumed the attack, sending his corps forward in "oblique order" from right to left. The Federal left held, but on the right one of those accidents that can occur in battle opened an inviting gap to the Confederates. Rosecrans, acting on the basis of incorrect information that he was too excited to check, ordered a division transferred to support another point on the line. Longstreet poured his troops through the hole and collapsed the whole Federal flank. The sudden turn of events also collapsed Rosecrans; he and two of his corps generals joined the flight to Chattanooga. Meanwhile, the Federal left under George H. Thomas continued to fight, but it could not withstand very long the forces now gathering against it. That night Thomas, under orders from Rosecrans, withdrew, and by the next day the whole Federal army was back within the Chattanooga defenses.

For the Confederates, however, Chickamauga had been a dearly bought victory. Their casualties were an appalling 25 percent of the total engaged. The losses undoubtedly accounted for Bragg's failure to attack the Federals in the city; he did not want to waste his depleted army assailing a foe that, although beaten, was behind entrenchments. Instead, he advanced and occupied heights south of the river and, mounting artillery there, was able to interdict the supply routes coming into Chattanooga. The Federal army was under a form of siege, and soon its supplies ran dangerously short. Rosecrans was so unstrung by the recent debacle that he could give no intelligent direction. His condition was aptly described by Lincoln, who said that the general was acting like "a duck hit on the head."

Although the beleaguered army seemed to be in desperate straits, it actually was in little danger. The Federal government had ample resources in the West to raise the siege. Grant's army was standing virtually idle on the Mississippi line, and with the Virginia front inactive, troops could be spared from the East for Tennessee. Lincoln appointed Grant commander of all forces in the West and authorized him to remove Rosecrans, who was replaced by Thomas. Then Grant went to Chattanooga to examine a situation that was improving. The government had moved over 20,000 troops from the East by rail to near Chattanooga, carrying them 1,200 miles in less than two weeks in one of the great transportation feats of the war. With the aid of these reinforcements the supply lines had been partially reopened, and provisions were again coming into the city. Realizing that the army was no longer in danger, Grant characteristically began to think of a way to turn the situation into a victory, of going over to the offensive. To build up Thomas's striking power, he brought part of his own army by rail to Chattanooga, giving the Federals a strength of 60,000.

While affairs on the Federal side were proceeding smoothly under Grant's direction, dissension racked the Confederate command. Most of the corps generals were openly critical of Bragg's conduct of the recent battle, and he responded by blaming them for the failure to achieve a greater success. The recriminations became so bitter that President Davis felt it necessary to journey to Bragg's camp to try to mediate the dispute. He failed. The generals stated to Davis in Bragg's presence that they distrusted the competence of their commander. In a curious demonstration of perversity, Davis retained Bragg in command, offering as a lame excuse that he could find no adequate successor. The only result of the conference was to weaken the size of the Confederate army. Longstreet had been one of the principal critics of Bragg and was obviously unhappy in his present service. At Davis's suggestion, and with Bragg's hearty approval, Longstreet was allowed to go off on what proved to be a fruitless expedition against Knoxville. His departure left Bragg with fewer than 50,000 men to meet Grant's blow.

Grant was ready to strike by late November. After clearing Confederate troops off Lookout Mountain, he moved on the main enemy position on Missionary Ridge on November 25. His plan was to use Thomas's army to hold the attention of the Confederates in front while the force from his own army under Sherman turned the enemy right. But the battle of Chattanooga did not go according to plan. Sherman ran into tough opposition and had to call for help. Thereupon Grant directed Thomas to seize the rifle pits at the foot of the ridge and await further orders. Thomas's men were aware that Grant regarded them as inferior soldiers, and they were determined to show their mettle. Sweeping past the line of rifle pits, they continued up the ridge in a mad charge. Although they were encouraged by their officers, they seemed to be animated by a mass will, the privates taking over temporarily from the generals. As the attackers came over the crest, the Confederates broke in disorder. Bragg retired all the way to Dalton, Georgia, where he asked to be relieved. Davis granted the request and appointed as his successor the officer demanded by military and public opinion, Joe Johnston.

Chattanooga was a third turning point. The Federals now held that vital base and from it could launch an offensive to divide the South again. After 1863 the South could not hope to win the war militarily. It could only pray that the North would tire of fighting and quit.

BY 1864 ALL THE PORTENTS favored the North. Northern manpower and industrial might were apparently inexhaustible, while Southern resources were running down. Northern armies had overrun and occupied large areas of Southern territory. On water the Northern navy was drawing its blockade tighter and tighter. Later in the year and early in 1865 the navy would seal off the principal remaining ports of entry by seizing the harbors of Mobile, Alabama, and Wilmington, North Carolina. Only Charleston continued open to blockade runners, and it was kept under siege by army and naval forces.

One of the great advantages possessed by the North was that now all its land forces were to be directed by one man. Grant had been appointed general in chief early in the year and had gone to Washington to discuss his position and plans with Lincoln. He proposed to move all Federal forces, large and small, against the Confederacy simultaneously, or as he expressed it, to work the armies toward "a common center." The Confederates could not meet every attack, and at one or several points would have to give way. This was the strategy Lincoln had long favored, and at last he had found a general who would execute it.

Grant planned three major offensives, each one to jump off in early May. In the East the Army of the Potomac, then resting north of the Rappahannock River, would cross and head south. Its objective was not to take Richmond but to engage and destroy Lee's army. Grant's instructions to Meade had a simple but steely ring: "Wherever Lee goes, there you will go also." Grant announced he would accompany the army. Although he gave several reasons for not remaining in Washington, he undoubtedly wanted to direct the Eastern army personally. He had discovered to his dismay that many officers believed Lee was invincible, and he was determined to overcome the psychological advantage that the Confederate commander had acquired.

Two offensives were planned in the large Western theater. One army of 100,000, under Sherman, was to move from Chattanooga into northern Georgia, engage and defeat the Confederate army under Johnston, and seize the industrial center of Atlanta. Another force of approximately 30,000 under

Banks was to advance from New Orleans to Mobile and turn northward toward Montgomery so as to be in position to cooperate with Sherman.

Banks's part in the grand offensive had to be canceled. In March, six weeks before the armies were to start moving, Banks launched an offensive of his own up the Red River. His expedition had been planned before Grant took over the chief command and had the blessing of Lincoln and Halleck. The object was to capture Shreveport, in northwestern Louisiana, and if possible to enter Texas; Lincoln and Halleck thought it was important to "show the flag" in Texas to deter the French in Mexico from moving northward. A secondary aim was to seize needed supplies of cotton in the Red River Valley. A number of cotton speculators accompanied the expedition, and several ranking officers were suspected of themselves engaging in cotton buying.

The expedition lacked a clear focus; it had too many objectives. Moreover, it was poorly led; Banks was an aggressive general but an indifferent handler of troops. Grant had small hope that the movement would succeed but was forced to consent to it. His doubts were more than confirmed. Marching northward, Banks encountered only light opposition and took almost no security precautions. But near Mansfield, below Shreveport, a smaller Confederate force under Richard Taylor was waiting in the woods, and on April 8 it struck the Federals in a surprise attack, sweeping them from the field. Shaken beyond reason by the setback, Banks retired all the way back to New Orleans. His army was so exhausted by marching up and down the state that it was useless for months. Grant had lost almost a third of his punch.

The two remaining offensives began during the first week in May. In Virginia the army under Grant and Meade, numbering approximately 120,000 men, crossed the Rappahannock and plunged into the Wilderness, where Hooker had met disaster. At the same time smaller Federal armies demonstrated on the James River east of Richmond and in the Valley. Lee had about 63,000 troops to meet Grant's thrust; for reserves he could draw only on forces in the Valley and the Richmond defenses.*

When Grant crossed the Rappahannock, he inaugurated a campaign of a kind not previously known in the war. Other battles had lasted only a day or two, or at the most, in the fighting before Richmond in 1862, seven days. But in this campaign there would be movement and battle extending over a period of forty-four days, from early May to mid-June. The battle of Virginia, as the series of clashes should be called, anticipated the drawn-out engagements of World War I and World War II.

Grant had not intended to fight an extended campaign. He hoped to bring Lee to a showdown battle and end the war in one blow. Specifically, he planned to hold his rival's front and envelop his right, turning the Confederates away

---

*The total number of Federals in the state was about 176,000, the Confederates numbered about 98,000.

from Richmond and forcing them to fight for their communications. But it did not work out that way. Lee confronted the Federals in the Wilderness and in two days of savage actions held his lines. Grant then sidled off to his left, leaving the field to Lee. The Confederate commander probably thought his enemy was retiring to regroup, as previous Federal generals had done after a repulse. Instead, Grant turned south and headed toward Spotsylvania. Lee moved to meet him, and in that critical moment Grant won the campaign. He had refused to let Lee impose his will on him. Now, having the stronger force, he would impose his will on Lee. Henceforth, the initiative would rest with Grant.

At Spotsylvania the armies fought for four bloody days. The Federals almost broke through at one point, but the Confederates managed to plug the breach. Again Grant broke off action and shifted to his left, and again Lee moved to meet him. Maneuvering in this manner, the opposing forces came to Cold Harbor, just northeast of Richmond, by the first week in June. Here Grant made another massive effort to smash through the Confederate lines. In a fierce frontal attack he lost 7,000 men, and recognizing failure, he called off the battle.

The month of fighting that ended at Cold Harbor signaled a new phase in the war. In the almost daily encounters both armies had suffered sickening losses, the casualty rates reaching over a third of the total number of men engaged. The war in the East was settling into a conflict of attrition. Recognizing the imminence of death, soldiers in each army sought even the slightest shelter, both attackers and defenders throwing up earthworks before a battle. Gone were the days of the grand flanking movements; the armies now seemed to disappear into the ground.

Near the beginning of the campaign Grant informed the government he would not turn back. "I propose to fight it out on this line if it takes all summer," he wrote. But after Cold Harbor he had to alter his strategy. If he remained on his present line, Lee would retire into the Richmond defenses and force the Federals to resort to a long and costly siege. Grant resolved to make a different effort to bring his adversary to battle in the open.

On June 12 Grant disappeared from Lee's front, covering his withdrawal with cavalry and infantry demonstrations. He moved southward, crossing the James River, and headed for Petersburg, about 23 miles below Richmond and the hub of the railroads that served the capital and Lee's army. If he could grasp Petersburg, he would make Lee come out and fight for his communications.

The plan almost succeeded. For five days Lee was uncertain as to Grant's whereabouts and remained near Richmond. In the meantime, the vanguard of Grant's army arrived before Petersburg, which was defended by only 14,000 men under Beauregard. However, the Creole general put up a superb defense, giving the impression he was much stronger than he was, and the Federal commanders leading the advance fed their men in such piecemeal fashion that the attacks failed. Lee finally awoke to the threat developing to the south and moved his army to Petersburg. The first of his troops arrived on June 18, just as Beauregard's tired men were bracing for another assault. Petersburg, and Richmond, had been saved.

Grant now realized that he could not force a showdown battle. Lee's army was behind field fortifications and would not come out. The only recourse was to take Petersburg by siege, and Grant doggedly began operations. The Confederate line of works stretched from 50 miles above Richmond to below Petersburg, and a Federal line was constructed opposite it. Grant constantly sought to move his trenches closer to the enemy works and particularly to extend his left around the Confederate right so as to reach the vital railroads. Both sides engaged in incessant artillery firing and sniping, and the men in each army, standing in heat and cold and mud and filth, remembered the long siege as a form of torture. Especially for the outnumbered Confederates the daily harassment was an ordeal. One officer recalled: "It was endurance without relief; sleeplessness without excitement; inactivity without rest."

Lee recognized that his cause was hopeless if he could not break the siege. In a desperate effort to force Grant to detach part of his strength, he resorted to the old strategy of seeming to threaten Washington through the Valley route. He sent a part of his own army under Jubal Early westward, with orders to drive toward the Union capital. Lee hoped the raid would so alarm Federal authorities that they would order troops from Grant's army to return to defend the city, and he could then attack the weakened besiegers.

The gamble that had worked in 1862 would not work now. Early reached the outskirts of Washington, but he did not have sufficient strength to assault the works around the city. His appearance did not cause the high command to panic. Some troops from Grant's army were brought up to assist the local defense forces, but there was no large detachment. After skirmishing with the defenders, Early retired to the Valley.

Although Lincoln had not been alarmed at the presence of a hostile force in the Valley, he thought the Confederate ability to make mischief in this area should be removed. He suggested to Grant that all the forces around Washington be placed under one commander and that this general be ordered to smash Early's army beyond repair. Grant responded by naming to the command his aggressive cavalry leader, Philip Sheridan. Moving into the Valley with a force superior to Early's, Sheridan defeated the Confederate at Winchester, Fisher's Hill, and Cedar Creek. Early was left with only a skeleton of his original force and was no longer a threat. Lee's plan had failed, and Grant's hold on Petersburg remained.

At the same time Grant crossed the Rappahannock, Sherman moved into northwest Georgia. Confronting his army of 100,000 were 62,000 Confederates under Joe Johnston. The two opposing generals were much alike in temperament and thinking. Neither one during the war won a set battle; Sherman, indeed, did not, as an independent commander, fight a set battle. Both were masters of maneuver, and they now proceeded to demonstrate their skill. Sherman advanced and sought to envelop Johnston in flank. Johnston avoided entrapment by slipping back while watching for an opportunity to hit exposed fractions of his enemy. Moving and skirmishing in this fashion for 74 days, the two armies went back 100 miles almost to Atlanta. Johnston was later praised for keeping his army intact while delaying the enemy. But as a price for this accomplishment he had to abandon important territory. And if he had not let Sherman damage him, neither had he damaged Sherman.*

President Davis was disgusted at Johnston's failure to fight Sherman. Nor could Davis get from the general a statement as to when he would engage his adversary. Johnston was abnormally secretive about revealing his plans to civilians, fearing they would become known to the enemy. All he would say was that he would strike at the right moment. This was not enough for Davis. Abruptly the president removed Johnston and replaced him with John B. Hood, a corps commander. Hood previously served in the Virginia army, and in allowing him to be transferred west, Davis may have marked him as a possible successor to Johnston.

Hood had been an able and aggressive unit leader, but he did not possess the intellectual capacity to plan and direct the movements of a large army. He knew he had been put in to fight, and fight he would. Sherman was approaching Atlanta in separate columns, and Hood hit first one segment and then another. Although the attacks were fiercely delivered, they failed to halt the Federals, and Hood thereupon retired into the city's defenses. His purpose was to force Sherman to resort to a siege, but the Federal commander had no mind to be held up. Atlanta relied for supplies on a single railroad running in from the south, and Sherman wheeled part of his army around to seize this line. Hood had to evacuate quickly, pulling out to the northwest on September 3. A proud message went from Sherman to Washington: "So Atlanta is ours, and fairly won."

Sherman's boast was not entirely justified. He had seized Atlanta and its important economic resources, but he had not brought the enemy army to bay. That force was still intact and it now proceeded to give Sherman a great deal of trouble. Hood moved northward and struck damaging raids on the railroad bringing supplies to the Federals. When Sherman sent troops to run Hood

*The closest the opposing armies came to fighting an actual battle was at Kennesaw Mountain. However, the respective commanders broke off action before a decision was reached.

down, the Confederate retired. Sherman did not believe he could ever force Hood to battle and was little interested in trying to do so. His mind was fixed on a new operation.

Sherman was the most intellectual or philosophical general in the war, the closest student of developing ways of war. He had concluded that fighting, seeking the decisive battle, was not the only way to win a war. An alternative method was to break the will to resist of the enemy population behind the enemy armies by bringing the war home to civilians. Sherman was proposing to employ what later would be called "total war."

He put his plan before Grant. He proposed to ignore Hood and march with the bulk of his army on a broad front across Georgia, destroying all economic resources in his way that might be used by the enemy. Although he expected to deprive the Confederacy of needed supplies, he intended the main effect of his sweep to be psychological—the spectacle of a Federal army moving unimpeded through the heart of the South should convince even the most hardened rebels that their cause was lost. Sherman admitted that what he was going to do might not be war; rather, he said, it was "statesmanship." He would emerge at a point on the coast, probably Savannah, and the navy could meet him there and transport his army to Virginia to join Grant for a final thrust at Lee.

Realizing that Lincoln and Grant would worry about Hood's army being loose in his rear, Sherman attempted to reassure them. Hood would either have to follow him or invade Tennessee, he said. In the former event, he could turn back on his rival. To deal with the latter possibility he would return 30,000 troops under Thomas to Tennessee, and these, with other forces Thomas could collect, should be sufficient to hold the state. Grant, sensing the risk in the plan, agreed to it with some reluctance, and Lincoln also assented.

Sherman's prediction of Hood's probable moves was accurate. At the same time the Federal commander was completing his plan, Hood was developing a scheme to invade Tennessee. Lustrous possibilities occurred to Hood. He would force Sherman to follow him, and in the mountains he could turn on his pursuer and destroy him. That accomplished, he could march through Tennessee and Kentucky to the Ohio River. Or he might choose to move eastward to join Lee in a final victorious attack on Grant. This was grand planning for a general with slender resources. Casualties suffered in the recent campaign and detachments of troops to other areas had reduced Hood's army to only 40,000 or so.

As desperate as the plan was, Hood might have brought it off in part, might at least have forced Sherman to return. The only organized Federal resistance in Tennessee consisted of the 30,000 troops sent back by Sherman; this force, under General John M. Schofield, was guarding the approaches on the Alabama border. At Nashville, Thomas was just beginning to bring in other troops. If Hood moved fast enough, he might smash Schofield and prevent the Federal concentration.

Hood, however, was slow in beginning his movement. Having conceived an audacious plan, he seemed to draw back from executing it. Still, he entered Tennessee before Thomas completed his preparations. Advancing against delaying operations by Schofield, he caught up to the Federals at Franklin on November 30. Although they were strongly entrenched, he decided to attack them. In six furious charges he suffered over 6,000 casualties; eleven of his generals were killed or wounded. At the end of the bloody day the Federals retired intact to Nashville. Hood followed them and encamped south of the city. What he hoped he could accomplish now was known only to him. He said he expected Thomas to attack him and he would respond with a successful counterattack. This was the unrealistic dreaming of a general who could not admit failure.

In Nashville, Thomas was putting his forces together. The Northern commander was slow and careful in preparing for battle, but when he finally struck, he always struck hard. When he was ready he would have an army of 60,000. A formidable part of his force was a cavalry column of 12,000 troopers under James H. Wilson. Wilson had armed his men with repeating rifles and trained them to ride to the point of contact in a battle and then to fight on foot. No other cavalry leader had conceived such intelligent use of horsemen.

On December 15 Thomas came out of Nashville and attacked the Confederates. The infantry smashed the enemy front while the cavalry rode to envelop the left. Driven from the field, Hood attempted to set up another line on the following day. He was crushed again, and his army broke in a disorganized flight. Even then the Confederates were not safe. Wilson's cavalry harried the Confederates for 26 days, and 200 miles, all the way back to Tupelo, Mississippi, the most sustained pursuit of the war. The rebel remnants that reached Tupelo were not an army and could not be collected into one again. Thomas had won the most decisive victory of the war and eliminated any possible enemy threat in Sherman's rear.

In mid-November, while Hood was moving to his fatal rendezvous in Tennessee, Sherman and his army of over 60,000 left Atlanta on the first leg of the great "march to the sea." Before swinging out, Sherman ordered that a part of the city, including all public buildings, be burned to prevent the Confederates from returning to use it as a base. "Behind us lay Atlanta smouldering and in ruins," Sherman wrote in describing his departure.

Ahead lay the farmlands and towns of Georgia almost undefended and bursting with foods and other resources. Sherman's wagon trains carried only emergency supplies; he intended to subsist on the country. The army marched on a 60-mile front, preceded by foragers whose function was to locate properties to be destroyed. Sherman's orders limited the items to be burned or captured to those useful to the enemy. But his men knew he would understand if they went beyond the orders. A great deal of unauthorized and individual looting went on as the army ripped across the state, and it went unpunished. By late December Sherman was at Savannah, and here he proposed to Grant a change in plans. Instead of going to Grant by sea, he wished to march by land, destroying more supplies and tearing up railroad lines as he went. Grant gave his assent, and in January, 1865, Sherman plunged into South Carolina and then into North Carolina. There the Confederate government collected an army of 30,000 under Johnston to oppose him, but this small force could do little more than delay his onward march.

Sherman usually referred to his operation as a "raid," and his terminology was accurate. It was a gigantic demonstration of psycho-economic warfare, anticipating the strategic bombing of twentieth-century war, and it hurt the Confederacy badly. But this mode of warfare in itself would not force the Southern government or people to admit defeat. The end would not come until the principal resisting force, Lee's army, was destroyed, and this was a target beyond Sherman's reach, or his inclination. Only Grant, still pounding away at Petersburg during the spring of 1865, could deliver the death blow.

Grant had never ceased his efforts to work around the Confederate right, and in the first week of April he finally succeeded. He stood astride the railroad lines serving Petersburg and Richmond, and Lee could not remain in his lines. Evacuating both cities, the Confederate commander moved to the west. His only hope now was to reach a rail line going to North Carolina; if he could unite with Joe Johnston, perhaps the two of them could fight yet another battle. Pursuing Federals striking at his rear were hard at his heels as he crawled onward. He had left with about 50,000 men, but losses and desertions reduced his force to little over half that number. Eventually Federal troops got ahead of him and closed off the escape route. One of his officers begged that he permit the army to scatter through the countryside and continue resistance by guerrilla methods. Lee replied that this kind of warfare would bring only devastation and misery to the people the army had been defending. His answer was peculiarly American. Sustained irregular warfare was not a part of the national genius. On April 9 Lee surrendered his army to Grant at Appomattox.

The word that Lee had yielded traveled southward, and as if a signal had been given, other Confederate generals quit the struggle. Johnston surrendered to Sherman near Durham, North Carolina, and commanders in Alabama, Mississippi, and Louisiana sought out their Federal counterparts and gave up. All resistance ceased by the first week in June. It was a curious ending to a war. The Confederate generals, not the government, decreed that the fighting must stop. Jefferson Davis, defiant to the last, fled Richmond when Lee evacuated his lines and went south, still believing he could arouse his people to renewed endeavors. He was captured by Federal cavalry in Georgia and sent north as a prisoner.*

The greatest war that Americans had yet fought was at last over. In the future the nation would engage in conflicts that involved more men, more money, more effect, but none would be remembered as the Civil War has been. It still remains the "great" American war.

*The Federal authorities thought of trying Davis for treason. They eventually abandoned the plan and released him on realizing they had a shaky legal case. The United States had indirectly recognized the Confederacy as a government, and the head of an enemy government could not be accused of treason.

INTERLUDE

1865-1898

THE UNITED STATES IN 1865 was a major military power. The volunteer
armies that were called into being during the Civil War ranked in size
and efficiency with the forces available to any of the leading European nations,
and the navy, although its vessels did not compare with the largest ships in
foreign squadrons, could have held American shores against any attacker.
Slightly more than a year later, this imposing structure had virtually disappeared. The volunteers were demobilized, and the navy was being allowed to
fall into a state of disrepair. It was, at least for this time, a characteristically
American and democratic way to end a war—to dismantle the military structure and to assume that a similar structure would never be required again.

Although the war had been fought by citizen soldiers, no one in the
political or military hierarchy inferred from the experience that the United
States should in the future rely on such an army as its principal line of defense.
There was general agreement, instead, that the nation should return to the
practice of depending on a professional or regular army. But differences of
opinion existed as to the size of the regular force required. Ulysses S. Grant,
serving as general in chief, proposed an army of 80,000 men. This figure was
too large for an economy-minded Congress and a suddenly peace-minded
people. In 1867 Congress consented to an establishment of 54,000 troops, the
highest peacetime figure yet reached, but the number did not remain in effect
very long. Two years later Congress reduced the authorized strength to 37,000,
and during the 1870s the legislators settled on a strength of 28,000. This was
the size of the army in 1898, when the United States became involved in the
War with Spain.

Behind the small regular army was a kind of reserve force, the volunteer
militia organizations in the states. The descendants of the old compulsory
militia, those units were made up of young men who were attracted to martial
life or who enjoyed the fraternal or political rewards offered by membership.
Supported financially by their states or by contributions from officers and
wealthy enlistees, the militia had only a loose relationship to the federal
government, which supplied a modest annual grant for firearms. Nevertheless,

the organizations in most states took the name of the National Guard, and in all states it was assumed that, like the militia designated in the Constitution, they could be called into national service to repel invasion, suppress insurrection, or enforce federal laws. However, the training and hence the efficiency of the various units varied from state to state, and the volunteer militia was far from being a reserve ready for war duty.

The haste to convert to a peacetime establishment also affected the command system that evolved during the war. The most innovative features of that structure were abolished or allowed to fall into disuse. Eliminated was the office of chief of staff, the coordinating position in which General Halleck had served so capably. The Army Board, which consisted of the bureau heads reporting to the president and the secretary of war, simply passed out of use. The chiefs had never been comfortable acting in a collective capacity, and they returned happily to their prewar status as individual administrators pursuing individual objectives.

The remaining elements in the system had been present before the war—the president, the secretary of war, the general in chief, and the bureau heads of the General Staff. Below the president, the commander in chief, there was uncertainty, and raging rivalry. The competition for power among the lower echelons existed before the war, and now it became even more intense.

The division originated in the vagueness of the defined responsibilities of the secretary and the commanding general. As outlined in War Department regulations, the secretary, the civilian deputy of the president, had authority over administrative and "fiscal" affairs. The commanding general, the military deputy of the president, oversaw matters of "discipline and military control." This seemed reasonably clear—the secretary administered through the medium of the staff offices, and the general commanded the "line," the regiments of the army. The problem was that in peacetime the general had little to command and was inevitably led to try to administer, to extend his supervision over the staff. If an ambitious general came into conflict with an ambitious secretary, there were continuous quarrels.

Complicating this situation was the collective ambition of the individual bureau heads. These men were senior officers who had achieved what amounted to a life tenure in their jobs. Considering themselves experts in their chosen function, which, indeed, some of them were, they were not willing to accept supervision from a line general who was ignorant of staff work. They took the position that they were responsible only to the secretary, and they consented to only the loosest control from him. At times they acted as though they were subject only to the president himself.

The commanding general and other line officers regarded the staff heads as Washington bureaucrats who were ignorant of the problems of troops in the field. The chiefs could have leveled the same criticism in reverse: the line officers knew little of the problems of staff. Here was an unappreciated weakness in the command system, the lack of rotation between staff and line. It was a facet of a more serious weakness, the absence of a clearly designated authority to direct the army in peace and plan what it would do in war.

The result of not having a central planning agency was apparent in the slowness with which the army adopted new weapons. Breech-loading and repeating rifles had been used only in limited numbers in the Civil War, because the arsenals were not tooled to produce them. In peacetime the arsenals could have been retooled to turn out the new weapons—if the government had placed orders. But the army held back. For several years after the war the Ordnance Department was satisfied to convert its stock of muzzle-loading muskets into breech-loaders, and this modified weapon was the standard shoulder arm of the infantry. In the cavalry a shorter arm, a carbine, was required, and greater variety prevailed. Cavalrymen carried several breech-loading models, and some units had repeaters.

The army eventually realized that it needed a better weapon and in 1872 convened a board to make recommendations. In the following year the board decided on a single-shot breech-loader chambered for the .45–.70, a cartridge loaded with black powder. Known as the "trap-door Springfield," because the breech opened upward like an attic access door, this was the standard shoulder gun in the army during the next twenty-five years. But it was obsolete almost as soon as it was issued. In Europe at this time repeating rifles were in general use, and by the 1880s Europeans had adopted repeaters chambered for small bore (.26–.32 caliber) cartridges loaded with smokeless powder. These weapons did not emit a puff of smoke upon discharge as did black powder weapons, and therefore did not betray the position of the firer. More important, the higher velocity of the projectiles shot from these weapons, compared to black-powder guns, resulted in a tripling of the maximum effective range when exposed troops were the targets. In 1892 the American army convinced Congress to agree to the adoption of the Krag-Jörgensen, a five-shot repeater of .30 caliber that fired smokeless cartridges. Krags had been issued throughout the regular army by 1897, the year before war with Spain began. The National Guard, however, remained armed with the old Springfields.

New developments in artillery were accepted even more slowly than those in small arms. The muzzle-loading, smoothbore pieces that had served in the Civil War continued for twenty more years. In the meantime, European armies were being equipped with breech-loading rifled guns of hitherto unimagined range and accuracy, using smokeless powder. Not until the 1880s did the American army adopt some of the newer models in its field and siege artillery, and the relatively few breech-loaders that were built still relied on black powder.

DEVELOPMENTS IN THE NAVY were in dramatic contrast with those in the army. Initially, the navy, like the army, went through a period of neglect and decline. But beginning in the 1880s a national interest in the importance of sea power took form and was reflected in demands for a stronger navy. A burst of expansion followed, the new vessels incorporating the latest developments in European fleets.

In Europe the years after 1865 witnessed unparalleled innovations in naval technology. Important changes in armor, weapons, and propelling power occurred so quickly that a new-model vessel might become obsolete soon after it was launched. Not even the experts could predict what would come next. A British official once announced that a battleship about to be built would be "armed with the latest type of gun—whatever that may be next year."

These feverish activities left the United States Navy untouched; in 1880 it was still an assemblage of wooden and iron-plated cruisers and venerable monitors. In size it ranked about twelfth among the world's navies, but in total capacity it was inferior to the squadrons of even second-rate powers. Also unchanged was its higher administration, whose structure dated back before the Civil War. The commanding officer bore the title Admiral of the Navy and was awarded the position on the basis of seniority; David G. Farragut was the first admiral and was succeeded by another veteran of the Civil War, David D. Porter. The staff work was performed by eight bureaus roughly similar to those of the army. Only the Office of Naval Intelligence was concerned with planning, and it but peripherally through its coverage of developments in European navies. Intelligence officers led the drive for a stronger navy, but the naval people by themselves could not have aroused the public support required to launch an extensive program of construction. Adding their voices to the chorus were influential politicians, businessmen, and intellectuals who for patriotic or more mundane reasons thought the nation should have a big navy. Behind the agitation, and responsible for its success, was a dawning consciousness that a strong navy was needed to uphold national interests beyond the continental limits, and perhaps to extend those interests. The United States was no longer an isolated nation. In the Pacific Ocean it had acquired Alaska and the Midway Islands and was casting covetous eyes on Hawaii and Samoa. In Latin America the nation continued its historical mission of countering European imperialism. One of the naval officers advocating expansion caught the new mood. "Whether they will or no," he declared, "Americans must now begin to look outward."

The first naval expansion began modestly. In 1882 Congress authorized the construction of four light steel cruisers, the second class of war vessels. But the foundation of a modern navy of steel and steam had been laid. Other appropriations followed, and by the end of the decade the navy maintained thirty-eight cruisers. Even this rapid progress did not satisfy the growing number of "big navy" advocates. Now the cry was for the United States to have a navy "second to none," including a number of the largest vessels afloat, battleships. Accordingly, Congress in 1890 provided the funds to build three of the vessels that in the current system of rankings determined the strength of a navy. By 1898 the navy contained six battleships and in the ratings of the sea forces of the world had advanced to sixth place.

Officers in the expanding navy developed an expansive view of the strategic function of their service. Naval doctrine was more sharply defined than army doctrine, cast in a more philosophical form and related to what its spokesmen considered to be America's broadening world role. The officers who articulated the new theory received their inspiration in the navy's educational system.

In that system the Naval Academy at Annapolis continued to provide basic training for would-be officers. Although its curriculum was broadened somewhat after 1865, it remained primarily a technical institution concentrating on tactics. The restrictions of the program bothered some officers, who were persuaded that naval men should give more study to strategy. One who was especially troubled was Rear Admiral Stephen B. Luce. An individual of scholarly tastes and a veteran of the Civil War, Luce believed that in the late conflict the navy had not achieved full potential because its leaders had neglected the lessons in high command provided by history. Resolved to remedy the situation, Luce in 1884 persuaded the Navy Department to establish a postgraduate school, the Naval War College at Newport, Rhode Island. Luce headed the school, and to its faculty he brought a number of able junior officers who shared his opinions. One of them was Alfred Thayer Mahan, son of Dennis Mahan, the West Point instructor who had taught so many of the Civil War generals. And it was the younger Mahan, more than any other officer, who formulated an American naval strategy and set naval thinking in a direction it would hold to for generations.

Mahan expressed his views in lectures but most convincingly in numerous writings, the best known being a book published in 1890, *The Influence of Sea Power upon History.* Drawing examples from the past, Mahan contended that the great nations had been those with sea power. The components of sea power were a productive domestic economy, foreign commerce, a merchant marine to carry trade, a navy to defend the trade routes, and colonies to provide raw materials and markets, and bases for the navy. The United States had the potential to become a great nation, Mahan suggested. Like a huge island, it enjoyed many of the components of sea power. But to attain the ordained goal it had to acquire a strong navy and colonial bases.

Although Mahan always stressed the defensive function of a strong navy in guarding America's coasts, he also had in mind a force that could operate offensively far from the homeland. Battleships must lead the fleets, he insisted, for only they could ensure that "command of the sea" necessary to a great and expanding nation. And to maintain command, battle squadrons must operate and, if necessary, fight as units; "Never divide the fleet" was Mahan's most repeated maxim. He was telling the navy that it existed to win in war and that to win, it would probably have to fight a showdown battle. More important, he was urging the American public to support the creation of a navy large enough to win any war—and to achieve any policy objective.

The army also maintained an extensive educational system. In addition to the military academy at West Point, it operated a number of service or postgraduate schools, some of them dating back to the 1820s and others having sprung up in the years after 1865. The various centers gave officers opportunity to learn the latest developments in their branch of the service. But they did nothing more. Excellent technical schools, they were satisfied to teach tactics while ignoring theory and command. This neglect troubled the officer who succeeded Grant as general in chief, William T. Sherman. Always interested in newly developing ways of war, Sherman concluded that somewhere in the system there should be a school that dealt with strategy. His urging finally began to show results. In 1881 the School of Application for Infantry and Cavalry was instituted at Fort Leavenworth, Kansas. For a time Leavenworth was just another advanced tactical school. But beginning in the 1890s its faculty gave increasing attention to the subject of strategy, and it finally became what Sherman had hoped it would be—the capstone in the army's system.*

Army officers concerned with overall strategy had differing views as to the role of a land arm in a war with a foreign power. For a time after the Civil War practically all officers, following tradition, believed that any war would begin with an attack by a European power on America's coast or borders; they defined the army's task as cooperating with the navy in repelling the assault. But by the 1880s most experts had discarded the likelihood of a European offensive. No nation seemed to have the strength or the inclination to attack the United States, protected by her oceans and her growing naval might. It was more possible now that America herself might resort to offensive actions abroad, to protect her maritime and commercial interests in the Pacific Ocean and the Caribbean Sea or, if Mahan's doctrines were followed, to acquire colonial bases in those areas. The degree to which the army should participate in wars fought at a great distance from the mainland was the cause of disagreement among the strategists.

Many, probably most, officers thought the army should accept a secondary role in these conflicts. The navy should deliver the main offensive thrust, although the army might organize small expeditionary forces to help the sea arm take and hold points on foreign soil. Most army strategists apparently believed that such points would be held only temporarily, to force the payment of an indemnity or the granting of a commercial privilege. "Foreign conquest and permanent occupation are not a part of the policy of the country," one high-ranking general declared. Other officers envisioned larger offensive opera-

*In 1901 the name of the school was changed to the General Service and Staff College.

tions, on a scale equal to those of the navy, to attain other than temporary material objectives, ends that were disguised with such phrases as national honor and national rights. Thus, one officer proclaimed that the United States must be "prepared to go even to the ends of the earth, not only with ships but with powerful armies," and another declared that the nation must possess a "known preparedness to send an efficient military force wherever the exigencies of just war might demand."

The officer who provided the most comprehensive and most systematic expression of army thinking was General Emory Upton, who had been a unit commander in the Civil War and a protégé of Sherman. A soldier of scholarly tastes, Upton compiled a manual of infantry tactics and wrote a long study of Asiatic and European armies. Then he turned to composing what he considered would be his greatest work, *The Military Policy of the United States from 1775.* He had carried the story down to the middle of the Civil War at the time of his death in 1881. The book was not initially published, except for a few privately printed copies, but in manuscript form it was circulated in the army hierarchy and had a profound influence upon the officers who read it.*

Upton's announced purpose in writing the book was to expose what he called the "folly and criminality" of past and present American military policy. Drawing upon history, he argued that the United States had blundered unprepared into each of its wars and had fought every one with an inadequate command system. He blamed the fault in command upon the dominating position of the secretary of war, and to remedy the situation he recommended the creation of a general staff on the Prussian model, that could take the direction of war from the secretary. To prevent a repetition of past unpreparedness, Upton proposed the creation of a compact and "expansible" professional army, a force that in event of war could be rapidly increased to at least 100,000 troops. Only a professional army could fight a "modern" war, he contended. He did not seem to realize that the Civil War had been a modern conflict, and he appeared to have forgotten that he had led citizen soldiers to victory in that war.†

Upton's proposal of a large standing army was not acceptable to the public of the time. The people might be persuaded that a big navy was needed to accomplish the objectives of national policy, but they remained unconvinced that a substantial land force was also required. Upton was demanding an army strong enough to attain any goal. Although he failed to carry his views, he had anticipated the future.

---

*The manuscript was finally published in 1904 at the instigation of Secretary of War Elihu Root, who used Upton's ideas to support his reform of army structure.

†Despite his apparent devotion to historical scholarship, Upton's use of history was often misleading. He chose examples that supported his own views and warped them if they did not. For example, he greatly exaggerated the influence of Secretary of War Stanton in the Civil War command system.

NO FOREIGN NATION disturbed the United States during the years just after 1865, but a domestic adversary threatened to impede and delay the onward march of national progress. In their continuing sweep across the continent Americans were pressing onto the Great Plains and into the Rocky Mountain region, and in these areas they encountered Indian tribes who resisted the intrusion of whites. Various civilian agencies, special "peace" commissions, or the Bureau of Indian Affairs, located in the Department of the Interior, attempted to persuade the Indians to accept the ending of their way of life, to cede large parts of their hunting grounds and agree to live on reservations. When these efforts failed, as they inevitably did, the army was called in to repress the "hostiles." Beginning in the late 1860s and continuing throughout the 1880s the army fought numerous Indian "wars," engaged in more than 1,000 combat actions, and suffered 2,000 casualties while killing 6,000 Indians. If these wars are considered parts of a connected process, this was probably the most sustained operation in military history.

Although the frontier army was assigned the only combat mission of the time, it was always a small force. Other areas claimed their share of regular troops. During the late 1860s approximately a third of the army was stationed in the former Confederate states, to uphold the Republican governments that had been established as a part of the Reconstruction process. The number was reduced somewhat after 1870, but troops remained in the South until 1877. Additional contingents guarded coastal fortifications and the long border with Mexico. These requirements left only a modest number available to fight Indians, especially during the 1870s, when the size of the regular army was cut approximately in half. About 5,000 troops in scattered posts held the northern Great Plains, and 4,000, equally scattered, patrolled the southern plains.

The enlisted men who composed the frontier army were a varied lot. Veterans of the Civil War probably comprised a majority in the years immediately after 1865. But during the 1870s the number of seasoned soldiers dropped sharply. Most of the new volunteers were unemployed laborers, recent immigrants, or individuals who had reasons to disappear from society—in short, men who had no place to go but into the army. Many did not stay. Because the conditions of life were hard and the discipline was harsh, numerous desertions occurred, in some years one-third of the troops.

A unique element in the postwar army was the presence of black units. In 1866 Congress provided for four "colored" regiments, two of infantry and two of cavalry, thereby compelling the army to drop from its recruiting regulations the traditional restriction to "free white." The black enlistees were mostly former Union soldiers, including many who had once been slaves; they, like the white recruits, were looking for security. Sent to the frontier, the four regiments won respect from many of their white comrades and the Indians, who called them, in reference to their hair, the "buffalo soldiers." Although serving under white line officers and living in segregated quarters, the blacks obviously found conditions in the army preferable to those in civilian life. The rate of desertion in these regiments was lower than in white units, and the rate of reenlistment was much higher.

Approximately 270,000 Indians lived in the West in 1866. However, only a minority of this total can be taken into account in calculating the manpower reservoir of the Indians. Some tribes accommodated to the intrusion of whites among them, and others lacked the strength or the will to offer resistance. The population of the tribes that were determined to fight was about 100,000. The principal hostile tribes were, on the northern Great Plains, the Sioux; on the central and southern plains, the Kiowas, the Comanches, the Cheyennes, and the Arapahoes; and in the southwestern deserts and mountains, the Apaches.*

The Indians of the plains and the Southwest presented the sternest resistance that the whites had yet encountered in their march across the continent. In earlier conflicts east of the Mississippi, settlers and soldiers had encountered Indians who moved on foot. But the Western warriors were mounted, riding small but strong horses that were descendants of Spanish stock; this mobility brought a new factor into Indian warfare. Some frontier officers called the "horse Indians" the finest light cavalry in the world, and many later historians have accepted the verdict. The tribesmen were, in truth, a formidable foe, whether armed with their traditional weapons, bows and arrows and lances, or with rifles obtained in various ways from whites. Gifted with great physical endurance and schooled by their culture to take pride in individual feats of bravery, they excelled in stealth and surprise and slashing hit-and-run forays. If at all possible, they fought only on their own terms.

The emphasis on individualism in Indian culture made the warrior the redoubtable enemy that he was. But this same quality prevented the natives from engaging in effective or sustained warfare in groups. Indians owed their allegiance to a tribe or to a clan within a tribe, and rarely formed even temporary alliances with other tribes; indeed, they fought one another as often as they fought whites. A particular tribe might decide to resist white intrusion, but the absence of racial consciousness precluded intertribal resistance. Tribal cooperation itself was not easily achieved. Political authority was diffused among many persons, resembling actually an anarchic democracy, and so-called chiefs or war leaders often had trouble in assembling a band for joint action or enforcing discipline on the members after it was formed. The downfall of the Indians was therefore inevitable: it would have occurred even if the

---

*Other, smaller tribes in the Rocky Mountains and Basin-Plateau region also offered resistance, such as the Utes, the Modocs, and the Nez Percés.

white man had not possessed greater numbers and a superior technology.

The difference in numbers between the races, as well as their differing cultures, led inescapably to conflict. The few hundred thousand Indians of the plains maintained a nomadic existence, following and hunting the huge herds of buffalo that roamed over the expanse—an estimated 15 million of these animals were at large in 1866—and for them to continue to live as they insisted on living required unrestricted use of vast areas of land. Demanding entrance into what was to the white man territory going to waste were millions of prospective settlers. A democratic government like the United States could not possibly have restrained them.

ARMY OFFICERS fighting Indians knew they faced a courageous, skilled foe. Some of them respected the Indians for their martial qualities, and a few even commiserated the inevitable fate they saw awaiting the race. But the majority viewed the Indians generally with contempt and revulsion, as inferior primitives standing in the way of white advance, savages who mutilated the bodies of fallen enemies, tortured captives, and engaged in other uncivilized practices. General Sherman expressed a common army opinion in characterizing the Indians as "the enemies of our race and our civilization." These dangerous people had to be repressed, and the army was prepared to employ whatever methods were required. "We must act with vindictive earnestness against the Sioux," Sherman declared in 1866, "even to their extermination, men, women, and children." A frequent tactic of the army, one supported by Sherman, was to attack the Indians in their villages, destroying their food, shelter, and horses, and sometimes in these forays women and children were killed, often by chance but on occasion deliberately. This was not extermination, but it was a form of total war, an extension of the techniques Sherman and his principal lieutenant and successor as general in chief, Philip Sheridan, had employed in the Civil War.*

In addition to attacking the Indians in their villages, the army relied on two other tactical innovations, both of them related to the objective of striking the natives in fixed locations. One was the winter campaign when Indians were especially vulnerable. They had to remain stationary for a long period, lacking mobility because their grass-fed ponies were weak. Not expecting to be attacked, they were easily surprised. Another tactic was to move converging columns from different directions upon a collection of Indians. These units, assembled from troops in many posts, might number several hundred or 2,000

*Some modern historians have suggested that the war had conditioned the army to employing a strategy of annihilation. This is possible, but it is also true that in prewar Indian conflicts, the army resorted to attacking villages and engaging in indiscriminate killing of their inhabitants. Although a few officers condoned the killing of noncombatants, the majority tried to prevent this practice. In some encounters, Indian women joined the warriors in fighting back.

or more men, and if they could not always catch the enemy, they could keep him constantly on the move.*

OF ALL THE MANY "WARS" that the army fought against Indians, three deserve special attention. Each was conducted against a determined and militant tribe or a number of tribes collected in one area, each called forth the best efforts of the army, and each was followed by a decisive result.

The combative tribes of the southern Great Plains, the Kiowas, the Cheyennes, the Arapahoes, and the Comanches, were uniformly warlike, but they fought always as individual groups and were unable to present a united front. They were further weakened by the appearance among them of "peace" factions, composed of individuals who wanted to come to terms with the whites. Nevertheless, they were able to keep the area in turmoil and to spread terror in the settlements, and the government finally turned them over to the army in 1874. In what became known as the Red River War, 3,000 troops, moving in five converging columns, ran the Indians down and forced them to agree to remove to reservations in the Indian Territory, in present Oklahoma.

The war that broke the power of the tribes of the southern plains was concluded in little more than a year. No such easy success attended the struggle with the guardians of the northern plains, the Sioux. Actually a confederation of several tribes, the Sioux numbered 30,000 and roamed from Dakota to Wyoming. In the view of some historians the Sioux were the ablest and most dangerous Indians. They possessed the capacity, rare among Indians, to unite for common action and were able, on occasion, to mobilize large forces. They had the equally rare ability to engage in a sustained operation, even to hold a fort under siege. Their relatively sophisticated capabilities resulted in part from the emergence of three chiefs or war leaders who displayed real qualities of generalship and who commanded large personal followings—Red Cloud, Sitting Bull, and the man who was probably their greatest captain, Crazy Horse.

The Sioux first encountered white pressure in 1866, when the army undertook to build a road, the Bozeman Trail, from Fort Laramie, Wyoming, to the mining centers in Montana. Along the initial stretch of the route the army raised several forts, the most advanced one being Fort Phil Kearny. From Kearny the proposed road would cut through territory the Sioux considered theirs, and when the threat was realized, the Indians decided to block the passage. Under the leadership of Red Cloud, they so harried the road workers and the soldiers guarding them as to halt further construction. Not satisfied

*Because the army had to guard and patrol a huge area, its forces were widely dispersed —in 1880, there were over a hundred posts. Unless troops were brought together in a column, the average soldier never saw a unit larger than a company.

with this accomplishment, they laid Kearny itself under a modified siege, making fifty-one attacks on the walls and preventing the garrison from venturing very far from them. They maintained this investment for an incredible three years. In the end the government had to give in, agreeing to abandon construction of the Bozeman Trail. At the same time the Sioux accepted a reservation in southern Dakota but with rights to hunt as far as Wyoming.

After 1868 the Sioux remained in comparative peace for years, attacking only the mining parties looking for gold in their reserve, or other intruders. These incursions became more frequent, however, and the Sioux began to suspect the government of not keeping its promise to exclude whites from the reservation. Their fears seemed confirmed when gold was discovered in the Black Hills of Dakota in 1875. Thousands of miners stampeded into the area while the army stood by. Shortly thereafter large numbers of Sioux left the reserve and congregated in Montana under the leadership of Crazy Horse and Sitting Bull. They refused to return, and many of them believed they were going into their last fight.

The government and the army appeared to welcome the pretext for a showdown. Early in 1876 three columns of infantry and cavalry moved from separated bases to converge upon the Indians. One unit under General George Crook came up from the south, one under General Alfred Terry pushed in from the east, and one under General John Gibbon marched from the west. The total force comprised over 3,000 and the leaders confidently expected to crush the Sioux between them. However, Crook's column, numbering something over 1,000, never got into the campaign. Confronted on the Rosebud River by warriors under Crazy Horse, Crook attempted to fight his way past and was handled so roughly that he had to retire to regroup. Terry and Gibbon continued on, however, and finally united their forces. Learning that the Sioux were encamped on the Little Bighorn River, they put their troops in motion toward what they thought was a waiting village. In the advance was Colonel George A. Custer and the Seventh Cavalry Regiment. Custer, a veteran of the plains wars, was an inveterate seeker of glory and contemptuous of the ability of Indians to fight.

The action on the Rosebud should have warned Custer and the generals that they were not dealing with an ordinary Indian enemy. Crazy Horse's warriors had engaged the soldiers for six hours, fighting what amounted to a pitched battle, an almost unheard-of feat for Indians. And the camp toward which Custer was riding so blithely was probably the largest assemblage of Indians ever brought together. The lowest estimated total was 10,000, the highest 15,000. At least 2,500 and possibly 4,000 warriors were there, the greatest concentration of Indian military might in history. The congregation of so many of these natives was a reflection of the desperation felt by many of them, and a tribute to the leadership appeal of Crazy Horse and Sitting Bull.

Custer and his 600 riders came upon the camp on June 25, his approach marked by Indian scouts. He did not realize its size, and even if he had, he probably would not have stopped. "I can whip all the Indians on the Continent with the Seventh Cavalry," he exclaimed as he prepared to attack. His plan was to converge on the village in three columns, the largest, about 230 troopers, going in under his command. Not one of the three forces went very far. One of the two smaller columns was stopped by Indian fire and after uniting with the other had to retreat to a defensive position. Custer was engulfed by over 1,000 Indians led by Crazy Horse, and in a fight lasting two hours his force was wiped out to a man. More than a hundred soldiers in one of the other columns were killed or wounded, raising the total casualties of the Seventh Cavalry to 50 percent.

Terry and Gibbon reached the field on June 27, to find the bodies of Custer's dead. But there were no Indians. The great village moved off to the south immediately after the battle, and soon its component clans broke away and drifted off in bands. The approach of the main force had something to do with the exodus, but the Indians also lacked the governmental structure to maintain a large force in the field very long. The authority of the chiefs was insufficient to enforce obedience, and the individualism of warriors was so pronounced as to prevent sustained collective action. Nor did the Indians possess a commissary that could have supported a large army indefinitely. They depended for their food on the buffalo, and to hunt the buffalo they had to roam—in separate bands. At the Little Bighorn the Sioux won their greatest victory, but in its aftermath they revealed their military weakness.

The destruction of Custer's force shocked the government and, indeed, the whole nation. From the chorus of outrage it could be concluded that the United States had suffered a major military setback. Reinforcements were dispatched to the northern plains, and the army was directed to hunt down the Indians. The task was not very difficult. Wandering in isolated bands and barely subsisting themselves, the Indians were easy victims of determined pursuers. Some chiefs brought in their hungry people voluntarily to army posts. By the spring of 1877 virtually all the Sioux had surrendered and had been herded onto reservations. Even Crazy Horse and Sitting Bull admitted defeat and became "agency Indians," depending on the white government for their daily sustenance.

The last Indians to concede defeat were the Apaches, a name given to a number of related small tribes who inhabited Arizona, New Mexico, and western Texas. Cunning, fierce, and possessed of great physical endurance, the Apaches were, in the opinion of some army officers, the most dangerous of all Indians. General Crook, who knew them well, called them the "tigers of the human race." They were never able, however, to present a united resistance, fighting usually as individual tribes. One of their ablest chiefs, Cochise, agreed to accept peace in 1872 and led his followers onto a reservation. Other leaders continued to loot and kill and elude the troops sent after them. Most obdurate of the irreconcilables was Geronimo, who was not officially a chief but who rose to leadership through his natural abilities.

Army officers assigned to hunt down the Apaches faced a difficult task, having to move their columns through a rugged terrain of deserts and mountains, every inch of which was known to their wily quarry. Crook had the greatest success against the Apaches. Having studied his enemy and his theater of operations thoroughly, he realized he must introduce new techniques to win. One of his innovations was to enlist large numbers of friendly Apaches to accompany his regular force, using them not only to scout and fight but also to interpret to him the probable intentions of the Indians. Second, he dispensed with wagon trains to carry his supplies and substituted mule trains, thereby investing himself with greater mobility. Last, he insisted that his men be ready to follow the Apaches wherever they went; once he pursued them across the international border into Mexico. He was not in the territory when Geronimo finally surrendered in 1886, but he was largely responsible for the result.

The capitulation of Geronimo marked the end of formal warfare between Indians and whites. Thereafter there were no more Indian "wars," although on some reservations individuals or groups within a tribe might at times become unruly and have to be disciplined. An incident occurring in 1890 on the Sioux reserve in South Dakota was the last action resembling an outbreak. Some of the Indians, excited by the preaching of a new religion that predicted a resurgence of Indian glory, left their agency. Intercepted by a party of soldiers at a place called Wounded Knee, they refused to yield their weapons, and a vicious fight at close quarters erupted. Approximately 200 Indians were killed or wounded, including a number of women and children, and over 50 soldiers fell. In the end the defectors were forced back to the agency, and quiet returned to the Sioux nation. Wounded Knee was a tragic ending to the tragic story of the attempt of the Indians to preserve their way of life.

The army played a large part in subjugating the Indians, but it was only one of several instruments. Commercial buffalo hunters, exploiting a suddenly developing market for hides, also had a role. Moving onto the plains in gangs, supported by the army and supplied by the railroads, they methodically slaughtered the herds. By 1888 only about 1,000 buffalo were left on the ranges, a dwindling source of food for the Indians. More important than anything done by the human actors, soldiers or hunters, were great impersonal forces —the transcontinental railroads pushing across the West, facilitating the coming of settlers as well as the quick movement of troops; the superior numbers of the pressing whites; and the superior quality of white technology. The outcome for the Indians had been foreordained.

CHAPTER XIII

The War with Spain

IN 1898 THE UNITED STATES became involved in its first conflict with a foreign power since engaging Mexico in 1846. Perhaps because a war with another nation seemed to represent a departure in national policy, the struggle took the name of the enemy country, the War with Spain or the Spanish-American War. It was a curious war, and in some of its aspects, a comic one. An American official with a role in getting the war started and who then was a participant said later: "It wasn't much of a war, but it was the best one we had." Another official, in a phrase that has endured, characterized it as "a splendid little war."

The "splendid" qualities of the war were easily apparent. For Americans it was a glorious and gratifying experience, an almost ideal war. Begun in April, it was over by August, and the most important land fighting, on the enemy's territory, the island of Cuba, lasted only a month. Victory followed victory, on sea and on land and in exotic places in the Caribbean Sea and the Pacific Ocean that few Americans had visited. Each action was extravagantly reported by the press—89 reporters followed the army of 17,000 men to Cuba —and the various engagements produced enough heroes and slogans to stock several larger wars. And to cap it all, the glory was achieved with small loss of life. Only about 385 men were killed in battle, although several thousand more died of disease.

If the war had some splendid aspects, it had others that were strange or ludicrous—the spectacle of an American naval squadron winning a great victory at Manila with only one casualty, and of a three-hundred-pound American general, William R. Shafter, leading in tropical Cuba an army clad in woolen uniforms. It offered examples of inefficiency in both the civilian and the military departments that seem incredible to the modern observer. Perhaps the oddest feature of the Spanish-American War was that the United States entered it without having a clear idea of the policy aims it expected to achieve.

Once proud and mighty, Spain had sunk during the nineteenth century to the status of a second-rate power. Afflicted with a backward economy and governed ineptly by an archaic monarchy, she spoke with but a feeble voice in the councils of Europe. Her one-time extensive colonial empire had dwindled to a few possessions, the only sizable ones left being the islands of Cuba and Puerto Rico in the Caribbean and the Philippine Islands in the Pacific. And in Cuba and the Philippines her rule was far from secure. Large numbers of the inhabitants in both areas desired independence and were willing to fight to accomplish their ends. A rebellion broke out in Cuba in 1895 and another in the Philippines in the following year.*

The uprising of the distant Filipinos went largely unnoticed in the United States. But the Cuban struggle excited public attention and sympathy. Cuba lay adjacent to the continental mainland, so close that possession of it by a European power seemed almost a threat. In 1895 there was support in America for rebels who were attempting to overthrow Spanish rule. There was also concern about reports that Spain was employing barbarous methods to repress the insurrection. These accounts emanated from the metropolitan press and particularly from certain papers that practiced a sensational kind of journalism. The "yellow press" publishers saw in the Cuban situation an opportunity to increase circulation. They sent swarms of reporters and artists to cover the conflict—and with orders to play up the atrocities. The idea that their exaggerations might inflame the public to demand American intervention apparently did not concern them. "You furnish the pictures," one publisher allegedly instructed a reluctant artist, "and I'll furnish the war."

The Cuban insurrection was, indeed, conducted with extreme savagery, but contrary to the impression given in the American press, the Spaniards were not the sole perpetrators. The Cubans were equally guilty. They were determined to win—they had announced they would accept no settlement except absolute independence—and they not only engaged the Spanish in constant guerrilla warfare but also attempted to deprive their oppressors of sustenance by devastating large parts of the island. The Spanish were determined to retain their authority, and they not only harried the rebels mercilessly but, in a countereffort to deny sustenance, laid waste whole provinces and removed the inhabitants to overcrowded prison camps where they died by thousands. By 1898 the contending sides had reduced much of the island to ruin, but neither was close to victory. The Spanish army, numbering about 150,000 regulars, held the seaport cities and controlled much of the countryside in the western provinces. The rebel forces, including at their peak strength some 40,000 men, dominated the eastern provinces except for the seaports and fought to maintain a precarious existence in the western provinces. Neither side seemed able to deliver a decisive blow, and the struggle threatened to continue indefinitely.

Only the Spanish excesses were reported in the American press, and as Americans read of them their anger mounted. Mingled with denunciations of

---

*The Cubans had long resented Spanish rule and previously had engaged in a ten-year attempt (1868–78) to overthrow it.

Spain were demands that the United States do something to stop the "killing," and the rising crescendo prompted Congress to state an official policy. Early in 1896 the houses adopted a concurrent resolution proposing that the United States grant belligerent status to the rebels and employ its good offices to induce Spain to recognize Cuban independence. Most of the members who voted for the resolution—the majorities in favor were overwhelming—were simply reflecting the wishes of their constituents; some hoped that by taking an aggressive position toward Spain they would further their chances of reelection. There was also one bloc of supporters who carefully concealed their ulterior motives, who cared little for the rebels but who discerned in the Cuban crisis an opportunity to extend American influence in the Caribbean, perhaps to acquire naval bases in the area. These men were Republicans, and although few in number they occupied key positions in the party. Outside the party structure they were allied with the "imperialists" in American society, the group for whom Alfred T. Mahan spoke, who wanted the United States to become a colonial and a world power. Whatever the motivation of the supporters of the resolution, whether they were idealists or imperialists, they were determined that Congress have a part in formulating foreign policy. Their action defies the current concept that the nation has always been led into its wars by bold presidents. Between 1896 and 1898 it was the Congress, not the president, who was in the forefront of defining foreign policy and who insisted on a posture that was almost certain to result in war.

At the time the resolutions passed the president was Grover Cleveland, a Democrat and an anti-imperialist. Convinced that the United States had no interest to be served by intervening in Cuba, Cleveland refused to exercise the authority offered in the resolution. But his days in the White House were almost at an end. Late in 1896 the country elected the Republican presidential candidate, William McKinley, and at the same time returned a majority of the party to Congress. One plank in the Republican platform committed the incoming president to use his influence to restore peace in Cuba and to ensure the island's independence.

On taking office in 1897, McKinley showed restraint in implementing the platform pledge. Although he protested to Spain against its "uncivilized and inhuman" conduct of operations in Cuba, he proposed no practical action except to offer American services in mediating the conflict. The Spanish government rejected the mediation offer but, worried that McKinley's approach might portend a more positive American policy, agreed to soften some of its methods in Cuba. The response encouraged the president to believe that by patiently applying pressure he could achieve a peace satisfactory to both sides.

The kind of limited solution sought by McKinley was impossible to realize. Under American urging Spain might agree to make various concessions in her policy, as when she consented to close the prison camps and to establish an armistice. But she was not going to grant Cuba complete independence. The rebels were even more recalcitrant. They would not accept any result short of independence, and they refused to consider an armistice to discuss any of the reforms Spain proffered. McKinley, in intervening, only encouraged the rebels to prolong their resistance. He also incited his own countrymen, already angry about Spain, to expect the government to do more, to intervene actively in Cuba and expel the foreign oppressors.

McKinley's hopes of achieving a diplomatic settlement received a rude jolt in February, 1898. Two incidents that occurred within a short time of each other made war almost inevitable. First, an American newspaper secured and published a private letter written by the Spanish minister in Washington that was highly critical of the president, calling him, among other epithets, a weak bidder for popular admiration. Although the minister resigned and the Spanish government apologized for his action, indignation swept the country; the arrogant Spaniards had insulted the national honor. Second, and more serious, the battleship *Maine,* which had been sent to Havana, ostensibly on a courtesy visit but actually to provide protection for American citizens in Cuba, blew up one night with a loss of 260 lives. Immediately the public concluded that the Spanish were responsible for the disaster, and this suspicion seemed confirmed when a naval investigative committee reported that the ship had been sunk as a result of an external explosion. Cries for revenge and war resounded throughout the United States, and "Remember the Maine" became a national chant.*

Even after the tragic event in Havana, McKinley did not abandon hope of inducing Spain to accept a peaceable solution. He realized, however, that the United States might be led into war, and accordingly his leaders in Congress introduced a measure to appropriate from surplus Treasury funds $50 million for the "National defense" to be expended at the "discretion of the President." The bill was passed in both houses by a unanimous vote, the enthusiastic response a warning that the legislators were running out of patience with the president's policy and were prepared to resort to war. McKinley knew he could not continue to resist the mounting pressure for direct action. Discouraged at his failure to persuade the Spanish and the Cubans to accept mediation, he resolved to take the ultimate step. On April 11 he asked Congress for authority to use military force to end the hostilities in Cuba, requesting it "in the name of humanity, in the name of civilization, in behalf of endangered American interests." Eight days later Congress by joint resolution authorized American intervention to expel the Spanish, proclaimed Cuba

---

*The Spanish contended that an internal explosion had ignited the magazine of the vessel. The actual cause of the explosion remains unknown to this day, but it does not seem likely that the Spanish authorities would have sanctioned an act almost certain to cause the United States to resort to war. Possibly some individual Spaniards acted on their own initiative. Or, more probably, the explosion may have been set off by Cuban rebels with the intention of provoking the United States to act against Spain.

to be independent, and disclaimed any intention on the part of the United States to annex the island. A breaking of diplomatic relations between the two nations followed, and on April 25 Congress formally declared war, the end to which American policy had pointed since the beginning of the rebellion.

The resolution authorizing American intervention in Cuba reflected the idealism and the confusion of purpose with which the nation embarked on war. What policy goal did the United States hope to attain? Clearly, one objective was to liberate Cuba. But was there anything else? To exact revenge for the *Maine*? Or to conquer new lands for the United States, as some of the imperialists advocated? McKinley never stated the policy aims of the country, nor did members of Congress. The president probably had only hazy ideas of the results he should seek. He said after the war that no nation could fix in advance what it hoped to attain by war, that the forces let loose by war would determine the consequences. Only the people seemed to know what they were fighting for. They wanted to free an oppressed people, overthrow a European tyranny, wave the Stars and Stripes, and demonstrate to the world and to themselves that the United States was a great power that other nations had to reckon with and respect.

THE COMBATANT POWERS offered an interesting study in national styles. Spain was an old and declining state, sunk in dreams of past greatness and striving to retain the scanty territorial remnants of that past. The United States was a young and rising nation, exhilarated by visions of future greatness and straining to break into that future.

If the contrast in spirit between the two nations seemed to weigh the balance in favor of the younger and more vigorous power, so also did the difference in their human and material resources. In both areas the United States was vastly superior. The American population, multiplying every decade, stood in 1898 at 75 million. The Spanish population, increasingly slightly, was only about 18 million. Just as preponderant was the American advantage in economic capacity, which was especially pronounced in the vital area of industrial potential. American industry had expanded phenomonally since 1865, and there had been equally sweeping progress in technology and invention. Within a relatively short time the United States had become the first manufacturing nation in the world. Spanish industry, in comparison, was antique and undeveloped. Spain imported many of its finished goods and relied on other nations for some of its weaponry. The United States not only produced sufficient weapons for its armed forces but could in time convert to creating whatever other matériel it might require.

Reconstituting its industrial system was only one of the problems the United States faced, and as it turned out, one of the easiest. A more difficult one was to raise an adequate land force out of the superior American manpower reservoir. Actually, despite the disparity in the population figures of the two sides, Spain possessed on the eve of the war a much larger army. Spain's Cuban force of 150,000 regulars was augmented by 50,000 Spanish volunteers and Cuban loyalists. Over 8,000 regulars were stationed in the nearby island of Puerto Rico, and at least 20,000 regulars were detailed to the Philippines. Back home in Spain were another 150,000 men. Against this array the United States had a regular army of approximately 28,000 and some 100,000 in the militia units of the states, the National Guard.

Neither army was organized or prepared to fight a modern war. The Spanish army was an ineffective instrument whose size was highly illusory. Tropical diseases rendered a large part of the colonial force unfit for duty. Thus, of the 150,000 in Cuba only a part were effectives, an estimated 80,000 at the most and perhaps only 50,000. And the usable troops were not concentrated but scattered all over the island in small garrisons trying to hold territory against the guerrillas. The Spaniards could not concentrate their forces, because the primitive rail and road system would not support moving large numbers of men and supplies to a few central points. The most serious deficiency of the Spanish army was its poor quality. The rank and file were conscripted young men who had been sent out to the colonies with little or no training and who received inadequate drill after arriving at their posts. Although the army had more officers in proportion to the number of troops than any force in Europe, one to every half-dozen soldiers and one general to every hundred men, these functionaries were usually of low competence. They knew little of tactics and training and were unable, or did not care, to transform the recruits under their control into an efficient force.

The American regular army was trained and disciplined. Composed of volunteers, many of them with several years' service, it had had actual war experience in fighting Indians. The quality of the officer corps was at least adequate, the generals having been volunteer officers in the Civil War and most of the junior officers having graduated from West Point. But for all its professional proficiency, the army was not fitted to fight a large-scale war. It was accustomed to operating in small units, employing tactics that worked very well against Indians but would not serve in a war with a foreign adversary. The largest permanent formation in the army was a regiment—there had not been a brigade formation for thirty years—and except for the veterans of the Civil War no officer had ever seen a larger force than a regiment assembled in one place. Even more unprepared for a modern war was the National Guard, whose members knew little more than the rudiments of close-order drill. The United States could easily call up from its manpower resources a much larger army—but it remained to be seen whether the government and the generals would be able to resolve the problems of directing troops in numbers.

If American land forces at the onset of war were inferior in numbers to those of Spain, American sea power was clearly superior. The United States navy, the sixth largest in the world, possessed five battleships, four of which were new and ranked in armor and guns as "first-class,"* over thirty cruisers, two of them powerfully armored and rating almost as battleships, and a number of vessels of other types. Spain had nothing to match this might. She could offer only one battleship, rated as "second-class," four armored cruisers, which were fast but imperfectly armed, and other assorted ships. American sea power remained ascendant throughout the war and helped to determine the outcome, enabling the landing and maintenance of armies in any of the Spanish colonies. The navy also prevented Spain from sending reinforcements and supplies to her threatened possessions. Thus, the 150,000 Spanish soldiers at home never got into the war.

WAR WAS ALMOST upon the nation before anybody in the government recognized that perhaps the little regular army of 28,000 officers and men could not take on Spain by itself. The first person to awaken to this possibility was the commanding general of the army, Nelson A. Miles, who was joined in his concern by certain officials in the War Department. Miles had entered the army as a volunteer officer in the Civil War and, remaining in the service at its close, had distinguished himself in the Indian conflicts before attaining the top command. Steeped in the tradition of the regular army, Miles saw no need to call out a host of citizen volunteers to deal with Spain. A strengthened regular army could do the small amount of fighting that would be required: to land in Cuba after a naval blockade had reduced the Spaniards to starvation, and to mop up remaining pockets of resistance. While the regulars were winning the war and the glory, National Guard units could man coastal defenses.

The thinking of Miles and his colleagues found favor with President McKinley and Secretary of War Russell A. Alger, and with the administration's blessing a bill was introduced in Congress in March to expand the regular army to slightly more than 100,000 officers and men. Supported by official sanction and approved widely in the press, the measure seemed headed for easy passage. But suddenly it encountered an opposition it could not surmount, an outraged resistance that was an expression of the democratic spirit applied to war. A martial fervor gripped the populace during the spring months of 1898, and all over the country volunteer and National Guard units were organizing and proffering their service to the government. As eager as they were to get into the prospective war, these men did not intend to enroll as anonymous regulars or to be commanded by unfamiliar regular officers. They demanded to be enlisted in their own units and under their own officers and to be given a prominent role in the fighting. Expressing their sentiments,

*If the *Maine* had not been lost, the navy would have had six battleships.

one congressman said: "Your constituents and my constituents do not want the standing army of the United States to fight this war."

Whatever its military deficiencies, the National Guard was a potent political lobby, and its influence stalled the administration's bill. In acting thusly, the Guardsmen were notifying the War Department that it had to frame a measure they would accept. The department quickly capitulated. A revised bill limited the expansion of the regular army to approximately 65,000 men and authorized the president to call upon the states for as many volunteers as he deemed necessary, to serve for two years or for the duration of hostilities, whichever was shorter.* In further deference to the National Guard, militia companies, battalions, and regiments could enlist as units and come in under their own officers. The measure became law on April 22, just as the war was beginning.

McKinley acted immediately to use the authority granted him. On April 23 he called for 125,000 volunteers, and in the following month he summoned 75,000 more. In convoking such a host, the president was in part responding to advice from certain military men who told him the country would need a large army to cope with the supposedly formidable Spanish forces. But he was primarily influenced by political considerations. The total number of volunteers exceeded the entire strength of the National Guard, and this inflation ensured that every state and every volunteer outfit would be able to share in the glory of the war.

Also expanding in numbers but at a more modest rate was the regular army. The enlistment rate rose dramatically as the war fervor increased, and the army could easily have attained its authorized strength. However, the officers running the recruitment process felt they could afford to be selective and rejected many applicants as not meeting certain physical and mental standards. Nevertheless, the army eventually reached a strength of about 59,000. The regulars, the volunteers called up by the president, and special volunteer units authorized by Congress brought the total American forces up to 275,000. Only a fraction of the troops raised were destined to see combat, the war ending before the majority could be brought into action. The largest single armies numbered but 17,000 and 15,000, respectively.

The troops were assembled quickly. By the end of May, 160,000 were in service and by the end of July, 270,000. As soon as the various units were mustered in, they were rushed off to camps in the Southern states, whence they could be moved to ports of embarkation for Cuba. The War Department had no previously prepared plan to mobilize such large bodies of troops, and the staff bureaus were unable to provide supplies for the thousands of men dumped suddenly in the camps. Scenes of incredible confusion occurred at all the

---

*The expansion in the regular army was limited to the period of the war; at the end of hostilities the army was to revert to its former peacetime strength.

assembly points, and the inefficiency became a scandal after the war. Actually, the performance of the bureaus was not quite as bad as contemporary critics charged or later historians have thought. A measure of order was eventually established, and within two months after the first call for troops, expeditionary forces were ready to embark for foreign destinations. This was a faster mobilization than would occur in the two world wars.

PRESIDENT MCKINLEY had served in the Civil War as a young volunteer officer. His experience possibly influenced him to believe that professionalism was required in the higher command posts. Certainly, his assignments of commissions revealed a preference to entrust command to professional soldiers. Of the 26 major generals that he appointed to lead volunteers, 19 were promoted regular army officers, and of the 102 brigadier generals he named, 66 were regulars. Even the officers from civilian life had some military experience, having served in the regular army or in the National Guard.

McKinley may also have remembered that in the Civil War black soldiers had made an important contribution to Union victory. At any rate, his administration showed a willingness to tap black manpower. The four Negro regiments in regular service in the West were transported to Southern camps to join the forces gathering to descend on Cuba. And when blacks protested that they were being excluded from the volunteer units because the National Guard did not accept Negroes, the government agreed to muster in several black regiments. Possibly as many as 10,000 Negroes served in volunteer units. None of the black volunteers saw combat service, remaining, like most of their white counterparts, in camp. But the black regulars fought well in Cuba. In one confused battle black and white soldiers became intermixed and charged up a hill together. This example of integration was so rare as to excite widespread comment.

THE FIRST MONEY to finance the war, $50 million appropriated by Congress in March, came out of surplus funds in the Treasury. The availability of such an amount testified to the wealth of the economy, which while bearing only light peacetime taxes, was producing more revenue than the government needed to meet its expenses. The administration experienced no difficulty in realizing additional sums. A War Revenue Act imposed by Congress provided for raising $100 million from internal taxes, and a bond issue authorizing $200 million was oversubscribed. Some of the revenues could not be spent before the war ended and were returned to the Treasury.

The ample finances should have provided abundant supplies for the armed forces. But success in financing was not translated into success in procuring matériel, and the failure in supply was one of the scandals of the war. The navy, with its small personnel, made few demands; it was reasonably well equipped at the beginning of the war and never experienced any serious lack of equipment. But the suddenly inflated army endured severe shortages during its mobilization, and some of the shortages continued for months after. The deprivations were in part the result of the excusable oversight of the War Department. Nobody in authority had foreseen the political pressures that forced the government to call up a large body of men, and the department was caught unprepared by the influx of men into the camps. The supply services had stockpiled only enough goods to equip a regular force of about 40,000, and for the gathering volunteers they could not provide such essential items as uniforms, shoes, socks, and underwear. Within a relatively short time the economy was able to furnish the supplies needed, but some of the materials did not start moving in volume to the camps until July, when the war was almost over.

Failure in procurement was not the only factor creating the crisis in supply. Equally to blame was faulty distribution. Even when supplies were available or became available, the staff bureaus of the War Department often were unable to place them where they were needed. The onus for this shortcoming was at the time laid on the shoulders of Secretary of War Alger, and historians have repeated the censure. Alger, a minor Michigan politician, was a mediocre administrator who took little initiative in supervising his department. But even if he had been a more active or dynamic director, he would have experienced trouble in getting his bureau chiefs to work together as an effective team. The chiefs were generally competent men who knew their business—but little else. Each was accustomed to running his own agency but not to cooperating with other agencies, and each preferred to operate in his separate sphere. The result was a diffusion of authority and effort in the distribution of supplies. One army critic, trying to sum up the shortcomings of the staff, wrote: "In a thousand ways there was a lack of coordination which not only led to miscarriage of plans but to extravagance in expenditures and lack of harmony in administration."

The lack of coordination also impressed a postwar commission that investigated the performance of the War Department. In restrained but biting language the commission concluded that the department had not demonstrated "that complete grasp of the situation" essential to the efficient conduct of war. If the United States was going to be involved in foreign wars in the future, it would have to create a special agency or staff to plan and coordinate operations.

The shortages in supply did not extend to weapons. American land forces were well armed, although no better than the Spaniards. The regulars were equipped with the recently introduced Krag-Jörgensen. The number of Krags on hand was not sufficient to furnish the National Guard, however, and the volunteers carried the .45–.70 Springfield.

The regular army also possessed ample stocks of artillery, including siege and field guns and lesser pieces. Indeed, the offensive expeditions to Cuba, Puerto Rico, and the Philippines carried more guns with them than they could use against the Spanish. However, the effectiveness of the artillery was limited. American developments had not kept pace with progress in Europe, and many of the guns were out of date. Some pieces were muzzle-loaders, and all of them fired black powder, which revealed their position to the enemy. The men manning the guns had no instruments to enable them to fire indirectly and had to see a target before they could engage it. In the forested terrain of Cuba, artillery usually came into action at a range of 1,000 yards or less, which was no longer than the distances covered during the Civil War.

DURING THE SPRING MONTHS OF 1898 ranking officers of the army and the navy gave a great deal of thought to preparing their services to fight Spain. It seemed obvious to them that the nation would soon be involved in war—the passage by Congress of the $50 million "national defense" bill in early March was a clear sign—and they wanted to be ready. But in attempting to devise strategic plans they were handicapped by not knowing what kind of war they would be called upon to wage. Were the services merely to aid the Cuban rebels to expel the Spaniards? Or would they be required to conquer parts or all of the Spanish empire? Although the lack of political guidance created problems for both services, it affected the navy less. Naval planners assumed that their function would be to seek out and destroy the Spanish fleet and to harry Spanish commerce, and they prepared a tentative strategy. For the army, however, the absence of direction from above posed a serious problem. Army planners did not know whether they would have to undertake a large or a modest effort, and until they were better informed, they could not make even tentative plans.

McKinley did not reveal his policy aims even to his cabinet. At this stage, as previously indicated, he probably had not decided on his ultimate objective. Not until war was formally declared did he take over active direction of the military machine. Then he set up a command post in the White House, establishing himself in a special "war room" adorned with wall maps on which colored pins showed the positions of land and naval forces. Another feature of the room was its communication facilities. Twenty-five telegraph wires and fifteen special telephone wires enabled McKinley to be in quick contact with officials in the military departments or officers in other cities; no previous commander in chief had possessed such a technological advantage.

In the war room McKinley met in frequent conference with Secretary of War Alger, Secretary of the Navy John D. Long, commanding general Nelson A. Miles, ranking naval officers, and other advisers. According to admiring colleagues, at these sessions the president decided on broad matters of strategy, ensured cooperation between the army and the navy, and provided a central-ized direction to the war effort. The claims were in part deserved. Insofar as central direction existed, McKinley provided it. He revised orders issuing from the War and the Navy departments and sometimes sent instructions directly to commanders in the field. However, his control was more apparent than real. He did not own a strong character, and he was likely to be swayed by whatever advisers he listened to at a particular time. His direction of strategy had a flaccid quality and was subject to sudden and disruptive changes.

McKinley's advisers constituted a makeshift command arrangement that evolved during the weeks preceding the outbreak of hostilities. In early March Secretary of the Navy Long created a new agency in his department, the Naval War Board, which was charged with the function of studying strategy and assisting the secretary in conducting operations. Composed of three officers, one of whom was Captain Alfred T. Mahan, the board took an active role in White House conferences and, according to army critics, came to exercise an undue influence on the president. No similar institution existed in the army. When McKinley sought counsel on land strategy, he turned to General Miles. However, an agency to advise on interservice planning was available to the president. Late in March, Alger and Long organized an Army-Navy Board, on which each service was represented by a single officer. Judged by modern standards, this command system lacked centrality and cohesion. But despite its defects, it provided a measure of coordination to the direction of the war, more than has been commonly realized.

To the navy's preparations for war McKinley gave comparatively little supervision. He trusted the abilities of Secretary Long, who was at least an adequate administrator, and the officers on the Naval War Board. But begin-ning in April he intervened constantly in the command of the army. Initially he felt compelled to act because he had increasing evidence of the incapacity of Secretary Alger to run his department efficiently. But he soon came to have an equal distrust of General Miles. The handsome and dashing general had made a good record fighting Indians, but when called upon to preside over a foreign war, he seemed out of his element. He vacillated over troop assembly points, over what training programs they should receive, and over the overseas objectives they should strike. At first he proposed that a force of 80,000 regulars invade Cuba, but not until the rainy season ended in October. This cautious plan found little favor with the president or the public, and Miles then insisted that the army's main effort be launched in Puerto Rico, 500 miles to the east of Cuba. Thereafter he was almost ignored by McKinley and spent much of his time away from Washington. The president turned for advice to former commanding general and now retired John M. Schofield, and eventu-ally to Adjutant General Henry C. Corbin, who although only a bureau chief became commanding general in all but name.

The navy had been prepared to act against Spain long before war with that country seemed probable. In 1896 officers on the faculty of the Naval War College, believing that Spain was a likely enemy, devised a strategy for the conflict. After discussing several plans, they settled on one that embodied the traditional offensive thrust of naval thinking. At the outbreak of war the navy would establish a blockade of Cuba to starve the Spanish forces on the island into submission, and simultaneously begin an attack on the squadron known to be at Manila, on Luzon Island in the Philippines. After these operations were completed, the navy could, if necessary, carry the war to the coasts of Spain itself.

None of the planners envisioned that either Cuba or the Philippines would be retained as American possessions. The blockade was to enable the army to occupy Cuba with a small force, in cooperation with the insurgents, and the attack on Manila was to deprive the Spanish fleet of a base from which to raid American commerce in the Pacific. Insofar as the planners thought in political terms, they believed that success in their offensives would force Spain to come to the peace table on American terms.

Secretary Long was apprised of the plan soon after he assumed office, and after consulting with ranking officers, he approved it. In the minds of some department officials the assault on Manila became the most important element in the strategy, either because they deemed it a military necessity or saw in it an opportunity to expand America's imperial horizons. One of them, Assistant Secretary Theodore Roosevelt, was particularly fascinated with Manila, so much so that he determined to expedite the attack on it. On February 25, a day when Long was absent from the office, Roosevelt sent a cablegram to the commander of the Asiatic Squadron, Commodore George Dewey, then cruising off the coast of China. Roosevelt's wire instructed Dewey to proceed to the British crown colony of Hong Kong, and on receiving word that the United States was at war with Spain, to undertake "offensive operations" at Manila. Long, on returning, reproved his subordinate for acting on his own initiative but permitted the order to stand, thus indicating that the government as a whole attached great importance to a strike at the Philippines.*

The navy's plan was approved by the Army-Navy Board. But the agency was not satisfied that the proposed blockade of Cuba would in itself force the Spaniards to leave the island. It recommended that a small army expedition be landed at a port on the southern coast from which supplies could be funneled to the insurgents. The board doubted that a large force would be required in Cuba, but if one was, it should not be employed there until the unhealthful rainy season ended. This suggestion accorded with the thinking of

---

*Roosevelt's wire has been widely misunderstood. It was believed at one time that he had committed the United States to act in an area where it had not intended to act, but he was clearly in line with official policy. However, he and other imperialists may have foreseen that intervention in the Philippines would lead to acquisition of the islands.

General Miles and found favor with McKinley. At this stage everybody concerned in strategic planning believed that the war, when it came, would be largely a naval affair. But the planners were not reckoning on the pressures being exerted by the National Guard lobby, which later in April would force Congress to agree to a huge volunteer army, or on the public demand to use this army against Spain.

The navy's dominant role was defined in specific detail after war was declared in late April. McKinley summoned his civilian and military advisers into strategy conferences, and out of these meetings came decisions to rely, at least for a time, on naval power alone. Admiral William T. Sampson, commander of the North Atlantic Squadron, was ordered to blockade the principal ports of Cuba, and Commodore Dewey at Hong Kong was directed to proceed to Manila and engage the Spanish fleet rumored to be in the harbor. Only one minor mission was allotted to the army. A force of 5,000 regulars was to be collected at Tampa, Florida, one of several camps in the Southern states where regulars and volunteers were being assembled, and from there to be landed briefly at a point on the southern Cuban coast to deliver supplies to the insurgents. The restricted nature of the expedition reflected the thinking of General Miles, who still insisted that the army was not yet sufficiently prepared to undertake a major operation.

This initial strategy had to be altered before it could be acted upon, one of several abrupt changes that the American planners felt compelled to make during the war. On April 29 it was learned that an enemy fleet under Admiral Pascual Cervera had left Spanish waters and was steaming westward. The strength of the squadron was not known in Washington, and its mission and destination were also uncertain. McKinley's naval advisers assumed that Cervera must command a formidable armada and that he either was coming to attack cities on the Atlantic coast or was heading for Cuba to attempt to break up the blockade. This unexpected development threw the American planners into a state of near-panic and caused them to take curious actions. First, the War Department called off the army's expedition to the Cuban coast, judging the movement unsafe if a Spanish fleet were approaching. Second, the Navy Department detached some of Sampson's blockading vessels to form a "flying squadron" under Commodore Winfield S. Schley to protect the eastern coast against the same fleet, thereby violating the Mahanian principle of concentration. All of this was done on the flimsiest of information. Cervera's mighty armada existed mainly in American imaginations. It actually consisted of but four armored cruisers, all of them only partly armed, and was no match for Sampson's squadron. The Spaniard's destination was Cuba, and his mission was entirely defensive; the Madrid government was sending him west in a pathetic hope that he might be able to help the army hold the island against the Americans.

While the American navy was scanning the Atlantic for Cervera's ships and the government was fumbling to readjust its strategy, a silence dropped over the Pacific theater. The calm was soon and sensationally shattered. Over the international cable came the news that on May 1 Commodore Dewey had steamed into Manila Bay and in a battle lasting only a few hours had destroyed the entire Spanish fleet. The country went wild with joy.

Dewey had left Hong Kong immediately on receipt of his orders, leading four armored cruisers and three smaller armed vessels. In an expectant mood, the commodore predicted that his ships would "make short work of the Spanish squadron." His confidence was not misplaced. From information supplied by American officials previously resident in the Philippines, Dewey had learned that the defending fleet was grossly unequal to his own. In the harbor were seven Spanish vessels classified as fighting craft, but their strength was deceptive. Only two of the ships, light cruisers, were armored; the remaining ones were antique wooden hulks. The Spanish mounted only thirty-one guns to Dewey's fifty-three heavier pieces. The Spanish admiral realized his inferiority and was resigned to defeat—but he felt he had to fight to sustain his and his nation's honor.

Dewey entered the harbor on the night of April 30, his ships easily evading the few shots directed at them by shore batteries. At dawn the next day the commodore led the flotilla toward the line of waiting Spanish vessels, his flagship *Olympia* in the van. As the American ships came within range, Dewey gave an order to his captain that became one of the popularly quoted slogans of the war: "You may fire when ready, Gridley." Shots from all the American ships followed the opening volley, the vessels moving westward and then retracing their course to maintain an incessant fire. The Spaniards returned the fire but without doing any apparent damage to Dewey's fleet. Nor could the commodore determine at first whether he had hurt the enemy. Dense smoke from the black powder used in the American guns hung over the scene and obscured vision. When it lifted, a welcome sight greeted Dewey's eyes. All seven of the Spanish ships had been sunk or were disabled, while the Americans were barely scratched. A later count disclosed that more than 400 Spaniards had been killed or wounded, as compared with only one American death, an engineer who died of heat stroke, and six men wounded. There was justice in the verdict of an English historian that Manila Bay was "a military execution rather than a real contest."

The victory elevated Dewey to the status of a national hero. Babies, horses, shirtwaists, hats, chewing gum ("Dewey's chewies"), and scores of other items were named after him, and a grateful government promoted him to the rank of admiral. The hero was, however, in a somewhat uncertain military position. There was no immediate danger from the Spaniards; he had silenced the land batteries that sniped at him by threatening to fire on the city, and he held the port under blockade. His problem was that he did not know what to do with his victory; his only instruction had been to reduce the Spanish fleet. He assumed that the government wished him to capture Manila City, the metropolis of the islands, but he realized that this task was beyond him, that a land force would be required to deal with the 10,000 or so Spanish troops reported to be in and around the city. He therefore cabled Washington asking that 5,000 men be sent out to cooperate with the navy. While awaiting their arrival, he provided material assistance to the principal insurgent leader, Emilio Aguinaldo, who was conducting guerrilla operations before the city.*

DEWEY'S VICTORY caused McKinley and his advisers to consider adopting a more aggressive strategy. From this easy success they realized they had overestimated the fighting capacity of the Spanish navy, that in planning operations in the Atlantic-Caribbean theater they had been too impressed by the threat of Cervera's still undiscovered squadron. Other factors also pushed the planners to think in bolder terms. The blockade was working hardships on the navy, wearing down both ships and men, and it was not having the anticipated effect of breaking Spanish resistance. Another presumption was also being proved false—the insurgents were making little headway against the Spaniards and obviously could not be relied upon to do the land fighting. Naval officers demanded of the president and the War Department that army forces be sent in to occupy one or more ports and thus relieve the navy of part of its burden. Even more insistent than pressure from the navy was the swelling clamor coming from the volunteer units and their political supporters that these brave citizen soldiers be given an opportunity to prove their fighting worth.

Impressed by these considerations, McKinley called another round of strategy conferences in early May. These discussions concerned mainly the possibility of organizing an invasion of Cuba. Encouraging information came from the commander of the Fifth Corps of regulars at Tampa, General William R. Shafter, who had been slated to head the aborted expedition to run in supplies to the rebels. Shafter reported his 15,000 troops ready for action and said that he could move quickly to seize a point on the coast to serve as a base for future operations. Emboldened to strike decisively, McKinley and his planners decided to attack the heart of Spanish resistance, the capital city of Havana on the northwestern coast. Shafter's corps was designated to form the vanguard of the offensive and to capture a port town near Havana. Once the base was secure, other regular units and some volunteer troops would be sent in, building up the force to a strength of 50,000 or perhaps 70,000 men. General Miles was to take command of the expedition and lead it against Havana.

*In urging the capture of Manila, Dewey had in mind only military objectives—securing a base for the fleet and a bargaining counter at the peace table.

The proposed commander was the only planner to dissent from the plan. Miles argued that in attacking Havana the army would be taking on the Spaniards in their strongest position. He recommended the proposed expedition be diverted to Puerto Rico; after reducing that island it could land on the eastern coast of Cuba and advance inland against weaker opposition. McKinley and Alger, becoming increasingly irritated with the general's fluctuations, brusquely overruled him.

Shafter was not able to launch his expedition at the promised time. Pleading that he needed more men and equipment, he delayed in Tampa. While he was still preparing, startling news arrived in Washington. The navy had at last located Cervera's squadron. Defying all the physical odds against them, the slow and inferior Spanish ships had crossed the Atlantic undetected by the American navy and entered the Caribbean Sea. Cervera was first sighted near Martinique on May 13, but he disappeared again. On May 19 he led his ships into the harbor of Santiago on the southern coast of Cuba, thankful to have found at least a temporary refuge. Not until ten days later did the Americans definitely establish his presence at Santiago. Then the combined squadrons of Sampson and Schley took up blockading positions off the harbor.

The information that Cervera was in the Caribbean and obviously heading for the southern coast of Cuba caused one of those disruptive changes that characterized the making of American strategy in the war. The planners suspended the attack on Havana and decided to direct Shafter's corps to Santiago. The force was to be landed at a point on the coast near the port, whence it would attack and aid the navy in destroying Cervera's squadron. After this was accomplished, the corps, reinforced by troops from the Southern camps, would proceed to occupy Puerto Rico. The offensive against Havana was postponed until autumn, when the War Department hoped to assemble another expedition to sail from the mainland. In making its arrangements for the Santiago movement, the War Department almost ignored Miles. The expedition was to be completely under the control of Shafter.

Shafter's Fifth Corps at Tampa was one of eight similar units that the War Department was organizing in hastily established Southern mobilization points. In selecting camps in the South, the War Department was guided by a simple principle—it seemed sensible to place troops presumably destined for Cuba in that part of the United States nearest to the island. Judged by these standards of proximity, Tampa seemed to be an ideal jumping-off site. A developing resort city of 26,000 on Florida's west coast, it lay less than 400 nautical miles from Havana and other possible objectives on Cuba's northwestern coast.

When Santiago was substituted for Havana as the army's first objective, Tampa lost some of its advantage of nearness. An expedition to the southern coast of the island could have been embarked from one of several Atlantic ports without having to travel a much greater distance. However, the War

Department gave no consideration to operating from any base but Tampa, partly because the Fifth Corps was already assembled there, the sole corps that was anywhere near battle fitness. In addition, army officials were still entranced with the idea that an invasion of Cuba could be launched most easily from a nearby Florida base, and Tampa was the only one available. They convinced themselves and their superiors that the Tampa facilities were adequate to support the embarkation of a large force. Theirs was one of the most incredible miscalculations of the war, and one that had distressing consequences.

The staff planners were correct in assuming that there would be no difficulty in subsisting troops at Tampa. The city was connected by rail routes to the north, and supplies for the base could be easily shipped down. But Tampa was merely a staging site in the operation. Supplies and then troops had to be moved thence to the sole point of embarkation available, Port Tampa, located nine miles to the south and linked to the city by only a single-track railroad. And to complicate the problem, Port Tampa possessed just two wharves, each of which could accommodate but two ships at a time. This frail line of communication was adequate to embark a small unit, such as the 5,000-man column that originally had been assigned to raid the Cuban coast. But it was sadly unequal to conveying the levies that the government poured into Tampa, regiments of regulars and volunteers that brought the total force up to 25,000 men. The effort to move this mass and its supplies through the bottleneck to Port Tampa turned into a nightmare.

The War Department's order to Shafter to move on Santiago reached the general on May 31. Already burdened with the task of organizing his augmented force, Shafter and his staff had to turn their efforts to the harder job of launching the expedition. The attempt was attended by scenes of wild confusion. Freight cars loaded with supplies were stacked up around Tampa, but nobody knew which supplies were on which cars because the invoices and bills of lading had not been received. A typical incident was reported by General Miles, after inspecting preparations: "Fifteen cars loaded with uniforms and ammunition were side-tracked twenty-five miles away from Tampa, and remained there for weeks while the troops were suffering for clothing. Five thousand rifles, which were discovered yesterday, were needed by several regiments."

Sorting out the equipment was only the beginning of the ordeal that awaited officers and staff. All the varied gear of a corps, including artillery pieces, had to be transported to Port Tampa on the single line of railroad, and the troops were carried in the same way. The movement turned into a massive traffic jam. Freight cars were backed up for miles and delayed for hours. Further delay occurred at the port. The mountain of supplies had to be unloaded and reloaded by hand onto the thirty-one transport vessels that the Quartermaster Department had leased from private owners. The troops were allowed to go on board in whatever order they arrived at the wharves. In view of the monumental disorder attending the confusion, it was a minor miracle that the expedition was ready to sail on June 8. But before it could take off, the War Department canceled the departure, on the basis of a navy report that Spanish cruisers were lurking in the area. The troops remained in the hot confines of the transports until the report was exposed as false. Not until June 14 did the transports and their naval convoy set forth on the voyage that would lead across the northern coast of Cuba and to Santiago.

Before embarking, Shafter discovered that the transports could not accommodate his entire corps. Therefore, he took with him what he considered the elite troops, all the regular regiments, two volunteer regiments, and one volunteer dismounted cavalry regiment known as the Rough Riders. (This last unit would win more newspaper attention in Cuba than all the other units combined, primarily because its colorful lieutenant colonel, Theodore Roosevelt, late of the Navy Department, was an expert in attracting attention.) The remaining volunteers stayed in Tampa, along with tons of supplies that would have overloaded the transports. Sailing for Santiago were approximately 17,000 officers and men, the largest military expedition that had ever left the United States.*

As the expedition plowed through the Caribbean waters, its commander pondered the problems he would face on landing. Shafter owed his position largely to seniority. Sixty-two years of age in 1898, he had first seen service as a volunteer officer in the Civil War. Remaining in the regular army, he fought against the Indians and held various garrison commands. He also became grossly fat, carrying three hundred pounds on a frame that was less than six feet in height. Irreverent observers called him "the floating tent," and one of his officers admitted he "couldn't walk two miles in an hour." Shafter had proved competent in every command that he had held, possessing great determination and strength of will. His most serious shortcoming was his lack of experience in handling troops in numbers; his largest previous command had been only a regiment.

The War Department allowed Shafter a wide latitude in determining his objective after landing. He could debark either east or west of Santiago as his judgment dictated and from his chosen point move onto the high ground overlooking the harbor or into the interior, taking whichever route would best enable him to capture the enemy fleet. Once he had secured Santiago, Shafter could remain there or transfer his force to Puerto Rico.

In allowing such an equivocal order, President McKinley was guilty of

---

*A somewhat larger number of troops served in Mexico during the war with that country. But these men had not departed from the United States as one force. Technically, the Mexican War was America's first overseas conflict in that some troops were transported by water to Vera Cruz. But the Spanish-American War was the first struggle to be waged in territory not contiguous to the United States.

a dereliction in command. The looseness of the language invited dispute between the army and the navy. The Navy Department and naval officers assumed that the sole reason for sending an army expedition was to enable Admiral Sampson to enter the harbor and attack the Spanish fleet. Therefore, the navy expected the army to assail the fortifications at the harbor's entrance and open the way to Sampson's ships. But the War Department's directive to Shafter allowed him the option of moving directly on Santiago, and in effect to ignore the wishes of the navy. Shafter, in fact, interpreted his orders as authorizing him to conduct a land campaign that would result in occupying eastern Cuba. The success of the campaign depended on interservice cooperation, but the services were not disposed to work in unison. And the only authority that could have enforced agreement, the president, was reluctant to impose his will.

Shafter's transports dropped anchor off Santiago on June 20. On the voyage out, the general studied possible plans of operation, and after arriving and conferring with Admiral Sampson and insurgent leaders, he came to a decision. He rejected Sampson's urging to land near the entrance to the harbor and storm the guarding works because this tactic would involve too great a loss of life. Instead, he proposed to debark at Daquiri, east of the bay, and move inland on Santiago itself. Seizing high ground east and north of the city and mounting artillery, he would command both the town and the harbor and force Cervera's fleet to run out to sea and into the hands of the waiting American squadron. Sampson argued against the movement but had no choice except to bow to Shafter's wishes.

The landing got under way on June 22, following naval shelling of the shore area to flush out unseen but presumed-to-be-present Spaniards. Scenes of confusion reminiscent of the Tampa departure delayed the operation. First, it was discovered that the Quartermaster Department had neglected to provide sufficient lighters to move the troops and supplies from the transports to the beach. Next, the captains of the private transports refused to bring their vessels close inshore, pleading possible damage from enemy fire. Finally the navy, realizing that without its help the troops might never get ashore, agreed to take over the landing. Sampson furnished a number of steam launches that pulled to the beach lines of small boats tied together. Most of the troops were debarked at Daquiri and the remaining units farther west at Siboney. The operation required four days to complete, and in its lack of coordination stood in unfavorable contrast to General Scott's landing of an only somewhat smaller army in one day in the Mexican War. If the Spaniards had chosen to fight, they undoubtedly could have inflicted heavy losses on the masses of troops struggling ashore. But probably out of fear of the naval guns, they chose to make their defense farther inland.

Shafter ordered his units to concentrate around Siboney, which he decided would be his main base of operations. From here he intended to push westward toward a series of ridges known as San Juan Hill that commanded the approaches to Santiago. In explaining his strategy, he said he simply meant to "rush it." He was oppressed by a fear that the tropical climate of Cuba would cause widespread disease in his army and wanted to complete his operation as soon as possible. While he was perfecting his plans and was still aboard ship, some of his advance units at Siboney tried to rush matters on their own, attacking without orders a Spanish outpost at Las Guasimas on the road to Santiago. In this rash little action the Americans forced the enemy to give way but suffered proportionately severe casualties. Back in the United States newspaper readers thrilled to accounts of the first land "battle" of the war.

The news prompted Shafter to come up to the front to take personal command of his forces. After hastily examining the terrain, he announced a plan that he promised would result in capturing Santiago in a day or so. Although his purpose was to break through the defenses on the San Juan heights, he proposed to begin the battle by attacking the fortified village of El Caney, two miles to the north, with 7,000 men. As soon as this division was engaged, 8,000 more troops were to advance on San Juan Hill. Shafter thought that El Caney, held by only 500 Spaniards, would fall quickly. The victors here would then swing south to join the right wing of the main assault force. Shafter anticipated little resistance at San Juan, which according to his intelligence branch was defended by only a small force. (For once, his staff was right, only about 2,000 Spaniards held the hill.) The general expected his combined column to brush the defenders aside and enter Santiago in triumph.*

The attack opened at dawn on July 1. Nothing went as Shafter had planned. The Spanish defenders at El Caney, armed with repeating rifles and fighting with tenacity, held off the Americans for nine hours. The attackers finally secured the village but too late in the day to join the main force moving on San Juan Hill. This column also encountered heavy resistance and did not carry the crest of the hill until late in the afternoon. In large part the Americans fought a small-unit battle, individual officers sending in men as their judgment dictated; General Shafter, prostrated by heat in the rear zone of the battle, gave little direction to the fighting. Officers and troops performed bravely and skillfully, but the American triumph was primarily the result of superior numbers. And it was only a partial victory. Shafter had not captured Santiago. At the end of the day the Spaniards retired to an inner defense line on the outskirts of the city.

The Americans had incurred over 1,000 casualties, most of them wounded. Although this was not an excessive total in relation to the number engaged, the result appalled many officers. Colonel Theodore Roosevelt, who

---

*Approximately 12,000 Spanish troops were in and around Santiago. However, they were disposed along an extensive defense perimeter. Some were detached to counter a diversionary move by a brigade that Shafter launched toward the fort at the eastern entrance to the bay.

had been in the forefront of the charge up San Juan Hill, wrote gloomily to a friend: "We are within measurable distance of a terrible military disaster." Also depressed was General Shafter, for reasons other than the losses in the battle. He observed that increasing numbers of his men were succumbing to sickness and that his ranks were thinning daily. Doubting that he possessed sufficient force to storm the Spanish second line of defense, he cabled the War Department for permission to withdraw closer to Siboney to await additional supplies and possible reinforcements. Secretary Alger, admonishing that a backward movement would have a bad "effect upon the country," replied that the general must hold his present position.

Not knowing anything else to do, Shafter turned to the navy for help. He asked Admiral Sampson to force an entrance into the harbor, promising that the army would at the same time move on the city. Sampson refused to act, claiming, as he had before, that his vessels could not safely penetrate the harbor until the army reduced the forts at its mouth. The two commanders wrangled in conferences without coming to a decision while McKinley remained aloof from the controversy. On July 3 Sampson took ship for Siboney to engage in another round in the discussions. Near shore, he heard a gun boom out at sea, and looking back he saw a sight that caused him to order his engines reversed. To the westward Cervera's squadron was emerging from the harbor of Santiago and heading for open waters.

Neither Shafter nor Sampson had realized the desperate condition of the Spaniards after the recent battle. The defending troops had suffered heavy casualties, in greater proportion than the Americans, and food and other supplies were running dangerously low. The Spanish commander, Jose Toral, had cabled his superior in Havana that his position was fast becoming "untenable" and that he might have to evacuate the city. Faced by this grim prospect, the Havana authorities ordered Cervera to leave the harbor and run for the open sea. What they expected him to do when he got out was not clear. Even if he escaped the American ships, he would eventually have to seek haven in another Cuban port, where he would be bottled up again. There is evidence to suggest that the authorities thought they had to order Cervera out as a gesture to national honor and that they knew he would be caught once he emerged from the harbor. That, at least, was the interpretation that Cervera and his officers placed upon the order. They assumed they were going to their doom.

As the four Spanish cruisers, accompanied by two smaller vessels, broke out of the harbor, they were sighted by spotters on the American ships, who sounded the alarm. Commodore Schley, realizing he was in temporary command, hoisted signals to follow his flagship in pursuit of the cruisers now running westward along the coast. The ensuing action, like the earlier one at Manila, was more of an execution than a battle. Although the American squadron was not at full strength—two vessels were off station and Sampson's ship was still miles to the rear—the remaining battleships and cruisers were superior in every way to Cervera's craft, in firepower, weight of arms, and speed. In a running fight of less than four hours the Americans destroyed all six Spanish ships, crippling them with shot and forcing them to run on shore as blazing hulls. American officers observed the devastation with satisfaction but also with pity. As one battleship went by a burning enemy cruiser, its captain cautioned his men: "Don't cheer, boys, the poor devils are dying." The Americans went to considerable effort to pick up survivors, and Cervera and other officers were received by the victors with great courtesy.

Admiral Sampson did not arrive on the scene until the battle had ended. Noting the approach of his superior, Schley signaled: "We have gained a great victory." Sampson, who did not like Schley, returned a curt reply: "Report your losses."* Schley had almost no losses to report, one man killed and two wounded (the Spaniards suffered over 400 casualties), and he had spoken truly in claiming a great victory. American naval power was now supreme in the Caribbean.

The importance of the naval victory was not lost on Shafter. Reasoning that the Spanish officers and troops in Santiago must be disheartened at the loss of their fleet, he summoned General Toral to surrender or endure a bombardment of the city. Toral knew the end was near, and he indicated an interest in negotiating terms. However, he held back on making a final decision, hoping to wring concessions from Shafter. In the end, both sides had to concede something. Toral agreed to surrender his garrison and all Spanish troops in eastern Cuba, a total of about 22,000 men. Shafter, with War Department approval, pledged that the United States would transport the prisoners back to Spain. On July 17 the American army marched into Santiago, and Shafter received the formal surrender of the city from Toral. The war was not over yet, but there would be no more fighting in Cuba. The Spanish government recognized that in the face of American naval command in the Caribbean it could do nothing to succor its troops in Havana and other posts.

Soon after Shafter landed in Cuba, the War Department agreed to let General Miles organize an expedition to occupy Puerto Rico, the objective that had intrigued his interest since the beginning of the war. At the start Miles was allowed only 3,400 troops, which he was to collect on the southern coast of Cuba; reinforcements were promised after he reached Puerto Rico. The decision to strike at another Spanish possession had McKinley's approval, and reflected the growing influence of the imperialists in the administration. These men advanced seductive reasons for acquiring Puerto Rico—the island would provide needed bases for the navy, would become a rich colony, and would constitute a deserved reward to the United States for freeing Cuba. McKinley

---

*This exchange marked the beginning of a controversy between the two officers and their partisans that raged for years and concerned the conduct of both men before and after the battle.

was becoming increasingly receptive to arguments that justified widening the war. "While we are conducting war . . . we must keep all we get," he remarked. "When the war is over we must keep what we want."

Miles sailed from Cuba on July 21. Landing on the south coast of Puerto Rico, he established a base and awaited his promised reinforcements. Over 10,000 troops reached him within three weeks, their expeditious arrival showing that the War Department bureaus had learned a great deal about transporting men and supplies. Thus strengthened, Miles advanced inland against virtually no opposition. Those Spaniards who did not surrender or were not captured retired to the capital of San Juan. In nineteen days Miles secured all the island except the capital. Before he could move on it, word arrived that Spain had asked the United States for peace.

WHILE MCKINLEY and his advisers were studying plans to attack Cuba, they were also considering the request of Admiral Dewey that 5,000 troops be sent to the Philippines to aid him in taking Manila. There was no opposition in the councils to sending troops. Dewey could not remain indefinitely before Manila, nor could he seek access to another port in the Far East, all of which were closed to him under international law. Unless he was given sufficient force to capture Manila, he would have to return home, a seeming retiral and a repudiation of his victory that was certain to enrage the public.

The question that occupied McKinley and the planners was how large a force to send out. Dewey reported that 10,000 Spanish troops were in Manila, and he indicated that the native insurgents who were "hemming in" the city were not completely sympathetic to the American presence. In the light of this information the administration decided that the 5,000-man force asked for by Dewey was insufficient to do the job required of it. They increased the number to 10,000 and finally to 20,000. The expedition was to be assembled at San Francisco and other Pacific coast ports and to consist predominantly of volunteer regiments from the Western states, plus a few regiments of regulars. Designated as the Eighth Corps, the force was to be commanded by General Wesley Merritt, a sixty-three-year-old Civil War veteran who was second in seniority in the regular army to Miles. Unlike most generals in the war, Merritt was a graduate of West Point.

Merritt met with McKinley several times to discuss the objectives of his mission. He was particularly concerned that the president would not indicate whether he desired the expedition merely to capture Manila or to occupy all the islands. In political and business circles and in many quarters of the public demands were being made that the United States annex the Philippines, either to acquire a valuable colony or to compensate itself for the cost of the war. McKinley seemed sympathetic to the imperialistic chorus, but he refused to commit himself to anybody, including Merritt, who favored annexation. The president's final letter of instruction stated merely that the expedition's purpose was that of "completing the reduction of the Spanish power in that quarter and of giving order and security to the islands while in the possession of the United States." The language could be read to mean much or little.

Departing for San Francisco, Merritt prepared his corps to sail within a relatively short time. A much better administrator than Shafter, he gave minute attention to coordinating every part of his operation, and the embarkation began with none of the confusion that had delayed the departure from Tampa. The vanguard left on May 25, the first American troops to sail for a destination beyond the western hemisphere, and reached Manila on June 30. Other contingents followed in scheduled progression, and by the end of July Merritt had about 11,000 troops landed in the vicinity of Manila. Later arrivals would build up his force to over 15,000.

On landing, Merritt's troops took a position behind the lines of the Filipino insurgent army of some 12,000 under Emilio Aguinaldo, who had proclaimed himself general and leader of the movement for independence. Merritt's orders enjoined him not to cooperate with the insurgents or to recognize their cause. He consequently had to tread a difficult course, to take Manila with the aid of Dewey's fleet and to deny the Filipinos a share in the victory without antagonizing them. Aguinaldo, for his part, hoped to use the Americans to further his goal of independence.

With the arrival of the American troops, the Spanish commander in Manila, Fermin Jaudenes, realized that his position was hopeless. He had only 13,000 poorly armed troops, he was short of vital supplies, and he was cut off from reinforcements by Dewey's squadron. Knowing that surrender was inevitable, he preferred to yield to the Americans rather than to the Filipinos, who, he feared, would commit avenging atrocities on his troops. Consequently, he entered into secret negotiations with Merritt and Dewey, through the medium of the Belgian consul. An elaborate sham battle was arranged. Jaudenes promised that if the Americans kept the Filipinos out of the city, he would make only a token resistance and then raise a white flag, whereupon Merritt's troops would enter the inner fortification and take possession of Manila.

The charade took place on August 13. Merritt's men passed through the insurgent lines, with the reluctant consent of Aguinaldo, and moved toward the Spanish outer works, while Dewey's fleet steamed toward shore firing harmlessly. Some shots were exchanged by troops on both sides, but otherwise the operation went off as planned. American casualties were only 17 killed and 105 wounded. The Americans occupied the city and on the following day received from Jaudenes the formal surrender. None of the participants knew that two days earlier Spain and the United States had agreed to an armistice.*

---

*August 12 was August 13 in Manila, the day of the sham battle. News of the armistice did not reach the city until the sixteenth.

The fall of Santiago convinced Spain that to continue the war was hopeless. In late July the government asked France to act as an intermediary in requesting the United States to grant an armistice. The American government accepted the offer, but on terms laid down by McKinley on August 12. Spain was to relinquish sovereignty over Cuba and cede to the United States Puerto Rico and a Pacific island in the Marianas (which turned out to be Guam). She was also to evacuate immediately all her troops in islands in the West Indies. The disposition of the Philippines was to be left to negotiations at a peace conference at Paris in October. Pending the conclusion of a formal treaty, the United States was to retain possession of Manila.

The principal terms of the treaty having already been determined, the only important question confronting representatives of the two countries at Paris was the fate of the Philippines. On the eve of the conference McKinley was still undecided as to what part of the islands the United States should demand. The only instruction he gave the American delegation was to ask for Luzon, the island on which Manila was located. But he was subjected to mounting pressure to claim the whole archipelago, not only from imperialist leaders but from the public. Soundings of opinion indicated unmistakably that a majority of Americans wanted the United States to acquire the Philippines.

McKinley had few choices in the matter. The United States could hardly return the islands to Spain. If it withdrew, certain European powers, then engaged in extending their power in the Far East, might take advantage of the vacuum created and annex the islands. A third alternative was to leave the Filipinos to work out their destiny themselves, but McKinley, in common with most American leaders, thought that they did not yet have a capacity for self-government. Feeling he had no other course, the president directed his negotiators to demand cession of all the islands in return for a money payment. Spain reluctantly agreed, accepting a compensation of $20 million. The formal treaty was signed on December 10.

McKinley justified the territorial acquisitions of the treaty on philosophical grounds. The war, he told the people, "has brought us new duties and responsibilities which we must meet and discharge as becomes a great nation." He spoke more truly than he could have known. The United States did indeed have new responsibilities. It was now a colonial and a world power and was launched on a new road that would demand of it duties never hitherto borne.

INTERLUDE

1898-1917

THE CONCLUSION of the treaty at Paris brought no peace to the Philippines. Spain's cession of the islands to the United States outraged Aguinaldo and other insurgent leaders, who from their "capital" near Manila proclaimed an independent Filipino republic. Aguinaldo had created a paramilitary organization that gradually extended his control throughout most of the archipelago, and he and his followers were determined to resist American control. They had not entered on their revolution merely to exchange one foreign master for another.*

In January, 1899, when the United States formally proclaimed possession of the Philippines, there were at least 30,000 insurgent soldiers in the Manila area. Only about half of them carried rifles, however, and the force had no artillery. Scattered throughout other islands were perhaps 20,000 more armed insurgents. American strength in the islands was restricted to Manila City, held by approximately 20,000 troops under General Elwell S. Otis, who replaced Merritt in command of the Eighth Corps. The Americans were well supplied with arms, including artillery, but Otis worried that in the event of an insurgent attack he could not commit his full force. Almost half of his men were volunteers and were scheduled for early discharge.

The attack that Otis feared came in February. A probing Filipino patrol fired on an American outpost, and the clash escalated into an assault on the city itself. In fighting that lasted several days the Americans drove the insurgents back and inflicted heavy losses. It was the beginning of another war— an undeclared war that would last until 1902 and occasion more American casualties than had the conflict with Spain.

Reports from Otis and Dewey of the assault on Manila struck Washington with chilling effect. Any hope the McKinley administration may have harbored of persuading Aguinaldo to acquiesce to the cession provision of

---

*By terms of the peace treaty, Spanish garrisons evacuated their posts in the islands, and in most places the insurgents took over as the Spaniards left. At this time there were no American troops available to replace the late occupants.

the peace treaty went quickly by the board. It was painfully clear that the rebels would oppose the American occupation and, what was worse, that they might be able to prevent it. Superior forces were required to overcome the insurgency, and the government acted vigorously to provide the necessary numbers. Additional regiments of volunteers were enlisted and shipped out to the islands in the company of reinforcements of regulars. By late 1899, 47,000 troops were in the Philippines, and the flow was just beginning. In the following year American commanders had over 70,000 at their disposal.

As the objective was to occupy the whole archipelago, the army had to establish bases on all the important islands. With the aid of the navy, ports were seized on various islands south of Luzon, and contingents were put ashore to hold them. From these places and from Manila, which continued to be the principal base of operations, columns of troops fanned out to secure key population centers and to break up or capture insurgent forces. The main effort was made in Luzon, where Aguinaldo commanded the greatest concentration of Filipino strength. The rebel general chose to meet the Americans on their terms, disposing his men in large formations. In this kind of fighting, his poorly armed and imperfectly disciplined troops were no match for the Americans and suffered one defeat after another. By autumn of 1899 Aguinaldo's army had apparently disintegrated, and the leader himself had fled into hiding in the mountains of northern Luzon. Otis and other officers felt that the American victory was so complete as to end Filipino resistance. The leader of one of the pursuing columns, General Arthur MacArthur, boasted that there was "no organized insurgent force left to strike it."

American officers were also proud of the progress they were making in persuading portions of the native population to detach themselves from the rebel cause and accept American rule. With Otis's blessing, a program of pacification was instituted in conjunction with the military campaigns. The army engaged in such activities as promoting public schools, establishing public-health facilities, and encouraging judicial reform. The word "reform" was a favorite of officers pushing the pacification policy and was a key to their objectives. Although they hoped to win substantial numbers of Filipinos over to their side, they were not animated entirely by military motives. They wanted to improve the lot of the natives, to uplift or, as they would have said, to "civilize" these backward people. Their efforts were an expression of the American sense of mission, and at the end of 1899 they seemed to be paying off. Increasing numbers of Filipinos, especially those who were relatively well to do, seemed to prefer efficient and benevolent American control to the iron hand of Aguinaldo.

The comforting belief of the American generals that the insurrection had been crushed was soon proved wrong. Also wrong was their opinion that the Filipino army had disintegrated. Aguinaldo and his fellow chiefs were as determined as ever to continue fighting until independence was achieved. But they realized now that they could not meet the Americans in open battle or in large formations. Consequently, they resolved on a major change in strategy —they would resort to guerrilla warfare conducted by small, dispersed bands. The perceived disappearance of the insurgent army was only a redistribution of its strength into irregular units. The rebel leaders had learned something about guerrilla tactics in resisting Spain, and they had apparently learned more from studying the methods of other guerrillas, such as the Cubans. Whatever the source of their knowledge, the leaders had a sound understanding of irregular warfare. They instructed their followers to avoid pitched battles but to subject the Americans to unceasing harassment—to attack small detachments and patrols, taking advantage of the jungle terrain they knew so well and relying always on the element of surprise. It was thought that this kind of warfare sustained for years would tire out the Americans and force them to leave.

As one element in their tactics, the insurgents employed a practice that would become standard in later guerrilla movements—terrorism. They terrorized both their own people and the invaders. In preying on their fellows, the insurgents had a double objective. They were determined to discourage any Filipinos who might be disposed to cooperate with the Americans, but more important, they wanted to demonstrate to people in a particular area that they ruled that area, that they could destroy inhabitants and villages which did not support the revolution. The most favored terroristic device was assassination of local leaders. During 1900 over three hundred political killings were carried out, usually in a manner calculated to horrify all beholders, by beheading the victims or burying them alive.

The motives of the insurgents in using terrorism against American military personnel were harder to fathom. Perhaps they felt they would so shock the invaders that they would leave the islands or, failing this, would be intimidated into remaining in their garrison posts. More probably, the guerrillas acted out of consuming hatred. They killed with primal abandon, their work facilitated by the bolo knives that many of them bore instead of rifles, and they delighted in mutilating the bodies of their victims. An American observer of the remains of one massacre wrote: "Captain Connell's head was slow-roasting in a fire. His body, naked and mutilated, was found crammed into the garrison latrine. A bolo slash across the face of Lt. Bumpus had been filled with strawberry jam. One of the Americans . . . had his abdomen slashed open and someone had dumped a sack of flour in the cavity."

The insurgent resort to guerrilla warfare set back American hopes of an early and victorious end to the war. Indeed, as the struggle wore on throughout the first half of 1900, some American officers feared the balance might be tipping in favor of the rebels. A large number of villages was under guerrilla control, providing havens from which the irregular fighters could issue and then fade back into hiding. American officers and troops felt they were under a form of siege in a land of enemies, and their sense of peril was heightened because they could never be sure who among the population was hostile. An apparently friendly peasant might turn in an instant into a murderer.

One result of the guerrilla war was to push the Americans into adopting harsher methods themselves, matching cruelty with cruelty, as their ancestors had responded in fighting Indians. This reaction was also an expression of the frustration that officers and men felt in their failure to end the war, in their inability to find a foe to strike at. Increasing numbers of them came to feel that almost all Filipinos were enemies and should be dealt with as enemies. One colonel predicted that the occupiers would be driven to employing "the Spanish method of dreadful general punishments on a whole community for the acts of its outlaws which the community shields and hides." His prophecy proved true in some areas, officers not hesitating to burn settlements suspected of harboring insurgents. The Americans also developed their own methods of terror. One was the torture of villagers to force them to reveal the whereabouts of guerrillas and their supplies; the most favored form of persuasion was the "water cure," in which the liquid was forced into the stomach of a person until he gasped out the desired information. In turning to retributive war, the Americans did not wholly abandon the program of pacification, but for a time they subordinated it. In its stead many soldiers preferred a policy summarized in a popular line: "Civilize 'em with a Krag."

Although American officers were frustrated by the guerrilla resistance, most of them remained confident that the rebellion could be subdued. Especially hopeful was Arthur MacArthur, who had replaced Otis in command in 1900. MacArthur led a large force, 70,000 troops, and he settled on a plan of operations. He believed that success depended upon the Americans' being able to isolate the guerrillas from their support in the villages. To accomplish this end, he proposed an extensive garrison system. Over five hundred posts were established throughout the islands, located in every important population center and strategic point. The natives around each post were ordered to move into a marked area that could be protected by the garrison; if they did not, their property was liable to destruction to prevent it from falling into the hands of the guerrillas.

Operating from the garrison posts, the Americans maintained a persistent offensive pressure on the guerrillas, following them into every recess and allowing them no rest. To facilitate the search, the pursuers employed native scouts who knew the terrain, as General Crook had earlier used Apaches to track down other Apaches. Harassed constantly and cut off from their former village havens, the guerrillas were unable to sustain their organization, and either broke up into tiny bands or simply gave up and went home. Aguinaldo himself was captured in 1901 by a party of Americans and native scouts who penetrated his camp, and on being returned to Manila, he issued a proclamation calling for peace. Increasing numbers of Filipinos were demanding the same end and announcing their willingness to accept American rule. Scattered resistance continued in isolated areas, but by the summer of 1902 the insurrection was essentially ended.

The struggle with the Filipinos was the first American guerrilla war since the Second Seminole War. The army in the islands finally won out over its opposition, as the army in Florida had eventually defeated the Indians. In the Philippines the Americans demonstrated more skill and imagination in devising tactics to deal with guerrillas than had their predecessors in Florida. However, the troops of Otis and MacArthur would have experienced vastly more trouble except for two advantages: the enemy had to operate in a restricted area, in isolated islands, and was prevented by the navy from importing weapons and other needed supplies; and, although the insurgents attempted to enlist help in Japan, no outside power intervened. These conditions would not prevail in some later guerrilla conflicts.

IN ACQUIRING THE PHILIPPINES the United States became a Pacific power. Enjoying longtime trade relations with the Far East, the nation now had to concern itself with the complexities of Oriental politics. The most immediate American concern was the ancient but enfeebled empire of China, on which the imperialistic nations of Europe and imperialistic Japan were casting covetous eyes. The outside powers desired to partition China into "spheres of influence," areas in which they could force the Chinese government to grant them special economic privileges. Fearing that partitioning would shut out American traders, the United States attempted to uphold an "open door" policy, giving all nations equal rights in any sphere. In an indirect way the American government was saying that it desired to maintain the territorial integrity of China.

In 1900 Chinese resentment against outside exploitation took a violent turn. A secret society known to Westerners as the Boxers organized to expel the aliens and, with the covert support of the government, killed a number of Christian missionaries and foreign diplomats. Those individuals who escaped fled to the British embassy in Peking, which was defended by a small force of retainers from other foreign legations. Immediately laid under siege by the Boxers, the diplomats and other persons in the embassy seemed destined for slaughter. Alarmed at this prospect, the nations with interests in China decided to send a relief expedition to Peking.

The United States, with large forces conveniently nearby in the Philippines, contributed troops to the reserve column, a total of 2,500 soldiers and marines. Although the government was concerned for the safety of American citizens in Peking, it participated primarily in order to secure a voice in the settlement of the episode, to be able to speak for U.S. interests in China. Seven other nations, also intent on serving their interests, provided additional troops, bringing the strength of the expedition up to 19,000. By August it had fought its way to Peking and raised the siege, whereupon the Chinese government asked for peace. During the negotiations the United States pressed the other powers to accept a money indemnity rather than to demand territorial concessions, and finally won their assent. The "open door" was apparently still open.

American participation in the relief expedition was a military first—the first time since the Yorktown campaign in the Revolution that the United States had engaged in an allied operation. More important, it was a military-diplomatic innovation—the debut of the nation on the stage of world politics, a new actor entering somewhat hesitantly into an old drama.

IN ASSUMING even a limited role in global affairs, the United States was acknowledging that it had important interests transcending its own boundaries. The admission represented more than a simple repudiation of physical insularity. It was, rather, the expression of an evolving popular consciousness that the United States was being forced into closer relationship with other nations, that as an imperial and colonial power it had to venture into new areas of foreign involvement. Or put in the language of the military historian, Americans for the first time in their history realized, however imperfectly, that they had a national policy, and that to execute it, they needed a national strategy.

The outlines of a strategy were visible in 1900, and details were filled in during the early years of the century. Some of the elements were as old or almost as old as the republic itself. Thus, defense of the continental mainland remained a cardinal principle; indeed, in the thinking of most military men, as well as in that of civilians, the ability to defend loomed in importance above all other requirements. Also inherited from the past was a conviction that the Monroe Doctrine had to be upheld, a belief that now took on added intensity because of growing American investments in Latin America. New components in the strategy were developed following the territorial acquisitions of 1898. The United States was now a Caribbean power, owning Puerto Rico, exercising a "protective" influence over Cuba, and retaining naval bases on that island, and a Pacific power, holding sway over Hawaii, part of Samoa, Guam, and the Philippines. At all times it had to be able to defend these far-flung possessions. It had also to stand behind American traders and investors who were carrying their activities not only into the Pacific colonies but into China and other lands in the Orient.

Faced with the problem of upholding American interests in distant and scattered areas, leaders developed a version of the balance-of-power policy long associated with Great Britain. They believed it was necessary for the United States to throw its influence against any nation that threatened to acquire undue ascendancy in an area in which American interests were important. Maintaining the open door in China was one application of the policy. Of all the areas involved, American concern was keenest in the Far East because of its commitment in the Philippines; in this area Russia was at first perceived to be the dangerous nation, and later, Japan. The United States had no colonial stake in Europe, but it feared the ambitions of one European nation, Germany. Already a land power and aspiring to be also a sea power, Germany was suspected of harboring dreams of overshadowing friendly Britain and possibly of planning to seize American possessions in the Caribbean.

Although political and military leaders admitted to having a national strategy, they did not consider that the commitments implied in it required the nation to alter its foreign policy. The United States, they believed, could continue to avoid entering into "entangling" alliances with other nations. American objectives were wholly defensive and could be upheld by American might alone, or, if worse came to worse, by enlisting the temporary support of a favorably disposed nation, probably that other devotee of balanced power, Great Britain.

In persuading themselves that a go-it-alone strategy was feasible, the policy makers were engaging in some romantic thinking and permitting the past to impose its influence upon the present. But they were sufficiently realistic to recognize that the United States could not defend its varied commitments with the modest military forces that had prevailed in the past. To safeguard America's new international interests, they advocated a greatly expanded navy and army.

Most political leaders who thought about strategy reflected a popular opinion when they considered the navy to be the more important of the two services, to be, in a later phrase, the nation's "first line of defense." No one accepted this idea more completely than the man who was president during the first eight years of the century, Theodore Roosevelt. A passionate "big navy" advocate, Roosevelt agreed with Admiral Dewey and other officers who wanted a fleet second to none, and pressed Congress to appropriate money to provide an armada of over forty battleships. He was not able to obtain everything he desired—many legislators balked at voting the huge sums asked for —but he got a good part. At the end of the Roosevelt era the navy contained twenty-five battleships and ten heavy cruisers and ranked in total size behind only the fleets of Britain and Germany. In modernity of equipment it would not have ranked so high. Some of its vessels were of the new "dreadnought" class introduced by the British, all big-gun ships, but others were of the old mixed-gun type. All of the fighting vessels, however, were provided with the latest advances in gunnery, telescopic sights and rangefinders that enabled ships to fire at ranges of 8,000 yards.*

*In the Spanish-American War the maximum range was only 2,000 yards.

Roosevelt soon found use for this new and improved navy in an attempt to maintain a balance of power in the Orient during the Russo-Japanese War. His primary aim was to hold Russia in check by encouraging Japan to halt her drive. But by 1905, when the Japanese had destroyed Russia's two fleets, Roosevelt became apprehensive. He did not want the Japanese to be entirely victorious, fearing that victory might "possibly mean a struggle between them and us in the future." However, the United States had no reason for immediate concern. After the victories, Japan found herself almost bankrupt and asked the president to mediate. Agreeing to the request, he called a conference at Portsmouth, New Hampshire, in 1905. Although he approved Japan's territorial gains—control over Korea and South Manchuria and the annexation of the southern half of Sakhalin Island—he opposed her demands for an enormous indemnity.

From then on, the traditionally harmonious relations between Americans and Japanese steadily worsened. Californians began to react against the annual arrival of between 500 to 1,000 immigrants from Japan. Fanned by articles in the newspapers, resentment toward Japan became intense. In October, 1906, the San Francisco school board ordered the segregation of Oriental schoolchildren. Roosevelt, however, was able to bring this situation under control. He persuaded San Francisco to desegregate its schools, and entered into the so-called gentleman's agreement with Japan whereby Tokyo promised to halt the entry of Japanese agricultural laborers into the United States.

Hoping to show sufficient naval strength to restore an unsteady balance in Asiatic waters, Roosevelt sent the navy on a 45,000-mile voyage around the world. The Japanese invited the "Great White Fleet" to visit Yokohama and gave it a warm welcome. By 1908 Japan and the United States had agreed to support the Open Door in China, negotiated the Root-Takahira Agreement, and agreed on Japan's role in Manchuria. All seemed quiet in the Pacific— at least, for the time being.

IN CONTRAST to the high-ranking status attained by the navy, the regular army remained small by European standards. Congress in 1901 established its minimum size at 60,000, allowing a maximum of only 100,000. The average size during the following ten years was never greater than about 75,000. As though recognizing that the nation might require a larger land force, the legislators attempted to improve the efficiency of the reserve behind the army, the National Guard. The Dick Act of 1903 provided a new federal supervision of the state organizations, authorizing the War Department to set up standards of training and to detail regular officers to furnish instruction. However, the supervision was more apparent than real. Washington could fix standards but could not enforce them, and as a result the quality of the militia outfits varied from state to state. The purely defensive function assigned to the Guard was reflected in a provision of the Dick Act restricting the length of its federal service to nine months.

Although small in comparison with European forces, the regular army was very large by American criteria, its authorized maximum strength of 100,000 being almost four times its numbers on the eve of the war with Spain and its average strength of 75,000 constituting the largest aggregation yet to exist in peacetime. It was by any standards well armed, boasting the most modern weapons. Recent technical developments had made the Krag-Jörgensen rifle obsolete, and the War Department equipped the infantry with a new piece called the 1903 Springfield. This weapon, patterned after the 1898 Mauser, was chambered for the new .30 caliber cartridge of even higher velocity than the .30–.40 in the Krag-Jörgensen. In all respects it was the equal of any military rifle in the world. Improvements in the artillery almost kept pace. The standard fieldpiece was a 3-inch gun that used smokeless power and employed optical rangefinders. Not quite so good as the famous "French 75," it was still the equal of guns in other European armies. In only one area of weaponry did the United States lag behind other advanced countries: the machine gun, an American invention, was in short supply in the army, not because officers did not value it, but because Congress was niggardly in appropriating money to procure this rapid-firing instrument that within a few years would dominate the Great War.

The receptivity that army officers displayed in accepting the latest weapons indicated a knowledge in the officer corps of the latest developments in the study of war itself, an awareness that was largely the result of an improved system of education. Reforms of a far-reaching import were made in that system during the first years of the century. West Point and the various service schools were retained to provide basic and tactical instruction, but one of the existing schools was given a new name and an enlarged function. The School of Application for Infantry and Cavalry at Fort Leavenworth became the General Service and Staff College and was charged with the task of training officers to command combined-arms or large units. The Staff College, as the Leavenworth institution was usually known, was also to prepare its students to enter a new and still more advanced school, the Army War College, which was quartered in Washington. The War College, receiving already educated and experienced officers, would instruct these men in strategy and command at the highest level in the field. Officers who exercised high command of any kind in the future, line or staff, were likely to have had experience in both areas as a result of a new War Department directive abolishing permanent staff assignments and requiring interchangeable staff and line service.

These developments—an enlarged regular army, federal supervision of the National Guard, and improved educational facilities—were largely the doing of Elihu Root, who was appointed secretary of war by McKinley in 1899 and who continued in the office under Roosevelt. A devoted public servant—

he later headed the State Department—Root deserves to be ranked as one of the great secretaries of war. The changes he brought about in his department and in the army were of such a magnitude and owed so much to his efforts that they have ever since borne his name, the Root reforms.

Root took over the War Department at the height of the controversy over its performance in the recently ended war with Spain, when charges of military inefficiency were reverberating throughout the country. His mission, as defined by McKinley, was to determine the cause of the wartime debacle and to recommend changes in organization that would prevent a repetition in future conflicts and would place the nation's land forces on an equal footing with those of the most advanced military states.

A careful investigator, Root read everything he could find on the conduct of the late war, including the lengthy report of the Dodge Commission, an agency that had exposed in detail the transgressions of the War Department. He also interviewed a number of younger officers, who gave him unvarnished accounts of the confusion that had marked many of the wartime operations. The accumulated findings left the secretary in a state of shock and dismay.

What troubled Root most was the lack of coordination so evident in the higher levels of command. This failure he ascribed to the fact that no agency in the army was charged with supervising the execution of "detailed plans made beforehand." Carrying his analysis further, he concluded that the army had not been really organized "for the purpose of war" but only for what he called "present utility."

Persuaded that the existing system was defective, Root considered what to put in its place. In seeking a model, he gave no attention to any arrangement in the American past, such as the excellent Union command system of 1864. He was, in fact, uninformed or misinformed on many aspects of that past, as were other individuals concerned in framing military policy in these years, and he scorned suggestions that historical experience might offer guidance to planners in the present. He conceded that in earlier wars Americans had been remarkably adept at getting up "jury-rigged, extempore" command organizations. But this genius for improvisation could not be depended upon in future wars. These would be modern conflicts that demanded a "system."

Root studied the command arrangements of European countries, particularly those of Germany and France, the leading land powers of the continent. Both had general staffs, and Root decided that this kind of organization was an important reason for their preeminence. He was reinforced in his conviction when he happened on the writings of General Emory Upton, the military scholar of the previous century. Highly impressed by the force of Upton's thinking, Root adopted most of the general's ideas: the enlarged standing army was an Uptonian contribution. Among other reforms, Upton had recommended that the United States establish a general staff on the German model, and Root took up the suggestion. However, in urging Congress to authorize a staff structure, the secretary did not ask that it duplicate the German example. The American staff, he stressed, should be "organized in our own way."*

The German system that Root thought might be adapted to American requirements was the most admired command arrangement of the time, widely believed to be responsible for the empire's victories over France and Austria in earlier wars and for its later emergence as the top military power in Europe. The heart of the system was an agency called the Great General Staff, which was presided over by a chief of staff. The Great General Staff was completely and only a planning body, occupying itself with studying and formulating strategy for war. No burden of administration rested upon it; other agencies supervised such matters as personnel and supply. Not until the outbreak of war did the staff become an active and functioning organization. Then it took over the direction of operations, acting as the combat command, and the chief of staff became general in chief, executing plans that he had helped to frame.

Root's recommendations for a staff system were enacted into law by Congress in 1903. One clause of the act abolished the office of general in chief, which Root considered to be a useless irritant in the chain of command. In the new system the principal elements were the chief of staff and the War Department General Staff. The latter agency consisted of a group of officers divided into three sections, one of which was concerned with planning strategy. The chief of staff was the immediate adviser of the secretary of war. All orders issued by the chief had to be in the secretary's name, thus ensuring that civilian control of the army would be maintained.

In structure the new American system resembled closely the German model. Both organizations were headed by a chief of staff, and the War Department General Staff seemed to be a duplicate of the Great General Staff. These were surface similarities, however. Behind the façade the American system was different in significant ways, having an unlike mission and method of operation and, more important, representing a distinctive concept of organization.

The most striking deviation was that the American chief of staff could not take the field in war as supreme combat commander, having to stay in Washington to comply with his assignment to advise the secretary of war. It was not clear that even from Washington he could command anybody. The law creating his office vested in him power to "supervise" the entire land establishment, including the line, but avoided saying he could command. Another important divergence was that the General Staff was not purely a planning agency. In addition to examining strategy, it was charged with a multitude of

---

*As indicated previously, Root had Upton's manuscript on the military policy of the United States published at government expense.

administrative duties, including the task of overseeing the bureaus of the War Department. Its powers, too, were defined in an elastic word—it was to "coordinate" the land establishment.

Supervise and *coordinate*—these were words that were coming to be used almost reverently in the world of American government, business, and education. But what did they mean when applied in the practice of war? Root never explained clearly why he chose them instead of *command* and *control.* Perhaps he simply did not understand the difference between supervision and command, a suspicion that is supported in part by his far-from-precise descriptions of how supervision would work. Or he may have wished to ensure that no officer holding the position of chief of staff could in time of peace impede a secretary as generals in chief had done in the past. In all of his arguments detailing the advantages of having a chief of staff instead of a commanding general, he seemed to be thinking only of peacetime conditions. This preoccupation invested his general staff system with a weakness. Although the setup was clearly superior to the one it had replaced, offering at least possibilities for planning and coordinating, it left the question of command in war unresolved. In failing to define the authority of the chief of staff, Root had sown seeds of trouble that would sprout in the future.

At the same time Root began to study ways to reorganize the army, ranking naval officers were mulling over improvements in their own system. Like Root, they recognized the necessity of having an agency to consider strategy and naval policy. They did not, however, conclude that a coordinating staff organization was required, nor did they seek congressional authorization of their proposed agency. Content to accept a more modest reform, these officers in 1900 persuaded Secretary John D. Long to create a body named the General Board. Consisting of the Admiral of the Navy, who was still George Dewey, and three other officers, the board was charged with the function of preparing war plans and advising the secretary on such matters as construction programs and bases. Although often referred to as a counterpart of the Root system, the naval organization was not a general staff in Root's concept. No officer in the navy compared to the chief of staff of the army, and the General Board had no supervisory power over the naval establishment. If the General Board could be compared with any other agency, it was an anemic imitation of the German Great General Staff.*

The establishment of the General Board and the General Staff suggested the possibility of joint strategic planning, and in 1903 the two secretaries acted to create an interservice agency. By executive order they organized the Joint Army and Navy Board, consisting of four principal officers of each service.

---

*Not until 1915 did Congress authorize the creation of an office in the navy similar to the chief of staff—the chief of naval operations—and this official was not provided with a staff of assistants.

Their directive charged the members to discuss and reach "common conclusions regarding all matters calling for the cooperation of the two services." This was Rootian language, but the officers, accustomed to bureaucratic jargon, were able to interpret it. They understood that they were to prepare strategic plans involving joint action of the army and the navy, and this was what they set themselves to do. Operating on the principle that the United States had to be ready to defend its mainland, its colonial possessions, and the Western Hemisphere, they devised color-coded plans to deal with probable enemies. Two plans were discussed above all others—Orange for Japan, which was thought to have designs on the Philippines, and Black for Germany, which was believed to have ambitions in the Caribbean.

All of the plans of the Joint Board were defensive in nature, being designed merely to repel attacks on the United States or on areas in which it had an interest. For this passive outlook the board was criticized, and its plans were called unrealistic. None of its designs were of much use in the World War. The critics speak with the advantage of a hindsight not available to the planners —during the early years of the century nobody dreamed that the nation would be involved in a war in Europe. National policy was completely defensive, and national strategy could be no other than it was.

ONE OF THE DEFENSIVE COMMITMENTS involved American forces in interventions in various countries of Latin America, an irony that was not perceived by national leaders, who insisted that the United States had no aggressive designs against any power. Pledged to uphold the Monroe Doctrine, the United States now saw new interests it had to uphold—ensuring its possession of Puerto Rico and suzerainty over Cuba, guarding the isthmian canal it had constructed across Panama, and protecting American and foreign economic investments in the countries to the south. The American government claimed, in fact, that under the guise of the Monroe Doctrine it could intervene in a Latin country simply to preserve order.

The American interventions occurred under both Republican and Democratic administrations, indicating a continuity of policy regardless of party, and were carried out by army and marine forces backed up by naval support. On one pretext or another expeditions, sometimes made up of several thousand men, were landed in Cuba, Santo Domingo, Haiti, and Nicaragua. These were relatively small efforts aimed at small countries, but one sizable force was directed at one of the larger Latin countries—America's immediate neighbor to the south, Mexico.

After 1910 Mexico entered on a period of internal conflict. Rival political leaders competed for influence and the office of president, using their own armed bands to achieve their ends and throwing much of the country into turmoil. Disorder also prevailed on the U.S. border, as outlaw chiefs took advantage of the absence of central authority to conduct raids into the southwestern American states. In order to deal with these incursions President William Howard Taft mobilized in Texas in 1911 the largest aggregation of troops since the Filipino insurrection, some 13,000 men of a new provisional organization called the "maneuver division."*

In 1913 Woodrow Wilson became president, and at the same time General Victoriano Huerta seized power in Mexico. Huerta and his followers shortly became involved in conflict with rival leader Venustiano Carranza and his followers, the conflict eventually enveloping the whole country. Wilson refused to recognize Huerta's government, on the grounds that its leader had not taken office in a constitutional manner—the first time that the United States had withheld recognition of a government for moral reasons. Wilson also abetted Carranza's cause with material aid, permitting him to buy arms from American suppliers. In a more direct move against Huerta, Wilson used the pretext of a clash between American sailors and Huertistan troops at Tampico in 1914 to blockade the port and to occupy Vera Cruz with 8,000 soldiers and marines. Partly because of American pressure Huerta agreed to resign, and Carranza assumed the presidency.

Carranza was barely settled in office when one of his important supporters, Francisco "Pancho" Villa, rebelled and set up his own authority in northern Mexico. Resenting Wilson's recognition of the Carranza government, Villa instigated raids on the border and finally sent a force into New Mexico that attacked an army post and killed a number of soldiers. Determined to stop the border incursions, and also to uphold Carranza, Wilson resolved to send a "punitive expedition" into Mexico to capture Villa and disperse his followers. He won Carranza's reluctant consent to let American troops enter the country.

Mobilized at Columbus, New Mexico, in 1916, the expedition comprised 15,000 troops under the command of General John J. Pershing, one of the army's rising officers. It was by American standards a formidable force, combining infantry, cavalry, and artillery and carrying such extra and modern complements as a motorized truck company, a field radio unit, and several machine-gun companies. As an additional innovation, it was accompanied by eight airplanes.

The expedition crossed the border in March, 1916, and remained in Mexico almost a year. Although it chased Villa for over 300 miles and dispersed most of his followers, the Mexican rebel remained at large. Carranza, who was also trying to catch Villa, became increasingly resentful of the presence of the foreign troops and finally insisted that they be withdrawn. The departing

---

*The largest permanent unit of the army in peacetime continued to be the regiment. However, the War Department was experimenting with larger units of combined arms, and the maneuver division was one of these self-contained groups.

Americans could take with them the satisfaction that they had ended the possibility of serious border incidents.

The Mexican adventure demonstrated a new American policy. The government, speaking through the president, had for the first time indicated that it considered the nature of another government, its goodness or its badness, to be a ruling factor in determining policy. And it had moved with boldness against the power that was deemed evil. The commander of the punishing American column, General Pershing, would shortly be called upon to lead a mightier force against a nation that to Americans seemed the incarnation of evil.

CHAPTER XIV

The World War:
Origins and the American
Reaction

I N 1917 THE UNITED STATES became involved in a war that had broken out in Europe three years before and raged unabated since. Americans had never been in a war like this one, nor, indeed, had any other people. It was an immense struggle of global proportions. Originating in Europe, it spread ultimately to other areas and drew in finally twenty-eight countries.* The principal campaigns were fought in Europe, but operations were also mounted in the Middle East, Africa, and China, and the navies of the leading powers clashed on all the oceans. The people of the time, awed by the scope of the struggle, called it the World War, or the Great War, believing that in magnitude it would never be equaled. But only two decades after it ended, an even greater and more nearly universal war erupted, and participants, as though unable to conceive of a more descriptive title, called their struggle World War II. The earlier contest thereupon became World War I, and has so remained.

World War I has received much less attention in military literature than its successor. The relative lack of emphasis is understandable in American writing, because the participation of the United States in I was short and limited in comparison with the mighty endeavor put forth in II. The reasons for this neglect in other countries are not so apparent. Although not as encompassing as World War II, World War I was nonetheless a momentous event, influencing the future course of European history and, though to a lesser

---

*Not all the nations officially involved in the war put forward a military effort. For example, a number of Latin American countries declared war on Germany at the request of the United States, but did not participate directly in the conflict.

degree, of American history. The greatest conflict since the Civil War, it was even more engrossing, demanding a supreme effort of the powers principally involved. World War I was the first total war.

Totality, or mass effort, is apparent in almost any aspect of the war that one studies. Frequently cited as a prominent example is the mobilization of manpower by the principal participants, the huge armies dramatically dwarfing those in previous conflicts that were called into being and sustained for years. Thus, in 1914, in the opening battles, 1 million Frenchmen advanced to meet 1.5 million Germans on the "Western Front" in France. And the outpouring was only a beginning. Within the next two years on this front France and her ally England built up their forces to 3 million, and Germany assembled and consistently maintained over 2 million, growing in 1918 to 3.5 million. The United States, after entering the war in 1917, assembled an army of 3.5 million and transported more than 2 million of these overseas to France, a total twice as large as the number serving in the Union armies during the Civil War.*

The raising of these hosts was a remarkable demonstration of mass effort, and even more impressive was the mobilizing of economic resources. Above any previous conflict World War I was a war of matériel, an enormous devourer of supplies. The major industrial nations were required to regiment their systems to an unprecedented degree to produce the needed goods. A revealing example is afforded by comparing the expenditure of artillery ammunition with that in the Civil War, which previously stood as the greatest artillery conflict in history. In a year of heavy firing in the Civil War the Union artillery got off almost 2 million rounds. But in a like period in World War I the American artillery fired 8 million rounds, and all the Allied guns, combined, discharged 160,615,000 rounds. The expenditure in a single engagement shows a similar disproportion. In three days at Gettysburg the Union artillery fired 32,700 rounds, whereas in four days at Saint Mihiel (in 1917) the American artillery alone shot 1,093,000 rounds.

All the contending armies in World War I fired sustained artillery barrages before venturing to attack, believing that sheer volume would soften up the enemy and make him a more vulnerable target. This dependence on artillery underlines an important fact about this war, and about the changing nature of war. Matériel was becoming more important than men—machines and weapons were taking over the direction of battle from humans. And the weapons were making war infinitely more destructive. The massive artillery pieces could destroy everything within their sweep—soldiers, civilians, homes, vegetation—converting large areas into literal deserts, and they could strike

---

*Approximately 1.5 million served in the Northern armies for three years. It should be noted, however, that the ratio of soldiers to total population was larger in the Civil War than in World War I.

with almost equal effect unseen targets. Another fearful weapon was the recently developed machine gun, which with its rapid rate of fire spewed death across a wide front, making significant advances impossible and for a time turning operations on the Western Front into a tactical nightmare.

Nothing so marked the growing dominance of the machine as the new weapons introduced during the war. Developed experimentally, they were not so destructive as the established weapons, but they heralded an even more lethal warfare in the future. Two of them gave added dimensions to war, carrying its operations into the air and under the seas. The airplane, a fragile and crude instrument compared with later craft, was used by both sides, being employed first to conduct reconnaissance, then to fight enemy planes and attack enemy ground troops, and finally to bomb enemy installations and cities. The submarine also was used by both sides but more extensively by Germany, which sought to counter Allied naval supremacy by interdicting trade with England and France—and almost succeeded. A third weapon, the armored tank, was initially viewed with skepticism by both sides and never won favor with the Germans. However, the Allies were finally persuaded to put a number of tanks into action on the Western Front and, in so doing, were able to restore a measure of mobility to operations.*

The cost of the war to the major European powers was staggering. They expended probably $160 billion in direct monetary outlays, and more serious, endured grave physical damages in the shape of shelled cities and ravaged farmlands. The devastation was restrained in comparison with the mass destruction of World War II, as it left the fabric of European civilization relatively unimpaired. Still, many of the scars remained and could be seen a generation later.

The United States did not suffer any physical damage, but it had to raise and disburse huge sums of money to support its war effort and to sustain the effort of its allies. Treasury expenditures from 1917 to 1919 amounted to $23.5 billion, and in addition the government extended loans of almost $9 billion to various Allied nations. An official accounting estimated that the war cost the United States more than $1 million an hour for two years and that the total cost was equal to the amount required to operate the government from 1791 to 1914.

The human costs of the war to the principal European powers were appalling. Nearly 9 million soldiers and more than 13 million civilians died within a span of four years. The number of battle deaths included 1,700,000 Russians, 1,600,000 Germans, 1,385,000 Frenchmen, and 900,000 Englishmen. The 50,000 American battle deaths and 125,000 deaths of all causes paled in comparison.

---

*A fourth weapon was introduced, first by the Germans: chlorine or "poison" gas. However, it has not been used in later wars.

THE PRINCIPAL POWERS of the continent were aligned in two rival blocs. On one side was the Triple Alliance, composed of Germany, Austria-Hungary, and Italy. Opposed was the Triple Entente, made up of France, Great Britain, and Russia. Various smaller nations were associated loosely or informally with one combination or the other.

The existence of the blocs was public knowledge, but less well known was the complex set of treaty arrangements linking the powers together, the obligations that each had assumed to go to the aid of its allies in a crisis. Consequently, even the most informed Americans were shocked at the lightning chain of events in the summer of 1914 that plunged most of Europe into war.

The incident that set the war off seemed minor. A young Serbian nationalist assassinated the heir to the throne of Austria-Hungary. The government of that polyglot empire, fearful of Serbian influence upon its Slavic minority, served an unanswerable ultimatum on Serbia and then declared war. Russia, announcing itself the protector of the Slavs, came to the support of Serbia, and this action brought Germany to the side of Austria. Germany demanded of France its intentions and, on receiving a defiant reply, declared war and struck at its western neighbor through Belgium. Britain thereupon declared war on Germany and Austria, and the holocaust was on.

Other nations joined in the fray then or shortly thereafter. Italy, which had territorial grievances against Austria, won promises of support for its ambitions from Britain and France and switched to the Entente. The latter, which also took in Rumania and Greece, became known as the Allied Powers. Japan also adhered to the Allied side, hoping to capture German possessions in the Pacific area. Germany and Austria-Hungary, left alone, took on the designation of the Central Powers, and later won the support of Bulgaria and Turkey.

The causes of the war have been debated endlessly by historians. The principal issue of difference has been whether one nation or alliance was unduly aggressive in pursuing its ambitions and hence bore a primary responsibility for starting the conflict. However, most scholars have avoided fixing war guilt on one nation or alliance, preferring to believe that the Great War sprang from a multiplicity of causes and that all the major powers were in some degree responsible. Among the inciting factors they see economic rivalry, a competition for international markets; imperialistic contention, a reaching out to acquire colonies; balance-of-power politics, a fear of other countries exemplified in the opposing alliances; and extreme nationalism, a conviction in each people that they were different from, and superior to, other peoples. The combined effect of these influences was to cause the nations to engage in an armaments race that created huge military machines, and some scholars have seen in these machines another origin of the war—because the weapons existed, there was always a temptation to use them. The latent power in weaponry was recognized by an American observer who visited Europe in the fateful summer of 1914. He characterized the situation as "militarism run stark mad."

Something else was running strongly that summer, perhaps affecting peoples more deeply than governments but ruling both—an intense consciousness of group identity, of the uniqueness of a group's culture, and an equally intense determination to preserve that culture against perceived enemies. It was as though the crowding together of many peoples of different languages and customs within the small space of Europe made each one excessively aware of its singularity, and of its superiority. A British historian, A. J. P. Taylor, has said that the powers fought for no clearly formulated aims, but "simply for victory, to decide Humpty Dumpty's question: 'Who's to be master?' " His judgment ignores some known facts of the story. Most of the powers did have defined objectives, including the acquisition of territory. But it is also true that the major nations fought to be "master"; each one wanted to ensure that the values of its culture prevailed over those of the enemy. Primarily, World War I was a conflict of ideologies. And when belief in those ideologies was stirred to a higher pitch by the propaganda of governments, popular hatreds were aroused that prevented any government from seeking a negotiated peace. The struggle had to continue until one side was totally defeated.

Before 1914 each of the major powers had developed plans of strategy to be put into operation when war came. In every nation it was assumed that the war would last but a short time, would, indeed, be decided in the first battles. Germany intended to invade France, encircle the French armies, and then turn eastward to conquer Russia. France hoped to advance in the Alsace-Lorraine area, destroy the German forces there, and cross the Rhine River in triumph. Austria meant to defeat Serbia at once and then move eastward against Russia. The Russians, after mobilizing their huge armies, planned offensives that would crush both Germany and Austria. The reasons for the obsession of each nation with a short war were several. Contempt for the enemy had something to do with it, plus the fact that no war in recent times had lasted more than a year or so; the American Civil War had been the only recent long war. But above all, it was assumed that an extensive war was now impossible—modern armies had such mobility and destructive capacity that the strongest could attain victory immediately. Nobody on the planning staffs of either side paused to consider what might happen if forces of equal capacity collided.

In 1914 Germany was able first to put her plan into action. Better prepared to move quickly than her enemies or her ally Austria—the German railroad system had been built to accommodate a rapid mobilization—her armies were on the march soon after war was declared. The German plan had been drawn up years before by a former chief of staff, Alfred von Schlieffen, and bore his name. Schlieffen assumed that Germany would have to fight a two-front war, against France, and probably Britain, on the west and against Russia on the east. His problem was to decide which enemy could be defeated more quickly, and he concluded that France, with its smaller land space, was the obvious victim. The Schlieffen Plan called for a massive sweep through the Low Countries (Holland and Belgium) into northern France, a great wheel that would turn west of Paris and envelop the French armies in a campaign of not more than six weeks. Concurrently, smaller German armies would have to stand on the defensive in Alsace-Lorraine and on the border with Russia—but not for long. The main blow was expected to knock France out of the war, and the united German armies could then deal with Russia. So convinced was Schlieffen of the success of his plan that he died adjuring those around him to "keep the right strong."

The execution of the plan in 1914 fell to chief of staff Helmut von Moltke, who altered some of the details. Moltke, hoping to keep Holland neutral and an outlet for German trade, confined the invasion route to Belgium, crowding two of the armies through a narrow fortified passage. Fearful of giving ground at the Rhine crossing to the French and in East Prussia to the Russians, he shifted troops from the vital right wing to those areas.

Although weakened by Moltke's tinkering, the offensive got off to a smashing start. Exploiting speed and surprise, the Germans had by August driven the French and the British back to the Marne River, east of Paris. But there the defenders rallied and held. Not only that, in September they were able to organize a counteroffensive that forced the Germans back forty miles, to the Aisne River. During the remainder of the year the tempo of the fighting lulled somewhat. Both sides dug into trenches and extended their flanks northward and southward, the line of entrenchments extending eventually from the North Sea to the Swiss border, a distance of 500 miles. The Schlieffen Plan had not achieved its objective of ending the war on the Western Front. But the plan did not fail because, as some have charged, Moltke altered it. It had been formulated too long in the past and did not take account of developments in weaponry that gave the defense an advantage. The German attack would undoubtedly have stalled even if the right had been stronger. In the outcome was a lesson for strategists—a nation may risk peril in not having a prewar plan, but risk equal peril in adhering too rigidly to it.

During 1915 and 1916 and extending into the early months of 1917, both sides engaged in repeated offensives. Because there were no flanks on this front, the attackers had to crash straight ahead, trying to break into and through the enemy trenches. The British, holding the northern sector of the Allied line, struck through Flanders, the French, to the south, thrust on the Aisne, and the two powers undertook a combined assault in the great battle of the Somme in 1916. The Germans were content to rely on more limited attacks, although in 1916 they made a sustained effort to "bleed France to death" at Verdun. Every offensive failed to achieve the result predicted by the general who had planned it; even the most formidable ones accomplished advances of only two to three miles. By 1917 the war in France had settled into a bloody stalemate, into what a British military writer, Correlli Barnett, has called "mutual paralysis." The constant fighting for no apparent purpose was having a disquieting effect on the troops. Mutiny spread through fifty-four French divisions, and a new commander, Henri Philippe Pétain, warned the government that if the army had to engage in another great offensive, it might disintegrate.

A state of equilibrium also existed on the Eastern Front. In the vast spaces on the German-Russian border, deeper and wider advances were possible than in France, and operations never settled into trench warfare. But even the most fully organized offensives ended in qualified success and without decision. The Germans repulsed the Russians in East Prussia and, after occupying Poland, pushed into Russia proper. They could not, however, destroy the Russian armies. Farther to the south the Russians undertook an offensive against the Austrians that carried almost to the Carpathian Mountains. The effort cost Russia a million casualties and, coming after failure to achieve success elsewhere, caused a collapse of morale in the army and among the populace. A revolution in 1917 overthrew the government of Tsar Nicholas II and established a government that was soon taken over by a communist minority, the Bolsheviks. The latter group, intent on cementing its position, asked Germany for peace and took Russia out of the war. The result was a victory for Germany, but it came about because of war weariness in Russia, not because Russia lost the field. On both fronts alike the two sides were in such balance of strength that neither was able to achieve permanent superiority. And no general on either side seemed able to devise tactics to break the impasse and bring victory.*

ALLIED COMMANDERS on the Western Front had been educated in the doctrine that wars were won by the tactical offensive—the mass charge driven through the enemy line with utmost physical shock. French manuals pronounced that the object of all attacks was "to charge the enemy with the bayonet in order to destroy him," and General Robert Nivelle, who directed one of the great French offensives, declared that by exercising "violence" and "brutality" troops could carry any German position. British generals held to the same tenets. Douglas Haig, who commanded British forces during the greater part of the war, disparaged the effect of artillery and machine-gun fire on attacking troops. He predicted that if his infantry were supported adequately by their own artillery they could "walk through" the German lines,

*The closest thing to a smashing success occurred in 1917 on the front between Austria and Italy. Here the Austrians almost broke up an Italian army and advanced 100 miles. However, the British and the French rushed reinforcements to the danger point, and this offensive too was contained.

and he never ceased to believe that a massive cavalry charge could ride down the enemy.

The Allied generals saw no reason to alter their tactics after being confronted by trench warfare. They believed that mass force would still carry a field, and that there was no need to think about such matters as surprise and deception. The planning of a battle followed a set routine. The generals and the staffs, headquartered far behind the lines, studied their maps and decided which enemy position should be hit and a time to move. Troops, guns, and supplies were moved forward to the designated point, and when all was ready, an artillery barrage was opened to pulverize the enemy trenches and force the defenders deep into their shelters. The firing might continue for days—Haig once bombarded the opposing trenches for a full week—and was a spectacle of deafening fury, a "whirlwind of fire and steel let loose," in the words of a French general.

The barrage was lifted after being judged to have done its work (later, "creeping barrages," a French invention, were used in front of the advancing infantry), and officers gave the signal to the assault divisions to move out. A British poet-soldier, Siegfried Sassoon, has described this moment:

> *The barrage roars and lifts. Then, clumsily bowed*
> *With bombs and guns and shovels and battle-gear,*
> *Men jostle and climb to meet the bristling fire.*
> *They leave their trenches, going over the top.*

"Going over the top" was a phrase that became one of the stock expressions of the war, and the men were, as Sassoon said, bowed as they went, each one bearing a pack of sixty-six pounds. They set forth in waves about a hundred yards apart and with a distance of about six feet between each man in a wave. They moved at a walk, and in theory were supposed to keep their lines symmetrical in order to have a maximum shock effect when they struck the enemy line. And in theory they were walking toward an adversary who was dazed by the opening artillery barrage and would break at their approach.

Things never happened as the planners envisioned. The Germans knew where the attack would fall and were prepared to receive it. The movement of the assault troops into position and the artillery barrage revealed the danger point and made surprise impossible. The Germans retired into their reserve trenches during the bombardment and emerged only when the firing ceased, bringing their machine guns into position while their artillery in the rear was unlimbering. Also, the opening barrage did not appreciably ease the way of the attackers. It might chew up the first line of enemy trenches, but it rarely did extensive damage to the second or third line. Moreover, the shells tore up the ground over which the infantry had to move, impeding the soldiers' progress and digging craters into which advance parties of German machine-gunners piled to open fire. The attackers had little chance from the start. Forced to move in a sheet of flame, not only from machine guns but also from rifles and artillery, they incurred fearful casualties; the British lost 60,000 men killed and wounded in one day on the Somme. And even if survivors broke into the enemy trenches, they could not go very far. As they advanced the men tended to shrink from the fire into a formless crowd and to hit the opposing line in the shape of a wedge. The point of the wedge was contained, and the attackers were left in a salient and exposed to enfilading fire if they chose to remain.*

German generals were also schooled in the doctrine that an offensive pressed with total violence would carry any field, and they employed the same tactics as the Allied commanders did. Some German officers, as the war settled into a stalemate, attempted to vary their arrangements, bringing up their assault divisions by night to avoid detection and permitting the leading infantry to infiltrate through weak spots without waiting for support. These and other tactics showed a degree of imagination not often found on the Allied side, but they were not sufficiently original to change the nature of the fighting. The best-organized German offensives usually achieved no deeper penetrations than did Allied thrusts.

The failure of commanders on either side to devise methods to break the impasse of trench warfare can be attributed in part to the conditions of the war. Both sides were approximately equal in armaments and, before American entrance into the conflict, in men. The balance favored the army on the defensive; an entrenched force could pour forth a fire that would stall any attack. This much can be said in extenuation of the commanders. But it has also to be said that the generals were singularly backward in experimenting with ways to circumvent the restrictions laid upon them. They did not consider, for example, that infantry might be trained to reach enemy machine-gun positions immediately behind a barrage and before the enemy guns could go into action, and they were, as will be seen, reluctant to accept armored tanks, which were impervious to machine-gun fire. Their conservatism stemmed possibly from ignorance. High-ranking generals placed their headquarters far in the rear—many junior British officers testified to having never seen an officer above the grade of brigade commander—and knew little of the situation at the front. But physical insulation is not a complete explanation. The plain truth is that the commanders were incapable of contriving new tactics. Educated to a belief in brute force, they could conceive of no other way of fighting a war. Douglas Haig in 1917 summed up the thinking of all the generals. "It is no longer a question of aiming at breaking through the enemy's front," he de-

---

*A commander rarely gave up a salient, even though the men in it suffered proportionately heavier losses than those on other parts of the line. Generals alleged that to abandon ground would impair the morale of the troops, but most of them were obviously thinking of their own reputations.

clared. "It is now a question of wearing down and exhausting the enemy's resistance." War, it appeared, had become merely a process of attrition.

OLIVER WENDELL HOLMES, son of the poet, served as a volunteer officer in the Civil War. He later achieved distinction as a legal scholar and an associate justice of the Supreme Court, but he always recalled with special pride his experience as a soldier. His generation had reason to be grateful to the war, Holmes thought, for in their youth their "hearts had been touched with fire." Rutherford B. Hayes had also been a volunteer officer in the war, and he later became governor of Ohio, congressman, and president of the United States, but he too remembered his war experiences as "the golden years."

Men like Holmes and Hayes were certainly aware that war entailed suffering and death. But even though the Civil War was more destructive than any previous struggle, it did not change the way individuals thought about war. The officers and also the ordinary soldiers could still view war as a romantic experience, a release from the bland routine of their peacetime lives. They regarded combat as an opportunity to engage in individual heroics, and even though one might die in battle, he would die in individual action, heroically and nobly. The men who fought the Civil War had to ignore some things to believe all of this, but their beliefs had some basis. War in the nineteenth century in both the United States and Europe was on occasion an exciting, exhilarating, and even an ennobling experience.

This romantic image of war persisted into the following century and influenced young men, and older ones, in all the Western world as the Great War began. It was especially prevalent in Britain and the United States, or so the extant expressions of individuals in those countries indicate. Many educated Britons welcomed the advent of the war, professing to see in the act of conflict something that was ennobling to men and nations. An officer wrote in his diary that fortunately once in every generation a "mysterious wish for war passes through the people. Their instinct tells them that *there is no other way* of progress and of escape from habits that no longer fit them." A rising politician, Winston Churchill, was elated by the sheer fury of the war, deriving satisfaction even from the death of a young acquaintance in battle. The man died heroically, and in Churchill's view this was reason for others to rejoice, to remember that the fallen warrior was an exemplar of that "nobility" of spirit that animated all British "youth in arms." A young soldier on reaching the front wrote: "It is all the most *wonderful* fun. I hope it goes on a nice long time."

Young Americans felt a similar exhilaration and could hardly wait for their country to get into the fighting. "We had spent our boyhood in the peaceful afterglow of the 19th century," recalled John Dos Passos, later a novelist. "What was war like? We wanted to see with our own eyes." Many who eventually went to France felt a kind of fulfillment on their arrival at the front. "I have always thirsted for this kind of thing, to be present where the pulsations are liveliest," wrote the poet Alan Seeger. "Every minute here is worth weeks of ordinary existence."

The young men who rushed so eagerly to enlist soon had their dreams of glory dashed. On the Western Front the armies of the Allies and of Germany, their ambitions of mobility thwarted, went into trenches at the end of 1914 and remained underground for almost three years, and the Americans, on arriving at the front, also had to go into trenches. As the men on both sides soon discovered, war in the trenches was not like the wars they had read about in military histories and heard recounted by veterans of previous conflicts. Trench warfare was not romantic or picturesque, and most frustrating of all, it was not individualistic or heroic.*

Accounts of the war nearly always refer to the trenches as running in a line from the Swiss border to the Belgian coast, giving the impression that only one line existed. Actually, in most areas there were three lines. The front-line trench might be situated as close to its enemy counterpart as fifty yards, or as far away as a mile. Several hundred yards back was the support line, and several hundred yards behind it was the reserve line. These three were called "firing trenches," and in addition there were two other kinds: "communication trenches," running perpendicular to the lines and connecting them, and "saps," shallower indentations pushed ahead of the front line to serve as observation posts or machine-gun positions. A firing trench was normally six to eight feet deep and four to five feet wide, and usually it did not run straight for any distance but zigzagged at frequent intervals to avoid enfilading fire.

The firing trenches were the center of operation in both armies. From them men went "over the top," if ordered to take the offensive, or filtered out at night in small patrols to rush an enemy position and bring back prisoners for interrogation. And in and behind them soldiers stood to meet an enemy attack, firing rifles and throwing hand grenades. But active operations on a large scale occurred only on separated occasions and consumed but a small part of the war. Most of the men, most of the time, did not stand to charge the enemy or to repel him. Instead, they sat, squatted, or lay down, taking any posture that promised safety from enemy fire, or merely rest. Troops in a particular trench might have to endure such an existence for weeks before being relieved. "The war was mainly a matter of holes and ditches," a British officer recalled.

Troops at the front had to bear many things. One of the greatest miseries

---

*The closest parallel in history to the trench warfare of World War I was the campaign in Virginia in 1864–65, culminating in the siege of Petersburg. European and British students of the American war had ignored this campaign, preferring to discuss the sweeping movements of Lee and Jackson.

was the constant, pervading stench that hung over the trenches, the smell of rotting, unburied dead men and horses, of stagnant mud, of human excrement, and of the chloride of lime sprinkled everywhere to combat the various odors. Another trial was the presence of the rats that came out at night, and even in day, to feed on the corpses, bloated creatures described as being as big as cats. A British officer recounted a particularly grisly experience involving these predators. Newly arrived, the officer after retiring heard scuffling on his bed. Turning on his flashlight, he found "two rats on his blanket tussling for the possession of a severed hand."

The men who sat in the trenches during a quiet period, one in which active operations were not in progress, might not see an enemy soldier for weeks. But they were always conscious of the enemy's presence, for at any moment of the day or night a shell from across the way might land in the trench. British narratives are replete with instances of this kind of enemy firing. A group of men are lolling around in a dugout making tea or playing cards when a shell explodes in their midst—and then death. "There came a shattering clang," an officer recalled of one such incident. "A complete silence fell. Then from the passage came one sigh, the simultaneous passing of life from the wounded men lying there." This was a new way of killing in war—random and without apparent reason, unless attrition be reckoned as an end in itself, and worst of all, anonymous, done by an unseen foe. In a very real sense the men who charged the enemy or who met his charge were more fortunate. They, at least, could see some of the men they were fighting, and the act of killing or dying retained an individual quality.

The romantic concept of the pre-1914 generation that war was a glorious spectacle dominated by individual heroes was obliterated in the trenches. That dream went down in the mire of the Western Front and under the weight of impersonal technology. The loss of the vision was described by a saddened British officer: "The spring, which had driven the battalion, was worn," he wrote sadly. "The last flickers of our early credulous idealism had died in the Arras battles. The men, though docile, willing, and biddable, were tired beyond hope. Indeed, they knew now too well to hope, though despair had not overthrown them. They lived from hand to mouth, expecting nothing, and so disappointed nowhere."

THE HISTORICAL LITERATURE on the causes of U.S. intervention has been marked by the same kind of disagreement that characterizes discussions of other American wars. One school of interpretation or another has prevailed at a particular time, its opinions reflecting current views of the causes of war, only to fall in favor to a newer school. The debate continues, and even as yet a consensus has not been reached.

Two of the earlier explanations may be dismissed quickly. They were peculiarly the product of their time, being advanced during the postwar years, when many Americans were disillusioned with the results of the war and ready to believe that their country had been inveigled into the conflict by its designing allies. Answering a contemporary need, these explanations enjoyed a contemporary vogue but have since been largely ignored. To the modern student of war they seem simplistic and inadequate.

One of these explanations reflected the postwar generation's fascination with propaganda. The governments of the principal nations had created agencies to engage in mass persuasion, to paint their cause as just and that of the enemy as evil, and this new development in war-making became an object of concentrated study. American writers, and their readers, believed that the making of propaganda had a sinister intention, even when it was done by their own government, which had its Committee on Public Information. They concluded, in fact, that British propaganda had been largely instrumental in persuading the United States to enter the war. The British, it appeared, had been very clever. Exploiting American sympathy for the Allies and antipathy to Germany, and using American pawns to express their message, they succeeded in depicting the war to a willing American audience as a struggle between good and evil, and so induced the United States to intervene on the good side.*

The second explanation propounded an economic reason for American involvement. In 1914 the United States was in the beginning stage of a business recession, but the war abruptly reversed this decline. The Allies, now dependent on American factories and farms for many products, placed huge orders that turned the recession into a boom. The Central Powers too wished to buy in the United States but could not—Britain proclaimed a blockade of ports under German control and enforced it with her naval might. The Allies at first were able to pay for their purchases in cash, but as they ran out of that commodity, they sought credit, specifically in the form of loans from American bankers, a practice that the State Department, after some hesitation, condoned. In these unfolding events the proponents of the economic thesis saw an ominous pattern developing. The United States had permitted its prosperity to come to rest on trade with the Allies, and thus had a tremendous stake in the Allied victory, for an Allied defeat would shut off this trade and make repayment of the loans doubtful. Therefore, the United States had to enter the

---

*Government, or individuals in government, have engaged in some form of propaganda since war began: any announcement of the purpose in fighting, even if made to but a small percentage of a population, may be defined as propaganda. But organized attempts at mass persuasion are a phenomenon of modern war. The first example occurred in the Civil War, in the North, the making of propaganda being performed by volunteer groups or individuals but mainly by existing agencies of government, the War Department, or committees of Congress. World War I was the first conflict in which governments created agencies charged specifically and solely with manufacturing propaganda.

war to protect its economic interests and, in the most extreme extension of this interpretation, to preserve the investments of its bankers.

These first analyses of the causes of American involvement get but short shrift in later writing about the war. Subsequent students concede that British propaganda had some influence on American thinking, but they believe that the effect was minimal and that the efforts did little more than intensify an already existing American desire to see the Allies triumph. They also admit that the United States came to have a close economic liaison with the Allies, but they reject, as lacking evidence, the charge that the government decided on war to guarantee the loans of the bankers or to preserve domestic prosperity. The real consequence of the economic connection, in their view, was to make the United States unneutral, to cause its resources to be thrown in the scale on one side. German leaders complained publicly that U.S. neutrality was a sham, but American leaders refused to acknowledge the fact publicly.

This partiality to the Allies was revealed unmistakably in the Wilson administration's attitude toward violations of American shipping rights by the belligerents. British searches or seizures of vessels headed for German ports stirred only restrained protests. But German interventions aroused the government and the public to expressions of outrage. These different responses were not caused wholly by sympathy to one side. Germany, hard-pressed by the British blockade, introduced into sea warfare the submarine, a new weapon that in American opinion flouted international law and rules of civilized war.

Germany's use of the submarine has seemed to many historians to be the primary cause of American entrance into the war. Even those scholars who find other causes of American involvement concede that the German resort to submarine warfare had a shocking impact upon American opinion. In analyzing the American reaction, it is helpful to remember that the United States was in the high tide of what has been called its "age of innocence." Americans believed in such things as international morality and humanity, ideals that the Germans, in sending out their undersea vessels, seemed to be mocking.

The submarine was a new weapon in that it had never before been employed extensively in war, but the dream of an undersea craft that could sink surface vessels had inspired the minds of inventors since antiquity. Usually cited as the first "practical" submarine was a crude contrivance possessed by the Americans during the Revolution. Somewhat more sophisticated models were developed during the early years of the nineteenth century, and two submarines were operated by the Confederates during the Civil War. However, all of these first models had grave technical deficiencies that limited their use to a few, usually futile, forays, and the submarine found little favor with naval planners. Not until after 1900 did designers come up with usable models, aided, among other factors, by the introduction of the Diesel engine as a source of propulsion, and only then did the principal naval powers begin to add "U-boats" to their arsenals. Germany had twenty or so of these boats in 1914 and stood only fifth in the world rankings. But her leaders saw possibilities in the submarine and embarked on a crash construction program. By 1917, Germany possessed well over a hundred submarines and ranked ahead of every other power.

German strategists viewed their submarine armada as a means of bringing Great Britain to her knees, and hence of winning the war, for if Britain could be forced out of the conflict, France too would have to yield. The German plan was simple and ruthless: Britain had to import huge amounts of supplies to sustain her military effort and support her population, and the U-boats would cut off these supplies. Operating in packs around the British Isles, they would attempt to sink all Allied vessels and, if necessary, neutral ships, heading for British ports. The submarine campaign was unleashed in February, 1915, amidst confident predictions that within a short time Britain would have to sue for peace.

The instructions to the submarine commanders were to sink ships in the interdicted zone on sight. The language of the orders revealed the limitations of the submarine as a weapon. The U-boat was actually a frail and vulnerable craft. On the surface it could be easily sunk by even the light guns of armed merchant ships. A submarine captain encountering an enemy merchant vessel simply could not follow the practice outlined in international law and adhered to by British destroyers—to fire a warning shot at the other vessel to make it halt and then to search and possibly seize it. To be effective, the German commander had to remain submerged and direct one or more torpedoes at the trader, unsure whether he was firing on an enemy or a neutral ship. Once his work of destruction was accomplished, he had to flee the scene quickly to avoid possible attack by nearby warships, without bothering to pick up survivors of the sinking vessel, another injunction of international law.

The German use of submarines shocked and angered American opinion. Every aspect of this method of waging war seemed to violate accepted canons of humanity and decency—the apparently cynical disregard of international law, the attack without warning, and, above all, the subsequent loss of lives. Public outrage mounted with each sinking and became particularly strident when Americans traveling on Allied ships went down with other passengers. President Woodrow Wilson protested to Germany on three occasions that submarine warfare was illegal and barbarous. In a note delivered after a sinking that had been particularly costly in lives, he warned that another such atrocity would be regarded by the United States as a "deliberately unfriendly act," and when Germany persisted in her policy, he threatened to "sever diplomatic relations," a recourse that in international affairs was usually a prelude to war.

Wilson's threat forced Germany to modify her use of submarines. Early in 1916 the government pledged to the United States that henceforth no merchant vessels would be sunk without warning. Germany observed the promise for nine months, and the crisis appeared to have passed. However, the calm was deceptive. In the meantime Germany was building up her submarine fleet to greater strength, and powerful elements within the nation were demanding that unrestricted warfare be resumed. These proponents argued persuasively that the U-boats had to be used, that they offered the surest chance of victory. As for their effect on the United States, that country was already in the war economically, and before it could enter openly the conflict would be over. Responding to the mounting pressures, the German government announced in January, 1917, that it was inaugurating the most unrestrained kind of submarine warfare—in designated zones around the British Isles and in the Mediterranean Sea all vessels, belligerent or neutral, armed or unarmed, were to be sunk on sight. Shortly thereafter, Wilson suspended diplomatic relations with Germany. The United States was not yet in the war, but it had drawn closer to the brink.

Recent students of World War I, although admitting the influence of submarine warfare upon American sensibilities, have doubted that the submarine issue alone caused the United States to enter the war. They have posed some questions that deserve consideration: Why did Americans react so angrily to German violations of neutral rights and so mildly to those of Britain? Can the difference be attributed solely to the nature of the acts, to the fact that the German practice was new and seemingly barbaric, resulting in loss of lives, whereas the British methods were conventional and caused no deaths? Or were not Americans previously disposed to believe that Germany was an evil and dangerous nation and, so believing, were they not easily led to conclude that Germany's use of the submarine was only one manifestation of her malignity? The questions indicate the trend of thinking in modern scholarship. Most historians now conclude that submarine warfare was only an immediate cause of American intervention and that the fundamental or underlying reasons have to be sought elsewhere.

Anyone looking for reasons will be struck immediately by the intense sympathy for the Allied side that existed from the beginning of the war. The great majority of Americans wanted to stay out of the war, but they also wanted the Allies, and especially Britain and France, to win. Britain and France were "good" nations, democratic and peace-loving, much like the United States. Germany, on the other hand, was a "bad" nation, autocratic in form of government, militaristic in spirit, and imperialistic in foreign policy. In American eyes Germany was guilty of starting the war. Her rapid mobilization and execution of the Schlieffen Plan were not the result of superior efficiency but ruthless determination to strike first. Her invasion of neutral little Belgium was cited as clear proof of her disregard of principles of law and morality. An indication of the depth of American dislike of Germany was afforded in an outburst of President Wilson to members of his cabinet in 1915. Ordinarily an unusually self-contained man, Wilson exclaimed that the Allies were fighting "wild beasts." As the war went on, he and his colleagues had to consider what the position of the United States would be if the "beasts" seemed on the point of winning.*

By 1917 the prospects of a German victory seemed very real. Germany controlled a large part of northern France that was rich in natural resources, and most of Belgium and Poland. With her ally Austria she occupied Serbia and Rumania. At sea the submarine campaign was inflicting frightful losses on Allied, and especially British, shipping. The sinkings had averaged 190,000 tons a month during 1916 but in February, 1917, they rose to the staggering total of 780,000 tons, and Britain reeled under the blow. It appeared that she might be starved into submission even though her navy remained afloat.

The crisis forced Americans to face up to the results of a German victory, and in their response some historians see the underlying cause of American intervention. If Britain and France went down, Germany would stand as the dominant power in Europe. More serious in American opinion, naval supremacy would in all likelihood pass from Britain to Germany, and this aggressive nation would become also the dominant power in the Atlantic Ocean, and thus be positioned to threaten the security of the United States. Recognizing this danger, the American people supported entrance into the war to protect legitimate national interests. The historians who espouse this interpretation are saying that the United States intervened simply to preserve a balance of power in the Atlantic community. They can produce ample contemporary quotations to support their view. Certainly the threat implied in a German triumph was recognized by many Americans. Their perceptions were expressed cogently by former Secretary of State Elihu Root. "If we had stayed out of the war, and Germany had won," Root said, "there would no longer have been a balance of power in Europe, or a British fleet to support the Monroe Doctrine and to protect America."

The government official charged with conducting foreign policy, the president, agreed with those of his countrymen who were contending that the United States had a stake in the result of the war. Indeed, in 1917 Woodrow Wilson placed himself at the head of the movement for intervention. But he advocated intervention for reasons very different from those advanced by other supporters of the war. He did not think the United States should fight to preserve a balance of power or even to foster its own national interest. These objectives, in fact, he repudiated. The United States should have higher aims

---

*The American analysis of the moral and political values represented by the warring powers was obviously simplistic, and overlooked some pertinent facts. Russia, for example, was far from being a democratic nation. After the United States entered the war, American leaders and propagandists found it embarrassing to defend fighting on the side of Russia. They therefore welcomed the overthrow of the czarist government in the revolution of 1917. However, their relief was short-lived. The Bolsheviks took over the revolutionary government and removed Russia from the war.

if it entered the conflict—to serve the needs of all humanity and to ensure a new and peaceful world.

A Southern Democrat with a deeply religious upbringing, Wilson usually defined issues and situations in moral terms, and once having taken a position he found it difficult if not impossible to retreat, to compromise what he knew to be right. His view of America's relation to other countries was simple—the United States had to act as moral leader, as a kind of international conscience. He said in 1914: "America will come into the full light of day when all shall know that she puts human rights above all other rights and that her flag is the flag not only of America but of humanity."

Wilson sympathized with the Allies from the beginning of the war, having a special feeling for Britain, whose system of government he admired. However, he was sufficiently realistic to acknowledge that both sides had selfish interests, and that the winners would impose harsh conditions of peace on the defeated side, conditions that could precipitate another war in the future. Only the United States could avert a punitive settlement, Wilson decided. Early in 1917 he proposed what he called "a peace without victory" and outlined its terms, some of which were international recognition of freedom of the seas, limitation of armaments, open diplomacy, and a league of nations to enforce peace.

In making his proposal, Wilson was telling the warring powers that the United States was willing to act as a mediator at the peace table. He received polite replies to his offer but no acceptances. Obsessed now with the idea that the United States had to determine the peace, he decided that it could have a voice in the negotiations only by joining the war. In his thinking, as in that of most Americans, there was no doubt as to which side the nation should support. Britain and France might not be as idealistic as Wilson wished them to be, but they were democratic nations and were therefore susceptible to good influences, to American influences. Germany, in contrast, could not be swayed to do good. She was a lawless nation and would accept nothing short of a complete victory. Germany's decision to use submarines was the final act that persuaded Wilson of her evil character, but he might have arrived at the same conclusion even had the submarines not been employed as they were.

Determined to place his country on the side of the good powers, Wilson went before Congress on April 2, 1917, to ask for a declaration of war. He asked for it to achieve the loftiest of ideals. The day had come, he declared, "when America is privileged to spend her blood and her might for the principles that gave her birth and happiness and the peace which she has treasured," and in a sentence that seized the imagination of the war generation, and that in the postwar era seemed ironic, he proclaimed: "The world must be made safe for democracy." Congress responded to the president's request with overwhelming approval. The vote in the Senate was 82 to 6 for war, and 373 to 50 in the House.

Wilson's appeal to American idealism evoked a wide and deep response. It was the kind of exhortation calculated to move an innocent people—they had always known they were good, and now they were told it was their duty to make the peoples of Europe good. This sense of mission was clearly a basic cause of American involvement, and it was not in conflict with the balance-of-power question. Americans could at the same time want to strike down Germany and to reform Europe; indeed, they could not save Europe unless they first crushed Germany. Their exuberant readiness to extend their ministrations to friends and foes alike perplexed and dismayed some individuals on the Allied side. "There is an element of pathos in the simple and serious faith of these people," an English observer wrote. "They are like the early Christians in some well known picture, standing white-robed in the arena, and hemmed in by wild beasts and shouting crowds. The unpleasant reflection is these early Christians destroyed the Roman empire and plunged Europe into the shadows of the Dark Ages."

THE LARGE MAJORITIES by which Congress declared war did not reflect with complete accuracy the opinions of its members or of the public. Some who voted for war doubted the wisdom or the rightness of American entry, but hesitated to oppose the administration or to bring on themselves the charge of being German sympathizers. Many ordinary citizens also questioned whether the United States had reason to become involved, and others, generally persons of German ancestry, had feelings of friendship to the Central Powers. A small band of pacifists and socialists opposed the war simply because they were against mass violence.

The divisions on the desirability of American involvement were not serious—the great majority were clearly willing to support the war effort. But Wilson and his advisers decided that in a total war no division could be permitted. They also believed that support for the war had to be more than passive or perfunctory: it had to be fervent, unquestioning, and built on hatred of the enemy. To achieve these dual objectives, Wilson created by executive order the agency called the Committee on Public Information.

The CPI was a propaganda agency designed to mobilize popular opinion. Tireless in its activities, it utilized all the means of mass persuasion then known: pamphlets, to the number of 75 million; "canned" editorials for distribution to small-town newspapers; posters, to bring the message to those who could not read or did not wish to read; motion pictures, a new medium; and prepared speeches for 75,000 volunteer orators. The various efforts of the agency were successful—in fact, in the view of later students, too successful, an example of what came to be called "overkill." The majority of citizens were persuaded not merely to back the war but to seek out and harass those who did not support it, or who might be suspected on the flimsiest of evidence of not supporting it. A number of pacifists and liberals were tarred and feathered, beaten, or subjected to other indignities, and German-Americans experienced constant surveillance by their neighbors. In some communities the German language was dropped from schools and German books were removed from libraries.

Not content to rely on official propaganda, the government also employed official restraint to silence opponents or even critics of the war. The Espionage Act, passed by a willing Congress at the request of the administration, prescribed a heavy fine and a prison term of up to twenty years for anyone who interfered with the draft or encouraged disloyalty. Congress followed with the Sedition Act, which set the same penalty but imposed it for a larger number of offenses. Sedition was defined broadly. A person was guilty, for example, if he should "wilfully utter, print, write or publish any disloyal, profane, scurrilous, or abusive language" about the form of government, the flag, or the uniforms of the services, or if he said or did anything calculated to bring the government or the Constitution into "contempt." Under the terms of these laws over 1,500 persons were arrested and imprisoned, and 450 conscientious objectors who refused to accept alternative service were jailed. Hardly anyone saw the irony in what was happening. Americans were going overseas to carry out their president's determination to make the world safe for democracy. In the meantime democracy at home was suffering.

THE OUTBREAK OF WAR in Europe did not cause the United States to strengthen its own armaments. In 1914 the conflict seemed far removed from American interests—leaders and the public might sympathize with the Allied side, but the nation appeared to have no direct concern in the outcome. None of the warring powers seemed disposed to question America's neutral position, and no enemy in any other quarter of the globe was likely to threaten American security. According to this analysis, there was simply no reason to increase the existing military capability. In the unlikely event that an enemy materialized, it was assumed that that establishment was adequate to deal with the danger.

The prevailing estimate was realistic—up to a point. The military force was competent to defend the nation against an attack by a second- or third-rate power, and it probably could have fended off an assault by a first-rate power. But it would have been hard put to conduct an offensive war against any but a secondary enemy and could not possibly have attacked a major enemy. The regular army had an authorized strength of only 100,000 men and was not up even to that number, a minuscule total in comparison to the armies of other great powers; France, for example, had 1.5 million troops available in 1914, and Germany 2 million. The navy on paper was formidable, being the third largest of the world's fleets, but it was far from being in seaworthy condition. Over 60 percent of the ships were in need of some kind of repair, and not more than

10 percent were fully manned. The modest size of the military was in remarkable contrast to the status of the United States as a major power, a nation boasting huge territorial limits, a population of 82 million, and the most productive industrial system in the world.

Shortcomings in strength were not the only weaknesses in the military services. Command arrangements at the highest level were inadequate to conduct a major war. In the army the Root reforms had provided a basis for more centralized control, but the new system was still struggling to establish itself. The chief of staff and the General Staff, handicapped by Root's imprecise language, were unable to assert a clear line of authority. Seeking to "supervise" and to "coordinate," they encountered stubborn resistance on all sides. Especially determined to evade staff control were the powerful heads of the War Department bureaus; the supply chiefs, for example, continued to do their own competitive and hence costly buying. The bureaus were not content merely to thwart control. Hoping to emasculate the General Staff, they used their considerable lobbying influence in Congress to secure legislation in 1912 reducing the number of staff officers. The number had been pitifully small from the beginning, a mere forty-five as compared with the several hundreds on the staffs of major European powers, and as a result of bureau intervention the total was reduced to thirty-six.

Even after this depletion, the army had more staff officers available than the navy, which, in fact, did not possess a true general staff. The General Board, in existence since 1900, advised the secretary of the navy on policy but had no supervisory powers. Congress in 1915 authorized a new command office, the chief of naval operations, but neglected to provide this functionary with staff assistants. Actually, the command personnel in either service was inadequate to exercise effective control or to perform the most important function expected of a staff—planning for possible wars.

The state of the military establishment did not alarm national leaders until 1915. In that year, for the first time, the war in Europe impinged on American interests. Germany and her allies, if not winning the land conflict, were far from losing it, and, indeed, to some observers the balance seemed to be swaying toward the Central Powers. On the high seas the submarine campaign was taking a deadly toll of Allied commerce and threatening British naval hegemony in the Atlantic—and angering and frightening America. Faced by the possibility of a German victory, President Wilson and his advisers turned to considering whether the nation was prepared to fight a major enemy. They began to speak out on the necessity of strengthening American defenses, and officers in the army and the navy hastened to draw up plans to enlarge their services.

Late in 1915 the army General Staff submitted to the War Department a study entitled "A Proper Military Policy for the United States." The authors of the plan proposed to rely mainly on a citizen army to defend the country.

Although they recommended that the regular army be more than doubled, bringing it up to 280,000, they emphasized the creation of a 400,000-man volunteer force, to be called the Continental Army, a partly trained reserve like the National Guard but under federal control. The existing National Guard received only perfunctory attention in the plan. The staff planners suggested increased federal support for the state troops but obviously thought they were too remote from federal control to be useful in a crisis.

The scheme won partial support from Wilson. The president refused to accept the recommended increase in the regular army, agreeing only to a force of about 140,000, but he embraced the concept of a Continental Army and recommended creation of such an organization in his message to Congress in December, 1915. His proposal brought the potent National Guard lobby down on Washington in loud wrath, crying that the state troops constituted an already existing citizen army. Responding to this pressure, influential congressmen introduced a bill providing increased federal support of the Guard but requiring it to accept federal training standards and to respond to a presidential call to mobilize. Wilson, anxious to get a preparedness bill adopted, accepted the congressional plan, which when enacted became known as the National Defense Act of 1916.

In framing the act, the legislators rejected the argument of followers of Emory Upton that the United States required for its defense a large standing army. The bill allowed an increase in the peacetime strength of the regular army to only 175,000, to be accomplished over five years, and permitted a wartime strength of 285,000. In place of professionals, the nation was to rely mainly on citizen forces. The National Guard, now federally obligated, was provided with augmented financial support and was authorized to increase its strength to 475,000. In another effort to encourage citizen participation in the army, the act authorized the creation of a "reserve corps" of officers and enlisted men, to be drawn from individuals who had taken officer training in the colleges or who had finished their active duty enlistment in the regular army. The authors of the measure went finally a step beyond mobilizing manpower. Impressed by the capacity of the war in Europe to devour supplies, they empowered the president to place orders for defense materials and to compel affected industries to comply, authorizing the War Department to make a survey of all industries concerned with producing arms and ammunition.

The National Defense Act is usually referred to admiringly by those connected with the military establishment: the most "comprehensive" military legislation yet passed by Congress is the stock encomium. It is not completely clear what there is to praise. If scholars believe that the act provided for raising a greater land force than any in previous history, and one with a greater variety of troops, the term "comprehensive" is justified. It is entirely another matter whether the measure was calculated to serve the needs of national policy, to meet the threat of rising German power. Viewed in this larger perspective, the act was deficient and unrealistic. It should have been obvious, from even rudimentary planning, that the place to defeat Germany was in Europe, that the United States would have to dispatch a force abroad to fight with allies—while it still had allies. But none of the persons concerned with planning—the president, his advisers, or the General Staff—grasped this conclusion; they all assumed that the United States should prepare to act alone in defending against a German attack. And this was all that the National Defense Act was designed to do, to provide a force capable of repelling an attack on the eastern seaboard. The reasoning that went into the act was hardly comprehensive.

Wilson may be excused for thinking in narrow terms. He rarely sought advice from military professionals, and even if he had been otherwise disposed, he probably would not have received very helpful counsel. The men on the General Staff who produced the paper that formed the basis of the Act of 1916 could conceive of doing nothing else than to await an attack. Nor did the act promise to provide the president with improved sources of advice. It allowed only a modest increase in the General Staff, from thirty-six to fifty-five officers, to come in five annual increments. Moreover, it was stipulated that not more than half of the total could serve in or near Washington. In 1917, when the United States finally entered the war, there were but twenty staff officers on duty in the capital. Nine were involved in supervising the bureaus and the line, leaving only eleven officers to study policy and plans.

In his message to Congress proposing an increase in the land forces, Wilson also recommended an expanded program of naval construction. His proposal revealed the same defensive cast of mind apparent in his suggestions on an army—he and whoever was advising him on naval matters clearly believed that the United States should prepare to fend off alone a German attack. The most effective means of preventing an attack would have been to destroy German naval might, which was in her submarines, and the best way to do this would have been to build a fleet of destroyers to operate with British destroyers. This strategy did not occur to Wilson. He asked Congress to appropriate money to construct ten battleships, six battle cruisers, and assorted lesser types of vessels, including only fifty destroyers. This was a program calculated to defend the eastern coast against a conventional naval assault, but it bore little relation to the needs of the moment. Nevertheless, a willing Congress acceded to his request.*

The United States entered the war in 1917 with its potential strength unmobilized. The regular army, counting that part of the National Guard that had been federalized for duty on the Mexican border, numbered about only 210,000 men. The navy was more ready for war, although many of its ships

---

*Most of the vessels provided for were never built. In 1917 construction was suspended to allow concentration on producing destroyers and other antisubmarine weapons.

had to be placed into commission without being fully manned. Considering their lack of prior preparation, both services put units into the war zones quickly. By early May, a month after the declaration of war, over thirty American destroyers were engaging in antisubmarine patrol in the north Atlantic. And in June an American division embarked for France. Scraped together hurriedly, the division was only a token force, sent to bolster Allied morale. But it was a harbinger of more to come.

When fully organized the might of the United States would be decisive in winning the war. America's industrial capacity, joined to American technological skills, swung the economic balance heavily in favor of the Allies. The American navy, adding its strength to the British blockade of ports open to the enemy, helped to draw an ever tighter grip on the Central Powers, whose people by 1918 were in a condition of near famine. And finally, the arrival in France of an American army, fresh, eager, and unshaken, enabled the Allied generals to mount a last offensive that crushed Germany.

CHAPTER XV

The World War:
The American Experience

AMERICA'S ENTRANCE into the war was like a catalyst on officers in the services concerned with planning—they were told at last what the policy objective of the nation was and were exhorted to accomplish it. Before 1917 the government lacked a precise foreign policy, and that which was defined was not coordinated with military policy. President Wilson and other leaders had warned that the nation might have to confront an unnamed enemy, presumed to be Germany, and in 1916 the administration had sponsored legislation to prepare a defense. But Wilson and his advisers went no further. The president had in fact resisted efforts to plan for war. Told that officers on the General Staff, as part of their work, were making plans for war with one or several nations, he went "white with passion," according to a reliable source, and said he thought these exercises should be stopped. All this evasion of reality ceased when Wilson decided on war. In his message to Congress he declared that the United States would throw its full might into the conflict— it would not only employ its powerful navy but would also raise and dispatch to Europe large ground forces. The government finally announced a military policy, and the planners now knew what they had to do.

Preparing the navy for an all-out effort was not a particularly difficult task; it mainly involved putting an existing fleet in fighting condition. But to organize an army of the proportions envisioned by the president was a different matter—the existing land force was inadequate to a large mission, and an entirely new one had to be created. Fortunately, the General Staff had foreseen early in 1917 the possibility of war and had drawn up plans to enable the government to raise from 500,000 to 1,500,000 troops. One of the plans proposed conscription, and the War Department recommended this method to Congress after war was declared. Congress accepted the argument that only a draft could raise the necessary number of men, and enacted the Selective

Service Act in May. For the second time in its history, and for the first time since the Civil War, the United States was to mobilize a conscript army.

The experience of the Civil War draft strongly influenced the staff officers who wrote the plan that became the basis of the Selective Service Act. Determined to avoid previous mistakes, the authors eliminated exemption by purchase or substitution and denied the offering of bounties. All males between the ages of twenty-one and thirty, later between eighteen and forty-five, had to register for service. The process of selection was vested in local boards of citizens nominated by the governors of the states—in order to relieve the military of the onus of administration—and the boards were empowered to grant defined exemptions, or to select some men to go into the army and others to remain out. Exemptions were allowed only to those engaged in essential service in industry or agriculture or who had dependents or were physically unfit.

The civilian boards registered over 24 million men. This job of paperwork was in itself a considerable feat, but the boards did much more. Placing the registrants in classes of eligibility, they first selected unmarried men with no dependents and within less than eighteen months delivered 2,810,000 inductees to the armed forces. These men represented 67 percent of the land forces serving in the war. The remaining portion consisted of men in the regular army and the National Guard, which together comprised about 750,000 troops when the Selective Act went into operation.* Thus, the total American force raised was approximately 3,685,000. The War Department found it necessary to mingle together in units men of all three classifications, draftees, regulars, and Guardsmen, and as a consequence designated all the ground forces as the United States Army.

Preparing these masses of men to serve in France was a herculean and time-consuming task. The troops had first to be assembled in camps to receive basic training, which consumed four months. Then they were taken to ports of embarkation and placed on whatever vessels were available to carry them across the Atlantic, whether American or, often, British transports. Under these conditions, it was remarkable that large American forces arrived in France as soon as they did. Over 1 million men had been landed by the summer of 1918, and before the end of the year the number had grown to slightly more than 2 million, organized in forty-two divisions.† These troops were designated as the American Expeditionary Forces and were under the command of General John J. Pershing. Even this large force did not satisfy Pershing. He was convinced that the Americans would have to bear the brunt of crushing

---

*The regular army and the National Guard had been raised to near their authorized wartime strength, 285,000 men and 475,000 men.

†An American combat division comprised about 28,000 men and was almost twice the size of an Allied or a German division. It was a mark of the increasing influence of technology on war that a unit of division size required almost as many men in support as were on the line.

Germany, and he asked the War Department to provide him with eighty divisions. Although the department questioned the size of Pershing's requisition, it set out to fulfill his request and had organized nineteen additional divisions when German resistance collapsed. German awareness that more and more American troops were on the way was a major factor in that nation's defeat.

As the size of the army increased, there developed an acute need for officers to train and lead men and units. The War Department estimated that 200,000 officers were required—and wondered where to find them. There were only about 9,000 officers in the regular army and approximately the same number in the National Guard, and even if all of these men were distributed among the conscript masses, they would be inadequate to the task. The only solution was to train new officers, and this the War Department proceeded to do by establishing officer-training camps throughout the country, many of them located in colleges and universities. Out of these camps came 96,000 graduates, or almost half of the officer corps of the war. Another 40 percent were commissioned from the ranks or the reserve. The only commissions given directly to men from civilian life were to doctors and other specialists. The practice in former wars of awarding commissions to prominent politicians was eliminated completely.

THERE WERE FOUR black regiments in the regular army at the outbreak of the war, comprising some 10,000 troops. Another 10,000 blacks were enlisted in segregated National Guard units. Black leaders demanded that other Negroes be allowed to prove their ability in the enlarging army. One spokesman declared that his people, held in second-class status, had no stake in the war's outcome, but this was not the prevailing black opinion. The National Association for the Advancement of Colored People urged blacks to join in "this fight for eventual world liberty," and one of the most militant leaders, W. E. B. DuBois, proclaimed: "If this is our country, then this is our war."

Even without conscription, blacks would have been admitted in some form into the army; the need for manpower was too great to exclude them. The problem was the basis on which they were admitted. Regular army officers were almost universally agreed that Negroes would not fight unless led by white officers, and some felt they would not fight under any conditions, being fitted only for labor duties. Consequently, although the army was willing to receive blacks and, indeed, under the conscription law had to take them, it was determined to keep them in segregated units and to restrict their duties.

Approximately 400,000 Negroes entered the army, practically all of them through the draft. Only 200,000 were selected by the War Department to serve in France, and of these about 150,000 were held in rear zones as labor troops.

There were only five black combat units: four separate infantry regiments and one division, the Ninety-second. Soon after arriving in France the infantry regiments were dispersed to serve with the French on a hard-pressed section of the front and acquitted themselves with great credit. The Ninety-second Division, on the other hand, became a part of the AEF, and in the opinion of white officers was a poor unit. Believed to lack fighting spirit, it brought bitter criticism on itself in the principal American offensive; at the height of the battle one of its regiments disintegrated, officers and men running from the enemy.

The indifferent conduct of the division can be explained by several factors. It had received only partial training, and many of its officers of both races were not competent.* But the primary cause of black soldiers' failure was the attitude of their high-ranking white officers. These men believed that Negroes were inferior as a race and hence were inferior soldiers. The corps commander of the Ninety-second filled his diary with laments of its lack of quality. "Poor Negroes!" he wrote in a typical passage. "They are hopelessly inferior. I have been talking with them about their division's success. That success is not troubling them. With everyone feeling and saying that they are worthless as soldiers, they are going on quite unconcernedly." If their commander expected them to fail, why should they disappoint him?

The Civil War, modern and almost total, had been the first conflict in which womanpower had augmented manpower. The World War, much more total, saw a greater participation of women in the war effort. For the first time in an American conflict a systematic effort was made through organizations like the National League for Women's Service and the Women's Committee of the Council of National Defense to enlist the talents of women. Women served in various volunteer capacities, making bandages, serving as hostesses at canteens and the like, but some took over important jobs in industry. Out of their experience many women gained a measure of economic independence and also a vision of life in which women would possess more social freedoms and political rights. In a similar development, blacks, although disappointed that their contribution to the war had not brought them greater recognition, came out of the conflict determined to seek more of the benefits of democracy. In a way that few had foreseen, the war was a harbinger of change.

THE OFFICERS of the principal naval powers had been educated to believe that a fleet existed but for one purpose: to engage and destroy an enemy fleet. This was the strategic doctrine that Alfred Thayer Mahan had made popular with

---

*The War Department, in response to black pressure, had admitted Negroes to the officer-training camps. Approximately 1,200 blacks were commissioned, but none above the rank of captain.

naval thinkers, and in the years preceding the war it had become naval gospel. So enshrined was the Mahanian concept that other uses of sea power, such as interdicting commerce, were almost ignored.

Given the prevailing doctrine, it might have been expected that the opposing navies would engage one another in constant battle, seeking the final showdown that would determine supremacy at sea. In actual fact, almost the exact opposite strategy was followed. The dominant British navy concerned itself with guarding the vital supply lines to the home ports and watching the German fleet, and the German navy aimed at trying to reduce British strength in attacks on individual ships. Only once did the two fleets meet in battle, with indecisive results. There were several reasons for the reluctance on both sides to engage, but the principal one was their leaders' realization of naval vulnerability: an army may be defeated and survive to fight another day, but a fleet can be destroyed in one short clash. It was said truly of the admiral of the British Grand Fleet that he "was the only man on either side who could lose the war in an afternoon."

At the beginning of the war the British navy was markedly superior to the German navy in number of ships. Britain possessed twenty-nine big-gun battleships to Germany's eighteen, and had more of every class of lesser vessels. On a ship-to-ship basis, the two forces were approximately equal. A German capital ship was at least as good as its British counterpart, and in ability to resist the impact of shellfire was probably superior.

Both navies deployed vessels in widely separated areas of the globe. Britain had to maintain ships in the Atlantic Ocean and the Mediterranean Sea to protect her sea communications. Germany broke cruisers through the British blockade to raid Allied commerce in the Atlantic, Pacific, and Indian oceans, and the British dispatched ships to hunt the raiders down. In all these theaters battles between individual ships or small squadrons occurred, but the actions were isolated and involved only a minor part of each fleet. The strength of the navies was concentrated closer to home.

The British Grand Fleet had its principal base at Scapa Flow, in the Orkney Islands, just off the northern tip of Scotland, with secondary forces operating out of ports on the eastern coast of England. From these positions the British could close the North Sea to German trade and, more important, keep vigil on the German High Seas Fleet, which was based in the southeastern corner of the North Sea at an anchorage known as the Jade. The High Seas Fleet, for its part, blockaded the entrance to the Baltic Sea, thus preventing the Allies from sending supplies to Russia, and occasionally diverted one ship or several ships into the North Sea to strike at detached British vessels or to bombard British coastal towns.

The two fleets played this cat-and-mouse game for the first two years of the war. The routine was broken only once. On May 31, 1916, virtually the entire High Seas Fleet left the Jade and emerged into the North Sea. The

German commander hoped to attack Allied shipping off Norway and lure a portion of the Grand Fleet to chase him; at the right moment he intended to turn and destroy the pursuers, thus reducing the rival fleet to such a level that he could later give it battle with good chance of success. But even before the Germans left their anchorage, the Grand Fleet put to sea to intercept them; the British were in possession of the German code and had read the orders. The fleets made contact in the battle that the British called Jutland, after a peninsula nearby on the Danish coast.* Both forces suffered serious losses, and in the end the Germans broke off action and retired to the Jade.

The fighting involved 250 ships on both sides, the largest number ever engaged in a naval encounter, and Jutland still stands as the greatest naval battle in history. But it was indecisive. The losses to both sides were severe but not crippling, and the two forces continued at their previous proportional level of strength. The Germans, however, never ventured again to risk a showdown. The first great surface engagement of the war was the last. Germany now concentrated its naval efforts on the submarine campaign, while Britain attempted to intensify its blockade. This was the situation when the United States navy threw its strength into the struggle.

THE SECRETARY OF THE NAVY was Josephus Daniels, a North Carolina politician and journalist. A man of fair ability, Daniels was devoted to the service he administered, but he had an almost obsessive fear of being dominated by its ranking officers. He revealed this in 1915, when Congress was considering a bill to create the office of chief of naval operations, the holder of which would be assisted by fifteen staff officers. Daniels did not object to the new position, but he saw the proposed general staff as a manifestation of militarism, or in his words, of "Prussianism," and he used his influence with Congress to eliminate this section of the bill. He gave renewed evidence of his determination to hold the coordinating authority of the department in his own hands when he chose the first chief of naval operations. Passing over several admirals who were aspirants, he appointed a captain, William S. Benson, who as a sudden admiral proved as compliant as Daniels hoped he would be.

During the war Daniels and Benson supervised a substantial and, on the whole, intelligent expansion of the navy. Realizing that the principal naval effort would have to be directed against German submarines, the secretary suspended construction of capital ships that had been authorized in 1916 and concentrated on building destroyers and lesser antisubmarine craft. Contracts were let to commission 250 destroyers and 400 submarine "chasers," smaller patrol boats equipped with listening devices to detect submarines at distances

*The Germans named the battle "Skaggerak." The Skaggerak was an arm of the North Sea between Denmark and Norway.

of up to 20 miles.* Not all these vessels had been completed when the war ended, but the sea arm had attained its greatest strength ever. The navy was operating over 2,000 ships of all types and had increased its total personnel to more than 500,000.†

The concentration on destroyers was forced by the situation in Europe and showed the extent to which previous developments in the war had limited American strategy. The United States entered a war in progress and was forced to adopt its actions to the needs of its allies and to fit its strategic purposes into already formulated plans. The navy had to make this adjustment in European waters, and so did the army in France.

Shortly before the United States joined the war, the Navy Department sent to London Admiral William S. Sims to discuss with British officers the problems involved in coping with the submarine campaign. Arriving in England after his country declared war, Sims was shocked to learn the toll of Allied shipping being taken by the Germans. "They will win," he was told, "unless we can stop these losses, and stop them soon." Sims was known in his own navy as being unusually receptive to new ideas, and now he was impressed by the arguments of those British officers who were pressing for convoys of fast destroyers to protect shipping in the Atlantic. He joined his voice to theirs and helped persuade the British Admiralty to adopt a convoy system. He cabled his government to dispatch to England immediately whatever destroyers it could spare.

This was the beginning of the principal American naval contribution to the Allied war effort. Sims was appointed commander of "U.S. Naval Forces Operating in European Waters," and eventually his force consisted of 370 ships of all types, including 79 destroyers. Because his escorts had to guard far-flung convoys, he stationed them in three separated bases: Queenstown, in southern Ireland; Brest, on the northwestern coast of France; and the British crown colony of Gibraltar, at the Atlantic entrance to the Mediterranean Sea. And in order to give these squadrons central direction he maintained his headquarters in London. It was a mark of the growing influence of technology on war that he chose to direct operations from a desk instead of from the quarter deck of a warship.

The convoy system proved a great success. By the close of the war 90 percent of Allied shipping was sailing in convoys, and less than one percent of the ships thus protected were lost to the enemy. The submarine menace was at last contained, and for their part in the accomplishment the Americans

*The detection device, a forerunner of sonar, consisted of a tube, or tubes, suspended in the water.

†As part of the manpower expansion, the Marine Corps grew during the war from 10,000 to over 70,000 men. Some marine officers had long contended that their men were as able to fight on land as to serve on ships, and during the war about 30,000 marines served in France as both support and combat troops.

received generous credit. A British admiral admitted the result would not have been possible but for "the entry of the United States into the war." But as important as the American role was, it was throughout a subordinate role. As compared with Sims's 79 destroyers in the Atlantic, the British had 100. The American vessels acted under British supervision, as did the five U.S. battleships that joined the Grand Fleet at Scapa Flow. The Americans accepted the position of a junior partner willingly, knowing they were inferior to the British in ships, guns, and knowledge of sea ways, and the latter assumed superiority as being their proper due. These roles would be reversed in World War II.

ONE OF THE GREAT technological breakthroughs before the war was the internal-combustion engine. Developed for peacetime use but sparingly adopted, this device received its first extensive application during the war. In the form of a truck it introduced a new element in military transportation, lessening dependence on railroads and horses.* In the form of a tank it provided a new offensive weapon. And in the form of an airplane the engine added a new dimension to war: men could now fly above the battlefield in heavier-than-air vehicles, and war managers could join to the conventional forces of land and sea an air force.

The first American air corps consisted of the observation balloons that the Union army operated in the Civil War. As instruments to obtain intelligence about the enemy, the lighter-than-air craft were thought to have proved their value. In 1892 the War Department established a balloon section in the Signal Corps, and at least one balloon was used in the war with Spain.

After the turn of the century, inventors and designers shifted their attention from balloons to heavier-than-air craft. In 1903 the Wright brothers, Orville and Wilbur, made the first successful airplane flight in history and, following their feat, went into the business of manufacturing planes. They did not have the field to themselves. Competition appeared in the person of Glenn Curtiss, a pilot and designer who set up a rival plant. It was apparent that a new industry was about to develop—but one with a limited market. Planes were so costly that only governments could afford to buy them.

The American aviation industry received only slight encouragement from Washington. In 1907 an Aeronautical Division was established in the Signal Corps, and two years later the army acquired its first plane, purchasing it from the Wright brothers and ordering four more. Another two years went by before Congress provided a special appropriation for aviation, a sum of $125,000, and up to 1914 a total of only about $430,000 was spent on military aviation. In the international rankings of funds expended on aviation the United States stood

---

*Horses were widely employed in the war, however, being used to pull supply vehicles and artillery pieces.

fourteenth, below even small nations like Greece and Bulgaria. At the same time the principal European powers were appropriating millions of dollars to buy planes from American builders and to foster their own aircraft industries.

After 1914 the army attempted to redress these shortcomings. An Aviation Section took the place of the Aeronautical Division in the Signal Corps, and this agency endeavored to persuade Congress to increase appropriations to commission more planes and recruit more pilots. The results of its labors were disappointing. Congress provided somewhat larger sums, but financial support was still inadequate. And even when money was available, planes were not always forthcoming; the young aviation industry, deprived of governmental patronage previously, was not geared to turn out planes in large numbers. On the eve of American entrance into the war the air establishment numbered but about 130 officers, of whom 26 were qualified pilots, and some 1,100 enlisted men. Only 224 planes had been acquired, and not one of these was by European standards a combat type. At the army's two flying fields there were 55 planes, "trainer" and observation models, and all of these were, according to General Pershing, either "obsolete" or "obsolescent."

After war was declared, the government gave closer attention and greater support to its air arm. As a first step in creating an adequate air force, President Wilson by executive order removed army aviation from the control of the Signal Corps. A new agency was created and given a title to indicate its semi-independent status: the Air Service, U.S. Army. This was a forward move but authority within the agency was divided between two components. Administration of training and operating procedures was vested in a director of military aeronautics, the first occupant of the office being William L. Kenly, a former major general of artillery. Responsibility for acquiring planes, engines, and other equipment was placed in a Bureau of Aircraft Production. The two departments reported separately to the secretary of war and followed no common policy. The result was a ruinous lag in the whole program and particularly in production. In an effort to bring order to the situation the War Department created the office of second assistant secretary of war, naming its holder director of the Air Service with authority over both agencies, those making planes and those using them.

Under the reorganized system aircraft production increased significantly, partly due to improved administration and partly to improved techniques in the aviation industry. By the end of the war American plants had turned out over 11,000 planes and were accelerating their rate of production. If the fighting had lasted another year the American air force would have become one of the largest in the world. As it was, production reached a peak too late to enable the United States to play a major part in the air war. The American role had, in fact, to be played largely with borrowed equipment. The air service in France consisted of some 2,900 planes and 5,000 pilots of a total of 11,425 officers enlisted. But only 696 of the planes were of American make. The remainder were acquired from the French—and it was to French and British officers that the American pilots looked for their first instructions in aerial tactics.

The Americans learned their lessons quickly and well, and the AEF's air corps developed into an effective fighting group. One reason for its rapid progress was that General Pershing appointed able officers to administer the program. As his senior aerial adviser and chief of air service, Pershing named Major General Mason M. Patrick, an engineer who had never been in an airplane but was an adept organizer. Under Patrick were two assistants, Brigadier General Benjamin D. Foulois supervising training and supply, and Brigadier General William Mitchell in charge of operations. It was Billy Mitchell who had the most direct contact with the pilots, and it was Mitchell who had the greatest influence upon the fledgling air force and pointed the thinking of airmen toward future goals.

Under Mitchell the air service engaged in the same kind of activities that occupied the forces of other countries—conducting reconnaissance flights, engaging enemy planes and strafing ground troops (a plane was armed with a machine gun), and bombing behind enemy lines. The record of American planes in individual battles was impressive, 781 shot down with a loss of only 289, causing Mitchell to exult: "We Americans had developed the best system of air fighting that the world had ever seen."* Although the general was proud of the victories, he foresaw a larger role for air power than reporting on enemy movements or battling enemy planes. He had become acquainted with General Hugh Trenchard, commander of the British Royal Air Force, and was profoundly impressed with Trenchard's views of air power. Trenchard believed that the primary function of an air force was to bomb enemy installations behind the lines, and he wanted to organize an inter-Allied air force to strike deep into Germany. Mitchell frequently quoted Trenchard's dictum that "an airplane is an offensive and not a defensive weapon," and he approved the Briton's idea that an air force should be separate from the other services and under a unified command. Mitchell's opinion on these matters would be heard again.†

Going contrary to Mitchell's dictum on unity, and arousing his anger, the navy insisted on developing its own air service. During the war the naval aviation force was increased from 54 to over 2,000 planes, and from 39 to more than 1,600 aviators. The naval planes were employed against enemy submarines and surface ships and generally operated from land bases. However, before the war, there were experiments in the American navy and in other

---

*The statement was exaggerated in view of the fact that the world had thus far seen very little air fighting.

†Britain alone among the major powers established its air force on an equal status with the army and the navy. France and Germany retained their air arms as parts of their armies and navies.

navies of having a plane land on and take off from a ship. And as the war continued, battleships and cruisers began to carry one or more light planes. Finally, in October, 1918, one month before the war ended, the British commissioned the first aircraft carrier in history. A big step into the warfare of the future had been taken.

The airplane proved successful as a reconnaissance instrument during World War I, but as a combat weapon it had exerted little effect on the course of the ground action. The individual battles that Mitchell and others gloried in and that created a mystique among aviators were of no importance except to the individual combatants. The existing bombers were too small or had too limited a range to carry out the raids envisioned by Trenchard and Mitchell. But the idea of strategic bombing had been born in the minds of airmen, and the promise, or the threat, would remain.

THE UNITED STATES had little difficulty in financing its war effort. Huge sums of money had to be raised, and raised quickly, but the government managed the feat, while at the same time contributing support to its allies. In addition to mobilizing money, the government mobilized the productive facilities of industry and agriculture to provide supplies for the armed forces, while satisfying the needs of the civilian population. It brought off this feat without disturbing seriously the routine or the tempo of civilian life. The achievement can be attributed to several factors. The economy was rich and resourceful and was able to sustain the strains placed upon it. Men in government and banking knew more about how to finance a war than their predecessors, and were prepared to adopt more sophisticated techniques. Perhaps most important, the United States was in the war for but a short time and was not subjected to severe economic burdens. It is hard to predict what might have happened if the struggle had gone on into another year. Probably the government would have been forced to impose direct controls on the economy in the form of price fixing and rationing of certain supplies.

Some economists advocated that the government raise the monies it needed by instituting a network of taxes. The Treasury Department rejected the idea as impractical—it would take too long to establish machinery to collect the taxes, and more important, it was obvious that taxes alone could not provide the vast sums that would be required. Instead, the government elected to borrow its principal revenues, but also to impose special war taxes. Four great "bond drives" to sell "Liberty Loans" were conducted in 1917 and 1918, and a fifth sale of "Victory" bonds were held after the armistice. In transacting these sales, Treasury officials had in mind the largest previous example of wartime borrowing, that of the Union government in the Civil War, and they were resolved to avoid what they considered mistakes in the earlier experience. Thus, they insisted that the government market the bonds directly instead of following Salmon Chase's practice of depending on bankers to take the bonds and recall them. They retained, however, an important innovation of Civil War financing, offering bonds to small as well as to large investors. The offerings to the citizenry were presented with all of the persuasive techniques that were coming to be associated with modern advertising, and in many localities they were accompanied by instances of intense pressure on reluctant buyers, and even by intimidation. Every bond drive was oversubscribed, and the government realized over $21 billion by borrowing.

Three taxation acts were imposed by Congress during the war. The most productive of these was the War Revenue Act of 1917. Sweeping in range, the bill doubled the existing income-tax rates, increased levies on corporate earnings, imposed an excess-profits tax on industries producing war goods, and provided a number of excise taxes, most of them on luxury items. More than $11 billion came into the government coffers as a result of the various tax laws.

Treasury officials who formed financial policy did not seem concerned at the inflation of prices that occurred during the war. The costs of most commodities rose substantially, but the government made no serious attempt to arrest the increases. A possible reason for the inaction was that officials were resigned to inflation as an inevitable accompaniment of modern war; they realized that the demands of war create full employment, and that with more buyers seeking fewer civilian goods, prices must spurt upward. A more probable reason for their passivity was that inflation did not seem to threaten the well-being of the economy. Prices kept climbing, but the real earnings of the largest consuming groups went up even faster. Thus, increases in the wages of labor outstripped the rise in prices, and the net income of workers jumped by 4 percent by the close of the war. Farmers, urged by the government to produce more of everything, experienced an even more spectacular increase, their real earnings swelling by 25 percent. Americans, in short, were enjoying prosperity, probably a greater prosperity than they had ever known, despite inflation. This happy state probably would not have endured if the war had gone into 1919. Continuing inflation would have eroded real income, and the government would have been forced to act to curb the increases.*

IN HIS HANDLING of relations with other countries before America's entrance into the war President Wilson betrayed a certain bumbling quality, a tendency to ignore the realities in a situation and to avoid meeting the requirements of that situation. His greatest failure was in refusing to realize the relationship

---

*Business shared in the wartime prosperity. Large profits were returned in war-related industries despite the higher corporate levies. In dealing with such industries, the government negotiated cost-plus contracts, guaranteeing a company profits of from 2 1/2 to 15 percent of the cost of production.

between foreign policy and military policy. His foreign policy led inevitably to war with Germany, but he had resisted advocacy of a military policy that would have enabled the nation to fight the war in the most favorable circumstances—by throwing its strength on the side of the nations already resisting Germany. His preparedness program of 1916 was based on an assumption that a victorious Germany would attack the Atlantic seaboard, but the forces he called for might not have been sufficient to repel any invasion.

Wilson shed his uncertainties when war was declared. It was as though the decision to fight altered something in his character. In an abrupt shift of roles, he became a purposeful and perceptive director of war. Better than most of his advisers, he understood that the United States had to do more than mobilize military forces, that it had to mobilize its whole economic resources to perform the task at hand. "It is not an army that we must shape and train for war," he proclaimed, "it is a nation." Not even Abraham Lincoln issued such a call to total effort.

In mobilizing the economy for war, Wilson decided that existing government agencies would have to be dispensed with: burdened with already prescribed functions, they could not take on additional wartime tasks. He therefore created a number of new departments and charged each one with supervising a specific area of production. He based his authority to establish these agencies on his inherent powers as president and commander in chief, but relied also on an act of Congress, passed at his instigation, that allowed him during the war emergency to consolidate existing agencies or to institute new ones. Using the authorization in both sources to the hilt, he brought about what has been called the most sweeping administrative reorganization in the federal government.

Wilson's creations are said to have coordinated the mobilization process, to have speeded up production dramatically, and hence to have contributed mightily to Allied victory. However, the agencies have also been viewed as something other than administrative successes—as exercises in power. Critics claim they constituted the greatest concentration of authority yet attempted in American history, representing a "dictatorship" over the economy. Some have gone so far as to assert that because of the agencies democracy in the United States ceased temporarily to exist. These allegations are exaggerated. It is true that the government extended its authority into areas it never before reached, but the interventions seem restrained in comparison with powers assumed by governments, including democratic ones, in later wars and times. Those who charged dictatorship by the World War I agencies were writing in the era between the world conflicts, before real dictators appeared.

In carrying through the administrative reorganization Wilson often sought advice from a group set up by Congress in 1916 to study economic mobilization, the Council of National Defense. Composed of six secretaries of the cabinet and seven representatives of business and labor, the Council acquired information about the economy possessed by no other body, and its recommendations as to what agencies were needed to prosecute the war had great influence on the president. It continued to function after war was declared, but inevitably took a secondary position in relation to the more active agencies.

Wilson created five major mobilization agencies and a number of lesser boards. The principal bodies were the War Industries Board, which wielded more power over the economy than any of the others, the Shipping Board, the Food Administration, the Fuel Administration, and the Railroad Administration. The heads of the several agencies met once a week with the president to discuss matters of common interest, and as a collective body they constituted a supercabinet very similar to the National Security Council established after World War II.

The Shipping Board was charged with obtaining sufficient transport and cargo vessels to carry American troops and supplies to British and French ports. It could build, buy, or rent ships, and utilizing all three methods, it acquired and operated the largest merchant marine yet developed, over 600 vessels, representing 3,500,000 tons.

The Food Administration had the dual function of encouraging farmers to increase their production of food and of persuading the public to consume less. To the farmers the agency could offer a material inducement. Vested with statutory authority to set prices, it fixed prices of wheat and other crops at high levels and so caused a great expansion of acreage and hence of production. The agency had no authority to limit consumption, or to ration food, as was done in World War II. It could only attempt to persuade people to augment their larders by planting "victory gardens" or to conserve food by observing a "meatless" or a "wheatless" day every week. Results were varied. Some people were willing to sacrifice, and others were not. Food stocks available remained sufficient to care for military and civilian requirements, but if the war had lasted much longer, a form of rationing might have been necessary.

The Fuel Administration was charged with increasing production and trying to reduce household consumption of fuels, especially of coal, which at that time was used more than oil in operating factories and heating homes. Like the Food Administration, the agency had statutory authority to set prices, and it fixed high prices on coal to encourage mine owners to work their pits to the limit or to reopen marginal pits that had been losing money; it also had authority to favor plants producing war materials in allotting supplies of coal and oil. In attempting to reduce consumption, the agency, like its food counterpart, relied on voluntary compliance, an appeal to ordinary people to demonstrate their patriotism by observing a "coal-less" day every week. As with the appeals to conserve food, the results were varied, but the fuel supply remained at adequate levels.

The Railroad Administration came into being because the various privately owned rail companies proved unable to handle the transportation burden imposed on them by the war; accustomed to acting separately, they could not coordinate their efforts to bring troops and supplies to the East Coast seaports for transshipment to France. The resulting snarl-ups pointed to the need for a consolidated system, under the operation of the government. Wilson did not flinch at this prospect of state socialism. By proclamation he took possession of the lines and put them into the hands of the Railroad Administration. The agency operated the roads for the duration of the war, paying the owners a generous annual rental on their properties.

Important as each new agency was, its influence was limited to a single area of the economy. Only one agency had supervisory power over a wide segment of production, the War Industries Board, which, as its name suggests, was concerned with industries turning out war materials. The board's function was described aptly by Wilson in referring to its chairman, Bernard Baruch, who came into government service from the world of business. Baruch, said Wilson, was "the general eye of all supply departments in the field of industry."

The mission of the War Industries Board was to coordinate the production and purchasing of all supplies required in the war effort. It became in the words of the historian Russell Weigley the "chief agency of economic mobilization."* Under its direction the economy produced vast amounts of supplies for the American and the Allied armies. The board's accomplishment was especially remarkable in view of the fact that it possessed few statutory powers; it could not, for instance, set prices or make direct purchasing agreements. Its success was due in part to Baruch's ability to secure cooperation from industry. More important, the agency could compel cooperation by exercising a great indirect authority, granted to it by Wilson, to fix priorities, which Baruch defined as "the power to determine who gets what and when." The giving of priorities, or the withholding of them, invested the WIB with life-or-death power over industry. By controlling supplies it could force a plant to convert to making war goods, compel another to cease making its usual goods, or even dictate the creation of additional industrial facilities. Priorities provided government with a new coercive power, and their use would not be forgotten. They were, in Baruch's words, an "absolutely essential" wartime device.†

---

*Members of the agency were businessmen who volunteered their services and were known as "dollar-a-year men."

†In addition to the various official agencies engaged in carrying on or aiding in the war effort, a number of private and volunteer groups appeared to minister to one aspect or another of the military machine—the Red Cross, the Young Men's Christian Association, the Salvation Army, and others. Similar groups had emerged in the Civil War, illustrating the totality of modern war, and its propensity to involve noncombatants.

THE WAR DEMANDED and devoured supplies, and then demanded and devoured still more. The cycle seemed to have no end, and the recurring requirements placed severe strains on the supply departments of both the army and the navy. The army departments bore by far the heavier burden. They had to provide for a much larger personnel and to serve that personnel over a long line of ocean communication. The task proved to be beyond the capacity of the War Department bureaus, and a crisis in supply was averted only by reorganizing the logistical services.

Several agencies in the War Department were concerned directly or indirectly with supply. Two of them having major responsibilities were the Quartermaster Corps, which saw to clothing, subsistence, construction, and transportation, and the Ordnance Department, which provided arms and ammunition. The chiefs of these bureaus were elderly officers who had served for many years and were accustomed to administering their affairs by a rigid routine. Their methods worked well enough in peacetime but were inadequate to meet the demands of the war. Some of the supply problems might have been alleviated if the chiefs had been willing to alter their methods. But this they were unable to do; wedded to their particular routines, they insisted on maintaining the old ways. The head of ordnance, for example, refused to accept the recommendations of combat officers as to what arms the fighting troops needed, declaring that his staff officers would determine the weaponry to be used.

The reorganization of the supply departments was accomplished under the direction of the chief of staff, General Peyton C. March, who took over the office early in 1918 and reorganized the entire General Staff. The problem in the Ordnance Department was solved by the simple expedient of appointing a new chief, an official who believed that his function was to satisfy the requests of the combat forces. He reportedly said: "If the fighting men want elephants, we get them elephants." The situation in the Quartermaster Corps was more complex, and here March decided on a more drastic change. Acting under authority conferred on him by the secretary of war, he transferred most of the functions of the corps to a newly created and more inclusive agency, Purchase, Storage, and Traffic. The reform provided the army for the first time with a centralized system of supply. March's creation was part of his plan to reorganize the General Staff and to extend its authority over the bureau chiefs, who were now instructed to report to the secretary of war only through the chief of staff. He established three additional offices on the General Staff: Operations, Military Intelligence, and War Plans.

March's reorganization of the supply service helped to ensure a steady flow of war matériel to the army in France, which was also facilitated by the expanding capacity of the industrial system to produce weapons, ammunition, and all the other implements of war. Many of the required items were manufactured in private industry, but large numbers of them were turned out in the government's own arsenals. In addition to operating its conventional establishments, the government built or financed approximately fifty new plants to produce war goods, a significant part of the vast industrial complex called into being by the war.

The combined private-governmental complex was able early to supply American troops with most of the weapons they needed, if not in the first year of the war, then in the opening months of 1918. The standard small arms of the infantryman was the 1903 model Springfield rifle, and government arsenals could turn out this weapon in mass amounts. Several private plants had been making the Enfield model for the British army, and this piece was modified to take American ammunition, thus providing another mass-processed small arm. The situation in respect to machine guns and automatic rifles was not so fortunate, the army never having adopted a standard model of either weapon. However, tests had indicated the superior quality of models developed by designer John M. Browning, and soon Browning water-cooled machine guns and automatic rifles were being manufactured in large numbers.

American production of rifles and machine guns eventually surpassed that of either England or France. The United States also exceeded or equaled its allies in making smokeless powder and rifle and machine-gun ammunition and almost equaled them in high explosives. Only in turning out artillery did the United States lag behind. Production facilities were limited, and rather than try to expand them, American leaders decided to take advantage of a French offer to supply the heavy pieces. Of the 2,250 fieldguns used by the army in France, only 100 were of American make.

The wartime logistical feat was of epic proportions. More than 2 million soldiers were transported across the Atlantic Ocean to France, and nearly 6 million tons of supplies and equipment were sent to subsist them. A historian of logistics, James A. Huston, has properly emphasized that never before in history had a nation attempted to transport and supply so large a force at such a distance from its home bases.

UNITED STATES POLICY objectives have been a subject of perplexing interest to historians. What troubles the scholars is that the objectives were never sharply defined. Indeed, it has seemed to some observers that the nation had no concrete war aims. It did not want to conquer any territory for itself; and it did not profess much interest in even aiding its allies to reconquer territory lost to the Germans. What then did the United States hope to secure as a result of the war? Many believe that American leaders wanted only to win a military victory, to force the "unconditional surrender" of Germany. In this view, the leaders were at fault in not looking to the shape of the postwar world. Obsessed with winning for the sake of winning, they forgot that war is always fought to achieve a political objective.

A determination to beat Germany to her knees did rule the thinking of American leaders, and the same resolve engaged most ordinary citizens. But this feeling did not originate in narrow military considerations—Americans did not want to whip Germany just to show that they could. A pervading fear of Germany had developed after 1914, and the prospect that this aggressive nation might come to dominate Europe was a factor impelling American entrance into the war. Germany had to be put down, but the act of putting her down seemed to most Americans to be in itself a political end: it was necessary to ensure U.S. security. A generation later other Americans would resolve to crush another Germany, that of Adolf Hitler, and for a like end, to preserve the safety of the nation.

The central figure in the command system, Woodrow Wilson, agreed with his countrymen that Germany must be defeated. Wilson too feared the ambitions of Germany, and to avert the danger she posed to the United States, he was willing to employ against her "force without stint or limit." But to the president, defeating Germany was not an end in itself. He regarded an Allied victory only as a means to achieve a just peace, the kind of idealistic peace he held out to the combatants before American entrance into the war. This was the reason he led the United States to the Allied side, so that he, as the representative of the United States at the negotiating table, could have a voice in the settlement. As the culmination of his quest, he proposed to secure the establishment of a league of nations to prevent future wars. It remained to be seen if he could persuade his Allied colleagues to accept his dream, or even his own people.

Although his position was far from assured, Wilson was still the official voice of the nation in the realm of foreign affairs, and no matter how imperfectly he may have represented popular opinion, he spoke with presidential authority. His goal of a just peace must, therefore, be judged a political objective for which the United States was fighting.

The president might differ with many of his countrymen as to why it was necessary to defeat Germany, but they agreed that a military victory was necessary to attain American policy ends, regardless of how those ends were defined. There was no debate over strategy; the United States had, in fact, no choice of strategy. It had entered a war nearly three years old and one with an already fixed theater, in France. It was, moreover, participating as a member of a coalition, an important member but not a dominating one: the American army was not expected to equal the French and British forces in size until 1919.* Faced by these constraints, Wilson and other war managers recognized that they had to conform American strategy to the needs of their allies. Secretary of War Newton D. Baker expressed the problem precisely. The

---

*Wilson's situation differed from that of Roosevelt and Truman in World War II and in the Korean War. In those conflicts the United States was the primary member of its coalition.

United States could not indulge in such intellectual exercises as devising an ideal plan of campaign or selecting an ideal theater of operations, Baker said. The war was in France, where the opposing forces faced each other across the trenches. On one side of the line was the German enemy, and the job of the Americans was "to get over there and get him."

EARLIER IN HIS CAREER President Wilson had been Doctor and Professor Wilson, an academic scholar of some distinction in the disciplines of history and political science. His writings on the evolution of political institutions were much esteemed for their lucidity. A reader looking for similar enlightenment on the development of military institutions, however, would have found little to reward him. Dr. Wilson usually gave war but scant attention, leaving an impression that the subject was unimportant to him and perhaps repellent. When he did discuss war, he did so unrealistically. Thus, in a long history of the American people his volume on the Civil War described in fair detail the great campaigns of the war, but he neglected to state who determined the strategy behind the campaigns or why particular movements were decided upon. Anyone reading his pages might have concluded that the war strategy was the product of unseen and mechanistic forces. The curiously impersonal quality of the narrative revealed much about Wilson's attitude toward war. Fascinated with political forms, he regarded military forms as unimportant. He was not interested in the structure of command systems or in the process by which men in command positions arrived at conclusions. It was an attitude he carried into his presidency.

Forced during the war to become commander in chief, Wilson endeavored to avoid exercising the powers of his position. He was no Polk or Lincoln, not even a McKinley. He did not set up a command post in the White House or follow closely the course of the fighting. He did not supervise the appointments of officers, or try to influence strategic planning. These and other responsibilities that had occupied previous presidents were delegated to selected persons in the command apparatus. He left to Secretary of War Baker the task of overseeing the operations of the General Staff and other agencies of the army; indeed, to Baker, who proved to be a competent administrator, Wilson entrusted even the direction of the huge economic mobilization program. The president assigned the job of organizing and ordering the American army in France to the commander of that army, General John J. Pershing. Pershing had only one meeting with Wilson before leaving for France, and during that meeting, much to Pershing's surprise, the president said nothing about the army's part in the war.

Wilson's passive role has usually been explained as resulting from lack of interest in, or ignorance of, military affairs. This is probably correct, but there may have been a more important reason. By refusing to interfere in the conduct of a coalition war, he avoided commitments to his allies and hence was in a stronger position to demand an American-dictated peace.* That he had political considerations in mind is apparent in his reaction to Allied attempts to create a unified command. The first effort in this direction came in November, 1917, at the instigation of British Prime Minister David Lloyd George, who was disheartened by the lack of military success and disturbed by the resistance of some of his generals to civilian control. Hoping to assert his ideas of strategy, he won agreement from the heads of the principal Allied powers to set up a Supreme War Council to coordinate movements and allotments of troops. European members of the council were to be the prime ministers of Great Britain, France, and Italy, or representatives of them, and a military delegate of each power. Wilson welcomed the promise of improved military direction held out in the new agency. He named as his military representative the chief of the General Staff, General Tasker H. Bliss. But he refused to appoint a permanent political representative. He seemed to be saying to his confederates that while allowing military cooperation, he would not be drawn directly into the making of joint strategic decisions.

The Supreme War Council, partly because it was a pluralistic agency, was unable to unify direction of the war, and in March, 1918, following a German advance, the Allied governments agreed to name one man to command all forces in France. The officer chosen was French General Ferdinand Foch. Although Foch was given the title of general in chief, his powers were limited. He was charged only with the "strategic direction of military operations." The commanders of the British, French, and American armies retained control of the "tactical employment" of their forces. Any leader of a national army could appeal to his government if he thought that the safety of his troops was compromised by an order of Foch.

The commanders of the armies, Douglas Haig of Britain, Henri Philippe Pétain of France, and John J. Pershing of the United States, were difficult subordinates. Foch handled them with tact and generally with success. One of his most sustained controversies was with Pershing, and concerned a problem that had developed before he assumed command.

The American army had arrived in France with its training incomplete and had been stationed in a relatively quiet sector of the front to enable it to continue preparations. Meanwhile, German attacks in other areas bled the British and French armies and on occasion seemed to threaten the Allied line. Alarmed by the depletions in their ranks, British and French commanders asked that American troops be fed into their forces as replacements, arguing

---

*The suggestion that Wilson wanted to leave himself free to concentrate on the peace is that of Ernest R. May. Wilson was less successful in delegating authority in naval affairs. Conflict between the Navy Department in Washington and Admiral Sims in England as to the course to be pursued against submarines forced Wilson to intervene in favor of Sims.

that they could gain experience by serving with veterans. Still later, the Supreme War Council requested Pershing to detach American units to serve with Allied armies. Pershing refused the demands for individual replacements, and he resisted detaching his units. In so doing he was following to the letter his orders, which directed him to preserve a separate army, and for a time he had the support of Wilson. However, the "amalgamation" controversy, as the issue was known, continued, and with Foch's accession it came to a head. The Allies' pressures for American support forced Wilson to intervene in the relations between Pershing and Foch, and to act for the first time as commander in chief.

The president recognized that he had to limit Pershing's discretion to decide on the allocation of American troops. If he did not, the Allied coalition would be weakened, perhaps to the point of losing the war, certainly to the point of losing British and French support for his peace plans. Wilson acted, but in a characteristic way—in effect, he delegated some of his authority to Foch. Newton Baker was instructed to tell Pershing that Foch would again broach the subject of using American troops and that the American commander was expected to "approach any such interviews as sympathetically as possible." In other words, the president desired Pershing to serve at Foch's command.

Wilson had downgraded Pershing in the command system, but not seriously. A good politician in his own right, Pershing recognized authority and bowed to the president's wish that he cooperate with Foch. Thereafter he responded to calls from Foch for assistance or offered to place American units at the latter's disposal. Nevertheless, he maintained his army as a separate entity, and when that army was ready for action, he recovered most of his independence. He was, after Wilson and Baker, the most important figure in the command apparatus.

Pershing had a wide experience behind him when he was appointed commander of the army in France. Following graduation from West Point in 1886, he had risen steadily in grade, partly because of political "pull" (his father-in-law was an influential senator) but mainly because in all his assignments he performed ably. He served in the West in minor Indian campaigns, in the War with Spain, and in the Philippines, and he led the "punitive expedition" into Mexico. In appointing him to command the gathering army, Wilson and Baker ignored the claims of five major generals of senior commission. These officers were passed over on grounds of age or health, and because Pershing's record seemed superior. He had served in both line and staff and was thought to be the general most likely to organize victory.

Pershing was able to inspire confidence in civilians and military men alike. Strongly built and martial in manner, he looked like a commander. He obviously knew his business, and he went about it with an energy that convinced all about him that he would get the job done. He radiated determination, and to sensitive observers something more, a strain of ruthlessness. One of his subordinates wrote admiringly but apprehensively: "He is looking for results. He intends to have them. He will sacrifice any man who does not bring them."

As a field commander, Pershing did not quite come up to expectations. Students of the war give him good but not high marks. It is universally agreed that he was a superb organizer and administrator. He molded the largely raw American army into an efficient fighting force. However, he came up with no original strategic or tactical ideas, no innovative proposal to break the impasse of trench warfare. His only tactical contribution was to insist that well-trained riflemen could again dominate the battlefield and restore openness to warfare. Although he was perhaps right in thinking that the British and the French were too wedded to the protection of trenches, he was wrong in supposing that the rifle could displace artillery or the machine gun. The war never assumed the fluid quality he hoped for, even in the final moment of Allied victory.

As a subordinate in a command system, Pershing was difficult to handle, perpetually sensitive to the rights of his position. He commanded the only American army in the war, and he therefore saw himself as general in chief. As such, he was subject to but one authority, the president, or the president's civilian deputy, the secretary of war: no person or agency should be allowed to interpose between the highest political authority and the highest military authority. He reiterated his claims to Secretary Baker in peremptory dispatches. "The whole must remain absolutely under one head," he wrote. "Please let us not make the mistake of handicapping our army here by attempting to control these things from Washington, or by introducing any co-ordinate authority." The "co-ordinate" authority he was rejecting was the chief of staff and the General Staff.

THE GENERAL STAFF underwent a sensational expansion in numbers after war was declared. The statutory limit of 55 officers was repealed, and the agency increased in size to over 1,000. It also underwent an extensive reorganization that invested it with new functions and powers, including authority over the bureau chiefs. The reorganization was accomplished under the direction of a dominating chief of staff, Peyton C. March. General March was a dedicated soldier and as determined as Pershing to subordinate everything to winning the war. He was equally determined to make the office he held superior to that of field general Pershing. The resulting controversy between March and Pershing provided the first serious test of the command system devised by Elihu Root.

The office of chief of staff was lightly regarded at the time of American entrance into the war. The current occupant, Hugh Scott, soon retired and was succeeded by Tasker Bliss. Bliss was detached to serve on the Supreme War Council, and for a period in 1918 the position was held by an acting chief.

However, Newton Baker was convinced of the importance of the office and that it should be filled by a "big" man. He asked Pershing to send an officer from France, and Pershing returned March, his chief of artillery.

Soon after March took office, Baker issued orders defining the position and powers of the chief of staff. The secretary acted at the height of the controversy over amalgamation, and one of his motives may have been to ensure that War Department directives to Pershing on allotment of troops would be obeyed. But more probably, he was attempting to elevate the office in the command structure, to give it a firm institutional basis. He described the chief of staff as the "immediate adviser" of the secretary on "all matters" relating to the military establishment, charged with the "planning, development, and execution of the Army program." The chief of staff had "rank and precedence" over all other officers and was to issue in the name of the secretary such orders as to ensure that the policies of the War Department were "harmoniously executed" and that the army's program was carried out "speedily and efficiently."

This seemed clear enough—but was it? The language of the order was reminiscent of Elihu Root. To March, the words "rank and precedence" meant that he could command all personnel in the army, that he could command even Pershing. They could also have been interpreted to mean that March was only to "supervise" the establishment. But could a staff officer supervise without commanding? Pershing thought that supervision denoted control, and he insisted that only the president, through the secretary of war, could control him. His pretensions enraged March, and controversy between the two generals continued throughout the war. "General Pershing's inability to function in teamwork with his legal and authorized superiors increased," March wrote bitterly. "He wanted a rubber stamp for Chief of Staff at home, so he could be entirely independent of any supervision or control."

Elihu Root's command arrangement had serious flaws. It notably lacked structure, and Baker's efforts to provide it with form had failed. The location of power within the system remained to be defined.

As the first American troops arrived in France, Pershing had to consider where he would assemble them and the larger numbers that were soon to come. In choosing a sector in which to gather his troops Pershing always kept in mind his instructions to maintain the American army as a "separate and distinct component" of the Allied forces, situated to cooperate with the British and the French but to be physically apart from them.

He also wanted to place his troops, only partially trained, in a relatively quiet zone so that he could give them additional drills before sending them into battle.

Pershing's choice of a location was further limited by the current location of the British and French armies on the battle line. The British, in order to cover the English Channel ports linking them to the home bases, occupied the northern flank of the Allied line, beginning in Belgium and extending into northeastern France. The French, determined to protect Paris, concentrated most of their troops in positions north and east of the city, with smaller bodies stationed to the south. The Americans might have occupied a sector between the British and the French, but Pershing rejected proposals for this as likely to restrict his army's area of operations. The injection of another army into this area would create serious supply problems—the channel ports and the northern railroads were already strained to serve the British and the French forces.

Allowed by the high command to decide his theater, Pershing chose an area southeast of Paris, between the Argonne Forest and the Vosges Mountains, known as the Lorraine sector. It met most of his requirements. Although the Germans occupied a line opposite, including a salient driven into the Allied area at Saint-Mihiel, they had committed the bulk of their forces farther north. In this sector the American army could train and, when ready for battle, it could operate as an independent force, striking at the Saint-Mihiel salient and coal and iron mines at Briey and in the Saar. For supplies the Americans were able to use ports on the western coast of France and railroads not heavily committed to the British or the French. When finally assembled, the American army would thus hold the southern or right flank of the Allied line.

The gradually gathering American divisions underwent an intensive training routine after arriving in Lorraine. The four months of training in the United States the troops had experienced, an amount considered sufficient in previous wars, was not long enough to satisfy Pershing. He believed that in this war not only were special skills required but special training was required to impart them. Even the infantry, the mass of the troops, had to be taught new techniques—how to survive in trench warfare, for example, and how to handle such weapons of the trenches as the machine gun and the hand grenade. Consequently, Pershing put his arriving divisions through an intensive training program, often utilizing the services of experienced British and French officers. As a part of the procedure, some battalions were fed into French divisions, to gain a sight of trench fighting before returning to their divisions to receive still more instruction. The entire schedule might require six months to complete, a time span that Pershing thought none too long. He wanted to educate his men in something other than trench warfare, the defensive tactics that seemed to dominate the thinking of the British and the French. At some point the Allied armies would have to break into the open in offensive warfare. To prepare his men for that day, he insisted they become proficient in using the rifle and the bayonet.

In addition to training his troops, Pershing had to ensure that they receive adequate logistical support. This was a gigantic task as the AEF expanded rapidly in size during 1918, going from 200,000 men in January to a peak strength, including support troops, of 2 million by October. Determined to keep supply operations in his own hands and out of the hands of the General Staff, Pershing created a line of communications headquarters under an officer responsible directly to him. Later designated the Services of Supply, this agency consisted of nine "base sections" organized around the ports receiving supplies from the United States. From these ports, supplies were moved by train to storage depots in an "intermediate" zone, and finally in wagons or trucks to the troops in the "zone of operations." The Services of Supply, commanded by General James G. Harbord, after getting over some initial problems, performed with reasonable efficiency. It remained, however, under Pershing's supervision. The general's insistence on controlling his line of communications placed an additional and heavy command burden on him.

IT WAS NOT EVIDENT YET, but by the beginning of 1918 the European combatants were approaching exhaustion. Shaken by severe losses in the failed offensive of 1917, the British and French armies were content to remain on the defensive while waiting for the Americans to arrive. The German army seemed in better shape, its numbers increased by troops shifted from the Eastern Front after Russia's withdrawal from the war.* But German strength was also being sapped. Many of the men now being called up were physically inferior to their predecessors, and on the home front, morale was sagging as food became scarcer due to the Allied naval blockade. Military leaders worried about a possible collapse of civilian support of the war, but they worried more about the American army that was beginning to arrive in France. That army, if allowed to complete its build-up, would swing the balance of strength and the odds of victory to the Allies. The men planning Germany's strategy decided to launch an offensive to smash the British and French armies before the Americans could fully mass their strength.

The German general ostensibly in charge of developing strategy was Paul von Hindenburg, who had become chief of the General Staff in 1916 after commanding victories over the Russians on the Eastern Front. But the victories were ascribed in some quarters to the genius of his deputy, General Erich von Ludendorff, and it was considered significant that Ludendorff accompanied the seventy-one-year-old Hindenburg to General Staff headquarters in France. If the deputy had not dominated his aging superior before, he clearly did so now. It was Ludendorff who did the actual strategic planning in 1918, and who directed the movements after they were approved by Hindenburg.

*The number of German troops moved from east to west would have been greater if the revolutionary government in Russia had not hesitated on its decision to get out of the war. Germany maintained approximately a million men in the east during the first half of 1918.

The civilian government was hardly more than a spectator to the planning, offering no objections to the decisions reached by the two generals.

By stripping other areas, Ludendorff assembled 3.5 million troops on the Western Front. With this host, he proposed to attack the British and the French and force a victorious peace. According to theory, he should have delivered one gigantic blow with the bulk of his force, but it was beyond German resources to organize that many men to advance on so wide a front. Instead, Ludendorff intended to throw a series of offensives at the British and the French over a period of months, with the aim of damaging if not destroying their armies and eroding their will to resist, and so rendering them impotent before the Americans could enter the fighting.

For his first attack Ludendorff hoped to hit the British army in Flanders, which was cramped into a narrow space on the extreme northern flank of the Allied line. However, the ground in this area had not yet dried from the winter rains, and Ludendorff was forced to delay the operation. He decided instead to strike the British on the Somme River, driving them back onto the Channel ports and separating them from the French to the south. This accomplished, he would then turn to smash the French.

The Germans advanced on March 21, using tactics developed by General von Hutier in 1916–17 on the Eastern Front. After a short but intensive artillery barrage, specially trained assault groups rushed forward behind a rolling artillery fire. These groups infiltrated through or past enemy strong points to attack his artillery. After the assault groups came a second wave of infantry that captured the strong points and attempted to break into the rear and the open. Both waves, to increase their firepower, carried machine guns and, in an innovation in trench warfare, were accompanied by light, horse-drawn artillery.

On the first day the Germans apparently achieved an astonishing success. They broke through on a 50-mile front, with a penetration of over 5 miles. Ludendorff continued to attack and at the end of 8 days had advanced 40 miles, threatening the town of Amiens, the possession of which would enable him to split the forces of the British and the French. But the British, with tardy assistance from the French, managed to stem the drive, and at the end of March Ludendorff had to halt the attack. He held a salient toward Amiens, but he had not achieved a breakthrough. And although he had badly chewed up the British, he had not driven them to the Channel or separated them from the French. His own losses had been heavy, especially in the trained shock troops that he could not readily replace.

Ludendorff did not seem to realize the limitation of his success. Early in April he returned to the attack, this time striking at the British on the Lys River line in Flanders. Again he broke through the first line of enemy trenches, but the British, although suffering heavy casualties, finally managed to contain the assault. At the end of April Ludendorff called off the offensive. He had driven another salient into the enemy line, but he had still not been able to force the British against the Channel and destroy them. His salient in Flanders was separated from the one pointing at Amiens.

Destroying the British in Flanders became an obsession with Ludendorff. He has been called a military gambler, and criticized for wasting his strength in continued attacks when it was evident that they were not achieving victory. Although he had an element of the gambler in him, he did not think he was betting on a long shot. On the contrary, he believed he was winning, that his next blow would force the Allies to accept peace. He was the victim of his own apparent successes. The German advances in the first two offensives had not been great enough to bring victory but were sufficient to tempt Ludendorff to continue. With less success he might have retired to a shortened defensive line and conserved his manpower. But he saw victory waiting on one more attack. He had damaged the British in Flanders, and he would yet destroy them. As a preliminary to the final thrust, he proposed to draw off British reserves from Flanders by making a diversionary attack on another section of the Allied line.

For his target Ludendorff chose a position held by the French, a ridge northeast of Paris called the Chemin des Dames. Although obviously of strategic importance, the ridge was occupied by a relatively thin defense, the French believing in its natural strength to preclude attack. When Ludendorff struck on May 27, they suffered a shocking surprise. The Germans easily knifed through the outer line and penetrated 13 miles, the longest advance made by any attacking force in one day since the beginning of trench warfare. The extent of the breakthrough astonished even Ludendorff. Although he had designed the attack as a diversion, intending to halt it at Soissons, he could not resist the temptation to exploit his success. Bringing in additional troops, he continued to attack, and though held to shorter advances, he still gained ground. By May 30 the Germans had reached the Marne River at Château-Thierry and stood less than 50 miles from Paris.

The German approach caused consternation in the Allied high command. It also aroused recriminations, one of which was that the Americans, with over 600,000 men in France, were not pulling their weight in the Allied defense. Pershing had offered to place American troops at Foch's disposal during the Somme battle, and in this greater crisis he tendered five divisions for use on the Marne line. Foch accepted the gesture, and two American divisions, one of which included a brigade of marines, were quickly moved up to positions around Château-Thierry. As they came into the line, British and French observers were impressed above all by their youth, their "magnificent youth," in the words of a British writer. Eager to meet the foe and confident they could beat him, they were like the innocents who composed the Allied armies in 1914, before the carnage of trench warfare set in.

The situation was not as perilous as it seemed. Ludendorff's deep salient —the Marne salient, as it became known—was narrow in width. Crowded into a small space, Ludendorff was having trouble bringing in supplies and rein-forcements. He needed both, but particularly men to replace his heavy losses. That the German offensive was losing much of its punch soon became evident. Ludendorff tried to force a crossing of the Marne during the first days of June, but the Americans, although not fully trained, threw back his every effort. They displayed great coolness under fire and delivered a rifle and machine-gun fire that impressed Allied observers with its accuracy. Not satisfied to stop the German attacks, they went over to the offensive during the rest of June, attacking and capturing enemy positions in Belleau Wood and the villages of Bouresches and Vaux. In this kind of fighting they demonstrated unusual technical skills for untried troops but also a tendency, apparent earlier among the British and French, to attempt to rush a position by headlong attack. Their tactics resulted in heavy losses, almost 10,000 total casualties, including 1,800 dead. Before the Americans on the Marne began their assaults, a division serving with the French to the north attacked and took the town of Cantigny in the Amiens salient, thus achieving the distinction of being the first unit to launch an offensive.

His Marne offensive stalled, Ludendorff should have pulled back to a more defensible line. But he could not give up the dream of victory. He tried two more offensives. One, launched in June, was a two-pronged movement designed to merge the Amiens and Marne salients. The second, and the last, German effort, came in July, an attempt to take the railroads around Reims and widen the Marne salient. Both offensives were contained by the French and American defenders, and Ludendorff finally admitted failure. He had achieved startling tactical successes, but he had not been able to gain his strategic purpose, to smash the British and the French armies before the Americans arrived in force. Ten American divisions served with the Allies during the summer battles, and without their presence it is doubtful that the German tide could have been stemmed. Now it was the turn of the Allies to attack, and in their offensive the Americans would again play a vital role.

Planning for an Allied offensive was going on even while the Germans were making their push. Foch, in consultation with his army commanders—Haig, Pétain, and Pershing—determined to attack as soon as the German advance was contained. The first Allied thrust began, in fact, on July 18, two days after the last German offensive ended. Seldom if ever in military history has such a dramatic reversal of roles occurred. Within the space of a few days the defender became the attacker and, having seized the initiative, never relinquished it. Several factors accounted for the switch. The Germans were exhausted not only physically but psychologically; they had fought their hearts out and, although gaining ground, were no closer to victory than before. The Allies, in contrast, were stronger. They had superiority in tanks, airplanes, guns, and all other form of supplies, and thanks to the arriving Americans, they had superiority in numbers. Their edge in the last category was not great, even by autumn, after the entire American force was assembled, but it was still an advantage, one of the several that lifted Allied morale. Superiority of morale was, in fact, the Allies' strongest weapon. They could hope for victory, whereas the Germans could not.

Foch planned to strike the Germans in a grand offensive along the whole line. But before beginning the movement, he felt he had to erase three German targets: the Marne salient in the French sector, the Amiens salient in the British sector, and the Saint-Mihiel salient opposite the Americans. As his first objective he chose the Marne, this being the attack that moved out on July 18.

The attacking force was primarily French, but included eight American divisions. On the first day the thrust carried from two to five miles and threatened Soissons, which dominated the German supply line into the salient. The danger was apparent to Ludendorff, who immediately ordered a planned withdrawal. Fighting a stubborn delaying action, the Germans retired behind the Vesle and Aisne rivers, a distance of 20 miles. Here they held, and at the end of the first week in August Foch halted the attack.* Both sides suffered heavily in the fighting, the attackers realizing the greater losses. The Americans charged with their usual courage, and with what Allied observers considered their usual lack of tactical skill. These observers were struck by the fact that the American dead were always found "lying in regular lines," which was the way that so many Union and Confederate soldiers had fallen in the Civil War.

The next Allied attack was directed at the Amiens salient. It called for moves by British and French armies converging on each side of the salient. The British, assisted by an American division, led off the assault on August 8, with the French following. At almost the first contact the German front collapsed, and the Allies broke 9 miles into the rear of the enemy line. This was, in Ludendorff's words, the "black day" of the German army.

The debacle resulted in part from Allied superiority in numbers but mainly from the armored tanks, over 400 of them, that the British flung into the battle. The British introduced tanks in 1916 and used them with limited success in actions at Cambrai and other places. Since then the British army, and to a lesser extent the French and American armies, had been equipped with tanks. In the Amiens operation the British for the first time massed tanks to lead an attack and achieved the first armored breakthrough in modern war. The iron monsters were impervious to rifle and machine-gun fire, although vulnerable to artillery, and they imparted such a feeling of irresistible power as they advanced that the German infantry fled. The tanks lost some of their effectiveness after the first day, as the Germans stiffened their defense, but the Allies still ground ahead. By the end of August the Germans had been forced

---

*This operation is sometimes called the "Aisne-Marne offensive"; and also, in reference to the earlier German offensive, the "second Marne."

back to the Hindenburg Line, whence they had begun their first offensive in March. The Amiens salient was eliminated, and at the same time another British force, supported by two American divisions, was beginning to erase the smaller Lys salient to the north.

The third great salient, Saint-Mihiel, was a logical objective for the Americans. They held the sector of the line adjacent to the bulge and could most easily mobilize forces to attack it. Moreover, they now had the strength to mount an assault. As more and more troops poured in, Pershing organized his divisions into corps and gave his aggregation a name, the First Army. Foch was willing to entrust the erasure of Saint-Mihiel to the Americans, but he and Pershing differed as to how the operation should be conducted. Pershing wanted to push through the salient to the communications center of Metz, whereas Foch wanted merely to eliminate the salient and then to divide the American forces for a drive northward, with some of the Americans operating under French command. Pershing objected violently to dividing his army, and the two generals finally compromised. The First Army would fight as an army but would stop after seizing the base of the salient and would then be at Foch's disposal in the grand offensive.

The American attack jumped off on September 12. The assault column was the largest single American force yet assembled, 550,000 troops. It was supported by over 260 tanks, many of them manned by French crews, and by 1,500 planes, of which 600 were piloted by Americans. The Germans knew that the attack was coming, and believing that Saint-Mihiel was not worth a hard fight, they had started to withdraw their heavy equipment and to thin their units before the Americans moved in. As a consequence, the attackers met only slight resistance and at the end of four days had occupied the salient. They had not, however, been able to catch the retiring Germans, who escaped to fight elsewhere. Nevertheless, the Americans could feel satisfied with their accomplishment. They had competently conducted a limited offensive, and they were confident of taking their place in the greater offensive that Foch was planning.

The French commander had been maturing his offensive plan for months, changing it in detail as developing events seemed to dictate alterations. The recent victories in the salients convinced him that a determined push could end the war in 1918. Doubting that he could destroy the German armies, he hoped at the most to punish them severely. But he did think he could force them to retire rapidly within their own frontiers, so rapidly they would have to abandon the immense stores they had built up in France. Deprived of this sustenance, the Germans would have to make peace, on Allied terms. Only one fear gnawed at Foch, that the Germans would be able to carry off their supplies and thus retain the capacity to prolong the war into 1919. His overriding purpose, therefore, was to prevent the Germans from conducting an orderly withdrawal. As an important first step to this end, he decided to cut the great lateral railroad serving the Germans behind the Hindenburg Line, seizing the key junctions of Aulnoye and Mézières and forcing the enemy into retreat.

The plan called for advances by all parts of the Allied force beginning on September 26 and continuing through the following three days—a classic example of a cordon offensive. "Everyone in the fight" was Foch's exhortation to the armies in his command. The British on the north, supported by the French left, was to attack on the Cambrai-Saint-Quentin front toward Aulnoye. The Americans on the south were to drive toward Mézières. In the meantime the French in the center were to strike at the Aisne River line, maintaining pressure on the front and preventing the Germans from detaching troops to other sectors. The British and the Americans were expected to act like a giant pair of pincers, crushing German forces between them. In addition to these major attacks, Foch organized a minor thrust in Flanders to be delivered by a combined Belgian, French, and British force under the titular command of the Belgian monarch, Albert.

The Americans, who were to lead off the offensive, had to overcome vexatious difficulties before they could move. One problem was that of time. Pershing had begun to plan his army's participation in the offensive even while he was preparing the Saint-Mihiel operation. He was thus committing himself to try what no other single army had yet attempted, to mount two offensives within a few weeks of each other—the Saint-Mihiel attack scheduled to start on September 12 and the larger offensive, to begin fourteen days later. Necessarily, preparations for the latter movement were precipitous. Another problem was that of space. In the grand offensive the Americans, with Pershing's acquiescence, were to take over a new sector of the Allied line, a sector around Verdun and 50 miles to the north and west of Saint-Mihiel. Transfer of American troops and supplies to the new area began ten days before the Saint-Mihiel battle, 600,000 troops being shifted, some of them in French trucks, some on rail lines, some marching. The concentration was completed only on the eve of battle. Left behind to come on later were the 500,000 men who fought in the salient.

The sector was bounded on the right by the Meuse River and on the left, 24 miles distant, by the rugged Argonne Forest. It was a difficult and desolate area in which to have to fight, especially hard in the Argonne Forest, described by British historian John Keegan as "that awful wilderness of shredded woods and choked up streams." But here the Americans would fight, in the operation known in World War I literature as the Meuse-Argonne offensive.

The attack was a massive and complex operation, the greatest battle to its time in American history. The U.S. Army, when assembled in its entirety, comprised 1,250,000 troops, a host that dwarfed any single army in previous wars; that was, indeed, larger than the total number of men called up in any previous conflict except the Civil War. This force advanced on a front of 24 miles that was gradually widened to one of 90 miles, a space that exceeded by far the fighting area in any earlier war.* The soldiers fought for forty-seven days, not in set battles with intervals, but every day, often in unplanned encounters, wherever they met the enemy. Only once before had there been a campaign that compared in sustained ferocity with the Meuse-Argonne, the Virginia campaign of 1864–65 in the Civil War.

The attack opened on schedule. Following a three-hour artillery bombardment, the infantry stepped off confidently; at the same time one of the French armies of the center advanced on the American left. The troops soon discovered they were not going to experience another easy Saint-Mihiel kind of advance; the Germans were prepared to fight. Dug in, in four defensive lines, they resisted stubbornly and, at the end of the day, had held the Americans to an advance that averaged only three miles. The going was particularly rough in the Argonne Forest. Here tanks were of no use, and the infantry had to bear the fighting alone.

The next few days were a repetition of the first. The attack went ahead, breaking through the second line of defense, but it remained badly behind the schedule Pershing had set. Part of the trouble was that the American commander had packed too many divisions into the battle area, which became literally choked. Tremendous traffic jams of men and trucks slowed down every attempted advance. Moreover, Pershing and his staff were unable to exercise consistent control over the various parts of the army—units became lost, guns failed to move up in support, and supplies failed to arrive. The poor staff work was criticized at General Pétain's headquarters, but the French were actually making little more progress. Only the British on the northern sector scored significant penetrations.

Although distressed at the slowness of the advance, Pershing continued to push the attack. By October 10 the Americans finally cleared the Argonne Forest, which Pershing originally hoped to seize on the third day of the battle. There was still a long way to go before reaching the German rail line, and Pershing paused to reorganize his forces. He recognized that the unsatisfactory American performance was in part his fault, that he had tried to exercise too direct a control over too large an army. As one phase of his reorganization he therefore divided his force, giving the First Army to General Hunter Liggett and creating the Second Army under General Robert L. Bullard. Thereafter Pershing acted as army group commander.

After the reorganization the Americans fought their way toward the Meuse River crossings. The going was still slow because of increased German resistance. Ludendorff, alarmed by the persistent advance, committed twenty-seven of his dwindling reserve divisions to the southern sector, thereby weakening his forces on other parts of the line. Nevertheless, the Americans pushed

---

*General Sherman in the Georgia campaign in the Civil War marched on a 60-mile front, but, meeting virtually no opposition, he did not have to fight his way forward.

ahead, as did the French on their left. They carried the third German defensive line on the last day of October, and on November 5 they crossed the Meuse. Subsequently the advance was more rapid, covering 24 miles on either side of the Meuse during the first week of November. Mézières fell to the French— Aulnoye went to the British on November 5—and the Americans and the French rolled eastward to Sedan, which the French were allowed to enter first to erase the stigma of a defeat by the Germans in 1870. All along the line, from north to south, German resistance was collapsing. In the homeland civilian demands for peace were becoming more insistent, and revolutionary councils were appearing in the army and the navy. It was obvious that the end of the war was near.

The German government had recognized earlier that its cause was probably lost. On October 8 it asked President Wilson for an armistice, thinking it could negotiate more lenient terms with Wilson than with the heads of other Allied governments. Wilson stated certain conditions, emphasizing political results that he hoped to see incorporated in a peace treaty, but his British and French colleagues objected to unilateral American action or to prescribing political conditions of peace. He thereupon referred the question of peace to the Allies jointly and informed Germany there could be no peace negotiations but only "surrender."

Now events moved quickly. The German imperial government fell, and a republican government was proclaimed. Ludendorff resigned, and his successor, with the consent of other officers, asked for an armistice. The Allied government demanded the following terms: evacuation of all occupied territory, retirement of the German army to the east bank of the Rhine River, evacuation of key bridgeheads over the Rhine, and surrender of vast military supplies, including all submarines and the bulk of the German navy. The Germans complied, and the armistice was signed on November 11. General Pershing thought the Allies had made a mistake in granting the armistice: the war should have been continued until Germany was forced into "unconditional surrender." It is doubtful, however, that the Allies could have achieved such a result. France and England were exhausted by their efforts, and a demand for unconditional surrender might have reunited the Germans. Although severely punished, the German army had not been destroyed, and it might have been able to maintain a defense of the frontier for an indefinite time.

THE VICTORS GATHERED at Versailles near Paris to make a peace that would confirm the results of the war. President Wilson attended the conference to put into the peace treaty the ideals he had proclaimed, which would constitute a "peace without victory" and end the possibility of future wars. He was able to get but few of his ideals into the treaty. His Allied colleagues, boasting of their "realism," disdained most of his proposals. He did manage to incorporate in the treaty his concept of an international organization to maintain peace, a League of Nations, only to see his own country reject adherence to the League. He retired into private life in 1921 a broken man, to die a few years later.

The principal European victors—Britain, France, and to a lesser extent Italy—gained various rewards from the war: lands, colonies, and financial reparations, all exacted from the defeated side. These exactions would become the great German myth in the postwar years—Germany would claim that she had been subjected to a harsh and punitive peace. Actually, relatively little was taken from Germany. She remained essentially a united nation, potentially the strongest power in Europe.

The apparent victors in truth won very little. Indeed, it can be said accurately that they were more losers than winners. They suffered heavy human casualties, severe physical damage, and harm to their social structures that cannot be calculated. Rightly considered, there was only one victor in the war: the United States. The American nation had endured light human losses and no physical suffering. Its economy had been immensely stimulated by the war; and, supplanting Britain, it emerged as the financial center of the West, the creditor of all the other belligerents. Although this was not recognized immediately at home or abroad, the United States was now in fact the greatest power in the postwar world.

BIBLIOGRAPHY

ADAMS, Henry. *The War of 1812.* Edited by H. A. DeWeerd. Charles Scribner's Sons, 1944.

ALDEN, Carroll Storrs and Allan Westcott. *The United States Navy.* Lippincott, 1943.

ALDEN, John R. *A History of the American Revolution.* Alfred A. Knopf, 1969.

ALFOLDI, Laszlo M. "The Hutier Legend," *Parameters: Journal of the U.S. Army War College,* V, Number 2 (1976), 69–74.

AMBROSE, Stephen E. *Crazy Horse and Custer.* Doubleday, 1975.

APPLEGATE, Howard Lewis. "The Medical Administrators of the American Revolutionary Army," *Military Affairs,* XXV (Spring, 1961), 1–10.

AUSTIN, Anthony. *The President's War.* Lippincott, 1971.

BAILEY, John W. "Pacifying the Plains: General Alfred Terry and the Decline of the Sioux, 1866–1890," *Military History,* Number 17.

BARBEAU, Arthur E. and Florette Henri. *The Unknown Soldier: Black American Troops in World War I.* Temple University Press, 1974.

BASS, Herbert J., ed. *America's Entry Into World War I: Submarines, Sentiment, or Security.* Holt, Rinehart and Winston, 1964.

BAUER, K. Jack. *The Mexican War, 1846–1848.* Macmillan, 1974.

———. *Surfboats and Horse Marines: U.S. Naval Operations in the Mexican War, 1846–1848.* United States Naval Institute, 1969.

BEIRNE, Francis F. *The War of 1812.* E. P. Dutton, 1949.

BELL, J. Bowyer. *The Myth of the Guerrilla.* Alfred A. Knopf, 1971.

BERNATH, Stuart L. *Squall Across the Atlantic.* University of California Press, 1970.

BIGELOW, John, Jr. *Reminiscences of the Santiago Campaign.* Harper & Brothers, 1899.

BLAINEY, Geoffrey. *The Causes of War.* The Free Press, 1973.

BLAKE, Robert, ed. *The Private Papers of Douglas Haig, 1914–1919.* Eyre & Spottiswoode, 1952.

BLUNDEN, Edmund. *Undertones of War.* Doubleday, 1929.

BRAISTED, William Reynolds. *The United States Navy in the Pacific, 1909–1922.* University of Texas Press, 1971.

BROWN, Alvin. *The Armor of Organization: A Rational Plan of Organization for the Armed Forces and as a Preliminary Thereto an Inquiry Into the Origins of Existing Military Organization.* Hibbert Printing Co., 1953.

BUCHAN, John. *The Battle of the Somme.* Grosset, 1917.

BULLARD, Robert Lee. *Personalities and Reminiscences of the War.* Doubleday, Page, 1925.

CABLE, Frank T. *The Birth and Development of the American Submarine.* Harper & Brothers, 1924.

CALLWELL, Charles Edward. *Field Marshal Henry Wilson, His Life and Diaries.* Cassell, 1927.

CASE, Lynn M. and Warren F. Spencer. *The United States and France: Civil War Diplomacy.* University of Pennsylvania Press, 1970.

CATTON, Bruce. *Glory Road.* Doubleday & Company, 1952.

CHAPMAN, Guy. *A Passionate Prodigality.* Holt, Rinehart and Winston, 1966.

CHITWOOD, Oliver Perry. *A History of Colonial America.* Harper & Brothers, 1931.

Civil War and Miscellaneous Papers, "American Tactics in the Present War," in the *Papers of Military History Society of Massachusetts,* XIV, pp. 437–457.

COFFMAN, Edward M. *The War to End All Wars.* Oxford University Press, 1968.

CONNER, Seymour V. and Odie B. Faulk. *North America Divided: The Mexican War, 1846–1848.* Oxford University Press, 1971.

COSMAS, Graham A. *An Army for Empire.* University of Missouri Press, 1971.

CROOK, D. P. *The North, The South, and The Powers, 1861–1865.* John Wiley, 1974.

CRUTTWELL, C. R. M. *A History of the Great War, 1914–1918.* Clarendon Press, 1934.

CULLOP, Charles P. *Confederate Propaganda in Europe, 1861–1865.* University of Miami Press, 1969.

CUNLIFFE, Marcus. *Soldiers & Citizens (1775–1865).* Little, Brown, 1968.

DAVIS, Carl L. *Arming the Union: Small Arms in the Union Army.* Kennikat Press, 1973.

DEWEERD, Harvey A. *President Wilson Fights His War.* Macmillan, 1968.

DILLON, Richard. *We Have Met the Enemy: Oliver Hazard Perry, Wilderness Commodore.* McGraw-Hill, 1978.

DOWNEY, Fairfax. *Sound of the Guns.* David McKay, 1956.

DULL, J. R. *The French Navy and American Independence.* Princeton University Press, 1975.

DYER, Brainerd. *Zachary Taylor.* Louisiana State University Press, 1946.

EARLE, Edward Mead, ed. *Makers of Modern Strategy: Military Thought from Machiavelli to Hitler.* Princeton University Press, 1943.

ESTHUS, Raymond A. "Naval Limitations and Domestic Political Imperatives," *Reviews in American History,* VI (March, 1978), 109–113.

FALLS, Cyril. *The Great War.* G. P. Putnam's Sons, 1959.

FINNEGAN, John Patrick. *Against the Specter of a Dragon: The Campaign for American Military Preparedness, 1914–1917.* Greenwood Press, 1974.

FLETCHER, Marvin E. *The Black Soldier and Officer in the United States Army, 1891–1917.* University of Missouri Press, 1974.

FOCH, Ferdinand. *The Memoirs of Marshal Foch.* Translated by T. Bentley Mott. Doubleday, 1931.

FONER, Jack D. *Blacks and the Military in American History.* Praeger, 1974.

———. *The United States Soldier Between Two Wars: Army Life and Reforms, 1865–1898.* Humanities Press, 1970.

FONER, Philip S. *The Spanish–Cuban American War, and the Birth of American Imperialism, 1895–1902.* Monthly Review Press, 1972.

FORESTER, C. S. *The Age of Fighting Sail.* Doubleday, 1956.

———. *The General.* Michael Joseph, 1958.

FORMAN, Sidney. "Why the United States Military Academy Was Established in 1802," *Military Affairs,* XXIX (Spring, 1965), 16–28.

FREIDEL, Frank. *The Splendid Little War.* Little, Brown, 1958.

———. *Over There.* Little, Brown, 1964.

FROTHINGHAM, Thomas C. *The Naval History of the World War: Offensive Operations, 1914–1915.* Harvard University Press, 1924.

———. *The Naval History of the World War: The United States in the War, 1917–1918.* Harvard University Press, 1927.

FULLER, J. F. C. *A Military History of the Western World,* Vol. 3. Funk & Wagnalls, 1956.

FUSSELL, Paul. *The Great War and Modern Memory.* Oxford University Press, 1975.

GABRIEL, Richard and Paul L. Savage. *Crisis in Command: Mismanagement in the Army.* Hill and Wang, 1978.

GATES, John M. *Schoolbooks and Krags: The United States Army in the Philippines, 1898–1902.* Greenwood Press, 1973.

GATEWOOD, Willard B., Jr. "Negro Troops in Florida, 1898," *The Florida Historical Quarterly,* XLIX (July, 1970), 1–15.

GOETZMAN, William H. *Army Exploration in the American West, 1803–1863.* Yale University Press, 1959.

GRAVES, Robert. *Good-Bye to All That.* Jonathan Cape & Harrison Smith, 1930.

GRAY, John S. *Centennial Campaign: The Sioux War of 1876.* Old Army, 1976.

GRIFFITH, Samuel B., II. *In Defense of the Public Liberty: Britain, America, and the Struggle for Independence—From 1760 to the Surrender at Yorktown in 1781.* Doubleday, 1976.

HAGAN, Kenneth J., ed. *In Peace and War: Interpretations of American Naval History, 1775–1978.* Greenwood Press, 1978.

HALLE, Louis J. "Does War Have a Future?", *Foreign Affairs,* LII (October, 1973), 20–34.

———. "1898: The United States in the Pacific," *Military Affairs,* XX (Summer, 1956), 76–80.

HAMILTON, Holman. *Zachary Taylor.* Bobbs-Merrill, 1941.

HARBORD, James G. *Leaves From a War Diary.* Dodd, Mead, 1925.

HENRY, Robert Selph. *The Story of the Mexican War.* Bobbs-Merrill, 1950.

HIGGINBOTHAM, Don. *The War of American Independence.* Macmillan, 1971.

HIGHAM, Robin and Carol Brandt, eds. *The United States Army in Peacetime: Essays in Honor of the Bicentennial, 1775–1975.* Published for the Freedom Park Foundation by Military Affairs/Aerospace Historian Publishing Co., 1975.

HITMAN, J. Mackay. *The Incredible War of 1812.* University of Toronto Press, 1965.

HORSMAN, Reginald. *The War of 1812.* Alfred A. Knopf, 1969.

HOUSE, Jonathan M. "The Decisive Attack: A New Look at French Infantry Tactics on the Eve of World War I," *Military Affairs,* XXX (December, 1976), 164–168.

HUSTON, James A. "The Logistics of Arnold's March to Quebec," *Military Affairs,* XXII (December, 1968), 110–123.

———. *The Sinews of War: Army Logistics, 1775–1953.* U.S. Government Printing Office, 1966.

INFANTRY JOURNAL. *Americans Vs. Germans: Personal Battle Experiences of Six American Fighters Against Germans in World War I.* Penguin Books, 1942.

JACOBS, James Ripley. *The Beginning of the U.S. Army, 1783–1812.* Princeton University Press, 1947.

JAMESON, Hugh. "Equipment for the Militia of Middle States, 1775–1781," *The Journal of the American Military Institute,* III (Spring, 1939), 26–38.

JENKINS, Brian. *Britain & The War for the Union,* Vol. I. McGill-Queen's University Press, 1974.

JOHNSON, Virginia W. *The Unregimented General: A Biography of Nelson A. Miles.* Houghton Mifflin, 1962.

KALB, Marvin and Elie Abel. *Roots of Involvement: The United States in Asia, 1784–1917.* W. W. Norton, 1971.

KEEGAN, John. *The Face of Battle.* The Viking Press, 1976.

KEENAN, George. *Campaigning in Cuba, 1899.* Kennikat Press, 1899.

KENNEDY, David M. "War & The American Character," *The Stanford Magazine,* III (Spring/Summer, 1975), 14–18.

KENNETT, Lee. *The French Forces in America, 1780–1783.* Greenwood Press, 1977.

KIMBALL, Jeffrey Philip. *Strategy on the Northern Frontier: 1814.* (Thesis, Ph.D., Louisiana State University, 1969), University Microfilms, Inc., 1970.

KING, Jere Clemans, ed. *The First World War.* Harper & Row, 1972.

KINNARD, Douglas. *The War Managers.* University Press of New England, 1977.

KOHN, Richard H. *Eagles & Swords: The Federalists and the Creation of the Military Establishment in America, 1783–1802.* Free Press, 1975.

KORB, Lawrence J. *The Joint Chiefs of Staff.* Indiana University Press, 1976.

KREIDBERG, Marvin A. and Merton G. Henry. *History of Military Mobilization in the United States Army, 1775–1945.* Department of the Army, 1955.

KUTGER, Joseph P. "Irregular Warfare in Transition," *Military Affairs,* XXIV (Fall, 1960), 113–123.

LANE, Jack C. *Armed Progressive: General Leonard Wood.* Presidio Press, 1978.

LEACH, Douglas Edward. *Arms for Empire: A Military History of the British Colonies in North America, 1607–1763.* Macmillan, 1973.

LEECH, Margaret. *In the Days of McKinley.* Harper & Brothers, 1959.

LERWILL, Leonard L. *The Personnel Replacement System in the United States Army.* Department of the Army, 1954.

LEWIS, George G. and John Mewha. *History of Prisoner of War Utilization by the United States Army, 1776–1945.* Department of the Army, 1955.

LIDDELL HART, B. H. *The War in Outline, 1914–1918.* Random House, 1936.

LIGGETT, Hunter. *Commanding an American Army: Recollections of the World War.* Houghton Mifflin, 1925.

LINDERMAN, Gerald F. *The Mirror of War: American Society and the Spanish-American War.* University of Michigan Press, 1924.

MACK, John E. *A Prince of Our Disorder.* Little, Brown, 1976.

MAHON, John K. *The War of 1812.* University of Florida Press, 1972.

_____. "Anglo-American Methods of Indian Warfare, 1676–1794," *Mississippi Valley Historical Review* (September, 1958), 254–275.

MANUCY, Albert. *Artillery Through the Ages.* U.S. Government Printing Office, 1949.

MARWICK, Arthur. *War and Social Change in the Twentieth Century.* St. Martin's Press, 1974.

MOSLEY, Nicholas. *Julian Grenfell: His Life and the Times of His Death, 1881–1915.* Holt, Rinehart and Winston, 1976.

MURDOCK, Eugene C. *One Million Men: The Civil War Draft in the North.* The State Historical Society of Wisconsin, 1971.

NELSON, Otto L., Jr. *National Security and the General Staff.* The Infantry Journal Press, 1946.

NELSON, P. D. *General Horatio Gates.* Louisiana State University Press, 1976.

NORMAN, Albert. *Operation Overload, Design and Reality: The Allied Invasion of Western Europe.* Military Service Publishing Co., 1952.

OFFNER, Arnold A. *The Origins of the Second World War: American Foreign Policy and World Politics, 1917–1941.* Praeger, 1975.

PALMER, Dave Richard. *The Way of the Fox: American Strategy in the War for America, 1775–1783.* Greenwood Press, 1975.

PALMER, Frederic. *Newton D. Baker,* Vol. I. Dodd, Mead, 1931.

PARKMAN, Francis. *The Battle for North America.* Edited by John Tebbel. Doubleday, 1948.

PAULLIN, Charles Oscar. *Paullin's History of Naval Administration, 1775–1911: A Collection of Articles from the U.S. Naval Institute Proceedings.* U.S. Naval Institute, 1968.

PAXSON, Frederic L. *America at War, 1917–1918.* Houghton Mifflin, 1939.

PECKHAM, Howard H. *The Colonial Wars, 1689–1762.* University of Chicago Press, 1964.

_____. *The War for Independence.* University of Chicago Press, 1958.

PITT, Barrie. *1918: The Last Act.* W. W. Norton, 1963.

PLETCHER, David M. *The Diplomacy of Annexation: Texas, Oregon & The Mexican War.* University of Missouri Press, 1973.

POGUE, Forrest C. *The European Theater of Operations: The Supreme Command.* Office of the Chief of Military History, Department of the Army, 1954.

PORTER, Kenneth Wiggins. "Florida Slaves and Free Negroes in the Seminole War, 1835–1842," *The Journal of Negro History,* XXVIII (October, 1943), 390–420.

POTTER, E. B. *The United States and World Sea Power.* Prentice-Hall, 1955.

PUSEY, Merlo J. *The Way We Go to War.* Houghton Mifflin, 1971.

QUARLES, Benjamin. "The Colonial Militia and Negro Manpower," *Mississippi Valley Historical Review,* XLV (March, 1959), 643–652.

RADABOUGH, Jack S. "The Militia of Colonial Massachusetts," *Military Affairs,* XVIII (Spring, 1954), 1–18.

REILLY, Robin. *The British at the Gates: The New Orleans Campaign in The War of 1812.* G. P. Putnam's Sons, 1974.

RICHARDSON, James D. *A Compilation of the Messages and Papers of the Presidents, 1789–1897,* 10 vols. U.S. Government Printing Office, 1896–1899.

RICKEY, Don, Jr. "The Enlisted Men of the Indian Wars," *Military Affairs,* XXIII (Summer, 1959), 91–96.

ROBINSON, Donald L. *Slavery in the Structure of American Politics, 1765–1820.* Harcourt Brace Jovanovich, 1971.

ROBSON, Eric. *The American Revolution in Its Political and Military Aspects, 1763–1783.* Oxford University Press, 1955.

ROOT, Elihu. *The Military and Colonial Policy of the United States: Addresses and Reports by Elihu Root.* Collected and edited by Robert Bacon and James Brown Scott. Harvard University Press, 1916.

ROPP, Theodore. *War in the Modern World.* Duke University Press, 1959.

ROSSIE, Jonathan G. *The Politics of Command in the American Revolution.* Syracuse University Press, 1974.

ROSTOW, W.W. *The Diffusion of Power: An Essay in Recent History.* Macmillan, 1972.

RUIZ, Roman Eduardo, ed. *The Mexican War.* Holt, Rinehart and Winston, 1963.

SAJER, Guy. *The Forgotten Soldier.* Translated from the French by Lily Emmet. Harper & Row, 1971.

SASSOON, Siegfried. *The Memoirs of George Sherston.* Doubleday, 1937.

SCHMIDT, Hans. *The United States Occupation of Haiti, 1915–1934.* Rutgers University Press, 1971.

SCHNEIDER, George A., ed. *The Freeman Journal: The Infantry in the Sioux Campaign of 1876.* Presidio Press, 1978.

SCHROEDER, John H. *Mr. Polk's War.* University of Wisconsin Press, 1973.

SEAGER, Robert, II. *Alfred Thayer Mahan: The Man and His Letters.* U.S. Naval Institute, 1977.

SEEGER, Alan. *Letters and Diary.* Charles Scribner's Sons, 1917.

SHULIMSON, Jack. "The First to Fight: Marine Corps Expansion, 1914–18," *Prologue* VIII (Spring, 1976), 5–16.

SHY, John. *Toward Lexington: The Role of the British Army in the Coming of the American Revolution.* Princeton University Press, 1965.

SINGLETARY, Otis A. *The Mexican War*. University of Chicago Press, 1960.

SKELTON, William B. "The Commanding General and the Problem of Command in the United States Army, 1821–1841," *Military Affairs*, XXXIV (December, 1970), 117–122.

SPECTOR, Ronald. *Admiral of the New Empire: The Life and Career of George Dewey*. Louisiana State University Press, 1974.

SPRAGUE, John T. *The Origins, Progress and Conclusion of the Florida War*. University of Florida Press, 1964.

STOWE, Gerald and Jac Weller. "Revolutionary West Point: 'The Key to the Continent,'" *Military Affairs*, XIV (Summer, 1955), 81–98.

SWORD, Wiley. *Shiloh: Bloody April*. William Morrow, 1974.

TAYLOR, A.J.P. *The Origins of the Second World War*, 2nd ed. Fawcett, 1969.

TERRAINE, John. *The Western Front, 1914–1918*. Lippincott, 1965.

UPTON, Emory. *Military Policy of the United States*. 64th Congress, 1st Session, December 6, 1915–September 8, 1916. Senate Documents, Vol. 13. U.S. Government Printing Office, 1916.

UTLEY, Robert M. *Frontiersmen in Blue: The United States Army and the Indian, 1848–1865*. Macmillan, 1967.

———. *Frontier Regulars: The United States Army and the Indian, 1866–1890*. Macmillan, 1973.

VANDIVER, Frank. "Haig, Nevelle, and Third Ypres," *Rice University Studies*, LVII (Winter, 1971), 77–85.

WALLACE, Willard M. *Appeal to Arms: A Military History of the American Revolution*. Harper & Brothers, 1951.

WARD, Christopher and John Richard Alden, eds. *The War of the Revolution*, 2 vols. Macmillan, 1952.

WEEMS, John Edward. *To Conquer a Peace: The War Between the United States and Mexico*. Doubleday, 1974.

WEIGLEY, Russell F. *The American Way of War*. Macmillan, 1973.

———. *History of the United States Army*. Macmillan, 1967.

WELLER, Jac. "Guns of Destiny," *Military Affairs*, XX (Spring, 1956), 15.

WELLMAN, Paul I. *The Indian Wars of the West*. Doubleday, 1967.

WILLCOX, William B. *Portrait of a General*. Alfred A. Knopf, 1964.

WOLFF, Leon. *In Flanders Fields*. The Viking Press, 1958.

WRIGHT, Monte D. and Lawrence J. Paszek, eds. *Soldiers and Statesmen*. United States Air Force Academy, 1973.

INDEX

Adams, John, 30, 88–90
Aguinaldo, Emilio, 332, 341, 343–5; captured, 346–7
Air Force, U.S., 389–90
Alger, Russell A., 323, 326, 327
Amherst, Gen. Jeffrey, 18
Ampudia, Gen. Pedro de, 172
Anderson, Maj. Robert, 212
Annapolis, 307
Arista, Gen. Mariano, 169–70
Armstrong, John, 122; as secretary of war, 108–9; as strategist, 124, 125, 126–7
army, American: early, 4–6; in Revolution, 40–5; in War of 1812, 97–101; after 1812, 136–7, 139; in Mexican War, 168–9; after Mexican War, 186–8, 192, 193; in Indian wars, 189–90, 310–16; in Civil War, 213, 221–2, 225–7, 247, 251–2, 260; after Civil War, 303–4, 308–11; in War with Spain, 322, 323–4, 343–4; and China, 347–8; in early 1900s, 350–2; in World War I, 377–84, 405–8
army, British, 23–5, 88, 97
army, Confederate, 221–2, 226–7, 247; see also Civil War
Army War College (Washington), 351
Arnold, Gen. Benedict, 53–4, 57–8, 68–9; desertion of, 73–4
Articles of Confederation, 83–4
Atkinson, Henry, 141

Bainbridge, William, 113
Baker, Newton D., 402–3; as strategist, 399–400
Banks, Gen. Nathaniel P., 277, 288
Baruch, Bernard, 396
battles: Antietam, 282–3; (Second) Bull Run, 280–1; Bunker Hill, 51–2; Cedar Hill, 297; Cerro Gordo, 180–1; Chancellorsville, 284–5; Chapultepec, 183–4; Château-Thierry, 408; Chattanooga, 293–4; Chickamauga, 292; Churubusco, 183; Cold Harbor, 296; Corinth, 271; Cowpens, 79; Eutaw Springs, 80; Fair Oaks, 278; Fisher's Hill, 297; Fort Donelson, 268–9; Fort Henry, 268–9; Franklin, 299–300; Fredericksburg, 282–3; Gettysburg, 289–91; Harper's Ferry, 278; Hobkirk's Hill, 80; Lexington-Concord, 49–50; Lundy's Lane, 127; Malvern Hill, 279; Manila, 329–32; Marne, 408–10; Meuse, 412–14; Monmouth, 72; Murfreesboro, 273–4; New Orleans, 131–3; Pea Ridge, 269; Perryville, 273; Petersburg, 296–7; Port Hudson, 288; Saint-Mihiel, 410–11; Saratoga, 38, 70; Seven Days, 278–81; Shiloh, 269–71; Somme, 363–4, 407; Spotsylvania, 296; Vicksburg, 286–8; Wilderness, 284; Winchester, 297; Yorktown, 81
Beaumarchais, Caron de, 38
Beauregard, Gen. P. G. T.: in Mexico, 184; and Fort Sumter, 212; at Second Bull Run, 261–4; at Corinth, 269–71; relieved of command, 272; at Petersburg, 297
Bell, John, 207–8
Benson, William S., 287–8
Black Hawk War, 140–1
Bliss, Gen. Tasker H., 401, 403
blockade: in Civil War, 217, 249–50, 265–6; in World War I, 370–1
Bonhomme Richard, 49
Braddock, Gen. Edward, 17
Bragg, Gen. Braxton: relieved of

Bragg, Gen. Braxton (*cont.*)
command, 254–5, 293; appointed
commander, 272; at Chattanooga,
272–3, 292, 294; at Perryville, 273;
as strategist, 273; at Chickamauga,
292
Breckinridge, John C., 207–8
Brock, Gen. Isaac, 115, 118
Brown, Gen. Jacob, 124, 126–7, 138
Brown, Joseph E., 238
Buchanan, James, 211
Buell, Gen. Don Carlos, 267, 269, 273,
282
Bullard, Gen. Robert L., 413
Burgoyne, General Sir John, 50, 63–70,
80
Burnside, Gen. Ambrose E., 282–3, 292

Calhoun, John C., 98, 155–6; as
secretary of war, 137–8
Canada: in colonial wars, 14–19 *passim;*
in Revolution, 52–4, 63–6; in War of
1812, 96–9, 105, 107–9, 114–29
Carleton, Sir Guy, 55, 57, 58, 63–4
Carlisle Barracks, Pennsylvania, 192
Carranza, Venustiano, 356
Cervera, Adm. Pascual, 330, 332, 333,
338–9
Chase, Salmon P., 230
Chauncey, Capt. Isaac, 121, 122, 126
Churchill, Winston, 367
Clark, Col. George Rogers, 74
Clausewitz, Karl von, 195, 197
Clay, Henry, 95, 149
Cleveland, Grover, 319
Clinton, Gen. Henry, 50, 56, 58, 69; at
Bunker Hill, 52; at Monmouth, 72–3;
at Yorktown, 80–2
Cochise, 316
Cochrane, Adm. Alexander, 131, 132
colonial system, 12–14, 16, 19
command system: American, 9, 29–30;
British, 30–2; *see also* General Staff,
American
Conner, Com. David, 172, 178–9
Constitution, U.S.S., 111, 113
Continental Congress, First, 26
Continental Congress, Second, 26, 30,

40; and Articles of Confederation, 27,
83–4; and logistics, 28, 34–6; and
military staff, 28–30, 35; financial
policy of, 32–4, 37
Corbin, Henry C., 328
Cornwallis, Charles, Lord, 61, 62–3, 76,
77–82; surrender of, 81–2
Crazy Horse, 313–15
Crook, George, 314
Curtis, Samuel, 267, 269

Daniels, Josephus, 387–8
Davis, Jefferson, 191, 193, 200, 229–30,
238–9; manpower policy of, 219–25;
and command system, 248, 253–5; as
strategist, 248–9, 254–5, 277; and
Manassas, 262–3; and Richmond, 277;
and Vicksburg, 288; and Bragg, 293;
removes Johnston, 298; capture of,
301–2 and *n.*
Dearborn, Henry, 100, 108, 118–19, 122,
123, 124
Declaration of Independence, 22–3, 27
Dewey, Adm. George, 329, 349; victory
at Manila, 330–1
Dix, Dorothea, 227
Doniphan, Col. Alfred W., 174
Dos Passos, John, 367–8
Douglas, Stephen A., 207–8
Drummond, Sir Gordon, 127–8
Dunmore, Lord, *see* Murray, John
Duportail, Louis, 39

Early, Gen. Jubal, 297
Estaing, Charles Hector, Comte d', 73,
75
Eustis, William, 108, 115–16
Ewell, Gen. Richard S., 290

Farragut, Adm. David G., 271, 272, 306
Federalists, 89–90, 104–5; and Hartford
Convention, 106–7
Ferguson, Maj. Patrick, 78

financing: for Revolution, 32–4, 37; for War of 1812, 103; for Mexican War, 166–7; for Civil War, 200, 203–4; for War with Spain, 325–6; for World War I, 360, 392–3
Five Civilized Tribes, 188
Foch, Gen. Ferdinand, 401–2, 409–14
Foote, Capt. Andrew, 268
foreign policy: in Civil War, 242–4; in 1916, 348, 356; under Wilson, 373–6, 382
Foulois, Gen. Benjamin D., 391
Franklin, Benjamin, 37–8
Frémont, Gen. John C., 153, 174–5, 277–8

Gage, Gen. Thomas, 50–1, 55
Gallatin, Albert, 89, 94, 103
Gates, Maj. Gen. Horatio, 46, 67, 69, 76–8
General Service and Staff College (Leavenworth), 351
General Staff, American, 102–3, 137; in Mexican War, 145, 168; structure of, 247–8; in Civil War, 248–9, 304; Root reforms, 353; in World War I, 378–80, 382, 403–4
General Staff, Great (German), 353
George III, King, 30–1, 115
Germain, Lord George, 31; strategy of, 63–4, 72, 74
Geronimo, 316
Ghent, treaty of, 133, 140
Gibbon, John, 314
Goodwin, Richard, 187–8
Gorgas, Gen. Josiah, 229
Grant, Gen. Ulysses S.: as general in chief, 252–3, 294; as strategist, 253, 268, 294, 296, 301; and Halleck, 267, 269–70; at Fort Henry, 268; at Shiloh, 269–71; at Vicksburg, 286–8; at Chattanooga, 293–4; at Appomattox, 301
Graves, Adm. Thomas, 81
Greene, Gen. Nathanael, 46, 78
Grierson, Col. Benjamin H., 287
Guadalupe Hidalgo, treaty of, 184–5

Haig, Gen. Douglas, 364–7, 401
Halleck, Gen. Henry W., 279; manual of, 196–7; as general in chief, 252–3, 272; as commander in West (1862), 267; and Grant, 267, 269–70; at Corinth, 271
Hamilton, Paul, 110, 113
Hamlin, Hannibal, 241
Hampton, Maj. Gen. Wade, 124–5
Harbord, Gen. James G., 406
Hardee's Tactics, 192
Harmar, Josiah, 86
Harrison, William Henry, 120–2
Hartford Convention, 106–7
Hayes, Rutherford B., 367
Hill, Gen. A. P., 290
Hindenburg, Gen. Paul von, 406
Holmes, Oliver Wendell, 367
Hood, Gen. John B., 298–300
Hooker, Gen. Joseph, 283–5, 289
Hopkins, Esek, 48
Howe, Adm. Richard, 56, 59, 71
Howe, Gen. William, 50; at Bunker Hill, 51–2; evacuates Boston, 54; succeeds Gates, 55–6; at battle for New York, 59–63; Canadian campaign, 63–6; peace offer, 71; relieved of command, 72
Huerta, Victoriano, 356
Hull, Isaac, 113
Hull, William, 108, 115–18
Humphreys, Joshua, 111

Indians (as antagonists), 86, 87–9, 310
Indian wars: in 17th and 18th centuries, 10–11, 86–7; in 19th century, 139–43, 189–90, 310–16
Izard, Maj. Gen. George, 126, 128

Jackson, Andrew, 131, 132, 148; and Indian wars, 139–41; as expansionist, 147
Jackson, Gen. Thomas J. (Stonewall), 277–8, 280–2, 285
Jaudenes, Fermin, 341

Jay's Treaty, 88–9
Jefferson, Thomas, 91–2, 95
Jefferson Barracks (St. Louis), 192
Jeffersonians, *see* Republicans
Johnson, Andrew, 241
Johnston, Gen. Albert Sidney, 268–71
Johnston, Gen. Joseph E., 261–3, 278, 287, 301; as strategist, 276; replaces Bragg, 294; removed from command, 298
Jomini, Henri Antoine, 195–6
Jones, John Paul, 88–9
Jones, William, 110

Kearny, Gen. Stephen, 163, 173–5
Kenly, William L., 390
King George's War, 13, 16
King Philip, 11
King William's War, 13–14
Knox, Henry, 46, 54, 85, 87

Lafayette, Gilbert Motier, Marquis de, 38, 80
Larkin, Thomas, 153
Lawrence, James, 113
Lee, Maj. Gen. Charles, 46, 61, 72
Lee, Gen. Robert E.: appointed general in chief, 254; at Second Bull Run, 262–3; and defense of Richmond, 276–80; as strategist, 278, 280, 285, 288, 290, 297; at Antietam, 281–3; at Chancellorsville, 284–5; at Gettysburg, 288–91; mystique of, 289, 294; at Cold Harbor, 296; at Appomattox, 301
Lincoln, Abraham, 200, 206; election of, 1860, 207–8; on secession, 211; and Fort Sumter, 211–13; manpower policy of, 213, 219–20; congressional message of 1864, 227, 229–30; war policy of, 238–9; opposition to, 239–40; and habeas corpus, 241; and election of 1864, 241–2; as strategist, 248, 251–2, 277–8, 279; and command system, 248–53; and McClellan, 250–2, 274–6,

281, 282; and Buell, 282; and Hooker, 283–4
Lincoln, Gen. Benjamin, 75
Lloyd George, David, 401
logistics: in Revolution, 34–6; in War of 1812, 102; in Mexican War, 145, 167–8; in Civil War, 201, 215–16, 227–9; in War with Spain, 326, 334–5; in World War I, 396–7, 398, 405–6
Long, John D., 327–9, 354–5
Longstreet, Gen. James, 281, 288, 290, 292, 293
Louisbourg, 3, 16
Luce, Rear Adm. Stephen B., 307
Ludendorff, Gen. Erich von, 406–11, 413–14
Lyon, Gen. Nathaniel, 259

MacArthur, Gen. Arthur, 344, 346
Macdonough, Thomas, 129
Macomb, Brig. Gen. Alexander, 129, 138
McClellan, Gen. George B., 260; and election of 1864, 241–2; as strategist, 250–1, 274–5; and Lincoln, 250–2, 274–6, 281, 282; replaces McDowell, 264; threatens Richmond, 275–80; at Antietam, 281–2; relieved of command, 282
McDowell, Gen. Irvin, 261–4, 276, 277–8
McKinley, William: and Cuba, 319–21, 335–6; and army, 320, 324–5; as strategist, 327–8, 330, 332, 340; and Miles, 328–30; and Puerto Rico, 339–41; and Merritt, 340–1
Madison, James, 91–2, 94, 95, 101, 115–16, 126; as strategist, 108–9; and treaty of Ghent, 133
Maine, U.S.S., 320
Mahan, Alfred T., 307–8, 319, 328
Mahan, Dennis Hart, manual of, 196–7
Mallory, Stephen R., 264–6
"Manifest Destiny," 149, 156
March, Gen. Peyton C., 397, 403–4
Marcy, William L., 157, 158, 171
Marion, Francis, 76
Meade, Gen. George C., 289–91, 294–6

Memminger, Christopher G., 231
Merrimack (Confederate vessel), 265
Merritt, Wesley, 340–1, 343
Miles, Gen. Nelson A., 323; and McKinley, 327, 330; as strategist, 328–9; and Cuba, 332–4; and Puerto Rico, 339–40
militia, origins of, 8; pre-Revolutionary, 8–10, 14, 22; in Revolution, 40–1; Law of 1792, 86; in War of 1812, 98–9; after War of 1812, 136; in Civil War, 213, 219–20; after Civil War, 303–4; in War with Spain, 322
Monitor, U.S.S., 265
Monroe Doctrine, 135–6, 195, 355
Montagu, John, Earl of Sandwich, 31
Montcalm, Louis Joseph, Marquis de, 19
Montgomery, Richard, 46, 53, 54
Montreal, 15, 19; in Revolution, 53, 54, 68; in War of 1812, 107, 109, 114, 117, 124–5
Mordecai, Alfred, artillery manual of, 193
Morgan, Gen. Daniel, 69, 78–9
Morris, Robert, 34, 36–7
Murray, John, Earl of Dunmore, 12

National Guard: in 18th century, 19; in Civil War, 304; in War with Spain, 322–4; lobby of, 330; in early 1900s, 351–2; in World War I, 379–80
Naval War College (Newport), 307
navy, American: in Revolution, 47–8, 88; in War of 1812, 97, 110–11; after 1812, 136; after Mexican War, 186–7; in Civil War, 216–17, 264–5, 268, 271–2, 286–8; after Civil War, 303, 306, 307; in War with Spain, 328–32, 354–5; in early 1900s, 349–51; in World War I, 380–3, 385–8, 391
navy, British, 14, 23–4, 48, 97, 374, 386–7
navy, Confederate, 264–5
navy, German, 374, 386–7
Negroes in armed services: in colonies, 9; in Continental army, 45–6; in War of 1812, 130, 132; in Civil War, 204–6,

214, 223, 225–7, 236–7, 239–40; after Civil War, 310; in War with Spain, 325; in World War I, 384–5
Nicholas II, Tsar, 364
Nicholson, Sir Francis, 15

Osceola, 142
Otis, Gen. Elwell, 343

Pakenham, Sir Edward, 131–3
Paredes, Marian, 154
Parrott, Robert, 192
Patrick, Gen. Mason M., 391
Patterson, Gen. Robert, 261
Peace Democrats, 240
Pemberton, Gen. John C., 286–8
Perry, Com. Matthew, 180
Perry, Com. Oliver Hazard, 121–2
Pershing, Gen. John J., 356; and AEF, 383–4, 404–6, 409–14; and Foch, 401–3; as field commander, 402–3; and March, 404
Pétain, Gen. Henri Philippe, 364, 401
Phips, Sir William, 15
Pickens, Andrew, 76
Pickett, Gen. George, 290
Pillow, Gen. Gideon, 164, 181, 183
Pinckney, Thomas, 100
Polk, James K., 144, 164, 177; as commander in chief, 145; as expansionist, 149, 150–1; as strategist, 152–6; and Mexican War, 155–60, 162, 172–3, 184
Pontiac, 11
Pope, Gen. John, 279–81
Porter, Com. David, 113, 287, 306
Prevost, Lt. Gen. Sir George, 115, 123, 128, 129, 134
Procter, Col. Henry, 120, 122
propaganda, World War I, 370, 371, 376–7

Quakers, 8
Quebec (City), 14–15, 18–19, 53–4, 107, 115

Queen Anne's War, 13, 15–16
Quitman, John A., 164

Radical Republicans, 239, 241–2
Rawdon, Lord Francis, 80
Red Cloud, 313–15
Republicans (Jeffersonian era), 89–91
Riall, Gen. Phineas, 127–8
Rochambeau, Jean Baptiste, Comte de, 74, 81
Rodgers, Com. John, 112
Roosevelt, Theodore, 329, 335; and navy, 349; in Cuba, 335, 337–8
Root, Elihu, 351–4
Rosecrans, Gen. William S., 273, 291–2
Ross, Gen. Robert, 129–30

Sackett's Harbor, 109, 121–8 *passim*
St. Clair, Arthur, 87, 138
St. Leger, Col. Barry, 67–9
Sampson, Adm. William T., 326, 336–9
Sandwich, Earl of, *see* Montagu
Santa Anna, Antonio Lopez de (Mexican leader), 148; and Mexican War, 162, 176–8, 182–3
Schley, Adm. Winfield S., 330, 338–9
Schlieffen, Alfred von, 362–3
Schlieffen Plan, 362–3, 373–4
Schofield, Gen. John M., 299, 328
School of Application for Infantry and Cavalry (Leavenworth), 308
Schuyler, Philip, 53, 58, 67, 68–9
Scott, Maj. Gen. Hugh, 403
Scott, Gen. Winfield, 124, 126, 138; as strategist, 123; manual of, 138–9; as Indian fighter, 141–2; and Mexican War, 157–8, 162, 163, 176–85; as military leader, 164–6; and secession, 245; and Anaconda Plan, 249–50
Seeger, Alan, 368
Seminole Wars: First, 139–40; Second, 141–3
Shafter, Gen. William R., 317; and Cuba, 332–9; as strategist, 336–7
Sheridan, Gen. Philip, 297
Sherman, Gen. William T., 215, 293–5, 308, 312
Sims, William S., 388–9

Sitting Bull, 313–15
slavery, *see* Negroes
Slidell, John, 154
Sloat, Com. J. D., 173, 175
Smith, Gen. Edmund Kirby, 273
Smith, Samuel, 130
Smyth, Brig. Gen. Alexander, 118–19
Stanton, Edwin M., 251, 279
Stark, Gen. John, 68
states rights' party (Confederate), 237–8
Stephens, Alexander H., 235, 237
Steuben, Friedrich Wilhelm von, 71
Stockton, Comm. Robert, 175
strategy, American: in Revolution, 53–4, 59–60, 63, 73, 81; in War of 1812, 108–9, 114, 124–7; after War of 1812, 136; in Mexican War, 145, 152–6; of annihilation, 197; in Civil War, 245–6, 249–53, 257–8, 262–3, 268, 273–6, 279, 282–3, 286–7, 289–90, 293–6, 299–301, 306–7; after Civil War, 308; in War with Spain, 323, 327–8, 330, 336–7, 344, 346; in early 1900s, 348–9, 350, 354–5, 362; in World War I, 382, 391, 399–402, 409–14
strategy, British: in Revolution, 31–2, 63–4, 72, 74; in War of 1812, 114–15
strategy, Confederate, 246–7, 254–5, 257–8, 265–6, 268, 278, 284, 287, 289–90, 297, 299, 365
strategy, German (World War I), 362–3, 407
strategy, Indian, 311–12
Strong, Caleb, 104
Stuart, Gen. J. E. B., 289
submarines, 371–3
Sumter, Thomas, 76

tactics, American: origins, 5–6; colonial, 10–11, 17; in Revolution, 22, 50; in Indian wars (1850), 189–90; in Mexican War, 192–5; in Civil War, 258–9, 279, 290, 295–8, 300; after Civil War, 307–9, 312–13; in War with Spain, 344–7; in World War I, 359–60, 363, 364–7, 407
Taft, William Howard, 355
Tarleton, Col. Banastre, 76, 79

Taylor, Gen. Zachary: as strategist, 142, 176; in Texas, 153–4, 158; and Mexican War, 154–5, 163, 164, 169–73, 176–8; elected president, 186

Tecumseh, 122

Terry, John, 314

Thayer, Sylvanus, 139

Thomas, Gen. George H., 292–4, 299, 300

Toombs, Robert, 208–9

Toral, Jose, 338, 339

Tories (Loyalists), 24, 66–8, 74, 76–8

Trenchard, Gen. Hugh, 391

trench warfare (World War I), 365–6, 368–9

Trist, Nicholas P., 182–3, 184

Twiggs, David E., 164, 180, 182

Tyler, John, as expansionist, 147–9, 150

Upton, Gen. Emory, 309

Valley Forge, 36, 66, 70

Van Buren, Martin, 149

Van Dorn, Gen. Earl, 268, 269

Van Rensselaer, Stephen, 118–19

Vauban, Sebastien, 6–7

Versailles, Treaty of, 414

Villa, Francisco "Pancho," 356

Ward, Gen. Artemas, 42, 50

War Department: established, 86; in Civil War, 247–8, 251–3; after Civil War, 304–5; in War with Spain, 326; early 1900's, 353–4; *see also* General Staff

War Department, Confederate, 253–5

War Hawks, 98, 107

Washington, George, 17, 61, 65; named commander, 26–8; as citizen soldier, 29; develops army, 40–4; as general, 46, 62; as strategist, 53–4, 59–60, 63, 73, 81; crosses Delaware, 62; at Valley Forge, 66, 70–1; at Monmouth, 72–3; at Yorktown, 81–2; and postwar army, 84, 85–6; and Indian danger, 86–7

Wayne, Gen. Anthony, 87, 88, 138

weaponry: in 17th century, 4–5, 8, 10–11; in Revolution, 34–5; in Mexican War, 168–9, 191; in Indian wars (1850), 190–1; in Civil War, 255–7, 300, 305; in War with Spain, 326–7, 343; in early 1900s, 349, 351; in World War I, 360, 364–5, 371–3, 389–90, 398

Welles, Gideon, 265

Wellington, Arthur Wellesley, Duke of, 131–2

West Point, 100, 139

Wilkinson, Brig. Gen. James, 88, 89, 100, 124–6, 131

Wilson, James H., 300

Wilson, Woodrow: and Mexico, 356; and submarine warfare, 372–3; and foreign policy, 373–6, 393–4; as moral leader, 375; and military policy, 382, 394–6, 399–403; and air force, 390; at Versailles, 414–15

Winchester, James, 120

Winder, Gen. William, 129

Wolfe, Gen. James, 18–19

women: in Civil War, 227; in World War I, 385

Wool, John, 163, 164, 173

A NOTE ABOUT THE AUTHOR

T. Harry Williams died in 1979, before he could bring *The History of American Wars* through the Vietnam War, as he had intended. Since the 1940s he had taught history at Louisiana State University, where he was Boyd Professor of History. Among his many books were *Lincoln and His Generals* (1952), a Book-of-the-Month Club selection; a biography of the Civil War general P. G. T. Beauregard (1955); and his classic biography of Huey Long, which won both a Pulitzer Prize and a National Book Award in 1970. At the time of his death he was writing a biography of Lyndon Johnson.

A NOTE ON THE TYPE

THE TEXT OF THIS BOOK was set via computer-driven cathode ray tube in a face called Times Roman, designed by Stanley Morison for *The Times* (London) and first introduced by that newspaper in 1932.

Among typographers and designers of the twentieth century, Stanley Morison has been a strong influence, as typographical adviser to the English Monotype Corporation, as a director of two distinguished English publishing houses, and as a writer of sensibility, erudition, and keen practical sense.

Composed, printed and bound by
The Haddon Craftsmen, Inc., Scranton, Pennsylvania
Typography based on a design by
GUY FLEMING